Contents

Contents

M-PER

External and intra-European Union trade —

Statistical yearbook

NOW WITH A CHAPTER ON
CANDIDATE COUNTRIES

Data 1958-2002

6

EUROPEAN
COMMISSION

THEME 6
External
trade

·········· Immediate access to **harmonised statistical data**

Eurostat Data Shops

A personalised data retrieval service

In order to provide the greatest possible number of people with access to high-quality statistical information, Eurostat has developed an extensive network of Data Shops (¹).

Data Shops provide a wide range of **tailor-made services:**

- ★ immediate information searches undertaken by a team of experts in European statistics,
- ★ rapid and personalised response that takes account of the specified search requirements and intended use,
- ★ a choice of data carrier depending on the type of information required.

Information can be requested by phone, mail, fax or e-mail.

(¹) See the list of Eurostat Data Shops at the end of this publication.

Internet

Essentials on Community statistical news

- ★ Euro indicators: more than 100 indicators on the euro zone; harmonised, comparable, and free of charge.
- ★ About Eurostat: what it does and how it works.
- ★ Products and databases: a detailed description of what Eurostat has to offer.
- ★ Indicators on the European Union: convergence criteria; euro yield curve and further main indicators on the European Union at your disposal.
- ★ Press releases: direct access to all Eurostat press releases.

For further information, visit us on the Internet: **www.europa.eu.int/comm/eurostat/**

Europe Direct is a service to help you find answers to your questions about the European Union

New freephone number:
00 800 6 7 8 9 10 11

A great deal of additional information on the European Union is available on the Internet.
It can be accessed through the Europa server (http://europa.eu.int).

Cataloguing data can be found at the end of this publication.

Luxembourg: Office for Official Publications of the European Communities, 2003

ISBN 92-894-4302-2
ISSN 1606-3481

EUROSTAT

L-2920 Luxembourg — Tel. (352) 43 01-1 — Telex COMEUR LU 3423

Eurostat is the Statistical Office of the European Communities. Its task is to provide the European Union with statistics, at a European level, that allow comparisons to be made between countries and regions. Eurostat consolidates and harmonises the data collected by the Member States.

To ensure that the vast quantity of accessible data is made widely available and to help each user make proper use of the information, Eurostat has set up a publications and services programme.

This programme makes a clear distinction between general and specialist users and particular collections have been developed for these different groups. The collections *Press releases*, *Statistics in focus*, *Panorama of the European Union*, *Pocketbooks* and *Catalogues* are aimed at general users. They give immediate key information through analyses, tables, graphs and maps.

The collections *Methods and nomenclatures* and *Detailed tables* suit the needs of the specialist who is prepared to spend more time analysing and using very detailed information and tables.

All Eurostat products are disseminated through the Data Shop network or the sales agents of the Office for Official Publications of the European Communities. Data Shops are available in 13 of the 15 Member States as well as in Switzerland, Norway and the United States. They provide a wide range of services from simple database extracts to tailor-made investigations. The information is provided on paper and/or in electronic form via e-mail, on diskette or on CD-ROM.

As part of the new programme, Eurostat has developed its web site. It includes a broad range of online information on Eurostat products and services, newsletters, catalogues, online publications and indicators on the euro zone.

Eurostat

Contents

Foreword

1. Introduction

Trade statistics - both detailed and global results - have now proved their worth. They are an instrument of prime importance for both public and private users. For instance, they enable Community authorities to prepare multilateral and bilateral negotiations on common trade policy; they help European businesses to carry out market surveys and thus improve their competitiveness; they are an essential source of information for statistics on the balance of payments, the national accounts and short-term economic studies. This non-exhaustive list highlights the variety of users and their requirements.

The environment in which trade statistics are collected has changed radically in recent years, leading to a detailed revision of the regulations. For statistics on trade with non-member countries, the introduction in 1988 of the Combined Nomenclature of goods (CN) and the Single Administrative Document had already led to considerable methodological changes. However, the major changes were brought about by the introduction of the single market on 1 January 1993. This led to the abolition of customs formalities between the Member States which had served as the traditional source of trade statistics, and the introduction of a special collection system called INTRASTAT. The accession of three new member states in 1995 led Eurostat to recalculate its historical series for the European Union to include Austria, Finland and Sweden; therefore figures published here concern the fifteen Members unless stated otherwise.

The yearbook on external and intra-European Union trade sets out to provide data on long-term trends in the trade of the European Union (EU) and its Member States. It contains data on the trade flows, broken down by major product group, of the EU with its main trading partners on one hand and between the Member States on the other.

In view of the next enlargements of the European Union and taking into account the importance of trade by members of the European Free Trade Association (Iceland, Liechtenstein, Norway and Switzerland) with the Union, a description of trade with the candidate countries (chapter 7) and the EFTA countries (chapter 8) has been added to that usually given for Member States only.

Statistics on external trade and Intra-EU trade at the most detailed classification level are published monthly on CD-ROM. They are also available on-line from the Eurostat's databases (Comext, Newcronos).

2. Intra-EU trade

Statistics on trade between the Member States are based on Council Regulation (EC) N^O 3330/91 of 7 November 1991 and on the various implementation regulations which have supplemented it or laid down rules on methodology, thresholds and forms. The system set up for the collection of information on trade between the Member States as from 1 January 1993 is commonly known as Intrastat. Its main features are:

- Monthly statistical declarations sent directly by businesses to the competent national authorities;

- A system of thresholds abolishing all statistical formalities for almost two thirds of businesses;

- A close link with the tax system.

With the introduction of this new system, the comparability of Intra-EU results before and after 1 January 1993 is limited, owing to a degree of under-estimation of flows. This is because of some businesses' failure to respond and the introduction of thresholds which exclude the smallest businesses. To correct this under-estimation, which varies according to the Member State, some countries make adjustments at an aggregate level (in general by partner country). Arrivals, i.e. imports from other EU countries, are particularly under-estimated. Consequently, Eurostat considers dispatches now to be the most reliable gauge of Intra-EU trade.

If the dispatches of a given Member State are compared with the corresponding arrivals of its partners, differences may emerge, mainly for the following reasons:

- Non-response by certain businesses;

- Errors or omissions.

For these reasons, figures on intra-EU trade should be interpreted with caution. They are also subject to frequent revision.

3.   *Extra-EU trade*

For data relating to the years 1978 to 1995, the Member States forwarded statistics on trade outside the European Union in accordance with a uniform methodology provided for in Council Regulation (EEC) N° 1736/75 and the regulations deriving from it. Since the beginning of 1996, data have been collected, transmitted and diffused in accordance with Council Regulation (EC) N° 1172/95 and its implementing rules (Council Regulation (EC) N° 840 196) which however retain the former methodological principles.

External trade statistics are usually recorded on the basis of customs declarations submitted by the declarant when clearing customs. The Single Administrative Document is used for this purpose. In some Member States, certain businesses are allowed to make a summary declaration.

Statistics on external trade and intra-EU trade are compiled on the basis of Community regulations. The same regulations are generally the basis for the compilation of statistics published nationally by each Member State. Nevertheless, methodological differences do arise, as a result of which Community statistics and national statistics do not match exactly.

Methodological notes and sources

1. Data sources

The tables in this publication on EU trade and that of the Member States were compiled by Eurostat using the detailed data forwarded by the Member States. Eurostat would like to take the opportunity to thank the departments concerned in the Member States for their cooperation, which makes it possible to compile these harmonized statistics and guarantee their quality.

Some of the tables of the first chapter describe the development of external trade as declared by the EU's most important trading partners. With the exception of table 1C and the results concerning the EU, these tables were compiled from data transmitted each month by the International Monetary Fund. Information in table 1C are taken from the Comtrade database that is managed by the United Nations.

2. Coverage

Series concerning the European Union were recalculated to include Austria, Finland and Sweden and therefore relate to the Union of 15 members unless stated otherwise.

2.1. Statistical territory

The statistical territory of the European Union corresponds to the customs territory of the European Union. From 1 January 1997 the statistical territories of France and Spain were modified to include respectively the French overseas departments (Guadeloupe, Guyana, Martinique and Reunion) and the Canary Islands.

That modification has lead to a growth in intra-EU trade and a reduction in extra-EU trade that amounted to 10.6 billion ecu for exports and 1.6 billion ecu for imports in 1995. The overall effect of this change on the European Union trade balance with the rest of the world will be a reduction in the trade surplus of almost 9 billion ecu.

Likewise, Greenland, Ceuta and Melilla are not covered, nor are the overseas countries and territories that are not part of the EU customs territory.

2.2 Intra-EU trade

Statistics on trade between the Member States cover the arrivals and dispatches of movable goods recorded by each Member State. Arrivals and dispatches are defined as follows:

- *arrivals* are goods in free circulation within the European Union which enter the statistical territory of a given Member State;

- *dispatches* are goods in free circulation within the European Union which leave the statistical territory of a given Member State to enter another Member State.

Goods placed under the customs arrangements of inward processing or processing under customs control (for working, processing, or repairs) are also regarded as arrivals or dispatches.

Consequently, statistics on trade between the Member States do not cover goods in transit or trade between Member States and the French overseas departments or the Canary Islands.

2.3 Extra-EU trade

Statistics on trade with third countries cover movable property imported and exported by the European Union. The definitions are as follows:

- *Imports* are goods which enter the statistical territory of the European Union from a third country and are placed under the customs procedure for free circulation (as a general rule goods intended for consumption), inward processing or processing under customs control (goods for working, processing or repair) immediately or after bonded warehousing;

- *Exports* are goods which leave the statistical territory of the European Union for a third country after being placed under the customs procedure for exports (definitive export) or outward processing (goods for working, processing) or repair or following inward processing.

Statistics on trade with third countries do not, therefore, include goods in transit or those placed under a customs procedure for bonded warehousing or temporary entry (for fairs, exhibitions, tests, etc.) nor do they include re-export following entry under one of these procedures.

The field covered by statistics on trade with third countries corresponds to "special" trade. This method of accounting differs from that of "general" trade, which includes all goods entering the statistical territory and those leaving it, with the exception of goods in transit. Goods placed in bonded warehouses and exports of goods after bonded warehousing are included in the definition of general trade.

3. Statistical data

3.1. Trading partners: countries and economic areas

The results are broken down by country and area in accordance with the "Country nomenclature for statistics on European Union external trade and trade between its Member States", referred to as the Geonomenclature (Geonom). For the purposes of presenting the results, Eurostat has defined geographical and economic areas.

In the case of exports (or dispatches), *the country* (or Member State) *of final destination* of the goods is the partner country.

The trading partner in the case of an Intra-European Union arrival is always the *country of consignment* of the goods, even when the goods originate in third countries and have been placed in free circulation in the country of consignment. For imports (Extra-EU trade) the statistics show, except in certain cases (returned goods, works of art, etc.), *the country of origin*. Where two or more countries were involved in the production of certain goods, the country where the final processing or substantial working took place is considered to be the country of origin.

3.2. Goods classification

The most detailed results published by Eurostat are broken down according to the subheadings of the Combined Nomenclature (CN). This tariff and statistical nomenclature is based on the international nomenclature of the Harmonized System (HS) and comprises around 10 000 eight-digit codes.

In this publication, the results are broken down by the sections and divisions of the UN Standard International Trade Classification (SITC Rev. 3 since 1988) by means of conversion tables drawn up by Eurostat on the basis of the CN.

3.3. Estimate of the statistical value

Although the data are collected in units of national currency, the values set out in this bulletin have been expressed, after monthly conversion, in euros. The Annex to the bulletin contains a table showing the conversion rates used. The reader should note that annual exchange rates are given for information only. Annual values are equal to the sum of monthly values expressed in euros.

3.3.1 Intra-European Union trade

The statistical value is based on the assessment basis for taxation purposes or the transaction value of the goods. It is the FOB (free on board) value for dispatches and the CIF (cost, insurance, freight) value for arrivals. It comprises only those subsidiary costs (freight and insurance) which relate, for dispatches, to the journey within the territory of the Member State from which the goods are dispatched and, for arrivals, to the journey outside the territory of the Member State into which the goods enter.

In the case of arrivals or dispatches under an inward or outward processing arrangement and those for outside processing, it is always the total value of the goods that is recorded and not simply the added value.

3.3.2 Extra-European Union trade

The statistical value is based on the customs value or, failing that, the transaction value of the goods. It is the FOB value for exports and the CIF value for imports. It comprises only those subsidiary costs (freight and insurance) which relate, for exports, to the journey within the territory of the Member State from which the goods are exported and, for imports, to the journey outside the territory of the Member State into which the goods are imported.

In the case of imports or exports under an inward or outward processing arrangement and those for outside processing, it is always the total value of the goods that is recorded and not simply the added value.

3.4 Statistical secrecy

Most Member States take measures to guarantee the confidentiality of certain flows of goods. The legislation, the procedures for implementing it and the range of goods subject to secrecy vary from one Member State to another.

This confidentiality applies to the most detailed level of the classification used for collecting the data: it may therefore refer to all or only part of a subheading of the Combined Nomenclature. Similarly, confidentiality may apply to imports only or to exports only and to only some of the variables recorded (value, statistical procedure, quantities, partner country, etc.).

Measures are taken during collection and during processing by Eurostat to minimize the effect of these headings on the results; therefore trade data under these headings are included at higher levels of aggregation and in totals.

4. Indices

4.1. Introduction

Changes over time in the value of trade are influenced by changes in prices and the quantities marketed. Eurostat calculates Fisher's annual chain indices to measure these two effects. This publication sets out the indices calculated according to the SITC for each Member State on a strictly comparable basis.

4.2. Methodology

The data transmitted for external trade and Intra-European Union trade statistics are used at the most detailed level for calculating the indices. The indices of unit values (values divided by quantities) are used as price change indicators.

The computer programs contain a system for automatically identifying extreme unit values.

Products having unlikely price movements are not included in the calculation of indices.

Three rules are applied to exclude unlikely price behavior. The first one consists in excluding the products for which historical data have not shown a significant correlation between the trade values and the quantities. The second rule is based on the hypothesis that, given the general level of inflation, the price of a product can not vary significantly from one year to another. The third rule - which is more restrictive - is that the change in the price of a product compared with the closest month available will not differ significantly from the average change in the price of similar products. The application of these rules prevents extreme changes due to factors unrelated to prices which, otherwise, would lead to a distortion of the unit value index. For products whose unit values are rejected, the changes are drawn up according to those of similar products.

Symbols and abbreviations used

EU	Total of the 15 EU Member States
USA	United States of America
CEEC	Countries of Central and Eastern Europe
MEDA	Countries of the Euro-mediterranean partnership
CIS	Commonwealth of Independent States
ACP	Countries of Africa, the Caribbean and the Pacific which signed the Lomé Convention
EFTA	Countries of the European Free Trade Association
NAFTA	Countries of the North American Free Trade Agreement
MERCOSUR	Countries of the Southern Common Market (South America)
OPEC	Organization of Petroleum Exporting Countries
DAE	Dynamic Asian Economies
OECD	Organization for Economic Co–operation and Development
IMF	International Monetary Fund
0	Data less than half the unit used
:	Data not available
^	Variation greater than, absolute value, 999.9%
Mio	Million
Bn	1000 million
ECU	European Currency Unit
Eurostat	Statistical Office of the European Communities
SITC	Standard International Trade Classification

Data sources

B	Belgique	Banque Nationale de Belgique
DK	Danmark	Danmarks Statistik, København
D	Deutschland	Statistisches Bundesamt, Wiesbaden
EL	Ελλάδα	Εθνική Στατιστική Υπηρεσία Ελλάδας, Αθήνα
E	España	Dirección General de Aduanas e Impuestos Especiales, Madrid
F	France	Direction générale des douanes et droits indirects, Paris
IRL	Ireland	Central Statistics Office, Dublin
I	Italia	Istituto centrale di statistica, Roma
L	Luxembourg	STATEC, Luxembourg
NL	Nederland	Centraal Bureau voor de statistiek, Heerlen
A	Österreich	Österreichisches Statistisches Zentralamt, Wien
P	Portugal	Instituto Nacional de Estatística, Lisboa
FIN	Suomi / Finland	National Board of Customs, Helsinki
S	Sverige	Statistika Centralbyran, Stockholm
UK	United Kingdom	HM Customs and Excise, Southend-on-Sea
IS	Iceland	Statistics Iceland, Reykjavik
NO	Norway	Statistik sentralbyrå, Oslo
CH	Suisse	Direction générale des douanes, Berne
BG	Bulgaria	National Statistical Institute, Sofia
CY	Cyprus	Statistical Service of Cyprus, Nicosia
CZ	Česká republika	Český statistický úřad, Praha
EE	Eesti	Eesti Statistikaamet, Tallinn
HU	Magyarország	Központi Statisztikai Hivatal, Budapest
LV	Latvija	Latvijas Republikas Centrālā statistikas pārvalde, Riga
LT	Lietuva	Statistics Lithuania, Vilnius
MT	Malta	Uffiċċju Nażżjonali ta' l-Istatistika, Valletta
PL	Polska	Glowny Urzad Statystyczny, Warszawa
RO	România	Institutul Național de Statistic, Bucureşti
SI	Slovenija	Statistični urad Republike Slovenije, Ljubljana
SK	Slovenska Republika	Štatistický úrad Slovenskej republiky, Bratislava
TR	Türkiye	Devlet İstatistik Enstitüsü, Ankara

Other countries :   International Monetary Fund, Washington D.C.

TRENDS IN WORLD TRADE

EXPORTS

Year	Main countries in 2002												
	World (1)	EU (Extra EU)	USA	Japan	China	Canada	Hong Kong	South Korea	Mexico	Singapore	USSR / Russia (3)	Malaysia	Switzer-land (4)
Value (Bn ECU/Euro)(2)													
1958	68.3	20.7	17.8	2.8	:	5.3	0.1	0.0	0.7	:	:	:	1.5
1960	82.6	24.4	20.5	3.9	:	5.8	0.7	0.0	0.8	0.2	0.1	:	1.9
1970	205.9	52.0	43.2	18.9	:	16.7	2.5	0.8	1.3	1.6	:	1.7	5.2
1978	683.5	167.2	112.8	77.2	7.6	38.0	9.0	9.9	4.7	8.0	:	5.8	18.5
1979	801.1	184.0	132.8	74.6	10.0	42.5	11.1	11.0	6.6	10.4	:	8.1	21.8
1980	987.4	212.1	158.6	93.7	13.0	48.6	14.2	12.5	11.2	13.9	:	9.3	21.3
1981	1,370.2	277.6	209.4	135.7	19.2	65.1	19.5	19.1	17.4	18.8	34.7	10.5	24.2
1982	1,426.9	297.3	216.7	141.3	22.3	72.7	21.3	22.3	21.6	21.2	37.8	12.3	26.5
1983	1,523.7	313.1	225.3	165.1	24.8	86.2	24.7	27.5	25.1	24.5	41.1	15.9	28.7
1984	1,844.6	365.0	276.1	215.1	31.5	114.4	35.9	37.1	30.9	30.5	51.7	21.0	32.8
1985	1,923.4	394.0	279.3	232.2	35.8	119.0	39.6	39.7	29.0	29.9	58.3	20.2	36.0
1986	1,528.7	333.1	220.9	214.2	31.9	91.2	36.0	35.4	16.4	22.9	44.1	14.2	38.1
1987	1,513.5	327.0	219.1	200.4	34.2	85.0	42.0	41.0	17.8	24.9	40.9	15.5	39.4
1988	1,714.2	311.4	273.5	224.6	40.5	101.9	53.9	52.3	17.3	33.5	41.5	17.9	42.8
1989	1,926.4	354.3	334.0	247.1	46.8	111.3	66.2	55.0	20.9	40.2	45.6	22.5	46.7
1990	1,849.4	355.2	300.5	213.7	50.2	99.0	61.7	50.2	21.3	39.9	38.5	22.6	49.7
1991	1,964.3	364.8	330.7	240.1	57.9	101.5	77.0	57.4	34.6	46.3	35.8	27.1	49.7
1992	2,004.8	377.5	334.3	246.3	65.7	102.5	89.0	58.0	35.6	47.1	12.9	30.4	50.1
1993	2,312.3	430.2	383.9	291.1	77.5	119.7	112.7	71.3	44.3	60.9	37.5	39.0	53.3
1994	2,607.1	476.7	416.8	312.4	99.1	134.7	124.0	82.8	51.5	78.1	52.7	47.8	59.1
1995	2,707.8	573.3	431.9	316.4	111.3	144.5	129.2	97.3	60.8	86.6	58.9	54.6	62.2
1996	2,929.2	626.3	476.5	303.9	117.1	156.9	139.0	105.4	75.7	94.8	65.8	59.1	62.6
1997	3,515.1	721.1	589.2	348.0	158.9	187.0	162.1	123.2	97.5	105.7	74.9	66.6	67.2
1998	3,375.3	733.4	591.4	323.5	160.5	188.1	151.5	113.1	104.8	94.0	63.7	62.8	70.3
1999	3,779.5	760.2	632.0	367.2	180.3	222.5	159.8	128.8	128.2	102.8	68.1	76.0	75.4
2000	5,064.9	942.0	814.2	480.8	266.3	298.2	214.9	178.8	181.2	141.5	111.8	102.8	87.4
2001	5,004.1	985.3	795.9	423.5	292.2	291.1	207.2	161.5	176.7	129.0	91.9	94.8	91.7
2002	4,841.9	993.8	713.6	412.9	337.5	266.1	128.6	164.6	158.0	125.8	112.9	98.5	93.0

Variation (%)
Average annual variation over 10 years

	World (1)	EU (Extra EU)	USA	Japan	China	Canada	Hong Kong	South Korea	Mexico	Singapore	USSR / Russia (3)	Malaysia	Switzer-land (4)
1970/1960	9.5	7.8	7.7	17.0	:	11.1	14.3	38.7	5.5	23.5	:	:	10.5
1980/1970	16.9	15.0	13.8	17.3	:	11.2	18.9	30.9	23.8	24.5	:	18.6	15.2
1990/1980	6.4	5.2	6.5	8.5	14.4	7.3	15.8	14.8	6.6	11.1	:	9.2	8.8
2002/1992	9.2	10.1	7.8	5.3	17.7	10.0	3.7	11.0	16.0	10.3	24.2	12.4	6.3

Annual variation

	World (1)	EU (Extra EU)	USA	Japan	China	Canada	Hong Kong	South Korea	Mexico	Singapore	USSR / Russia (3)	Malaysia	Switzer-land (4)
1998/1997	-3.9	1.7	0.3	-7.0	0.9	0.5	-6.5	-8.1	7.4	-11.1	-14.9	-5.6	4.6
1999/1998	11.9	3.6	6.8	13.5	12.3	18.3	5.4	13.8	22.3	9.3	6.9	20.9	7.2
2000/1999	34.0	23.9	28.8	30.9	47.7	34.0	34.4	38.8	41.3	37.6	64.1	35.3	15.9
2001/2000	-1.2	4.5	-2.2	-11.9	9.7	-2.4	-3.6	-9.7	-2.4	-8.8	-17.8	-7.7	4.8
2002/2001	-3.2	0.8	-10.3	-2.4	15.4	-8.5	-37.9	1.9	-10.6	-2.4	22.8	3.8	1.4

Share (%)

	World (1)	EU (Extra EU)	USA	Japan	China	Canada	Hong Kong	South Korea	Mexico	Singapore	USSR / Russia (3)	Malaysia	Switzer-land (4)
1960	100.0	29.5	24.8	4.7	:	7.0	0.7	0.0	0.9	0.2	0.1	:	2.2
1970	100.0	25.2	20.9	9.1	:	8.1	1.2	0.4	0.6	0.7	:	0.8	2.5
1980	100.0	21.4	16.0	9.4	1.3	4.9	1.4	1.2	1.1	1.4	:	0.9	2.1
1990	100.0	19.2	16.2	11.5	2.7	5.3	3.3	2.7	1.1	2.1	2.0	1.2	2.6
1996	100.0	21.3	16.2	10.3	3.9	5.3	4.7	3.5	2.5	3.2	2.2	2.0	2.1
1997	100.0	20.5	16.7	9.8	4.5	5.3	4.6	3.5	2.7	3.0	2.1	1.8	1.9
1998	100.0	21.7	17.5	9.5	4.7	5.5	4.4	3.3	3.1	2.7	1.8	1.8	2.0
1999	100.0	20.1	16.7	9.7	4.7	5.8	4.2	3.4	3.3	2.7	1.8	2.0	1.9
2000	100.0	18.5	16.0	9.4	5.2	5.8	4.2	3.5	3.5	2.7	2.2	2.0	1.7
2001	100.0	19.6	15.9	8.4	5.8	5.8	4.1	3.2	3.5	2.5	1.8	1.8	1.8
2002	100.0	20.5	14.7	8.5	6.9	5.4	2.6	3.3	3.2	2.5	2.3	2.0	1.9

(1) Excluding intra EU.
(2) From 1958 to 1970 included, the convention is 1 ECU = 1 US$.
(3) Relates to the external trade of the USSR until 1991 and from 1992 to the external trade of Russia.
(4) Switzerland including Liechtenstein up to 1994.

EXPORTS

Australia	Thaïland	Brazil	India	Saudi Arabia	Indonesia	Norway	Poland	United Arab Emirates	Turkey	Czech Republic (5)	Philippines	Hungary	Year
				Main countries in 2002									Year

Value (Bn ECU/Euro)

Australia	Thaïland	Brazil	India	Saudi Arabia	Indonesia	Norway	Poland	United Arab Emirates	Turkey	Czech Republic (5)	Philippines	Hungary	Year
1.6	0.3	1.2	1.2	:	:	0.7	:	:	0.2	:	0.5	:	1958
2.0	0.3	1.3	1.3	:	0.6	0.9	0.0	:	0.3	0.0	0.5	0.2	1960
4.8	0.7	2.7	2.0	2.4	1.1	2.4	3.5	:	0.6	:	1.0	1.7	1970
11.3	3.2	9.9	5.2	29.7	9.3	8.5	11.1	7.2	1.8	:	2.7	5.0	1978
13.6	3.9	11.1	5.7	42.8	11.4	9.9	11.9	10.0	1.6	:	3.4	5.8	1979
15.8	4.7	14.5	6.1	73.3	15.7	13.3	12.2	15.5	2.1	10.7	4.2	6.2	1980
19.5	6.3	20.9	6.1	101.4	21.4	16.3	11.9	19.0	4.2	13.2	5.1	7.8	1981
22.5	7.1	20.6	8.4	77.4	22.8	17.9	11.4	17.2	5.9	12.0	5.1	9.0	1982
23.2	7.2	24.5	8.8	51.5	23.8	20.2	13.0	16.5	6.4	13.8	5.5	9.8	1983
30.3	9.4	34.2	10.4	47.6	27.7	24.0	14.9	18.0	9.0	14.2	6.8	10.9	1984
29.6	9.3	33.6	10.8	36.0	24.4	26.2	15.7	18.4	10.4	14.9	6.0	11.2	1985
22.9	9.0	22.8	9.3	20.5	15.1	18.8	12.3	12.6	7.6	13.3	4.9	9.3	1986
23.0	10.0	22.7	9.4	19.6	14.9	18.8	10.6	11.7	8.9	12.6	4.9	8.3	1987
28.1	13.5	28.4	11.1	19.2	16.4	19.0	11.5	11.0	9.9	12.4	6.0	8.4	1988
33.1	18.1	29.3	13.8	24.7	19.4	24.5	12.4	14.8	10.5	12.8	7.0	8.8	1989
29.6	17.8	24.4	14.0	33.4	19.4	26.5	10.6	16.8	10.2	9.1	6.3	7.5	1990
32.5	23.0	25.1	14.3	37.5	22.7	26.9	12.0	18.6	11.2	8.8	6.9	8.1	1991
31.4	24.6	28.1	14.7	37.9	25.3	26.8	10.1	17.3	11.2	8.5	7.4	8.3	1992
34.8	31.5	32.6	17.7	35.1	30.3	26.2	11.9	17.9	12.8	10.1	9.4	7.4	1993
38.2	37.9	36.3	20.2	34.8	32.4	28.7	14.3	17.9	15.2	12.0	10.9	8.9	1994
38.7	43.8	35.3	23.1	37.1	34.9	31.9	17.4	18.1	16.4	13.1	12.8	9.8	1995
45.4	43.4	37.4	25.2	46.7	38.1	38.5	19.1	21.5	18.2	17.4	16.4	10.4	1996
53.1	50.2	47.3	29.0	52.2	46.5	42.1	22.6	27.1	23.1	19.8	21.3	16.9	1997
47.6	47.9	45.4	29.8	33.8	42.3	36.1	25.2	22.7	24.1	23.5	24.8	20.4	1998
50.4	53.1	45.2	33.4	44.9	44.1	42.3	25.7	26.0	26.1	24.7	30.4	23.3	1999
65.6	72.4	60.7	45.9	79.8	65.0	63.0	34.3	43.2	30.1	31.4	38.5	30.5	2000
67.7	70.6	64.7	50.4	74.7	69.8	64.8	40.2	42.6	34.8	33.5	33.5	33.6	2001
66.1	70.7	65.8	52.2	69.2	67.6	64.1	38.6	39.2	37.1	35.7	38.9	35.5	2002

Variation (%)
Average annual variation over 10 years

Australia	Thaïland	Brazil	India	Saudi Arabia	Indonesia	Norway	Poland	United Arab Emirates	Turkey	Czech Republic (5)	Philippines	Hungary	Year
8.9	7.5	7.9	4.4	:	6.7	10.4	94.8	:	6.3	:	6.8	23.0	1970/1960
12.7	20.7	18.1	11.5	41.0	30.3	18.8	13.1	:	13.5	:	14.8	13.6	1980/1970
6.4	14.3	5.3	8.6	-7.5	2.1	7.0	-1.3	0.8	17.1	-1.5	4.2	1.8	1990/1980
7.7	11.1	8.8	13.5	6.2	10.3	9.1	14.3	8.4	12.7	15.3	18.0	15.6	2002/1992

Annual variation

Australia	Thaïland	Brazil	India	Saudi Arabia	Indonesia	Norway	Poland	United Arab Emirates	Turkey	Czech Republic (5)	Philippines	Hungary	Year
-10.3	-4.5	-4.0	2.8	-35.1	-8.8	-14.2	11.3	-16.1	3.9	18.7	16.3	21.1	1998/1997
5.8	10.8	-0.3	12.1	32.8	4.2	17.0	2.0	14.4	8.3	4.7	22.8	14.1	1999/1998
30.1	36.2	34.3	37.2	77.7	47.2	49.1	33.5	66.1	15.3	27.5	26.5	30.8	2000/1999
3.2	-2.4	6.4	9.8	-6.4	7.4	2.7	17.2	-1.4	15.5	6.4	-12.9	10.1	2001/2000
-2.3	0.2	1.7	3.6	-7.4	-3.1	-1.0	-4.1	-8.1	6.8	6.7	15.9	5.5	2002/2001

Share (%)

Australia	Thaïland	Brazil	India	Saudi Arabia	Indonesia	Norway	Poland	United Arab Emirates	Turkey	Czech Republic (5)	Philippines	Hungary	Year
2.4	0.4	1.5	1.5	:	0.7	1.0	0.0	:	0.3	0.0	0.6	0.2	1960
2.3	0.3	1.3	0.9	1.1	0.5	1.1	1.7	:	0.2	:	0.5	0.8	1970
1.6	0.4	1.4	0.6	7.4	1.5	1.3	1.2	1.5	0.2	1.0	0.4	0.6	1980
1.5	0.9	1.3	0.7	1.8	1.0	1.4	0.5	0.9	0.5	0.4	0.3	0.4	1990
1.5	1.4	1.2	0.8	1.5	1.2	1.3	0.6	0.7	0.6	0.5	0.5	0.3	1996
1.5	1.4	1.3	0.8	1.4	1.3	1.1	0.6	0.7	0.6	0.5	0.6	0.4	1997
1.4	1.4	1.3	0.8	1.0	1.2	1.0	0.7	0.6	0.7	0.6	0.7	0.6	1998
1.3	1.4	1.1	0.8	1.1	1.1	1.1	0.6	0.6	0.6	0.6	0.8	0.6	1999
1.2	1.4	1.1	0.9	1.5	1.2	1.2	0.6	0.8	0.5	0.6	0.7	0.6	2000
1.3	1.4	1.2	1.0	1.4	1.3	1.2	0.8	0.8	0.6	0.6	0.6	0.6	2001
1.3	1.4	1.3	1.0	1.4	1.3	1.3	0.7	0.8	0.7	0.7	0.8	0.7	2002

(5) Czechoslovakia before 1993.

TRENDS IN WORLD TRADE

IMPORTS

Year	World (1)	EU (Extra EU)	USA	Japan	China	Canada	Hong Kong	South Korea	Mexico	Singapore	USSR / Russia (3)	Malaysia	Switzer- land (4)
								Main countries in 2002					

Value (Bn ECU/Euro)(2)

Year	World (1)	EU (Extra EU)	USA	Japan	China	Canada	Hong Kong	South Korea	Mexico	Singapore	USSR / Russia (3)	Malaysia	Switzer- land (4)
1958	74.7	23.1	14.5	2.8	:	5.4	0.5	0.4	1.0	:	:	:	1.7
1960	90.1	28.2	16.2	4.2	:	5.9	1.0	0.3	1.1	0.4	0.2	:	2.2
1970	221.7	60.1	42.7	18.8	:	13.8	2.9	2.0	2.1	2.5	:	1.4	6.5
1978	738.7	181.4	146.0	62.7	8.6	35.3	10.5	11.8	5.4	10.2	:	4.7	18.7
1979	847.6	222.0	162.2	80.1	11.4	40.4	12.5	14.7	8.0	12.9	:	5.7	19.3
1980	1,046.2	281.1	184.6	101.5	14.0	43.8	16.1	15.8	12.7	17.2	:	7.8	26.1
1981	1,442.1	328.4	244.8	128.0	19.4	60.9	22.2	23.4	19.6	24.7	42.3	10.4	27.5
1982	1,513.2	346.7	260.2	134.3	19.3	57.9	23.9	24.8	14.0	28.8	45.9	12.7	29.3
1983	1,604.7	351.9	303.2	142.1	23.9	71.0	27.0	29.4	9.2	31.6	49.1	14.9	32.8
1984	1,950.5	403.5	432.4	172.5	32.9	96.2	36.2	38.8	13.1	36.3	58.8	17.8	37.4
1985	2,049.7	421.4	473.9	171.0	55.7	103.1	38.9	40.7	17.6	34.4	71.5	16.1	40.2
1986	1,627.9	321.9	393.5	129.8	44.0	84.7	35.9	32.3	11.7	25.9	53.2	11.0	41.7
1987	1,587.0	326.0	367.3	130.7	37.4	78.3	42.0	35.5	11.1	28.3	47.0	11.0	43.9
1988	1,813.4	339.9	390.5	158.8	48.4	102.7	54.3	46.2	18.3	37.2	52.4	14.1	47.8
1989	2,037.2	393.5	448.3	189.1	53.2	119.6	64.6	55.8	22.8	44.4	61.1	20.0	52.8
1990	1,943.7	404.4	387.7	177.7	40.9	101.5	58.8	53.7	25.9	45.8	49.9	21.6	54.5
1991	2,055.9	434.7	392.8	183.4	48.9	105.6	73.6	67.3	44.2	51.4	39.0	28.2	53.0
1992	2,088.2	428.5	406.7	172.6	58.9	104.4	86.6	63.1	52.3	53.2	12.3	29.1	50.4
1993	2,392.1	431.7	492.7	198.3	78.2	125.1	108.2	72.8	60.8	69.8	22.6	37.0	51.6
1994	2,681.6	474.3	555.6	221.4	85.1	138.3	124.1	84.4	72.2	82.9	32.3	47.4	57.2
1995	2,783.8	545.3	566.2	245.8	89.5	135.6	134.4	101.2	60.3	91.1	35.4	56.3	61.1
1996	3,027.0	581.0	620.0	263.7	96.9	145.6	143.9	116.2	76.8	99.3	35.0	58.7	61.6
1997	3,608.5	672.6	764.2	287.8	111.3	187.4	170.1	125.5	105.7	112.2	46.3	66.4	67.0
1998	3,518.1	710.5	812.5	241.9	110.1	193.1	153.0	81.3	121.4	87.4	38.6	49.5	71.4
1999	3,970.5	779.8	952.0	280.3	138.0	218.2	156.9	109.5	145.4	100.4	28.5	58.4	75.0
2000	5,364.5	1,033.4	1,303.0	393.6	217.7	281.5	215.0	169.3	206.7	140.2	36.8	84.5	89.6
2001	5,363.2	1,028.0	1,278.9	373.9	241.4	268.5	209.4	152.7	203.1	124.0	41.0	77.2	93.9
2002	5,289.9	987.5	1,235.9	342.2	273.1	255.0	195.2	155.7	159.5	117.5	47.9	81.9	88.7

Variation (%)
Average annual variation over 10 years

Year	World (1)	EU (Extra EU)	USA	Japan	China	Canada	Hong Kong	South Korea	Mexico	Singapore	USSR / Russia (3)	Malaysia	Switzer- land (4)
1970/1960	9.4	7.8	10.1	16.2	:	8.9	10.8	21.6	7.0	18.7	:	:	11.2
1980/1970	16.7	16.6	15.7	18.3	:	12.2	18.7	23.0	19.6	21.5	:	18.7	14.9
1990/1980	6.3	3.7	7.7	5.7	11.3	8.7	13.8	12.9	7.3	10.2	:	10.7	7.6
2002/1992	9.7	8.7	11.7	7.0	16.5	9.3	8.4	9.4	11.7	8.2	14.5	10.9	5.8

Annual variation

Year	World (1)	EU (Extra EU)	USA	Japan	China	Canada	Hong Kong	South Korea	Mexico	Singapore	USSR / Russia (3)	Malaysia	Switzer- land (4)
1998/1997	-2.5	5.6	6.3	-15.9	-1.0	3.0	-10.0	-35.1	14.8	-22.1	-16.5	-25.5	6.6
1999/1998	12.8	9.7	17.1	15.8	25.2	13.0	2.5	34.6	19.7	14.9	-26.3	18.0	5.0
2000/1999	35.1	32.5	36.8	40.4	57.7	29.0	37.0	54.5	42.1	39.5	29.3	44.6	19.4
2001/2000	0.0	-0.5	-1.8	-4.9	10.9	-4.6	-2.6	-9.7	-1.7	-11.5	11.4	-8.5	4.8
2002/2001	-1.3	-3.9	-3.3	-8.4	13.1	-5.0	-6.8	1.9	-21.4	-5.2	16.8	6.0	-5.5

Share (%)

Year	World (1)	EU (Extra EU)	USA	Japan	China	Canada	Hong Kong	South Korea	Mexico	Singapore	USSR / Russia (3)	Malaysia	Switzer- land (4)
1960	100.0	31.3	17.9	4.6	:	6.5	1.1	0.3	1.1	0.4	0.1	:	2.4
1970	100.0	27.1	19.2	8.4	:	6.2	1.3	0.8	0.9	1.1	:	0.6	2.9
1980	100.0	26.8	17.6	9.6	1.3	4.1	1.5	1.5	1.2	1.6	:	0.7	2.4
1990	100.0	20.8	19.9	9.1	2.1	5.2	3.0	2.7	1.3	2.3	2.5	1.1	2.8
1996	100.0	19.1	20.4	8.7	3.1	4.8	4.7	3.8	2.5	3.2	1.1	1.9	2.0
1997	100.0	18.6	21.1	7.9	3.0	5.1	4.7	3.4	2.9	3.1	1.2	1.8	1.8
1998	100.0	20.1	23.0	6.8	3.1	5.4	4.3	2.3	3.4	2.4	1.0	1.4	2.0
1999	100.0	19.6	23.9	7.0	3.4	5.4	3.9	2.7	3.6	2.5	0.7	1.4	1.8
2000	100.0	19.2	24.2	7.3	4.0	5.2	4.0	3.1	3.8	2.6	0.6	1.5	1.6
2001	100.0	19.1	23.8	6.9	4.5	5.0	3.9	2.8	3.7	2.3	0.7	1.4	1.7
2002	100.0	18.6	23.3	6.4	5.1	4.8	3.6	2.9	3.0	2.2	0.9	1.5	1.6

(1) Excluding intra EU.
(2) From 1958 to 1970 included, the convention is 1 ECU = 1 US$.
(3) Relates to the external trade of the USSR until 1991 and from 1992 to the external trade of Russia.
(4) Switzerland including Liechtenstein up to 1994.

IMPORTS

Australia	Thaïland	Brazil	India	Saudi Arabia	Indonesia	Norway	Poland	United Arab Emirates	Turkey	Czech Republic (5)	Philippines	Hungary	Year
					Main countries in 2002								Year

Value (Bn ECU/Euro)

Australia	Thaïland	Brazil	India	Saudi Arabia	Indonesia	Norway	Poland	United Arab Emirates	Turkey	Czech Republic (5)	Philippines	Hungary	Year
1.7	0.4	1.0	1.8	:	:	1.3	:	:	0.3	:	0.6	:	1958
2.3	0.4	1.4	2.2	:	0.6	1.5	0.0	:	0.5	0.0	0.7	0.3	1960
4.5	1.3	2.8	2.1	0.7	1.0	3.7	4.0	0.3	0.9	:	1.2	2.4	1970
11.1	4.2	11.8	6.1	16.0	5.3	9.0	13.9	4.2	3.6	:	4.0	6.2	1978
12.1	5.2	14.4	7.2	17.7	5.3	10.0	14.1	5.1	3.7	:	4.8	6.3	1979
14.6	6.6	17.9	10.6	21.7	7.8	12.2	15.1	6.2	5.5	12.0	6.0	6.6	1980
21.3	8.9	21.6	13.0	31.6	11.9	14.0	15.2	8.4	8.0	14.4	7.6	8.2	1981
24.6	8.7	21.5	16.0	41.5	17.2	15.8	11.5	9.6	9.0	12.8	8.4	9.0	1982
21.8	11.6	18.9	15.6	44.0	18.4	15.1	13.1	9.4	10.3	14.5	8.8	9.6	1983
29.7	13.2	19.3	19.2	42.7	17.6	17.6	14.9	8.9	13.5	15.1	7.9	10.3	1984
30.8	12.1	18.8	21.4	31.0	13.5	20.4	16.5	8.5	14.8	16.1	7.0	10.8	1985
24.2	9.3	15.8	15.3	19.4	10.9	20.6	12.5	6.5	11.2	14.9	5.3	9.8	1986
23.4	11.3	14.4	14.6	17.4	11.1	19.6	10.3	6.0	12.7	14.1	6.0	8.5	1987
31.2	17.3	15.0	16.0	17.8	11.5	19.4	11.7	7.2	12.4	13.5	7.4	7.9	1988
40.2	22.0	20.0	17.2	18.6	14.0	21.1	10.5	8.7	15.1	14.1	9.9	8.1	1989
32.7	24.8	19.2	18.5	18.5	16.0	20.9	7.0	9.1	17.8	11.8	9.6	7.0	1990
33.2	29.3	20.4	15.6	23.1	19.9	19.7	13.7	11.2	17.4	9.1	9.6	9.0	1991
33.3	29.7	17.4	17.7	25.3	20.1	19.7	11.7	13.5	17.6	8.2	10.5	8.6	1992
38.5	37.8	26.3	18.3	23.7	23.1	19.2	15.9	16.7	24.9	11.9	14.2	10.6	1993
44.5	44.0	30.0	21.2	19.4	25.8	22.5	17.9	17.2	19.5	13.7	17.9	12.0	1994
46.7	56.2	40.9	26.1	20.7	31.4	25.0	22.0	15.6	27.0	17.4	20.4	11.7	1995
51.6	56.7	45.8	28.1	21.6	32.5	27.0	29.0	17.3	33.1	24.0	26.2	12.7	1996
58.1	53.4	59.5	34.0	24.8	36.0	31.2	37.0	19.6	42.6	26.0	32.9	18.6	1997
57.9	37.1	55.8	37.3	26.4	23.5	32.6	41.6	21.5	40.6	28.1	26.8	22.7	1998
65.7	45.2	51.0	44.7	26.0	21.9	31.7	42.7	32.9	38.7	29.1	29.4	25.9	1999
78.2	64.3	66.5	54.1	32.7	35.0	36.6	52.7	43.5	58.8	37.9	32.0	34.6	2000
72.7	66.4	67.4	62.1	46.7	41.5	36.3	55.6	48.8	45.9	42.2	31.2	36.8	2001
78.8	65.4	60.8	65.4	48.9	40.6	36.8	57.4	51.2	52.1	43.9	43.2	38.5	2002

Variation (%)
Average annual variation over 10 years

Australia	Thaïland	Brazil	India	Saudi Arabia	Indonesia	Norway	Poland	United Arab Emirates	Turkey	Czech Republic (5)	Philippines	Hungary	Year
7.0	11.5	7.0	-0.7	:	5.0	9.7	97.9	:	6.6	:	6.2	24.9	1970/1960
12.4	17.6	20.1	17.6	40.7	22.6	12.6	14.2	36.6	20.0	:	17.3	10.5	1980/1970
8.3	14.1	0.6	5.6	-1.5	7.5	5.5	-7.4	3.9	12.4	-0.1	4.8	0.5	1990/1980
9.0	8.2	13.3	13.9	6.8	7.2	6.4	17.2	14.2	11.4	18.2	15.1	16.1	2002/1992

Annual variation

Australia	Thaïland	Brazil	India	Saudi Arabia	Indonesia	Norway	Poland	United Arab Emirates	Turkey	Czech Republic (5)	Philippines	Hungary	Year
-0.4	-30.5	-6.0	9.7	6.5	-34.5	4.4	12.3	9.4	-4.6	8.0	-18.7	21.9	1998/1997
13.4	21.8	-8.6	19.6	-1.4	-7.0	-2.7	2.7	53.3	-4.6	3.4	10.0	14.2	1999/1998
19.1	42.2	30.3	21.0	25.4	60.3	15.4	23.2	32.3	51.9	30.1	8.8	33.2	2000/1999
-7.0	3.2	1.2	14.7	42.9	18.5	-1.0	5.6	11.9	-22.0	11.5	-2.5	6.6	2001/2000
8.3	-1.5	-9.6	5.2	4.8	-2.2	1.3	3.1	4.8	13.6	4.0	38.3	4.6	2002/2001

Share (%)

Australia	Thaïland	Brazil	India	Saudi Arabia	Indonesia	Norway	Poland	United Arab Emirates	Turkey	Czech Republic (5)	Philippines	Hungary	Year
2.5	0.4	1.6	2.4	:	0.6	1.6	0.0	:	0.5	0.0	0.7	0.2	1960
2.0	0.5	1.2	0.9	0.3	0.4	1.6	1.7	0.1	0.4	:	0.5	1.0	1970
1.3	0.6	1.7	1.0	2.0	0.7	1.1	1.4	0.5	0.5	1.1	0.5	0.6	1980
1.6	1.2	0.9	0.9	0.9	0.8	1.0	0.3	0.4	0.9	0.6	0.4	0.3	1990
1.7	1.8	1.5	0.9	0.7	1.0	0.8	0.9	0.5	1.0	0.7	0.8	0.4	1996
1.6	1.4	1.6	0.9	0.6	0.9	0.8	1.0	0.5	1.1	0.7	0.9	0.5	1997
1.6	1.0	1.5	1.0	0.7	0.6	0.9	1.1	0.6	1.1	0.7	0.7	0.6	1998
1.6	1.1	1.2	1.1	0.6	0.5	0.7	1.0	0.8	0.9	0.7	0.7	0.6	1999
1.4	1.1	1.2	1.0	0.6	0.6	0.6	0.9	0.8	1.0	0.7	0.5	0.6	2000
1.3	1.2	1.2	1.1	0.8	0.7	0.6	1.0	0.9	0.8	0.7	0.5	0.6	2001
1.4	1.2	1.1	1.2	0.9	0.7	0.6	1.0	0.9	0.9	0.8	0.8	0.7	2002

(5) Czechoslovakia before 1993.

TRENDS IN WORLD TRADE

TRADE BALANCE

Year	Main countries in 2002											
	EU (Extra EU)	USA	Japan	China	Canada	Hong Kong	South Korea	Mexico	Singapore	USSR / Russia (3)	Malaysia	Switzer- land (4)
Value (Bn ECU/Euro)(2)												
1958	-2.4	3.3	-0.1	:	-0.2	-0.4	-0.4	-0.3	:	:	:	-0.2
1960	**-3.8**	**4.4**	**-0.3**	**:**	**-0.1**	**-0.4**	**-0.2**	**-0.3**	**-0.3**	**-0.0**	**:**	**-0.3**
1970	**-8.1**	**0.5**	**0.2**	**:**	**2.9**	**-0.4**	**-1.1**	**-0.8**	**-0.9**	**:**	**0.3**	**-1.3**
1978	-14.2	-33.2	14.5	-0.9	2.7	-1.5	-1.9	-0.7	-2.3	:	1.2	-0.2
1979	-38.0	-29.4	-5.5	-1.5	2.2	-1.4	-3.8	-1.5	-2.5	:	2.4	2.4
1980	**-69.0**	**-26.0**	**-7.8**	**-1.0**	**4.8**	**-1.9**	**-3.3**	**-1.5**	**-3.3**	**:**	**1.5**	**-4.8**
1981	-50.9	-35.5	7.7	-0.1	4.2	-2.6	-4.4	-2.3	-5.9	-7.6	0.2	-3.3
1982	-49.4	-43.5	7.0	3.0	14.8	-2.6	-2.5	7.7	-7.5	-8.1	-0.4	-2.7
1983	-38.9	-77.9	23.0	0.9	15.3	-2.3	-2.0	15.9	-7.1	-8.0	1.0	-4.1
1984	-38.4	-156.2	42.6	-1.4	18.2	-0.3	-1.7	17.8	-5.8	-7.1	3.2	-4.6
1985	-27.4	-194.6	61.2	-19.9	15.9	0.6	-1.0	11.4	-4.5	-13.2	4.1	-4.3
1986	11.2	-172.6	84.4	-12.1	6.5	0.1	3.1	4.7	-3.1	-9.1	3.2	-3.7
1987	1.0	-148.3	69.7	-3.3	6.6	0.0	5.4	6.7	-3.4	-6.1	4.5	-4.5
1988	-28.5	-116.9	65.9	-7.8	-0.8	-0.4	6.0	-1.0	-3.8	-11.0	3.8	-5.0
1989	-39.2	-114.3	58.0	-6.4	-8.3	1.6	-0.8	-1.8	-4.2	-15.5	2.5	-6.1
1990	**-49.2**	**-87.2**	**36.0**	**9.3**	**-2.5**	**2.9**	**-3.5**	**-4.6**	**-5.9**	**-11.4**	**1.0**	**-4.8**
1991	-69.9	-62.0	56.6	9.0	-4.2	3.4	-9.8	-9.6	-5.1	-3.2	-1.1	-3.3
1992	-51.1	-72.4	73.6	6.7	-1.8	2.4	-5.2	-16.7	-6.2	0.6	1.3	-0.3
1993	-1.4	-108.8	92.8	-0.7	-5.4	4.5	-1.5	-16.5	-8.9	14.8	2.0	1.7
1994	2.4	-138.8	91.0	14.0	-3.6	-0.1	-1.6	-20.7	-4.8	20.4	0.4	1.9
1995	28.0	-134.3	70.6	21.8	8.9	-5.2	-3.9	0.5	-4.5	23.6	-1.7	1.0
1996	45.3	-143.6	40.1	20.2	11.4	-4.9	-10.8	-1.1	-4.5	30.8	0.4	1.0
1997	48.6	-174.9	60.2	47.7	-0.4	-8.0	-2.2	-8.2	-6.4	28.6	0.2	0.2
1998	22.9	-221.1	81.6	50.3	-5.1	-1.5	31.8	-16.6	6.6	25.1	13.4	-1.1
1999	-19.6	-320.0	87.0	42.3	4.3	2.9	19.2	-17.2	2.4	39.6	17.6	0.4
2000	**-91.4**	**-488.7**	**87.2**	**48.6**	**16.7**	**-0.1**	**9.5**	**-25.6**	**1.4**	**75.0**	**18.4**	**-2.2**
2001	-42.6	-482.9	49.5	50.8	22.5	-2.3	8.7	-26.4	5.0	50.9	17.6	-2.2
2002	**6.3**	**-522.4**	**70.7**	**64.3**	**11.1**	**-66.6**	**8.9**	**-1.5**	**8.3**	**65.0**	**16.6**	**4.3**

(2) From 1958 to 1970 included, the convention is 1 ECU = 1 US$.

(3) Relates to the external trade of the USSR until 1991 and from 1992 to the external trade of Russia.

(4) Switzerland including Liechtenstein up to 1994.

TRADE BALANCE

Australia	Thaïland	Brazil	India	Saudi Arabia	Indonesia	Norway	Poland	United Arab Emirates	Turkey	Czech Republic (5)	Philippines	Hungary	Year
						Main countries in 2002							Year

Value (Bn ECU/Euro)

Australia	Thaïland	Brazil	India	Saudi Arabia	Indonesia	Norway	Poland	United Arab Emirates	Turkey	Czech Republic (5)	Philippines	Hungary	Year
-0.1	-0.1	0.2	-0.6	:	:	-0.6	:	:	-0.1	:	-0.1	:	1958
-0.3	-0.1	-0.2	-0.9	:	-0.0	-0.6	0.0	:	-0.1	0.0	-0.1	-0.0	**1960**
0.2	-0.6	-0.1	-0.1	1.6	0.1	-1.3	-0.4	:	-0.3	:	-0.2	-0.7	**1970**
0.2	-1.0	-1.9	-0.9	13.7	4.0	-0.5	-2.8	2.9	-1.8	:	-1.3	-1.2	1978
1.5	-1.4	-3.3	-1.6	25.1	6.1	-0.1	-2.2	4.9	-2.0	:	-1.5	-0.6	1979
1.2	-1.9	-3.5	-4.6	51.6	8.0	1.2	-2.9	9.4	-3.4	-1.3	-1.8	-0.4	**1980**
-1.8	-2.6	-0.7	-6.9	69.9	9.5	2.3	-3.4	10.6	-3.8	-1.2	-2.5	-0.4	1981
-2.0	-1.6	-0.9	-7.5	35.9	5.6	2.1	-0.0	7.6	-3.1	-0.8	-3.3	-0.0	1982
1.4	-4.4	5.7	-6.8	7.5	5.4	5.1	-0.1	7.1	-3.9	-0.7	-3.3	0.2	1983
0.6	-3.8	15.0	-8.7	4.8	10.2	6.4	0.0	9.1	-4.5	-0.9	-1.2	0.6	1984
-1.2	-2.8	14.8	-10.6	5.1	10.9	5.9	-0.8	9.9	-4.3	-1.2	-1.0	0.4	1985
-1.3	-0.3	7.0	-6.0	1.1	4.2	-1.9	-0.3	6.0	-3.6	-1.7	-0.4	-0.4	1986
-0.4	-1.2	8.4	-5.2	2.2	3.7	-0.8	0.2	5.7	-3.8	-1.5	-1.1	-0.3	1987
-3.1	-3.8	13.4	-4.9	1.4	4.9	-0.5	-0.2	3.8	-2.5	-1.2	-1.4	0.5	1988
-7.1	-3.8	9.3	-3.4	6.1	5.4	3.4	1.9	6.1	-4.5	-1.3	-3.0	0.7	1989
-3.1	-7.0	5.2	-4.5	14.8	3.4	5.6	3.7	7.8	-7.6	-2.6	-3.3	0.5	**1990**
-0.7	-6.3	4.7	-1.3	14.4	2.8	7.2	-1.7	7.4	-6.2	-0.2	-2.7	-0.9	1991
-1.9	-5.1	10.7	-3.0	12.6	5.1	7.1	-1.6	3.8	-6.4	0.4	-3.1	-0.3	1992
-3.7	-6.3	6.3	-0.6	11.4	7.1	7.0	-4.0	1.2	-12.1	-1.8	-4.9	-3.2	1993
-6.3	-6.1	6.3	-1.1	15.5	6.6	6.2	-3.6	0.7	-4.3	-1.8	-7.0	-3.2	1994
-8.1	-12.3	-5.6	-3.0	16.5	3.5	6.9	-4.6	2.5	-10.6	-4.3	-7.6	-1.9	1995
-6.2	-13.3	-8.5	-2.9	25.1	5.5	11.5	-9.8	4.2	-14.9	-6.6	-9.8	-2.4	1996
-5.0	-3.2	-12.2	-5.0	27.4	10.5	10.8	-14.4	7.5	-19.4	-6.2	-11.6	-1.8	1997
-10.2	10.9	-10.5	-7.5	7.4	18.8	3.5	-16.4	1.3	-16.6	-4.6	-2.0	-2.3	1998
-15.2	7.9	-5.8	-11.3	18.9	22.3	10.5	-17.0	-6.9	-12.6	-4.4	1.0	-2.6	1999
-12.6	8.1	-5.8	-8.2	47.2	29.9	26.4	-18.3	-0.3	-28.7	-6.4	6.5	-4.0	**2000**
-5.0	4.2	-2.7	-11.7	28.1	28.3	28.5	-15.4	-6.1	-11.1	-8.8	2.3	-3.2	2001
-12.7	5.4	4.9	-13.1	20.2	27.0	27.4	-18.8	-12.0	-15.0	-8.2	-4.3	-3.0	**2002**

(5) Czechoslovakia before 1993.

SHARE OF TRADE WITH THE EUROPEAN UNION, THE UNITED STATES AND JAPAN

EXPORTS

Value (Mio ECU/Euro)[1]

Year	World excluding intra EU	EU (extra EU)	USA	Japan	Switzerland [2]	China	Norway	USSR / Russia [3]	Hungary	Poland	Czech Republic [4]	South Korea	Hong Kong
						Main countries in 2002							

Exports to EU

Year	World excluding intra EU	EU (extra EU)	USA	Japan	Switzerland [2]	China	Norway	USSR / Russia [3]	Hungary	Poland	Czech Republic [4]	South Korea	Hong Kong
1960	44,080	:	6,478	420	1,118	:	629	:	126	:	5	5	148
1970	123,830	:	13,083	2,507	3,107	:	1,925	:	340	736	73	73	593
1980	542,824	:	44,239	14,225	12,976	1,791	11,134	:	1,654	3,353	2,106	2,106	3,498
1990	1,150,283	:	81,267	46,097	32,142	4,928	21,228	18,532	3,416	5,864	7,874	7,874	11,961
1997	1,717,433	:	124,775	58,077	40,172	21,130	32,064	24,716	12,017	14,590	14,930	14,930	24,469
1998	1,813,428	:	133,824	63,956	43,869	25,109	27,883	20,599	14,940	17,214	15,388	15,388	24,445
1999	2,013,052	:	142,549	70,034	44,525	28,526	30,150	22,659	17,813	18,163	18,271	18,271	26,355
2000	2,450,133	:	179,078	85,052	49,604	41,610	46,192	40,137	22,981	24,065	25,533	25,533	33,609
2001	2,474,454	:	177,987	72,028	53,099	45,797	47,512	35,703	25,049	27,907	21,978	21,978	30,655
2002	2,416,213	:	152,346	64,815	52,900	51,000	46,419	39,574	26,151	25,994	22,976	22,976	21,344

Exports to the United States

Year	World excluding intra EU	EU (extra EU)	USA	Japan	Switzerland [2]	China	Norway	USSR / Russia [3]	Hungary	Poland	Czech Republic [4]	South Korea	Hong Kong
1960	13,810	3,742	:	1,108	189	:	61	:	2	:	4	4	134
1970	38,580	10,408	:	6,027	462	:	141	:	26	93	395	395	897
1980	162,864	29,543	:	22,918	1,542	706	397	:	81	305	3,321	3,321	3,704
1990	368,763	76,495	:	71,533	4,014	4,153	1,752	828	264	296	15,271	15,271	15,528
1997	737,246	141,373	:	104,526	7,035	29,015	2,636	4,370	546	599	19,315	19,315	36,265
1998	779,685	161,545	:	106,838	7,716	33,833	2,231	5,355	929	685	20,591	20,591	36,312
1999	923,021	183,016	:	122,415	9,327	39,614	3,403	6,062	1,224	714	27,885	27,885	39,082
2000	1,249,601	232,470	:	156,509	11,435	56,913	5,037	8,687	1,610	1,092	41,239	41,239	51,392
2001	1,203,559	239,904	:	137,000	10,646	60,734	5,191	6,637	1,669	953	35,012	35,012	47,356
2002	1,136,134	239,938	:	127,090	11,104	74,081	5,531	6,891	1,736	1,126	34,832	34,832	25,519

Exports to Japan

Year	World excluding intra EU	EU (extra EU)	USA	Japan	Switzerland [2]	China	Norway	USSR / Russia [3]	Hungary	Poland	Czech Republic [4]	South Korea	Hong Kong
1960	3,220	329	1,451	:	30	:	2	:	0.0	:	20	20	40
1970	13,290	1,512	4,653	:	163	:	19	:	3	30	236	236	178
1980	81,489	5,232	14,932	:	547	2,896	106	:	9	57	2,183	2,183	653
1990	156,562	22,727	38,201	:	2,390	7,166	442	2,395	86	87	9,890	9,890	3,659
1997	258,009	36,097	57,947	:	2,711	28,168	850	2,599	90	52	13,037	13,037	10,075
1998	215,616	31,567	51,752	:	2,707	26,476	821	1,935	84	41	10,940	10,940	8,149
1999	248,595	35,374	54,207	:	3,033	30,561	1,108	1,986	73	41	14,959	14,959	8,850
2000	352,509	44,936	70,213	:	3,710	45,482	1,071	3,018	175	67	22,267	22,267	12,207
2001	339,256	44,920	64,356	:	3,564	50,331	987	2,722	189	73	18,429	18,429	12,561
2002	308,762	42,279	54,389	:	3,530	51,263	1,039	1,892	242	79	16,011	16,011	6,030

Recapitulation of exports to the European Community with 6, 9, 10 and 12 Member States

Year	World excluding intra EU	EU (extra EU)	USA	Japan	Switzerland [2]	China	Norway	USSR / Russia [3]	Hungary	Poland	Czech Republic [4]	South Korea	Hong Kong
1960 EU-6	25,340	:	3,987	174	775	:	227	:	74	:	3	3	34
1970 EU-6	81,830	:	8,423	1,303	1,924	:	729	:	250	432	52	52	259
1973 EU-6	123,631	:	10,248	2,315	2,786	:	814	:	423	862	209	209	482
1973 EU-9	158,639	:	13,601	3,581	3,535	:	1,803	:	466	1,123	270	270	970
1980 EU-9	463,604	:	38,561	12,022	10,704	1,657	9,470	:	1,209	2,653	1,826	1,826	3,152
1981 EU-9	542,532	:	46,297	16,106	11,628	2,161	11,426	11,785	1,281	2,205	2,360	2,360	3,588
1981 EU-10	554,964	:	46,902	16,870	11,799	2,174	11,515	12,053	1,333	2,247	2,417	2,417	3,616
1986 EU-10	716,755	:	50,730	30,071	20,018	3,996	12,102	11,903	1,596	2,567	4,200	4,200	5,050
1986 EU-12	759,808	:	54,037	31,640	20,881	4,083	12,269	12,228	1,613	2,615	4,388	4,388	5,243
1990 EU-12	1,055,545	:	77,025	42,467	29,090	4,708	17,302	15,356	2,670	5,003	6,964	6,964	10,987
1995 EU-12	1,343,213	:	89,658	50,526	34,229	14,156	20,471	16,929	5,040	11,174	11,303	11,303	18,390

(1) From 1958 to 1970 included, the convention is 1 ECU = 1 US$.
(2) Including Liechtenstein before 1995.
(3) Relates to the external trade of the USSR until 1991 and from 1992 to the external trade of Russia.
(4) Czechoslovakia before 1993.

SHARE OF TRADE WITH THE EUROPEAN UNION, THE UNITED STATES AND JAPAN

EXPORTS

Value (Mio ECU/Euro)

Turkey	Singapore	South Africa (5)	Brazil	Algeria	Malaysia	India	Saudi Arabia	Canada	Thailand	Indonesia	Romania	Slovakia	Year
Exports to EU													
166	72	603	423	367	:	492	:	1,458	57	142	137	:	1960
308	275	1,094	1,194	811	352	396	1,049	2,768	138	168	538	:	1970
989	1,839	3,572	4,651	4,960	1,670	1,436	30,118	6,332	1,240	1,036	2,399	:	1980
5,652	6,231	4,887	8,025	6,026	3,552	3,876	6,386	8,261	4,105	2,430	1,540	:	1990
10,814	15,401	8,493	12,866	7,673	10,015	7,368	10,260	9,321	8,115	7,796	4,199	4,006	1997
12,231	15,522	7,918	13,212	5,728	10,581	8,070	6,512	9,207	8,640	7,129	4,793	5,316	1998
13,491	16,375	9,184	13,042	7,678	12,507	8,709	7,712	9,814	9,258	6,661	5,245	5,705	1999
15,745	19,911	11,621	16,311	14,979	14,608	11,026	14,429	13,335	11,816	9,439	7,212	7,619	2000
17,997	18,174	12,977	16,628	14,473	13,379	11,948	11,929	12,771	11,729	9,996	8,638	8,451	2001
20,050	16,574	15,896	15,162	12,946	12,536	11,955	11,189	11,144	10,792	9,511	9,376	8,633	2002
Exports to the United States													
58	19	83	564	1	:	214	:	3,110	57	216	1	:	1960
56	172	181	676	8	219	274	21	10,438	96	144	13	:	1970
91	1,741	1,527	2,521	5,394	1,522	695	11,345	29,496	591	3,091	335	:	1980
757	8,812	1,450	6,099	1,670	3,925	2,126	8,251	75,097	4,111	2,645	270	:	1990
1,781	20,447	1,527	8,308	1,930	12,878	5,682	8,168	156,454	9,870	6,327	276	139	1997
2,003	19,531	1,718	8,842	1,389	14,162	6,349	5,674	163,153	10,866	6,285	286	115	1998
2,294	20,769	1,860	10,241	1,686	17,452	7,607	7,500	195,535	11,929	6,491	299	140	1999
3,414	26,061	2,721	14,562	2,765	21,962	9,866	14,185	261,556	16,011	9,248	413	184	2000
3,490	20,941	2,742	16,055	2,949	19,892	10,445	14,631	255,676	14,789	11,071	399	181	2001
3,614	20,201	4,150	16,073	2,461	21,496	11,967	13,353	233,980	14,297	9,983	716	260	2002
Exports to Japan													
1	12	43	31	0.0	:	71	:	182	73	64	:	:	1960
17	118	253	145	3	309	281	499	777	181	452	6	:	1970
27	1,120	1,114	885	348	2,124	557	12,788	2,694	705	7,752	81	:	1980
184	3,603	1,308	1,835	79	3,525	1,304	6,518	5,623	3,111	8,522	74	:	1990
127	7,805	1,429	2,716	68	8,793	1,641	9,249	6,381	7,703	11,007	33	11	1997
100	6,454	1,179	1,972	53	6,884	1,532	5,179	4,280	6,676	8,145	21	11	1998
115	8,024	1,127	2,066	61	9,263	1,571	7,199	4,949	7,767	9,797	18	13	1999
162	11,340	1,488	2,682	42	13,921	1,919	14,053	6,450	11,041	15,691	17	13	2000
139	10,430	1,442	2,218	63	13,141	2,245	12,501	5,809	11,125	15,107	20	13	2001
159	9,447	2,822	2,564	39	11,114	2,009	11,187	5,448	10,574	13,625	49	147	2002
Recapitulation of exports to the European Community with 6, 9, 10 and 12 Member States													
108	14	201	250	339	:	102	:	449	32	121	94	:	1960 EU-6
238	129	395	771	742	209	131	716	1,153	113	152	376	:	1970 EU-6
400	305	611	1,538	892	331	288	2,114	1,238	186	239	632	:	1973 EU-6
496	505	1,479	1,866	991	530	546	2,703	2,561	215	265	721	:	1973 EU-9
891	1,625	3,388	3,840	4,449	1,569	1,362	23,965	5,767	1,200	998	1,937	:	1980 EU-9
1,304	1,880	3,604	5,258	5,627	1,600	1,112	31,969	6,437	1,360	925	1,962	:	1981 EU-9
1,346	1,979	3,623	5,314	5,635	1,605	1,127	33,977	6,492	1,363	1,009	2,217	:	1981 EU-10
3,239	2,467	3,728	5,457	5,031	1,996	1,917	5,768	5,624	1,862	1,356	2,753	:	1986 EU-10
3,318	2,550	3,955	5,979	5,463	2,062	1,970	6,393	5,834	1,930	1,408	2,791	:	1986 EU-12
5,429	5,972	4,819	7,794	5,812	3,455	3,693	6,182	7,842	3,910	2,380	1,451	:	1990 EU-12
8,151	11,722	5,451	9,597	5,298	7,775	6,082	7,422	8,198	6,268	4,921	3,201	2,053	1995 EU-12

(5)   Including Namibia up to 31.12.1989.

SHARE OF TRADE WITH THE EUROPEAN UNION, THE UNITED STATES AND JAPAN

eurostat

IMPORTS

Value (Mio ECU/Euro)[1]

Year	World excluding intra EU	EU (extra EU)	USA	Switzer-land [2]	Japan	China	Poland	Czech Republic [3]	Canada	Turkey	Norway	Hungary	Hong Kong
Main countries in 2002													
Imports from EU													
1960	45,700	:	4,143	1,651	357	:	:	:	948	246	1,035	189	212
1970	125,390	:	11,055	5,016	1,725	:	830	:	1,737	428	2,530	495	546
1980	503,243	:	30,583	19,452	6,547	2,207	3,659	2,109	3,900	1,859	8,606	2,033	2,056
1990	1,152,631	:	81,202	42,831	29,695	7,183	3,624	4,968	12,771	7,795	14,054	3,312	6,720
1997	1,704,393	:	143,679	51,604	39,930	16,995	23,828	13,591	18,755	21,969	21,719	11,696	20,272
1998	1,791,308	:	162,479	54,828	35,075	18,395	27,693	18,002	18,699	21,846	22,597	14,688	17,591
1999	1,976,523	:	187,726	56,112	40,238	24,033	28,042	18,669	22,281	20,180	21,020	16,918	15,433
2000	**2,370,194**	:	**243,096**	**63,912**	**50,841**	**33,618**	**32,522**	**23,844**	**29,672**	**29,037**	**22,585**	**20,415**	**20,332**
2001	2,435,916	:	252,489	68,659	49,770	39,945	34,466	30,443	30,417	20,411	23,406	21,637	21,724
2002	**2,467,733**	:	**245,496**	**66,462**	**46,340**	**40,060**	**39,964**	**31,588**	**28,739**	**26,081**	**23,754**	**22,751**	**20,120**
Imports from the United States													
1960	19,830	6,448	:	255	1,554	:	:	:	3,770	121	123	2	126
1970	45,360	14,293	:	552	5,564	:	64	:	9,465	172	267	36	382
1980	169,493	50,706	:	1,762	17,645	2,751	608	243	29,591	317	1,019	181	1,905
1990	311,280	84,946	:	3,364	41,546	5,163	114	65	64,938	1,784	1,657	178	5,240
1997	651,897	137,847	:	5,602	67,016	14,401	1,686	1,007	128,109	3,839	2,103	705	14,303
1998	657,208	152,019	:	5,082	60,418	15,126	1,587	1,059	133,118	3,641	2,400	888	12,305
1999	707,566	160,588	:	5,307	63,357	18,382	1,558	1,148	148,280	2,904	2,310	908	11,962
2000	**897,269**	**199,024**	:	**7,033**	**78,831**	**24,358**	**2,373**	**1,697**	**183,530**	**4,224**	**2,971**	**1,333**	**15,791**
2001	855,078	195,655	:	6,308	71,137	29,277	1,916	868	173,291	3,641	2,562	1,575	15,057
2002	**772,466**	**174,656**	:	**5,866**	**61,948**	**28,353**	**799**	**761**	**161,740**	**3,613**	**2,274**	**1,298**	**13,782**
Imports from Japan													
1960	3,770	436	1,248	27	:	:	:	:	113	5	8	0.0	165
1970	16,880	2,312	6,256	143	:	:	23	:	556	25	162	15	691
1980	89,634	15,428	23,682	858	:	3,712	181	49	1,712	81	434	96	3,693
1990	230,722	46,086	73,120	2,410	:	5,976	161	55	6,970	867	922	141	10,385
1997	375,481	59,876	109,738	1,872	:	25,661	650	508	8,756	1,809	1,355	613	25,308
1998	352,845	66,042	111,704	1,900	:	25,207	814	519	9,281	1,826	1,500	881	20,813
1999	390,797	71,911	126,002	2,148	:	31,877	872	588	10,449	1,307	1,282	1,060	19,778
2000	**514,075**	**87,133**	**162,649**	**2,517**	:	**45,238**	**1,140**	**736**	**13,337**	**1,770**	**1,647**	**1,858**	**27,874**
2001	472,195	76,298	144,823	2,245	:	47,799	1,102	321	11,710	1,460	1,275	1,715	25,351
2002	**450,476**	**68,485**	**131,779**	**1,785**	:	**54,774**	**469**	**389**	**11,418**	**989**	**1,128**	**1,504**	**27,558**
Recapitulation of imports from the European Community with 6, 9, 10 and 12 Member States													
1960 EU-6	**28,130**	:	**2,457**	**1,371**	**209**	:	:	:	**300**	**166**	**480**	**123**	**87**
1970 EU-6	**85,760**	:	**7,056**	**3,789**	**1,118**	:	**414**	:	**769**	**305**	**919**	**292**	**266**
1973 EU-6	135,159	:	9,730	5,776	1,880	:	1,517	:	1,131	721	1,440	393	403
1973 EU-9	166,213	:	13,453	6,518	2,581	:	1,903	:	2,015	905	2,289	457	691
1980 EU-9	**438,488**	:	**27,307**	**17,484**	**5,657**	**1,960**	**2,862**	**1,554**	**3,386**	**1,583**	**5,795**	**1,460**	**1,938**
1981 EU-9	536,692	:	38,758	18,008	7,639	2,349	2,358	1,615	4,670	2,237	6,477	1,865	2,546
1981 EU-10	542,290	:	39,102	18,049	7,673	2,359	2,416	1,672	4,710	2,256	6,487	1,906	2,551
1986 EU-10	762,339	:	77,226	29,804	13,934	7,472	2,375	3,547	8,876	4,417	9,953	2,146	4,028
1986 EU-12	798,916	:	80,841	30,495	14,409	7,888	2,421	3,596	9,254	4,592	10,331	2,195	4,126
1990 EU-12	**1,052,204**	:	**75,042**	**39,251**	**27,776**	**6,606**	**2,997**	**3,684**	**11,540**	**7,348**	**9,874**	**2,492**	**6,335**
1995 EU-12	1,322,393	:	96,308	44,500	33,817	14,624	12,686	7,478	11,246	12,087	12,751	5,600	14,919

(1) From 1958 to 1970 included, the convention is 1 ECU = 1 US$.

(2) Including Liechtenstein before 1995.

(3) Czechoslovakia before 1993.

SHARE OF TRADE WITH THE EUROPEAN UNION, THE UNITED STATES AND JAPAN

 1B

IMPORTS

Value (Mio ECU/Euro)

USSR / Russia (4)	Australia	South Korea	Mexico	Brazil	Saudi Arabia	United Arab Emirates	India	Singapore	Israel	South Africa(5)	Romania	Malaysia	Year
	Main countries in 2002												Year

Imports from EU

USSR / Russia (4)	Australia	South Korea	Mexico	Brazil	Saudi Arabia	United Arab Emirates	India	Singapore	Israel	South Africa(5)	Romania	Malaysia	Year
:	1,136	61	203	466	:	:	896	159	231	793	133	:	1960
:	1,729	210	495	932	228	101	395	404	745	1,855	639	344	1970
:	3,698	1,220	2,033	3,144	8,539	2,311	2,443	2,134	2,097	4,960	1,941	1,337	1980
20,606	8,607	7,119	4,519	4,543	6,848	2,935	6,153	6,585	6,176	6,673	1,740	3,646	1990
17,336	14,617	16,720	9,626	15,893	8,523	6,171	9,067	16,316	13,115	11,927	5,172	9,881	1997
14,001	14,178	9,350	11,475	16,498	8,751	7,198	9,578	12,604	11,923	11,549	6,084	6,174	1998
10,433	15,428	11,439	13,174	15,947	8,821	10,560	10,266	13,293	13,528	10,801	6,042	7,180	1999
12,173	17,538	17,170	17,701	16,856	9,917	13,453	11,502	16,584	16,799	13,054	8,069	9,646	2000
16,597	16,830	16,664	19,854	18,204	14,208	15,167	13,401	15,281	15,557	12,977	9,971	10,601	2001
19,173	18,592	18,100	17,122	16,585	15,926	15,351	14,692	14,581	14,332	14,063	12,396	9,522	2002

Imports from the United States

USSR / Russia (4)	Australia	South Korea	Mexico	Brazil	Saudi Arabia	United Arab Emirates	India	Singapore	Israel	South Africa(5)	Romania	Malaysia	Year
:	432	118	779	443	:	:	624	46	144	293	6	:	1960
:	1,156	585	1,303	918	126	29	614	266	323	593	60	120	1970
:	3,185	3,513	7,821	3,328	4,338	833	1,339	2,434	1,113	1,815	701	1,172	1980
2,746	8,170	13,329	17,155	4,081	3,136	825	2,066	7,701	2,139	1,901	379	3,873	1990
3,604	13,296	26,439	79,944	13,964	5,664	2,291	3,026	19,775	4,801	3,680	389	11,689	1997
3,645	13,393	18,153	91,547	13,316	5,702	2,209	3,265	16,800	4,816	3,477	448	10,244	1998
2,240	14,259	23,472	108,992	12,278	5,001	2,801	3,365	17,876	5,935	3,431	350	10,733	1999
2,916	16,127	31,861	152,900	15,587	6,324	2,757	3,425	22,071	7,204	3,910	430	14,882	2000
3,571	13,699	25,045	139,726	16,013	7,333	3,242	4,623	21,392	7,486	3,830	548	13,218	2001
3,091	14,829	24,436	113,435	14,432	5,558	4,185	4,766	17,557	8,187	3,063	289	13,431	2002

Imports from Japan

USSR / Russia (4)	Australia	South Korea	Mexico	Brazil	Saudi Arabia	United Arab Emirates	India	Singapore	Israel	South Africa(5)	Romania	Malaysia	Year
:	138	58	16	38	:	:	118	96	9	63	:	:	1960
:	577	813	78	178	70	38	97	476	32	310	27	245	1970
:	2,497	4,207	646	856	3,886	1,069	585	3,096	86	1,199	152	1,775	1980
2,220	6,320	14,548	1,103	1,170	2,887	1,285	1,417	9,618	427	1,465	68	5,518	1990
870	8,223	24,557	4,212	3,500	1,679	1,997	1,611	20,571	911	2,072	114	15,330	1997
729	8,224	15,021	4,466	3,198	2,297	2,324	2,130	15,214	871	2,008	76	10,252	1998
430	9,103	22,775	5,263	2,658	2,422	2,620	2,371	17,449	1,031	1,954	110	12,856	1999
621	10,629	34,567	7,750	3,557	3,455	3,021	2,173	25,238	1,291	2,576	189	18,859	2000
908	9,676	29,737	9,931	3,763	4,413	3,147	2,382	17,966	1,130	2,139	171	15,867	2001
1,030	9,980	31,568	4,380	2,111	4,380	3,432	2,174	15,412	898	1,853	22	14,607	2002

Recapitulation of imports from the European Community with 6, 9, 10 and 12 Member States

USSR / Russia (4)	Australia	South Korea	Mexico	Brazil	Saudi Arabia	United Arab Emirates	India	Singapore	Israel	South Africa(5)	Romania	Malaysia	Year
:	277	49	125	295	:	:	406	49	142	295	94	:	1960 EU-6
:	605	174	349	630	167	29	229	185	443	922	430	129	1970 EU-6
:	741	180	393	1,313	273	88	436	344	897	1,149	676	209	1973 EU-6
:	1,690	236	477	1,568	391	201	711	588	1,306	1,915	788	413	1973 EU-9
:	3,234	1,107	1,665	2,759	7,282	2,163	2,219	1,895	1,926	4,648	1,520	1,208	1980 EU-9
8,600	4,110	1,685	2,450	2,925	10,367	2,546	2,728	2,415	2,504	6,779	1,628	1,438	1981 EU-9
8,674	4,126	1,725	2,466	2,926	10,689	2,546	2,768	2,417	2,524	6,785	1,705	1,438	1981 EU-10
10,514	5,824	3,310	1,531	3,307	6,636	2,318	4,602	2,964	4,885	4,655	793	1,588	1986 EU-10
10,835	5,946	3,378	1,724	3,506	6,986	2,390	4,774	3,019	5,032	4,759	835	1,611	1986 EU-12
16,555	7,668	6,604	4,170	4,192	6,458	2,809	5,769	6,143	5,934	6,415	1,587	3,376	1990 EU-12
11,035	9,527	12,519	4,875	10,687	6,980	5,026	6,520	11,601	10,644	8,684	3,389	8,254	1995 EU-12

(4) Relates to the external trade of the USSR until 1991 and from 1992 to the external trade of Russia.
(5) Including Namibia up to 31.12.1989.

FROM EU-6 TO EU-15: EXTERNAL TRADE TRENDS WITH MAIN PARTNER COUNTRIES

eurostat

EXPORTS

This table presents trade exchange trends of EU-6 from 1958 to 1972, EU-9 from 1973 to 1980, EU-10 from 1981 to 1985, EU-12 from 1986 to 1994 and EU-15 from 1995.

| Year | Total extra EU | Partner | | | | | | | | | | | | |
| | | EUROPE | | | | | | | | | AFRICA | | | |
		Norway	Switzerland (1)	Turkey	Poland	Czech Republic (2)	Slovakia	Hungary	Romania	Russia (3)	Maghreb	Egypt	Nigeria	South Africa (4)
Value (Bn ECU/Euro) (*)														
1958 EU-6	11.7	0.4	1.0	0.2	0.1	0.1	:	0.1	0.0	0.2	1.4	0.2	0.1	0.3
1960	**14.0**	**0.5**	**1.5**	**0.2**	**0.1**	**0.1**	**:**	**0.1**	**0.1**	**0.4**	**1.6**	**0.2**	**0.1**	**0.3**
1970	**32.1**	**0.9**	**4.0**	**0.4**	**0.4**	**0.5**	**:**	**0.3**	**0.4**	**1.1**	**1.6**	**0.3**	**0.2**	**1.0**
1979 EU-9	158.5	4.4	17.8	1.6	2.5	1.3	:	1.5	1.7	6.3	10.2	2.3	3.6	3.3
1980	**183.4**	**5.1**	**22.3**	**1.8**	**2.8**	**1.3**	**:**	**1.6**	**1.6**	**7.5**	**19.7**	**3.1**	**6.0**	**5.0**
1981 EU-10	242.7	6.1	21.8	2.2	2.3	1.4	:	2.0	1.7	7.9	26.7	4.3	8.0	6.9
1985	341.0	9.3	28.5	5.0	2.7	1.9	:	2.4	1.1	11.9	26.7	5.9	4.3	5.5
1986 EU-12	300.7	10.1	31.5	4.7	2.4	1.9	:	2.4	1.0	9.9	21.8	4.6	2.9	4.7
1987	295.8	9.5	32.8	5.6	2.3	2.1	:	2.4	0.7	9.2	18.4	3.7	2.2	5.0
1988	358.5	8.5	35.9	5.2	2.8	2.2	:	2.4	0.6	10.1	11.2	3.7	2.2	6.4
1989	413.2	8.6	40.1	5.6	3.9	2.4	:	3.0	0.7	12.6	13.6	3.8	2.2	6.5
1990	**415.4**	**9.3**	**41.3**	**7.7**	**4.4**	**2.6**	**:**	**2.9**	**1.2**	**11.2**	**14.4**	**4.1**	**2.5**	**4.1**
1991	423.5	9.7	40.2	8.2	7.9	3.8	:	3.5	1.3	14.2	14.2	4.1	2.9	5.8
1992	436.1	9.9	38.6	8.3	8.2	6.3	:	4.1	1.9	11.7	13.8	3.6	3.4	5.4
1993	487.5	10.2	39.5	11.8	10.0	6.1	1.2	5.0	2.3	11.5	15.0	4.4	2.9	5.6
1994	541.6	11.5	43.0	8.9	11.0	7.9	1.8	6.2	2.6	12.2	15.1	4.6	2.1	7.1
1995 EU-15	573.3	17.5	51.0	13.4	15.3	11.7	3.2	8.7	3.8	16.1	16.1	5.0	2.1	8.7
1998	733.4	25.1	57.2	22.2	28.2	17.2	5.8	16.9	6.3	21.2	20.7	7.6	2.8	10.5
1999	760.2	23.2	62.6	20.6	29.0	18.4	5.5	18.4	6.3	14.7	20.4	7.9	3.0	9.7
2000	**942.0**	**25.6**	**70.8**	**30.0**	**33.8**	**24.0**	**6.6**	**23.0**	**8.7**	**19.9**	**24.0**	**7.9**	**3.9**	**11.7**
2001	985.3	26.2	74.8	20.3	35.7	27.7	8.0	23.9	10.5	28.0	26.3	6.9	5.1	12.5
2002	**993.8**	**26.5**	**70.6**	**24.2**	**37.3**	**29.2**	**8.8**	**25.0**	**11.4**	**30.4**	**26.8**	**6.3**	**5.1**	**12.4**
Share (%)														
1958 EU-6	100.0	3.7	8.9	1.2	1.2	0.9	:	0.4	0.4	1.7	12.2	1.3	0.6	2.2
1960	**100.0**	**3.2**	**10.4**	**1.6**	**1.0**	**0.9**	**:**	**0.7**	**0.6**	**2.9**	**11.5**	**1.4**	**0.7**	**2.0**
1970	**100.0**	**2.7**	**12.5**	**1.2**	**1.2**	**1.4**	**:**	**1.0**	**1.2**	**3.4**	**4.9**	**0.8**	**0.7**	**3.1**
1979 EU-9	100.0	2.7	11.2	1.0	1.5	0.8	:	0.9	1.1	3.9	6.4	1.4	2.2	2.0
1980	**100.0**	**2.8**	**12.1**	**0.9**	**1.5**	**0.7**	**:**	**0.8**	**0.8**	**4.0**	**10.7**	**1.6**	**3.2**	**2.7**
1981 EU-10	100.0	2.4	8.9	0.9	0.9	0.5	:	0.8	0.7	3.2	11.0	1.7	3.3	2.8
1985	100.0	2.7	8.3	1.4	0.7	0.5	:	0.7	0.3	3.4	7.7	1.7	1.2	1.6
1986 EU-12	100.0	3.3	10.4	1.5	0.7	0.6	:	0.8	0.3	3.2	7.1	1.5	0.9	1.5
1987	100.0	3.2	11.0	1.8	0.7	0.7	:	0.8	0.2	3.1	6.1	1.2	0.7	1.6
1988	100.0	2.3	10.0	1.4	0.7	0.6	:	0.6	0.1	2.8	3.1	1.0	0.6	1.7
1989	100.0	2.0	9.7	1.3	0.9	0.5	:	0.7	0.1	3.0	3.2	0.9	0.5	1.5
1990	**100.0**	**2.2**	**9.9**	**1.8**	**1.0**	**0.6**	**:**	**0.6**	**0.2**	**2.7**	**3.4**	**0.9**	**0.6**	**0.9**
1991	100.0	2.2	9.4	1.9	1.8	0.9	:	0.8	0.3	3.3	3.3	0.9	0.6	1.3
1992	100.0	2.2	8.8	1.8	1.8	1.4	:	0.9	0.4	2.6	3.1	0.8	0.7	1.2
1993	100.0	2.0	8.0	2.4	2.0	1.2	0.2	1.0	0.4	2.3	3.0	0.9	0.5	1.1
1994	100.0	2.1	7.9	1.6	2.0	1.4	0.3	1.1	0.4	2.2	2.7	0.8	0.3	1.3
1995 EU-15	100.0	3.0	8.9	2.3	2.6	2.0	0.5	1.5	0.6	2.8	2.8	0.8	0.3	1.5
1998	100.0	3.4	7.7	3.0	3.8	2.3	0.7	2.2	0.8	2.8	2.8	1.0	0.3	1.4
1999	100.0	3.0	8.2	2.7	3.8	2.4	0.7	2.4	0.8	1.9	2.6	1.0	0.3	1.2
2000	**100.0**	**2.7**	**7.5**	**3.1**	**3.5**	**2.5**	**0.7**	**2.4**	**0.9**	**2.1**	**2.5**	**0.8**	**0.4**	**1.2**
2001	100.0	2.6	7.5	2.0	3.6	2.8	0.8	2.4	1.0	2.8	2.6	0.7	0.5	1.2
2002	**100.0**	**2.6**	**7.1**	**2.4**	**3.7**	**2.9**	**0.8**	**2.5**	**1.1**	**3.0**	**2.7**	**0.6**	**0.5**	**1.2**

(*) From 1958 to 1970 included, the convention is 1 ECU = 1 US$.

(1) Switzerland including Liechtenstein up to 1994.

(2) Czechoslovakia before 1993.

(3) Relates to the external trade of the USSR until 1991 and from 1992 to the external trade of Russia.

(4) South Africa includes Namibia up to 31.12.1989.

EXPORTS

This table presents trade exchange trends of EU-6 from 1958 to 1972, EU-9 from 1973 to 1980, EU-10 from 1981 to 1985, EU-12 from 1986 to 1994 and EU-15 from 1995.

Year	AMERICA					ASIA									OCEANIA	Total for all reported countries
	USA	Canada	Mexico	Brazil	Argentina	Iran	Israel	Saudi Arabia	United Arab Emirates	India	Indonesia	China	DAE [5]	Japan	Australia	
Value (Bn ECU/Euro) [*]																
1958 EU-6	1.7	0.2	0.1	0.3	0.3	0.2	0.1	0.1	0.0	0.4	0.1	0.3	0.2	0.1	0.2	8.5
1960	2.2	0.3	0.1	0.3	0.3	0.2	0.1	0.0	0.0	0.3	0.1	0.2	0.3	0.2	0.3	10.5
1970	6.6	0.7	0.4	0.6	0.5	0.6	0.4	0.2	0.0	0.3	0.2	0.3	0.9	1.0	0.6	24.4
1979 EU-9	25.0	3.4	1.5	2.4	1.7	2.3	1.8	6.4	1.8	2.0	0.8	2.1	6.9	4.6	2.9	122.0
1980	26.6	3.4	2.2	2.5	2.2	3.2	1.7	7.3	2.1	2.3	1.3	1.7	7.4	4.6	3.1	149.4
1981 EU-10	37.2	4.4	3.2	2.5	2.2	4.2	2.2	10.4	2.7	3.4	2.0	1.9	9.2	5.6	4.0	186.3
1985	81.7	9.5	2.5	2.6	1.4	4.9	3.8	10.4	3.2	5.6	2.1	6.5	16.2	10.1	7.0	273.0
1986 EU-12	75.2	9.1	2.0	3.5	1.7	3.7	4.3	8.3	2.5	5.7	1.9	6.5	15.4	11.4	5.8	255.0
1987	71.9	9.0	1.8	3.4	1.8	3.1	4.7	7.7	2.5	5.7	1.7	5.5	17.9	13.6	5.6	249.7
1988	71.8	10.1	2.3	3.1	1.3	2.9	4.7	7.6	2.3	5.6	1.9	5.8	23.1	17.0	6.4	257.1
1989	78.0	10.6	3.5	3.8	1.2	3.3	5.1	8.8	3.1	7.1	2.0	6.4	27.7	21.2	8.3	293.1
1990	76.6	9.3	3.9	3.6	1.2	5.0	5.2	7.7	3.6	6.0	2.8	5.3	29.2	22.7	6.8	294.7
1991	71.2	9.3	4.8	4.0	1.7	7.5	5.9	10.0	4.1	5.2	3.2	5.6	32.4	22.2	6.2	309.1
1992	73.8	8.5	5.7	3.6	2.7	8.2	6.6	10.0	4.5	5.2	4.1	6.9	34.6	20.6	6.3	316.4
1993	85.1	8.6	5.9	5.4	3.4	5.6	7.6	9.5	5.5	6.3	4.1	11.3	43.4	22.8	7.0	356.6
1994	96.4	9.6	6.8	7.0	4.9	3.7	9.0	8.8	6.0	7.1	4.3	12.5	52.6	26.6	8.5	397.8
1995 EU-15	103.3	10.3	4.5	11.4	4.6	3.5	9.7	8.6	6.5	9.4	5.9	14.7	65.6	32.9	10.5	473.9
1998	161.5	14.9	9.3	15.7	7.6	4.4	10.9	12.0	8.8	9.6	3.9	17.4	60.1	31.6	13.0	622.3
1999	183.0	16.6	10.4	14.2	6.4	3.9	12.9	10.2	9.6	10.4	3.3	19.4	62.0	35.4	13.7	651.3
2000	232.5	20.6	14.0	16.6	6.2	5.2	15.8	12.0	11.8	13.4	4.5	25.5	81.6	44.9	15.7	810.3
2001	239.9	21.9	15.0	18.3	5.0	6.6	14.4	13.2	13.8	12.6	4.5	30.1	81.9	44.9	15.5	843.4
2002	239.9	22.3	15.0	15.4	2.1	8.0	13.4	14.5	14.2	14.0	4.5	34.1	78.0	42.3	16.6	848.7
Share (%)																
1958 EU-6	14.2	2.0	1.1	2.2	2.6	1.7	0.9	0.4	0.0	3.7	1.0	2.6	2.0	1.1	1.4	71.6
1960	16.0	2.0	1.0	1.9	2.4	1.5	1.0	0.3	0.0	2.4	0.9	1.7	2.2	1.4	1.9	73.5
1970	20.6	2.2	1.2	1.7	1.4	1.7	1.3	0.5	0.0	0.8	0.5	1.0	2.8	3.0	1.7	74.5
1979 EU-9	15.8	2.1	0.9	1.4	1.0	1.4	1.1	4.0	1.1	1.2	0.5	1.3	4.3	2.9	1.8	75.9
1980	14.4	1.8	1.1	1.3	1.2	1.7	0.9	3.9	1.1	1.2	0.6	0.9	4.0	2.4	1.6	79.8
1981 EU-10	15.3	1.8	1.3	1.0	0.9	1.7	0.9	4.3	1.1	1.3	0.8	0.7	3.7	2.3	1.6	75.8
1985	23.9	2.7	0.7	0.7	0.4	1.4	1.1	3.0	0.9	1.6	0.6	1.9	4.7	2.9	2.0	78.7
1986 EU-12	24.9	3.0	0.6	1.1	0.5	1.2	1.4	2.7	0.8	1.8	0.6	2.1	5.1	3.7	1.9	83.2
1987	24.3	3.0	0.6	1.1	0.5	1.0	1.5	2.6	0.8	1.9	0.5	1.8	6.0	4.6	1.8	83.1
1988	20.0	2.8	0.6	0.8	0.3	0.8	1.3	2.1	0.6	1.5	0.5	1.6	6.4	4.7	1.7	70.6
1989	18.8	2.5	0.8	0.9	0.2	0.7	1.2	2.1	0.7	1.7	0.4	1.5	6.7	5.1	1.9	69.4
1990	18.4	2.2	0.9	0.8	0.2	1.2	1.2	1.8	0.8	1.4	0.6	1.2	7.0	5.4	1.6	69.5
1991	16.8	2.2	1.1	0.9	0.4	1.7	1.3	2.3	0.9	1.2	0.7	1.3	7.6	5.2	1.4	71.6
1992	16.9	1.9	1.3	0.8	0.6	1.8	1.5	2.3	1.0	1.2	0.9	1.5	7.9	4.7	1.4	71.3
1993	17.4	1.7	1.2	1.0	0.6	1.1	1.5	1.9	1.1	1.2	0.8	2.3	8.8	4.6	1.4	71.5
1994	17.8	1.7	1.2	1.2	0.9	0.6	1.6	1.6	1.1	1.3	0.7	2.3	9.7	4.9	1.5	72.1
1995 EU-15	18.0	1.8	0.7	1.9	0.7	0.6	1.6	1.5	1.1	1.6	1.0	2.5	11.4	5.7	1.8	81.4
1998	22.0	2.0	1.2	2.1	1.0	0.5	1.4	1.6	1.2	1.3	0.5	2.3	8.1	4.3	1.7	83.4
1999	24.0	2.1	1.3	1.8	0.8	0.5	1.6	1.3	1.2	1.3	0.4	2.5	8.1	4.6	1.8	84.3
2000	24.6	2.1	1.4	1.7	0.6	0.5	1.6	1.2	1.2	1.4	0.4	2.7	8.6	4.7	1.6	84.5
2001	24.3	2.2	1.5	1.8	0.5	0.6	1.4	1.3	1.3	1.2	0.4	3.0	8.3	4.5	1.5	84.2
2002	24.1	2.2	1.5	1.5	0.2	0.8	1.3	1.4	1.4	1.4	0.4	3.4	7.8	4.2	1.6	84.2

(*)   From 1958 to 1970 included, the convention is 1 ECU = 1 US$.

(5)   Dynamic Asian Economies = Thailand + Malaysia + Singapore + South Korea + Hong Kong + Taiwan.

FROM EU-6 TO EU-15: EXTERNAL TRADE TRENDS WITH MAIN PARTNER COUNTRIES

IMPORTS

This table presents trade exchange trends of EU-6 from 1958 to 1972, EU-9 from 1973 to 1980, EU-10 from 1981 to 1985, EU-12 from 1986 to 1994 and EU-15 from 1995.

Year	Total extra EU	Partner												
		EUROPE									AFRICA			
		Norway	Switzer-land [1]	Turkey	Poland	Czech Republic [2]	Slovakia	Hungary	Romania	Russia [3]	Maghreb	Egypt	Nigeria	South Africa [4]
Value (Bn ECU/Euro) (*)														
1958 EU-6	12.8	0.2	0.6	0.1	0.1	0.1	:	0.1	0.1	0.3	0.9	0.1	0.1	0.2
1960	**15.2**	**0.2**	**0.8**	**0.1**	**0.1**	**0.1**	**:**	**0.1**	**0.1**	**0.4**	**1.0**	**0.1**	**0.2**	**0.2**
1970	**35.6**	**0.8**	**1.9**	**0.3**	**0.4**	**0.4**	**:**	**0.3**	**0.4**	**1.0**	**3.2**	**0.2**	**0.5**	**0.6**
1979 EU-9	187.1	6.2	12.4	0.9	2.4	1.3	:	1.3	1.6	8.4	9.6	1.2	5.3	7.0
1980	**235.5**	**8.1**	**15.1**	**1.0**	**2.7**	**1.4**	**:**	**1.4**	**1.7**	**10.8**	**19.1**	**1.7**	**7.9**	**6.5**
1981 EU-10	279.4	10.3	16.5	1.3	2.1	1.6	:	1.5	1.8	13.5	24.3	3.3	5.4	7.1
1985	362.2	17.4	22.9	3.1	3.4	2.2	:	2.0	2.8	20.2	38.1	3.9	10.1	9.1
1986 EU-12	295.8	12.2	25.4	3.1	2.9	2.1	:	1.9	2.5	13.2	23.8	1.8	4.6	8.0
1987	298.6	12.1	26.7	3.8	2.9	2.1	:	2.0	2.4	13.1	23.1	2.1	3.0	5.4
1988	380.5	12.5	29.5	4.3	3.4	2.2	:	2.2	2.2	13.0	14.1	1.6	2.9	12.5
1989	447.4	15.4	32.1	5.5	3.9	2.6	:	2.6	2.5	15.2	17.1	2.4	3.5	8.2
1990	**461.6**	**16.4**	**34.3**	**5.9**	**5.2**	**2.7**	**:**	**2.9**	**1.6**	**16.2**	**20.4**	**2.3**	**4.4**	**5.9**
1991	494.1	17.4	34.5	6.2	6.2	4.1	:	3.6	1.5	18.5	21.4	2.2	4.6	8.4
1992	487.1	17.2	35.0	6.6	7.1	5.5	:	4.0	1.4	15.6	19.8	2.5	4.0	9.1
1993	487.4	17.8	35.7	6.5	7.6	4.8	1.2	4.0	1.7	15.5	18.6	2.2	3.1	8.6
1994	538.6	20.0	38.7	7.5	9.1	6.4	1.9	4.9	2.5	18.4	18.8	2.8	4.1	6.7
1995 EU-15	545.3	25.5	43.2	9.2	12.3	9.0	3.1	7.6	3.4	21.5	18.3	2.2	3.4	7.8
1998	710.5	28.1	49.5	13.6	16.2	14.7	5.4	14.7	5.1	23.2	22.4	2.5	2.8	9.7
1999	779.8	29.6	52.9	15.1	17.6	16.8	6.0	17.6	5.8	26.0	25.3	2.4	2.8	10.5
2000	**1,033.4**	**46.1**	**60.0**	**17.5**	**23.3**	**21.6**	**6.9**	**22.0**	**7.6**	**45.7**	**41.3**	**3.4**	**6.4**	**14.5**
2001	1,028.0	45.1	60.8	20.2	26.6	25.1	8.2	24.8	9.4	47.7	40.3	3.1	6.5	16.0
2002	**987.5**	**45.8**	**58.8**	**22.0**	**28.2**	**27.5**	**9.7**	**25.3**	**10.4**	**47.7**	**36.4**	**3.2**	**5.0**	**15.6**
Share (%)														
1958 EU-6	100.0	1.6	4.6	0.7	0.9	0.8	:	0.4	0.4	2.1	7.2	0.5	0.8	1.7
1960	**100.0**	**1.5**	**5.0**	**0.9**	**0.9**	**0.8**	**:**	**0.5**	**0.6**	**2.8**	**6.2**	**0.5**	**1.0**	**1.5**
1970	**100.0**	**2.1**	**5.3**	**0.7**	**1.2**	**1.0**	**:**	**0.8**	**1.0**	**2.7**	**8.9**	**0.4**	**1.4**	**1.5**
1979 EU-9	100.0	3.3	6.6	0.5	1.3	0.6	:	0.6	0.8	4.4	5.1	0.6	2.8	3.7
1980	**100.0**	**3.4**	**6.4**	**0.4**	**1.1**	**0.6**	**:**	**0.5**	**0.7**	**4.6**	**8.0**	**0.7**	**3.3**	**2.7**
1981 EU-10	100.0	3.6	5.8	0.4	0.7	0.5	:	0.5	0.6	4.8	8.6	1.1	1.9	2.5
1985	100.0	4.8	6.3	0.8	0.9	0.6	:	0.5	0.7	5.5	10.4	1.0	2.7	2.5
1986 EU-12	100.0	4.1	8.5	1.0	0.9	0.7	:	0.6	0.8	4.4	7.9	0.6	1.5	2.7
1987	100.0	4.0	8.9	1.2	0.9	0.6	:	0.6	0.8	4.3	7.6	0.7	1.0	1.8
1988	100.0	3.2	7.7	1.1	0.8	0.5	:	0.5	0.5	3.4	3.6	0.4	0.7	3.2
1989	100.0	3.4	7.1	1.2	0.8	0.5	:	0.5	0.5	3.3	3.8	0.5	0.7	1.8
1990	**100.0**	**3.5**	**7.4**	**1.2**	**1.1**	**0.5**	**:**	**0.6**	**0.3**	**3.5**	**4.4**	**0.4**	**0.9**	**1.2**
1991	100.0	3.5	6.9	1.2	1.2	0.8	:	0.7	0.2	3.7	4.3	0.4	0.9	1.6
1992	100.0	3.5	7.1	1.3	1.4	1.1	:	0.8	0.2	3.1	4.0	0.5	0.8	1.8
1993	100.0	3.6	7.3	1.3	1.5	0.9	0.2	0.8	0.3	3.1	3.8	0.4	0.6	1.7
1994	100.0	3.7	7.1	1.3	1.6	1.1	0.3	0.9	0.4	3.4	3.4	0.5	0.7	1.2
1995 EU-15	100.0	4.6	7.9	1.6	2.2	1.6	0.5	1.3	0.6	3.9	3.3	0.4	0.6	1.4
1998	100.0	3.9	6.9	1.9	2.2	2.0	0.7	2.0	0.7	3.2	3.1	0.3	0.4	1.3
1999	100.0	3.7	6.7	1.9	2.2	2.1	0.7	2.2	0.7	3.3	3.2	0.3	0.3	1.3
2000	**100.0**	**4.4**	**5.8**	**1.6**	**2.2**	**2.0**	**0.6**	**2.1**	**0.7**	**4.4**	**3.9**	**0.3**	**0.6**	**1.4**
2001	100.0	4.3	5.9	1.9	2.5	2.4	0.7	2.4	0.9	4.6	3.9	0.3	0.6	1.5
2002	**100.0**	**4.6**	**5.9**	**2.2**	**2.8**	**2.7**	**0.9**	**2.5**	**1.0**	**4.8**	**3.6**	**0.3**	**0.5**	**1.5**

(*) From 1958 to 1970 included, the convention is 1 ECU = 1 US$.
(1) Switzerland including Liechtenstein up to 1994.
(2) Czechoslovakia before 1993.
(3) Relates to the external trade of the USSR until 1991 and from 1992 to the external trade of Russia.
(4) South Africa includes Namibia up to 31.12.1989.

FROM EU-6 TO EU-15: EXTERNAL TRADE TRENDS WITH MAIN PARTNER COUNTRIES

IMPORTS

This table presents trade exchange trends of EU-6 from 1958 to 1972, EU-9 from 1973 to 1980, EU-10 from 1981 to 1985, EU-12 from 1986 to 1994 and EU-15 from 1995.

Year	Partner															OCEANIA	Total for all reported countries
	AMERICA					ASIA											
	USA	Canada	Mexico	Brazil	Argentina	Iran	Israel	Saudi Arabia	United Arab Emirates	India	Indonesia	China	DAE [5]	Japan	Australia	
Value (Bn ECU/Euro) (*)																	
1958 EU-6	2.8	0.4	0.1	0.2	0.4	0.2	0.0	0.3	0.0	0.1	0.2	0.1	0.2	0.1	0.4	8.5
1960	3.8	0.4	0.1	0.3	0.5	0.3	0.1	0.3	0.0	0.1	0.1	0.1	0.4	0.2	0.4	10.6
1970	9.0	1.3	0.1	0.9	0.8	0.7	0.2	1.0	0.3	0.2	0.2	0.3	0.9	1.2	0.6	27.4
1979 EU-9	33.8	5.1	0.4	3.6	2.1	4.3	1.3	14.3	3.1	1.8	1.1	1.3	9.8	9.7	2.4	151.6
1980	43.5	6.1	1.1	4.1	1.8	2.8	1.6	24.5	4.4	1.8	1.2	1.9	12.5	12.3	2.5	199.4
1981 EU-10	49.6	6.7	2.0	5.2	1.8	2.6	1.7	36.8	4.6	1.9	1.1	2.3	13.3	16.2	2.7	237.3
1985	64.0	7.3	3.1	9.5	2.8	5.5	2.6	7.8	1.5	2.7	1.8	3.8	18.8	27.1	4.7	298.5
1986 EU-12	56.6	6.5	2.2	7.4	2.3	3.0	2.5	8.6	0.8	2.4	1.6	4.2	20.7	33.2	4.1	257.6
1987	56.2	6.9	2.9	7.3	1.9	3.9	2.6	5.6	1.4	2.8	1.7	5.2	25.3	34.8	4.3	261.4
1988	68.4	8.4	2.5	9.3	2.6	3.1	2.9	5.5	0.6	3.3	2.1	7.0	30.3	41.6	4.9	292.9
1989	83.7	9.8	2.8	10.5	2.8	5.4	3.2	6.7	1.6	4.2	2.6	9.1	33.5	46.4	5.3	338.1
1990	85.2	9.4	3.0	9.2	3.5	5.8	3.5	8.2	1.5	4.5	2.9	10.6	33.8	46.2	4.8	350.5
1991	92.0	9.9	3.1	9.4	3.8	6.3	3.4	11.2	1.7	4.8	3.6	15.0	40.0	51.8	4.5	388.9
1992	86.8	9.0	2.9	9.1	3.3	5.4	3.3	9.6	1.4	4.9	4.3	16.8	39.8	51.5	4.7	380.8
1993	84.3	7.9	2.3	8.2	3.1	5.9	3.4	9.3	0.9	5.9	5.0	19.6	42.8	47.7	3.9	377.7
1994	92.6	9.1	2.6	10.3	3.5	5.3	4.1	8.8	0.9	6.9	5.9	22.7	46.9	48.5	4.6	414.6
1995 EU-15	103.7	11.7	3.2	10.8	3.7	5.4	4.7	8.8	0.9	7.8	6.1	26.3	54.4	54.3	5.0	473.3
1998	152.0	12.7	4.0	13.2	4.2	3.7	6.9	6.6	1.6	9.8	9.0	42.0	77.9	66.0	7.5	625.2
1999	160.6	13.5	4.7	13.3	4.8	4.7	7.6	8.5	1.8	10.0	8.8	49.7	85.2	71.9	6.9	680.5
2000	199.0	18.4	7.0	17.6	5.4	8.4	10.0	15.9	2.5	12.4	10.9	70.3	109.4	87.1	8.9	899.9
2001	195.7	18.0	7.4	18.3	5.5	6.7	9.6	13.1	2.8	12.9	10.9	75.9	98.1	76.3	9.3	894.3
2002	174.7	15.9	6.2	17.3	6.1	5.6	8.5	12.3	2.8	13.0	10.3	81.8	91.8	68.5	8.9	859.5
Share (%)																	
1958 EU-6	22.0	3.3	0.8	1.8	2.7	1.8	0.2	2.5	0.0	0.8	1.2	0.8	1.8	0.9	2.9	65.2
1960	25.1	2.9	0.9	1.8	2.9	1.8	0.3	2.2	0.0	0.7	0.8	0.9	2.4	1.0	2.7	68.5
1970	25.3	3.5	0.3	2.4	2.2	1.9	0.5	2.7	0.8	0.5	0.5	0.7	2.4	3.4	1.5	75.5
1979 EU-9	18.0	2.7	0.2	1.9	1.1	2.3	0.7	7.6	1.6	0.9	0.5	0.7	5.2	5.1	1.2	79.9
1980	18.4	2.5	0.4	1.7	0.7	1.1	0.6	10.4	1.8	0.7	0.5	0.7	5.3	5.2	1.0	83.4
1981 EU-10	17.7	2.3	0.7	1.8	0.6	0.9	0.6	13.1	1.6	0.6	0.4	0.8	4.7	5.7	0.9	83.3
1985	17.6	2.0	0.8	2.6	0.7	1.5	0.7	2.1	0.4	0.7	0.5	1.0	5.1	7.4	1.2	81.0
1986 EU-12	19.1	2.1	0.7	2.4	0.7	1.0	0.8	2.9	0.2	0.8	0.5	1.4	6.9	11.2	1.3	85.7
1987	18.8	2.3	0.9	2.4	0.6	1.2	0.8	1.8	0.4	0.9	0.5	1.7	8.4	11.6	1.4	86.0
1988	17.9	2.2	0.6	2.4	0.6	0.8	0.7	1.4	0.1	0.8	0.5	1.8	7.9	10.9	1.2	75.4
1989	18.7	2.1	0.6	2.3	0.6	1.1	0.7	1.4	0.3	0.9	0.5	2.0	7.4	10.9	1.1	74.0
1990	18.4	2.0	0.6	1.9	0.7	1.2	0.7	1.7	0.3	0.9	0.6	2.2	7.3	10.0	1.0	74.5
1991	18.6	1.9	0.6	1.8	0.7	1.2	0.6	2.2	0.3	0.9	0.7	3.0	8.0	10.4	0.9	77.2
1992	17.8	1.8	0.6	1.8	0.6	1.1	0.6	1.9	0.2	1.0	0.8	3.4	8.1	10.5	0.9	76.6
1993	17.3	1.6	0.4	1.6	0.6	1.2	0.7	1.9	0.1	1.2	1.0	4.0	8.7	9.7	0.8	76.2
1994	17.1	1.6	0.4	1.9	0.6	0.9	0.7	1.6	0.1	1.2	1.0	4.2	8.7	8.9	0.8	75.2
1995 EU-15	19.0	2.1	0.5	1.9	0.6	0.9	0.8	1.6	0.1	1.4	1.1	4.8	9.9	9.9	0.9	85.3
1998	21.3	1.7	0.5	1.8	0.5	0.5	0.9	0.9	0.2	1.3	1.2	5.9	10.9	9.2	1.0	86.4
1999	20.5	1.7	0.6	1.7	0.6	0.6	0.9	1.0	0.2	1.2	1.1	6.3	10.9	9.2	0.8	85.9
2000	19.2	1.7	0.6	1.7	0.5	0.8	0.9	1.5	0.2	1.1	1.0	6.8	10.5	8.4	0.8	85.7
2001	19.0	1.7	0.7	1.7	0.5	0.6	0.9	1.2	0.2	1.2	1.0	7.3	9.5	7.4	0.9	85.7
2002	17.6	1.6	0.6	1.7	0.6	0.5	0.8	1.2	0.2	1.3	1.0	8.2	9.3	6.9	0.8	85.6

(*) From 1958 to 1970 included, the convention is 1 ECU = 1 US$.
(5) Dynamic Asian Economies = Thailand + Malaysia + Singapore + South Korea + Hong Kong + Taiwan.

FROM EU-6 TO EU-15: EXTERNAL TRADE TRENDS WITH MAIN PARTNER COUNTRIES

TRADE BALANCE

This table presents trade exchange trends of EU-6 from 1958 to 1972, EU-9 from 1973 to 1980, EU-10 from 1981 to 1985, EU-12 from 1986 to 1994 and EU-15 from 1995.

Value (Bn ECU) (*)

Year	Total extra EU	Partner												
		EUROPE									AFRICA			
		Norway	Switzer-land (1)	Turkey	Poland	Czech Republic (2)	Slovakia	Hungary	Romania	Russia (3)	Maghreb	Egypt	Nigeria	South Africa (4)
Value (Bn ECU/Euro) (*)														
1958 EU-6	-1.1	0.2	0.5	0.1	0.0	0.0	:	0.0	-0.0	-0.1	0.5	0.1	-0.0	0.0
1960	**-1.2**	**0.2**	**0.7**	**0.1**	**-0.0**	**0.0**	**:**	**0.0**	**-0.0**	**-0.0**	**0.7**	**0.1**	**-0.0**	**0.1**
1970	**-3.6**	**0.1**	**2.1**	**0.1**	**-0.1**	**0.1**	**:**	**0.0**	**0.0**	**0.1**	**-1.6**	**0.1**	**-0.3**	**0.4**
1979 EU-9	-28.6	-1.8	5.4	0.6	0.0	-0.0	:	0.2	0.2	-2.1	0.7	1.1	-1.8	-3.7
1980	**-52.1**	**-3.0**	**7.2**	**0.8**	**0.1**	**-0.1**	**:**	**0.2**	**-0.1**	**-3.3**	**-5.1**	**1.4**	**-1.9**	**-1.5**
1981 EU-10	-36.7	-4.3	21.6	0.8	0.2	-0.2	:	0.5	-0.1	-5.7	0.7	0.9	2.6	-0.2
1985	-21.2	-8.2	5.6	1.9	-0.7	-0.3	:	0.4	-1.7	-8.4	-2.1	2.0	-5.7	-3.6
1986 EU-12	4.8	-2.0	6.2	1.6	-0.6	-0.2	:	0.6	-1.5	-3.3	0.4	2.7	-1.7	-3.3
1987	-2.8	-2.6	6.1	1.8	-0.6	0.0	:	0.4	-1.8	-3.9	-0.9	1.6	-0.8	-0.4
1988	-22.0	-4.0	6.4	0.9	-0.6	-0.0	:	0.2	-1.6	-2.9	-2.8	2.0	-0.7	-6.2
1989	-34.2	-6.8	8.0	0.1	0.1	-0.2	:	0.4	-1.9	-2.6	-3.4	1.3	-1.3	-1.7
1990	**-46.1**	**-7.2**	**7.0**	**1.8**	**-0.8**	**-0.1**	**:**	**-0.1**	**-0.4**	**-4.9**	**-6.0**	**1.8**	**-1.9**	**-1.8**
1991	-70.6	-7.8	5.7	2.0	1.7	-0.2	:	-0.1	-0.1	-4.3	-7.2	1.9	-1.6	-2.6
1992	-51.0	-7.4	3.7	1.7	1.1	0.7	:	0.1	0.5	-2.7	-5.9	1.1	-0.6	-3.7
1993	0.1	-7.7	3.7	5.2	2.4	1.2	0.1	1.0	0.6	-4.0	-3.6	2.2	-0.3	-3.0
1994	3.0	-8.5	4.3	1.3	1.9	1.6	-0.1	1.2	0.1	-6.2	-3.8	1.8	-1.9	0.4
1995 EU-15	28.0	-8.0	7.8	4.1	3.1	2.7	0.1	1.1	0.4	-5.4	-2.1	2.8	-1.4	0.9
1998	22.9	-3.0	7.7	8.6	12.0	2.5	0.4	2.2	1.2	-2.0	-1.7	5.1	-0.0	0.8
1999	-19.6	-6.4	9.7	5.5	11.4	1.6	-0.4	0.8	0.6	-11.2	-4.8	5.5	0.2	-1.0
2000	**-91.4**	**-20.5**	**10.8**	**12.4**	**10.5**	**2.4**	**-0.3**	**1.0**	**1.1**	**-25.8**	**-17.3**	**4.4**	**-2.6**	**-2.8**
2001	-42.6	-19.0	13.9	0.0	9.1	2.5	-0.2	-0.9	1.1	-19.7	-14.0	3.8	-1.4	-3.5
2002	**6.3**	**-19.3**	**11.9**	**2.2**	**9.1**	**1.7**	**-1.0**	**-0.3**	**1.0**	**-17.3**	**-9.5**	**3.1**	**0.1**	**-3.2**

(*)   From 1958 to 1970 included, the convention is 1 ECU = 1 US$.

(1)   Switzerland including Liechtenstein up to 1994.

(2)   Czechoslovakia before 1993.

(3)   Relates to the external trade of the USSR until 1991 and from 1992 to the external trade of Russia.

(4)   South Africa includes Namibia up to 31.12.1989.

FROM EU-6 TO EU-15: EXTERNAL TRADE TRENDS WITH MAIN PARTNER COUNTRIES

TRADE BALANCE

This table presents trade exchange trends of EU-6 from 1958 to 1972, EU-9 from 1973 to 1980,

EU-10 from 1981 to 1985, EU-12 from 1986 to 1994 and EU-15 from 1995.

Value (Bn ECU) (*)

Year	Partner																
	AMERICA					ASIA									OCEANIA	Total for all reported countries
	USA	Canada	Mexico	Brazil	Argentina	Iran	Israel	Saudi Arabia	United Arab Emirates	India	Indonesia	China	DAE (5)	Japan	Australia	
Value (Bn ECU/Euro) (*)																
1958 EU-6	-1.1	-0.2	0.0	0.0	-0.0	-0.0	0.1	-0.3	-0.0	0.3	-0.0	0.2	0.0	0.0	-0.2	0.0
1960	-1.6	-0.2	0.0	-0.0	-0.1	-0.1	0.1	-0.3	0.0	0.2	-0.0	0.1	-0.0	0.0	-0.2	-0.2
1970	-2.4	-0.5	0.3	-0.3	-0.3	-0.1	0.2	-0.8	-0.3	0.1	-0.0	0.1	0.0	-0.2	-0.0	-3.0
1979 EU-9	-8.7	-1.7	1.1	-1.2	-0.4	-2.1	0.4	-7.9	-1.3	0.2	-0.3	0.8	-2.9	-5.0	0.6	-29.6
1980	-16.9	-2.7	1.1	-1.6	0.5	0.4	0.1	-17.2	-2.3	0.5	0.1	-0.1	-5.1	-7.7	0.6	-55.7
1981 EU-10	-12.4	-2.2	1.2	-2.7	0.4	1.6	0.5	-26.4	-2.0	1.5	0.9	-0.4	-4.1	-10.6	1.3	-36.3
1985	17.7	2.2	-0.6	-7.0	-1.4	-0.6	1.2	2.6	1.7	2.9	0.3	2.7	-2.6	-17.0	2.3	-16.3
1986 EU-12	18.5	2.6	-0.2	-3.9	-0.6	0.8	1.8	-0.4	1.8	3.3	0.2	2.3	-5.2	-21.8	1.7	-0.1
1987	15.7	2.1	-1.1	-3.9	-0.1	-0.8	2.1	2.1	1.1	2.9	0.0	0.3	-7.4	-21.1	1.3	-7.9
1988	3.5	1.7	-0.2	-6.2	-1.3	-0.2	1.8	2.1	1.6	2.4	-0.2	-1.2	-7.1	-24.6	1.5	-35.8
1989	-5.6	0.8	0.8	-6.6	-1.6	-2.1	1.9	2.1	1.6	2.9	-0.5	-2.8	-5.8	-25.2	3.0	-45.0
1990	-8.7	-0.1	0.9	-5.6	-2.2	-0.8	1.8	-0.5	2.0	1.5	-0.0	-5.3	-4.6	-23.5	2.0	-55.8
1991	-20.8	-0.5	1.8	-5.4	-2.1	1.2	2.5	-1.2	2.3	0.5	-0.4	-9.4	-7.6	-29.7	1.7	-79.8
1992	-13.0	-0.5	2.8	-5.5	-0.6	2.8	3.2	0.4	3.0	0.4	-0.3	-9.9	-5.2	-31.0	1.6	-63.2
1993	0.8	0.7	3.6	-2.8	0.3	-0.3	4.1	0.2	4.5	0.4	-0.9	-8.3	0.6	-24.9	3.0	-21.1
1994	3.8	0.5	4.2	-3.4	1.4	-1.6	4.9	-0.1	5.1	0.2	-1.5	-10.2	5.7	-21.8	3.9	-16.8
1995 EU-15	-0.4	-1.4	1.3	0.6	0.9	-2.0	5.0	-0.2	5.6	1.6	-0.3	-11.7	11.2	-21.4	5.5	0.7
1998	9.5	2.1	5.3	2.4	3.5	0.7	4.0	5.4	7.2	-0.2	-5.1	-24.6	-17.8	-34.5	5.4	-2.9
1999	22.4	3.1	5.7	0.9	1.6	-0.9	5.2	1.8	7.8	0.3	-5.4	-30.3	-23.2	-36.5	6.8	-29.3
2000	33.4	2.2	7.0	-1.0	0.7	-3.2	5.9	-3.9	9.4	1.0	-6.5	-44.8	-27.9	-42.2	6.9	-89.6
2001	44.2	4.0	7.7	-0.0	-0.5	-0.1	4.9	0.1	11.0	-0.3	-6.4	-45.8	-16.2	-31.4	6.3	-50.9
2002	65.3	6.4	8.7	-1.9	-3.9	2.4	4.9	2.2	11.3	0.9	-5.8	-47.7	-13.9	-26.2	7.7	-10.9

(*)   From 1958 to 1970 included, the convention is 1 ECU = 1 US$.

(5)   Dynamic Asian Economies = Thailand + Malaysia + Singapore + South Korea + Hong Kong + Taiwan.

European Union trading partners

MAIN TRADING PARTNERS

EXPORTS

Partner	Value (Bn ECU/Euro)						%						Annual rank		
	1980	1990	1999	2000	2001	2002	1980	1990	1999	2000	2001	2002	1980	1990	2002
Extra EU	**212.1**	**355.2**	**760.2**	**942.0**	**985.3**	**993.8**	**100.0**	**100.0**	**100.0**	**100.0**	**100.0**	**100.0**			
USA	29.5	76.5	183.0	232.5	239.9	239.9	13.9	21.5	24.0	24.6	24.3	24.1	1	1	1
Switzerland[1]	24.3	41.3	62.6	70.8	74.8	70.6	11.4	11.6	8.2	7.5	7.5	7.1	2	2	2
Japan	5.2	22.7	35.4	44.9	44.9	42.3	2.4	6.3	4.6	4.7	4.5	4.2	8	3	3
Poland	3.5	4.4	29.0	33.8	35.7	37.3	1.6	1.2	3.8	3.5	3.6	3.7	15	19	4
China	2.0	5.3	19.4	25.5	30.1	34.1	0.9	1.4	2.5	2.7	3.0	3.4	25	14	5
Russia[2]	10.2	11.2	14.7	19.9	28.0	30.4	4.8	3.1	1.9	2.1	2.8	3.0	3	4	6
Czech Republic[3]	1.7	2.6	18.4	24.0	27.7	29.2	0.7	0.7	2.4	2.5	2.8	2.9	30	31	7
Norway	8.0	9.3	23.2	25.6	26.2	26.5	3.7	2.6	3.0	2.7	2.6	2.6	5	6	8
Hungary	2.0	2.9	18.4	23.0	23.9	25.0	0.9	0.8	2.4	2.4	2.4	2.5	21	28	9
Turkey	2.0	7.7	20.6	30.0	20.3	24.2	0.9	2.1	2.7	3.1	2.0	2.4	22	8	10
Canada	3.9	9.3	16.6	20.6	21.9	22.3	1.8	2.6	2.1	2.1	2.2	2.2	12	5	11
Hong Kong	2.2	6.6	15.7	20.5	21.5	19.9	1.0	1.8	2.0	2.1	2.1	2.0	19	10	12
South Korea	1.0	6.1	11.5	16.5	15.6	17.3	0.4	1.7	1.5	1.7	1.5	1.7	35	11	13
Australia	3.5	6.8	13.7	15.7	15.5	16.6	1.6	1.9	1.8	1.6	1.5	1.6	14	9	14
Brazil	2.9	3.6	14.2	16.6	18.3	15.4	1.3	1.0	1.8	1.7	1.8	1.5	16	23	15
Mexico	2.7	3.9	10.4	14.0	15.0	15.0	1.2	1.0	1.3	1.4	1.5	1.5	17	22	16
Saudi Arabia	8.3	7.7	10.2	12.0	13.2	14.5	3.9	2.1	1.3	1.2	1.3	1.4	4	7	17
Singapore	2.0	5.7	11.8	14.8	14.6	14.2	0.9	1.5	1.5	1.5	1.4	1.4	24	13	19
United Arab Emirates	2.2	3.5	9.6	11.8	13.8	14.2	1.0	0.9	1.2	1.2	1.3	1.4	20	25	18
India	2.5	6.0	10.4	13.4	12.6	14.0	1.1	1.6	1.3	1.4	1.2	1.4	18	12	20
Israel	1.8	5.2	12.9	15.8	14.4	13.4	0.8	1.4	1.6	1.6	1.4	1.3	28	15	21
South Africa[4]	5.0	4.1	9.7	11.7	12.5	12.4	2.3	1.1	1.2	1.2	1.2	1.2	9	21	22
Taiwan	0.9	4.9	11.8	14.9	13.3	11.6	0.4	1.3	1.5	1.5	1.3	1.1	37	18	23
Romania	2.0	1.2	6.3	8.7	10.5	11.4	0.9	0.3	0.8	0.9	1.0	1.1	23	37	24
Slovakia	:	:	5.5	6.6	8.0	8.8	:	:	0.7	0.7	0.8	0.8	:	:	25
Slovenia	:	:	6.9	8.1	8.5	8.7	:	:	0.9	0.8	0.8	0.8	:	:	26
Malaysia	1.2	2.4	6.4	8.4	9.3	8.2	0.5	0.6	0.8	0.8	0.9	0.8	34	33	27
Algeria	5.3	5.0	5.2	6.1	7.5	8.1	2.4	1.3	0.6	0.6	0.7	0.8	7	17	28
Iran	3.9	5.0	3.9	5.2	6.6	8.0	1.8	1.4	0.5	0.5	0.6	0.8	11	16	29
Morocco	1.8	3.6	6.6	7.7	7.5	7.7	0.8	1.0	0.8	0.8	0.7	0.7	27	24	30
Tunisia	1.8	3.0	6.0	7.3	8.0	7.6	0.8	0.8	0.7	0.7	0.8	0.7	29	27	31
Thailand	0.8	3.4	4.7	6.5	7.6	6.8	0.3	0.9	0.6	0.6	0.7	0.6	38	26	32
Croatia	:	:	4.0	4.6	5.5	6.5	:	:	0.5	0.4	0.5	0.6	:	:	33
Egypt	3.6	4.2	7.9	7.9	6.9	6.3	1.7	1.1	1.0	0.8	0.7	0.6	13	20	34
Ukraine	:	:	2.6	3.7	5.0	5.5	:	:	0.3	0.3	0.5	0.5	:	:	35
Nigeria	6.5	2.5	3.0	3.9	5.1	5.1	3.0	0.7	0.3	0.4	0.5	0.5	6	32	36
Indonesia	1.4	2.8	3.3	4.5	4.5	4.5	0.6	0.7	0.4	0.4	0.4	0.4	32	29	37
Bulgaria	0.9	0.9	2.7	3.2	4.0	4.2	0.4	0.2	0.3	0.3	0.4	0.4	36	41	38
Lithuania	:	:	2.1	2.6	3.4	4.0	:	:	0.2	0.2	0.3	0.4	:	:	39
Estonia	:	:	2.4	3.2	3.0	3.5	:	:	0.3	0.3	0.3	0.3	:	:	40
Philippines	0.7	1.2	3.3	4.5	4.5	3.3	0.3	0.3	0.4	0.4	0.4	0.3	40	36	41
Libya	4.7	2.6	2.3	2.5	3.0	3.1	2.2	0.7	0.3	0.2	0.2	0.3	10	30	42
Chile	0.7	1.2	2.5	3.5	3.7	3.1	0.3	0.3	0.3	0.3	0.3	0.3	39	39	43
Venezuela	1.9	1.7	2.7	3.2	3.7	3.1	0.9	0.4	0.3	0.3	0.3	0.3	26	34	44
Federal Republic of Yugoslavia	:	:	1.2	1.8	2.5	3.0	:	:	0.1	0.1	0.2	0.3	:	:	45
Liban	1.2	0.8	2.7	2.9	3.1	3.0	0.5	0.2	0.3	0.3	0.3	0.2	33	42	46
Kuwait	1.6	1.0	2.0	2.3	2.7	2.9	0.7	0.2	0.2	0.2	0.2	0.2	31	40	47
Cyprus	0.6	1.3	2.4	3.1	3.0	2.9	0.2	0.3	0.3	0.3	0.3	0.2	41	35	48
Malta	0.5	1.2	2.1	2.8	2.5	2.7	0.2	0.3	0.2	0.2	0.2	0.2	42	38	49
Latvia	:	:	1.7	2.0	2.4	2.6	:	:	0.2	0.2	0.2	0.2	:	:	50
Total for all 50	**168.6**	**302.2**	**685.8**	**855.3**	**895.5**	**905.1**	**79.4**	**85.0**	**90.2**	**90.7**	**90.8**	**91.0**			

(1) Including Liechtenstein up to 1994.
(2) Relates to the external trade of USSR until 1991 and from 1992 to the external trade of Russia.
(3) Czechoslovakia before 1993.
(4) South Africa includes Namibia up to 31.12.1989.

IMPORTS

Partner	Value (Bn ECU/Euro)						%						Annual rank		
	1980	1990	1999	2000	2001	2002	1980	1990	1999	2000	2001	2002	1980	1990	2002
Extra EU	**281.1**	**404.4**	**779.8**	**1,033.4**	**1,028.0**	**987.5**	**100.0**	**100.0**	**100.0**	**100.0**	**100.0**	**100.0**			
USA	50.7	84.9	160.6	199.0	195.7	174.7	18.0	21.0	20.5	19.2	19.0	17.6	1	1	1
China	2.1	10.6	49.7	70.3	75.9	81.8	0.7	2.6	6.3	6.8	7.3	8.2	22	6	2
Japan	15.4	46.1	71.9	87.1	76.3	68.5	5.4	11.3	9.2	8.4	7.4	6.9	4	2	3
Switzerland[1]	17.3	34.3	52.9	60.0	60.8	58.8	6.1	8.4	6.7	5.8	5.9	5.9	3	3	4
Russie[2]	15.0	16.2	26.0	45.7	47.7	47.7	5.3	4.0	3.3	4.4	4.6	4.8	5	5	5
Norway	9.8	16.3	29.6	46.1	45.1	45.8	3.5	4.0	3.7	4.4	4.3	4.6	7	4	6
Poland	3.4	5.2	17.6	23.3	26.6	28.2	1.1	1.2	2.2	2.2	2.5	2.8	17	18	7
Czech Republic[3]	2.0	2.7	16.8	21.6	25.1	27.5	0.7	0.6	2.1	2.0	2.4	2.7	26	31	8
Hongrie	1.8	2.9	17.6	22.0	24.8	25.3	0.6	0.7	2.2	2.1	2.4	2.5	31	29	9
South Korea	2.0	6.5	18.4	24.9	21.6	22.3	0.7	1.6	2.3	2.4	2.1	2.2	27	13	10
Turkey	1.1	5.9	15.1	17.5	20.2	22.0	0.4	1.4	1.9	1.6	1.9	2.2	38	14	11
Taiwan	2.1	9.1	20.0	26.7	24.2	21.1	0.7	2.2	2.5	2.5	2.3	2.1	21	9	12
Brazil	5.1	9.2	13.3	17.6	18.3	17.3	1.8	2.2	1.7	1.7	1.7	1.7	13	8	13
Canada	6.8	9.4	13.5	18.4	18.0	15.9	2.4	2.3	1.7	1.7	1.7	1.6	10	7	14
South Africa[4]	6.5	5.9	10.7	14.5	16.0	15.6	2.3	1.4	1.3	1.4	1.5	1.5	11	15	15
Algeria	4.6	7.0	7.8	16.4	16.0	14.2	1.6	1.7	0.9	1.5	1.5	1.4	14	12	17
Malaysia	2.0	3.6	13.3	17.4	15.8	14.4	0.7	0.8	1.7	1.6	1.5	1.4	25	24	16
India	1.9	4.5	10.0	12.4	12.9	13.0	0.6	1.1	1.2	1.1	1.2	1.3	30	21	19
Singapore	2.0	4.7	12.8	15.9	13.9	13.1	0.6	1.1	1.6	1.5	1.3	1.3	29	20	18
Saudi Arabia	29.7	8.3	8.5	15.9	13.1	12.3	10.5	2.0	1.0	1.5	1.2	1.2	2	10	20
Thailand	1.3	4.1	10.1	12.9	12.4	11.2	0.4	1.0	1.2	1.2	1.2	1.1	37	23	21
Romania	2.0	1.6	5.8	7.6	9.4	10.4	0.6	0.3	0.7	0.7	0.9	1.0	28	37	22
Indonesia	1.3	2.9	8.8	10.9	10.9	10.3	0.4	0.7	1.1	1.0	1.0	1.0	36	30	23
Hong Kong	4.0	5.9	10.7	11.6	10.3	9.7	1.4	1.4	1.3	1.1	0.9	0.9	15	16	25
Slovaquia	:	:	6.0	6.9	8.2	9.7	:	:	0.7	0.6	0.7	0.9	:	:	24
Libya	7.9	7.9	6.9	13.0	11.5	9.4	2.8	1.9	0.8	1.2	1.1	0.9	9	11	26
Australia	2.7	4.8	6.9	8.9	9.3	8.9	0.9	1.1	0.8	0.8	0.9	0.8	18	19	27
Israel	1.8	3.5	7.6	10.0	9.6	8.5	0.6	0.8	0.9	0.9	0.9	0.8	32	26	28
Philippines	0.9	1.3	6.4	8.9	7.6	7.6	0.3	0.3	0.8	0.8	0.7	0.7	40	40	29
Slovenia	:	:	5.3	6.3	6.6	6.8	:	:	0.6	0.6	0.6	0.6	:	:	30
Morocco	1.4	3.1	5.6	6.0	6.2	6.3	0.4	0.7	0.7	0.5	0.6	0.6	34	27	31
Mexico	2.1	3.0	4.7	7.0	7.4	6.2	0.7	0.7	0.6	0.6	0.7	0.6	24	28	32
Argentina	2.1	3.5	4.8	5.4	5.5	6.1	0.7	0.8	0.6	0.5	0.5	0.6	23	25	33
Tunisia	1.4	2.3	4.8	5.5	6.2	6.0	0.4	0.5	0.6	0.5	0.6	0.6	35	34	34
Iran	3.9	5.8	4.7	8.4	6.7	5.6	1.3	1.4	0.6	0.8	0.6	0.5	16	17	35
Nigeria	8.7	4.4	2.8	6.4	6.5	5.0	3.0	1.0	0.3	0.6	0.6	0.5	8	22	36
Chile	1.5	2.6	3.6	5.1	5.1	4.8	0.5	0.6	0.4	0.4	0.4	0.4	33	32	37
Vietnam	0	0.1	3.2	4.0	4.5	4.4	0.0	0.0	0.4	0.3	0.4	0.4	44	44	38
Ukraine	:	:	2.1	3.0	3.6	4.2	:	:	0.2	0.2	0.3	0.4	:	:	39
Syria	0.9	1.2	2.2	3.4	4.1	4.1	0.3	0.3	0.2	0.3	0.4	0.4	39	41	40
Bulgaria	0.6	0.6	2.3	3.1	3.5	3.6	0.1	0.1	0.2	0.2	0.3	0.3	41	42	41
Kazakhstan	:	:	1.8	3.2	3.0	3.6	:	:	0.2	0.3	0.2	0.3	:	:	42
Egypt	2.4	2.3	2.4	3.4	3.1	3.2	0.8	0.5	0.3	0.3	0.3	0.3	20	33	43
Bangladesh	0.2	0.5	2.1	3.1	3.3	3.2	0.0	0.1	0.2	0.2	0.3	0.3	43	43	44
Estonia	:	:	1.9	3.2	3.0	3.0	:	:	0.2	0.3	0.2	0.3	:	:	45
Pakistan	0.5	1.5	2.2	2.6	2.8	2.9	0.1	0.3	0.2	0.2	0.2	0.2	42	39	46
United Arab Emirates	5.5	1.5	1.8	2.5	2.8	2.8	1.9	0.3	0.2	0.2	0.2	0.2	12	38	47
Irak	10.4	2.2	3.7	6.3	3.6	2.8	3.6	0.5	0.4	0.6	0.3	0.2	6	35	48
Lithuania	:	:	1.6	2.2	2.6	2.7	:	:	0.2	0.2	0.2	0.2	:	:	49
Venezuela	2.6	1.8	1.8	2.7	2.9	2.7	0.9	0.4	0.2	0.2	0.2	0.2	19	36	50
Total for all 50	**247.1**	**361.6**	**720.2**	**956.6**	**950.3**	**915.6**	**87.9**	**89.4**	**92.3**	**92.5**	**92.4**	**92.7**			

(1) Including Liechtenstein up to 1994.
(2) Relates to the external trade of USSR until 1991 and from 1992 to the external trade of Russia.
(3) Czechoslovakia before 1993.
(4) South Africa includes Namibia up to 31.12.1989.

TRENDS IN EU TRADE BY PARTNER COUNTRY

eurostat

EXPORTS

Main partners	Value (Mio ECU/Euro)											
	1980	**1990**	1993	1994	1995	1996	1997	1998	1999	**2000**	2001	**2002**
Extra EU	212,111	355,164	430,247	476,689	573,277	626,294	721,128	733,428	760,192	942,044	985,326	993,796
Europe excluding EU	62,475	155,434	171,208	189,310	166,701	190,348	224,177	237,373	235,057	287,603	304,965	317,627
of which Iceland	412	638	646	603	812	923	1,137	1,248	1,391	1,733	1,553	1,349
Norway	8,005	9,296	10,154	11,486	17,475	19,755	23,361	25,088	23,243	25,598	26,154	26,524
Liechtenstein	:	:	:	:	448	534	551	714	652	885	834	743
Switzerland(1)	24,315	41,288	39,464	89,808	51,041	51,457	53,024	57,180	62,556	70,782	74,761	70,645
Faroe Islands	124	131	122	135	165	194	194	212	246	270	339	310
Andorra	322	874	727	685	722	688	850	840	890	974	1,012	1,093
Poland	3,467	4,390	9,984	10,975	15,315	19,971	25,081	28,207	28,973	33,810	35,681	37,327
Hungary	2,037	2,876	4,967	6,153	8,731	10,028	13,596	16,863	18,442	23,039	23,878	25,004
Romania	1,990	1,227	2,320	2,647	3,795	4,473	5,015	6,300	6,332	8,743	10,515	11,435
Bulgaria	930	901	1,347	1,597	2,053	1,695	1,847	2,436	2,706	3,237	4,012	4,229
Albania	70	118	400	426	518	744	566	555	693	802	1,094	1,082
Czech Republic(2)	1,683	2,606	6,082	7,928	11,657	14,008	15,909	17,214	18,433	24,003	27,674	29,222
Slovakia	:	:	1,222	1,794	3,194	4,003	4,818	5,809	5,517	6,598	7,959	8,754
Estonia	:	:	210	309	1,350	1,693	2,388	2,697	2,413	3,209	3,047	3,537
Latvia	:	:	311	487	942	1,115	1,535	1,819	1,664	2,026	2,447	2,586
Lithuania	:	:	478	726	1,021	1,460	2,155	2,395	2,098	2,582	3,412	4,014
Ukraine	:	:	1,475	1,668	2,250	2,627	3,442	3,543	2,607	3,655	4,951	5,518
Belarus	:	:	553	577	886	902	1,233	1,175	1,024	1,137	1,393	1,508
Russia(3)	10,243	11,177	11,528	12,172	16,133	19,132	25,539	21,170	14,727	19,917	27,961	30,439
Serbia and Montenegro(4)	4,914	8,491	83	129	190	1,251	1,768	1,793	1,224	1,806	2,522	3,017
Slovenia	:	:	3,061	3,675	5,178	5,388	6,338	6,773	6,918	8,143	8,467	8,659
Croatia	:	:	2,058	2,915	3,739	3,897	4,786	4,421	4,023	4,631	5,492	6,481
Form. Yug. Rep. Maced.	:	:	676	738	880	809	849	891	1,173	1,326	1,184	1,021
Gibraltar	88	294	454	593	401	647	687	480	766	1,242	1,131	1,408
Malta	515	1,208	1,761	1,867	2,016	1,870	1,999	1,978	2,078	2,787	2,501	2,692
Cyprus	629	1,276	1,879	1,999	2,015	1,933	1,959	2,130	2,368	3,123	2,956	2,896
Turkey	2,033	7,718	11,780	8,875	13,391	18,320	22,377	22,187	20,580	29,953	20,266	24,217
Africa	39,548	44,930	44,680	45,766	51,592	53,387	52,077	58,673	56,919	66,112	69,915	69,383
of which **North Africa**	17,213	22,820	23,869	24,130	25,985	26,740	24,531	28,651	28,871	32,498	33,757	33,655
of which Canary Islands	:	4,037	4,120	4,185	4,483	4,767	:	:	:	:	:	:
Ceuta and Melilla	:	495	605	573	596	521	30	656	779	1,008	948	875
Morocco	1,825	3,570	4,237	4,373	4,728	4,699	5,329	6,603	6,627	7,736	7,476	7,671
Algeria	5,285	4,955	4,116	4,612	4,727	4,075	4,357	5,268	5,220	6,107	7,508	8,074
Tunisia	1,774	2,967	3,631	3,784	4,156	4,345	5,285	5,784	6,031	7,283	7,965	7,564
Libya	4,710	2,644	2,739	2,037	2,279	2,505	2,772	2,743	2,286	2,496	2,954	3,133
Egypt	3,619	4,150	4,422	4,567	5,017	5,827	6,758	7,597	7,927	7,868	6,905	6,339
Sudan	509	337	271	297	280	295	361	531	474	440	612	542
Mauritania	152	221	239	248	233	261	278	283	276	377	382	396
Senegal	467	684	527	534	715	797	882	991	999	1,027	1,036	1,177
Guinea	173	252	262	285	270	281	314	316	325	335	356	436
Liberia	474	965	664	598	1,240	454	531	1,944	734	2,074	1,556	1,363
Ivory Coast	1,214	831	845	734	1,187	1,180	1,284	1,473	1,400	1,425	1,323	1,261
Ghana	329	499	631	658	744	985	1,110	1,148	1,110	1,257	941	1,026
Benin	294	166	286	205	271	303	387	428	502	553	545	554
Nigeria	6,479	2,516	2,858	2,124	2,054	2,371	2,713	2,804	3,004	3,861	5,054	5,139
Cameroon	775	736	550	433	564	636	732	874	780	921	1,142	1,093
Gabon	403	545	786	821	719	971	1,138	959	1,127	1,114	1,153	802
Congo	265	350	347	292	478	923	420	441	295	401	523	528
Zaire	538	731	264	305	358	370	294	283	177	276	278	372
Angola	530	831	698	576	800	778	1,055	985	841	1,018	1,363	1,400
Ethiopia	190	414	428	417	469	451	488	442	461	433	406	367
Kenya	795	825	549	724	857	880	910	879	894	931	1,037	918
Uganda	119	153	115	128	182	174	181	198	165	196	194	198
Tanzania	458	400	359	332	318	303	401	315	310	339	410	382
Madagascar	313	259	199	234	248	262	320	367	331	385	435	269
Reunion	398	1,176	1,210	1,421	1,483	1,484	:	:	:	:	:	:
Mauritius	110	391	434	647	651	589	653	546	739	860	842	739
Zimbabwe	84	336	300	347	371	420	440	372	348	257	226	184
Namibia	:	1,668	107	75	138	129	189	153	152	149	168	165
South Africa(5)	5,042	4,090	5,601	7,092	8,689	8,869	9,742	10,475	9,731	11,715	12,480	12,438
CEEC(6)	15,091	20,610	33,286	40,598	58,722	71,062	87,413	99,026	101,575	125,100	138,608	147,711
ACP(7)	15,683	18,290	16,505	14,940	17,573	18,665	20,447	32,681	31,514	38,318	40,178	40,419
DOM	1,232	4,132	4,366	4,577	5,868	5,427	:	:	:	:	:	:
Mediterranean Basin	41,768	45,547	53,620	55,079	64,552	73,159	83,821	87,173	88,191	109,615	102,056	106,949

(1) Including Liechtenstein up to 1994.
(2) Czechoslovakia before 1993.
(3) Relates to the external trade of the USSR until 1991 and from 1992 to the external trade of Russia.
(4) In 1992, Serbia, Montenegro and Macedonia. Since 1993, Serbia and Montenegro.

EXPORTS

Annual variation (%)					Share (%)						Main partners
98/97	99/98	00/99	01/00	02/01	1980	1990	1999	2000	2001	2002	
1.7	3.6	23.9	4.5	0.8	100.0	100.0	100.0	100.0	100.0	100.0	**Extra EU**
5.8	-0.9	22.3	6.0	4.1	29.4	43.7	30.9	30.5	30.9	31.9	**Europe excluding EU**
9.7	11.4	24.5	-10.3	-13.1	0.1	0.1	0.1	0.1	0.1	0.1	*of which* Iceland
7.3	-7.3	10.1	2.1	1.4	3.7	2.6	3.0	2.7	2.6	2.6	Norway
29.5	-8.7	35.7	-5.7	-10.9	:	:	0.0	0.0	0.0	0.0	Liechtenstein
7.8	9.4	13.1	5.6	-5.5	11.4	11.6	8.2	7.5	7.5	7.1	Switzerland[1]
9.3	15.7	9.7	25.6	-8.3	0.0	0.0	0.0	0.0	0.0	0.0	Faroe Islands
-1.1	5.9	9.3	3.9	7.9	0.1	0.2	0.1	0.1	0.1	0.1	Andorra
12.4	2.7	16.6	5.5	4.6	1.6	1.2	3.8	3.5	3.6	3.7	Poland
24.0	9.3	24.9	3.6	4.7	0.9	0.8	2.4	2.4	2.4	2.5	Hungary
25.6	0.5	38.0	20.2	8.7	0.9	0.3	0.8	0.9	1.0	1.1	Romania
31.8	11.0	19.6	23.9	5.4	0.4	0.2	0.3	0.3	0.4	0.4	Bulgaria
-1.8	24.7	15.7	36.4	-1.1	0.0	0.0	0.0	0.0	0.1	0.1	Albania
8.2	7.0	30.2	15.2	5.5	0.7	0.7	2.4	2.5	2.8	2.9	Czech Republic[2]
20.5	-5.0	19.5	20.6	9.9	:	:	0.7	0.7	0.8	0.8	Slovakia
12.9	-10.5	32.9	-5.0	16.0	:	:	0.3	0.3	0.3	0.3	Estonia
18.5	-8.5	21.7	20.7	5.6	:	:	0.2	0.2	0.2	0.2	Latvia
11.1	-12.4	23.0	32.1	17.6	:	:	0.2	0.2	0.3	0.4	Lithuania
2.9	-26.4	40.2	35.4	11.4	:	:	0.3	0.3	0.5	0.5	Ukraine
-4.6	-12.8	11.0	22.4	8.2	:	:	0.1	0.1	0.1	0.1	Belarus
-17.1	-30.4	35.2	40.3	8.8	4.8	3.1	1.9	2.1	2.8	3.0	Russia[3]
1.4	-31.7	47.5	39.6	19.6	2.3	2.3	0.1	0.1	0.2	0.3	Serbia and Montenegro[4]
6.8	2.1	17.7	3.9	2.2	:	:	0.9	0.8	0.8	0.8	Slovenia
-7.6	-8.9	15.1	18.5	18.0	:	:	0.5	0.4	0.5	0.6	Croatia
4.8	31.6	13.1	-10.7	-13.7	:	:	0.1	0.1	0.1	0.1	Form. Yug. Rep. Maced.
-30.1	59.7	62.1	-8.9	24.4	0.0	0.0	0.1	0.1	0.1	0.1	Gibraltar
-1.0	5.0	34.1	-10.2	7.6	0.2	0.3	0.2	0.2	0.2	0.2	Malta
8.7	11.1	31.8	-5.3	-2.0	0.2	0.3	0.3	0.3	0.3	0.2	Cyprus
-0.8	-7.2	45.5	-32.3	19.4	0.9	2.1	2.7	3.1	2.0	2.4	Turkey
12.6	-2.9	16.1	5.7	-0.7	18.6	12.6	7.4	7.0	7.0	6.9	**Africa**
16.7	0.7	12.5	3.8	-0.3	8.1	6.4	3.7	3.4	3.4	3.3	*of which* **North Africa**
:	:	:	:	:	:	1.1	:	:	:	:	*of which* Canary Islands
2,084.1	18.8	29.3	-5.8	-7.7	:	0.1	0.1	0.1	0.0	0.0	Ceuta and Melilla
23.9	0.3	16.7	-3.3	2.6	0.8	1.0	0.8	0.8	0.7	0.7	Morocco
20.9	-0.9	17.0	22.9	7.5	2.4	1.3	0.6	0.6	0.7	0.8	Algeria
9.4	4.2	20.7	9.3	-5.0	0.8	0.8	0.7	0.7	0.8	0.7	Tunisia
-1.0	-16.6	9.1	18.3	6.0	2.2	0.7	0.3	0.2	0.2	0.3	Libya
12.4	4.3	-0.7	-12.2	-8.2	1.7	1.1	1.0	0.8	0.7	0.6	Egypt
47.0	-10.7	-7.1	39.1	-11.4	0.2	0.0	0.0	0.0	0.0	0.0	Sudan
1.9	-2.4	36.2	1.3	3.7	0.0	0.0	0.0	0.0	0.0	0.0	Mauritania
12.4	0.7	2.8	0.7	13.6	0.2	0.1	0.1	0.1	0.1	0.1	Senegal
0.5	2.7	3.0	6.3	22.4	0.0	0.0	0.0	0.0	0.0	0.0	Guinea
266.4	-62.2	182.8	-25.0	-12.3	0.2	0.2	0.0	0.2	0.1	0.1	Liberia
14.6	-4.9	1.8	-7.1	-4.6	0.5	0.2	0.1	0.1	0.1	0.1	Ivory Coast
3.4	-3.3	13.2	-25.1	9.1	0.1	0.1	0.1	0.1	0.0	0.1	Ghana
10.5	17.2	10.2	-1.5	1.6	0.1	0.0	0.0	0.0	0.0	0.0	Benin
3.3	7.1	28.5	30.9	1.6	3.0	0.7	0.3	0.4	0.5	0.5	Nigeria
19.3	-10.6	18.0	23.9	-4.2	0.3	0.2	0.1	0.0	0.1	0.1	Cameroon
-15.7	17.5	-1.1	3.4	-30.4	0.1	0.1	0.1	0.1	0.1	0.0	Gabon
5.1	-33.1	35.8	30.5	0.9	0.1	0.0	0.0	0.0	0.0	0.0	Congo
-3.6	-37.6	55.9	0.8	33.9	0.2	0.2	0.0	0.0	0.0	0.0	Zaire
-6.6	-14.6	21.0	33.9	2.7	0.2	0.2	0.1	0.1	0.1	0.1	Angola
-9.3	4.3	-6.1	-6.2	-9.4	0.0	0.1	0.0	0.0	0.0	0.0	Ethiopia
-3.3	1.7	4.0	11.4	-11.5	0.3	0.2	0.1	0.0	0.1	0.0	Kenya
9.4	-16.6	18.6	-0.9	2.0	0.0	0.0	0.0	0.0	0.0	0.0	Uganda
-21.3	-1.6	9.0	21.0	-6.9	0.2	0.1	0.0	0.0	0.0	0.0	Tanzania
14.6	-10.0	16.3	12.9	-38.0	0.1	0.0	0.0	0.0	0.0	0.0	Madagascar
:	:	:	:	:	0.1	0.3	:	:	:	:	Reunion
-16.4	35.4	16.3	-2.1	-12.1	0.0	0.1	0.0	0.0	0.0	0.0	Mauritius
-15.2	-6.6	-26.1	-11.9	-18.6	0.0	0.0	0.0	0.0	0.0	0.0	Zimbabwe
-18.7	-0.9	-2.0	12.5	-1.4	:	0.4	0.0	0.0	0.0	0.0	Namibia
7.5	-7.0	20.3	6.5	-0.3	2.3	1.1	1.2	1.2	1.2	1.2	South Africa[5]
13.2	2.5	23.1	10.7	6.5	7.1	5.8	13.3	13.2	14.0	14.8	**CEEC[6]**
59.8	-3.5	21.5	4.8	0.5	7.3	5.1	4.1	4.0	4.0	4.0	**ACP[7]**
:	:	:	:	:	0.5	1.1	:	:	:	:	**DOM**
3.9	1.1	24.2	-6.8	4.7	19.6	12.8	11.6	11.6	10.3	10.7	**Mediterranean Basin**

(5) South Africa includes Namibia up to 31.12.1989.
(6) Including Estonia Latvia and Lithuania since 1.1.1992.
(7) Including Eritrea since 1.1.1994 and Namibia since 1.1.1990.

TRENDS IN EU TRADE BY PARTNER COUNTRY

EXPORTS

Main partners	Value (Mio ECU/Euro)											
	1980	1990	1993	1994	1995	1996	1997	1998	1999	2000	2001	2002
North America	**33,642**	**86,030**	**93,986**	**106,360**	**113,962**	**125,891**	**155,787**	**176,766**	**199,960**	**253,489**	**262,219**	**262,584**
of which USA	29,543	76,495	85,137	96,431	103,315	114,877	141,373	161,545	183,016	232,470	239,904	239,938
Canada	3,893	9,300	8,582	9,614	10,342	10,708	14,107	14,880	16,591	20,643	21,939	22,284
Central America and Antilles	**6,302**	**9,601**	**13,722**	**14,582**	**13,279**	**15,064**	**15,956**	**18,493**	**21,502**	**28,049**	**28,541**	**28,367**
of which Mexico	2,668	3,882	5,883	6,790	4,511	5,119	7,430	9,341	10,422	14,042	15,034	14,957
Bermuda	58	216	623	610	772	1,057	1,083	656	1,127	1,724	2,487	1,841
Guatemala	172	183	283	285	301	332	382	443	491	479	557	638
El Salvador	75	111	147	176	222	207	348	432	385	667	690	435
Costa Rica	119	166	300	270	340	303	392	472	570	669	814	819
Panama	492	564	753	710	879	1,323	1,101	1,458	1,687	1,584	1,139	1,471
Cuba	628	594	475	570	712	792	931	1,157	1,207	1,419	1,428	1,143
Bahamas	161	306	1,213	539	523	812	593	447	878	1,010	678	1,175
Dominican Republic	132	216	347	373	341	399	520	657	672	1,165	1,114	1,036
Guadeloupe	380	1,060	982	1,070	1,145	1,225	:	:	:	:	:	:
Martinique	359	987	969	1,018	1,122	1,091	:	:	:	:	:	:
Cayman Islands	49	35	156	233	299	480	692	817	939	1,363	1,214	1,515
Jamaica	95	172	186	166	241	221	311	306	261	405	432	486
Trinidad and Tobago	306	139	172	174	267	301	422	401	461	410	604	425
Netherlands Antilles	247	297	383	401	403	403	480	510	605	628	574	515
South America	**10,574**	**10,750**	**17,008**	**20,730**	**27,058**	**28,705**	**34,023**	**35,693**	**30,169**	**34,493**	**36,062**	**28,623**
Colombia	738	807	1,325	1,732	1,816	1,980	2,389	2,418	1,567	1,913	2,124	1,846
Venezuela	1,912	1,691	2,026	1,587	1,865	1,748	2,395	2,996	2,661	3,221	3,686	3,068
French Guiana	95	909	1,205	1,068	2,118	1,627	:	:	:	:	:	:
Guina	69	45	73	57	73	85	81	72	66	72	78	101
Ecuador	353	325	504	523	629	548	723	688	429	529	811	929
Peru	528	334	438	687	985	1,011	1,118	1,145	934	1,015	978	942
Brazil	2,877	3,623	5,351	6,986	11,373	11,755	14,907	15,657	14,220	16,604	18,313	15,446
Chile	737	1,173	1,699	1,907	2,392	2,738	3,449	3,321	2,535	3,468	3,691	3,125
Uruguay	277	233	580	752	642	690	888	907	780	862	751	450
Argentina	2,679	1,234	3,396	4,936	4,576	5,839	7,327	7,646	6,373	6,154	5,020	2,139
Near and Middle East	**27,168**	**29,104**	**37,717**	**37,649**	**39,350**	**43,131**	**51,219**	**49,492**	**49,363**	**59,398**	**65,556**	**67,793**
of which Lebanon	1,200	755	1,744	2,198	2,471	2,722	3,095	2,823	2,666	2,856	3,063	2,971
Syria	1,245	840	1,362	1,611	1,378	1,402	1,354	1,534	1,665	1,760	2,089	2,095
Iraq	4,525	2,074	100	49	26	33	194	484	611	1,124	1,931	1,763
Iran	3,903	4,983	5,591	3,729	3,452	3,869	4,918	4,399	3,869	5,208	6,578	8,038
Israel	1,814	5,234	7,572	8,971	9,663	10,444	11,512	10,892	12,866	15,846	14,449	13,425
Jordan	803	829	953	1,039	1,046	1,194	1,200	1,139	1,244	1,622	1,830	1,957
Saudi Arabia	8,311	7,726	9,453	8,756	8,647	10,380	13,178	12,021	10,231	11,981	13,230	14,467
Kuwait	1,644	1,017	2,382	1,823	2,424	2,195	2,294	2,163	2,008	2,330	2,747	2,901
Bahrain	344	512	613	585	529	883	667	770	1,058	896	934	933
Qatar	424	455	742	790	1,167	1,096	2,118	1,503	1,085	1,344	1,937	1,893
United Arab Emirates	2,198	3,504	5,470	6,021	6,491	6,668	7,917	8,839	9,615	11,838	13,781	14,178
Oman	407	694	1,011	1,352	1,300	1,138	1,308	1,433	1,166	1,128	1,441	1,366
Other Asian coutries	**22,060**	**70,197**	**95,233**	**111,729**	**137,149**	**149,045**	**163,066**	**133,425**	**141,006**	**182,909**	**187,766**	**185,655**
of which Uzbekistan	:	:	201	389	420	697	762	592	498	484	534	437
Kazakhstan	:	:	634	680	447	566	1,394	1,256	976	1,244	1,590	1,625
Pakistan	978	1,427	2,035	2,061	2,045	2,148	2,054	1,595	1,656	1,918	2,020	2,166
India	2,505	5,985	6,289	7,058	9,440	9,891	10,248	9,576	10,353	13,384	12,610	13,967
Bangladesh	352	402	433	453	495	603	670	567	587	701	850	742
Sri Lanka	298	347	563	803	720	674	884	799	1,146	1,580	985	885
China	1,962	5,268	11,339	12,529	14,690	14,752	16,482	17,411	19,351	25,498	30,087	34,139
Indonesia	1,364	2,812	4,145	4,314	5,854	7,000	8,284	3,866	3,346	4,474	4,532	4,516
Philippines	665	1,247	1,733	1,958	2,291	3,251	5,095	3,147	3,257	4,453	4,548	3,274
Thailand	838	3,407	5,044	6,104	8,492	8,502	7,805	5,217	4,699	6,487	7,573	6,762
Vietnam	213	128	487	616	750	1,297	1,158	1,062	1,052	1,236	1,778	1,833
Malaysia	1,189	2,425	3,986	5,773	7,939	7,542	8,763	5,480	6,437	8,381	9,317	8,198
Brunei	54	383	589	786	625	1,094	1,064	695	261	272	162	154
Singapore	1,973	5,677	7,685	8,873	10,904	12,298	13,520	10,911	11,836	14,798	14,605	14,165
South Korea	953	6,059	7,677	10,059	12,331	14,366	14,475	9,100	11,499	16,482	15,588	17,323
Japan	5,232	22,727	22,764	26,606	32,896	35,770	36,097	31,567	35,374	44,936	44,920	42,279
Taiwan	872	4,912	7,584	8,733	10,112	9,985	12,657	12,056	11,835	14,888	13,264	11,631
Hong Kong	2,238	6,597	11,392	13,087	15,796	17,509	20,441	17,320	15,691	20,536	21,533	19,906
Macao	7	50	61	104	137	170	216	208	187	178	175	329
Oceania	**4,590**	**9,091**	**9,205**	**10,886**	**13,500**	**14,487**	**16,366**	**15,945**	**17,172**	**19,314**	**19,747**	**21,032**
Australia	3,515	6,804	6,962	8,520	10,497	11,535	13,135	12,988	13,737	15,727	15,531	16,574
New Zealand	715	1,285	1,204	1,466	1,775	1,889	1,965	1,783	2,042	2,138	2,339	2,374
New Caledonia and dep.	129	408	386	368	389	411	462	461	470	582	593	692
Latin America	**11,748**	**15,618**	**24,084**	**28,999**	**32,395**	**35,601**	**45,177**	**49,740**	**45,753**	**54,689**	**56,984**	**49,222**
OPEC	**36,618**	**35,246**	**40,911**	**37,187**	**38,988**	**41,941**	**51,139**	**47,085**	**43,936**	**53,985**	**63,938**	**67,170**
DAE	**7,420**	**29,076**	**43,367**	**52,629**	**65,574**	**70,203**	**77,661**	**60,084**	**61,997**	**81,572**	**81,879**	**77,984**

EXPORTS

Annual variation (%)					Share (%)						Main partners
98/97	99/98	00/99	01/00	02/01	1980	1990	1999	2000	2001	2002	
13.4	13.1	26.7	3.4	0.1	15.8	24.2	26.3	26.9	26.6	26.4	**North America**
14.2	13.2	27.0	3.1	0.0	13.9	21.5	24.0	24.6	24.3	24.1	*of which* USA
5.4	11.4	24.4	6.2	1.5	1.8	2.6	2.1	2.1	2.2	2.2	Canada
15.9	16.2	30.4	1.7	-0.6	2.9	2.7	2.8	2.9	2.8	2.8	**Central America and Antilles**
25.7	11.5	34.7	7.0	-0.5	1.2	1.0	1.3	1.4	1.5	1.5	*of which* Mexico
-39.4	71.8	52.9	44.2	-25.9	0.0	0.0	0.1	0.1	0.2	0.1	Bermuda
16.0	10.8	-2.4	16.2	14.5	0.0	0.0	0.0	0.0	0.0	0.0	Guatemala
23.9	-10.7	73.0	3.4	-36.9	0.0	0.0	0.0	0.0	0.0	0.0	El Salvador
20.2	20.7	17.4	21.7	0.6	0.0	0.0	0.0	0.0	0.0	0.0	Costa Rica
32.4	15.6	-6.1	-28.1	29.1	0.2	0.1	0.2	0.1	0.1	0.1	Panama
24.2	4.2	17.5	0.6	-19.9	0.2	0.1	0.1	0.1	0.1	0.1	Cuba
-24.6	96.5	14.9	-32.9	73.4	0.0	0.0	0.1	0.1	0.0	0.1	Bahamas
26.3	2.2	73.4	-4.3	-6.9	0.0	0.0	0.0	0.1	0.1	0.1	Dominican Republic
:	:	:	:	:	0.1	0.2	:	:	:	:	Guadeloupe
:	:	:	:	:	0.1	0.2	:	:	:	:	Martinique
18.1	15.0	45.0	-10.9	24.8	0.0	0.0	0.1	0.1	0.1	0.1	Cayman Islands
-1.7	-14.6	55.4	6.6	12.4	0.0	0.0	0.0	0.0	0.0	0.0	Jamaica
-4.9	14.9	-11.0	47.3	-29.6	0.1	0.0	0.0	0.0	0.0	0.0	Trinidad and Tobago
6.3	18.6	3.6	-8.5	-10.2	0.1	0.0	0.0	0.0	0.0	0.0	Netherlands Antilles
4.9	-15.4	14.3	4.5	-20.6	4.9	3.0	3.9	3.6	3.6	2.8	**South America**
1.2	-35.1	22.0	11.0	-13.0	0.3	0.2	0.2	0.2	0.2	0.1	Colombia
25.1	-11.1	21.0	14.4	-16.7	0.9	0.4	0.3	0.3	0.3	0.3	Venezuela
:	:	:	:	:	0.0	0.2	:	:	:	:	French Guiana
-10.2	-9.3	9.6	8.3	29.4	0.0	0.0	0.0	0.0	0.0	0.0	Guina
-4.8	-37.6	23.2	53.1	14.5	0.1	0.0	0.0	0.0	0.0	0.0	Ecuador
2.4	-18.4	8.6	-3.6	-3.7	0.2	0.0	0.1	0.1	0.0	0.0	Peru
5.0	-9.1	16.7	10.2	-15.6	1.3	1.0	1.8	1.7	1.8	1.5	Brazil
-3.7	-23.6	36.7	6.4	-15.3	0.3	0.3	0.3	0.3	0.3	0.3	Chile
2.2	-14.0	10.5	-12.9	-40.0	0.1	0.0	0.1	0.0	0.0	0.0	Uruguay
4.3	-16.6	-3.4	-18.4	-57.3	1.2	0.3	0.8	0.6	0.5	0.2	Argentina
-3.3	-0.2	20.3	10.3	3.4	12.8	8.1	6.4	6.3	6.6	6.8	**Near and Middle East**
-8.7	-5.5	7.1	7.2	-3.0	0.5	0.2	0.3	0.3	0.3	0.2	*of which* Lebanon
13.3	8.5	5.6	18.7	0.2	0.5	0.2	0.2	0.1	0.2	0.2	Syria
149.0	26.4	83.9	71.7	-8.7	2.1	0.5	0.0	0.1	0.1	0.1	Iraq
-10.5	-12.0	34.6	26.3	22.1	1.8	1.4	0.5	0.5	0.6	0.8	Iran
-5.3	18.1	23.1	-8.8	-7.0	0.8	1.4	1.6	1.6	1.4	1.3	Israel
-5.0	9.1	30.3	12.8	6.9	0.3	0.2	0.1	0.1	0.1	0.1	Jordan
-8.7	-14.8	17.1	10.4	9.3	3.9	2.1	1.3	1.2	1.3	1.4	Saudi Arabia
-5.7	-7.1	16.0	17.8	5.6	0.7	0.2	0.2	0.2	0.2	0.2	Kuwait
15.3	37.4	-15.3	4.2	0.0	0.1	0.1	0.1	0.0	0.0	0.0	Bahrain
-29.0	-27.7	23.8	44.0	-2.2	0.1	0.1	0.1	0.1	0.1	0.1	Qatar
11.6	8.7	23.1	16.4	2.8	1.0	0.9	1.2	1.2	1.3	1.4	United Arab Emirates
9.5	-18.6	-3.2	27.7	-5.2	0.1	0.1	0.1	0.1	0.1	0.1	Oman
-18.1	5.6	29.7	2.6	-1.1	10.4	19.7	18.5	19.4	19.0	18.6	**Other Asian coutries**
-22.4	-15.7	-2.9	10.3	-18.1	:	:	0.0	0.0	0.0	0.0	*of which* Uzbekistan
-9.9	-22.2	27.5	27.7	2.1	:	:	0.1	0.1	0.1	0.1	Kazakhstan
-22.3	3.8	15.7	5.3	7.2	0.4	0.4	0.2	0.2	0.2	0.2	Pakistan
-6.5	8.1	29.2	-5.7	10.7	1.1	1.6	1.3	1.4	1.2	1.4	India
-15.2	3.5	19.3	21.2	-12.7	0.1	0.1	0.0	0.0	0.0	0.0	Bangladesh
-9.7	43.5	37.8	-37.6	-10.1	0.1	0.0	0.1	0.1	0.0	0.0	Sri Lanka
5.6	11.1	31.7	17.9	13.4	0.9	1.4	2.5	2.7	3.0	3.4	China
-53.3	-13.4	33.7	1.2	-0.3	0.6	0.7	0.4	0.4	0.4	0.4	Indonesia
-38.2	3.5	36.7	2.1	-28.0	0.3	0.3	0.4	0.4	0.4	0.3	Philippines
-33.1	-9.9	38.0	16.7	-10.7	0.3	0.9	0.6	0.6	0.7	0.6	Thailand
-8.2	-1.0	17.5	43.8	3.0	0.1	0.0	0.1	0.1	0.1	0.1	Vietnam
-37.4	17.4	30.2	11.1	-12.0	0.5	0.6	0.8	0.8	0.9	0.8	Malaysia
-34.6	-62.4	4.4	-40.7	-4.9	0.0	0.1	0.0	0.0	0.0	0.0	Brunei
-19.2	8.4	25.0	-1.3	-3.0	0.9	1.5	1.5	1.5	1.4	1.4	Singapore
-37.1	26.3	43.3	-5.4	11.1	0.4	1.7	1.5	1.7	1.5	1.7	South Korea
-12.5	12.0	27.0	0.0	-5.8	2.4	6.3	4.6	4.7	4.5	4.2	Japan
-4.7	-1.8	25.7	-10.9	-12.3	0.4	1.3	1.5	1.5	1.3	1.1	Taiwan
-15.2	-9.4	30.8	4.8	-7.5	1.0	1.8	2.0	2.1	2.1	2.0	Hong Kong
-3.6	-10.1	-4.6	-1.8	88.1	0.0	0.0	0.0	0.0	0.0	0.0	Macao
-2.5	7.6	12.4	2.2	6.5	2.1	2.5	2.2	2.0	2.0	2.1	**Oceania**
-1.1	5.7	14.4	-1.2	6.7	1.6	1.9	1.8	1.6	1.5	1.6	Australia
-9.2	14.5	4.7	9.3	1.4	0.3	0.3	0.2	0.2	0.2	0.2	New Zealand
-0.1	1.9	23.8	1.8	16.7	0.0	0.1	0.0	0.0	0.0	0.0	New Caledonia and dep.
10.1	-8.0	19.5	4.1	-13.6	5.5	4.3	6.0	5.8	5.7	4.9	**Latin America**
-7.9	-6.6	22.8	18.4	5.0	17.2	9.9	5.7	5.7	6.4	6.7	**OPEC**
-22.6	3.1	31.5	0.3	-4.7	3.4	8.1	8.1	8.6	8.3	7.8	**DAE**

TRENDS IN EU TRADE BY PARTNER COUNTRY

IMPORTS

Main partners	Value (Mio ECU/Euro)											
	1980	1990	1993	1994	1995	1996	1997	1998	1999	2000	2001	2002
Extra EU	**281,117**	**404,351**	**431,689**	**474,284**	**545,253**	**581,015**	**672,568**	**710,538**	**779,825**	**1,033,436**	**1,027,955**	**987,479**
Europe excluding EU	**57,263**	**153,912**	**162,169**	**187,502**	**152,236**	**159,518**	**183,951**	**192,621**	**210,348**	**281,204**	**300,905**	**309,383**
of which Iceland	382	936	821	877	920	974	1,058	1,225	1,327	1,643	1,698	1,757
Norway	9,845	16,313	17,846	19,961	25,518	27,863	33,711	28,134	29,594	46,101	45,112	45,800
Liechtenstein	:	:	:	:	268	448	578	634	739	858	935	910
Switzerland[1]	17,335	34,273	35,736	80,533	43,222	42,750	45,130	49,460	52,881	60,018	60,835	58,794
Faroe Islands	111	294	276	246	235	298	316	345	379	404	526	480
Andorra	15	35	31	35	33	29	41	43	42	45	49	60
Poland	3,369	5,153	7,583	9,107	12,256	12,249	14,228	16,176	17,582	23,307	26,623	28,201
Hungary	1,779	2,934	3,953	4,923	7,610	8,847	11,684	14,655	17,624	22,046	24,817	25,276
Romania	1,959	1,605	1,690	2,509	3,390	3,590	4,428	5,138	5,775	7,650	9,374	10,430
Bulgaria	560	583	951	1,343	1,836	1,712	2,091	2,238	2,257	3,083	3,492	3,615
Albania	67	81	81	123	151	198	191	217	229	277	352	335
Czech Republic[2]	1,995	2,688	4,843	6,364	8,997	9,766	11,755	14,670	16,844	21,638	25,136	27,531
Slovakia	:	:	1,161	1,874	3,089	3,419	3,982	5,373	5,961	6,942	8,160	9,717
Estonia	:	:	181	266	889	1,087	1,504	1,670	1,891	3,176	3,032	2,965
Latvia	:	:	618	735	1,126	1,141	1,281	1,342	1,408	1,901	1,910	1,949
Lithuania	:	:	641	750	971	1,119	1,314	1,417	1,620	2,169	2,623	2,720
Ukraine	:	:	934	1,254	1,544	1,457	1,885	2,235	2,084	2,953	3,647	4,190
Belarus	:	:	265	426	562	416	436	464	539	742	690	867
Russia[3]	15,013	16,184	15,540	18,398	21,492	23,397	27,038	23,173	25,977	45,724	47,688	47,700
Serbia and Montenegro[4]	2,399	7,670	3	4	32	490	1,029	1,073	570	808	1,098	1,311
Slovenia	:	:	2,866	3,422	4,245	4,271	4,668	5,227	5,297	6,284	6,577	6,840
Croatia	:	:	1,646	1,808	1,893	1,742	1,777	1,826	1,914	2,215	2,500	2,457
Form. Yug. Rep. Maced.	:	:	534	661	664	429	492	598	593	747	646	562
Gibraltar	5	37	46	62	60	65	66	42	133	86	126	85
Malta	268	649	864	1,031	1,077	797	701	765	851	1,035	1,171	1,120
Cyprus	278	578	719	619	737	564	373	434	605	1,004	955	715
Turkey	1,131	5,940	6,545	7,539	9,245	10,184	11,872	13,624	15,071	17,547	20,217	22,029
Africa	**43,736**	**49,757**	**43,830**	**46,302**	**46,894**	**52,349**	**56,752**	**53,122**	**57,029**	**83,937**	**87,057**	**81,433**
of which **North Africa**	**17,625**	**23,570**	**22,050**	**22,778**	**21,301**	**24,268**	**27,382**	**24,630**	**27,376**	**44,428**	**43,107**	**39,276**
of which Canary Islands	:	1,095	1,452	1,334	1,086	1,039	:	:	:	:	:	:
Ceuta and Melilla	:	10	23	48	12	8	0.0	11	21	25	33	37
Morocco	1,394	3,050	3,394	3,701	4,017	4,233	4,750	5,334	5,553	6,015	6,241	6,296
Algeria	4,552	6,970	6,321	5,919	4,844	5,509	8,361	6,807	7,776	16,424	16,034	14,249
Tunisia	1,387	2,252	2,492	3,036	3,352	3,633	4,017	4,290	4,774	5,495	6,188	6,041
Libya	7,883	7,896	6,135	5,956	5,799	7,066	7,618	5,662	6,857	13,033	11,473	9,409
Egypt	2,409	2,298	2,232	2,785	2,190	2,780	2,637	2,527	2,394	3,436	3,138	3,244
Sudan	199	160	136	176	172	168	234	241	185	255	304	265
Mauritania	160	239	221	235	257	266	317	319	312	346	376	373
Senegal	215	411	238	286	370	337	349	427	444	409	451	407
Guinea	152	308	219	318	310	352	378	439	397	515	586	477
Liberia	492	702	171	370	637	578	433	430	414	434	737	873
Ivory Coast	1,622	1,666	1,386	1,740	2,068	2,008	1,990	2,276	2,080	1,959	2,057	2,529
Ghana	436	730	514	779	839	877	940	1,218	1,186	1,159	1,069	1,116
Benin	45	43	46	63	58	68	64	56	41	79	65	58
Nigeria	8,703	4,446	3,137	4,055	3,443	5,018	4,544	2,847	2,795	6,413	6,458	4,998
Cameroon	768	1,382	966	1,124	1,175	1,197	1,537	1,423	1,320	1,694	1,735	1,547
Gabon	964	1,092	787	858	799	851	947	846	1,023	1,034	1,174	607
Congo	410	602	314	564	718	890	715	388	293	367	411	504
Zaire	1,340	1,142	553	761	842	850	733	780	876	1,026	1,035	1,244
Angola	250	1,103	446	562	561	683	606	588	769	1,530	2,010	2,264
Ethiopia	123	129	148	144	230	250	260	283	178	243	173	190
Kenya	506	519	527	590	647	745	821	777	840	831	924	853
Uganda	181	131	82	234	356	375	365	283	267	251	250	263
Tanzania	230	177	167	186	202	208	246	256	233	412	408	434
Madagascar	142	151	222	307	346	365	415	476	497	584	602	503
Reunion	100	125	124	121	123	118	:	:	:	:	:	:
Mauritius	320	757	826	824	1,020	1,071	1,081	1,107	1,157	1,206	1,289	1,342
Zimbabwe	211	578	417	561	639	719	825	700	752	766	783	613
Namibia	:	1,727	226	418	370	290	325	385	509	510	884	739
South Africa[5]	6,546	5,922	8,618	6,736	7,752	8,218	9,089	9,724	10,700	14,475	16,018	15,626
CEEC[6]	**12,128**	**20,715**	**26,780**	**33,900**	**47,172**	**50,129**	**60,586**	**71,868**	**79,925**	**102,778**	**116,949**	**124,541**
ACP[7]	**18,893**	**21,903**	**14,945**	**18,615**	**19,893**	**22,033**	**23,047**	**31,153**	**32,566**	**43,330**	**47,629**	**46,067**
DOM	**241**	**495**	**428**	**446**	**447**	**480**	**:**	**:**	**:**	**:**	**:**	**:**
Mediterranean Basin	**33,001**	**42,312**	**39,360**	**42,630**	**44,980**	**49,613**	**57,342**	**57,384**	**63,185**	**88,779**	**91,523**	**88,447**

(1) Including Liechtenstein up to 1994.
(2) Czechoslovakia before 1993.
(3) Relates to the external trade of the USSR until 1991 and from 1992 to the external trade of Russia.
(4) In 1992, Serbia, Montenegro and Macedonia. Since 1993, Serbia and Montenegro.

IMPORTS

Annual variation (%)					Share (%)						Main partners
98/97	99/98	00/99	01/00	02/01	1980	1990	1999	2000	2001	2002	
5.6	9.7	32.5	-0.5	-3.9	100.0	100.0	100.0	100.0	100.0	100.0	**Extra EU**
4.7	9.2	33.6	7.0	2.8	20.3	38.0	26.9	27.2	29.2	31.3	**Europe excluding EU**
15.7	8.3	23.8	3.3	3.4	0.1	0.2	0.1	0.1	0.1	0.1	*of which* Iceland
-16.5	5.1	55.7	-2.1	1.5	3.5	4.0	3.7	4.4	4.3	4.6	Norway
9.7	16.6	16.0	8.9	-2.6	:	:	0.0	0.0	0.0	0.0	Liechtenstein
9.5	6.9	13.4	1.3	-3.3	6.1	8.4	6.7	5.8	5.9	5.9	Switzerland[1]
9.1	9.8	6.5	30.1	-8.7	0.0	0.0	0.0	0.0	0.0	0.0	Faroe Islands
5.7	-2.7	6.2	8.5	22.2	0.0	0.0	0.0	0.0	0.0	0.0	Andorra
13.6	8.6	32.5	14.2	5.9	1.1	1.2	2.2	2.2	2.5	2.8	Poland
25.4	20.2	25.0	12.5	1.8	0.6	0.7	2.2	2.1	2.4	2.5	Hungary
16.0	12.4	32.4	22.5	11.2	0.6	0.3	0.7	0.7	0.9	1.0	Romania
7.0	0.8	36.6	13.2	3.5	0.1	0.1	0.2	0.2	0.3	0.3	Bulgaria
13.3	5.8	20.9	26.8	-4.9	0.0	0.0	0.0	0.0	0.0	0.0	Albania
24.8	14.8	28.4	16.1	9.5	0.7	0.6	2.1	2.0	2.4	2.7	Czech Republic[2]
34.9	10.9	16.4	17.5	19.0	:	:	0.7	0.6	0.7	0.9	Slovakia
11.0	13.2	67.9	-4.5	-2.1	:	:	0.2	0.3	0.2	0.3	Estonia
4.7	4.8	34.9	0.4	2.0	:	:	0.1	0.1	0.1	0.1	Latvia
7.8	14.2	33.8	20.9	3.6	:	:	0.2	0.2	0.2	0.2	Lithuania
18.5	-6.7	41.6	23.5	14.8	:	:	0.2	0.2	0.3	0.4	Ukraine
6.4	16.2	37.6	-7.0	25.5	:	:	0.0	0.0	0.0	0.0	Belarus
-14.2	12.1	76.0	4.2	0.0	5.3	4.0	3.3	4.4	4.6	4.8	Russia[3]
4.1	-46.8	41.8	35.7	19.4	0.8	1.8	0.0	0.0	0.1	0.1	Serbia and Montenegro[4]
11.9	1.3	18.6	4.6	4.0	:	:	0.6	0.6	0.6	0.6	Slovenia
2.7	4.7	15.7	12.8	-1.7	:	:	0.2	0.2	0.2	0.2	Croatia
21.5	-0.8	26.0	-13.5	-13.0	:	:	0.0	0.0	0.0	0.0	Form. Yug. Rep. Maced.
-36.6	219.6	-35.6	46.5	-32.1	0.0	0.0	0.0	0.0	0.0	0.0	Gibraltar
9.0	11.2	21.6	13.1	-4.3	0.0	0.1	0.1	0.1	0.1	0.1	Malta
16.4	39.3	65.9	-4.8	-25.2	0.0	0.1	0.0	0.0	0.0	0.0	Cyprus
14.7	10.6	16.4	15.2	8.9	0.4	1.4	1.9	1.6	1.9	2.2	Turkey
-6.3	7.3	47.1	3.7	-6.4	15.5	12.3	7.3	8.1	8.4	8.2	**Africa**
-10.0	11.1	62.2	-2.9	-8.8	6.2	5.8	3.5	4.2	4.1	3.9	*of which* **North Africa**
:	:	:	:	:	:	0.2	:	:	:	:	*of which* Canary Islands
81,392.3	102.2	18.6	29.3	13.8	:	0.0	0.0	0.0	0.0	0.0	Ceuta and Melilla
12.2	4.0	8.3	3.7	0.8	0.4	0.7	0.7	0.5	0.6	0.6	Morocco
-18.5	14.2	111.2	-2.3	-11.1	1.6	1.7	0.9	1.5	1.5	1.4	Algeria
6.7	11.2	15.0	12.6	-2.3	0.4	0.5	0.6	0.5	0.6	0.6	Tunisia
-25.6	21.1	90.0	-11.9	-17.9	2.8	1.9	0.8	1.2	1.1	0.9	Libya
-4.1	-5.2	43.5	-8.6	3.3	0.8	0.5	0.3	0.3	0.3	0.3	Egypt
2.6	-23.3	38.1	19.2	-12.8	0.0	0.0	0.0	0.0	0.0	0.0	Sudan
0.7	-2.2	10.7	8.6	-0.7	0.0	0.0	0.0	0.0	0.0	0.0	Mauritania
22.3	3.8	-7.9	10.4	-9.7	0.0	0.1	0.0	0.0	0.0	0.0	Senegal
16.3	-9.7	29.7	13.9	-18.5	0.0	0.0	0.0	0.0	0.0	0.0	Guinea
-0.7	-3.5	4.8	69.7	18.4	0.1	0.1	0.0	0.0	0.0	0.0	Liberia
14.3	-8.6	-5.8	5.0	22.9	0.5	0.4	0.2	0.1	0.2	0.2	Ivory Coast
29.5	-2.6	-2.2	-7.7	4.3	0.1	0.1	0.1	0.1	0.1	0.1	Ghana
-12.3	-26.9	92.8	-17.2	-10.6	0.0	0.0	0.0	0.0	0.0	0.0	Benin
-37.3	-1.8	129.4	0.7	-22.6	3.0	1.0	0.3	0.6	0.6	0.5	Nigeria
-7.4	-7.2	28.3	2.4	-10.8	0.2	0.3	0.1	0.1	0.1	0.1	Cameroon
-10.7	20.9	1.1	13.5	-48.2	0.3	0.2	0.1	0.1	0.1	0.0	Gabon
-45.6	-24.5	25.3	11.9	22.6	0.1	0.1	0.0	0.0	0.0	0.0	Congo
6.4	12.3	17.0	0.9	20.1	0.4	0.2	0.1	0.0	0.1	0.1	Zaire
-3.0	30.9	98.8	31.3	12.6	0.0	0.2	0.0	0.1	0.1	0.2	Angola
9.2	-37.1	36.7	-29.0	10.1	0.0	0.0	0.0	0.0	0.0	0.0	Ethiopia
-5.4	8.0	-1.0	11.2	-7.7	0.1	0.1	0.1	0.0	0.0	0.0	Kenya
-22.3	-5.7	-5.7	-0.7	5.5	0.0	0.0	0.0	0.0	0.0	0.0	Uganda
4.2	-8.9	76.8	-0.8	6.3	0.0	0.0	0.0	0.0	0.0	0.0	Tanzania
14.6	4.5	17.4	3.0	-16.4	0.0	0.0	0.0	0.0	0.0	0.0	Madagascar
:	:	:	:	:	0.0	0.0	:	:	:	:	Reunion
2.3	4.4	4.2	6.8	4.1	0.1	0.1	0.1	0.1	0.1	0.1	Mauritius
-15.1	7.3	1.9	2.2	-21.7	0.0	0.1	0.0	0.0	0.0	0.0	Zimbabwe
18.4	32.2	0.2	73.3	-16.4	:	0.4	0.0	0.0	0.0	0.0	Namibia
6.9	10.0	35.2	10.6	-2.4	2.3	1.4	1.3	1.4	1.5	1.5	South Africa[5]
18.6	11.2	28.5	13.7	6.4	4.3	5.1	10.2	9.9	11.3	12.6	**CEEC[6]**
35.1	4.5	33.0	9.9	-3.2	6.7	5.4	4.1	4.1	4.6	4.6	**ACP[7]**
:	:	:	:	:	0.0	0.1	:	:	:	:	**DOM**
0.0	10.1	40.5	3.0	-3.3	11.7	10.4	8.1	8.5	8.9	8.9	**Mediterranean Basin**

(5)   South Africa includes Namibia up to 31.12.1989.
(6)   Including Estonia Latvia and Lithuania since 1.1.1992.
(7)   Including Eritrea since 1.1.1994 and Namibia since 1.1.1990.

TRENDS IN EU TRADE BY PARTNER COUNTRY

IMPORTS

Main partners	Value (Mio ECU/Euro)											
	1980	1990	1993	1994	1995	1996	1997	1998	1999	2000	2001	2002
North America	57,597	94,693	92,406	101,996	115,594	124,890	150,607	164,945	174,297	217,645	213,869	190,859
of which USA	50,706	84,946	84,334	92,625	103,674	113,140	137,847	152,019	160,588	199,024	195,655	174,656
Canada	6,776	9,404	7,883	9,114	11,707	11,511	12,537	12,736	13,507	18,398	17,978	15,911
Central America and Antilles	5,853	6,270	6,076	7,120	8,695	9,487	10,926	10,683	12,187	17,318	16,832	15,863
of which Mexico	2,051	2,956	2,333	2,628	3,208	3,153	3,818	4,018	4,695	7,042	7,382	6,215
Bermuda	15	86	485	454	780	924	1,023	443	677	745	1,343	925
Guatemala	332	139	190	240	370	343	457	427	404	461	346	268
El Salvador	269	117	108	255	278	270	371	236	165	183	112	114
Costa Rica	254	433	471	717	813	813	881	1,343	1,729	2,658	2,027	2,487
Panama	212	487	264	258	384	423	439	350	358	410	480	502
Cuba	365	318	242	304	344	400	454	446	499	682	581	621
Bahamas	692	213	307	207	232	245	321	322	471	636	612	617
Dominican Republic	91	117	154	191	223	227	256	254	223	321	315	351
Guadeloupe	75	97	114	118	90	71	:	:	:	:	:	:
Martinique	61	196	136	143	127	163	:	:	:	:	:	:
Cayman Islands	2	9	46	179	178	462	633	602	785	909	899	788
Jamaica	227	276	329	335	368	470	464	516	546	527	571	510
Trinidad and Tobago	303	178	164	219	227	215	436	377	320	511	486	504
Netherlands Antilles	454	55	127	238	326	369	311	254	186	283	190	130
South America	14,536	21,169	18,415	22,520	24,825	24,617	27,896	28,333	29,165	37,083	38,671	37,805
Colombia	1,444	1,457	1,522	1,906	2,247	2,181	2,534	2,507	2,039	2,342	2,405	2,271
Venezuela	2,566	1,782	1,152	1,273	1,622	1,527	1,757	1,419	1,756	2,739	2,938	2,707
French Guiana	5	75	54	65	107	128	:	:	:	:	:	:
Guina	122	118	142	149	146	174	190	162	186	207	204	183
Ecuador	238	351	577	729	818	878	945	892	937	870	941	1,087
Peru	596	796	863	1,275	1,316	1,305	1,438	1,164	1,427	1,699	2,084	2,339
Brazil	5,146	9,194	8,180	10,339	10,820	10,442	12,581	13,225	13,323	17,630	18,321	17,309
Chile	1,486	2,609	2,057	2,405	3,175	3,184	3,467	3,514	3,607	5,113	5,108	4,834
Uruguay	264	567	317	352	344	409	495	444	468	425	472	566
Argentina	2,085	3,468	3,057	3,529	3,705	3,882	3,846	4,164	4,751	5,412	5,531	6,058
Near and Middle East	58,609	25,536	24,100	23,245	23,664	25,808	30,060	24,249	31,696	52,509	45,718	41,256
of which Lebanon	48	91	64	90	111	123	154	154	209	245	305	185
Syria	927	1,234	1,666	1,572	1,735	2,025	2,027	1,465	2,158	3,426	4,136	4,055
Iraq	10,357	2,222	25	1	1	1	1,386	1,866	3,681	6,289	3,555	2,754
Iran	3,853	5,781	5,870	5,323	5,441	5,762	5,189	3,711	4,743	8,426	6,675	5,594
Israel	1,776	3,465	3,423	4,093	4,658	5,260	6,274	6,921	7,648	9,957	9,568	8,543
Jordan	21	92	277	151	135	167	174	159	169	180	151	294
Saudi Arabia	29,727	8,284	9,298	8,818	8,847	9,331	10,913	6,641	8,456	15,900	13,085	12,316
Kuwait	4,236	1,808	1,805	1,707	1,367	1,589	1,480	710	1,474	3,202	2,380	1,810
Bahrain	53	90	116	111	136	95	215	267	259	434	522	385
Qatar	1,755	77	188	112	113	117	235	288	234	373	669	461
United Arab Emirates	5,461	1,535	938	872	851	955	1,480	1,614	1,839	2,470	2,813	2,829
Oman	380	154	129	159	117	172	181	181	140	185	284	434
Other Asian coutries	36,816	102,868	129,083	140,043	159,058	168,361	199,257	222,393	245,050	317,259	300,266	291,935
of which Uzbekistan	:	:	416	519	500	519	541	466	393	506	630	806
Kazakhstan	:	:	293	271	359	468	1,442	937	1,775	3,206	3,002	3,566
Pakistan	491	1,461	1,677	1,894	1,979	2,068	2,283	2,321	2,221	2,621	2,835	2,922
India	1,908	4,539	5,878	6,887	7,796	8,594	9,485	9,795	10,022	12,372	12,911	13,039
Bangladesh	157	501	904	1,097	1,260	1,474	1,772	1,978	2,122	3,091	3,349	3,213
Sri Lanka	240	440	730	886	930	990	1,145	1,192	1,290	1,907	1,552	1,437
China	2,096	10,589	19,631	22,688	26,343	30,044	37,490	41,974	49,655	70,275	75,915	81,843
Indonesia	1,310	2,863	5,032	5,857	6,109	7,107	8,330	8,955	8,759	10,949	10,885	10,297
Philippines	915	1,258	1,910	2,099	2,420	3,474	4,374	6,086	6,391	8,869	7,633	7,636
Thailand	1,305	4,101	5,533	6,265	6,625	7,596	8,616	9,337	10,121	12,879	12,379	11,198
Vietnam	13	83	544	858	1,151	1,436	2,246	2,613	3,155	4,026	4,485	4,429
Malaysia	2,016	3,605	6,260	7,526	9,156	9,419	10,799	12,243	13,307	17,368	15,769	14,437
Brunei	3	225	397	314	263	416	544	299	101	174	55	81
Singapore	1,956	4,686	6,441	7,753	8,760	9,276	11,510	12,535	12,765	15,947	13,919	13,115
South Korea	1,971	6,548	7,751	8,560	10,925	11,108	13,125	16,009	18,353	24,934	21,597	22,260
Japan	15,428	46,086	47,673	48,453	54,299	52,556	59,876	66,042	71,911	87,133	76,298	68,485
Taiwan	2,128	9,136	10,387	10,309	11,756	13,272	15,698	18,089	20,017	26,654	24,177	21,128
Hong Kong	3,973	5,909	6,438	6,493	7,156	7,262	8,371	9,718	10,681	11,650	10,271	9,704
Macao	261	519	520	549	532	569	667	643	654	866	825	714
Oceania	4,567	6,931	5,909	6,852	7,454	7,830	9,105	10,521	9,911	12,028	12,874	12,361
Australia	2,687	4,806	3,941	4,644	4,971	5,227	6,263	7,540	6,922	8,856	9,265	8,867
New Zealand	1,176	1,564	1,432	1,568	1,696	1,879	2,074	2,225	2,197	2,403	2,700	2,675
New Caledonia and dep.	238	189	145	169	189	185	189	147	143	251	253	207
Latin America	13,579	25,633	22,117	27,024	30,430	30,240	34,651	35,569	37,228	48,985	49,944	48,367
OPEC	67,233	45,106	41,264	41,479	38,437	43,981	51,292	40,517	48,370	86,217	76,966	67,422
DAE	12,503	33,985	42,809	46,905	54,378	57,934	68,118	77,931	85,244	109,431	98,112	91,841

IMPORTS

Annual variation (%)					Share (%)						Main partners
98/97	99/98	00/99	01/00	02/01	1980	1990	1999	2000	2001	2002	
9.5	5.6	24.8	-1.7	-10.7	20.4	23.4	22.3	21.0	20.8	19.3	**North America**
10.2	5.6	23.9	-1.6	-10.7	18.0	21.0	20.5	19.2	19.0	17.6	*of which* USA
1.5	6.0	36.2	-2.2	-11.4	2.4	2.3	1.7	1.7	1.7	1.6	Canada
-2.2	14.0	42.1	-2.8	-5.7	2.0	1.5	1.5	1.6	1.6	1.6	**Central America and Antilles**
5.2	16.8	49.9	4.8	-15.8	0.7	0.7	0.6	0.6	0.7	0.6	*of which* Mexico
-56.7	52.9	10.0	80.2	-31.1	0.0	0.0	0.0	0.0	0.1	0.0	Bermuda
-6.6	-5.3	14.1	-24.9	-22.5	0.1	0.0	0.0	0.0	0.0	0.0	Guatemala
-36.4	-30.0	10.9	-38.5	1.6	0.0	0.0	0.0	0.0	0.0	0.0	El Salvador
52.3	28.7	53.7	-23.7	22.6	0.0	0.1	0.2	0.2	0.1	0.2	Costa Rica
-20.3	2.4	14.5	17.1	4.6	0.0	0.1	0.0	0.0	0.0	0.0	Panama
-1.8	11.9	36.6	-14.8	6.9	0.1	0.0	0.0	0.0	0.0	0.0	Cuba
0.3	46.1	35.0	-3.6	0.7	0.2	0.0	0.0	0.0	0.0	0.0	Bahamas
-1.0	-12.2	44.1	-1.9	11.3	0.0	0.0	0.0	0.0	0.0	0.0	Dominican Republic
:	:	:	:	:	0.0	0.0	:	:	:	:	Guadeloupe
:	:	:	:	:	0.0	0.0	:	:	:	:	Martinique
-4.9	30.4	15.8	-1.0	-12.3	0.0	0.0	0.1	0.0	0.0	0.0	Cayman Islands
11.4	5.7	-3.5	8.3	-10.7	0.0	0.0	0.0	0.0	0.0	0.0	Jamaica
-13.5	-15.0	59.5	-4.9	3.7	0.1	0.0	0.0	0.0	0.0	0.0	Trinidad and Tobago
-18.2	-26.7	51.9	-32.8	-31.4	0.1	0.0	0.0	0.0	0.0	0.0	Netherlands Antilles
1.5	2.9	27.1	4.2	-2.2	5.1	5.2	3.7	3.5	3.7	3.8	**South America**
-1.0	-18.7	14.8	2.6	-5.5	0.5	0.3	0.2	0.2	0.2	0.2	Colombia
-19.2	23.7	56.0	7.2	-7.8	0.9	0.4	0.2	0.2	0.2	0.2	Venezuela
:	:	:	:	:	0.0	0.0	:	:	:	:	French Guiana
-14.6	14.9	10.9	-1.2	-10.6	0.0	0.0	0.0	0.0	0.0	0.0	Guina
-5.5	5.0	-7.1	8.1	15.4	0.0	0.0	0.1	0.0	0.0	0.1	Ecuador
-19.0	22.5	19.0	22.6	12.2	0.2	0.1	0.1	0.1	0.2	0.2	Peru
5.1	0.7	32.3	3.9	-5.5	1.8	2.2	1.7	1.7	1.7	1.7	Brazil
1.3	2.6	41.7	-0.1	-5.3	0.5	0.6	0.4	0.4	0.4	0.4	Chile
-10.3	5.4	-9.1	11.0	20.0	0.0	0.1	0.0	0.0	0.0	0.0	Uruguay
8.2	14.0	13.9	2.2	9.5	0.7	0.8	0.6	0.5	0.5	0.6	Argentina
-19.3	30.7	65.6	-12.9	-9.7	20.8	6.3	4.0	5.0	4.4	4.1	**Near and Middle East**
0.4	35.4	17.2	24.2	-39.3	0.0	0.0	0.0	0.0	0.0	0.0	*of which* Lebanon
-27.7	47.3	58.7	20.7	-1.9	0.3	0.3	0.2	0.3	0.4	0.4	Syria
34.6	97.2	70.8	-43.4	-22.5	3.6	0.5	0.4	0.6	0.3	0.2	Iraq
-28.4	27.8	77.6	-20.7	-16.2	1.3	1.4	0.6	0.8	0.6	0.5	Iran
10.3	10.5	30.1	-3.8	-10.7	0.6	0.8	0.9	0.9	0.9	0.8	Israel
-8.5	6.1	6.2	-15.8	94.0	0.0	0.0	0.0	0.0	0.0	0.0	Jordan
-39.1	27.3	88.0	-17.7	-5.8	10.5	2.0	1.0	1.5	1.2	1.2	Saudi Arabia
-52.0	107.7	117.1	-25.6	-23.9	1.5	0.4	0.1	0.3	0.2	0.1	Kuwait
24.0	-3.0	67.8	20.0	-26.1	0.0	0.0	0.0	0.0	0.0	0.0	Bahrain
22.3	-18.7	59.5	79.1	-31.1	0.6	0.0	0.0	0.0	0.0	0.0	Qatar
9.0	13.9	34.3	13.9	0.5	1.9	0.3	0.2	0.2	0.2	0.2	United Arab Emirates
0.1	-22.7	32.5	53.0	52.9	0.1	0.0	0.0	0.0	0.0	0.0	Oman
11.6	10.1	29.4	-5.3	-2.7	13.0	25.4	31.4	30.6	29.2	29.5	**Other Asian coutries**
-13.9	-15.6	28.7	24.6	27.8	:	:	0.0	0.0	0.0	0.0	*of which* Uzbekistan
-35.0	89.4	80.5	-6.3	18.7	:	:	0.2	0.3	0.2	0.3	Kazakhstan
1.6	-4.2	18.0	8.1	3.0	0.1	0.3	0.2	0.2	0.2	0.2	Pakistan
3.2	2.3	23.4	4.3	0.9	0.6	1.1	1.2	1.1	1.2	1.3	India
11.5	7.3	45.6	8.3	-4.0	0.0	0.1	0.2	0.2	0.3	0.3	Bangladesh
4.1	8.2	47.8	-18.6	-7.3	0.0	0.1	0.1	0.1	0.1	0.1	Sri Lanka
11.9	18.2	41.5	8.0	7.8	0.7	2.6	6.3	6.8	7.3	8.2	China
7.5	-2.1	25.0	-0.5	-5.4	0.4	0.7	1.1	1.0	1.0	1.0	Indonesia
39.1	4.9	38.7	-13.9	0.0	0.3	0.3	0.8	0.8	0.7	0.7	Philippines
8.3	8.3	27.2	-3.8	-9.5	0.4	1.0	1.2	1.2	1.2	1.1	Thailand
16.3	20.7	27.6	11.3	-1.2	0.0	0.0	0.4	0.3	0.4	0.4	Vietnam
13.3	8.6	30.5	-9.2	-8.4	0.7	0.8	1.7	1.6	1.5	1.4	Malaysia
-45.0	-66.1	71.8	-68.3	47.0	0.0	0.0	0.0	0.0	0.0	0.0	Brunei
8.9	1.8	24.9	-12.7	-5.7	0.6	1.1	1.6	1.5	1.3	1.3	Singapore
21.9	14.6	35.8	-13.3	3.0	0.7	1.6	2.3	2.4	2.1	2.2	South Korea
10.2	8.8	21.1	-12.4	-10.2	5.4	11.3	9.2	8.4	7.4	6.9	Japan
15.2	10.6	33.1	-9.2	-12.6	0.7	2.2	2.5	2.5	2.3	2.1	Taiwan
16.0	9.9	9.0	-11.8	-5.5	1.4	1.4	1.3	1.1	0.9	0.9	Hong Kong
-3.6	1.7	32.3	-4.6	-13.4	0.0	0.1	0.0	0.0	0.0	0.0	Macao
15.5	-5.7	21.3	7.0	-3.9	1.6	1.7	1.2	1.1	1.2	1.2	**Oceania**
20.3	-8.2	27.9	4.6	-4.2	0.9	1.1	0.8	0.8	0.9	0.8	Australia
7.2	-1.2	9.3	12.3	-0.9	0.4	0.3	0.2	0.2	0.2	0.2	New Zealand
-22.0	-2.5	75.0	1.0	-18.4	0.0	0.0	0.0	0.0	0.0	0.0	New Caledonia and dep.
2.6	4.6	31.5	1.9	-3.1	4.8	6.3	4.7	4.7	4.8	4.8	**Latin America**
-21.0	19.3	78.2	-10.7	-12.4	23.9	11.1	6.2	8.3	7.4	6.8	**OPEC**
14.4	9.3	28.3	-10.3	-6.3	4.4	8.4	10.9	10.5	9.5	9.3	**DAE**

TRENDS IN EU TRADE BY PARTNER COUNTRY

eurostat

TRADE BALANCE

Main partners	Value (Mio ECU/Euro)											
	1980	**1990**	1993	1994	1995	1996	1997	1998	1999	**2000**	2001	**2002**
Extra EU	**-69,006**	**-49,187**	**-1,442**	**2,405**	**28,024**	**45,279**	**48,561**	**22,890**	**-19,633**	**-91,391**	**-42,629**	**6,317**
Europe excluding EU	**5,212**	**1,522**	**9,039**	**1,807**	**14,465**	**30,831**	**40,227**	**44,751**	**24,709**	**6,399**	**4,060**	**8,244**
of which Iceland	30	-299	-175	-274	-109	-52	79	23	65	90	-145	-408
Norway	-1,840	-7,017	-7,691	-8,475	-8,043	-8,108	-10,350	-3,045	-6,351	-20,503	-18,958	-19,275
Liechtenstein	:	:	:	:	180	86	-27	80	-88	27	-101	-167
Switzerland[1]	6,980	7,015	3,727	1,208	7,819	8,707	7,894	7,720	9,675	10,764	13,926	11,850
Faroe Islands	0.0	-163	-154	-111	-70	-104	-122	-133	-133	-134	-187	-170
Andorra	307	839	696	650	689	659	809	797	848	929	964	1,034
Poland	98	-763	2,400	1,868	3,058	7,722	10,852	12,030	11,391	10,503	9,058	9,126
Hungary	258	-58	1,014	1,230	1,120	1,181	1,912	2,208	817	993	-939	-272
Romania	32	-378	630	139	405	883	587	1,162	557	1,093	1,141	1,006
Bulgaria	370	318	396	255	217	-17	-244	198	449	154	520	614
Albania	3	37	319	303	367	546	375	339	463	524	742	747
Czech Republic[2]	-312	-82	1,239	1,564	2,660	4,242	4,154	2,544	1,589	2,365	2,537	1,691
Slovakia	:	:	60	-80	105	585	836	436	-444	-344	-201	-964
Estonia	:	:	29	43	461	606	883	1,027	522	33	15	572
Latvia	:	:	-307	-247	-184	-27	254	477	256	125	537	638
Lithuania	:	:	-163	-24	50	341	841	978	478	413	788	1,294
Ukraine	:	:	541	414	706	1,170	1,556	1,308	523	702	1,304	1,328
Belarus	:	:	288	150	324	486	797	711	485	395	703	641
Russia[3]	-4,769	-5,007	-4,012	-6,226	-5,358	-4,264	-1,498	-2,002	-11,250	-25,807	-19,727	-17,261
Serbia and Montenegro[4]	2,515	822	80	125	159	761	739	720	654	998	1,424	1,706
Slovenia	:	:	195	253	934	1,116	1,670	1,547	1,621	1,860	1,890	1,819
Croatia	:	:	413	1,107	1,846	2,155	3,009	2,595	2,109	2,416	2,992	4,024
Form. Yug. Rep. Maced.	:	:	141	78	216	380	358	293	580	579	538	459
Gibraltar	83	257	408	531	341	582	621	438	633	1,156	1,005	1,323
Malta	248	560	897	836	939	1,074	1,297	1,214	1,227	1,752	1,331	1,572
Cyprus	351	698	1,161	1,380	1,278	1,369	1,586	1,696	1,763	2,119	2,001	2,181
Turkey	902	1,778	5,235	1,337	4,146	8,136	10,505	8,563	5,510	12,407	49	2,188
Africa	**-4,188**	**-4,827**	**850**	**-536**	**4,698**	**1,039**	**-4,675**	**5,551**	**-110**	**-17,825**	**-17,143**	**-12,049**
of which **North Africa**	**-413**	**-751**	**1,819**	**1,352**	**4,684**	**2,472**	**-2,851**	**4,021**	**1,495**	**-11,931**	**-9,350**	**-5,622**
of which Canary Islands	:	2,942	2,667	2,850	3,397	3,729	:	:	:	:	:	:
Ceuta and Melilla	:	485	582	525	584	513	30	645	758	982	916	837
Morocco	431	520	843	672	711	467	579	1,269	1,075	1,720	1,236	1,375
Algeria	733	-2,015	-2,205	-1,307	-118	-1,434	-4,004	-1,539	-2,556	-10,317	-8,526	-6,175
Tunisia	387	715	1,138	748	803	712	1,269	1,495	1,257	1,788	1,777	1,523
Libya	-3,173	-5,251	-3,396	-3,918	-3,520	-4,561	-4,846	-2,919	-4,571	-10,537	-8,520	-6,276
Egypt	1,210	1,853	2,190	1,782	2,827	3,047	4,121	5,070	5,533	4,432	3,767	3,094
Sudan	311	177	135	121	108	127	126	290	289	185	308	277
Mauritania	-7	-18	19	13	-24	-5	-40	-36	-36	31	6	23
Senegal	252	273	289	248	345	460	533	564	555	619	584	769
Guinea	21	-56	43	-33	-40	-70	-63	-123	-72	-180	-230	-41
Liberia	-18	263	493	228	603	-124	98	1,515	319	1,640	818	490
Ivory Coast	-409	-835	-541	-1,007	-881	-828	-706	-804	-680	-534	-735	-1,268
Ghana	-108	-230	117	-121	-95	108	170	-69	-76	98	-129	-90
Benin	249	123	240	143	213	235	324	373	461	475	480	496
Nigeria	-2,224	-1,930	-279	-1,931	-1,389	-2,648	-1,831	-42	209	-2,552	-1,404	141
Cameroon	8	-646	-416	-691	-611	-561	-805	-549	-539	-772	-593	-454
Gabon	-561	-547	-1	-37	-79	121	191	113	104	80	-22	194
Congo	-144	-253	33	-272	-240	33	-295	53	2	34	113	25
Zaire	-803	-411	-289	-456	-484	-480	-439	-497	-700	-750	-757	-872
Angola	281	-272	252	14	238	95	449	398	71	-512	-646	-864
Ethiopia	67	285	280	272	239	200	228	158	283	190	233	177
Kenya	289	306	22	134	211	136	88	102	55	99	113	65
Uganda	-62	21	32	-106	-174	-201	-183	-85	-101	-55	-55	-65
Tanzania	228	223	192	146	115	95	156	60	77	-73	2	-53
Madagascar	171	109	-23	-74	-98	-103	-95	-108	-167	-199	-167	-234
Reunion	299	1,050	1,087	1,300	1,359	1,366	:	:	:	:	:	:
Mauritius	-210	-366	-392	-177	-370	-482	-428	-561	-418	-346	-447	-602
Zimbabwe	-127	-242	-117	-214	-268	-299	-386	-328	-404	-510	-557	-429
Namibia	:	-59	-119	-344	-232	-162	-136	-231	-357	-361	-717	-574
South Africa[5]	-1,504	-1,832	-3,017	356	937	651	653	751	-969	-2,760	-3,538	-3,188
CEEC[6]	**2,963**	**-105**	**6,506**	**6,698**	**11,550**	**20,933**	**26,827**	**27,158**	**21,650**	**22,323**	**21,659**	**23,170**
ACP[7]	**-3,210**	**-3,613**	**1,560**	**-3,675**	**-2,320**	**-3,368**	**-2,601**	**1,528**	**-1,052**	**-5,013**	**-7,451**	**-5,648**
DOM	**992**	**3,638**	**3,938**	**4,130**	**5,420**	**4,947**	**:**	**:**	**:**	**:**	**:**	**:**
Mediterranean Basin	**8,767**	**3,234**	**14,260**	**12,450**	**19,572**	**23,546**	**26,479**	**29,789**	**25,006**	**20,836**	**10,533**	**18,503**

(1) Including Liechtenstein up to 1994.
(2) Czechoslovakia before 1993.
(3) Relates to the external trade of the USSR until 1991 and from 1992 to the external trade of Russia.
(4) In 1992, Serbia, Montenegro and Macedonia. Since 1993, Serbia and Montenegro.

TRADE BALANCE

Main partners	Value (Mio ECU/Euro)											
	1980	**1990**	**1993**	**1994**	**1995**	**1996**	**1997**	**1998**	**1999**	**2000**	**2001**	**2002**
North America	**-23,954**	**-8,662**	**1,581**	**4,364**	**-1,633**	**1,001**	**5,180**	**11,821**	**25,663**	**35,844**	**48,350**	**71,725**
of which USA	-21,162	-8,451	803	3,806	-358	1,737	3,527	9,526	22,428	33,446	44,248	65,282
Canada	-2,883	-104	699	500	-1,365	-803	1,570	2,144	3,084	2,245	3,961	6,373
Central America and Antilles	**448**	**3,331**	**7,647**	**7,462**	**4,584**	**5,577**	**5,030**	**7,809**	**9,315**	**10,731**	**11,709**	**12,503**
of which Mexico	617	926	3,550	4,162	1,303	1,966	3,612	5,323	5,727	7,001	7,651	8,741
Bermuda	44	131	139	156	-8	133	59	213	450	979	1,144	916
Guatemala	-160	44	93	45	-69	-10	-75	17	88	18	212	371
El Salvador	-194	-5	38	-78	-56	-63	-22	196	220	484	577	321
Costa Rica	-135	-267	-171	-447	-473	-510	-489	-871	-1,159	-1,989	-1,212	-1,667
Panama	280	77	489	452	495	900	662	1,109	1,329	1,174	659	969
Cuba	263	276	233	267	368	392	477	712	708	737	847	522
Bahamas	-531	93	905	333	291	567	272	125	408	374	65	559
Dominican Republic	41	99	193	182	118	172	264	403	449	844	799	686
Guadeloupe	305	962	868	953	1,055	1,154	:	:	:	:	:	:
Martinique	298	791	833	875	995	929	:	:	:	:	:	:
Cayman Islands	47	26	110	54	121	18	59	215	155	454	315	727
Jamaica	-132	-104	-144	-169	-127	-249	-153	-211	-285	-121	-139	-24
Trinidad and Tobago	3	-39	7	-45	40	86	-14	24	141	-101	118	-79
Netherlands Antilles	-207	242	256	163	77	34	169	256	419	345	384	385
South America	**-3,962**	**-10,419**	**-1,407**	**-1,790**	**2,233**	**4,088**	**6,127**	**7,360**	**1,003**	**-2,589**	**-2,609**	**-9,182**
Colombia	-707	-650	-197	-174	-431	-202	-145	-89	-472	-428	-281	-425
Venezuela	-654	-91	874	315	244	221	637	1,577	905	482	749	361
French Guiana	90	834	1,151	1,002	2,011	1,498	:	:	:	:	:	:
Guina	-53	-74	-69	-93	-74	-89	-109	-90	-121	-135	-126	-82
Ecuador	115	-27	-73	-206	-189	-330	-222	-204	-508	-341	-130	-158
Peru	-68	-462	-425	-588	-331	-294	-321	-19	-492	-684	-1,106	-1,397
Brazil	-2,269	-5,571	-2,828	-3,353	553	1,313	2,326	2,431	897	-1,026	-9	-1,864
Chile	-749	-1,436	-358	-499	-783	-446	-18	-194	-1,072	-1,645	-1,417	-1,709
Uruguay	13	-334	262	399	298	282	393	463	312	437	279	-117
Argentina	594	-2,235	339	1,408	871	1,957	3,481	3,482	1,622	742	-512	-3,919
Near and Middle East	**-31,441**	**3,568**	**13,616**	**14,404**	**15,686**	**17,323**	**21,159**	**25,243**	**17,667**	**6,889**	**19,838**	**26,537**
of which Lebanon	1,152	664	1,680	2,108	2,361	2,599	2,941	2,669	2,457	2,611	2,758	2,786
Syria	318	-394	-304	39	-357	-623	-673	69	-493	-1,667	-2,047	-1,959
Iraq	-5,831	-148	75	48	25	33	-1,192	-1,382	-3,069	-5,165	-1,624	-991
Iran	50	-798	-279	-1,594	-1,989	-1,893	-271	688	-874	-3,218	-97	2,444
Israel	38	1,769	4,149	4,878	5,005	5,184	5,238	3,971	5,218	5,890	4,880	4,882
Jordan	782	737	676	888	911	1,027	1,026	980	1,075	1,442	1,679	1,663
Saudi Arabia	-21,416	-558	155	-62	-200	1,050	2,265	5,380	1,774	-3,919	144	2,151
Kuwait	-2,592	-791	577	116	1,057	606	813	1,453	534	-871	367	1,092
Bahrain	291	422	497	474	393	788	452	503	799	461	412	548
Qatar	-1,332	378	554	679	1,055	978	1,883	1,215	851	971	1,268	1,433
United Arab Emirates	-3,263	1,969	4,532	5,148	5,640	5,714	6,437	7,226	7,775	9,368	10,968	11,349
Oman	27	540	883	1,192	1,183	966	1,127	1,252	1,026	942	1,157	932
Other Asian coutries	**-14,756**	**-32,672**	**-33,851**	**-28,314**	**-21,909**	**-19,316**	**-36,192**	**-88,968**	**-104,044**	**-134,350**	**-112,500**	**-106,280**
of which Uzbekistan	:	:	-214	-130	-79	178	221	126	106	-22	-96	-369
Kazakhstan	:	:	340	409	88	98	-49	319	-799	-1,961	-1,412	-1,941
Pakistan	488	-35	358	167	67	80	-229	-726	-565	-704	-815	-757
India	597	1,446	412	171	1,644	1,297	762	-219	331	1,012	-301	927
Bangladesh	195	-99	-471	-644	-765	-871	-1,102	-1,410	-1,535	-2,390	-2,499	-2,472
Sri Lanka	59	-93	-167	-84	-210	-316	-260	-393	-143	-326	-567	-553
China	-134	-5,320	-8,292	-10,159	-11,653	-15,292	-21,008	-24,563	-30,304	-44,776	-45,828	-47,704
Indonesia	53	-51	-887	-1,543	-254	-106	-46	-5,089	-5,413	-6,475	-6,353	-5,782
Philippines	-250	-11	-177	-142	-129	-223	721	-2,940	-3,133	-4,415	-3,085	-4,361
Thailand	-467	-694	-489	-160	1,867	906	-811	-4,120	-5,422	-6,391	-4,806	-4,436
Vietnam	200	45	-57	-241	-401	-139	-1,088	-1,550	-2,103	-2,790	-2,707	-2,596
Malaysia	-827	-1,181	-2,274	-1,754	-1,217	-1,876	-2,036	-6,763	-6,870	-8,987	-6,453	-6,239
Brunei	51	158	192	472	362	678	520	396	160	98	106	73
Singapore	17	990	1,244	1,121	2,144	3,022	2,010	-1,624	-929	-1,149	686	1,050
South Korea	-1,018	-489	-74	1,498	1,407	3,258	1,350	-6,909	-6,854	-8,452	-6,009	-4,937
Japan	-10,196	-23,359	-24,908	-21,847	-21,403	-16,787	-23,779	-34,475	-36,537	-42,197	-31,378	-26,206
Taiwan	-1,256	-4,223	-2,803	-1,576	-1,643	-3,287	-3,040	-6,032	-8,182	-11,766	-10,913	-9,497
Hong Kong	-1,735	688	4,955	6,594	8,640	10,248	12,070	7,602	5,010	8,886	11,262	10,201
Macao	-253	-469	-459	-445	-395	-399	-452	-435	-467	-688	-651	-385
Oceania	**24**	**2,160**	**3,296**	**4,034**	**6,045**	**6,657**	**7,261**	**5,424**	**7,261**	**7,286**	**6,873**	**8,670**
Australia	828	1,999	3,021	3,876	5,526	6,308	6,871	5,447	6,815	6,872	6,266	7,707
New Zealand	-461	-279	-228	-102	78	10	-109	-442	-155	-265	-361	-301
New Caledonia and dep.	-109	219	241	199	201	226	273	314	327	331	340	486
Latin America	**-1,831**	**-10,014**	**1,966**	**1,975**	**1,965**	**5,360**	**10,526**	**14,171**	**8,525**	**5,705**	**7,040**	**855**
OPEC	**-30,615**	**-9,860**	**-353**	**-4,292**	**551**	**-2,041**	**-153**	**6,568**	**-4,434**	**-32,232**	**-13,028**	**-252**
DAE	**-5,083**	**-4,909**	**559**	**5,724**	**11,196**	**12,270**	**9,543**	**-17,847**	**-23,247**	**-27,859**	**-16,233**	**-13,857**

(5)   South Africa includes Namibia up to 31.12.1989.
(6)   Including Estonia Latvia and Lithuania since 1.1.1992.
(7)   Including Eritrea since 1.1.1994 and Namibia since 1.1.1990.

PRODUCT BREAKDOWN OF EU TRADE
BY MAIN PARTNER COUNTRY

eurostat

EXPORTS

Value (Mio ECU/Euro)

Year	TOTAL	Food, beverages and tobacco	Crude materials	Energy	Chemicals	Machinery and transport equipment	Other manufactured products	Breakdown by product as % of total					
	SITC 0-9	SITC 0+1	SITC 2+4	SITC 3	SITC 5	SITC 7	SITC 6+8	0+1	2+4	3	5	7	6+8
EXTRA EU													
1980	212,111	17,540	5,911	12,191	24,227	83,745	67,817	8.2	2.7	5.7	11.4	39.4	31.9
1990	355,164	27,946	6,967	9,478	41,980	142,962	108,084	7.8	1.9	2.6	11.8	40.2	30.4
1998	733,428	43,878	14,562	14,014	95,949	345,503	202,726	5.9	1.9	1.9	13.0	47.1	27.6
1999	760,192	43,636	15,363	16,593	106,651	351,833	206,123	5.7	2.0	2.1	14.0	46.2	27.1
2000	942,044	49,917	18,780	30,250	129,610	439,142	253,170	5.2	1.9	3.2	13.7	46.6	26.8
2001	985,326	51,565	18,183	25,943	142,460	461,603	264,532	5.2	1.8	2.6	14.4	46.8	26.8
2002	993,796	52,446	19,832	26,338	152,523	451,376	268,000	5.2	1.9	2.6	15.3	45.4	26.9
NORWAY													
1980	8,005	351	344	833	594	2,513	3,060	4.3	4.2	10.4	7.4	31.3	38.2
1990	9,296	505	218	298	839	3,367	3,335	5.4	2.3	3.2	9.0	36.2	35.8
1998	25,088	1,024	853	612	2,215	10,857	8,302	4.0	3.4	2.4	8.8	43.2	33.0
1999	23,243	1,105	805	768	2,236	9,711	7,705	4.7	3.4	3.3	9.6	41.7	33.1
2000	25,598	1,167	951	1,013	2,536	10,978	8,005	4.5	3.7	3.9	9.9	42.8	31.2
2001	26,154	1,243	879	1,079	2,651	11,421	8,111	4.7	3.3	4.1	10.1	43.6	31.0
2002	26,524	1,387	882	849	2,773	11,165	8,624	5.2	3.3	3.2	10.4	42.0	32.5
SWITZERLAND(1)													
1980	24,315	1,207	623	1,421	1,919	5,085	12,062	4.9	2.5	5.8	7.8	20.9	49.6
1990	41,288	2,125	905	1,969	5,040	13,033	16,552	5.1	2.1	4.7	12.2	31.5	40.0
1998	57,180	2,731	1,072	2,329	9,117	19,771	20,129	4.7	1.8	4.0	15.9	34.5	35.2
1999	62,556	2,912	1,063	2,214	9,883	23,520	20,425	4.6	1.7	3.5	15.7	37.5	32.6
2000	70,782	3,020	1,212	3,379	10,923	25,437	23,580	4.2	1.7	4.7	15.4	35.9	33.3
2001	74,761	3,224	1,213	3,310	12,518	25,500	25,518	4.3	1.6	4.4	16.7	34.1	34.1
2002	70,645	3,441	1,285	3,001	13,609	22,636	23,691	4.8	1.8	4.2	19.2	32.0	33.5
POLAND													
1980	3,467	616	165	35	491	1,102	881	17.7	4.7	1.0	14.1	31.7	25.4
1990	4,390	552	126	132	492	1,630	1,276	12.5	2.8	2.9	11.2	37.1	29.0
1998	28,207	1,383	618	520	3,827	11,929	9,151	4.9	2.1	1.8	13.5	42.2	32.4
1999	28,973	1,259	567	538	4,230	12,237	9,348	4.3	1.9	1.8	14.5	42.2	32.2
2000	33,810	1,515	683	603	5,050	14,263	10,778	4.4	2.0	1.7	14.9	42.1	31.8
2001	35,681	1,611	752	420	5,666	14,910	11,372	4.5	2.1	1.1	15.8	41.7	31.8
2002	37,327	1,622	904	434	6,082	15,759	11,684	4.3	2.4	1.1	16.2	42.2	31.3
CZECH REPUBLIC(2)													
1980	1,683	151	137	20	320	556	379	8.9	8.1	1.1	19.0	33.0	22.5
1990	2,606	131	115	18	401	1,213	580	5.0	4.4	0.6	15.3	46.5	22.2
1998	17,214	781	351	226	2,111	7,778	5,504	4.5	2.0	1.3	12.2	45.1	31.9
1999	18,433	793	361	321	2,204	8,296	5,942	4.3	1.9	1.7	11.9	45.0	32.2
2000	24,003	895	457	474	2,635	11,424	7,406	3.7	1.9	1.9	10.9	47.5	30.8
2001	27,674	1,014	487	556	2,970	13,349	8,359	3.6	1.7	2.0	10.7	48.2	30.2
2002	29,222	1,105	506	484	3,450	13,503	9,239	3.7	1.7	1.6	11.8	46.2	31.6
HUNGARY													
1980	2,037	91	135	25	415	546	720	4.4	6.6	1.2	20.3	26.8	35.3
1990	2,876	98	88	4	420	1,097	1,046	3.4	3.0	0.1	14.6	38.1	36.3
1998	16,863	394	219	109	1,606	9,324	4,907	2.3	1.2	0.6	9.5	55.2	29.1
1999	18,442	348	207	104	1,721	10,436	5,246	1.8	1.1	0.5	9.3	56.6	28.4
2000	23,039	455	256	155	2,060	13,505	6,054	1.9	1.1	0.6	8.9	58.6	26.2
2001	23,878	550	274	200	2,356	13,514	6,437	2.3	1.1	0.8	9.8	56.5	26.9
2002	25,004	628	310	226	2,640	14,047	6,752	2.5	1.2	0.9	10.5	56.1	27.0

(*)   The SITC rev. 2 nomenclature of products has been replaced by the SITC rev. 3 nomenclature since 1.1.1988.

(1)   Switzerland including Liechtenstein up to 1994

(2)   Relates to the external trade of Czechoslovakia up to 1992 and to the external trade of the Czech Republic from 1993 onwards.

PRODUCT BREAKDOWN OF EU TRADE
BY MAIN PARTNER COUNTRY

IMPORTS

SITC rev. 2 and 3(*)

Year	TOTAL	Food, beverages and tobacco	Crude materials	Energy	Chemicals	Machinery and transport equipment	Other manufactured products	Breakdown by product as % of total					
	SITC 0-9	SITC 0+1	SITC 2+4	SITC 3	SITC 5	SITC 7	SITC 6+8	0+1	2+4	3	5	7	6+8
EXTRA EU													
1980	281,117	28,214	29,276	109,811	12,048	40,389	57,057	10.0	10.4	39.0	4.2	14.3	20.2
1990	404,351	34,699	31,819	68,802	26,442	113,054	107,565	8.5	7.8	17.0	6.5	27.9	26.6
1998	710,538	49,937	42,363	61,690	55,570	267,170	211,382	7.0	5.9	8.6	7.8	37.6	29.7
1999	779,825	50,153	40,266	78,275	58,913	305,956	224,102	6.4	5.1	10.0	7.5	39.2	28.7
2000	1,033,436	54,808	50,349	149,091	71,366	394,660	279,555	5.3	4.8	14.4	6.9	38.1	27.0
2001	1,027,955	58,289	48,908	144,978	77,533	379,951	286,128	5.6	4.7	14.1	7.5	36.9	27.8
2002	987,479	58,593	45,639	137,490	80,934	356,787	277,213	5.9	4.6	13.9	8.1	36.1	28.0
NORWAY													
1980	9,845	529	561	3,477	567	856	2,195	5.3	5.7	35.3	5.7	8.6	22.2
1990	16,313	1,040	847	8,118	859	1,116	3,513	6.3	5.1	49.7	5.2	6.8	21.5
1998	28,134	2,218	1,033	11,336	1,823	3,204	6,054	7.8	3.6	40.2	6.4	11.3	21.5
1999	29,594	2,256	1,035	12,903	1,905	3,088	6,232	7.6	3.4	43.5	6.4	10.4	21.0
2000	46,101	2,387	1,259	26,148	2,230	3,533	7,036	5.1	2.7	56.7	4.8	7.6	15.2
2001	45,112	2,178	1,343	24,186	2,337	3,394	6,930	4.8	2.9	53.6	5.1	7.5	15.3
2002	45,800	2,192	1,282	24,205	2,271	3,074	6,474	4.7	2.7	52.8	4.9	6.7	14.1
SWITZERLAND(1)													
1980	17,335	432	366	233	2,149	3,680	5,452	2.4	2.1	1.3	12.3	21.2	31.4
1990	34,273	707	561	303	6,544	9,670	11,473	2.0	1.6	0.8	19.0	28.2	33.4
1998	49,460	1,032	689	372	11,727	14,520	16,997	2.0	1.3	0.7	23.7	29.3	34.3
1999	52,881	1,119	788	414	12,423	16,017	18,763	2.1	1.4	0.7	23.4	30.2	35.4
2000	60,018	1,166	1,099	491	13,390	18,435	21,473	1.9	1.8	0.8	22.3	30.7	35.7
2001	60,835	1,251	1,030	1,288	15,300	17,811	19,516	2.0	1.6	2.1	25.1	29.2	32.0
2002	58,794	1,287	828	1,613	17,451	15,050	18,487	2.1	1.4	2.7	29.6	25.5	31.4
POLAND													
1980	3,369	423	333	910	125	408	994	12.5	9.8	27.0	3.7	12.1	29.4
1990	5,153	965	486	537	444	579	2,041	18.7	9.4	10.4	8.6	11.2	39.5
1998	16,176	1,045	564	1,018	779	4,324	8,231	6.4	3.4	6.2	4.8	26.7	50.8
1999	17,582	1,113	572	893	715	5,347	8,695	6.3	3.2	5.0	4.0	30.4	49.4
2000	23,307	1,269	724	1,184	1,092	8,188	10,616	5.4	3.1	5.0	4.6	35.1	45.5
2001	26,623	1,497	715	1,550	1,066	9,738	11,744	5.6	2.6	5.8	4.0	36.5	44.1
2002	28,201	1,555	763	1,392	1,144	10,767	12,251	5.5	2.7	4.9	4.0	38.1	43.4
CZECH REPUBLIC(2)													
1980	1,995	100	303	364	169	244	790	5.0	15.1	18.2	8.4	12.2	39.5
1990	2,688	192	294	153	299	413	1,282	7.1	10.9	5.6	11.1	15.3	47.6
1998	14,670	242	705	360	781	6,452	5,895	1.6	4.8	2.4	5.3	43.9	40.1
1999	16,844	264	812	352	794	7,800	6,581	1.5	4.8	2.0	4.7	46.3	39.0
2000	21,638	347	922	444	1,013	10,681	7,929	1.6	4.2	2.0	4.6	49.3	36.6
2001	25,136	407	896	448	1,065	13,108	8,928	1.6	3.5	1.7	4.2	52.1	35.5
2002	27,531	437	912	467	1,013	14,847	9,556	1.5	3.3	1.6	3.6	53.9	34.7
HUNGARY													
1980	1,779	418	172	118	170	193	681	23.5	9.6	6.6	9.5	10.8	38.2
1990	2,934	616	231	85	285	443	1,227	20.9	7.8	2.8	9.7	15.1	41.8
1998	14,655	904	390	253	640	8,497	3,824	6.1	2.6	1.7	4.3	57.9	26.0
1999	17,624	943	392	275	806	10,913	4,129	5.3	2.2	1.5	4.5	61.9	23.4
2000	22,046	989	501	327	1,154	13,991	4,920	4.4	2.2	1.4	5.2	63.4	22.3
2001	24,817	1,143	472	387	1,442	15,851	5,345	4.6	1.9	1.5	5.8	63.8	21.5
2002	25,276	1,229	527	305	1,488	16,019	5,559	4.8	2.0	1.2	5.8	63.3	21.9

(*) The SITC rev. 2 nomenclature of products has been replaced by the SITC rev. 3 nomenclature since 1.1.1988.

(1) Switzerland including Liechtenstein up to 1994

(2) Relates to the external trade of Czechoslovakia up to 1992 and to the external trade of the Czech Republic from 1993 onwards.

PRODUCT BREAKDOWN OF EU TRADE
BY MAIN PARTNER COUNTRY

EXPORTS

Value (Mio ECU/Euro)

Year	TOTAL	Food, beverages and tobacco	Crude materials	Energy	Chemicals	Machinery and transport equipment	Other manufactured products	Breakdown by product as % of total					
	SITC 0-9	SITC 0+1	SITC 2+4	SITC 3	SITC 5	SITC 7	SITC 6+8	0+1	2+4	3	5	7	6+8
TURKEY													
1980	2,033	95	78	132	346	867	380	4.6	3.8	6.4	17.0	42.6	18.7
1990	7,718	423	349	81	1,054	3,380	1,795	5.4	4.5	1.0	13.6	43.7	23.2
1998	22,187	503	819	272	3,214	11,263	4,996	2.2	3.6	1.2	14.4	50.7	22.5
1999	20,580	404	628	388	3,466	10,150	4,446	1.9	3.0	1.8	16.8	49.3	21.6
2000	29,953	478	896	763	4,570	16,041	6,139	1.5	2.9	2.5	15.2	53.5	20.4
2001	20,266	321	825	311	3,931	9,014	5,045	1.5	4.0	1.5	19.3	44.4	24.8
2002	24,217	415	1,101	340	4,622	10,853	5,953	1.7	4.5	1.4	19.0	44.8	24.5
RUSSIA(1)													
1980	10,243	1,359	281	55	1,311	2,889	4,054	13.2	2.7	0.5	12.8	28.2	39.5
1990	11,177	1,469	134	73	1,417	4,906	2,670	13.1	1.1	0.6	12.6	43.8	23.8
1998	21,170	3,679	506	86	2,332	7,949	6,114	17.3	2.3	0.4	11.0	37.5	28.8
1999	14,727	2,417	519	63	1,693	5,396	4,211	16.4	3.5	0.4	11.4	36.6	28.5
2000	19,917	2,263	587	99	2,707	7,661	6,007	11.3	2.9	0.4	13.5	38.4	30.1
2001	27,961	2,792	740	109	3,844	11,843	7,902	9.9	2.6	0.3	13.7	42.3	28.2
2002	30,439	2,948	762	138	3,973	13,533	8,455	9.6	2.5	0.4	13.0	44.4	27.7
SOUTH AFRICA(2)													
1980	5,042	88	71	25	515	3,093	977	1.7	1.4	0.4	10.2	61.3	19.3
1990	4,090	72	85	19	545	2,233	960	1.7	2.0	0.4	13.3	54.6	23.4
1998	10,475	305	125	158	1,501	5,852	2,245	2.9	1.1	1.5	14.3	55.8	21.4
1999	9,731	332	112	58	1,551	5,279	2,128	3.4	1.1	0.5	15.9	54.2	21.8
2000	11,715	293	139	82	1,728	6,549	2,606	2.5	1.1	0.7	14.7	55.9	22.2
2001	12,480	289	113	86	1,783	7,111	2,742	2.3	0.9	0.6	14.2	56.9	21.9
2002	12,438	316	120	121	1,673	7,101	2,526	2.5	0.9	0.9	13.4	57.0	20.3
USA													
1980	29,543	2,058	498	1,681	2,132	12,099	9,264	6.9	1.6	5.6	7.2	40.9	31.3
1990	76,495	4,170	870	3,574	6,888	33,948	23,367	5.4	1.1	4.6	9.0	44.3	30.5
1998	161,545	6,788	1,609	2,887	21,460	83,493	41,651	4.2	0.9	1.7	13.2	51.6	25.7
1999	183,016	7,792	1,755	4,689	27,237	92,333	45,535	4.2	0.9	2.5	14.8	50.4	24.8
2000	232,470	8,982	2,271	11,043	34,983	112,362	58,659	3.8	0.9	4.7	15.0	48.3	25.2
2001	239,904	9,362	2,246	8,922	38,783	117,686	58,371	3.9	0.9	3.7	16.1	49.0	24.3
2002	239,938	10,084	2,529	9,369	44,365	112,821	55,800	4.2	1.0	3.9	18.4	47.0	23.2
CANADA													
1980	3,893	373	84	74	314	1,538	1,278	9.5	2.1	1.9	8.0	39.5	32.8
1990	9,300	736	143	809	837	3,409	2,972	7.9	1.5	8.6	9.0	36.6	31.9
1998	14,880	1,059	259	187	1,999	7,129	3,853	7.1	1.7	1.2	13.4	47.9	25.8
1999	16,591	1,128	254	207	2,191	8,139	4,187	6.8	1.5	1.2	13.2	49.0	25.2
2000	20,643	1,363	343	542	2,634	9,898	5,278	6.6	1.6	2.6	12.7	47.9	25.5
2001	21,939	1,417	292	989	3,410	10,282	5,084	6.4	1.3	4.5	15.5	46.8	23.1
2002	22,284	1,480	325	1,267	3,428	10,035	5,308	6.6	1.4	5.6	15.3	45.0	23.8
BRAZIL													
1980	2,877	107	33	23	489	1,488	546	3.7	1.1	0.7	16.9	51.7	18.9
1990	3,623	196	66	23	690	1,860	579	5.4	1.8	0.6	19.0	51.3	15.9
1998	15,657	531	191	258	2,384	8,753	2,961	3.3	1.2	1.6	15.2	55.9	18.9
1999	14,220	378	184	198	2,495	7,841	2,444	2.6	1.2	1.3	17.5	55.1	17.1
2000	16,604	471	218	152	2,856	9,198	3,058	2.8	1.3	0.9	17.2	55.3	18.4
2001	18,313	443	186	154	3,130	10,594	3,176	2.4	1.0	0.8	17.0	57.8	17.3
2002	15,446	372	182	230	2,920	8,613	2,618	2.4	1.1	1.4	18.9	55.7	16.9

(*) The SITC rev. 2 nomenclature of products has been replaced by the SITC rev. 3 nomenclature since 1.1.1988.
(1) Relates to the external trade with the USSR until 1991 and to the external trade with Russia from 1992 onwards.
(2) South Africa includes Namibia up to 31.12.1989.

PRODUCT BREAKDOWN OF EU TRADE
BY MAIN PARTNER COUNTRY

IMPORTS

SITC rev. 2 and 3[*]

Year	TOTAL	Food, beverages and tobacco	Crude materials	Energy	Chemicals	Machinery and transport equipment	Other manufactured products	Breakdown by product as % of total					
	SITC 0-9	SITC 0+1	SITC 2+4	SITC 3	SITC 5	SITC 7	SITC 6+8	0+1	2+4	3	5	7	6+8
TURKEY													
1980	1,131	494	254	12	12	14	313	43.6	22.4	1.0	1.0	1.2	27.7
1990	5,940	905	343	258	175	423	3,789	15.2	5.7	4.3	2.9	7.1	63.7
1998	13,624	1,731	499	81	275	2,617	8,328	12.7	3.6	0.5	2.0	19.2	61.1
1999	15,071	1,770	594	128	298	3,295	8,900	11.7	3.9	0.8	1.9	21.8	59.0
2000	17,547	1,807	571	192	386	3,958	10,554	10.2	3.2	1.0	2.2	22.5	60.1
2001	20,217	1,993	600	246	420	4,947	11,839	9.8	2.9	1.2	2.0	24.4	58.5
2002	22,029	1,878	547	214	462	6,044	12,757	8.5	2.4	0.9	2.0	27.4	57.9
RUSSIA[1]													
1980	15,013	101	1,280	9,450	723	366	831	0.6	8.5	62.9	4.8	2.4	5.5
1990	16,184	194	1,464	8,741	669	514	1,944	1.1	9.0	54.0	4.1	3.1	12.0
1998	23,173	517	2,619	8,172	1,462	414	5,558	2.2	11.3	35.2	6.3	1.7	23.9
1999	25,977	458	2,339	11,799	1,529	443	5,327	1.7	9.0	45.4	5.8	1.7	20.5
2000	45,724	577	2,875	22,874	2,036	577	8,599	1.2	6.2	50.0	4.4	1.2	18.8
2001	47,688	744	2,498	24,811	2,078	516	7,604	1.5	5.2	52.0	4.3	1.0	15.9
2002	47,700	1,007	2,200	26,480	1,904	492	6,301	2.1	4.6	55.5	3.9	1.0	13.2
SOUTH AFRICA[2]													
1980	6,546	590	910	583	293	43	2,316	9.0	13.9	8.9	4.4	0.6	35.3
1990	5,922	507	844	828	203	115	1,635	8.5	14.2	13.9	3.4	1.9	27.6
1998	9,724	1,217	1,186	1,083	324	1,101	2,857	12.5	12.1	11.1	3.3	11.3	29.3
1999	10,700	1,234	1,139	1,047	324	1,762	3,099	11.5	10.6	9.7	3.0	16.4	28.9
2000	14,475	1,338	1,508	1,462	399	2,025	5,565	9.2	10.4	10.1	2.7	13.9	38.4
2001	16,018	1,669	1,470	2,111	377	2,573	5,347	10.4	9.1	13.1	2.3	16.0	33.3
2002	15,626	1,710	1,410	1,830	407	2,522	4,170	10.9	9.0	11.7	2.6	16.1	26.6
USA													
1980	50,706	5,918	7,540	2,267	4,520	15,722	10,207	11.6	14.8	4.4	8.9	31.0	20.1
1990	84,946	4,110	6,045	3,137	8,388	39,708	16,942	4.8	7.1	3.6	9.8	46.7	19.9
1998	152,019	5,563	6,986	2,008	19,272	81,391	30,897	3.6	4.5	1.3	12.6	53.5	20.3
1999	160,588	5,290	6,030	1,582	20,317	90,938	31,459	3.2	3.7	0.9	12.6	56.6	19.5
2000	199,024	5,816	7,894	2,140	25,721	112,149	39,243	2.9	3.9	1.0	12.9	56.3	19.7
2001	195,655	5,874	7,221	2,228	28,432	106,827	40,128	3.0	3.6	1.1	14.5	54.5	20.5
2002	174,656	5,381	6,644	1,784	29,743	92,216	34,519	3.0	3.8	1.0	17.0	52.7	19.7
CANADA													
1980	6,776	975	2,735	245	309	488	1,395	14.3	40.3	3.6	4.5	7.2	20.5
1990	9,404	738	3,674	243	340	1,846	1,873	7.8	39.0	2.5	3.6	19.6	19.9
1998	12,736	1,029	3,078	326	600	4,452	2,684	8.0	24.1	2.5	4.7	34.9	21.0
1999	13,507	1,098	2,949	348	659	5,145	2,869	8.1	21.8	2.5	4.8	38.0	21.2
2000	18,398	1,233	4,045	429	731	7,645	3,795	6.7	21.9	2.3	3.9	41.5	20.6
2001	17,978	1,193	3,641	624	791	7,406	3,570	6.6	20.2	3.4	4.4	41.1	19.8
2002	15,911	956	3,252	481	887	6,760	2,935	6.0	20.4	3.0	5.5	42.4	18.4
BRAZIL													
1980	5,146	2,563	1,428	19	78	300	722	49.8	27.7	0.3	1.5	5.8	14.0
1990	9,194	3,200	2,208	47	427	1,153	2,080	34.8	24.0	0.5	4.6	12.5	22.6
1998	13,225	4,200	3,745	20	497	2,008	2,637	31.7	28.3	0.1	3.7	15.1	19.9
1999	13,323	4,247	3,612	30	467	2,320	2,538	31.8	27.1	0.2	3.5	17.4	19.0
2000	17,630	5,128	4,921	84	629	3,403	3,309	29.0	27.9	0.4	3.5	19.3	18.7
2001	18,321	5,790	5,422	229	638	2,831	3,256	31.6	29.5	1.2	3.4	15.4	17.7
2002	17,309	5,449	5,070	272	694	2,296	3,284	31.4	29.2	1.5	4.0	13.2	18.9

(*) The SITC rev. 2 nomenclature of products has been replaced by the SITC rev. 3 nomenclature since 1.1.1988.

(1) Relates to the external trade with the USSR until 1991 and to the external trade with Russia from 1992 onwards.

(2) South Africa includes Namibia up to 31.12.1989.

PRODUCT BREAKDOWN OF EU TRADE
BY MAIN PARTNER COUNTRY

EXPORTS

Value (Mio ECU/Euro)

Year	TOTAL	Food, beverages and tobacco	Crude materials	Energy	Chemicals	Machinery and transport equipment	Other manufactured products	Breakdown by product as % of total					
	SITC 0-9	SITC 0+1	SITC 2+4	SITC 3	SITC 5	SITC 7	SITC 6+8	0+1	2+4	3	5	7	6+8
ISRAEL													
1980	1,814	101	60	6	174	531	787	5.5	3.3	0.3	9.5	29.2	43.3
1990	5,234	265	81	32	637	1,413	2,637	5.0	1.5	0.6	12.1	27.0	50.3
1998	10,892	479	177	39	1,444	3,357	5,115	4.4	1.6	0.3	13.2	30.8	46.9
1999	12,866	444	187	111	1,528	3,909	5,918	3.4	1.4	0.8	11.8	30.3	45.9
2000	15,846	521	199	318	1,751	5,439	7,055	3.2	1.2	2.0	11.0	34.3	44.5
2001	14,449	588	171	131	1,820	5,263	5,971	4.0	1.1	0.9	12.5	36.4	41.3
2002	13,425	550	198	89	1,758	4,167	5,511	4.0	1.4	0.6	13.0	31.0	41.0
SAUDI ARABIA													
1980	8,311	767	135	282	458	3,118	2,957	9.2	1.6	3.3	5.5	37.5	35.5
1990	7,726	1,023	61	17	911	1,946	1,972	13.2	0.7	0.2	11.7	25.1	25.5
1998	12,021	1,143	155	30	1,480	5,534	3,112	9.5	1.2	0.2	12.3	46.0	25.8
1999	10,231	1,429	160	20	1,505	3,949	2,707	13.9	1.5	0.1	14.7	38.5	26.4
2000	11,981	1,688	209	35	1,761	4,818	3,195	14.0	1.7	0.2	14.7	40.2	26.6
2001	13,230	1,417	184	38	1,796	5,853	3,388	10.7	1.3	0.2	13.5	44.2	25.6
2002	14,467	1,362	255	30	2,382	6,605	3,585	9.4	1.7	0.2	16.4	45.6	24.7
INDIA													
1980	2,505	79	70	123	312	764	869	3.1	2.7	4.9	12.4	30.5	34.7
1990	5,985	23	180	108	553	1,965	2,564	0.3	3.0	1.8	9.2	32.8	42.8
1998	9,576	53	289	38	903	3,582	4,237	0.5	3.0	0.4	9.4	37.4	44.2
1999	10,353	117	391	91	1,020	3,201	5,167	1.1	3.7	0.8	9.8	30.9	49.9
2000	13,384	54	451	422	1,240	3,927	6,396	0.4	3.3	3.1	9.2	29.3	47.7
2001	12,610	80	496	62	1,266	3,934	5,833	0.6	3.9	0.4	10.0	31.1	46.2
2002	13,967	126	436	63	1,327	4,350	6,205	0.9	3.1	0.4	9.5	31.1	44.4
THAILAND													
1980	838	55	14	12	141	384	140	6.5	1.6	1.4	16.7	45.7	16.7
1990	3,407	235	38	9	447	1,694	776	6.9	1.1	0.2	13.1	49.7	22.7
1998	5,217	205	89	11	598	2,950	1,079	3.9	1.7	0.2	11.4	56.5	20.6
1999	4,699	285	115	13	775	1,909	1,278	6.0	2.4	0.2	16.4	40.6	27.1
2000	6,487	402	118	19	964	2,928	1,572	6.2	1.8	0.2	14.8	45.1	24.2
2001	7,573	401	97	21	1,021	3,920	1,628	5.2	1.2	0.2	13.4	51.7	21.4
2002	6,762	366	155	18	1,050	3,244	1,694	5.4	2.2	0.2	15.5	47.9	25.0
MALAYSIA													
1980	1,189	80	6	3	113	640	203	6.6	0.4	0.2	9.5	53.8	17.0
1990	2,425	128	44	7	264	1,329	496	5.2	1.8	0.2	10.8	54.8	20.4
1998	5,480	222	104	6	484	3,709	773	4.0	1.8	0.1	8.8	67.6	14.0
1999	6,437	218	90	10	584	4,405	941	3.3	1.3	0.1	9.0	68.4	14.6
2000	8,381	296	137	9	739	5,773	1,141	3.5	1.6	0.1	8.8	68.8	13.6
2001	9,317	325	127	13	716	6,600	1,290	3.4	1.3	0.1	7.6	70.8	13.8
2002	8,198	296	187	11	772	5,424	1,226	3.6	2.2	0.1	9.4	66.1	14.9
SINGAPORE													
1980	1,973	90	15	44	205	991	496	4.5	0.7	2.2	10.3	50.2	25.1
1990	5,677	301	29	85	643	2,810	1,455	5.3	0.5	1.5	11.3	49.5	25.6
1998	10,911	513	41	68	1,153	6,507	2,332	4.7	0.3	0.6	10.5	59.6	21.3
1999	11,836	525	48	183	1,478	6,845	2,438	4.4	0.4	1.5	12.4	57.8	20.5
2000	14,798	659	63	177	1,673	8,760	3,068	4.4	0.4	1.1	11.3	59.1	20.7
2001	14,605	590	47	176	1,685	8,750	2,944	4.0	0.3	1.2	11.5	59.9	20.1
2002	14,165	539	54	251	1,893	7,871	3,004	3.8	0.3	1.7	13.3	55.5	21.2

(*) The SITC rev. 2 nomenclature of products has been replaced by the SITC rev. 3 nomenclature since 1.1.1988.

PRODUCT BREAKDOWN OF EU TRADE
BY MAIN PARTNER COUNTRY

IMPORTS

SITC rev. 2 and 3(*)

Year	TOTAL	Food, beverages and tobacco	Crude materials	Energy	Chemicals	Machinery and transport equipment	Other manufactured products	Breakdown by product as % of total					
	SITC 0-9	SITC 0+1	SITC 2+4	SITC 3	SITC 5	SITC 7	SITC 6+8	0+1	2+4	3	5	7	6+8
ISRAEL													
1980	1,776	436	257	82	203	78	660	24.5	14.4	4.6	11.4	4.3	37.1
1990	3,465	629	275	50	590	408	1,285	18.1	7.9	1.4	17.0	11.7	37.0
1998	6,921	543	380	102	1,122	1,741	2,843	7.8	5.4	1.4	16.2	25.1	41.0
1999	7,648	548	317	85	1,252	1,993	3,271	7.1	4.1	1.1	16.3	26.0	42.7
2000	9,957	603	397	201	1,547	3,008	4,003	6.0	3.9	2.0	15.5	30.2	40.2
2001	9,568	642	371	168	1,672	2,768	3,698	6.7	3.8	1.7	17.4	28.9	38.6
2002	8,543	587	345	111	1,659	2,092	3,423	6.8	4.0	1.3	19.4	24.4	40.0
SAUDI ARABIA													
1980	29,727	1	:	29,333	0	129	28	0.0	:	98.6	0.0	0.4	0.0
1990	8,284	34	45	7,097	443	308	121	0.4	0.5	85.6	5.3	3.7	1.4
1998	6,641	8	45	4,846	444	901	370	0.1	0.6	72.9	6.6	13.5	5.5
1999	8,456	9	39	6,636	432	803	306	0.1	0.4	78.4	5.1	9.4	3.6
2000	15,900	7	58	13,634	839	859	481	0.0	0.3	85.7	5.2	5.4	3.0
2001	13,085	6	57	10,756	994	863	349	0.0	0.4	82.1	7.5	6.5	2.6
2002	12,316	8	62	9,608	1,026	1,084	355	0.0	0.5	78.0	8.3	8.8	2.8
INDIA													
1980	1,908	429	118	14	29	42	1,240	22.4	6.1	0.7	1.5	2.1	64.9
1990	4,539	477	295	90	183	172	3,235	10.5	6.5	1.9	4.0	3.7	71.2
1998	9,795	895	524	8	814	881	6,627	9.1	5.3	0.0	8.3	8.9	67.6
1999	10,022	931	565	12	805	1,017	6,649	9.2	5.6	0.1	8.0	10.1	66.3
2000	12,372	1,125	652	38	1,064	1,158	8,264	9.0	5.2	0.3	8.5	9.3	66.8
2001	12,911	1,096	564	147	1,079	1,233	8,698	8.4	4.3	1.1	8.3	9.5	67.3
2002	13,039	1,045	532	93	1,201	1,311	8,752	8.0	4.0	0.7	9.2	10.0	67.1
THAILAND													
1980	1,305	667	113	:	6	11	504	51.1	8.6	:	0.4	0.8	38.6
1990	4,101	1,415	141	0	15	537	1,963	34.4	3.4	0.0	0.3	13.1	47.8
1998	9,337	1,418	303	2	149	3,743	3,262	15.1	3.2	0.0	1.5	40.0	34.9
1999	10,121	1,410	316	3	160	4,320	3,547	13.9	3.1	0.0	1.5	42.6	35.0
2000	12,879	1,554	426	3	264	5,536	4,487	12.0	3.3	0.0	2.0	42.9	34.8
2001	12,379	1,586	346	0	183	5,470	4,338	12.8	2.7	0.0	1.4	44.1	35.0
2002	11,198	1,288	308	0	176	5,294	4,085	11.5	2.7	0.0	1.5	47.2	36.4
MALAYSIA													
1980	2,016	153	1,253	:	3	193	381	7.5	62.1	:	0.1	9.5	18.8
1990	3,605	266	1,069	19	36	1,159	1,004	7.3	29.6	0.5	1.0	32.1	27.8
1998	12,243	228	1,274	13	267	8,076	2,103	1.8	10.4	0.1	2.1	65.9	17.1
1999	13,307	273	1,142	9	260	8,713	2,190	2.0	8.5	0.0	1.9	65.4	16.4
2000	17,368	313	1,240	75	321	10,551	2,638	1.8	7.1	0.4	1.8	60.7	15.1
2001	15,769	295	1,213	49	406	9,288	2,537	1.8	7.6	0.3	2.5	58.9	16.0
2002	14,437	284	1,265	69	298	9,940	2,498	1.9	8.7	0.4	2.0	68.8	17.3
SINGAPORE													
1980	1,956	39	188	71	13	568	385	1.9	9.6	3.6	0.6	29.0	19.6
1990	4,686	68	111	0	136	3,482	821	1.4	2.3	0.0	2.9	74.3	17.5
1998	12,535	123	76	10	897	9,548	929	0.9	0.6	0.0	7.1	76.1	7.4
1999	12,765	106	66	3	1,472	9,592	934	0.8	0.5	0.0	11.5	75.1	7.3
2000	15,947	116	105	7	1,538	12,056	1,090	0.7	0.6	0.0	9.6	75.6	6.8
2001	13,919	106	134	18	1,849	9,406	1,096	0.7	0.9	0.1	13.2	67.5	7.8
2002	13,115	115	79	236	2,151	9,352	1,054	0.8	0.5	1.7	16.3	71.3	8.0

(*) The SITC rev. 2 nomenclature of products has been replaced by the SITC rev. 3 nomenclature since 1.1.1988.

PRODUCT BREAKDOWN OF EU TRADE
BY MAIN PARTNER COUNTRY

EXPORTS

Value (Mio ECU/Euro)

Year	TOTAL	Food, beverages and tobacco	Crude materials	Energy	Chemicals	Machinery and transport equipment	Other manufactured products	Breakdown by product as % of total					
	SITC 0-9	SITC 0+1	SITC 2+4	SITC 3	SITC 5	SITC 7	SITC 6+8	0+1	2+4	3	5	7	6+8
CHINA													
1980	1,962	20	105	4	397	847	471	1.0	5.3	0.2	20.2	43.1	24.0
1990	5,268	254	280	9	505	3,193	778	4.8	5.3	0.1	9.5	60.6	14.7
1998	17,411	308	585	19	1,427	11,985	2,668	1.7	3.3	0.1	8.1	68.8	15.3
1999	19,351	354	1,012	216	1,657	12,683	3,035	1.8	5.2	1.1	8.5	65.5	15.6
2000	25,498	428	1,337	162	2,368	16,390	4,202	1.6	5.2	0.6	9.2	64.2	16.4
2001	30,087	436	1,223	132	2,674	19,861	5,131	1.4	4.0	0.4	8.8	66.0	17.0
2002	34,139	451	1,237	314	3,200	22,003	6,250	1.3	3.6	0.9	9.3	64.4	18.3
SOUTH KOREA													
1980	953	15	25	2	124	527	160	1.6	2.6	0.2	13.0	55.3	16.8
1990	6,059	150	164	10	928	2,801	1,458	2.4	2.7	0.1	15.3	46.2	24.0
1998	9,100	366	163	15	1,360	4,228	1,918	4.0	1.7	0.1	14.9	46.4	21.0
1999	11,499	644	300	39	1,815	4,849	2,777	5.5	2.6	0.3	15.7	42.1	24.1
2000	16,482	788	416	9	2,447	7,924	4,005	4.7	2.5	0.0	14.8	48.0	24.3
2001	15,588	811	323	12	2,519	7,150	4,201	5.2	2.0	0.0	16.1	45.8	26.9
2002	17,323	975	438	28	2,694	7,881	4,696	5.6	2.5	0.1	15.5	45.4	27.1
JAPAN													
1980	5,232	642	165	23	925	1,427	1,729	12.2	3.1	0.4	17.6	27.2	33.0
1990	22,727	2,104	450	54	3,263	8,154	7,918	9.2	1.9	0.2	14.3	35.8	34.8
1998	31,567	3,296	945	50	5,379	11,790	9,102	10.4	2.9	0.1	17.0	37.3	28.8
1999	35,374	3,474	1,258	49	6,639	13,035	9,629	9.8	3.5	0.1	18.7	36.8	27.2
2000	44,936	3,938	1,465	78	8,186	17,559	12,286	8.7	3.2	0.1	18.2	39.0	27.3
2001	44,920	3,941	1,373	54	8,339	17,305	12,382	8.7	3.0	0.1	18.5	38.5	27.5
2002	42,279	3,735	1,437	125	8,013	15,847	11,663	8.8	3.3	0.2	18.9	37.4	27.5
TAIWAN													
1980	872	49	13	6	155	436	130	5.5	1.5	0.6	17.7	50.0	14.9
1990	4,912	225	116	32	719	2,377	1,053	4.5	2.3	0.6	14.6	48.3	21.4
1998	12,056	544	258	51	1,627	6,566	2,381	4.5	2.1	0.4	13.4	54.4	19.7
1999	11,835	599	309	43	1,815	5,984	2,372	5.0	2.6	0.3	15.3	50.5	20.0
2000	14,888	691	419	50	2,058	7,558	3,300	4.6	2.8	0.3	13.8	50.7	22.1
2001	13,264	675	366	56	1,870	6,836	2,726	5.0	2.7	0.4	14.1	51.5	20.5
2002	11,631	664	368	58	1,954	5,404	2,799	5.7	3.1	0.5	16.8	46.4	24.0
HONG KONG													
1980	2,238	137	18	2	249	735	978	6.1	0.7	0.1	11.1	32.8	43.6
1990	6,597	570	135	11	919	1,745	2,924	8.6	2.0	0.1	13.9	26.4	44.3
1998	17,320	844	802	14	1,747	7,881	5,677	4.8	4.6	0.0	10.0	45.5	32.7
1999	15,691	755	692	16	1,831	6,064	5,839	4.8	4.4	0.1	11.6	38.6	37.2
2000	20,536	863	863	25	2,137	8,691	7,301	4.2	4.2	0.1	10.4	42.3	35.5
2001	21,533	881	807	17	2,041	9,621	7,572	4.0	3.7	0.0	9.4	44.6	35.1
2002	19,906	695	746	17	2,061	8,564	7,359	3.4	3.7	0.0	10.3	43.0	36.9
AUSTRALIA													
1980	3,515	155	47	27	369	1,572	1,088	4.4	1.3	0.7	10.5	44.7	30.9
1990	6,804	354	88	54	951	2,707	2,107	5.2	1.2	0.7	13.9	39.7	30.9
1998	12,988	535	133	17	2,335	5,970	3,586	4.1	1.0	0.1	17.9	45.9	27.6
1999	13,737	626	151	17	2,726	6,179	3,631	4.5	1.0	0.1	19.8	44.9	26.4
2000	15,727	762	182	34	2,738	7,485	4,140	4.8	1.1	0.2	17.4	47.5	26.3
2001	15,531	750	152	18	3,109	7,300	3,841	4.8	0.9	0.1	20.0	47.0	24.7
2002	16,574	811	188	19	3,275	7,750	4,152	4.8	1.1	0.1	19.7	46.7	25.0

(*) The SITC rev. 2 nomenclature of products has been replaced by the SITC rev. 3 nomenclature since 1.1.1988.

PRODUCT BREAKDOWN OF EU TRADE
BY MAIN PARTNER COUNTRY

IMPORTS

SITC rev. 2 and 3(*)

Year	TOTAL	Food, beverages and tobacco	Crude materials	Energy	Chemicals	Machinery and transport equipment	Other manufactured products	Breakdown by product as % of total					
	SITC 0-9	SITC 0+1	SITC 2+4	SITC 3	SITC 5	SITC 7	SITC 6+8	0+1	2+4	3	5	7	6+8
CHINA													
1980	2,096	359	468	118	191	16	907	17.1	22.3	5.6	9.1	0.7	43.2
1990	10,589	608	807	131	623	1,547	6,780	5.7	7.6	1.2	5.8	14.6	64.0
1998	41,974	1,038	1,101	339	1,987	12,300	24,925	2.4	2.6	0.8	4.7	29.3	59.3
1999	49,655	1,077	1,134	303	2,055	15,866	28,906	2.1	2.2	0.6	4.1	31.9	58.2
2000	70,275	1,372	1,443	393	2,587	25,682	38,276	1.9	2.0	0.5	3.6	36.5	54.4
2001	75,915	1,588	1,447	633	2,908	28,726	40,026	2.0	1.9	0.8	3.8	37.8	52.7
2002	81,843	1,341	1,311	505	3,070	32,566	42,757	1.6	1.6	0.6	3.7	39.7	52.2
SOUTH KOREA													
1980	1,971	87	19	1	18	284	1,548	4.4	0.9	0.0	0.9	14.4	78.5
1990	6,548	147	45	0	164	2,640	3,508	2.2	0.6	0.0	2.4	40.3	53.5
1998	16,009	154	171	8	903	10,616	3,759	0.9	1.0	0.0	5.6	66.3	23.4
1999	18,353	114	179	16	807	13,242	3,837	0.6	0.9	0.0	4.3	72.1	20.9
2000	24,934	118	263	8	1,069	18,768	4,569	0.4	1.0	0.0	4.2	75.2	18.3
2001	21,597	128	240	13	915	15,911	4,227	0.5	1.1	0.0	4.2	73.6	19.5
2002	22,260	123	223	34	915	17,035	3,835	0.5	1.0	0.1	4.1	76.5	17.2
JAPAN													
1980	15,428	107	193	10	602	10,003	4,389	0.6	1.2	0.0	3.8	64.8	28.4
1990	46,086	136	198	29	2,160	34,371	8,542	0.2	0.4	0.0	4.6	74.5	18.5
1998	66,042	95	330	51	4,184	48,909	11,739	0.1	0.4	0.0	6.3	74.0	17.7
1999	71,911	87	384	42	4,520	54,491	11,758	0.1	0.5	0.0	6.2	75.7	16.3
2000	87,133	115	470	46	5,321	66,131	14,215	0.1	0.5	0.0	6.1	75.8	16.3
2001	76,298	133	445	69	5,493	55,728	13,538	0.1	0.5	0.0	7.1	73.0	17.7
2002	68,485	113	398	73	5,438	49,682	12,061	0.1	0.5	0.1	7.9	72.5	17.6
TAIWAN													
1980	2,128	137	18	:	21	494	1,419	6.4	0.8	:	1.0	23.1	66.6
1990	9,136	56	54	6	180	4,820	3,952	0.6	0.5	0.0	1.9	52.7	43.2
1998	18,089	99	96	4	375	11,826	5,250	0.5	0.5	0.0	2.0	65.3	29.0
1999	20,017	61	91	3	328	13,387	5,568	0.3	0.4	0.0	1.6	66.8	27.8
2000	26,654	68	133	7	418	18,706	6,474	0.2	0.4	0.0	1.5	70.1	24.2
2001	24,177	98	115	0	397	17,335	5,627	0.4	0.4	0.0	1.6	71.6	23.2
2002	21,128	106	131	0	391	15,757	4,653	0.5	0.6	0.0	1.8	74.5	22.0
HONG KONG													
1980	3,973	14	84	0	4	493	3,149	0.3	2.1	0.0	0.0	12.3	79.2
1990	5,909	28	29	0	24	1,524	4,145	0.4	0.4	0.0	0.4	25.7	70.1
1998	9,718	54	79	3	59	3,459	5,456	0.5	0.8	0.0	0.6	35.5	56.1
1999	10,681	55	33	0	58	4,162	5,992	0.5	0.3	0.0	0.5	38.9	56.0
2000	11,650	60	39	0	52	4,573	6,418	0.5	0.3	0.0	0.4	39.2	55.0
2001	10,271	53	19	0	47	4,064	5,703	0.5	0.1	0.0	0.4	39.5	55.5
2002	9,704	54	14	0	43	3,787	5,345	0.5	0.1	0.0	0.4	39.0	55.0
AUSTRALIA													
1980	2,687	251	1,265	357	16	63	645	9.3	47.0	13.2	0.5	2.3	24.0
1990	4,806	324	2,146	814	128	387	790	6.7	44.6	16.9	2.6	8.0	16.4
1998	7,540	746	2,142	881	294	844	1,581	9.8	28.4	11.6	3.8	11.1	20.9
1999	6,922	882	1,816	1,018	357	916	1,410	12.7	26.2	14.7	5.1	13.2	20.3
2000	8,856	1,058	2,447	1,255	561	1,159	1,925	11.9	27.6	14.1	6.3	13.0	21.7
2001	9,265	1,208	2,389	1,608	578	1,040	1,907	13.0	25.7	17.3	6.2	11.2	20.5
2002	8,867	1,265	2,011	1,544	483	1,066	1,766	14.2	22.6	17.4	5.4	12.0	19.9

(*) The SITC rev. 2 nomenclature of products has been replaced by the SITC rev. 3 nomenclature since 1.1.1988.

EXTRA-EU TRADE INDICES BY PARTNER COUNTRY
2000 = 100

EXPORTS

Value

Year	Extra EU	USA	Japan	Switzerland	CEEC	Mediterranean Basin	Latin America	OPEC	DAE	ACP
1990	**41.3**	**36.0**	**57.1**	**64.5**	**19.6**	**44.8**	**30.9**	**67.6**	**39.6**	**71.3**
1992	43.9	34.8	51.8	60.4	26.3	44.7	40.5	80.4	47.0	68.0
1993	49.9	40.0	57.4	61.6	31.5	52.0	47.6	78.2	58.8	64.8
1994	55.1	44.8	66.9	67.2	38.4	53.4	57.2	71.1	71.4	58.3
1995	60.7	44.6	75.1	73.9	47.9	60.3	60.4	73.3	82.2	66.8
1996	66.5	49.6	80.0	74.0	57.6	67.7	65.2	78.2	86.8	70.4
1997	75.3	60.0	79.5	75.5	69.4	76.6	81.0	93.6	93.1	76.0
1998	78.5	69.6	70.8	81.9	79.9	80.6	91.2	87.9	74.2	85.7
1999	81.4	79.3	79.4	89.8	82.1	80.1	84.1	82.1	76.3	83.1
2000	**100.0**	**100.0**	**100.0**	**100.0**	**100.0**	**100.0**	**100.0**	**100.0**	**100.0**	**100.0**
2001	104.6	103.2	100.0	105.6	110.8	93.1	104.2	118.4	100.4	104.9
2002	**105.5**	**103.2**	**94.1**	**99.9**	**118.1**	**97.6**	**89.9**	**124.5**	**95.6**	**105.4**

Volume

Year	Extra EU	USA	Japan	Switzerland	CEEC	Mediterranean Basin	Latin America	OPEC	DAE	ACP
1990	**61.4**	**64.3**	**85.8**	**83.8**	**24.7**	**61.4**	**43.8**	**102.9**	**59.7**	**102.8**
1992	61.4	56.6	71.2	75.6	32.4	58.9	53.0	114.8	65.9	93.1
1993	66.7	61.2	74.0	74.0	37.6	66.7	59.2	107.4	78.0	85.2
1994	71.6	66.3	83.9	78.3	45.2	66.0	70.7	94.4	91.5	74.7
1995	75.5	63.4	93.0	81.8	53.1	70.0	72.2	94.0	102.0	81.2
1996	79.6	66.2	97.8	81.3	62.7	76.2	75.6	94.5	102.8	82.1
1997	86.1	74.0	93.4	83.2	74.9	83.6	90.3	106.6	104.8	84.0
1998	88.8	83.8	83.8	89.2	85.9	88.4	100.8	98.5	82.6	93.8
1999	89.2	90.1	86.2	96.2	87.2	87.4	89.9	89.6	83.9	90.6
2000	**100.0**	**100.0**	**100.0**	**100.0**	**100.0**	**100.0**	**100.0**	**100.0**	**100.0**	**100.0**
2001	103.7	102.0	102.0	102.2	109.6	92.0	103.7	116.8	100.1	103.7
2002	**105.7**	**103.4**	**98.7**	**96.6**	**117.3**	**97.6**	**91.5**	**124.2**	**96.2**	**105.3**

Unit Value

Year	Extra EU	USA	Japan	Switzerland	CEEC	Mediterranean Basin	Latin America	OPEC	DAE	ACP
1990	**67.2**	**56.0**	**66.6**	**77.0**	**79.2**	**73.0**	**70.5**	**65.7**	**66.3**	**69.4**
1992	71.5	61.4	72.8	79.9	81.1	75.9	76.4	70.0	71.3	73.0
1993	74.8	65.4	77.5	83.2	83.9	78.0	80.4	72.8	75.4	76.0
1994	76.9	67.5	79.7	85.8	84.9	80.9	80.9	75.3	78.0	78.0
1995	80.4	70.4	80.7	90.4	90.3	86.1	83.6	78.0	80.6	82.3
1996	83.5	74.9	81.8	91.0	91.9	88.8	86.3	82.8	84.4	85.8
1997	87.5	81.1	85.1	90.8	92.7	91.6	89.7	87.8	88.8	90.5
1998	88.4	83.0	84.5	91.8	93.0	91.2	90.5	89.2	89.8	91.4
1999	91.2	88.0	92.1	93.3	94.1	91.7	93.5	91.6	91.0	91.7
2000	**100.0**	**100.0**	**100.0**	**100.0**	**100.0**	**100.0**	**100.0**	**100.0**	**100.0**	**100.0**
2001	100.9	101.2	98.0	103.3	101.1	101.2	100.5	101.4	100.3	101.1
2002	**99.8**	**99.8**	**95.3**	**103.4**	**100.7**	**100.0**	**98.3**	**100.2**	**99.4**	**100.1**

The indices, which are manually linked, relate to reporter EU-12 until 1995 and EU-15 thereafter. They cover all the products.

EXTRA-EU TRADE INDICES BY PARTNER COUNTRY

2000 = 100

IMPORTS

Year	Extra EU	USA	Japan	Switzerland	CEEC	Mediterranean Basin	Latin America	OPEC	DAE	ACP
Value										
1990	**41.1**	**45.4**	**56.6**	**64.5**	**22.7**	**51.3**	**54.6**	**53.8**	**33.9**	**76.2**
1992	43.6	46.3	62.9	65.7	28.3	49.8	52.5	51.0	40.0	62.7
1993	43.6	44.6	57.7	67.1	29.2	47.0	47.1	48.7	42.8	52.0
1994	48.3	49.7	59.6	72.8	37.1	51.0	58.4	48.6	47.4	64.5
1995	52.6	52.6	62.8	75.6	46.3	53.3	62.7	47.5	52.6	68.4
1996	55.9	57.0	60.6	74.5	49.1	59.0	62.2	55.1	55.4	75.8
1997	63.9	67.9	68.1	76.8	58.9	65.8	70.3	60.2	63.5	77.6
1998	69.1	76.5	75.7	84.7	70.4	65.7	72.6	50.7	73.4	73.2
1999	75.0	80.3	80.8	90.8	77.9	72.5	74.7	56.3	79.5	73.6
2000	**100.0**	**100.0**	**100.0**	**100.0**	**100.0**	**100.0**	**100.0**	**100.0**	**100.0**	**100.0**
2001	99.5	98.3	87.6	101.4	113.8	103.1	102.0	89.3	89.7	109.9
2002	**95.5**	**87.8**	**78.5**	**98.0**	**121.2**	**99.7**	**98.3**	**78.3**	**83.8**	**106.5**
Volume										
1990	**61.3**	**90.1**	**101.0**	**91.5**	**29.9**	**74.5**	**71.9**	**81.3**	**46.4**	**93.4**
1992	65.5	86.4	98.7	88.7	36.9	74.8	74.9	92.2	51.3	88.8
1993	62.0	74.5	79.4	85.2	37.1	70.2	65.6	88.9	50.7	73.1
1994	66.2	78.6	74.4	87.4	45.2	74.9	75.8	92.1	54.9	86.3
1995	69.9	84.1	75.8	85.5	51.2	74.2	77.0	88.6	61.1	86.5
1996	72.0	85.6	75.6	83.1	54.0	77.1	76.1	89.2	63.9	94.9
1997	76.6	89.7	83.0	84.7	62.9	82.1	75.4	92.2	69.1	89.4
1998	87.3	98.8	95.3	90.7	75.0	90.7	84.4	100.9	85.8	90.5
1999	91.1	97.4	94.8	95.5	83.3	95.0	91.2	93.1	90.7	91.0
2000	**100.0**	**100.0**	**100.0**	**100.0**	**100.0**	**100.0**	**100.0**	**100.0**	**100.0**	**100.0**
2001	99.7	95.6	87.4	99.4	111.0	104.7	105.4	97.5	90.5	110.5
2002	**98.5**	**85.9**	**80.9**	**94.5**	**118.1**	**104.9**	**107.2**	**89.2**	**87.2**	**110.0**
Unit Value										
1990	**67.1**	**50.4**	**56.0**	**70.5**	**75.8**	**68.9**	**76.0**	**66.2**	**73.1**	**81.6**
1992	66.5	53.6	63.7	74.1	76.7	66.6	70.1	55.3	78.0	70.6
1993	70.4	59.9	72.7	78.7	78.6	67.0	71.8	54.8	84.5	71.1
1994	72.9	63.2	80.1	83.3	82.0	68.1	77.1	52.8	86.4	74.7
1995	75.2	62.5	82.8	88.4	90.5	71.8	81.4	53.6	86.1	79.1
1996	77.7	66.6	80.1	89.7	90.9	76.5	81.8	61.8	86.7	79.9
1997	83.4	75.7	82.0	90.7	93.7	80.1	93.2	65.3	91.9	86.8
1998	79.2	77.4	79.4	93.4	93.8	72.4	86.0	50.2	85.5	80.9
1999	82.3	82.4	85.2	95.1	93.5	76.3	81.9	60.5	87.6	80.9
2000	**100.0**	**100.0**	**100.0**	**100.0**	**100.0**	**100.0**	**100.0**	**100.0**	**100.0**	**100.0**
2001	99.8	102.8	100.2	102.0	102.5	98.5	96.7	91.6	99.1	99.5
2002	**97.0**	**102.2**	**97.0**	**103.7**	**102.6**	**95.1**	**91.7**	**87.8**	**96.1**	**96.8**

The indices, which are manually linked, relate to reporter EU-12 until 1995 and EU-15 thereafter. They cover all the products.

EXTRA-EU TRADE INDICES BY PARTNER COUNTRY
2000 = 100

Year	Extra EU	USA	Japan	Switzerland	CEEC	Mediterranean Basin	Latin America	OPEC	DAE	ACP
Cover Rate [1]										
1990	**100.4**	**79.2**	**100.8**	**100.0**	**86.3**	**87.3**	**56.5**	**125.6**	**116.8**	**93.5**
1992	100.6	75.1	82.3	91.9	92.9	89.7	77.1	157.6	117.5	108.4
1993	114.4	89.6	99.4	91.8	107.8	110.6	101.0	160.5	137.3	124.6
1994	114.0	90.1	112.2	92.3	103.5	104.7	97.9	146.2	150.6	90.3
1995	115.3	84.7	119.5	97.7	103.4	113.1	96.3	154.3	156.2	97.6
1996	118.9	87.0	132.0	99.3	117.3	114.7	104.8	141.9	156.6	92.8
1997	117.8	88.3	116.7	98.3	117.8	116.4	115.2	155.4	146.6	97.9
1998	113.6	90.9	93.5	96.6	113.4	122.6	125.6	173.3	101.0	117.0
1999	108.5	98.7	98.2	98.8	105.3	110.4	112.5	145.8	95.9	112.9
2000	**100.0**	**100.0**	**100.0**	**100.0**	**100.0**	**100.0**	**100.0**	**100.0**	**100.0**	**100.0**
2001	105.1	104.9	114.1	104.1	97.3	90.3	102.1	132.5	111.9	95.4
2002	**110.4**	**117.5**	**119.8**	**101.9**	**97.4**	**97.8**	**91.4**	**159.0**	**114.0**	**98.9**
Volume Ratio [2]										
1990	**100.1**	**71.3**	**84.9**	**91.5**	**82.6**	**82.4**	**60.9**	**126.5**	**128.6**	**110.0**
1992	93.7	65.5	72.1	85.2	87.8	78.7	70.7	124.5	128.4	104.8
1993	107.5	82.1	93.1	86.8	101.3	95.0	90.2	120.8	153.8	116.5
1994	108.1	84.3	112.7	89.5	100.0	88.1	93.2	102.4	166.6	86.5
1995	108.0	75.3	122.6	95.6	103.7	94.3	93.7	106.0	166.9	93.8
1996	110.5	77.3	129.3	97.8	116.1	98.8	99.3	105.9	160.8	86.5
1997	112.4	82.4	112.5	98.2	119.0	101.8	119.7	115.6	151.6	93.9
1998	101.7	84.8	87.9	98.3	114.5	97.4	119.4	97.6	96.2	103.6
1999	97.9	92.5	90.9	100.7	104.6	92.0	98.5	96.2	92.5	99.5
2000	**100.0**	**100.0**	**100.0**	**100.0**	**100.0**	**100.0**	**100.0**	**100.0**	**100.0**	**100.0**
2001	104.0	106.6	116.7	102.8	98.7	87.8	98.3	119.7	110.6	93.8
2002	**107.3**	**120.3**	**122.0**	**102.2**	**99.3**	**93.0**	**85.3**	**139.2**	**110.3**	**95.7**
Terms of Trade [3]										
1990	**100.1**	**111.1**	**118.9**	**109.2**	**104.4**	**105.9**	**92.7**	**99.2**	**90.6**	**85.0**
1992	107.5	114.5	114.2	107.8	105.7	113.9	108.9	126.5	91.4	103.3
1993	106.2	109.1	106.6	105.7	106.7	116.4	111.9	132.8	89.2	106.8
1994	105.4	106.8	99.5	103.0	103.5	118.7	104.9	142.6	90.2	104.4
1995	106.9	112.6	97.4	102.2	99.7	119.9	102.7	145.5	93.6	104.0
1996	107.4	112.4	102.1	101.4	101.1	116.0	105.5	133.9	97.3	107.3
1997	104.9	107.1	103.7	100.1	98.9	114.3	96.2	134.4	96.6	104.2
1998	111.6	107.2	106.4	98.2	99.1	125.9	105.2	177.6	105.0	112.9
1999	110.8	106.7	108.0	98.1	100.6	120.1	114.1	151.4	103.8	113.3
2000	**100.0**	**100.0**	**100.0**	**100.0**	**100.0**	**100.0**	**100.0**	**100.0**	**100.0**	**100.0**
2001	101.1	98.4	97.8	101.2	98.6	102.7	103.9	110.6	101.2	101.6
2002	**102.8**	**97.6**	**98.2**	**99.7**	**98.1**	**105.1**	**107.1**	**114.1**	**103.4**	**103.4**

(1) Cover rate is the export value index divided by the import value index.

(2) Volume ratio is the export volume index divided by the import volume index.

(3) Terms of trade is the unit value export index divided by the unit value import index.

The indices, which are manually linked, relate to reporter EU-12 until 1995 and EU-15 thereafter. They cover all the products.

TRADE BALANCE

Product list	Value (Mio ECU/Euro)				
SITC rev. 3	**1990**	**1999**	**2000**	**2001**	**2002**
0-9 **TOTAL**	**-49,187**	**-19,633**	**-91,391**	**-42,629**	**6,317**
0 **Food and live animals**	**-11,585**	**-14,390**	**-13,706**	**-15,501**	**-15,970**
00 Live animals	-336	188	100	16	145
01 Meat and meat preparations	251	985	759	-71	63
02 Dairy products and birds'eggs	2,790	3,478	4,190	4,036	3,785
03 Fish, crustaceans, molluscs	-5,246	-8,589	-9,633	-10,506	-10,045
04 Cereals and cereal preparations	3,474	3,291	4,099	3,446	2,237
05 Vegetables and fruit	-7,694	-9,037	-8,927	-9,037	-8,676
06 Sugar, sugar preparations, honey	799	346	802	854	86
07 Coffee, tea, cocoa, spices	-3,444	-5,211	-4,617	-3,526	-3,445
08 Feeding stuff for animals	-3,531	-2,650	-3,514	-4,188	-3,829
1 **Beverages and tobacco**	**4,832**	**7,874**	**8,815**	**8,778**	**9,824**
11 Beverages	5,581	7,879	8,819	8,910	9,726
12 Tobacco	-749	56	22	-104	131
2 **Crude materials, except fuels**	**-24,625**	**-24,433**	**-31,563**	**-30,496**	**-25,540**
21 Hides and skins, raw	-557	-93	-83	-141	143
22 Oil seeds and oleaginous fruits	-3,300	-3,850	-4,441	-5,362	-5,090
23 Crude rubber	-716	-938	-1,129	-1,027	-880
24 Cork and wood	-4,744	-4,607	-5,439	-4,952	-4,492
25 Pulp and waste paper	-3,240	-2,914	-4,962	-3,911	-3,184
26 Textile fibres and their wastes	-2,887	-1,568	-1,985	-1,899	-1,304
27 Crude fertilizers	-1,280	-1,598	-1,827	-1,782	-1,546
28 Metalliferous ores and metal scrap	-7,273	-8,465	-11,270	-11,018	-9,173
3 **Energy**	**-59,324**	**-61,682**	**-118,842**	**-119,035**	**-111,153**
32 Coal, coke and briquettes	-5,057	-5,794	-7,283	-9,918	-8,388
33 Petroleum and petroleum products	-50,092	-46,626	-94,914	-87,729	-82,020
34 Gas, natural and manufactured	-4,383	-9,669	-17,501	-21,483	-20,050
35 Electric current	208	462	629	59	-722
4 **Oils, fats and waxes**	**-226**	**-470**	**-6**	**-228**	**-267**
41 Animal oils and fats	-137	-32	14	20	76
42 Fixed vegetable fats and oils	-105	-462	-43	-250	-429
43 Animal or vegetable oils, and fats, waxes	16	10	15	-8	78
5 **Chemical products**	**15,538**	**47,738**	**58,244**	**64,927**	**71,588**
51 Organic chemicals	1,821	8,134	11,934	13,142	11,570
52 Inorganic chemicals	313	-363	-444	-875	-323
53 Tanning and colouring materials	2,248	4,390	4,984	5,047	5,778
54 Medicinal and pharmaceutical products	3,607	15,420	18,188	21,297	25,234
55 Essential oils, perfume mat., cosmetics	3,062	7,034	8,127	9,293	9,705
56 Fertilizers	-747	-841	-1,349	-1,304	-900
57 Plastics in primary forms	1,266	4,079	5,371	5,759	6,392
58 Plastics in non-primary forms	768	3,012	3,691	4,208	4,763
6 **Manufactured goods classif. by material**	**10,399**	**16,417**	**14,952**	**19,092**	**28,850**
61 Leather manufactures, dressed furskins	-241	1,258	1,479	1,170	1,288
62 Rubber manufactures	715	13	201	-54	-184
63 Cork and wood manufactures	-1,281	-1,762	-1,813	-1,496	-983
64 Paper, paperboard and articles thereof	519	7,282	9,522	9,083	9,963
65 Textile yarn, fabrics and related products	745	4,059	4,568	5,564	6,195
66 Non-metallic mineral manufactures	6,400	5,200	5,471	5,945	8,612
67 Iron and steel	6,582	4,762	4,996	5,900	7,209
68 Non-ferrous metals	-7,111	-8,922	-13,402	-11,414	-9,157
69 Manufactures of metals	3,739	4,345	3,774	4,191	5,675
7 **Machinery and transport equipment**	**29,908**	**45,877**	**44,482**	**81,652**	**94,589**
71 Power generating machinery and equipment	4,122	4,656	3,859	7,481	6,129
72 Machinery specialized for particular ind.	16,653	26,278	31,106	34,942	36,997
73 Metalworking machinery	1,936	2,398	1,667	3,022	4,009
74 General industry machinery and equipment	12,512	22,673	23,528	26,907	31,172
75 Office machines and computers	-14,291	-36,025	-40,222	-33,976	-33,237
76 Telecommunication, sound, TV, video	-8,076	-1,098	-4,999	-6,913	-9,131
77 Electrical machinery	-243	-4,672	-18,049	-6,491	-1,437
78 Road vehicles	15,142	25,655	39,298	46,300	53,233
79 Other transport equipment	129	3,617	6,691	8,017	3,852
8 **Miscellaneous manuf. articles**	**-9,880**	**-34,396**	**-41,337**	**-40,688**	**-38,063**
81 Prefabr. buildings, sanitary, heating, lighting	768	727	442	555	409
82 Furniture, bedding, mattresses	1,897	-147	-678	-1,087	-2,033
83 Travel goods, handbags and similar goods	-209	-1,367	-1,433	-1,084	-1,216
84 Clothing and clothing accessories	-11,772	-30,005	-35,363	-36,345	-36,394
85 Footwear	328	-2,370	-2,919	-3,323	-3,714
87 Professional, scientific, controlling material	488	2,166	1,353	2,555	5,468
88 Photogr. apparatus, optical goods, clocks	-2,450	-2,680	-2,322	-1,834	-252
89 Miscellaneous manufactured articles	1,013	-820	-481	-226	-435
9 **Articles non classified elsewhere**	**-4,224**	**-2,167**	**-12,431**	**-11,127**	**-9,444**

TRENDS IN EXTRA-EU TRADE BY PRODUCT

eurostat

EXPORTS

Product list SITC rev. 3	Value (Mio ECU/Euro)					Annual variation (%)					% of total	
	1990	1999	2000	2001	2002	90/89	99/98	00/99	01/00	02/01	1990	2002
0-9 TOTAL	355,164	760,192	942,044	985,326	993,796	0.2	3.6	23.9	4.5	0.8	100.0	100.0
0 Food and live animals	20,633	30,818	35,485	36,598	36,731	-4.8	-3.1	15.1	3.1	0.3	5.8	3.6
00 Live animals	366	813	974	856	940	19.6	25.1	19.7	-12.0	9.8	0.1	0.0
01 Meat and meat preparations	2,835	4,203	4,449	4,247	4,104	-6.4	4.8	5.8	-4.5	-3.3	0.7	0.4
02 Dairy products and birds'eggs	3,426	4,376	5,185	5,197	4,820	-16.2	-4.6	18.4	0.2	-7.2	0.9	0.4
03 Fish, crustaceans, molluscs	1,033	1,727	1,921	2,087	2,178	-4.9	6.2	11.1	8.6	4.3	0.2	0.2
04 Cereals and cereal preparations	4,701	5,153	6,208	5,847	5,724	-10.3	4.7	20.4	-5.8	-2.1	1.3	0.5
05 Vegetables and fruit	2,480	4,496	5,176	5,757	6,382	-2.6	-3.0	15.1	11.2	10.8	0.6	0.6
06 Sugar, sugar preparations, honey	2,052	1,930	2,387	2,616	2,067	18.4	-21.9	23.7	9.6	-21.0	0.5	0.2
07 Coffee, tea, cocoa, spices	1,352	2,463	2,791	3,100	3,222	2.3	-13.2	13.2	11.0	3.9	0.3	0.3
08 Feeding stuff for animals	773	1,711	1,935	2,000	2,240	-6.3	-9.9	13.0	3.3	12.0	0.2	0.2
1 Beverages and tobacco	7,313	12,818	14,432	14,967	15,715	7.1	6.2	12.5	3.7	4.9	2.0	1.5
11 Beverages	6,204	10,425	11,880	12,553	13,318	4.8	10.1	13.9	5.6	6.0	1.7	1.3
12 Tobacco	1,109	2,383	2,517	2,407	2,389	22.0	1.7	5.6	-4.3	-0.7	0.3	0.2
2 Crude materials, except fuels	5,634	12,955	16,206	15,773	17,019	-9.2	11.0	25.0	-2.6	7.9	1.5	1.7
21 Hides and skins, raw	375	626	1,059	1,105	1,197	-29.3	-20.7	69.1	4.3	8.3	0.1	0.1
22 Oil seeds and oleaginous fruits	26	445	262	171	317	-11.7	51.6	-41.1	-34.6	84.7	0.0	0.0
23 Crude rubber	441	615	782	778	893	-4.9	-6.9	27.1	-0.5	14.7	0.1	0.0
24 Cork and wood	383	2,449	2,900	2,683	2,879	3.3	22.4	18.3	-7.4	7.3	0.1	0.2
25 Pulp and waste paper	190	956	1,342	1,221	1,332	-12.1	42.3	40.4	-9.0	9.1	0.0	0.1
26 Textile fibres and their wastes	1,369	1,674	2,020	1,944	2,080	-9.1	6.9	20.6	-3.7	7.0	0.3	0.2
27 Crude fertilizers	760	1,481	1,742	1,798	1,866	-7.8	8.4	17.5	3.2	3.7	0.2	0.1
28 Metalliferous ores and metal scrap	987	2,128	3,116	3,063	3,261	-16.7	14.6	46.4	-1.6	6.4	0.2	0.3
3 Energy	9,478	16,593	30,250	25,943	26,338	14.2	18.4	82.3	-14.2	1.5	2.6	2.6
32 Coal, coke and briquettes	154	118	152	144	146	-48.9	-13.5	29.0	-5.4	1.3	0.0	0.0
33 Petroleum and petroleum products	8,671	14,720	27,470	22,996	23,843	15.8	20.8	86.6	-16.2	3.6	2.4	2.3
34 Gas, natural and manufactured	120	531	1,082	912	769	38.8	29.1	103.7	-15.7	-15.6	0.0	0.0
35 Electric current	534	1,192	1,309	1,638	1,540	24.2	-3.9	9.7	25.1	-5.9	0.1	0.1
4 Oils, fats and waxes	1,333	2,408	2,575	2,410	2,813	0.4	-16.7	6.9	-6.4	16.7	0.3	0.2
41 Animal oils and fats	62	113	164	205	230	-1.9	-18.4	45.3	24.5	12.4	0.0	0.0
42 Fixed vegetable fats and oils	1,138	1,892	2,003	1,807	2,085	2.1	-19.3	5.8	-9.7	15.3	0.3	0.2
43 Animal or vegetable oils, and fats, waxes	133	371	363	383	489	-11.3	0.2	-2.2	5.5	27.6	0.0	0.0
5 Chemical products	41,980	106,651	129,610	142,460	152,523	0.0	11.1	21.5	9.9	7.0	11.8	15.3
51 Organic chemicals	9,609	24,791	32,051	33,839	33,625	-4.1	22.0	29.2	5.5	-0.6	2.7	3.3
52 Inorganic chemicals	2,858	4,397	5,409	5,389	5,058	-1.9	9.0	22.9	-0.3	-6.1	0.8	0.5
53 Tanning and colouring materials	3,808	7,247	8,358	8,346	8,914	5.2	4.5	15.3	-0.1	6.8	1.0	0.8
54 Medicinal and pharmaceutical products	7,728	30,343	35,840	43,917	51,420	4.5	13.0	18.1	22.5	17.0	2.1	5.1
55 Essential oils, perfume mat., cosmetics	4,166	10,029	11,698	13,132	13,802	5.4	6.8	16.6	12.2	5.0	1.1	1.3
56 Fertilizers	562	750	765	778	908	-9.2	9.0	1.9	1.7	16.6	0.1	0.0
57 Plastics in primary forms	4,855	9,755	12,631	12,797	13,237	-6.1	6.2	29.4	1.3	3.4	1.3	1.3
58 Plastics in non-primary forms	2,240	6,172	7,465	7,929	8,455	-2.6	4.1	20.9	6.2	6.6	0.6	0.8
6 Manufactured goods classif. by material	59,932	113,427	140,032	144,408	146,491	-6.4	0.1	23.4	3.1	1.4	16.8	14.7
61 Leather manufactures, dressed furskins	1,694	3,311	4,533	4,913	4,741	-7.8	2.9	36.9	8.3	-3.5	0.4	0.4
62 Rubber manufactures	2,530	5,042	5,901	5,980	6,119	-8.8	2.5	17.0	1.3	2.3	0.7	0.6
63 Cork and wood manufactures	1,022	3,297	4,093	4,361	4,805	0.5	3.6	24.1	6.5	10.1	0.2	0.4
64 Paper, paperboard and articles thereof	3,988	13,763	17,055	17,198	17,791	-1.1	2.2	23.9	0.8	3.4	1.1	1.7
65 Textile yarn, fabrics and related products	10,758	20,128	23,471	24,742	24,465	2.2	-0.7	16.6	5.4	-1.1	3.0	2.4
66 Non-metallic mineral manufactures	13,529	25,203	31,378	31,556	32,750	-7.5	11.5	24.5	0.5	3.7	3.8	3.2
67 Iron and steel	12,142	14,958	19,503	19,976	20,133	-16.6	-15.4	30.3	2.4	0.7	3.4	2.0
68 Non-ferrous metals	4,732	8,234	11,930	11,938	11,052	-8.8	-0.2	44.8	0.0	-7.4	1.3	1.1
69 Manufactures of metals	9,204	19,310	22,011	23,541	24,403	0.2	-0.3	13.9	6.9	3.6	2.5	2.4
7 Machinery and transport equipment	142,962	351,833	439,142	461,603	451,376	5.0	1.8	24.8	5.1	-2.2	40.2	45.4
71 Power generating machinery and equipment	13,644	31,885	38,703	43,540	40,062	13.5	5.7	21.3	12.4	-7.9	3.8	4.0
72 Machinery specialized for particular ind.	24,231	40,662	48,547	51,841	52,129	6.5	-8.2	19.3	6.7	0.5	6.8	5.2
73 Metalworking machinery	5,384	8,264	8,905	10,062	9,547	-0.7	-5.2	7.7	12.9	-5.1	1.5	0.9
74 General industry machinery and equipment	21,778	45,701	52,283	56,693	59,098	6.3	-3.5	14.4	8.4	4.2	6.1	5.9
75 Office machines and computers	7,789	24,043	31,305	31,499	29,028	-0.6	12.1	30.2	0.6	-7.8	2.1	2.9
76 Telecommunication, sound, TV, video	5,969	31,283	44,295	41,879	34,723	7.3	11.3	41.5	-5.4	-17.0	1.6	3.4
77 Electrical machinery	17,690	56,776	75,336	75,544	71,452	3.5	6.4	32.6	0.2	-5.4	4.9	7.1
78 Road vehicles	31,108	69,263	87,761	95,070	104,497	4.1	1.1	26.7	8.3	9.9	8.7	10.5
79 Other transport equipment	13,347	41,561	50,407	53,111	47,838	2.0	3.1	21.2	5.3	-9.9	3.7	4.8
8 Miscellaneous manuf. articles	48,152	92,696	113,137	120,124	121,510	3.3	3.5	22.0	6.1	1.1	13.5	12.2
81 Prefabr. buildings, sanitary, heating, lighting	1,347	3,476	3,822	4,133	4,159	-1.3	1.2	9.9	8.1	0.6	0.3	0.4
82 Furniture, bedding, mattresses	3,858	8,602	10,243	10,519	10,464	0.2	4.2	19.0	2.6	-0.5	1.0	1.0
83 Travel goods, handbags and similar goods	1,247	1,973	2,638	3,004	2,763	1.0	9.4	33.6	13.9	-8.0	0.3	0.2
84 Clothing and clothing accessories	8,020	13,713	15,903	17,565	17,562	3.9	-3.0	15.9	10.4	0.0	2.2	1.7
85 Footwear	3,508	5,457	6,485	7,058	6,828	5.7	-6.2	18.8	8.8	-3.2	0.9	0.6
87 Professional, scientific, controlling material	8,647	19,893	24,359	26,995	27,795	3.6	7.3	22.4	10.8	2.9	2.4	2.7
88 Photogr. apparatus, optical goods, clocks	3,951	7,896	10,751	10,457	10,505	-1.4	5.9	36.1	-2.7	0.4	1.1	1.0
89 Miscellaneous manufactured articles	17,518	31,585	38,871	40,292	41,328	5.1	5.3	23.0	3.6	2.5	4.9	4.1
9 Articles non classified elsewhere	17,747	19,992	21,175	21,041	21,361	-16.4	19.0	5.9	-0.6	1.5	4.9	2.1

IMPORTS

Product list SITC rev. 3		Value (Mio ECU/Euro)					Annual variation (%)					% of total	
		1990	1999	2000	2001	2002	90/89	99/98	00/99	01/00	02/01	1990	2002
0-9	TOTAL	404,351	779,825	1033436	1027955	987,479	2.7	9.7	32.5	-0.5	-3.9	100.0	100.0
0	Food and live animals	32,218	45,208	49,191	52,099	52,701	-0.7	-0.5	8.8	5.9	1.1	7.9	5.3
00	Live animals	701	625	874	840	795	-1.7	9.3	39.8	-3.8	-5.3	0.1	0.0
01	Meat and meat preparations	2,584	3,217	3,690	4,318	4,041	-0.8	5.3	14.6	17.0	-6.4	0.6	0.4
02	Dairy products and birds'eggs	636	898	995	1,161	1,034	-7.5	6.8	10.7	16.6	-10.9	0.1	0.1
03	Fish, crustaceans, molluscs	6,279	10,316	11,554	12,593	12,223	9.8	-2.0	11.9	8.9	-2.9	1.5	1.2
04	Cereals and cereal preparations	1,227	1,862	2,108	2,400	3,487	-7.0	-3.0	13.2	13.8	45.2	0.3	0.3
05	Vegetables and fruit	10,174	13,533	14,102	14,794	15,058	15.2	6.9	4.2	4.9	1.7	2.5	1.5
06	Sugar, sugar preparations, honey	1,253	1,583	1,585	1,762	1,981	-2.9	1.4	0.1	11.1	12.4	0.3	0.2
07	Coffee, tea, cocoa, spices	4,795	7,675	7,408	6,626	6,668	-22.1	-13.3	-3.4	-10.5	0.6	1.1	0.6
08	Feeding stuff for animals	4,305	4,361	5,449	6,188	6,069	-12.2	-3.2	24.9	13.5	-1.9	1.0	0.6
1	Beverages and tobacco	2,481	4,944	5,617	6,190	5,891	8.4	10.5	13.6	10.1	-4.8	0.6	0.5
11	Beverages	622	2,546	3,061	3,643	3,591	28.8	18.2	20.2	19.0	-1.4	0.1	0.3
12	Tobacco	1,858	2,328	2,496	2,511	2,259	2.9	1.2	7.2	0.6	-10.0	0.4	0.2
2	Crude materials, except fuels	30,259	37,388	47,769	46,269	42,559	-10.8	-5.0	27.7	-3.1	-8.0	7.4	4.3
21	Hides and skins, raw	933	719	1,141	1,246	1,054	-24.9	-25.3	58.8	9.1	-15.3	0.2	0.1
22	Oil seeds and oleaginous fruits	3,327	4,295	4,703	5,533	5,406	-5.4	-13.3	9.5	17.6	-2.3	0.8	0.5
23	Crude rubber	1,157	1,554	1,911	1,805	1,773	-14.0	-7.7	23.0	-5.5	-1.8	0.2	0.1
24	Cork and wood	5,127	7,056	8,338	7,635	7,371	2.0	9.0	18.1	-8.4	-3.4	1.2	0.7
25	Pulp and waste paper	3,431	3,870	6,304	5,132	4,516	-14.2	0.7	62.9	-18.5	-11.9	0.8	0.4
26	Textile fibres and their wastes	4,256	3,242	4,005	3,843	3,384	-17.3	-17.0	23.5	-4.0	-11.9	1.0	0.3
27	Crude fertilizers	2,040	3,078	3,569	3,580	3,412	-13.1	-1.0	15.9	0.3	-4.6	0.5	0.3
28	Metalliferous ores and metal scrap	8,260	10,593	14,386	14,081	12,434	-13.4	-6.9	35.7	-2.1	-11.6	2.0	1.2
3	Energy	68,802	78,275	149,091	144,978	137,490	13.2	26.8	90.4	-2.7	-5.1	17.0	13.9
32	Coal, coke and briquettes	5,211	5,912	7,435	10,061	8,534	5.5	-8.6	25.7	35.3	-15.1	1.2	0.9
33	Petroleum and petroleum products	58,762	61,346	122,384	110,725	105,863	13.7	40.3	99.4	-9.5	-4.3	14.5	10.7
34	Gas, natural and manufactured	4,503	10,199	18,583	22,394	20,819	16.5	-5.5	82.1	20.5	-7.0	1.1	2.1
35	Electric current	326	730	680	1,579	2,262	12.9	7.9	-6.8	132.2	43.2	0.0	0.2
4	Oils, fats and waxes	1,559	2,878	2,580	2,638	3,080	-6.8	-3.6	-10.3	2.2	16.7	0.3	0.3
41	Animal oils and fats	199	145	151	185	155	-25.9	-20.8	3.7	22.8	-16.4	0.0	0.0
42	Fixed vegetable fats and oils	1,243	2,354	2,046	2,057	2,514	-2.4	-5.1	-13.0	0.5	22.2	0.3	0.2
43	Animal or vegetable oils, and fats, waxes	117	361	348	392	411	-10.8	12.2	-3.6	12.4	5.0	0.0	0.0
5	Chemical products	26,442	58,913	71,366	77,533	80,934	3.2	6.0	21.1	8.6	4.3	6.5	8.1
51	Organic chemicals	7,788	16,657	20,117	20,697	22,055	0.1	6.9	20.7	2.8	6.5	1.9	2.2
52	Inorganic chemicals	2,545	4,761	5,853	6,264	5,381	-14.5	-4.1	22.9	7.0	-14.0	0.6	0.5
53	Tanning and colouring materials	1,559	2,857	3,374	3,299	3,135	5.5	-2.6	18.1	-2.2	-4.9	0.3	0.3
54	Medicinal and pharmaceutical products	4,121	14,922	17,652	22,621	26,186	11.4	17.7	18.2	28.1	15.7	1.0	2.6
55	Essential oils, perfume mat., cosmetics	1,104	2,995	3,571	3,839	4,096	6.5	11.6	19.2	7.4	6.7	0.2	0.4
56	Fertilizers	1,309	1,592	2,113	2,083	1,808	-2.3	-8.7	32.7	-1.4	-13.1	0.3	0.1
57	Plastics in primary forms	3,589	5,676	7,260	7,038	6,845	14.5	-7.0	27.9	-3.0	-2.7	0.8	0.6
58	Plastics in non-primary forms	1,472	3,160	3,775	3,721	3,692	5.7	4.5	19.4	-1.4	-0.7	0.3	0.3
6	Manufactured goods classif. by material	49,533	97,010	125,080	125,316	117,640	-2.2	2.1	28.9	0.1	-6.1	12.2	11.9
61	Leather manufactures, dressed furskins	1,935	2,053	3,054	3,742	3,453	6.6	-17.8	48.7	22.5	-7.7	0.4	0.3
62	Rubber manufactures	1,815	5,029	5,701	6,034	6,302	3.3	9.0	13.3	5.8	4.4	0.4	0.6
63	Cork and wood manufactures	2,303	5,058	5,906	5,857	5,787	10.2	7.7	16.7	-0.8	-1.1	0.5	0.5
64	Paper, paperboard and articles thereof	3,469	6,481	7,533	8,115	7,828	2.5	4.2	16.2	7.7	-3.5	0.8	0.7
65	Textile yarn, fabrics and related products	10,014	16,069	18,904	19,178	18,270	6.3	-2.0	17.6	1.4	-4.7	2.4	1.8
66	Non-metallic mineral manufactures	7,130	20,003	25,908	25,611	24,149	-1.7	22.1	29.5	-1.1	-5.7	1.7	2.4
67	Iron and steel	5,560	10,196	14,507	14,076	12,924	-7.9	-17.2	42.2	-2.9	-8.1	1.3	1.3
68	Non-ferrous metals	11,843	17,156	25,332	23,351	20,210	-13.1	-3.6	47.6	-7.8	-13.4	2.9	2.0
69	Manufactures of metals	5,465	14,965	18,237	19,350	18,728	3.8	6.6	21.8	6.1	-3.2	1.3	1.8
7	Machinery and transport equipment	113,054	305,956	394,660	379,951	356,787	3.1	14.5	28.9	-3.7	-6.0	27.9	36.1
71	Power generating machinery and equipment	9,522	27,229	34,843	36,060	33,933	3.9	16.5	27.9	3.4	-5.8	2.3	3.4
72	Machinery specialized for particular ind.	7,579	14,384	17,441	16,898	15,132	1.0	8.4	21.2	-3.1	-10.4	1.8	1.5
73	Metalworking machinery	3,448	5,865	7,238	7,041	5,538	12.3	-1.2	23.4	-2.7	-21.3	0.8	0.5
74	General industry machinery and equipment	9,266	23,028	28,754	29,786	27,926	7.0	10.6	24.8	3.5	-6.2	2.2	2.8
75	Office machines and computers	22,080	60,069	71,526	65,476	62,264	0.2	10.6	19.0	-8.4	-4.9	5.4	6.3
76	Telecommunication, sound, TV, video	14,044	32,381	49,294	48,792	43,854	6.2	22.2	52.2	-1.0	-10.1	3.4	4.4
77	Electrical machinery	17,933	61,448	93,385	82,035	72,889	0.9	12.8	51.9	-12.1	-11.1	4.4	7.3
78	Road vehicles	15,965	43,609	48,462	48,770	51,264	6.8	18.4	11.1	0.6	5.1	3.9	5.1
79	Other transport equipment	13,217	37,944	43,716	45,094	43,986	-0.6	19.3	15.2	3.1	-2.4	3.2	4.4
8	Miscellaneous manuf. articles	58,032	127,092	154,475	160,812	159,573	7.7	9.1	21.5	4.1	-0.7	14.3	16.1
81	Prefabr. buildings, sanitary, heating, lighting	579	2,749	3,380	3,579	3,750	16.0	21.1	22.9	5.8	4.7	0.1	0.3
82	Furniture, bedding, mattresses	1,961	8,750	10,921	11,606	12,497	4.3	21.7	24.8	6.2	7.6	0.4	1.2
83	Travel goods, handbags and similar goods	1,456	3,340	4,071	4,088	3,979	5.8	10.1	21.8	0.4	-2.6	0.3	0.4
84	Clothing and clothing accessories	19,792	43,719	51,267	53,910	53,957	14.8	6.7	17.2	5.1	0.0	4.8	5.4
85	Footwear	3,180	7,826	9,405	10,380	10,542	11.1	12.0	20.1	10.3	1.5	0.7	1.0
87	Professional, scientific, controlling material	8,159	17,727	23,006	24,440	22,328	0.8	10.0	29.7	6.2	-8.6	2.0	2.2
88	Photogr. apparatus, optical goods, clocks	6,401	10,577	13,073	12,290	10,757	1.1	6.7	23.6	-5.9	-12.4	1.5	1.0
89	Miscellaneous manufactured articles	16,505	32,404	39,352	40,517	41,763	5.7	8.1	21.4	2.9	3.0	4.0	4.2
9	Articles non classified elsewhere	21,971	22,159	33,606	32,168	30,805	-2.7	-1.1	51.6	-4.2	-4.2	5.4	3.1

MAIN EU TRADING PARTNERS
FOOD PRODUCTS

EXPORTS

Ranking of EU main trading partners in 2002

Partner	Value (Mio ECU/euro)					Share (%)				
	1990	1999	2000	2001	2002	1990	1999	2000	2001	2002
Meat and meat preparations - SITC 01										
Extra EU-15	**2,835**	**4,203**	**4,449**	**4,247**	**4,104**	**100.0**	**100.0**	**100.0**	**100.0**	**100.0**
Japan	454	830	1,052	983	910	16.0	19.7	23.6	23.1	22.1
Russia[4]	351	991	670	862	749	12.3	23.5	15.0	20.2	18.2
United States	301	228	299	275	263	10.6	5.4	6.7	6.4	6.4
Switzerland[1]	148	175	204	197	220	5.2	4.1	4.5	4.6	5.3
Romania	101	17	43	104	125	3.5	0.4	0.9	2.4	3.0
South Korea	6	171	143	116	123	0.2	4.0	3.2	2.7	2.9
Saudi Arabia	148	170	160	118	95	5.2	4.0	3.5	2.7	2.3
Hong Kong	37	134	141	124	94	1.2	3.1	3.1	2.9	2.2
Poland	43	45	65	52	93	1.5	1.0	1.4	1.2	2.2
Hungary	2	21	61	89	88	0.0	0.4	1.3	2.1	2.1
Total for all 10	**1,590**	**2,783**	**2,838**	**2,920**	**2,760**	**56.0**	**66.2**	**63.7**	**68.7**	**67.2**
Dairy products and birds' eggs - SITC 02										
Extra EU-15	**3,426**	**4,376**	**5,185**	**5,197**	**4,820**	**100.0**	**100.0**	**100.0**	**100.0**	**100.0**
United States	235	443	478	533	546	6.8	10.1	9.2	10.2	11.3
Saudi Arabia	268	357	404	409	393	7.8	8.1	7.7	7.8	8.1
Russia[4]	116	214	231	259	285	3.3	4.8	4.4	4.9	5.9
Algeria	238	275	346	325	269	6.9	6.2	6.6	6.2	5.5
Japan	135	215	249	274	259	3.9	4.9	4.7	5.2	5.3
Switzerland[1]	171	241	254	265	255	4.9	5.5	4.9	5.1	5.2
Nigeria	46	53	85	153	152	1.3	1.2	1.6	2.9	3.1
United Arab Emirates	71	124	139	145	141	2.0	2.8	2.6	2.7	2.9
Mexico	273	96	190	93	103	7.9	2.1	3.6	1.7	2.1
Canada	42	65	88	94	96	1.2	1.4	1.6	1.8	1.9
Total for all 10	**1,594**	**2,082**	**2,464**	**2,551**	**2,499**	**46.5**	**47.5**	**47.5**	**49.0**	**51.8**
Cereals and cereal preparations - SITC 04										
Extra EU-15	**4,701**	**5,153**	**6,208**	**5,847**	**5,724**	**100.0**	**100.0**	**100.0**	**100.0**	**100.0**
United States	179	467	522	591	644	3.8	9.0	8.4	10.1	11.2
Algeria	332	240	360	379	358	7.0	4.6	5.7	6.4	6.2
Switzerland[1]	130	214	244	259	283	2.7	4.1	3.9	4.4	4.9
Russia[4]	806	321	220	270	269	17.1	6.2	3.5	4.6	4.6
Japan	90	188	227	252	251	1.9	3.6	3.6	4.3	4.3
Saudi Arabia	196	419	586	297	250	4.1	8.1	9.4	5.0	4.3
Egypt	276	54	59	113	234	5.8	1.0	0.9	1.9	4.0
Libya	202	115	164	214	225	4.2	2.2	2.6	3.6	3.9
Norway	58	167	174	200	219	1.2	3.2	2.8	3.4	3.8
Morocco	75	174	336	245	184	1.5	3.3	5.4	4.1	3.2
Total for all 10	**2,345**	**2,357**	**2,892**	**2,820**	**2,916**	**49.8**	**45.7**	**46.5**	**48.2**	**50.9**
Beverages - SITC 11										
Extra EU-15	**6,204**	**10,425**	**11,880**	**12,553**	**13,318**	**100.0**	**100.0**	**100.0**	**100.0**	**100.0**
United States	2,186	4,256	4,967	5,300	5,843	35.2	40.8	41.8	42.2	43.8
Japan	811	1,110	1,201	1,217	1,120	13.0	10.6	10.1	9.6	8.4
Switzerland[1]	517	787	764	826	842	8.3	7.5	6.4	6.5	6.3
Canada	334	525	641	695	722	5.3	5.0	5.3	5.5	5.4
South Korea	52	193	282	321	386	0.8	1.8	2.3	2.5	2.8
Australia	132	201	240	253	245	2.1	1.9	2.0	2.0	1.8
Singapore	101	188	244	201	231	1.6	1.8	2.0	1.5	1.7
Norway	53	171	190	192	217	0.8	1.6	1.5	1.5	1.6
Taiwan	51	186	219	186	200	0.8	1.7	1.8	1.4	1.5
Russia[4]	18	81	110	142	199	0.2	0.7	0.9	1.1	1.4
Total for all 10	**4,253**	**7,698**	**8,857**	**9,332**	**10,005**	**68.5**	**73.8**	**74.5**	**74.3**	**75.1**

(1) Switzerland including Liechtenstein up to 1994.
(4) Relates to the exteranl trade of the USSR until 1991 and from 1992 to the external trade of Russia.

MAIN EU TRADING PARTNERS
FOOD PRODUCTS

IMPORTS

Ranking of EU main trading partners in 2002

Partner	Value (Mio ECU/euro)					Share (%)				
	1990	1999	2000	2001	2002	1990	1999	2000	2001	2002
Fish, crustaceans, molluscs - SITC 03										
Extra EU-15	**6,279**	**10,316**	**11,554**	**12,593**	**12,223**	**100.0**	**100.0**	**100.0**	**100.0**	**100.0**
Norway	994	2,016	2,171	1,968	1,908	15.8	19.5	18.7	15.6	15.6
Iceland	718	819	858	914	882	11.4	7.9	7.4	7.2	7.2
Morocco	240	398	532	573	644	3.8	3.8	4.6	4.5	5.2
United States	323	465	434	572	634	5.1	4.5	3.7	4.5	5.1
Argentina	179	395	465	642	509	2.8	3.8	4.0	5.0	4.1
Russia[4]	127	402	474	540	467	2.0	3.8	4.1	4.2	3.8
Faroe Islands	274	341	362	438	432	4.3	3.3	3.1	3.4	3.5
Thailand	329	380	397	377	345	5.2	3.6	3.4	2.9	2.8
Canada	325	323	348	361	308	5.1	3.1	3.0	2.8	2.5
India	109	167	247	275	304	1.7	1.6	2.1	2.1	2.4
Total for all 10	**3,619**	**5,707**	**6,286**	**6,659**	**6,434**	**57.6**	**55.3**	**54.4**	**52.8**	**52.6**
Vegetables and fruit - SITC 05										
Extra EU-15	**10,174**	**13,533**	**14,102**	**14,794**	**15,058**	**100.0**	**100.0**	**100.0**	**100.0**	**100.0**
Turkey	734	1,424	1,418	1,600	1,443	7.2	10.5	10.0	10.8	9.5
United States	865	1,344	1,361	1,281	1,263	8.5	9.9	9.6	8.6	8.3
Brazil	588	972	1,070	934	1,045	5.7	7.1	7.5	6.3	6.9
South Africa[3]	372	804	795	958	988	3.6	5.9	5.6	6.4	6.5
Costa Rica	263	553	583	634	733	2.5	4.0	4.1	4.2	4.8
China	322	454	571	610	711	3.1	3.3	4.0	4.1	4.7
Poland	322	490	579	656	666	3.1	3.6	4.1	4.4	4.4
Morocco	473	580	537	574	662	4.6	4.2	3.8	3.8	4.3
Ecuador	157	427	428	491	595	1.5	3.1	3.0	3.3	3.9
Chile	336	460	398	488	522	3.3	3.3	2.8	3.2	3.4
Total for all 10	**4,432**	**7,509**	**7,740**	**8,226**	**8,629**	**43.5**	**55.4**	**54.8**	**55.6**	**57.3**
Coffee, tea, cocoa, spices - SITC 07										
Extra EU-15	**4,795**	**7,675**	**7,408**	**6,626**	**6,668**	**100.0**	**100.0**	**100.0**	**100.0**	**100.0**
Côte d'Ivoire	705	1,184	985	1,071	1,358	14.7	15.4	13.2	16.1	20.3
Brazil	599	1,142	1,138	980	881	12.4	14.8	15.3	14.7	13.2
Ghana	184	337	275	290	406	3.8	4.3	3.7	4.3	6.0
Colombia	643	638	560	455	370	13.4	8.3	7.5	6.8	5.5
Nigeria	113	196	122	194	286	2.3	2.5	1.6	2.9	4.2
Indonesia	218	329	356	246	281	4.5	4.2	4.8	3.7	4.2
Switzerland[1]	85	181	200	239	266	1.7	2.3	2.6	3.6	3.9
India	129	323	357	267	233	2.6	4.2	4.8	4.0	3.4
Kenya	269	320	294	269	222	5.6	4.1	3.9	4.0	3.3
Vietnam	18	345	319	260	213	0.3	4.4	4.3	3.9	3.2
Total for all 10	**2,962**	**4,994**	**4,606**	**4,270**	**4,515**	**61.7**	**65.0**	**62.1**	**64.4**	**67.7**
Feeding stuff for animals - SITC 08										
Extra EU-15	**4,305**	**4,361**	**5,449**	**6,188**	**6,069**	**100.0**	**100.0**	**100.0**	**100.0**	**100.0**
Argentina	652	1,379	1,762	1,893	2,030	15.1	31.6	32.3	30.5	33.4
Brazil	1,401	1,053	1,504	2,007	1,851	32.5	24.1	27.5	32.4	30.5
United States	1,105	905	954	970	842	25.6	20.7	17.5	15.6	13.8
Peru	103	118	202	191	165	2.3	2.7	3.7	3.0	2.7
Iceland	40	73	80	90	147	0.9	1.6	1.4	1.4	2.4
Norway	21	110	88	81	127	0.4	2.5	1.6	1.3	2.0
Malaysia	98	87	94	100	110	2.2	1.9	1.7	1.6	1.8
Indonesia	72	61	77	85	88	1.6	1.3	1.4	1.3	1.4
Poland	23	44	44	81	80	0.5	1.0	0.8	1.3	1.3
Hungary	26	31	45	52	70	0.5	0.7	0.8	0.8	1.1
Total for all 10	**3,542**	**3,861**	**4,849**	**5,550**	**5,512**	**82.2**	**88.5**	**88.9**	**89.6**	**90.8**

(1)   Switzerland including Liechtenstein up to 1994.

(3)   South Africa includes Namibia up to 31.12.1989.

(4)   Relates to the exteranl trade of the USSR until 1991 and from 1992 to the external trade of Russia.

MAIN EU TRADING PARTNERS
RAW MATERIALS

EXPORTS

Ranking of EU main trading partners in 2002

Partner	Value (Mio ECU/euro)					Share (%)				
	1990	1999	2000	2001	2002	1990	1999	2000	2001	2002
Cork and wood - SITC 24										
Extra EU-15	**383**	**2,449**	**2,900**	**2,683**	**2,879**	**100.0**	**100.0**	**100.0**	**100.0**	**100.0**
Japan	13	475	604	571	639	3.3	19.3	20.8	21.2	22.1
United States	16	153	246	330	500	4.0	6.2	8.4	12.2	17.3
Norway	16	269	309	297	311	4.0	10.9	10.6	11.0	10.7
Switzerland[1]	138	199	204	184	183	36.1	8.1	7.0	6.8	6.3
China	2	206	353	253	162	0.4	8.4	12.1	9.4	5.6
Egypt	8	190	200	130	118	1.9	7.7	6.8	4.8	4.0
Algeria	4	89	91	112	106	0.9	3.6	3.1	4.1	3.6
Saudi Arabia	2	62	84	73	93	0.6	2.5	2.8	2.7	3.2
Slovenia	:	50	61	56	62	:	2.0	2.0	2.0	2.1
Morocco	23	49	48	50	60	6.1	2.0	1.6	1.8	2.0
Total for all 10	**221**	**1,742**	**2,200**	**2,055**	**2,233**	**57.7**	**71.0**	**75.8**	**76.5**	**77.5**
Textile fibres and their wastes - SITC 26										
Extra EU-15	**1,369**	**1,674**	**2,020**	**1,944**	**2,080**	**100.0**	**100.0**	**100.0**	**100.0**	**100.0**
Turkey	85	218	288	237	243	6.2	13.0	14.2	12.1	11.6
China	124	102	191	148	187	9.0	6.0	9.4	7.6	8.9
Czech Republic[2]	24	68	109	117	119	1.7	4.0	5.3	6.0	5.7
Poland	28	79	91	97	112	2.0	4.7	4.4	4.9	5.3
United States	95	160	117	114	110	6.9	9.5	5.7	5.8	5.3
South Korea	32	34	45	42	67	2.3	2.0	2.2	2.1	3.2
Japan	72	60	78	67	66	5.2	3.5	3.8	3.4	3.1
Hungary	26	35	47	51	55	1.9	2.0	2.3	2.6	2.6
Tunisia	22	52	55	56	53	1.5	3.1	2.7	2.8	2.5
Lithuania	:	31	39	46	50	:	1.8	1.9	2.3	2.4
Total for all 10	**509**	**839**	**1,058**	**975**	**1,063**	**37.1**	**50.1**	**52.3**	**50.1**	**51.1**
Crude fertilizers - SITC 27										
Extra EU-15	**760**	**1,481**	**1,742**	**1,798**	**1,866**	**100.0**	**100.0**	**100.0**	**100.0**	**100.0**
Switzerland[1]	152	154	180	221	254	20.0	10.4	10.3	12.2	13.6
United States	92	182	257	242	220	12.0	12.2	14.7	13.4	11.8
China	4	55	83	93	100	0.5	3.7	4.7	5.1	5.3
Norway	44	89	89	89	87	5.8	5.9	5.1	4.9	4.6
Poland	7	71	79	81	86	0.9	4.7	4.5	4.4	4.5
Japan	67	77	92	87	81	8.7	5.1	5.2	4.8	4.3
South Korea	10	37	48	50	54	1.3	2.4	2.7	2.7	2.8
Czech Republic[2]	6	41	41	46	50	0.8	2.7	2.3	2.5	2.6
Turkey	17	37	41	37	40	2.2	2.5	2.3	2.0	2.1
Russia[4]	3	21	26	31	36	0.3	1.4	1.4	1.7	1.9
Total for all 10	**402**	**764**	**936**	**978**	**1,007**	**52.8**	**51.5**	**53.7**	**54.3**	**53.9**
Metalliferous ores and metal scrap - SITC 28										
Extra EU-15	**987**	**2,128**	**3,116**	**3,063**	**3,261**	**100.0**	**100.0**	**100.0**	**100.0**	**100.0**
China	27	220	400	417	392	2.7	10.3	12.8	13.6	12.0
Turkey	100	115	220	238	378	10.1	5.4	7.0	7.7	11.5
United States	97	291	372	324	283	9.8	13.6	11.9	10.5	8.6
India	121	151	222	270	222	12.2	7.0	7.1	8.8	6.8
Norway	63	214	260	231	195	6.3	10.0	8.3	7.5	5.9
Japan	110	214	193	172	184	11.1	10.0	6.1	5.6	5.6
Taiwan	48	101	175	172	171	4.8	4.7	5.6	5.6	5.2
Switzerland[1]	46	86	120	124	140	4.6	4.0	3.8	4.0	4.2
South Korea	27	79	131	79	135	2.7	3.6	4.1	2.5	4.1
Mexico	3	11	47	122	113	0.2	0.5	1.5	3.9	3.4
Total for all 10	**641**	**1,482**	**2,140**	**2,150**	**2,212**	**64.9**	**69.6**	**68.6**	**70.1**	**67.8**

(1) Switzerland including Liechtenstein up to 1994.
(2) Czechoslovakia before 1993.
(4) Relates to the exteranl trade of the USSR until 1991 and from 1992 to the external trade of Russia.

IMPORTS

Ranking of EU main trading partners in 2002

Partner	Value (Mio ECU/euro)					Share (%)				
	1990	1999	2000	2001	2002	1990	1999	2000	2001	2002
Oil seeds and oleaginous fruits - SITC 22										
Extra EU-15	**3,327**	**4,295**	**4,703**	**5,533**	**5,406**	**100.0**	**100.0**	**100.0**	**100.0**	**100.0**
Brazil	555	1,114	1,431	2,125	2,005	16.6	25.9	30.4	38.4	37.0
United States	1,480	1,455	1,750	1,614	1,798	44.4	33.8	37.2	29.1	33.2
Argentina	534	482	250	318	436	16.0	11.2	5.3	5.7	8.0
Canada	68	160	209	237	233	2.0	3.7	4.4	4.2	4.3
China	116	105	163	181	156	3.4	2.4	3.4	3.2	2.8
Hungary	23	78	102	95	136	0.6	1.8	2.1	1.7	2.5
Czech Republic[2]	2	80	103	88	84	0.0	1.8	2.1	1.5	1.5
Paraguay	277	133	91	147	58	8.3	3.0	1.9	2.6	1.0
Bulgaria	5	50	12	19	55	0.1	1.1	0.2	0.3	1.0
Uruguay	1	15	0	4	55	0.0	0.3	0.0	0.0	1.0
Total for all 10	**3,061**	**3,672**	**4,112**	**4,827**	**5,016**	**91.9**	**85.4**	**87.4**	**87.2**	**92.7**
Cork and wood - SITC 24										
Extra EU-15	**5,127**	**7,056**	**8,338**	**7,635**	**7,371**	**100.0**	**100.0**	**100.0**	**100.0**	**100.0**
Russia[4]	730	942	1,103	1,103	1,144	14.2	13.3	13.2	14.4	15.5
United States	680	846	1,008	867	728	13.2	11.9	12.0	11.3	9.8
Latvia	:	533	667	625	660	:	7.5	8.0	8.1	8.9
Canada	793	420	507	386	363	15.4	5.9	6.0	5.0	4.9
Cameroon	211	376	451	422	351	4.1	5.3	5.4	5.5	4.7
Estonia	:	313	345	317	340	:	4.4	4.1	4.1	4.6
Czech Republic[2]	132	366	334	318	322	2.5	5.1	4.0	4.1	4.3
Malaysia	506	322	446	327	301	9.8	4.5	5.3	4.2	4.0
Brazil	128	266	334	333	290	2.5	3.7	4.0	4.3	3.9
Poland	116	219	245	206	231	2.2	3.0	2.9	2.7	3.1
Total for all 10	**3,298**	**4,603**	**5,440**	**4,905**	**4,730**	**64.3**	**65.2**	**65.2**	**64.2**	**64.1**
Pulp and waste paper - SITC 25										
Extra EU-15	**3,431**	**3,870**	**6,304**	**5,132**	**4,516**	**100.0**	**100.0**	**100.0**	**100.0**	**100.0**
United States	1,226	1,035	1,593	1,397	1,280	35.7	26.7	25.2	27.2	28.3
Canada	1,272	1,221	1,916	1,479	1,160	37.0	31.5	30.3	28.8	25.6
Brazil	199	440	823	573	597	5.7	11.3	13.0	11.1	13.2
Chile	97	287	449	358	316	2.8	7.4	7.1	6.9	6.9
Norway	247	228	324	299	280	7.2	5.8	5.1	5.8	6.1
Indonesia	4	69	148	232	157	0.1	1.7	2.3	4.5	3.4
Czech Republic[2]	61	68	119	97	102	1.7	1.7	1.8	1.8	2.2
Russia[4]	142	70	179	139	100	4.1	1.8	2.8	2.7	2.2
Switzerland[1]	36	71	117	86	88	1.0	1.8	1.8	1.6	1.9
South Africa[3]	19	77	130	94	84	0.5	1.9	2.0	1.8	1.8
Total for all 10	**3,303**	**3,564**	**5,799**	**4,755**	**4,162**	**96.2**	**92.0**	**91.9**	**92.6**	**92.1**
Metalliferous ores and metal scrap - SITC 28										
Extra EU-15	**8,260**	**10,593**	**14,386**	**14,081**	**12,434**	**100.0**	**100.0**	**100.0**	**100.0**	**100.0**
Brazil	1,074	1,317	1,771	1,768	1,615	12.9	12.4	12.3	12.5	12.9
Canada	1,298	953	1,200	1,299	1,297	15.7	8.9	8.3	9.2	10.4
Australia	985	957	1,415	1,207	1,118	11.9	9.0	9.8	8.5	8.9
United States	1,009	889	1,438	1,322	1,020	12.2	8.3	9.9	9.3	8.2
South Africa[3]	343	607	857	834	771	4.1	5.7	5.9	5.9	6.2
Russia[4]	179	1,018	1,130	882	664	2.1	9.6	7.8	6.2	5.3
Indonesia	39	417	528	800	580	0.4	3.9	3.6	5.6	4.6
Chile	219	401	630	426	470	2.6	3.7	4.3	3.0	3.7
Switzerland[1]	163	333	502	498	349	1.9	3.1	3.4	3.5	2.8
Peru	200	189	154	179	289	2.4	1.7	1.0	1.2	2.3
Total for all 10	**5,509**	**7,083**	**9,625**	**9,215**	**8,172**	**66.6**	**66.8**	**66.9**	**65.4**	**65.7**

(1)   Switzerland including Liechtenstein up to 1994.

(2)   Czechoslovakia before 1993.

(3)   South Africa includes Namibia up to 31.12.1989.

(4)   Relates to the exteranl trade of the USSR until 1991 and from 1992 to the external trade of Russia.

MAIN EU TRADING PARTNERS
FUEL PRODUCTS AND OTHER COMBUSTIBLES

EXPORTS

Ranking of EU main trading partners in 2002

Partner	Value (Mio ECU/euro)					Share (%)				
	1990	1999	2000	2001	2002	1990	1999	2000	2001	2002
Petroleum oils, crude - SITC 333										
Extra EU-15	**2,804**	**3,470**	**7,282**	**5,501**	**6,439**	**100.0**	**100.0**	**100.0**	**100.0**	**100.0**
United States	1,950	2,676	6,111	4,514	5,048	69.5	77.0	83.9	82.0	78.4
Canada	694	63	328	738	998	24.7	1.8	4.5	13.4	15.4
China	:	178	126	65	239	:	5.1	1.7	1.1	3.7
Turkey	:	:	:	0	84	:	:	:	0.0	1.3
South Africa[3]	:	0	:	:	50	:	0.0	:	:	0.7
Norway	103	173	80	73	20	3.6	4.9	1.0	1.3	0.3
Morocco	:	:	:	0	0	:	:	:	0.0	0.0
Switzerland[1]	:	0	2	:	0	:	0.0	0.0	:	0.0
Côte d'Ivoire	0	:	:	0	0	0.0	:	:	0.0	0.0
Cameroon	:	:	:	:	0	:	:	:	:	0.0
Total for all 10	**2,747**	**3,090**	**6,647**	**5,391**	**6,439**	**97.9**	**89.0**	**91.2**	**97.9**	**99.9**
Petroleum products - SITC 334+335										
Extra EU-15	**8,352**	**14,211**	**26,798**	**22,297**	**23,102**	**100.0**	**100.0**	**100.0**	**100.0**	**100.0**
United States	3,515	4,579	10,855	8,706	9,176	42.0	32.2	40.5	39.0	39.7
Switzerland[1]	1,380	1,090	1,940	1,663	1,542	16.5	7.6	7.2	7.4	6.6
Canada	806	193	523	965	1,244	9.6	1.3	1.9	4.3	5.3
Norway	186	487	749	785	641	2.2	3.4	2.7	3.5	2.7
Gibraltar	83	349	721	436	502	0.9	2.4	2.6	1.9	2.1
Malta	60	243	426	390	442	0.7	1.7	1.5	1.7	1.9
Czech Republic[2]	15	300	442	519	374	0.1	2.1	1.6	2.3	1.6
Libya	182	148	308	374	310	2.1	1.0	1.1	1.6	1.3
Tunisia	156	214	379	418	306	1.8	1.5	1.4	1.8	1.3
Turkey	73	346	645	275	294	0.8	2.4	2.4	1.2	1.2
Total for all 10	**6,457**	**7,949**	**16,987**	**14,532**	**14,831**	**77.3**	**55.9**	**63.3**	**65.1**	**64.1**

(1) Switzerland including Liechtenstein up to 1994.

(2) Czechoslovakia before 1993.

(3) South Africa includes Namibia up to 31.12.1989.

MAIN EU TRADING PARTNERS
FUEL PRODUCTS AND OTHER COMBUSTIBLES

IMPORTS

Ranking of EU main trading partners in 2002

Partner	Value (Mio ECU/euro)					Share (%)				
	1990	1999	2000	2001	2002	1990	1999	2000	2001	2002
Coal, coke and briquettes - SITC 32										
Extra EU-15	5,211	5,912	7,435	10,061	8,534	100.0	100.0	100.0	100.0	100.0
South Africa[3]	818	1,023	1,430	2,082	1,801	15.6	17.3	19.2	20.6	21.1
Australia	792	1,017	1,254	1,601	1,536	15.2	17.2	16.8	15.9	17.9
Poland	420	739	936	1,211	1,032	8.0	12.4	12.5	12.0	12.0
United States	2,117	948	1,044	1,166	812	40.6	16.0	14.0	11.5	9.5
Colombia	328	516	752	880	692	6.3	8.7	10.1	8.7	8.1
Russia[4]	178	236	421	851	671	3.4	3.9	5.6	8.4	7.8
China	128	267	366	601	473	2.4	4.5	4.9	5.9	5.5
Indonesia	13	197	277	398	400	0.2	3.3	3.7	3.9	4.6
Canada	175	247	280	396	320	3.3	4.1	3.7	3.9	3.7
Czech Republic[2]	74	219	217	259	251	1.4	3.7	2.9	2.5	2.9
Total for all 10	5,043	5,408	6,977	9,445	7,988	96.7	91.4	93.8	93.8	93.6
Petroleum oils, crude - SITC 333										
Extra EU-15	46,187	51,167	103,013	91,377	86,726	100.0	100.0	100.0	100.0	100.0
Norway	5,922	10,300	21,648	19,219	19,531	12.8	20.1	21.0	21.0	22.5
Russia[4]	3,375	7,366	14,576	15,590	17,676	7.3	14.3	14.1	17.0	20.3
Saudi Arabia	6,119	6,352	13,018	9,917	9,153	13.2	12.4	12.6	10.8	10.5
Libya	6,380	5,463	10,648	9,362	7,565	13.8	10.6	10.3	10.2	8.7
Algeria	2,908	2,333	5,969	4,612	4,923	6.2	4.5	5.7	5.0	5.6
Iran	5,159	3,769	7,213	5,557	4,695	11.1	7.3	7.0	6.0	5.4
Nigeria	3,957	2,154	5,486	5,304	3,836	8.5	4.2	5.3	5.8	4.4
Syria	932	1,755	2,787	3,472	3,434	2.0	3.4	2.7	3.7	3.9
Iraq	2,015	3,679	6,288	3,552	2,752	4.3	7.1	6.1	3.8	3.1
Kazakhstan	:	843	2,136	1,999	2,706	:	1.6	2.0	2.1	3.1
Total for all 10	36,767	44,014	89,770	78,584	76,271	79.6	86.0	87.1	85.9	87.9
Petroleum products - SITC 334+335										
Extra EU-15	57,810	60,515	121,179	109,376	104,688	100.0	100.0	100.0	100.0	100.0
Russia[4]	7,539	10,312	20,313	21,442	23,717	13.0	17.0	16.7	19.6	22.6
Norway	6,739	11,084	22,975	20,242	20,534	11.6	18.3	18.9	18.5	19.6
Saudi Arabia	6,753	6,549	13,551	10,705	9,598	11.6	10.8	11.1	9.7	9.1
Libya	7,418	6,527	12,343	10,801	8,957	12.8	10.7	10.1	9.8	8.5
Algéria	4,074	3,214	7,584	6,194	6,154	7.0	5.3	6.2	5.6	5.8
Iran	5,188	3,781	7,229	5,579	4,701	8.9	6.2	5.9	5.1	4.4
Nigeria	3,972	2,208	5,493	5,311	3,925	6.8	3.6	4.5	4.8	3.7
Syria	1,096	1,832	2,983	3,666	3,593	1.8	3.0	2.4	3.3	3.4
Kazakhstan	:	865	2,218	2,045	2,767	:	1.4	1.8	1.8	2.6
Iraq	2,134	3,679	6,288	3,552	2,752	3.6	6.0	5.1	3.2	2.6
Total for all 10	44,913	50,051	100,976	89,536	86,700	77.6	82.7	83.3	81.8	82.8
Gas, natural and manufactured - SITC 34										
Extra EU-15	4,503	10,199	18,583	22,394	20,819	100.0	100.0	100.0	100.0	100.0
Algeria	1,782	2,419	4,354	4,692	4,439	39.5	23.7	23.4	20.9	21.3
Norway	1,283	1,623	2,848	3,757	3,237	28.5	15.9	15.3	16.7	15.5
Russia[4]	876	1,126	2,046	2,364	1,909	19.4	11.0	11.0	10.5	9.1
Nigeria	:	51	409	419	400	:	0.4	2.1	1.8	1.9
Qatar	2	72	46	103	224	0.0	0.7	0.2	0.4	1.0
Oman	:	:	16	112	217	:	:	0.0	0.4	1.0
Libya	126	116	176	197	134	2.8	1.1	0.9	0.8	0.6
United Arab Emirates	17	42	39	21	90	0.3	0.4	0.2	0.0	0.4
Trinidad and Tobago	:	41	142	52	72	:	0.4	0.7	0.2	0.3
Egypt	:	:	20	50	49	:	:	0.1	0.2	0.2
Total for all 10	4,087	5,490	10,094	11,768	10,771	90.7	53.8	54.3	52.5	51.7

(2) Czechoslovakia before 1993.
(3) South Africa includes Namibia up to 31.12.1989.
(4) Relates to the exteranl trade of the USSR until 1991 and from 1992 to the external trade of Russia.

MAIN EU TRADING PARTNERS
CHEMICALS

EXPORTS

Ranking of EU main trading partners in 2002

Partner	Value (Mio ECU/euro)					Share (%)				
	1990	1999	2000	2001	2002	1990	1999	2000	2001	2002
Organic chemicals - SITC 51										
Extra EU-15	**9,609**	**24,791**	**32,051**	**33,839**	**33,625**	**100.0**	**100.0**	**100.0**	**100.0**	**100.0**
United States	2,443	11,073	15,146	16,073	16,587	25.4	44.6	47.2	47.4	49.3
Switzerland[1]	1,291	2,098	2,544	3,065	3,219	13.4	8.4	7.9	9.0	9.5
Japan	887	2,042	2,705	2,783	2,518	9.2	8.2	8.4	8.2	7.4
Brazil	305	730	763	861	751	3.1	2.9	2.3	2.5	2.2
China	147	441	625	688	713	1.5	1.7	1.9	2.0	2.1
Mexico	184	403	522	620	636	1.9	1.6	1.6	1.8	1.8
Turkey	221	558	790	677	637	2.2	2.2	2.4	2.0	1.8
South Korea	258	487	670	597	601	2.6	1.9	2.0	1.7	1.7
Canada	200	504	577	744	553	2.0	2.0	1.7	2.1	1.6
Australia	155	460	465	497	429	1.6	1.8	1.4	1.4	1.2
Total for all 10	**6,091**	**18,797**	**24,806**	**26,605**	**26,643**	**63.3**	**75.8**	**77.3**	**78.6**	**79.2**
Medicinal and pharmaceutical products - SITC 54										
Extra EU-15	**7,728**	**30,343**	**35,840**	**43,917**	**51,420**	**100.0**	**100.0**	**100.0**	**100.0**	**100.0**
United States	994	8,364	10,370	12,914	17,556	12.8	27.5	28.9	29.4	34.1
Switzerland[1]	906	3,849	3,998	4,898	5,888	11.7	12.6	11.1	11.1	11.4
Japan	890	2,030	2,371	2,742	2,757	11.5	6.6	6.6	6.2	5.3
Canada	195	932	1,118	1,762	1,907	2.5	3.0	3.1	4.0	3.7
Australia	281	1,197	1,324	1,510	1,719	3.6	3.9	3.6	3.4	3.3
Poland	110	871	1,039	1,432	1,489	1.4	2.8	2.8	3.2	2.8
Saudi Arabia	250	522	610	658	1,168	3.2	1.7	1.7	1.4	2.2
Turkey	114	657	842	916	1,119	1.4	2.1	2.3	2.0	2.1
Czech Republic[2]	24	455	520	660	971	0.3	1.4	1.4	1.5	1.8
Russia[4]	147	310	627	1,023	908	1.9	1.0	1.7	2.3	1.7
Total for all 10	**3,913**	**19,187**	**22,819**	**28,513**	**35,483**	**50.6**	**63.2**	**63.6**	**64.9**	**69.0**
Essential oils, perfume mat., cosmetics - SITC 55										
Extra EU-15	**4,166**	**10,029**	**11,698**	**13,132**	**13,802**	**100.0**	**100.0**	**100.0**	**100.0**	**100.0**
United States	508	1,306	1,607	1,800	1,891	12.1	13.0	13.7	13.7	13.6
Switzerland[1]	468	857	914	979	1,027	11.2	8.5	7.8	7.4	7.4
Russia[4]	270	342	571	787	883	6.4	3.4	4.8	5.9	6.3
Japan	244	655	731	738	687	5.8	6.5	6.2	5.6	4.9
Poland	69	484	513	557	615	1.6	4.8	4.3	4.2	4.4
United Arab Emirates	84	259	312	358	423	2.0	2.5	2.6	2.7	3.0
Norway	115	338	394	409	413	2.7	3.3	3.3	3.1	2.9
Turkey	64	364	417	363	388	1.5	3.6	3.5	2.7	2.8
South Korea	51	196	288	338	383	1.2	1.9	2.4	2.5	2.7
Saudi Arabia	177	294	340	353	373	4.2	2.9	2.9	2.6	2.7
Total for all 10	**2,049**	**5,096**	**6,087**	**6,681**	**7,082**	**49.1**	**50.8**	**52.0**	**50.8**	**51.3**
Plastics in primary forms - SITC 57										
Extra EU-15	**4,855**	**9,755**	**12,631**	**12,797**	**13,237**	**100.0**	**100.0**	**100.0**	**100.0**	**100.0**
United States	483	1,202	1,516	1,452	1,480	9.9	12.3	11.9	11.3	11.1
Turkey	188	748	1,135	830	1,041	3.8	7.6	8.9	6.4	7.8
Poland	61	691	932	967	1,003	1.2	7.0	7.3	7.5	7.5
Switzerland[1]	706	879	1,027	1,024	926	14.5	9.0	8.1	8.0	6.9
China	53	253	395	516	623	1.0	2.5	3.1	4.0	4.7
Czech Republic[2]	84	296	427	470	512	1.7	3.0	3.3	3.6	3.8
Hong Kong	120	420	531	489	499	2.4	4.3	4.2	3.8	3.7
Japan	202	305	424	385	381	4.1	3.1	3.3	3.0	2.8
Russia[4]	271	165	256	345	372	5.5	1.6	2.0	2.6	2.8
Hungary	57	235	343	363	367	1.1	2.4	2.7	2.8	2.7
Total for all 10	**2,225**	**5,194**	**6,986**	**6,841**	**7,204**	**45.8**	**53.2**	**55.3**	**53.4**	**54.4**

(1) Switzerland including Liechtenstein up to 1994.
(2) Czechoslovakia before 1993.
(4) Relates to the exteranl trade of the USSR until 1991 and from 1992 to the external trade of Russia.

MAIN EU TRADING PARTNERS
CHEMICALS

IMPORTS

Ranking of EU main trading partners in 2002

Partner	Value (Mio ECU/euro)					Share (%)				
	1990	1999	2000	2001	2002	1990	1999	2000	2001	2002
Organic chemicals - SITC 51										
Extra EU-15	**7,788**	**16,657**	**20,117**	**20,697**	**22,055**	**100.0**	**100.0**	**100.0**	**100.0**	**100.0**
United States	2,400	4,953	6,408	6,046	6,431	30.8	29.7	31.8	29.2	29.1
Switzerland[1]	1,788	2,815	2,923	3,343	4,237	22.9	16.8	14.5	16.1	19.2
Japan	932	1,784	1,930	1,997	2,070	11.9	10.7	9.5	9.6	9.3
Singapore	109	1,314	1,290	1,493	1,711	1.3	7.8	6.4	7.2	7.7
China	198	746	820	939	1,034	2.5	4.4	4.0	4.5	4.6
Hungary	117	361	518	803	811	1.5	2.1	2.5	3.8	3.6
India	71	424	565	546	640	0.9	2.5	2.8	2.6	2.9
Norway	144	372	547	636	598	1.8	2.2	2.7	3.0	2.7
Russia[4]	225	299	649	598	535	2.8	1.7	3.2	2.8	2.4
Saudi Arabia	208	160	511	555	521	2.6	0.9	2.5	2.6	2.3
Total for all 10	**6,192**	**13,228**	**16,162**	**16,957**	**18,588**	**79.5**	**79.4**	**80.3**	**81.9**	**84.2**
Inorganic chemicals - SITC 52										
Extra EU-15	**2,545**	**4,761**	**5,853**	**6,264**	**5,381**	**100.0**	**100.0**	**100.0**	**100.0**	**100.0**
United States	640	893	1,368	1,446	943	25.1	18.7	23.3	23.0	17.5
Russia[4]	258	819	821	889	877	10.1	17.2	14.0	14.1	16.2
Norway	164	372	404	396	400	6.4	7.8	6.8	6.3	7.4
China	133	251	370	510	321	5.2	5.2	6.3	8.1	5.9
Canada	81	113	142	220	271	3.1	2.3	2.4	3.5	5.0
Japan	102	175	228	221	206	4.0	3.6	3.8	3.5	3.8
Israel	133	189	174	170	152	5.2	3.9	2.9	2.7	2.8
Turkey	25	124	132	129	141	1.0	2.6	2.2	2.0	2.6
Poland	52	129	161	153	135	2.0	2.7	2.7	2.4	2.5
Brazil	43	81	129	149	125	1.7	1.7	2.2	2.3	2.3
Total for all 10	**1,631**	**3,147**	**3,928**	**4,282**	**3,571**	**64.0**	**66.0**	**67.1**	**68.3**	**66.3**
Medicinal and pharmaceutical products - SITC 54										
Extra EU-15	**4,121**	**14,922**	**17,652**	**22,621**	**26,186**	**100.0**	**100.0**	**100.0**	**100.0**	**100.0**
United States	1,247	6,555	8,074	11,108	13,043	30.2	43.9	45.7	49.1	49.8
Switzerland[1]	2,106	5,352	5,972	7,351	8,599	51.1	35.8	33.8	32.4	32.8
Japan	268	789	947	1,108	1,054	6.5	5.2	5.3	4.8	4.0
China	123	410	488	536	678	2.9	2.7	2.7	2.3	2.5
Israel	13	260	411	569	548	0.3	1.7	2.3	2.5	2.0
Australia	18	233	397	374	296	0.4	1.5	2.2	1.6	1.1
Singapore	4	81	116	221	285	0.0	0.5	0.6	0.9	1.0
Canada	49	164	168	163	227	1.2	1.0	0.9	0.7	0.8
Norway	36	145	156	162	189	0.8	0.9	0.8	0.7	0.7
India	18	52	80	102	150	0.4	0.3	0.4	0.4	0.5
Total for all 10	**3,882**	**14,041**	**16,808**	**21,695**	**25,069**	**94.2**	**94.0**	**95.2**	**95.9**	**95.7**
Plastics in primary forms - SITC 57										
Extra EU-15	**3,589**	**5,676**	**7,260**	**7,038**	**6,845**	**100.0**	**100.0**	**100.0**	**100.0**	**100.0**
United States	1,207	1,852	2,209	2,199	2,015	33.6	32.6	30.4	31.2	29.4
Switzerland[1]	439	612	629	640	675	12.2	10.7	8.6	9.0	9.8
Japan	244	524	603	625	600	6.8	9.2	8.3	8.8	8.7
Saudi Arabia	226	231	286	414	477	6.2	4.0	3.9	5.8	6.9
Norway	239	401	480	456	433	6.6	7.0	6.6	6.4	6.3
South Korea	54	266	386	281	322	1.4	4.6	5.3	3.9	4.7
Hungary	75	197	341	289	260	2.0	3.4	4.6	4.1	3.8
Poland	84	115	256	230	216	2.3	2.0	3.5	3.2	3.1
Czech Republic[2]	72	173	243	221	177	2.0	3.0	3.3	3.1	2.5
China	11	56	69	78	141	0.2	0.9	0.9	1.1	2.0
Total for all 10	**2,650**	**4,426**	**5,502**	**5,433**	**5,316**	**73.8**	**77.9**	**75.7**	**77.1**	**77.6**

(1)   Switzerland including Liechtenstein up to 1994.

(2)   Czechoslovakia before 1993.

(4)   Relates to the exteranl trade of the USSR until 1991 and from 1992 to the external trade of Russia.

MAIN EU TRADING PARTNERS
MACHINERY AND EQUIPMENT

EXPORTS

Ranking of EU main trading partners in 2002

Partner	Value (Mio ECU/euro)					Share (%)				
	1990	1999	2000	2001	2002	1990	1999	2000	2001	2002
Power generating machinery and equipment - SITC 71										
Extra EU-15	**13,644**	**31,885**	**38,703**	**43,540**	**40,062**	**100.0**	**100.0**	**100.0**	**100.0**	**100.0**
United States	5,535	13,290	15,950	18,613	15,052	40.5	41.6	41.2	42.7	37.5
China	488	1,013	1,316	1,475	1,621	3.5	3.1	3.4	3.3	4.0
Canada	436	1,540	1,534	1,585	1,445	3.1	4.8	3.9	3.6	3.6
Switzerland[1]	682	1,355	1,520	1,442	1,306	5.0	4.2	3.9	3.3	3.2
Turkey	262	771	1,064	898	1,160	1.9	2.4	2.7	2.0	2.8
Poland	43	639	815	981	1,061	0.3	2.0	2.1	2.2	2.6
Hungary	30	722	809	866	940	0.2	2.2	2.0	1.9	2.3
Brazil	175	617	600	888	922	1.2	1.9	1.5	2.0	2.3
Singapore	287	558	858	968	813	2.1	1.7	2.2	2.2	2.0
Hong Kong	156	613	947	968	765	1.1	1.9	2.4	2.2	1.9
Total for all 10	**8,094**	**21,119**	**25,413**	**28,684**	**25,084**	**59.3**	**66.2**	**65.6**	**65.8**	**62.6**
Machinery specialized for particular ind. - SITC 72										
Extra EU-15	**24,231**	**40,662**	**48,547**	**51,841**	**52,129**	**100.0**	**100.0**	**100.0**	**100.0**	**100.0**
United States	4,851	10,003	11,350	10,511	9,333	20.0	24.6	23.3	20.2	17.9
China	751	2,092	2,887	3,927	5,059	3.1	5.1	5.9	7.5	9.7
Russia[4]	1,894	944	1,366	1,991	2,152	7.8	2.3	2.8	3.8	4.1
Turkey	823	1,161	1,752	1,236	1,986	3.3	2.8	3.6	2.3	3.8
Switzerland[1]	1,532	1,791	2,142	2,156	1,971	6.3	4.4	4.4	4.1	3.7
Poland	371	1,577	1,593	1,711	1,685	1.5	3.8	3.2	3.3	3.2
Japan	1,156	1,084	1,411	1,628	1,441	4.7	2.6	2.9	3.1	2.7
Norway	510	1,097	1,104	1,279	1,263	2.1	2.6	2.2	2.4	2.4
Czech Republic[2]	374	751	1,090	1,322	1,227	1.5	1.8	2.2	2.5	2.3
Australia	504	910	966	986	1,168	2.0	2.2	1.9	1.9	2.2
Total for all 10	**12,766**	**21,410**	**25,659**	**26,747**	**27,285**	**52.6**	**52.6**	**52.8**	**51.5**	**52.3**
General industry machinery and equipment - SITC 74										
Extra EU-15	**21,778**	**45,701**	**52,283**	**56,693**	**59,098**	**100.0**	**100.0**	**100.0**	**100.0**	**100.0**
United States	3,702	8,874	10,797	10,832	10,775	16.9	19.4	20.6	19.1	18.2
China	569	1,709	2,012	2,711	3,384	2.6	3.7	3.8	4.7	5.7
Switzerland[1]	2,132	2,773	3,095	3,265	3,202	9.7	6.0	5.9	5.7	5.4
Poland	370	2,069	2,511	2,526	2,549	1.6	4.5	4.8	4.4	4.3
Russia[4]	845	928	1,304	1,937	2,225	3.8	2.0	2.4	3.4	3.7
Czech Republic[2]	289	1,348	1,630	2,032	2,091	1.3	2.9	3.1	3.5	3.5
South Korea	770	944	1,262	1,447	1,755	3.5	2.0	2.4	2.5	2.9
Norway	645	1,636	1,449	1,571	1,681	2.9	3.5	2.7	2.7	2.8
Japan	761	1,237	1,617	1,766	1,679	3.4	2.7	3.0	3.1	2.8
Turkey	489	1,251	1,541	1,215	1,461	2.2	2.7	2.9	2.1	2.4
Total for all 10	**10,571**	**22,770**	**27,218**	**29,302**	**30,802**	**48.5**	**49.8**	**52.0**	**51.6**	**52.1**
Telecommunication, sound, TV, video - SITC 76										
Extra EU-15	**5,969**	**31,283**	**44,295**	**41,879**	**34,723**	**100.0**	**100.0**	**100.0**	**100.0**	**100.0**
United States	703	3,802	5,402	5,437	5,280	11.7	12.1	12.1	12.9	15.2
Russia[4]	65	532	900	1,474	1,861	1.0	1.6	2.0	3.5	5.3
Switzerland[1]	529	1,734	1,991	1,833	1,719	8.8	5.5	4.4	4.3	4.9
China	157	2,672	3,726	3,315	1,715	2.6	8.5	8.4	7.9	4.9
Hong Kong	79	1,057	1,778	1,723	1,653	1.3	3.3	4.0	4.1	4.7
United Arab Emirates	75	602	1,053	1,404	1,479	1.2	1.9	2.3	3.3	4.2
Poland	113	1,220	1,523	1,520	1,266	1.8	3.9	3.4	3.6	3.6
Hungary	60	1,151	1,521	1,430	1,188	1.0	3.6	3.4	3.4	3.4
Norway	165	964	1,146	1,082	1,011	2.7	3.0	2.5	2.5	2.9
Saudi Arabia	177	491	655	871	896	2.9	1.5	1.4	2.0	2.5
Total for all 10	**2,125**	**14,226**	**19,695**	**20,091**	**18,067**	**35.5**	**45.4**	**44.4**	**47.9**	**52.0**

(1)   Switzerland including Liechtenstein up to 1994.

(2)   Czechoslovakia before 1993.

(4)   Relates to the exteranl trade of the USSR until 1991 and from 1992 to the external trade of Russia.

IMPORTS

Ranking of EU main trading partners in 2002

Partner	Value (Mio ECU/euro)					Share (%)				
	1990	1999	2000	2001	2002	1990	1999	2000	2001	2002
Power generating machinery and equipment - SITC 71										
Extra EU-15	**9,522**	**27,229**	**34,843**	**36,060**	**33,933**	**100.0**	**100.0**	**100.0**	**100.0**	**100.0**
United States	5,772	14,292	18,718	18,428	16,008	60.6	52.4	53.7	51.1	47.1
Hungary	23	2,632	2,904	3,373	3,524	0.2	9.6	8.3	9.3	10.3
Japan	1,034	2,469	2,868	2,822	2,654	10.8	9.0	8.2	7.8	7.8
Poland	70	345	1,511	1,903	2,035	0.7	1.2	4.3	5.2	5.9
Switzerland[1]	558	1,088	1,266	1,372	1,160	5.8	3.9	3.6	3.8	3.4
Canada	399	1,040	1,119	1,131	1,126	4.1	3.8	3.2	3.1	3.3
China	59	549	785	933	958	0.6	2.0	2.2	2.5	2.8
Czech Republic[2]	42	442	570	667	847	0.4	1.6	1.6	1.8	2.4
Brazil	164	384	523	588	703	1.7	1.4	1.5	1.6	2.0
Turkey	36	221	315	472	471	0.3	0.8	0.9	1.3	1.3
Total for all 10	**8,157**	**23,464**	**30,578**	**31,688**	**29,485**	**85.6**	**86.1**	**87.7**	**87.8**	**86.8**
Machinery specialized for particular ind. - SITC 72										
Extra EU-15	**7,579**	**14,384**	**17,441**	**16,898**	**15,132**	**100.0**	**100.0**	**100.0**	**100.0**	**100.0**
United States	2,169	4,536	5,608	5,230	4,239	28.6	31.5	32.1	30.9	28.0
Switzerland[1]	2,375	2,897	3,243	3,322	2,828	31.3	20.1	18.5	19.6	18.6
Japan	1,803	2,658	3,363	2,829	2,331	23.7	18.4	19.2	16.7	15.4
Czech Republic[2]	79	566	746	873	944	1.0	3.9	4.2	5.1	6.2
South Korea	19	317	442	433	476	0.2	2.2	2.5	2.5	3.1
Poland	54	307	362	423	450	0.7	2.1	2.0	2.5	2.9
Hungary	80	278	349	398	448	1.0	1.9	2.0	2.3	2.9
China	11	210	299	355	416	0.1	1.4	1.7	2.0	2.7
Norway	179	426	375	408	405	2.3	2.9	2.1	2.4	2.6
Canada	145	399	456	373	391	1.9	2.7	2.6	2.2	2.5
Total for all 10	**6,913**	**12,594**	**15,244**	**14,644**	**12,928**	**91.2**	**87.5**	**87.4**	**86.6**	**85.4**
General industry machinery and equipment - SITC 74										
Extra EU-15	**9,266**	**23,028**	**28,754**	**29,786**	**27,926**	**100.0**	**100.0**	**100.0**	**100.0**	**100.0**
United States	3,407	7,384	9,204	8,872	7,552	36.7	32.0	32.0	29.7	27.0
Japan	2,019	4,368	5,485	4,992	4,364	21.7	18.9	19.0	16.7	15.6
Switzerland[1]	1,928	2,775	2,980	3,043	2,933	20.8	12.0	10.3	10.2	10.5
China	125	1,014	1,600	1,982	2,165	1.3	4.4	5.5	6.6	7.7
Czech Republic[2]	59	1,043	1,334	1,791	2,049	0.6	4.5	4.6	6.0	7.3
Poland	79	467	640	812	898	0.8	2.0	2.2	2.7	3.2
South Africa[3]	19	451	756	1,059	882	0.2	1.9	2.6	3.5	3.1
Hungary	83	430	557	692	692	0.8	1.8	1.9	2.3	2.4
South Korea	93	489	695	721	591	1.0	2.1	2.4	2.4	2.1
Taiwan	193	474	614	615	560	2.0	2.0	2.1	2.0	2.0
Total for all 10	**8,005**	**18,895**	**23,865**	**24,578**	**22,688**	**86.3**	**82.0**	**82.9**	**82.5**	**81.2**
Telecommunication, sound, TV, video - SITC 76										
Extra EU-15	**14,044**	**32,381**	**49,294**	**48,792**	**43,854**	**100.0**	**100.0**	**100.0**	**100.0**	**100.0**
China	868	3,537	6,297	7,380	8,728	6.1	10.9	12.7	15.1	19.9
Japan	6,573	5,793	8,103	7,335	6,916	46.8	17.8	16.4	15.0	15.7
United States	1,548	8,405	12,366	10,677	5,936	11.0	25.9	25.0	21.8	13.5
Hungary	30	1,613	2,686	3,631	3,567	0.2	4.9	5.4	7.4	8.1
South Korea	1,066	1,918	2,797	2,513	3,137	7.5	5.9	5.6	5.1	7.1
Malaysia	561	1,491	2,249	2,552	2,014	3.9	4.6	4.5	5.2	4.5
Taiwan	700	1,085	1,638	1,797	1,517	4.9	3.3	3.3	3.6	3.4
Turkey	162	633	891	964	1,422	1.1	1.9	1.8	1.9	3.2
Poland	25	613	774	1,018	1,223	0.1	1.8	1.5	2.0	2.7
Czech Republic[2]	5	205	502	1,004	985	0.0	0.6	1.0	2.0	2.2
Total for all 10	**11,537**	**25,294**	**38,305**	**38,871**	**35,446**	**82.1**	**78.1**	**77.7**	**79.6**	**80.8**

(1) Switzerland including Liechtenstein up to 1994.
(2) Czechoslovakia before 1993.
(3) South Africa includes Namibia up to 31.12.1989.

MAIN EU TRADING PARTNERS
MACHINERY AND EQUIPMENT

EXPORTS

Ranking of EU main trading partners in 2002

Partner	Value (Mio ECU/euro)					Share (%)				
	1990	1999	2000	2001	2002	1990	1999	2000	2001	2002
Office machines and computers - SITC 75										
Extra EU-15	**7,789**	**24,043**	**31,305**	**31,499**	**29,028**	**100.0**	**100.0**	**100.0**	**100.0**	**100.0**
United States	2,660	6,442	7,894	7,174	6,547	34.1	26.7	25.2	22.7	22.5
Switzerland[1]	1,162	2,757	3,271	3,402	2,968	14.9	11.4	10.4	10.7	10.2
Russia[4]	211	753	1,134	1,469	1,567	2.7	3.1	3.6	4.6	5.3
Japan	250	1,345	2,399	2,326	1,536	3.2	5.5	7.6	7.3	5.2
Norway	401	1,215	1,409	1,375	1,274	5.1	5.0	4.5	4.3	4.3
Czech Republic[2]	119	574	816	987	1,135	1.5	2.3	2.6	3.1	3.9
Poland	88	896	1,167	1,179	1,103	1.1	3.7	3.7	3.7	3.7
Hungary	55	1,162	1,503	1,346	1,045	0.7	4.8	4.8	4.2	3.6
Singapore	199	716	807	779	897	2.5	2.9	2.5	2.4	3.0
United Arab Emirates	38	490	600	697	749	0.4	2.0	1.9	2.2	2.5
Total for all 10	**5,184**	**16,350**	**21,000**	**20,735**	**18,822**	**66.5**	**68.0**	**67.0**	**65.8**	**64.8**
of which computer equipement - SITC 752										
Extra EU-15	**3,875**	**12,076**	**14,913**	**15,175**	**13,710**	**100.0**	**100.0**	**100.0**	**100.0**	**100.0**
United States	988	2,227	2,560	2,346	2,214	25.4	18.4	17.1	15.4	16.1
Switzerland[1]	752	1,890	1,999	2,122	1,772	19.4	15.6	13.4	13.9	12.9
Russia[4]	145	525	820	1,087	1,042	3.7	4.3	5.4	7.1	7.5
Norway	248	837	902	898	818	6.3	6.9	6.0	5.9	5.9
Japan	102	858	1,496	1,260	665	2.6	7.1	10.0	8.3	4.8
Poland	59	587	672	667	631	1.5	4.8	4.5	4.3	4.6
Czech Republic[2]	76	316	409	494	474	1.9	2.6	2.7	3.2	3.4
Hungary	30	251	432	501	465	0.7	2.0	2.8	3.3	3.3
United Arab Emirates	19	344	374	446	433	0.4	2.8	2.5	2.9	3.1
South Africa[3]	52	416	462	476	412	1.3	3.4	3.0	3.1	3.0
Total for all 10	**2,471**	**8,251**	**10,127**	**10,297**	**8,926**	**63.7**	**68.3**	**67.9**	**67.8**	**65.1**
Electrical machinery - SITC 77										
Extra EU-15	**17,690**	**56,776**	**75,336**	**75,544**	**71,452**	**100.0**	**100.0**	**100.0**	**100.0**	**100.0**
United States	3,476	10,914	14,647	13,901	13,650	19.6	19.2	19.4	18.4	19.1
China	249	1,727	2,690	3,313	3,481	1.4	3.0	3.5	4.3	4.8
Hungary	160	2,193	3,195	3,250	3,418	0.9	3.8	4.2	4.3	4.7
Czech Republic[2]	130	2,115	2,839	3,198	3,209	0.7	3.7	3.7	4.2	4.4
Malaysia	403	2,178	3,132	3,348	2,991	2.2	3.8	4.1	4.4	4.1
Switzerland[1]	1,783	2,827	3,214	3,338	2,990	10.0	4.9	4.2	4.4	4.1
Poland	162	2,121	2,354	2,639	2,804	0.9	3.7	3.1	3.4	3.9
Singapore	860	2,570	3,610	3,278	2,694	4.8	4.5	4.7	4.3	3.7
Japan	817	1,956	2,769	2,924	2,545	4.6	3.4	3.6	3.8	3.5
Hong Kong	500	1,842	2,514	2,212	2,188	2.8	3.2	3.3	2.9	3.0
Total for all 10	**8,541**	**30,443**	**40,964**	**41,400**	**39,969**	**48.2**	**53.6**	**54.3**	**54.8**	**55.9**
of which valves, transistors etc. - SITC 776										
Extra EU-15	**3,178**	**16,226**	**25,419**	**23,010**	**19,803**	**100.0**	**100.0**	**100.0**	**100.0**	**100.0**
United States	737	2,966	4,422	3,920	3,649	23.1	18.2	17.3	17.0	18.4
Malaysia	292	1,687	2,377	2,683	2,356	9.1	10.3	9.3	11.6	11.8
Singapore	468	1,739	2,531	2,271	1,763	14.7	10.7	9.9	9.8	8.9
Taiwan	240	1,106	1,738	1,209	1,196	7.5	6.8	6.8	5.2	6.0
Hungary	26	559	996	998	1,156	0.8	3.4	3.9	4.3	5.8
Hong Kong	134	768	1,056	868	961	4.2	4.7	4.1	3.7	4.8
China	6	410	825	873	934	0.1	2.5	3.2	3.7	4.7
Philippines	114	728	1,308	1,287	768	3.5	4.4	5.1	5.5	3.8
Japan	148	605	970	992	737	4.6	3.7	3.8	4.3	3.7
South Korea	95	550	1,526	1,005	723	2.9	3.3	6.0	4.3	3.6
Total for all 10	**2,259**	**11,117**	**17,750**	**16,107**	**14,243**	**71.0**	**68.5**	**69.8**	**69.9**	**71.9**

(1)   Switzerland including Liechtenstein up to 1994.
(2)   Czechoslovakia before 1993.
(4)   Relates to the exteranl trade of the USSR until 1991 and from 1992 to the external trade of Russia.

IMPORTS

Ranking of EU main trading partners in 2002

Partner	Value (Mio ECU/euro)					Share (%)				
	1990	1999	2000	2001	2002	1990	1999	2000	2001	2002
Office machines and computers - SITC 75										
Extra EU-15	**22,080**	**60,069**	**71,526**	**65,476**	**62,264**	**100.0**	**100.0**	**100.0**	**100.0**	**100.0**
United States	9,707	13,861	15,893	14,395	12,634	43.9	23.0	22.2	21.9	20.2
China	99	4,839	7,578	9,072	10,544	0.4	8.0	10.5	13.8	16.9
Taiwan	2,065	7,361	9,908	9,620	8,797	9.3	12.2	13.8	14.6	14.1
Japan	6,229	9,341	10,703	8,480	7,084	28.2	15.5	14.9	12.9	11.3
Singapore	1,434	5,494	5,646	4,868	4,468	6.4	9.1	7.8	7.4	7.1
South Korea	574	3,017	4,383	3,447	3,651	2.5	5.0	6.1	5.2	5.8
Malaysia	33	4,347	3,699	3,131	2,708	0.1	7.2	5.1	4.7	4.3
Philippines	15	2,581	2,626	2,503	2,169	0.0	4.2	3.6	3.8	3.4
Czech Republic[2]	3	188	296	843	1,770	0.0	0.3	0.4	1.2	2.8
Hungary	4	1,901	2,341	1,855	1,814	0.0	3.1	3.2	2.8	2.9
Total for all 10	**20,162**	**52,931**	**63,073**	**58,215**	**55,638**	**91.3**	**88.1**	**88.1**	**88.9**	**89.3**
of which computer equipement - SITC 752										
Extra EU-15	**13,181**	**31,538**	**38,052**	**35,843**	**36,388**	**100.0**	**100.0**	**100.0**	**100.0**	**100.0**
China	26	2,929	4,439	4,873	6,225	0.1	9.2	11.6	13.5	17.1
United States	5,422	6,408	6,846	6,213	6,096	41.1	20.3	17.9	17.3	16.7
Taiwan	1,540	3,900	5,593	5,674	5,582	11.6	12.3	14.6	15.8	15.3
Singapore	1,015	3,882	3,969	3,496	3,148	7.7	12.3	10.4	9.7	8.6
Japan	3,491	4,642	5,025	3,471	2,985	26.4	14.7	13.2	9.6	8.2
South Korea	461	1,724	2,581	2,557	2,290	3.4	5.4	6.7	7.1	6.2
Malaysia	14	1,805	2,081	2,014	1,815	0.1	5.7	5.4	5.6	4.9
Philippines	10	1,370	1,478	1,607	1,615	0.0	4.3	3.8	4.4	4.4
Czech Republic[2]	1	81	142	645	1,602	0.0	0.2	0.3	1.8	4.4
Hungary	1	1,335	1,774	1,471	1,491	0.0	4.2	4.6	4.1	4.0
Total for all 10	**11,982**	**28,077**	**33,928**	**32,022**	**32,850**	**90.8**	**89.0**	**89.1**	**89.3**	**90.2**
Electrical machinery - SITC 77										
Extra EU-15	**17,933**	**61,448**	**93,385**	**82,035**	**72,889**	**100.0**	**100.0**	**100.0**	**100.0**	**100.0**
United States	5,212	13,541	19,983	18,253	13,779	29.0	22.0	21.3	22.2	18.9
China	251	4,956	7,922	7,444	8,445	1.4	8.0	8.4	9.0	11.5
Japan	4,635	10,206	15,055	10,956	8,292	25.8	16.6	16.1	13.3	11.3
Malaysia	448	2,335	3,890	3,047	4,398	2.5	3.7	4.1	3.7	6.0
Singapore	797	2,370	4,048	2,909	3,551	4.4	3.8	4.3	3.5	4.8
Philippines	148	1,228	1,925	1,917	3,491	0.8	1.9	2.0	2.3	4.7
Taiwan	1,047	2,480	4,246	3,330	3,282	5.8	4.0	4.5	4.0	4.5
Hungary	163	2,062	2,605	2,858	3,033	0.9	3.3	2.7	3.4	4.1
South Korea	619	2,854	4,865	3,626	2,978	3.4	4.6	5.2	4.4	4.0
Switzerland[1]	1,872	2,983	3,274	3,363	2,961	10.4	4.8	3.5	4.0	4.0
Total for all 10	**15,192**	**45,014**	**67,815**	**57,702**	**54,209**	**84.7**	**73.2**	**72.6**	**70.3**	**74.3**
of which valves, transistors etc. - SITC 776										
Extra EU-15	**5,845**	**22,565**	**40,481**	**32,466**	**26,190**	**100.0**	**100.0**	**100.0**	**100.0**	**100.0**
United States	1,738	5,020	8,571	7,512	5,269	29.7	22.2	21.1	23.1	20.1
Malaysia	353	1,840	3,114	2,430	3,756	6.0	8.1	7.6	7.4	14.3
Philippines	135	850	1,403	1,516	3,097	2.3	3.7	3.4	4.6	11.8
Singapore	467	1,756	3,210	2,190	3,001	7.9	7.7	7.9	6.7	11.4
Japan	1,747	3,612	5,698	4,071	2,751	29.8	16.0	14.0	12.5	10.5
South Korea	285	1,727	3,109	2,148	1,628	4.8	7.6	7.6	6.6	6.2
Taiwan	363	1,000	2,054	1,467	1,556	6.2	4.4	5.0	4.5	5.9
Costa Rica	0	28	291	118	1,426	0.0	0.1	0.7	0.3	5.4
China	5	261	573	421	703	0.0	1.1	1.4	1.2	2.6
Thailand	45	319	537	348	503	0.7	1.4	1.3	1.0	1.9
Total for all 10	**5,138**	**16,412**	**28,559**	**22,221**	**23,689**	**87.9**	**72.7**	**70.5**	**68.4**	**90.4**

(1)   Switzerland including Liechtenstein up to 1994.

(2)   Czechoslovakia before 1993.

MAIN EU TRADING PARTNERS
TRANSPORT EQUIPMENT

EXPORTS

Ranking of EU main trading partners in 2002

Partner	Value (Mio ECU/euro)					Share (%)				
	1990	1999	2000	2001	2002	1990	1999	2000	2001	2002
Road vehicles - SITC 78										
Extra EU-15	**31,108**	**69,263**	**87,761**	**95,070**	**104,497**	**100.0**	**100.0**	**100.0**	**100.0**	**100.0**
United States	8,681	23,238	26,919	29,360	34,223	27.9	33.5	30.6	30.8	32.7
Japan	4,133	5,168	6,400	6,159	5,960	13.2	7.4	7.2	6.4	5.7
Switzerland[1]	3,863	5,024	5,337	6,055	5,659	12.4	7.2	6.0	6.3	5.4
Hungary	173	3,119	4,167	4,209	4,794	0.5	4.5	4.7	4.4	4.5
Poland	242	3,244	3,743	3,823	4,455	0.7	4.6	4.2	4.0	4.2
Czech Republic[2]	95	1,925	2,569	3,127	3,581	0.3	2.7	2.9	3.2	3.4
Russia[4]	163	722	1,168	2,307	2,658	0.5	1.0	1.3	2.4	2.5
Mexico	279	1,409	1,873	2,277	2,656	0.8	2.0	2.1	2.3	2.5
China	231	871	1,239	1,982	2,561	0.7	1.2	1.4	2.0	2.4
Norway	609	1,920	2,238	2,374	2,465	1.9	2.7	2.5	2.4	2.3
Total for all 10	**18,469**	**46,640**	**55,653**	**61,673**	**69,013**	**59.3**	**67.3**	**63.4**	**64.8**	**66.0**
of which passenger cars etc. - SITC 781										
Extra EU-15	**18,826**	**40,241**	**51,727**	**56,417**	**63,191**	**100.0**	**100.0**	**100.0**	**100.0**	**100.0**
United States	6,508	18,008	20,690	22,945	27,513	34.5	44.7	39.9	40.6	43.5
Japan	3,671	4,379	5,502	5,148	4,723	19.5	10.8	10.6	9.1	7.4
Switzerland[1]	2,596	3,586	3,565	4,174	3,983	13.7	8.9	6.8	7.3	6.3
Poland	104	1,087	1,453	1,733	1,870	0.5	2.7	2.8	3.0	2.9
Russia[4]	50	472	787	1,604	1,777	0.2	1.1	1.5	2.8	2.8
Australia	250	969	1,109	1,502	1,603	1.3	2.4	2.1	2.6	2.5
Norway	320	1,116	1,353	1,472	1,464	1.7	2.7	2.6	2.6	2.3
Canada	621	635	866	861	1,461	3.3	1.5	1.6	1.5	2.3
Mexico	26	207	609	1,077	1,460	0.1	0.5	1.1	1.9	2.3
Hungary	94	666	987	889	1,094	0.4	1.6	1.9	1.5	1.7
Total for all 10	**14,241**	**31,125**	**36,921**	**41,407**	**46,948**	**75.6**	**77.3**	**71.3**	**73.3**	**74.2**
Aircraft, spacecraft etc. - SITC 792										
Extra EU-15	**9,322**	**31,269**	**37,792**	**40,057**	**33,832**	**100.0**	**100.0**	**100.0**	**100.0**	**100.0**
United States	3,028	11,453	15,192	16,472	13,482	32.4	36.6	40.1	41.1	39.8
Canada	279	1,645	1,767	2,729	2,367	2.9	5.2	4.6	6.8	6.9
Brazil	182	965	1,587	1,681	1,746	1.9	3.0	4.1	4.1	5.1
Switzerland[1]	552	4,422	3,791	2,916	1,728	5.9	14.1	10.0	7.2	5.1
China	14	990	968	1,097	1,405	0.1	3.1	2.5	2.7	4.1
United Arab Emirates	436	581	983	1,279	956	4.6	1.8	2.6	3.1	2.8
Saudi Arabia	167	234	372	561	781	1.7	0.7	0.9	1.4	2.3
Hong Kong	3	204	405	1,590	760	0.0	0.6	1.0	3.9	2.2
Japan	381	354	675	276	714	4.0	1.1	1.7	0.6	2.1
South Korea	186	486	902	434	580	1.9	1.5	2.3	1.0	1.7
Total for all 10	**5,227**	**21,333**	**26,642**	**29,034**	**24,519**	**56.0**	**68.2**	**70.4**	**72.4**	**72.4**
Ships, boats etc. - SITC 793										
Extra EU-15	**3,542**	**8,329**	**10,287**	**10,724**	**11,450**	**100.0**	**100.0**	**100.0**	**100.0**	**100.0**
United States	284	1,558	1,121	2,446	1,868	8.0	18.7	10.8	22.8	16.3
Cayman Islands	9	560	955	1,052	1,430	0.2	6.7	9.2	9.8	12.4
Liberia	863	625	1,927	1,436	1,284	24.3	7.5	18.7	13.3	11.2
Bermuda	88	209	626	1,214	1,195	2.4	2.5	6.0	11.3	10.4
Bahamas	217	628	818	497	915	6.1	7.5	7.9	4.6	7.9
Gibraltar	27	211	266	405	602	0.7	2.5	2.5	3.7	5.2
Panama	162	744	643	211	602	4.5	8.9	6.2	1.9	5.2
Norway	212	523	826	947	373	5.9	6.2	8.0	8.8	3.2
Antigua and Barbuda	8	418	856	182	268	0.2	5.0	8.3	1.7	2.3
Marshall Islands	:	0	71	167	261	:	0.0	0.6	1.5	2.2
Total for all 10	**1,870**	**5,475**	**8,108**	**8,558**	**8,799**	**52.7**	**65.7**	**78.8**	**79.8**	**76.8**

(1) Switzerland including Liechtenstein up to 1994.
(2) Czechoslovakia before 1993.
(4) Relates to the exteranl trade of the USSR until 1991 and from 1992 to the external trade of Russia.

IMPORTS

Ranking of EU main trading partners in 2002

Partner	Value (Mio ECU/euro)					Share (%)				
	1990	1999	2000	2001	2002	1990	1999	2000	2001	2002
Road vehicles - SITC 78										
Extra EU-15	**15,965**	**43,609**	**48,462**	**48,770**	**51,264**	**100.0**	**100.0**	**100.0**	**100.0**	**100.0**
Japan	10,636	17,451	17,736	15,485	15,910	66.6	40.0	36.5	31.7	31.0
United States	1,751	5,282	5,572	6,343	6,491	10.9	12.1	11.4	13.0	12.6
Czech Republic[2]	127	3,032	4,158	4,546	4,760	0.7	6.9	8.5	9.3	9.2
South Korea	93	3,506	3,628	3,344	3,398	0.5	8.0	7.4	6.8	6.6
Poland	115	1,787	2,676	2,933	3,140	0.7	4.0	5.5	6.0	6.1
Slovakia	:	1,754	1,621	1,940	3,041	:	4.0	3.3	3.9	5.9
Hungary	30	1,870	2,383	2,818	2,767	0.1	4.2	4.9	5.7	5.3
Turkey	60	984	1,182	1,829	2,219	0.3	2.2	2.4	3.7	4.3
Slovenia	:	946	1,096	1,146	1,293	:	2.1	2.2	2.3	2.5
South Africa[3]	23	782	707	893	1,092	0.1	1.7	1.4	1.8	2.1
Total for all 10	**12,834**	**37,394**	**40,759**	**41,278**	**44,111**	**80.3**	**85.7**	**84.1**	**84.6**	**86.0**
of which passenger cars etc. - SITC 781										
Extra EU-15	**9,681**	**25,551**	**26,323**	**26,281**	**27,974**	**100.0**	**100.0**	**100.0**	**100.0**	**100.0**
Japan	7,393	11,584	11,068	9,343	9,873	76.3	45.3	42.0	35.5	35.2
United States	938	2,218	2,105	2,885	3,704	9.6	8.6	7.9	10.9	13.2
South Korea	70	3,164	3,258	2,970	3,076	0.7	12.3	12.3	11.3	10.9
Slovakia	:	1,428	1,260	1,516	2,541	:	5.5	4.7	5.7	9.0
Czech Republic[2]	85	1,750	2,530	2,617	2,444	0.8	6.8	9.6	9.9	8.7
Hungary	2	1,110	1,436	1,709	1,547	0.0	4.3	5.4	6.5	5.5
Poland	67	761	1,179	1,229	1,021	0.6	2.9	4.4	4.6	3.6
Slovenia	:	689	756	761	879	:	2.6	2.8	2.8	3.1
South Africa[3]	1	572	473	656	795	0.0	2.2	1.7	2.4	2.8
Turkey	9	480	505	691	649	0.0	1.8	1.9	2.6	2.3
Total for all 10	**8,565**	**23,755**	**24,570**	**24,377**	**26,529**	**88.4**	**92.9**	**93.3**	**92.7**	**94.8**
Aircraft, spacecraft etc. - SITC 792										
Extra EU-15	**11,313**	**31,881**	**34,825**	**35,795**	**33,402**	**100.0**	**100.0**	**100.0**	**100.0**	**100.0**
United States	9,246	21,900	22,345	22,466	23,978	81.7	68.6	64.1	62.7	71.7
Canada	261	854	1,591	2,282	2,585	2.3	2.6	4.5	6.3	7.7
Switzerland[1]	489	2,486	3,275	2,423	1,397	4.3	7.7	9.4	6.7	4.1
Bermuda	17	476	444	1,096	600	0.1	1.4	1.2	3.0	1.7
Brazil	88	694	1,434	1,108	546	0.7	2.1	4.1	3.0	1.6
Saudi Arabia	57	156	244	275	426	0.5	0.4	0.7	0.7	1.2
China	4	174	36	355	274	0.0	0.5	0.1	0.9	0.8
Turkey	31	456	368	303	266	0.2	1.4	1.0	0.8	0.7
Australia	28	73	123	104	221	0.2	0.2	0.3	0.2	0.6
Algeria	3	0	64	413	209	0.0	0.0	0.1	1.1	0.6
Total for all 10	**10,224**	**27,270**	**29,925**	**30,825**	**30,502**	**90.3**	**85.5**	**85.9**	**86.1**	**91.3**
Ships, boats etc. - SITC 793										
Extra EU-15	**1,778**	**4,561**	**6,902**	**6,962**	**8,167**	**100.0**	**100.0**	**100.0**	**100.0**	**100.0**
South Korea	68	749	1,399	1,270	2,285	3.8	16.4	20.2	18.2	27.9
Cayman Islands	0	445	633	800	786	0.0	9.7	9.1	11.4	9.6
Liberia	129	83	207	623	777	7.2	1.8	2.9	8.9	9.5
Antigua and Barbuda	20	1	479	341	772	1.0	0.0	6.9	4.9	9.4
Japan	420	521	549	686	539	23.6	11.4	7.9	9.8	6.6
Poland	20	265	277	277	350	1.1	5.8	4.0	3.9	4.2
Bermuda	49	167	268	223	301	2.7	3.6	3.8	3.2	3.6
United States	335	369	420	330	274	18.8	8.0	6.0	4.7	3.3
Panama	71	36	103	175	221	3.9	0.7	1.4	2.5	2.7
China	3	178	238	385	196	0.1	3.9	3.4	5.5	2.3
Total for all 10	**1,115**	**2,813**	**4,572**	**5,111**	**6,501**	**62.7**	**61.6**	**66.2**	**73.4**	**79.5**

(1)   Switzerland including Liechtenstein up to 1994.

(2)   Czechoslovakia before 1993.

(3)   South Africa includes Namibia up to 31.12.1989.

MAIN EU TRADING PARTNERS
OTHER MANUFACTURED GOODS

EXPORTS

Ranking of EU main trading partners in 2002

Partner	Value (Mio ECU/euro)					Share (%)				
	1990	1999	2000	2001	2002	1990	1999	2000	2001	2002
Papier, paperboard and articles thereof - SITC 64										
Extra EU-15	**3,988**	**13,763**	**17,055**	**17,198**	**17,791**	**100.0**	**100.0**	**100.0**	**100.0**	**100.0**
United States	639	1,933	2,556	2,346	2,394	16.0	14.0	14.9	13.6	13.4
Switzerland[1]	632	1,412	1,579	1,625	1,635	15.8	10.2	9.2	9.4	9.1
Poland	47	986	1,205	1,277	1,361	1.1	7.1	7.0	7.4	7.6
Russia[4]	100	448	651	829	868	2.5	3.2	3.8	4.8	4.8
Norway	133	723	777	721	720	3.3	5.2	4.5	4.1	4.0
Czech Republic[2]	23	430	546	620	670	0.5	3.1	3.2	3.6	3.7
Turkey	56	443	635	452	586	1.4	3.2	3.7	2.6	3.2
Hungary	56	431	519	572	584	1.3	3.1	3.0	3.3	3.2
Australia	218	503	631	522	513	5.4	3.6	3.6	3.0	2.8
China	40	280	358	373	498	0.9	2.0	2.1	2.1	2.7
Total for all 10	**1,944**	**7,588**	**9,456**	**9,337**	**9,830**	**48.7**	**55.1**	**55.4**	**54.2**	**55.2**
Non-metallic mineral manufactures - SITC 66										
Extra EU-15	**13,529**	**25,203**	**31,378**	**31,556**	**32,750**	**100.0**	**100.0**	**100.0**	**100.0**	**100.0**
United States	3,165	6,016	7,767	7,164	6,988	23.3	23.8	24.7	22.7	21.3
India	1,572	3,608	4,357	3,814	4,056	11.6	14.3	13.8	12.0	12.3
Israel	1,470	3,391	4,142	3,194	3,012	10.8	13.4	13.2	10.1	9.1
Switzerland[1]	1,397	1,526	2,266	3,112	1,825	10.3	6.0	7.2	9.8	5.5
Hong Kong	559	1,028	1,257	1,315	1,454	4.1	4.0	4.0	4.1	4.4
Japan	1,167	833	1,015	949	834	8.6	3.3	3.2	3.0	2.5
United Arab Emirates	90	394	587	823	816	0.6	1.5	1.8	2.6	2.4
China	53	364	541	586	733	0.3	1.4	1.7	1.8	2.2
Poland	50	677	725	714	728	0.3	2.6	2.3	2.2	2.2
Czech Republic[2]	39	339	397	479	557	0.2	1.3	1.2	1.5	1.7
Total for all 10	**9,562**	**18,177**	**23,055**	**22,150**	**21,003**	**70.6**	**72.1**	**73.4**	**70.1**	**64.1**
Iron and steel - SITC 67										
Extra EU-15	**12,142**	**14,958**	**19,503**	**19,976**	**20,133**	**100.0**	**100.0**	**100.0**	**100.0**	**100.0**
United States	2,436	3,241	4,698	4,049	3,282	20.0	21.6	24.0	20.2	16.2
Switzerland[1]	1,227	1,272	1,649	1,545	1,368	10.1	8.5	8.4	7.7	6.7
Poland	140	718	960	1,046	1,112	1.1	4.8	4.9	5.2	5.5
China	202	338	460	708	962	1.6	2.2	2.3	3.5	4.7
Czech Republic[2]	38	620	883	970	931	0.3	4.1	4.5	4.8	4.6
Norway	465	709	735	752	887	3.8	4.7	3.7	3.7	4.4
Turkey	445	479	881	668	814	3.6	3.2	4.5	3.3	4.0
Canada	333	511	726	578	648	2.7	3.4	3.7	2.8	3.2
Mexico	251	359	466	450	612	2.0	2.4	2.3	2.2	3.0
Hungary	79	336	439	471	469	0.6	2.2	2.2	2.3	2.3
Total for all 10	**5,617**	**8,584**	**11,895**	**11,236**	**11,085**	**46.2**	**57.3**	**60.9**	**56.2**	**55.0**
Non-ferrous metals - SITC 68										
Extra EU-15	**4,732**	**8,234**	**11,930**	**11,938**	**11,052**	**100.0**	**100.0**	**100.0**	**100.0**	**100.0**
United States	1,079	1,916	3,175	3,311	2,437	22.8	23.2	26.6	27.7	22.0
Switzerland[1]	960	973	1,285	1,373	1,405	20.2	11.8	10.7	11.5	12.7
Czech Republic[2]	24	327	474	505	566	0.5	3.9	3.9	4.2	5.1
Poland	14	384	501	517	548	0.2	4.6	4.1	4.3	4.9
Japan	399	499	831	623	540	8.4	6.0	6.9	5.2	4.8
China	22	149	231	271	303	0.4	1.8	1.9	2.2	2.7
Hungary	19	178	258	271	286	0.4	2.1	2.1	2.2	2.5
Norway	119	246	274	291	274	2.5	2.9	2.2	2.4	2.4
Turkey	152	180	253	197	265	3.2	2.1	2.1	1.6	2.3
Russia[4]	32	118	164	211	256	0.6	1.4	1.3	1.7	2.3
Total for all 10	**2,821**	**4,970**	**7,445**	**7,570**	**6,881**	**59.6**	**60.3**	**62.4**	**63.4**	**62.2**

(1) Switzerland including Liechtenstein up to 1994.

(2) Czechoslovakia before 1993.

(4) Relates to the exteranl trade of the USSR until 1991 and from 1992 to the external trade of Russia.

MAIN EU TRADING PARTNERS
OTHER MANUFACTURED GOODS

IMPORTS

Ranking of EU main trading partners in 2002

Partner	Value (Mio ECU/euro)					Share (%)				
	1990	1999	2000	2001	2002	1990	1999	2000	2001	2002
Papier, paperboard and articles thereof - SITC 64										
Extra EU-15	**3,469**	**6,481**	**7,533**	**8,115**	**7,828**	**100.0**	**100.0**	**100.0**	**100.0**	**100.0**
Switzerland[1]	600	1,196	1,320	1,407	1,375	17.2	18.4	17.5	17.3	17.5
United States	715	1,255	1,436	1,335	1,147	20.6	19.3	19.0	16.4	14.6
Norway	703	971	1,045	1,079	912	20.2	14.9	13.8	13.2	11.6
Poland	39	351	503	681	817	1.1	5.4	6.6	8.3	10.4
Canada	495	533	541	561	508	14.2	8.2	7.1	6.9	6.4
China	40	250	317	356	346	1.1	3.8	4.2	4.3	4.4
Russia[4]	23	218	277	352	328	0.6	3.3	3.6	4.3	4.1
Czech Republic[2]	55	188	250	283	312	1.5	2.9	3.3	3.4	3.9
Slovakia	:	114	157	250	222	:	1.7	2.0	3.0	2.8
Brazil	205	140	126	161	210	5.9	2.1	1.6	1.9	2.6
Total for all 10	**2,874**	**5,216**	**5,971**	**6,465**	**6,177**	**82.8**	**80.4**	**79.2**	**79.6**	**78.9**
Non-metallic mineral manufactures - SITC 66										
Extra EU-15	**7,130**	**20,003**	**25,908**	**25,611**	**24,139**	**100.0**	**100.0**	**100.0**	**100.0**	**100.0**
United States	787	1,918	2,715	2,998	2,524	11.0	9.5	10.4	11.7	10.4
Israel	469	1,422	1,982	1,706	1,749	6.5	7.1	7.6	6.6	7.2
China	136	967	1,331	1,426	1,526	1.9	4.8	5.1	5.5	6.3
India	560	1,048	1,386	1,357	1,496	7.8	5.2	5.3	5.2	6.1
South Africa[3]	667	806	2,237	2,198	1,318	9.3	4.0	8.6	8.5	5.4
Congo (Democratic Republic)	190	713	781	839	1,026	2.6	3.5	3.0	3.2	4.2
Switzerland[1]	552	4,227	4,599	1,899	1,023	7.7	21.1	17.7	7.4	4.2
Hong Kong	160	388	703	718	959	2.2	1.9	2.7	2.8	3.9
Czech Republic[2]	157	652	734	783	763	2.1	3.2	2.8	3.0	3.1
Turkey	176	414	538	668	747	2.4	2.0	2.0	2.6	3.0
Total for all 10	**3,854**	**12,554**	**17,008**	**14,592**	**13,130**	**54.0**	**62.7**	**65.6**	**56.9**	**54.3**
Iron and steel - SITC 67										
Extra EU-15	**5,560**	**10,196**	**14,507**	**14,076**	**12,924**	**100.0**	**100.0**	**100.0**	**100.0**	**100.0**
Russia[4]	328	845	1,519	1,313	1,451	5.9	8.2	10.4	9.3	11.2
Czech Republic[2]	359	611	761	820	839	6.4	5.9	5.2	5.8	6.4
Switzerland[1]	556	679	846	808	768	10.0	6.6	5.8	5.7	5.9
South Africa[3]	305	621	931	882	768	5.4	6.0	6.4	6.2	5.9
Norway	461	763	820	788	719	8.2	7.4	5.6	5.5	5.5
Turkey	242	593	791	905	686	4.3	5.8	5.4	6.4	5.3
Poland	271	514	773	772	614	4.8	5.0	5.3	5.4	4.7
United States	325	525	683	717	600	5.8	5.1	4.7	5.0	4.6
Brazil	414	488	705	516	554	7.4	4.7	4.8	3.6	4.2
Ukraine	:	364	412	555	530	:	3.5	2.8	3.9	4.0
Total for all 10	**3,261**	**6,003**	**8,240**	**8,075**	**7,527**	**58.6**	**58.8**	**56.8**	**57.3**	**58.2**
Non-ferrous metals - SITC 68										
Extra EU-15	**11,843**	**17,156**	**25,332**	**23,351**	**20,210**	**100.0**	**100.0**	**100.0**	**100.0**	**100.0**
Russia[4]	980	2,677	4,945	3,779	3,042	8.2	15.6	19.5	16.1	15.0
Norway	1,665	2,697	3,136	3,028	2,825	14.0	15.7	12.3	12.9	13.9
Chile	1,267	1,331	2,148	2,027	1,811	10.6	7.7	8.4	8.6	8.9
United States	818	1,595	2,091	2,439	1,554	6.9	9.2	8.2	10.4	7.6
Switzerland[1]	806	1,037	1,509	1,217	1,137	6.8	6.0	5.9	5.2	5.6
South Africa[3]	433	671	1,240	1,071	848	3.6	3.9	4.8	4.5	4.1
Poland	348	708	891	789	834	2.9	4.1	3.5	3.3	4.1
Australia	443	358	641	621	581	3.7	2.0	2.5	2.6	2.8
Canada	516	445	771	565	536	4.3	2.5	3.0	2.4	2.6
Mozambique	13	0	22	381	462	0.1	0.0	0.0	1.6	2.2
Total for all 10	**7,289**	**11,520**	**17,394**	**15,916**	**13,630**	**61.5**	**67.1**	**68.6**	**68.1**	**67.4**

(1) Switzerland including Liechtenstein up to 1994.

(2) Czechoslovakia before 1993.

(3) South Africa includes Namibia up to 31.12.1989.

(4) Relates to the exteranl trade of the USSR until 1991 and from 1992 to the external trade of Russia.

MAIN EU TRADING PARTNERS
OTHER MANUFACTURED GOODS

EXPORTS

Ranking of EU main trading partners in 2002

Partner	Value (Mio ECU/euro)					Share (%)				
	1990	1999	2000	2001	2002	1990	1999	2000	2001	2002
Textile yarn, fabrics and related products - SITC 65										
Extra EU-15	**10,758**	**20,128**	**23,471**	**24,742**	**24,465**	**100.0**	**100.0**	**100.0**	**100.0**	**100.0**
United States	1,431	2,388	2,924	2,830	2,718	13.2	11.8	12.4	11.4	11.1
Poland	403	1,843	2,021	2,104	2,031	3.7	9.1	8.6	8.5	8.3
Romania	147	1,149	1,429	1,661	1,816	1.3	5.7	6.0	6.7	7.4
Tunisia	537	1,326	1,421	1,594	1,504	4.9	6.5	6.0	6.4	6.1
Morocco	571	1,164	1,275	1,380	1,362	5.3	5.7	5.4	5.5	5.5
Turkey	273	859	1,064	978	1,203	2.5	4.2	4.5	3.9	4.9
Czech Republic[2]	100	797	931	1,012	1,063	0.9	3.9	3.9	4.0	4.3
Switzerland[1]	1,095	1,097	1,132	1,152	1,051	10.1	5.4	4.8	4.6	4.2
Hong Kong	323	748	887	942	893	3.0	3.7	3.7	3.8	3.6
Hungary	278	807	876	913	877	2.5	4.0	3.7	3.6	3.5
Total for all 10	**5,157**	**12,179**	**13,961**	**14,566**	**14,519**	**47.9**	**60.5**	**59.4**	**58.8**	**59.3**
Clothing and clothing accessories - SITC 84										
Extra EU-15	**8,020**	**13,713**	**15,903**	**17,565**	**17,562**	**100.0**	**100.0**	**100.0**	**100.0**	**100.0**
United States	1,505	2,342	2,872	3,031	2,593	18.7	17.0	18.0	17.2	14.7
Switzerland[1]	1,762	2,163	2,231	2,442	2,500	21.9	15.7	14.0	13.9	14.2
Japan	1,229	1,358	1,523	1,671	1,547	15.3	9.9	9.5	9.5	8.8
Russia[4]	93	492	770	1,071	1,184	1.1	3.5	4.8	6.0	6.7
Romania	51	454	563	693	733	0.6	3.3	3.5	3.9	4.1
Norway	533	684	684	679	720	6.6	4.9	4.3	3.8	4.0
Hong Kong	325	457	568	632	593	4.0	3.3	3.5	3.5	3.3
Tunisia	143	379	450	486	524	1.7	2.7	2.8	2.7	2.9
Poland	84	453	415	453	448	1.0	3.3	2.6	2.5	2.5
Czech Republic[2]	25	243	252	286	441	0.3	1.7	1.5	1.6	2.5
Total for all 10	**5,750**	**9,026**	**10,329**	**11,442**	**11,282**	**71.6**	**65.8**	**64.9**	**65.1**	**64.2**
Professional, scientific, controlling material - SITC 87										
Extra EU-15	**8,647**	**19,893**	**24,359**	**26,995**	**27,795**	**100.0**	**100.0**	**100.0**	**100.0**	**100.0**
United States	2,259	6,086	7,483	8,337	8,472	26.1	30.5	30.7	30.8	30.4
Japan	587	1,501	1,887	2,058	2,004	6.7	7.5	7.7	7.6	7.2
Switzerland[1]	705	1,212	1,366	1,432	1,480	8.1	6.0	5.6	5.3	5.3
China	150	465	654	835	1,061	1.7	2.3	2.6	3.0	3.8
South Korea	220	508	620	707	797	2.5	2.5	2.5	2.6	2.8
Norway	223	598	597	681	734	2.5	3.0	2.4	2.5	2.6
Czech Republic[2]	100	385	492	582	673	1.1	1.9	2.0	2.1	2.4
Canada	196	476	651	687	627	2.2	2.3	2.6	2.5	2.2
Russia[4]	334	305	470	624	614	3.8	1.5	1.9	2.3	2.2
Singapore	162	447	530	546	608	1.8	2.2	2.1	2.0	2.1
Total for all 10	**4,936**	**11,984**	**14,750**	**16,488**	**17,070**	**57.0**	**60.2**	**60.5**	**61.0**	**61.4**
Photogr. apparatus, optical goods, clocks - SITC 88										
Extra EU-15	**3,951**	**7,896**	**10,751**	**10,457**	**10,505**	**100.0**	**100.0**	**100.0**	**100.0**	**100.0**
United States	1,247	2,340	3,174	3,068	3,056	31.5	29.6	29.5	29.3	29.0
Switzerland[1]	719	971	1,113	1,160	1,075	18.2	12.2	10.3	11.0	10.2
Japan	254	473	651	713	650	6.4	5.9	6.0	6.8	6.1
Taiwan	37	317	824	451	564	0.9	4.0	7.6	4.3	5.3
South Korea	47	390	452	407	529	1.1	4.9	4.2	3.8	5.0
Hong Kong	215	362	510	553	502	5.4	4.5	4.7	5.2	4.7
Singapore	81	128	264	189	263	2.0	1.6	2.4	1.8	2.4
China	6	100	169	197	259	0.1	1.2	1.5	1.8	2.4
Russia[4]	41	107	200	240	247	1.0	1.3	1.8	2.2	2.3
Norway	81	162	174	169	181	2.0	2.0	1.6	1.6	1.7
Total for all 10	**2,729**	**5,351**	**7,530**	**7,147**	**7,325**	**69.0**	**67.7**	**70.0**	**68.3**	**69.7**

(1) Switzerland including Liechtenstein up to 1994.

(2) Czechoslovakia before 1993.

(4) Relates to the exteranl trade of the USSR until 1991 and from 1992 to the external trade of Russia.

IMPORTS

Ranking of EU main trading partners in 2002

Partner	Value (Mio ECU/euro)					Share (%)				
	1990	1999	2000	2001	2002	1990	1999	2000	2001	2002
Textile yarn, fabrics and related products - SITC 65										
Extra EU-15	10,014	16,069	18,904	19,178	18,270	100.0	100.0	100.0	100.0	100.0
China	797	1,417	1,987	2,048	2,231	7.9	8.8	10.5	10.6	12.2
Turkey	777	1,774	2,042	2,242	2,135	7.7	11.0	10.7	11.6	11.6
India	727	1,644	1,940	1,979	1,718	7.2	10.2	10.2	10.3	9.4
Pakistan	504	941	1,054	1,111	1,177	5.0	5.8	5.5	5.7	6.4
United States	990	1,350	1,521	1,412	1,121	9.8	8.4	8.0	7.3	6.1
Switzerland[1]	1,403	1,137	1,187	1,155	1,019	14.0	7.0	6.2	6.0	5.5
Czech Republic[2]	179	659	852	987	1,002	1.7	4.0	4.5	5.1	5.4
South Korea	360	739	937	900	840	3.5	4.5	4.9	4.6	4.5
Poland	85	454	589	658	666	0.8	2.8	3.1	3.4	3.6
Japan	701	699	738	659	566	7.0	4.3	3.9	3.4	3.0
Total for all 10	**6,525**	**10,814**	**12,847**	**13,151**	**12,476**	**65.1**	**67.2**	**67.9**	**68.5**	**68.2**
Clothing and clothing accessories - SITC 84										
Extra EU-15	19,792	43,719	51,267	53,910	53,957	100.0	100.0	100.0	100.0	100.0
China	2,054	7,407	8,860	9,472	10,332	10.3	16.9	17.2	17.5	19.1
Turkey	2,263	4,809	5,577	6,060	6,981	11.4	10.9	10.8	11.2	12.9
Romania	337	2,104	2,587	3,306	3,653	1.7	4.8	5.0	6.1	6.7
Tunisia	961	2,395	2,586	2,898	2,902	4.8	5.4	5.0	5.3	5.3
Bangladesh	236	1,781	2,571	2,796	2,710	1.1	4.0	5.0	5.1	5.0
India	1,112	2,029	2,464	2,655	2,677	5.6	4.6	4.8	4.9	4.9
Morocco	1,057	2,131	2,378	2,648	2,617	5.3	4.8	4.6	4.9	4.8
Hong Kong	2,396	2,842	3,182	2,608	2,329	12.1	6.5	6.2	4.8	4.3
Poland	507	1,810	1,852	1,954	1,733	2.5	4.1	3.6	3.6	3.2
Indonesia	448	1,440	1,851	1,816	1,492	2.2	3.2	3.6	3.3	2.7
Total for all 10	**11,371**	**28,748**	**33,908**	**36,212**	**37,426**	**57.4**	**65.7**	**66.1**	**67.1**	**69.3**
Professional, scientific, controlling material - SITC 87										
Extra EU-15	8,159	17,727	23,006	24,440	22,328	100.0	100.0	100.0	100.0	100.0
United States	4,477	9,483	12,518	13,182	11,415	54.8	53.4	54.4	53.9	51.1
Japan	1,246	2,064	2,731	2,702	2,409	15.2	11.6	11.8	11.0	10.7
Switzerland[1]	1,185	1,674	1,793	2,026	2,021	14.5	9.4	7.7	8.2	9.0
China	51	546	722	794	1,027	0.6	3.0	3.1	3.2	4.5
Hungary	12	170	288	440	472	0.1	0.9	1.2	1.8	2.1
Norway	129	345	392	419	443	1.5	1.9	1.7	1.7	1.9
Canada	114	356	615	562	432	1.3	2.0	2.6	2.3	1.9
Israel	94	387	524	567	310	1.1	2.1	2.2	2.3	1.3
Czech Republic[2]	7	178	217	296	285	0.0	1.0	0.9	1.2	1.2
Malaysia	60	140	189	240	274	0.7	0.7	0.8	0.9	1.2
Total for all 10	**7,375**	**15,343**	**19,989**	**21,227**	**19,088**	**90.3**	**86.5**	**86.8**	**86.8**	**85.4**
Photogr.apparatus, optical goods, clocks - SITC 88										
Extra EU-15	6,401	10,577	13,073	12,290	10,757	100.0	100.0	100.0	100.0	100.0
Switzerland[1]	1,572	2,426	2,789	3,050	2,885	24.5	22.9	21.3	24.8	26.8
Japan	2,253	2,326	2,865	2,608	1,995	35.1	21.9	21.9	21.2	18.5
China	184	1,470	2,012	2,014	1,948	2.8	13.8	15.3	16.3	18.1
United States	1,223	1,925	2,813	2,077	1,701	19.1	18.2	21.5	16.8	15.8
Hong Kong	531	732	665	577	477	8.3	6.9	5.0	4.6	4.4
Thailand	35	166	211	266	242	0.5	1.5	1.6	2.1	2.2
Taiwan	192	268	290	254	206	2.9	2.5	2.2	2.0	1.9
Hungary	4	44	85	113	131	0.0	0.4	0.6	0.9	1.2
South Korea	71	174	183	169	123	1.1	1.6	1.3	1.3	1.1
Indonesia	7	68	81	104	107	0.1	0.6	0.6	0.8	0.9
Total for all 10	**6,072**	**9,599**	**11,992**	**11,231**	**9,816**	**94.8**	**90.7**	**91.7**	**91.3**	**91.2**

(1) Switzerland including Liechtenstein up to 1994.
(2) Czechoslovakia before 1993.

EXTRA-EU TRADE INDICES BY PRODUCT
2000 = 100

eurostat

SITC rev. 3

Year	TOTAL	Food, beverages and tobacco	Crude materials	Energy	Manufactured products	Chemicals	Machinery and transport equipment	Other manufactured products
	0-9	0+1	2+4	3	5+6+7+8	5	7	6+8

EXPORTS
Value

Year	TOTAL	Food, beverages and tobacco	Crude materials	Energy	Manufactured products	Chemicals	Machinery and transport equipment	Other manufactured products
1990	41.3	57.3	43.9	30.7	39.6	33.8	36.5	47.9
1997	75.3	91.6	81.1	51.7	75.9	69.0	74.8	81.3
1998	78.5	87.7	77.1	46.2	78.8	74.1	78.9	80.7
1999	81.4	87.4	81.8	54.1	81.8	83.0	81.1	82.4
2000	100.0	100.0	100.0	100.0	100.0	100.0	100.0	100.0
2001	104.6	103.3	96.8	85.8	105.7	109.9	105.1	104.5
2002	105.5	105.1	105.8	87.0	106.1	117.8	102.7	105.9

Volume

Year	TOTAL	Food, beverages and tobacco	Crude materials	Energy	Manufactured products	Chemicals	Machinery and transport equipment	Other manufactured products
1990	61.4	75.2	53.3	71.5	59.1	53.9	59.7	60.2
1997	86.1	98.2	83.4	85.9	86.7	80.5	87.3	88.5
1998	88.8	94.9	82.0	95.0	88.1	84.3	89.7	86.9
1999	89.2	95.9	90.4	93.8	88.6	90.5	88.2	88.0
2000	100.0	100.0	100.0	100.0	100.0	100.0	100.0	100.0
2001	103.7	98.2	98.4	91.9	104.7	110.8	103.9	102.9
2002	105.7	101.1	108.1	95.7	106.2	121.7	102.0	105.6

Unit Value

Year	TOTAL	Food, beverages and tobacco	Crude materials	Energy	Manufactured products	Chemicals	Machinery and transport equipment	Other manufactured products
1990	67.2	76.2	82.4	42.9	67.0	62.8	61.1	79.5
1997	87.5	93.3	97.3	60.2	87.6	85.7	85.7	91.9
1998	88.4	92.4	94.0	48.6	89.4	87.9	88.0	92.9
1999	91.2	91.1	90.5	57.7	92.3	91.7	91.9	93.6
2000	100.0	100.0	100.0	100.0	100.0	100.0	100.0	100.0
2001	100.9	105.2	98.4	93.3	100.9	99.2	101.2	101.5
2002	99.8	104.0	97.8	90.9	99.9	96.8	100.7	100.3

IMPORTS
Value

Year	TOTAL	Food, beverages and tobacco	Crude materials	Energy	Manufactured products	Chemicals	Machinery and transport equipment	Other manufactured products
1990	41.1	65.4	67.3	48.3	35.2	39.1	30.5	40.8
1997	63.9	87.0	83.3	56.2	63.5	71.1	57.4	70.3
1998	69.1	90.1	84.0	43.4	71.5	77.8	67.5	75.6
1999	75.0	89.7	79.2	51.6	78.7	82.6	76.9	80.3
2000	100.0	100.0	100.0	100.0	100.0	100.0	100.0	100.0
2001	99.5	106.4	97.1	97.2	99.7	108.6	96.3	102.4
2002	95.5	107.1	90.7	92.3	95.9	113.6	90.3	99.2

Volume

Year	TOTAL	Food, beverages and tobacco	Crude materials	Energy	Manufactured products	Chemicals	Machinery and transport equipment	Other manufactured products
1990	61.3	84.2	89.0	76.6	54.9	61.6	52.9	56.5
1997	76.6	88.6	93.4	91.0	74.0	83.3	68.9	79.0
1998	87.3	92.8	96.5	95.2	84.4	89.6	82.5	86.0
1999	91.1	96.1	95.0	90.6	90.3	93.8	89.2	91.3
2000	100.0	100.0	100.0	100.0	100.0	100.0	100.0	100.0
2001	99.7	107.1	99.2	103.8	98.6	108.6	95.2	100.7
2002	98.5	110.4	95.8	104.3	96.9	118.4	90.6	100.6

Unit Value

Year	TOTAL	Food, beverages and tobacco	Crude materials	Energy	Manufactured products	Chemicals	Machinery and transport equipment	Other manufactured products
1990	67.1	77.7	75.6	63.0	64.1	63.4	57.6	72.2
1997	83.4	98.2	89.2	61.8	85.8	85.3	83.3	89.0
1998	79.2	97.1	87.0	45.6	84.7	86.8	81.8	87.9
1999	82.3	93.3	83.4	56.9	87.1	88.1	86.2	87.9
2000	100.0	100.0	100.0	100.0	100.0	100.0	100.0	100.0
2001	99.8	99.3	97.9	93.7	101.2	100.0	101.1	101.6
2002	97.0	97.0	94.6	88.5	98.9	95.9	99.7	98.6

The indices, which are manually linked, relate to reporter EU-12 until 1995 and EU-15 thereafter. They cover all the products.

EXTRA-EU TRADE INDICES BY PRODUCT
2000 = 100

SITC rev. 3

Year	TOTAL	Food, beverages and tobacco	Crude materials	Energy	Manufactured products	Chemicals	Machinery and transport equipment	Other manufactured products
	0-9	0+1	2+4	3	5+6+7+8	5	7	6+8
Cover Rate [1]								
1990	**100.4**	**87.6**	**65.2**	**63.5**	**112.5**	**86.4**	**119.6**	**117.4**
1997	117.8	105.2	97.3	91.9	119.5	97.0	130.3	115.6
1998	113.6	97.3	91.7	106.4	110.2	95.2	116.8	106.7
1999	108.5	97.4	103.2	104.8	103.9	100.4	105.4	102.6
2000	**100.0**	**100.0**	**100.0**	**100.0**	**100.0**	**100.0**	**100.0**	**100.0**
2001	105.1	97.0	99.6	88.2	106.0	101.1	109.1	102.0
2002	**110.4**	**98.1**	**116.6**	**94.2**	**110.6**	**103.6**	**113.7**	**106.7**
Volume Ratio [2]								
1990	**100.1**	**89.3**	**59.8**	**93.3**	**107.6**	**87.5**	**112.8**	**106.5**
1997	112.4	110.8	89.2	94.3	117.1	96.6	126.7	112.0
1998	101.7	102.2	84.9	99.7	104.3	94.0	108.7	101.0
1999	97.9	99.7	95.1	103.5	98.1	96.4	98.8	96.3
2000	**100.0**	**100.0**	**100.0**	**100.0**	**100.0**	**100.0**	**100.0**	**100.0**
2001	104.0	91.6	99.1	88.5	106.1	102.0	109.1	102.1
2002	**107.3**	**91.5**	**112.8**	**91.7**	**109.5**	**102.7**	**112.5**	**104.9**
Terms of Trade [3]								
1990	**100.1**	**98.0**	**108.9**	**68.0**	**104.5**	**99.0**	**106.0**	**110.1**
1997	104.9	95.0	109.0	97.4	102.0	100.4	102.8	103.2
1998	111.6	95.1	108.0	106.5	105.5	101.2	107.5	105.6
1999	110.8	97.6	108.5	101.4	105.9	104.0	106.6	106.4
2000	**100.0**	**100.0**	**100.0**	**100.0**	**100.0**	**100.0**	**100.0**	**100.0**
2001	101.1	105.9	100.5	99.5	99.7	99.2	100.0	99.9
2002	**102.8**	**107.2**	**103.3**	**102.7**	**101.0**	**100.9**	**101.0**	**101.7**

(1) Cover rate is the export value index divided by the import value index.
(2) Volume ratio is the export volume index divided by the import volume index.
(3) Terms of trade is the unit value export index divided by the unit value import index.

TRENDS IN INTRA-EU TRADE BY PRODUCT

eurostat

EXPORTS / DISPATCHES

Product list	Values (Mio ECU/Euro)					Annual variation (%)					% of total	
SITC rev. 3	1990	1999	2000	2001	2002	90/89	99/98	00/99	01/00	02/01	1990	2002
0-9 TOTAL	715,622	1,339,172	1,565,494	1,599,940	1,596,766	4.6	6.3	16.9	2.2	-0.1	100.0	100.0
0 Food and live animals	66,485	107,040	116,200	122,165	122,317	1.8	1.5	8.5	5.1	0.1	9.2	7.6
00 Live animals	3,034	3,467	3,929	3,375	3,608	-9.9	3.8	13.3	-14.0	6.8	0.4	0.2
01 Meat and meat preparations	12,705	16,656	18,773	19,808	19,239	1.9	0.5	12.7	5.5	-2.8	1.7	1.2
02 Dairy products and birds'eggs	10,036	15,460	16,634	17,795	16,373	-8.6	0.3	7.5	6.9	-7.9	1.4	1.0
03 Fish, crustaceans, molluscs	4,746	9,027	9,934	10,460	10,407	10.8	7.4	10.0	5.2	-0.5	0.6	0.6
04 Cereals and cereal preparations	8,809	12,424	13,119	13,513	13,765	8.8	2.1	5.5	3.0	1.8	1.2	0.8
05 Vegetables and fruit	14,903	25,159	26,439	28,361	28,733	7.9	0.8	5.0	7.2	1.3	2.0	1.7
06 Sugar, sugar preparations, honey	2,009	3,932	4,167	4,013	4,449	-18.0	4.1	5.9	-3.6	10.8	0.2	0.2
07 Coffee, tea, cocoa, spices	3,424	6,964	7,269	7,397	7,934	0.2	-1.4	4.3	1.7	7.2	0.4	0.4
08 Feeding stuff for animals	3,535	5,104	5,581	6,049	6,198	-2.9	-2.1	9.3	8.4	2.4	0.4	0.3
1 Beverages and tobacco	10,354	20,560	21,592	22,663	23,656	10.1	12.5	5.0	4.9	4.3	1.4	1.4
11 Beverages	7,633	14,326	14,775	15,415	15,756	9.7	11.4	3.1	4.3	2.2	1.0	0.9
12 Tobacco	2,722	5,824	6,456	6,772	7,643	11.1	13.3	10.8	4.9	12.8	0.3	0.4
2 Crude materials, except fuels	22,698	34,690	42,450	40,310	39,513	-7.9	-1.6	22.3	-5.0	-1.9	3.1	2.4
21 Hides and skins, raw	1,259	1,204	1,537	1,600	1,478	-14.5	-10.0	27.6	4.0	-7.6	0.1	0.0
22 Oil seeds and oleaginous fruits	1,582	1,154	1,284	1,424	1,398	-1.2	-29.1	11.1	10.8	-1.8	0.2	0.0
23 Crude rubber	1,241	1,545	1,857	1,846	1,683	4.4	-11.3	20.2	-0.6	-8.8	0.1	0.1
24 Cork and wood	2,134	6,167	6,984	6,409	6,386	4.5	4.1	13.2	-8.2	-0.3	0.2	0.3
25 Pulp and waste paper	1,539	3,544	5,888	4,560	4,243	-15.2	9.4	66.1	-22.5	-6.9	0.2	0.2
26 Textile fibres and their wastes	2,677	2,304	2,686	2,527	2,451	-10.8	-18.9	16.5	-5.9	-3.0	0.3	0.1
27 Crude fertilizers	2,370	3,378	3,739	3,644	3,536	0.3	2.3	10.7	-2.5	-2.9	0.3	0.2
28 Metalliferous ores and metal scrap	4,993	5,981	8,079	7,795	7,537	-23.4	-6.5	35.0	-3.5	-3.3	0.6	0.4
3 Energy	25,718	39,136	67,391	66,527	63,969	10.8	28.3	72.1	-1.2	-3.8	3.5	4.0
32 Coal, coke and briquettes	1,603	1,063	1,241	1,708	1,588	-5.6	-49.8	16.7	37.6	-7.0	0.2	0.0
33 Petroleum and petroleum products	19,337	29,602	54,321	49,575	47,259	10.2	38.1	83.5	-8.7	-4.6	2.7	2.9
34 Gas, natural and manufactured	3,162	5,009	8,104	10,521	10,209	21.2	25.7	61.7	29.8	-2.9	0.4	0.6
35 Electric current	1,615	3,108	3,487	4,218	4,723	19.4	10.9	12.1	20.9	11.9	0.2	0.2
4 Oils, fats and waxes	2,613	4,892	4,582	4,990	5,538	1.4	-4.7	-6.3	8.8	10.9	0.3	0.3
41 Animal oils and fats	322	394	396	389	452	-6.7	-18.7	0.5	-1.9	16.2	0.0	0.0
42 Fixed vegetable fats and oils	1,791	3,387	3,010	3,426	3,871	6.6	-2.8	-11.1	13.8	12.9	0.2	0.2
43 Animal or vegetable oils, and fats, waxes	500	999	1,009	1,001	1,104	-9.0	-7.0	1.0	-0.8	10.3	0.0	0.0
5 Chemical products	79,919	168,992	201,925	215,674	231,541	4.9	4.5	19.4	6.8	7.3	11.1	14.5
51 Organic chemicals	17,550	35,814	45,715	44,585	45,836	-2.8	0.7	27.6	-2.4	2.8	2.4	2.8
52 Inorganic chemicals	5,011	7,547	9,500	10,206	8,949	4.1	-0.2	25.8	7.4	-12.3	0.7	0.5
53 Tanning and colouring materials	5,643	9,965	11,151	11,137	11,186	9.4	2.4	11.8	-0.1	0.4	0.7	0.7
54 Medicinal and pharmaceutical products	8,375	33,653	39,150	52,586	68,943	12.2	15.9	16.3	34.3	31.1	1.1	4.3
55 Essential oils, perfume mat., cosmetics	6,546	16,016	17,623	19,094	20,557	14.0	9.2	10.0	8.3	7.6	0.9	1.2
56 Fertilizers	1,900	2,393	2,325	2,232	2,144	-3.9	-7.3	-2.8	-4.0	-3.9	0.2	0.1
57 Plastics in primary forms	16,654	26,673	33,587	32,779	30,866	4.3	3.2	25.9	-2.4	-5.8	2.3	1.9
58 Plastics in non-primary forms	7,902	14,672	16,377	16,165	16,215	7.7	-5.8	11.6	-1.2	0.3	1.1	1.0
6 Manufactured goods classif. by material	134,658	215,448	249,081	245,766	238,208	2.3	-0.7	15.6	-1.3	-3.0	18.8	14.9
61 Leather manufactures, dressed furskins	2,442	2,662	3,158	3,370	2,982	-3.2	-9.1	18.6	6.7	-11.5	0.3	0.1
62 Rubber manufactures	7,709	13,744	14,629	14,624	14,596	3.6	1.2	6.4	0.0	-0.1	1.0	0.9
63 Cork and wood manufactures	3,611	8,118	9,010	9,056	8,914	7.1	6.1	10.9	0.5	-1.5	0.5	0.5
64 Paper, paperboard and articles thereof	14,855	35,736	41,981	41,353	40,796	7.7	2.7	17.4	-1.4	-1.3	2.0	2.5
65 Textile yarn, fabrics and related products	25,766	31,862	33,870	32,847	30,758	6.1	-5.0	6.3	-3.0	-6.3	3.6	1.9
66 Non-metallic mineral manufactures	16,668	25,093	27,236	26,747	26,630	6.0	6.7	8.5	-1.7	-0.4	2.3	1.6
67 Iron and steel	28,441	38,252	47,434	45,214	45,069	-1.7	-9.5	24.0	-4.6	-0.3	3.9	2.8
68 Non-ferrous metals	14,738	22,396	29,330	28,873	25,970	-13.3	-2.5	30.9	-1.5	-10.0	2.0	1.6
69 Manufactures of metals	20,392	37,557	42,412	43,653	42,472	9.9	5.2	12.9	2.9	-2.7	2.8	2.6
7 Machinery and transport equipment	262,580	561,993	658,546	669,665	640,739	6.2	9.0	17.1	1.6	-4.3	36.6	40.1
71 Power generating machinery and equipment	14,727	35,150	37,361	40,353	40,569	3.8	10.2	6.2	8.0	0.5	2.0	2.5
72 Machinery specialized for particular ind.	24,637	35,864	38,919	38,548	36,015	3.5	4.9	8.5	-0.9	-6.5	3.4	2.2
73 Metalworking machinery	6,446	8,029	9,275	9,433	7,907	15.4	0.1	15.5	1.7	-16.1	0.9	0.4
74 General industry machinery and equipment	32,194	60,127	66,650	68,092	66,490	9.3	5.2	10.8	2.1	-2.3	4.4	4.1
75 Office machines and computers	28,237	73,036	86,101	82,706	72,499	1.3	9.9	17.8	-3.9	-12.3	3.9	4.5
76 Telecommunication, sound, TV, video	12,642	50,908	68,481	65,319	60,747	15.6	20.3	34.5	-4.6	-6.9	1.7	3.8
77 Electrical machinery	34,825	82,459	105,330	103,065	96,504	5.9	6.6	27.7	-2.1	-6.3	4.8	6.0
78 Road vehicles	90,630	178,477	195,353	204,308	207,943	8.7	7.5	9.4	4.5	1.7	12.6	13.0
79 Other transport equipment	18,012	37,570	50,697	57,647	51,773	-4.9	17.4	34.9	13.7	-10.1	2.5	3.2
8 Miscellaneous manuf. articles	87,566	154,330	171,580	177,585	175,139	10.4	5.4	11.1	3.4	-1.3	12.2	10.9
81 Prefabr. buildings, sanitary, heating, lighting	3,738	7,406	7,903	7,668	7,535	10.8	5.9	6.7	-2.9	-1.7	0.5	0.4
82 Furniture, bedding, mattresses	9,783	16,782	18,604	18,867	18,179	11.4	5.3	10.8	1.4	-3.6	1.3	1.1
83 Travel goods, handbags and similar goods	990	1,860	2,161	2,331	2,363	11.2	11.1	16.2	7.8	1.3	0.1	0.1
84 Clothing and clothing accessories	21,926	33,441	35,544	36,393	36,273	13.2	1.4	6.2	2.3	-0.3	3.0	2.2
85 Footwear	6,866	11,126	11,916	12,947	12,630	9.3	3.8	7.1	8.6	-2.4	0.9	0.7
87 Professional, scientific, controlling material	10,592	21,456	24,842	26,460	26,030	6.0	8.4	15.7	6.5	-1.6	1.4	1.6
88 Photogr. apparatus, optical goods, clocks	5,978	10,207	11,854	11,510	10,508	1.0	5.4	16.1	-2.9	-8.7	0.8	0.6
89 Miscellaneous manufactured articles	27,689	52,043	58,745	61,397	61,615	12.1	7.1	12.8	4.5	0.3	3.8	3.8
9 Articles non classified elsewhere	23,031	32,090	32,146	34,597	54,053	-6.4	34.0	0.1	7.6	56.2	3.2	3.3

INTRA-EU TRADE INDICES BY PRODUCT

2000 = 100

4B

EXPORTS/DISPATCHES

SITC rev. 3

Year	TOTAL	Food, beverages and tobacco	Crude materials	Energy	Manufactured products	Chemicals	Machinery and transport equipment	Other manufactured products
	0-9(1)	0+1	2+4	3	5+6+7+8	5	7	6+8
Value								
1990	50.5	58.0	68.5	38.8	49.2	42.5	44.0	61.1
1993	50.9	66.6	58.8	38.4	49.2	47.3	43.4	59.6
1994	57.9	73.3	72.8	41.0	56.9	57.1	50.5	67.2
1995	63.2	76.6	78.1	40.9	63.2	64.5	56.4	73.5
1996	63.9	80.8	73.3	52.6	62.9	62.3	58.2	70.8
1997	74.7	82.8	81.8	54.2	72.8	72.8	68.3	80.2
1998	80.3	86.1	80.1	43.4	79.8	79.0	77.2	84.6
1999	84.8	91.3	83.1	55.3	85.4	84.2	84.6	87.5
2000	**100.0**	**100.0**	**100.0**	**100.0**	**100.0**	**100.0**	**100.0**	**100.0**
2001	102.2	105.2	96.5	98.7	102.2	106.8	101.7	100.7
2002	**102.0**	**106.0**	**96.1**	**94.5**	**100.4**	**114.8**	**97.3**	**98.3**
Volume								
1990	67.5	66.4	82.2	71.4	66.8	60.2	63.1	75.5
1993	63.9	75.2	76.2	77.8	61.3	66.4	53.1	71.8
1994	70.3	81.2	85.1	87.6	68.5	76.4	59.9	78.1
1995	72.7	82.2	82.2	85.3	71.7	77.8	65.0	79.4
1996	72.4	85.4	81.0	93.6	70.6	76.5	65.0	76.6
1997	82.8	86.8	86.7	89.7	80.1	85.9	74.4	86.1
1998	89.1	90.6	87.3	90.0	87.0	91.1	84.2	89.3
1999	92.9	95.4	93.8	93.1	92.2	97.2	90.2	92.8
2000	**100.0**	**100.0**	**100.0**	**100.0**	**100.0**	**100.0**	**100.0**	**100.0**
2001	100.7	101.5	98.1	102.3	100.6	105.4	100.3	98.8
2002	**100.4**	**102.2**	**96.1**	**104.5**	**98.5**	**114.6**	**95.0**	**96.3**
Unit Value								
1990	74.8	87.4	83.3	54.4	73.7	70.6	69.7	80.9
1993	79.6	88.6	77.2	49.4	80.2	71.3	81.8	83.0
1994	82.3	90.3	85.5	46.8	83.1	74.8	84.3	86.0
1995	87.0	93.2	95.0	47.9	88.1	82.9	86.8	92.6
1996	88.3	94.6	90.5	56.2	89.1	81.4	89.6	92.4
1997	90.2	95.4	94.3	60.4	90.9	84.7	91.8	93.1
1998	90.1	95.0	91.8	48.2	91.7	86.7	91.7	94.7
1999	91.3	95.7	88.6	59.4	92.6	86.6	93.8	94.3
2000	**100.0**	**100.0**	**100.0**	**100.0**	**100.0**	**100.0**	**100.0**	**100.0**
2001	101.5	103.6	98.3	96.5	101.6	101.4	101.4	101.9
2002	**101.6**	**103.7**	**100.0**	**90.4**	**101.9**	**100.2**	**102.4**	**102.1**

(1) Adjustements included.

The indices, which are annually linked, relate to reporter EU-12 until 1995 and EU-15 thereafter.

INTRA-EU + EXTRA-EU (1)

Value (Mio ECU/Euro)

Year	B(2)	DK	D	EL	E	F	IRL	I	L	NL	A	P	FIN	S	UK
1980	-5,154	-1,911	3,545	-3,887	-9,368	-16,951	-1,897	-15,698	:	-2,184	-4,963	-3,310	-1,027	-1,689	-3,592
1990	-6,203	2,423	43,678	-9,349	-20,525	-16,739	2,334	-9,261	:	-1,124	-6,390	-6,668	-287	2,252	-32,015
1993	8,324	5,504	32,011	-11,589	-11,035	3,644	6,687	18,048	:	10,536	-7,175	-7,501	4,670	6,154	-23,858
1994	11,982	4,752	38,290	-10,175	-10,228	3,842	7,049	18,660	:	8,799	-8,665	-7,626	5,413	7,411	-24,378
1995	10,782	3,797	45,557	-11,349	-11,994	9,000	9,453	21,235	:	13,555	-6,498	-7,513	8,425	11,777	-22,398
1996	8,854	4,823	51,625	-13,016	-11,008	8,623	11,041	34,676	:	14,236	-8,099	-8,336	7,640	14,165	-22,685
1997	11,675	3,854	59,222	-13,751	-13,151	15,093	13,757	26,703	:	15,080	-5,251	-9,788	8,694	15,132	-23,908
1998	11,521	1,909	64,471	-17,327	-22,022	11,471	18,855	24,383	:	16,357	-4,834	-12,168	9,626	14,597	-42,175
1999	13,456	4,262	65,202	-18,258	-29,004	9,174	22,959	14,005	-2,829	11,651	-4,935	-14,480	9,504	15,302	-49,477
2000	11,758	6,210	59,130	-22,566	-44,274	-12,266	28,553	1,907	-3,140	16,092	-5,071	-16,878	12,624	15,432	-63,177
2001	13,047	7,127	95,495	-20,080	-42,419	-5,839	36,041	9,183	-2,872	24,807	-4,334	-16,731	11,834	13,896	-67,316
2002	17,511	8,046	126,226	-22,118	-37,609	2,598	38,395	8,478	-3,093	26,220	395	-13,545	11,556	15,504	-69,773

INTRA-EU

Value (Mio ECU/Euro)

Year	B(2)	DK	D	EL	E	F	IRL	I	L	NL	A	P	FIN	S	UK
1980	2,403	-1,442	9,215	-1,547	-73	-6,381	-1,473	-4,393	:	8,747	-3,934	-1,061	455	-1,222	1,624
1990	-206	1,403	32,739	-6,307	-10,353	-16,243	2,594	-4,651	:	17,259	-5,609	-3,637	-138	974	-16,860
1993	10,692	2,759	17,278	-7,596	-7,563	-6,453	5,793	7,249	:	22,324	-6,269	-4,876	2,728	2,342	-7,394
1994	11,833	1,731	18,209	-7,760	-6,641	-7,045	6,793	6,265	:	27,891	-7,271	-4,623	3,814	2,668	-8,091
1995	13,788	700	18,604	-8,799	-8,640	-6,438	9,296	6,538	:	34,512	-9,403	-4,484	3,140	2,503	-5,512
1996	11,977	1,813	18,998	-9,352	-8,841	-7,365	9,106	9,972	:	39,079	-10,724	-5,529	1,500	2,078	-5,454
1997	13,552	1,033	18,647	-10,354	-6,558	-417	11,101	3,430	:	46,341	-9,872	-6,512	1,519	1,369	-8,480
1998	16,545	-363	25,976	-12,516	-15,117	-7,081	16,033	3,766	:	49,212	-8,990	-8,651	2,569	1,583	-11,192
1999	19,499	1,632	36,258	-13,546	-17,434	-7,092	17,053	1,407	-2,023	56,348	-9,407	-10,139	3,191	2,944	-12,528
2000	19,860	3,497	42,042	-15,128	-24,637	-20,434	18,628	-2,160	-2,456	77,722	-8,947	-11,320	4,698	2,120	-7,759
2001	21,635	3,408	51,513	-12,322	-22,687	-19,632	21,259	-2,214	-1,534	82,523	-8,188	-11,179	2,787	-135	-10,767
2002	16,341	2,866	64,961	-12,457	-18,744	-14,576	24,214	-5,051	-1,642	76,765	-4,680	-9,693	2,331	-55	-18,106

EXTRA-EU

Value (Mio ECU/Euro)

Year	EU	B(2)	DK	D	EL	E	F	IRL	I	L	NL	A	P	FIN	S	UK
1980	-69,006	-7,557	-469	-5,670	-2,341	-9,295	-10,569	-425	-11,305	:	-10,931	-1,029	-2,249	-1,481	-467	-5,216
1990	-49,187	-5,997	1,020	10,939	-3,042	-10,172	-496	-260	-4,611	:	-18,383	-780	-3,031	-149	1,277	-15,155
1993	-1,442	-2,368	2,745	14,733	-3,993	-3,472	10,097	895	10,799	:	-11,788	-906	-2,625	1,942	3,811	-16,464
1994	2,405	149	3,021	20,081	-2,415	-3,587	10,887	256	12,395	:	-19,092	-1,394	-3,003	1,598	4,743	-16,287
1995	28,024	-3,006	3,097	26,953	-2,550	-3,355	15,438	158	14,697	:	-20,957	2,905	-3,029	5,285	9,274	-16,886
1996	45,279	-3,123	3,010	32,627	-3,664	-2,167	15,987	1,935	24,703	:	-24,843	2,625	-2,806	6,140	12,087	-17,232
1997	48,561	-1,877	2,821	40,574	-3,397	-6,594	15,510	2,656	23,273	:	-31,262	4,621	-3,276	7,175	13,764	-15,428
1998	22,890	-5,024	2,272	38,495	-4,812	-6,905	18,552	2,822	20,617	:	-32,855	4,156	-3,518	7,057	13,014	-30,982
1999	-19,633	-6,042	2,630	28,944	-4,713	-11,571	16,266	5,906	12,598	-806	-44,697	4,472	-4,341	6,313	12,358	-36,950
2000	-91,391	-8,102	2,713	17,088	-7,438	-19,637	8,168	9,926	4,067	-684	-61,630	3,876	-5,558	7,927	13,312	-55,418
2001	-42,629	-8,588	3,719	43,982	-7,758	-19,732	13,793	14,783	11,397	-1,339	-57,716	3,854	-5,552	9,046	14,031	-56,549
2002	6,317	1,170	5,180	61,265	-9,661	-18,865	17,174	14,181	13,529	-1,451	-50,544	5,075	-3,852	9,225	15,558	-51,667

(1)   Intra-EU and extra-EU statistics are collected using different methodologies since 1993 when INTRASTAT, the new system for statistics on trade exchanges between Member States, was introduced.

(2)   With Luxembourg until 1998.

Years	Reporter															
	EU	B(1)	DK	D	EL	E	F	IRL	I	L	NL	A	P	FIN	S	UK

EXPORTS / DISPATCHES
Value (Mio ECU/Euro)

1980	330,655	35,279	8,214	83,925	1,876	8,107	46,465	4,767	31,278	:	40,832	7,658	2,185	5,926	13,214	40,929
1990	715,622	72,850	19,094	199,231	4,242	30,869	114,108	14,513	83,566	:	85,189	22,315	10,261	12,652	28,008	81,698
1993	728,498	81,388	21,280	189,958	4,247	35,498	117,662	17,922	82,566	:	79,569	22,473	10,529	11,496	25,102	87,879
1994	825,777	89,127	23,089	208,169	4,516	42,970	133,624	20,994	92,528	:	99,445	24,543	12,092	14,575	26,907	99,224
1995	1,000,279	100,674	25,922	232,722	5,080	50,827	145,033	25,274	102,384	:	109,016	29,036	13,952	17,787	36,629	105,945
1996	1,068,952	105,290	26,981	237,061	4,975	57,287	150,299	27,110	110,161	:	131,647	29,405	15,623	17,651	38,196	117,268
1997	1,165,121	113,166	28,840	251,249	5,078	60,718	165,256	32,413	116,528	:	144,870	32,692	17,071	19,457	40,549	137,233
1998	1,258,920	123,724	29,050	274,108	5,216	71,002	178,385	39,777	124,669	:	150,659	36,686	18,135	21,889	43,815	141,805
1999	1,339,172	128,352	31,599	293,371	5,603	69,772	190,889	44,131	128,693	6,574	163,010	38,998	19,161	22,888	46,495	149,637
2000	1,565,494	151,813	37,164	337,380	5,698	87,666	219,074	53,008	144,411	7,636	198,566	44,985	21,173	27,780	52,772	176,370
2001	1,599,940	160,262	37,915	351,612	4,680	92,976	219,565	58,350	144,731	9,369	202,878	48,609	21,893	25,925	46,132	175,045
2002	1,596,766	164,305	39,974	354,792	4,791	87,949	215,411	60,746	141,106	9,263	199,383	51,087	21,576	25,717	46,419	174,245

Annual variation (%)

98/97	8.0	9.3	0.7	9.0	2.7	16.9	7.9	22.7	6.9	:	3.9	12.2	6.2	12.5	8.0	3.3
99/98	6.3	3.7	8.7	7.0	7.4	-1.7	7.0	10.9	3.2	:	8.1	6.3	5.6	4.5	6.1	5.5
00/99	16.9	18.2	17.6	15.0	1.6	25.6	14.7	20.1	12.2	16.1	21.8	15.3	10.5	21.3	13.5	17.8
01/00	2.2	5.5	2.0	4.2	-17.8	6.0	0.2	10.0	0.2	22.6	2.1	8.0	3.4	-6.6	-12.5	-0.7
02/01	-0.1	2.5	5.4	0.9	2.3	-5.4	-1.8	4.1	-2.5	-1.1	-1.7	5.0	-1.4	-0.7	0.6	-0.4

Share (%)

1980	100.0	10.6	2.4	25.3	0.5	2.4	14.0	1.4	9.4	:	12.3	2.3	0.6	1.7	3.9	12.3
1990	100.0	10.1	2.6	27.8	0.5	4.3	15.9	2.0	11.6	:	11.9	3.1	1.4	1.7	3.9	11.4
1996	100.0	9.8	2.5	22.1	0.4	5.3	14.0	2.5	10.3	:	12.3	2.7	1.4	1.6	3.5	10.9
1997	100.0	9.7	2.4	21.5	0.4	5.2	14.1	2.7	10.0	:	12.4	2.8	1.4	1.6	3.4	11.7
1998	100.0	9.8	2.3	21.7	0.4	5.6	14.1	3.1	9.9	:	11.9	2.9	1.4	1.7	3.4	11.2
1999	100.0	9.5	2.3	21.9	0.4	5.2	14.2	3.2	9.6	0.4	12.1	2.9	1.4	1.7	3.4	11.1
2000	100.0	9.6	2.3	21.5	0.3	5.5	13.9	3.3	9.2	0.4	12.6	2.8	1.3	1.7	3.3	11.2
2001	100.0	10.0	2.3	21.9	0.2	5.8	13.7	3.6	9.0	0.5	12.6	3.0	1.3	1.6	2.8	10.9
2002	100.0	10.2	2.5	22.2	0.3	5.5	13.4	3.8	8.8	0.5	12.4	3.1	1.3	1.6	2.9	10.9

IMPORTS / ARRIVALS
Value (Mio ECU/Euro)

1980	329,735	32,875	9,656	74,710	3,423	8,180	52,847	6,240	35,670	:	32,085	11,592	3,246	5,471	14,436	39,305
1990	719,885	73,056	17,691	166,492	10,549	41,222	130,351	11,919	88,217	:	67,931	27,924	13,898	12,790	27,033	98,559
1993	696,285	70,697	18,521	172,679	11,843	43,061	124,115	12,129	75,317	:	57,246	28,742	15,406	8,767	22,759	95,272
1994	787,216	77,294	21,359	189,960	12,276	49,611	140,669	14,202	86,263	:	71,553	31,814	16,716	10,760	24,239	107,315
1995	954,473	86,886	25,221	214,119	13,879	59,467	151,471	15,978	95,845	:	74,504	38,439	18,436	14,647	34,125	111,457
1996	1,021,693	93,313	25,169	218,063	14,328	66,128	157,663	18,004	100,188	:	92,568	40,129	21,152	16,150	36,118	122,722
1997	1,110,321	99,614	27,807	232,601	15,432	67,275	165,673	21,312	113,098	:	98,528	42,564	23,583	17,938	39,180	145,714
1998	1,207,146	107,179	29,414	248,132	17,732	86,119	185,466	23,744	120,903	:	101,447	45,676	26,786	19,320	42,232	152,998
1999	1,273,006	108,853	29,967	257,113	19,148	87,205	197,981	27,078	127,285	8,597	106,662	48,405	29,300	19,697	43,551	162,164
2000	1,489,770	131,953	33,667	295,338	20,826	112,303	239,508	34,380	146,571	10,092	120,844	53,932	32,494	23,082	50,652	184,129
2001	1,505,472	138,626	34,508	300,100	17,002	115,662	239,197	37,091	146,945	10,902	120,354	56,797	33,072	23,137	46,267	185,812
2002	1,494,292	147,964	37,108	289,831	17,248	106,693	229,987	36,532	146,157	10,905	122,618	55,767	31,270	23,387	46,474	192,351

Annual variation (%)

98/97	8.7	7.5	5.7	6.6	14.9	28.0	11.9	11.4	6.9	:	2.9	7.3	13.5	7.7	7.7	4.9
99/98	5.4	1.5	1.8	3.6	7.9	1.2	6.7	14.0	5.2	:	5.1	5.9	9.3	1.9	3.1	5.9
00/99	17.0	21.2	12.3	14.8	8.7	28.7	20.9	26.9	15.1	17.3	13.2	11.4	10.9	17.1	16.3	13.5
01/00	1.0	5.0	2.4	1.6	-18.3	2.9	-0.1	7.8	0.2	8.0	-0.4	5.3	1.7	0.2	-8.6	0.9
02/01	-0.7	6.7	7.5	-3.4	1.4	-7.7	-3.8	-1.5	-0.5	0.0	1.8	-1.8	-5.4	1.0	0.4	3.5

Share (%)

1980	100.0	9.9	2.9	22.6	1.0	2.4	16.0	1.8	10.8	:	9.7	3.5	0.9	1.6	4.3	11.9
1990	100.0	10.1	2.4	23.1	1.4	5.7	18.1	1.6	12.2	:	9.4	3.8	1.9	1.7	3.7	13.6
1996	100.0	9.1	2.4	21.3	1.4	6.4	15.4	1.7	9.8	:	9.0	3.9	2.0	1.5	3.5	12.0
1997	100.0	8.9	2.5	20.9	1.3	6.0	14.9	1.9	10.1	:	8.8	3.8	2.1	1.6	3.5	13.1
1998	100.0	8.8	2.4	20.5	1.4	7.1	15.3	1.9	10.0	:	8.4	3.7	2.2	1.6	3.4	12.6
1999	100.0	8.5	2.3	20.1	1.5	6.8	15.5	2.1	9.9	0.6	8.3	3.8	2.3	1.5	3.4	12.7
2000	100.0	8.8	2.2	19.8	1.3	7.5	16.0	2.3	9.8	0.6	8.1	3.6	2.1	1.5	3.3	12.3
2001	100.0	9.2	2.2	19.9	1.1	7.6	15.8	2.4	9.7	0.7	7.9	3.7	2.1	1.5	3.0	12.3
2002	100.0	9.9	2.4	19.3	1.1	7.1	15.3	2.4	9.7	0.7	8.2	3.7	2.0	1.5	3.1	12.8

(1)   With Luxembourg until 1998.

Year								Reporter								
	EU	B(1)	DK	D	EL	E	F	IRL	I	L	NL	A	P	FIN	S	UK

EXPORTS
Value (Mio ECU/Euro)

Year	EU	B(1)	DK	D	EL	E	F	IRL	I	L	NL	A	P	FIN	S	UK
1980	212,111	11,180	3,981	54,862	1,883	7,168	33,686	1,333	24,838	:	12,353	5,009	1,231	4,295	9,163	41,131
1990	355,164	19,399	8,818	112,669	1,995	14,789	60,532	3,957	49,578	:	20,292	10,573	2,376	8,348	17,094	60,760
1993	430,247	25,265	10,960	134,633	2,962	19,671	71,594	6,836	61,951	:	26,713	11,821	2,645	8,575	17,476	67,016
1994	476,689	29,958	12,508	150,745	3,389	21,507	77,025	7,586	68,346	:	29,414	13,310	3,031	10,352	20,900	73,181
1995	573,277	31,257	12,997	167,474	3,371	23,980	85,212	8,904	76,335	:	31,161	15,106	3,467	13,168	24,870	75,975
1996	626,294	32,512	13,511	176,130	4,247	27,173	90,307	10,960	88,534	:	32,952	16,448	3,765	14,737	28,680	86,337
1997	721,128	39,143	14,609	201,020	4,908	28,129	101,175	14,629	95,470	:	38,398	20,026	4,053	17,112	32,426	110,029
1998	733,428	38,538	14,668	210,913	4,478	28,877	107,615	17,605	94,582	:	40,206	20,477	3,980	17,137	31,797	102,554
1999	760,192	39,740	15,592	216,611	4,784	28,214	114,540	22,710	92,328	1,123	42,075	22,984	3,865	16,747	33,154	105,727
2000	942,044	52,140	18,372	260,076	6,705	37,119	135,637	30,809	116,002	1,435	53,848	28,327	5,205	22,136	41,568	132,666
2001	985,326	52,276	19,817	286,669	6,747	37,283	141,510	34,142	124,504	1,528	54,888	30,390	5,429	22,352	38,330	129,461
2002	993,796	61,919	20,358	293,454	6,155	38,013	135,392	32,659	124,259	1,551	58,717	32,112	5,528	22,025	39,638	122,017

Annual variation (%)

Year	EU	B(1)	DK	D	EL	E	F	IRL	I	L	NL	A	P	FIN	S	UK
98/97	1.7	-1.5	0.4	4.9	-8.7	2.6	6.3	20.3	-0.9	:	4.7	2.2	-1.7	0.1	-1.9	-6.7
99/98	3.6	3.1	6.2	2.7	6.8	-2.2	6.4	29.0	-2.3	:	4.6	12.2	-2.8	-2.2	4.2	3.0
00/99	23.9	31.2	17.8	20.0	40.1	31.5	18.4	35.6	25.6	27.8	27.9	23.2	34.6	32.1	25.3	25.4
01/00	4.5	0.2	7.8	10.2	0.6	0.4	4.3	10.8	7.3	6.4	1.9	7.2	4.3	0.9	-7.7	-2.4
02/01	0.8	18.4	2.7	2.3	-8.7	1.9	-4.3	-4.3	-0.1	1.5	6.9	5.6	1.8	-1.4	3.4	-5.7

Share (%)

Year	EU	B(1)	DK	D	EL	E	F	IRL	I	L	NL	A	P	FIN	S	UK
1980	100.0	5.2	1.8	25.8	0.8	3.3	15.8	0.6	11.7	:	5.8	2.3	0.5	2.0	4.3	19.3
1990	100.0	5.4	2.4	31.7	0.5	4.1	17.0	1.1	13.9	:	5.7	2.9	0.6	2.3	4.8	17.1
1996	100.0	5.1	2.1	28.1	0.6	4.3	14.4	1.7	14.1	:	5.2	2.6	0.6	2.3	4.5	13.7
1997	100.0	5.4	2.0	27.8	0.6	3.9	14.0	2.0	13.2	:	5.3	2.7	0.5	2.3	4.4	15.2
1998	100.0	5.2	1.9	28.7	0.6	3.9	14.6	2.4	12.8	:	5.4	2.7	0.5	2.3	4.3	13.9
1999	100.0	5.2	2.0	28.4	0.6	3.7	15.0	2.9	12.1	0.1	5.5	3.0	0.5	2.2	4.3	13.9
2000	100.0	5.5	1.9	27.6	0.7	3.9	14.3	3.2	12.3	0.1	5.7	3.0	0.5	2.3	4.4	14.0
2001	100.0	5.3	2.0	29.0	0.6	3.7	14.3	3.4	12.6	0.1	5.5	3.0	0.5	2.2	3.8	13.1
2002	100.0	6.2	2.0	29.5	0.6	3.8	13.6	3.2	12.5	0.1	5.9	3.2	0.5	2.2	3.9	12.2

IMPORTS
Value (Mio ECU/Euro)

Year	EU	B(1)	DK	D	EL	E	F	IRL	I	L	NL	A	P	FIN	S	UK
1980	281,117	18,737	4,450	60,532	4,223	16,463	44,256	1,758	36,143	:	23,284	6,038	3,480	5,776	9,630	46,347
1990	404,351	25,396	7,798	101,730	5,036	24,961	61,029	4,217	54,189	:	38,675	11,354	5,406	8,498	15,817	75,915
1993	431,689	27,633	8,216	119,900	6,956	23,143	61,496	5,942	51,152	:	38,501	12,728	5,271	6,633	13,665	83,480
1994	474,284	29,809	9,487	130,664	5,805	25,094	66,139	7,329	55,951	:	48,506	14,704	6,034	8,754	16,157	89,468
1995	545,253	34,263	9,900	140,521	5,921	27,335	69,774	8,746	61,638	:	52,118	12,201	6,495	7,883	15,596	92,861
1996	581,015	35,635	10,501	143,503	7,912	29,341	74,319	9,025	63,831	:	57,795	13,823	6,572	8,596	16,593	103,569
1997	672,568	41,020	11,788	160,446	8,306	34,723	85,665	11,974	72,197	:	69,659	15,405	7,328	9,937	18,663	125,457
1998	710,538	43,563	12,396	172,418	9,289	35,782	89,062	14,782	73,965	:	73,061	16,321	7,498	10,080	18,783	133,537
1999	779,825	45,782	12,962	187,667	9,496	39,785	98,274	16,804	79,730	1,928	86,772	18,512	8,206	10,435	20,795	142,676
2000	1,033,436	60,242	15,659	242,987	14,142	56,756	127,469	20,883	111,935	2,119	115,478	24,451	10,764	14,210	28,257	188,084
2001	1,027,955	60,865	16,097	242,687	14,505	57,015	127,717	19,359	113,107	2,866	112,604	26,536	10,982	13,306	24,300	186,010
2002	987,479	60,749	15,178	232,189	15,817	56,879	118,217	18,477	110,730	3,001	109,261	27,037	9,380	12,800	24,080	173,684

Annual variation (%)

Year	EU	B(1)	DK	D	EL	E	F	IRL	I	L	NL	A	P	FIN	S	UK
98/97	5.6	6.1	5.1	7.4	11.8	3.0	3.9	23.4	2.4	:	4.8	5.9	2.3	1.4	0.6	6.4
99/98	9.7	5.0	4.5	8.8	2.2	11.1	10.3	13.6	7.7	:	18.7	13.4	9.4	3.5	10.7	6.8
00/99	32.5	31.5	20.8	29.4	48.9	42.6	29.7	24.2	40.3	9.9	33.0	32.0	31.1	36.1	35.8	31.8
01/00	-0.5	1.0	2.7	-0.1	2.5	0.4	0.1	-7.2	1.0	35.2	-2.4	8.5	2.0	-6.3	-14.0	-1.1
02/01	-3.9	-0.1	-5.7	-4.3	9.0	-0.2	-7.4	-4.5	-2.1	4.7	-2.9	1.8	-14.5	-3.8	-0.9	-6.6

Share (%)

Year	EU	B(1)	DK	D	EL	E	F	IRL	I	L	NL	A	P	FIN	S	UK
1980	100.0	6.6	1.5	21.5	1.5	5.8	15.7	0.6	12.8	:	8.2	2.1	1.2	2.0	3.4	16.4
1990	100.0	6.2	1.9	25.1	1.2	6.1	15.0	1.0	13.4	:	9.5	2.8	1.3	2.1	3.9	18.7
1996	100.0	6.1	1.8	24.6	1.3	5.0	12.7	1.5	10.9	:	9.9	2.3	1.1	1.4	2.8	17.8
1997	100.0	6.0	1.7	23.8	1.2	5.1	12.7	1.7	10.7	:	10.3	2.2	1.0	1.4	2.7	18.6
1998	100.0	6.1	1.7	24.2	1.3	5.0	12.5	2.0	10.4	:	10.2	2.2	1.0	1.4	2.6	18.7
1999	100.0	5.8	1.6	24.0	1.2	5.1	12.6	2.1	10.2	0.2	11.1	2.3	1.0	1.3	2.6	18.2
2000	100.0	5.8	1.5	23.5	1.3	5.4	12.3	2.0	10.8	0.2	11.1	2.3	1.0	1.3	2.7	18.1
2001	100.0	5.9	1.5	23.6	1.4	5.5	12.4	1.8	11.0	0.2	10.9	2.5	1.0	1.2	2.3	18.0
2002	100.0	6.1	1.5	23.5	1.6	5.7	11.9	1.8	11.2	0.3	11.0	2.7	0.9	1.2	2.4	17.5

(1) With Luxembourg until 1998.

BREAKDOWN BY MEMBER STATE OF GOODS TRADED
INTRA-EU

EXPORTS / DISPATCHES

Reporter	SITC rev. 3	Value (Mio ECU/Euro)					Share of EU total by SITC (%)				
		1990	1999	2000	2001	2002	1990	1999	2000	2001	2002
EU											
TOTAL	0-9	715,622	1,339,172	1,565,494	1,599,940	1,596,766	100.0	100.0	100.0	100.0	100.0
Agricultural products	0+1	76,839	127,600	137,791	144,828	145,974	100.0	100.0	100.0	100.0	100.0
Crude materials	2+4	25,311	39,582	47,033	45,300	45,051	100.0	100.0	100.0	100.0	100.0
Energy	3	25,718	39,136	67,391	66,527	63,969	100.0	100.0	100.0	100.0	100.0
Chemicals	5	79,919	168,992	201,925	215,674	231,541	100.0	100.0	100.0	100.0	100.0
Machinery and transp. equipment	7	262,580	561,993	658,546	669,665	640,739	100.0	100.0	100.0	100.0	100.0
Other manufactured products	6+8	222,224	369,778	420,662	423,350	413,347	100.0	100.0	100.0	100.0	100.0
B[1]											
TOTAL	0-9	72,850	128,352	151,813	160,262	164,305	10.1	9.5	9.6	10.0	10.2
Agricultural products	0+1	7,380	14,302	15,231	16,269	16,407	9.6	11.2	11.0	11.2	11.2
Crude materials	2+4	2,187	3,616	4,439	4,148	4,065	8.6	9.1	9.4	9.1	9.0
Energy	3	2,153	3,662	7,308	6,855	7,250	8.3	9.3	10.8	10.3	11.3
Chemicals	5	10,301	24,785	29,856	32,617	40,621	12.8	14.6	14.7	15.1	17.5
Machinery and transp. equipment	7	20,986	40,832	47,624	52,469	49,461	7.9	7.2	7.2	7.8	7.7
Other manufactured products	6+8	26,969	40,215	46,173	46,463	45,856	12.1	10.8	10.9	10.9	11.0
DK											
TOTAL	0-9	19,094	31,599	37,164	37,915	39,974	2.6	2.3	2.3	2.3	2.5
Agricultural products	0+1	4,846	6,803	7,426	8,135	8,099	6.3	5.3	5.3	5.6	5.5
Crude materials	2+4	1,092	1,213	1,327	1,270	1,342	4.3	3.0	2.8	2.8	2.9
Energy	3	802	1,550	3,672	2,899	3,047	3.1	3.9	5.4	4.3	4.7
Chemicals	5	1,038	3,106	3,520	3,698	4,238	1.2	1.8	1.7	1.7	1.8
Machinery and transp. equipment	7	4,611	8,477	9,271	9,910	10,846	1.7	1.5	1.4	1.4	1.6
Other manufactured products	6+8	5,087	8,886	10,250	10,263	10,680	2.2	2.4	2.4	2.4	2.5
D											
TOTAL	0-9	199,231	293,371	337,380	351,612	354,792	27.8	21.9	21.5	21.9	22.2
Agricultural products	0+1	10,299	16,596	18,876	20,764	19,034	13.4	13.0	13.6	14.3	13.0
Crude materials	2+4	4,833	5,618	6,777	6,675	6,244	19.0	14.1	14.4	14.7	13.8
Energy	3	2,053	3,284	4,163	4,309	3,759	7.9	8.3	6.1	6.4	5.8
Chemicals	5	22,211	33,740	40,158	43,132	39,490	27.7	19.9	19.8	19.9	17.0
Machinery and transp. equipment	7	94,450	146,232	168,890	175,248	166,887	35.9	26.0	25.6	26.1	26.0
Other manufactured products	6+8	59,906	72,550	84,714	86,449	83,007	26.9	19.6	20.1	20.4	20.0
EL											
TOTAL	0-9	4,242	5,603	5,698	4,680	4,791	0.5	0.4	0.3	0.2	0.3
Agricultural products	0+1	1,130	1,456	1,333	1,195	1,171	1.4	1.1	0.9	0.8	0.8
Crude materials	2+4	423	746	514	425	383	1.6	1.8	1.0	0.9	0.8
Energy	3	182	108	231	174	82	0.7	0.2	0.3	0.2	0.1
Chemicals	5	101	313	468	451	441	0.1	0.1	0.2	0.2	0.1
Machinery and transp. equipment	7	147	450	458	310	474	0.0	0.0	0.0	0.0	0.0
Other manufactured products	6+8	2,140	2,422	2,692	2,124	2,135	0.9	0.6	0.6	0.5	0.5

(1)   With Luxembourg until 1998.

EXPORTS

Reporter	SITC rev. 3	Value (Mio ECU/Euro)					Share of EU total by SITC (%)				
		1990	1999	2000	2001	2002	1990	1999	2000	2001	2002
EU											
TOTAL	0-9	355,164	760,192	942,044	985,326	993,796	100.0	100.0	100.0	100.0	100.0
Agricultural products	0+1	27,946	43,636	49,917	51,565	52,446	100.0	100.0	100.0	100.0	100.0
Crude materials	2+4	6,967	15,363	18,780	18,183	19,832	100.0	100.0	100.0	100.0	100.0
Energy	3	9,478	16,593	30,250	25,943	26,338	100.0	100.0	100.0	100.0	100.0
Chemicals	5	41,980	106,651	129,610	142,460	152,523	100.0	100.0	100.0	100.0	100.0
Machinery and transp. equipment	7	142,962	351,833	439,142	461,603	451,376	100.0	100.0	100.0	100.0	100.0
Other manufactured products	6+8	108,084	206,123	253,170	264,532	268,000	100.0	100.0	100.0	100.0	100.0
B(1)											
TOTAL	0-9	19,399	39,740	52,140	52,276	61,919	5.4	5.2	5.5	5.3	6.2
Agricultural products	0+1	964	1,708	2,275	2,484	2,467	3.4	3.9	4.5	4.8	4.7
Crude materials	2+4	500	910	1,176	1,031	1,043	7.1	5.9	6.2	5.6	5.2
Energy	3	528	1,218	2,392	2,401	2,537	5.5	7.3	7.9	9.2	9.6
Chemicals	5	2,630	9,383	11,492	12,090	20,411	6.2	8.7	8.8	8.4	13.3
Machinery and transp. equipment	7	4,333	9,727	13,538	13,810	13,490	3.0	2.7	3.0	2.9	2.9
Other manufactured products	6+8	9,155	16,375	20,705	19,849	21,694	8.4	7.9	8.1	7.5	8.0
DK											
TOTAL	0-9	8,818	15,592	18,372	19,817	20,358	2.4	2.0	1.9	2.0	2.0
Agricultural products	0+1	2,218	3,100	3,488	3,671	3,603	7.9	7.1	6.9	7.1	6.8
Crude materials	2+4	254	649	814	830	815	3.6	4.2	4.3	4.5	4.1
Energy	3	110	267	428	491	642	1.1	1.6	1.4	1.8	2.4
Chemicals	5	626	2,110	2,528	3,075	3,124	1.4	1.9	1.9	2.1	2.0
Machinery and transp. equipment	7	2,831	4,783	5,566	6,112	6,250	1.9	1.3	1.2	1.3	1.3
Other manufactured products	6+8	1,933	3,776	4,549	4,622	4,739	1.7	1.8	1.7	1.7	1.7
D											
TOTAL	0-9	112,669	216,611	260,076	286,669	293,454	31.7	28.4	27.6	29.0	29.5
Agricultural products	0+1	3,607	5,692	6,636	6,830	6,702	12.9	13.0	13.2	13.2	12.7
Crude materials	2+4	1,367	2,605	3,114	3,072	3,420	19.6	16.9	16.5	16.8	17.2
Energy	3	951	1,725	2,678	2,293	2,505	10.0	10.3	8.8	8.8	9.5
Chemicals	5	13,657	30,204	35,118	38,548	35,212	32.5	28.3	27.0	27.0	23.0
Machinery and transp. equipment	7	59,241	118,876	145,986	164,599	170,448	41.4	33.7	33.2	35.6	37.7
Other manufactured products	6+8	29,059	51,662	60,536	64,523	66,714	26.8	25.0	23.9	24.3	24.8
EL											
TOTAL	0-9	1,995	4,784	6,705	6,747	6,155	0.5	0.6	0.7	0.6	0.6
Agricultural products	0+1	475	878	1,057	1,193	1,177	1.6	2.0	2.1	2.3	2.2
Crude materials	2+4	174	386	469	468	413	2.4	2.5	2.4	2.5	2.0
Energy	3	276	834	1,519	1,121	843	2.9	5.0	5.0	4.3	3.2
Chemicals	5	130	437	549	603	630	0.3	0.4	0.4	0.4	0.4
Machinery and transp. equipment	7	117	649	1,089	1,019	977	0.0	0.1	0.2	0.2	0.2
Other manufactured products	6+8	798	1,569	2,021	2,340	2,068	0.7	0.7	0.7	0.8	0.7

BREAKDOWN BY MEMBER STATE OF GOODS TRADED
INTRA-EU

EXPORTS / DISPATCHES

Reporter	SITC rev. 3	Value (Mio ECU/Euro)					Share of EU total by SITC (%)				
		1990	1999	2000	2001	2002	1990	1999	2000	2001	2002
E											
TOTAL	**0-9**	**30,869**	**69,772**	**87,666**	**92,976**	**87,949**	**4.3**	**5.2**	**5.5**	**5.8**	**5.5**
Agricultural products	0+1	4,224	10,161	12,360	14,089	13,382	5.4	7.9	8.9	9.7	9.1
Crude materials	2+4	1,503	1,883	2,833	2,876	2,771	5.9	4.7	6.0	6.3	6.1
Energy	3	860	1,311	2,673	2,122	1,670	3.3	3.3	3.9	3.1	2.6
Chemicals	5	2,186	5,704	7,785	8,738	8,682	2.7	3.3	3.8	4.0	3.7
Machinery and transp. equipment	7	13,582	32,541	39,140	40,695	38,601	5.1	5.7	5.9	6.0	6.0
Other manufactured products	6+8	8,442	17,574	22,499	24,047	22,442	3.7	4.7	5.3	5.6	5.4
F											
TOTAL	**0-9**	**114,108**	**190,889**	**219,074**	**219,565**	**215,411**	**15.9**	**14.2**	**13.9**	**13.7**	**13.4**
Agricultural products	0+1	17,743	24,210	24,679	24,350	25,417	23.0	18.9	17.9	16.8	17.4
Crude materials	2+4	4,971	4,439	5,435	5,168	5,002	19.6	11.2	11.5	11.4	11.1
Energy	3	2,587	3,841	5,475	5,089	4,846	10.0	9.8	8.1	7.6	7.5
Chemicals	5	14,052	26,782	30,781	30,882	31,633	17.5	15.8	15.2	14.3	13.6
Machinery and transp. equipment	7	44,427	85,140	101,105	103,118	97,394	16.9	15.1	15.3	15.3	15.2
Other manufactured products	6+8	29,822	45,180	50,363	49,816	49,546	13.4	12.2	11.9	11.7	11.9
IRL											
TOTAL	**0-9**	**14,513**	**44,131**	**53,008**	**58,350**	**60,746**	**2.0**	**3.2**	**3.3**	**3.6**	**3.8**
Agricultural products	0+1	3,140	4,548	4,942	4,974	5,159	4.0	3.5	3.5	3.4	3.5
Crude materials	2+4	568	619	791	791	713	2.2	1.5	1.6	1.7	1.5
Energy	3	107	106	149	205	262	0.4	0.2	0.2	0.3	0.4
Chemicals	5	1,956	12,690	15,065	17,778	24,343	2.4	7.5	7.4	8.2	10.5
Machinery and transp. equipment	7	4,699	17,159	21,333	24,139	21,200	1.7	3.0	3.2	3.6	3.3
Other manufactured products	6+8	3,567	6,482	7,417	7,032	6,041	1.6	1.7	1.7	1.6	1.4
I											
TOTAL	**0-9**	**83,566**	**128,693**	**144,411**	**144,731**	**141,106**	**11.6**	**9.6**	**9.2**	**9.0**	**8.8**
Agricultural products	0+1	5,685	9,705	10,010	10,556	11,065	7.3	7.6	7.2	7.2	7.5
Crude materials	2+4	1,130	1,726	1,909	1,798	1,807	4.4	4.3	4.0	3.9	4.0
Energy	3	1,346	1,016	1,894	2,134	1,872	5.2	2.5	2.8	3.2	2.9
Chemicals	5	5,102	11,519	14,040	15,305	16,086	6.3	6.8	6.9	7.0	6.9
Machinery and transp. equipment	7	31,027	49,806	56,003	54,225	51,633	11.8	8.8	8.5	8.0	8.0
Other manufactured products	6+8	38,420	53,847	59,158	58,426	56,258	17.2	14.5	14.0	13.8	13.6
L											
TOTAL	**0-9**	**:**	**6,574**	**7,636**	**9,369**	**9,263**	**:**	**0.4**	**0.4**	**0.5**	**0.5**
Agricultural products	0+1	:	486	569	611	642	:	0.3	0.4	0.4	0.4
Crude materials	2+4	:	88	91	105	168	:	0.2	0.1	0.2	0.3
Energy	3	:	5	8	16	54	:	0.0	0.0	0.0	0.0
Chemicals	5	:	437	475	492	542	:	0.2	0.2	0.2	0.2
Machinery and transp. equipment	7	:	1,832	2,492	3,783	3,662	:	0.3	0.3	0.5	0.5
Other manufactured products	6+8	:	3,571	3,867	4,218	4,069	:	0.9	0.9	0.9	0.9
NL											
TOTAL	**0-9**	**85,189**	**163,010**	**198,566**	**202,878**	**199,383**	**11.9**	**12.1**	**12.6**	**12.6**	**12.4**
Agricultural products	0+1	16,123	25,134	27,149	28,832	29,653	20.9	19.6	19.7	19.9	20.3
Crude materials	2+4	5,464	10,095	11,138	11,474	11,929	21.5	25.5	23.6	25.3	26.4
Energy	3	8,981	11,957	20,414	20,380	19,867	34.9	30.5	30.2	30.6	31.0
Chemicals	5	12,154	20,347	25,620	26,359	28,386	15.2	12.0	12.6	12.2	12.2
Machinery and transp. equipment	7	17,730	55,795	68,807	68,834	62,655	6.7	9.9	10.4	10.2	9.7
Other manufactured products	6+8	19,206	35,434	40,728	42,155	42,354	8.6	9.5	9.6	9.9	10.2

EXPORTS

Reporter	SITC rev. 3	Value (Mio ECU/Euro)					Share of EU total by SITC (%)				
		1990	1999	2000	2001	2002	1990	1999	2000	2001	2002
E											
TOTAL	0-9	14,789	28,214	37,119	37,283	38,013	4.1	3.7	3.9	3.7	3.8
Agricultural products	0+1	1,923	3,121	3,569	3,752	3,786	6.8	7.1	7.1	7.2	7.2
Crude materials	2+4	605	965	1,223	1,326	1,395	8.6	6.2	6.5	7.2	7.0
Energy	3	790	1,218	2,390	2,107	1,816	8.3	7.3	7.9	8.1	6.8
Chemicals	5	1,824	3,122	4,093	4,414	5,014	4.3	2.9	3.1	3.0	3.2
Machinery and transp. equipment	7	3,855	10,002	13,373	12,709	13,088	2.6	2.8	3.0	2.7	2.8
Other manufactured products	6+8	5,747	9,067	11,526	11,957	11,964	5.3	4.3	4.5	4.5	4.4
F											
TOTAL	0-9	60,532	114,540	135,637	141,510	135,392	17.0	15.0	14.3	14.3	13.6
Agricultural products	0+1	7,037	9,376	10,244	9,940	10,289	25.1	21.4	20.5	19.2	19.6
Crude materials	2+4	949	1,437	1,644	1,409	1,618	13.6	9.3	8.7	7.7	8.1
Energy	3	1,438	2,077	3,489	3,237	2,902	15.1	12.5	11.5	12.4	11.0
Chemicals	5	8,073	15,573	18,234	20,805	21,681	19.2	14.6	14.0	14.6	14.2
Machinery and transp. equipment	7	25,852	59,557	71,513	74,282	66,116	18.0	16.9	16.2	16.0	14.6
Other manufactured products	6+8	16,933	23,315	27,861	29,050	28,585	15.6	11.3	11.0	10.9	10.6
IRL											
TOTAL	0-9	3,957	22,710	30,809	34,142	32,659	1.1	2.9	3.2	3.4	3.2
Agricultural products	0+1	1,008	1,742	1,973	1,817	1,595	3.6	3.9	3.9	3.5	3.0
Crude materials	2+4	90	279	333	351	345	1.2	1.8	1.7	1.9	1.7
Energy	3	11	71	136	91	99	0.1	0.4	0.4	0.3	0.3
Chemicals	5	992	8,554	12,393	14,624	14,955	2.3	8.0	9.5	10.2	9.8
Machinery and transp. equipment	7	1,111	8,698	11,763	12,502	10,815	0.7	2.4	2.6	2.7	2.3
Other manufactured products	6+8	586	2,698	3,367	3,798	3,894	0.5	1.3	1.3	1.4	1.4
I											
TOTAL	0-9	49,578	92,328	116,002	124,504	124,259	13.9	12.1	12.3	12.6	12.5
Agricultural products	0+1	2,205	4,146	4,764	5,374	5,647	7.8	9.5	9.5	10.4	10.7
Crude materials	2+4	828	1,437	1,925	1,866	1,956	11.8	9.3	10.2	10.2	9.8
Energy	3	1,293	2,086	3,700	3,140	2,960	13.6	12.5	12.2	12.1	11.2
Chemicals	5	3,645	8,282	10,517	10,891	11,542	8.6	7.7	8.1	7.6	7.5
Machinery and transp. equipment	7	19,106	35,827	44,046	47,892	47,873	13.3	10.1	10.0	10.3	10.6
Other manufactured products	6+8	21,716	39,224	49,328	54,036	52,680	20.0	19.0	19.4	20.4	19.6
L											
TOTAL	0-9	:	1,123	1,435	1,528	1,551	:	0.1	0.1	0.1	0.1
Agricultural products	0+1	:	8	14	17	15	:	0.0	0.0	0.0	0.0
Crude materials	2+4	:	3	2	2	2	:	0.0	0.0	0.0	0.0
Energy	3	:	0.0	0.0	1	1	:	0.0	0.0	0.0	0.0
Chemicals	5	:	70	90	89	82	:	0.0	0.0	0.0	0.0
Machinery and transp. equipment	7	:	323	504	528	581	:	0.0	0.1	0.1	0.1
Other manufactured products	6+8	:	689	817	838	821	:	0.3	0.3	0.3	0.3
NL											
TOTAL	0-9	20,292	42,075	53,848	54,888	58,717	5.7	5.5	5.7	5.5	5.9
Agricultural products	0+1	4,119	5,691	6,752	7,002	7,614	14.7	13.0	13.5	13.5	14.5
Crude materials	2+4	1,044	2,237	2,664	2,592	2,913	14.9	14.5	14.1	14.2	14.6
Energy	3	738	1,197	2,234	2,042	2,655	7.7	7.2	7.3	7.8	10.0
Chemicals	5	3,131	6,456	8,264	8,856	9,695	7.4	6.0	6.3	6.2	6.3
Machinery and transp. equipment	7	5,257	16,254	20,774	21,589	21,314	3.6	4.6	4.7	4.6	4.7
Other manufactured products	6+8	3,611	8,358	11,010	10,495	12,281	3.3	4.0	4.3	3.9	4.5

BREAKDOWN BY MEMBER STATE OF GOODS TRADED
INTRA-EU

EXPORTS / DISPATCHES

Reporter	SITC rev. 3	Value (Mio ECU/Euro)					Share of EU total by SITC (%)				
		1990	1999	2000	2001	2002	1990	1999	2000	2001	2002
A											
TOTAL	**0-9**	**22,315**	**38,998**	**44,985**	**48,609**	**51,087**	**3.1**	**2.9**	**2.8**	**3.0**	**3.1**
Agricultural products	0+1	563	2,251	2,594	2,861	3,096	0.7	1.7	1.8	1.9	2.1
Crude materials	2+4	1,297	1,569	1,754	1,729	1,802	5.1	3.9	3.7	3.8	3.9
Energy	3	248	321	499	926	1,246	0.9	0.8	0.7	1.3	1.9
Chemicals	5	1,685	2,965	3,409	3,654	3,909	2.1	1.7	1.6	1.6	1.6
Machinery and transp. equipment	7	8,656	16,185	19,587	21,152	22,723	3.2	2.8	2.9	3.1	3.5
Other manufactured products	6+8	9,862	15,674	17,106	18,130	18,100	4.4	4.2	4.0	4.2	4.3
P											
TOTAL	**0-9**	**10,261**	**19,161**	**21,173**	**21,893**	**21,576**	**1.4**	**1.4**	**1.3**	**1.3**	**1.3**
Agricultural products	0+1	603	1,158	1,305	1,369	1,439	0.7	0.9	0.9	0.9	0.9
Crude materials	2+4	911	810	1,001	863	771	3.5	2.0	2.1	1.9	1.7
Energy	3	231	183	273	202	253	0.8	0.4	0.4	0.3	0.3
Chemicals	5	497	885	1,140	1,098	1,189	0.6	0.5	0.5	0.5	0.5
Machinery and transp. equipment	7	2,123	6,920	7,486	8,068	8,048	0.8	1.2	1.1	1.2	1.2
Other manufactured products	6+8	5,893	9,193	9,941	10,269	9,857	2.6	2.4	2.3	2.4	2.3
FIN											
TOTAL	**0-9**	**12,652**	**22,888**	**27,780**	**25,925**	**25,717**	**1.7**	**1.7**	**1.7**	**1.6**	**1.6**
Agricultural products	0+1	156	300	353	351	367	0.2	0.2	0.2	0.2	0.2
Crude materials	2+4	1,520	1,924	2,347	1,946	1,983	6.0	4.8	4.9	4.2	4.4
Energy	3	278	637	1,199	1,200	1,118	1.0	1.6	1.7	1.8	1.7
Chemicals	5	604	1,354	1,607	1,555	1,616	0.7	0.8	0.7	0.7	0.6
Machinery and transp. equipment	7	3,200	8,221	10,444	9,353	9,457	1.2	1.4	1.5	1.3	1.4
Other manufactured products	6+8	6,886	10,142	11,530	11,162	10,824	3.0	2.7	2.7	2.6	2.6
S											
TOTAL	**0-9**	**28,008**	**46,495**	**52,772**	**46,132**	**46,419**	**3.9**	**3.4**	**3.3**	**2.8**	**2.9**
Agricultural products	0+1	415	1,177	1,294	1,397	1,527	0.5	0.9	0.9	0.9	1.0
Crude materials	2+4	3,151	3,166	4,125	3,571	3,471	12.4	7.9	8.7	7.8	7.7
Energy	3	1,077	1,321	2,336	1,959	1,842	4.1	3.3	3.4	2.9	2.8
Chemicals	5	2,132	4,363	4,743	4,946	4,918	2.6	2.5	2.3	2.2	2.1
Machinery and transp. equipment	7	10,571	19,387	21,276	15,849	15,945	4.0	3.4	3.2	2.3	2.4
Other manufactured products	6+8	10,419	13,662	15,509	15,195	15,435	4.6	3.6	3.6	3.5	3.7
UK											
TOTAL	**0-9**	**81,698**	**149,637**	**176,370**	**175,045**	**174,245**	**11.4**	**11.1**	**11.2**	**10.9**	**10.9**
Agricultural products	0+1	5,666	9,313	9,669	9,074	9,513	7.3	7.2	7.0	6.2	6.5
Crude materials	2+4	2,229	2,069	2,551	2,460	2,600	8.8	5.2	5.4	5.4	5.7
Energy	3	6,417	9,836	17,097	18,056	16,803	24.9	25.1	25.3	27.1	26.2
Chemicals	5	10,320	20,001	23,259	24,970	25,446	12.9	11.8	11.5	11.5	10.9
Machinery and transp. equipment	7	28,798	73,015	84,632	82,513	81,753	10.9	12.9	12.8	12.3	12.7
Other manufactured products	6+8	22,772	34,948	38,716	37,600	36,744	10.2	9.4	9.2	8.8	8.8

BREAKDOWN BY MEMBER STATE OF GOODS TRADED
EXTRA-EU

EXPORTS

Reporter	SITC rev. 3	Value (Mio ECU/Euro)					Share of EU total by SITC (%)				
		1990	1999	2000	2001	2002	1990	1999	2000	2001	2002
A											
TOTAL	0-9	10,573	22,984	28,327	30,390	32,112	2.9	3.0	3.0	3.0	3.2
Agricultural products	0+1	500	832	860	1,181	1,229	1.7	1.9	1.7	2.2	2.3
Crude materials	2+4	437	683	757	782	859	6.2	4.4	4.0	4.3	4.3
Energy	3	84	338	416	553	624	0.8	2.0	1.3	2.1	2.3
Chemicals	5	1,100	2,800	3,241	3,703	4,243	2.6	2.6	2.5	2.5	2.7
Machinery and transp. equipment	7	3,673	10,409	12,846	13,638	13,887	2.5	2.9	2.9	2.9	3.0
Other manufactured products	6+8	4,776	7,788	9,542	10,400	10,865	4.4	3.7	3.7	3.9	4.0
P											
TOTAL	0-9	2,376	3,865	5,205	5,429	5,528	0.6	0.5	0.5	0.5	0.5
Agricultural products	0+1	235	335	378	405	443	0.8	0.7	0.7	0.7	0.8
Crude materials	2+4	297	229	279	238	215	4.2	1.4	1.4	1.3	1.0
Energy	3	123	238	401	303	285	1.3	1.4	1.3	1.1	1.0
Chemicals	5	170	262	351	376	380	0.4	0.2	0.2	0.2	0.2
Machinery and transp. equipment	7	344	946	1,597	1,700	1,784	0.2	0.2	0.3	0.3	0.3
Other manufactured products	6+8	1,204	1,841	2,180	2,353	2,365	1.1	0.8	0.8	0.8	0.8
FIN											
TOTAL	0-9	8,348	16,747	22,136	22,352	22,025	2.3	2.2	2.3	2.2	2.2
Agricultural products	0+1	341	415	445	530	539	1.2	0.9	0.8	1.0	1.0
Crude materials	2+4	612	869	1,089	1,124	1,189	8.7	5.6	5.7	6.1	5.9
Energy	3	31	310	503	305	489	0.3	1.8	1.6	1.1	1.8
Chemicals	5	733	1,104	1,346	1,495	1,698	1.7	1.0	1.0	1.0	1.1
Machinery and transp. equipment	7	3,279	8,852	12,304	12,387	11,524	2.2	2.5	2.8	2.6	2.5
Other manufactured products	6+8	3,343	5,196	6,449	6,497	6,577	3.0	2.5	2.5	2.4	2.4
S											
TOTAL	0-9	17,094	33,154	41,568	38,330	39,638	4.8	4.3	4.4	3.8	3.9
Agricultural products	0+1	463	751	935	1,032	1,106	1.6	1.7	1.8	2.0	2.1
Crude materials	2+4	910	1,239	1,557	1,410	1,719	13.0	8.0	8.2	7.7	8.6
Energy	3	293	531	815	874	695	3.0	3.2	2.6	3.3	2.6
Chemicals	5	1,230	2,905	3,740	3,919	4,282	2.9	2.7	2.8	2.7	2.8
Machinery and transp. equipment	7	8,951	18,386	23,450	20,102	20,008	6.2	5.2	5.3	4.3	4.4
Other manufactured products	6+8	5,099	8,175	9,896	9,748	10,473	4.7	3.9	3.9	3.6	3.9
UK											
TOTAL	0-9	60,760	105,727	132,666	129,461	122,017	17.1	13.9	14.0	13.1	12.2
Agricultural products	0+1	4,156	5,842	6,527	6,336	6,234	14.8	13.3	13.0	12.2	11.8
Crude materials	2+4	859	1,435	1,736	1,682	1,931	12.3	9.3	9.2	9.2	9.7
Energy	3	3,220	4,482	9,149	6,986	7,282	33.9	27.0	30.2	26.9	27.6
Chemicals	5	7,100	15,390	17,652	18,972	19,574	16.9	14.4	13.6	13.3	12.8
Machinery and transp. equipment	7	20,914	48,543	60,791	58,734	53,218	14.6	13.7	13.8	12.7	11.7
Other manufactured products	6+8	17,341	26,389	33,383	34,024	32,281	16.0	12.8	13.1	12.8	12.0

BREAKDOWN BY MEMBER STATE OF GOODS TRADED
INTRA-EU

IMPORTS / ARRIVALS

Reporter	SITC rev. 3	Value (Mio ECU/Euro)					Share of EU total by SITC (%)				
		1990	1999	2000	2001	2002	1990	1999	2000	2001	2002
EU											
TOTAL	0-9	719,885	1,273,006	1,489,770	1,505,472	1,494,292	100.0	100.0	100.0	100.0	100.0
Agricultural products	0+1	76,716	125,507	132,951	140,233	140,316	100.0	100.0	100.0	100.0	100.0
Crude materials	2+4	31,593	39,938	47,665	46,329	45,670	100.0	100.0	100.0	100.0	100.0
Energy	3	26,478	35,168	65,102	63,168	60,771	100.0	100.0	100.0	100.0	100.0
Chemicals	5	84,819	168,964	200,892	213,916	229,868	100.0	100.0	100.0	100.0	100.0
Machinery and transp. equipment	7	255,091	527,638	616,247	623,600	586,879	100.0	100.0	100.0	100.0	100.0
Other manufactured products	6+8	228,685	341,622	390,795	390,073	377,580	100.0	100.0	100.0	100.0	100.0
B(1)											
TOTAL	0-9	73,056	108,853	131,953	138,626	147,964	10.1	8.5	8.8	9.2	9.9
Agricultural products	0+1	6,980	10,800	11,274	12,282	12,322	9.0	8.6	8.4	8.7	8.7
Crude materials	2+4	3,296	3,713	4,499	4,232	4,493	10.4	9.2	9.4	9.1	9.8
Energy	3	4,965	6,845	13,032	12,677	12,050	18.7	19.4	20.0	20.0	19.8
Chemicals	5	9,099	18,801	23,428	27,048	41,098	10.7	11.1	11.6	12.6	17.8
Machinery and transp. equipment	7	19,720	37,722	44,783	47,163	43,327	7.7	7.1	7.2	7.5	7.3
Other manufactured products	6+8	23,573	30,694	34,753	34,817	34,554	10.3	8.9	8.8	8.9	9.1
DK											
TOTAL	0-9	17,691	29,967	33,667	34,508	37,108	2.4	2.3	2.2	2.2	2.4
Agricultural products	0+1	1,509	2,921	3,120	3,362	3,702	1.9	2.3	2.3	2.3	2.6
Crude materials	2+4	807	1,136	1,228	1,237	1,292	2.5	2.8	2.5	2.6	2.8
Energy	3	663	523	761	784	778	2.5	1.4	1.1	1.2	1.2
Chemicals	5	2,327	3,705	4,065	4,278	4,763	2.7	2.1	2.0	1.9	2.0
Machinery and transp. equipment	7	5,741	11,856	13,481	13,594	14,957	2.2	2.2	2.1	2.1	2.5
Other manufactured products	6+8	6,203	9,314	10,549	10,613	10,965	2.7	2.7	2.6	2.7	2.9
D											
TOTAL	0-9	166,492	257,113	295,338	300,100	289,831	23.1	20.1	19.8	19.9	19.3
Agricultural products	0+1	17,876	25,131	26,202	27,717	25,399	23.3	20.0	19.7	19.7	18.1
Crude materials	2+4	8,276	8,467	10,250	10,040	9,525	26.1	21.2	21.5	21.6	20.8
Energy	3	8,058	8,901	17,562	17,958	14,777	30.4	25.3	26.9	28.4	24.3
Chemicals	5	17,793	31,627	36,945	42,056	39,251	20.9	18.7	18.3	19.6	17.0
Machinery and transp. equipment	7	54,189	94,513	107,872	115,306	99,517	21.2	17.9	17.5	18.4	16.9
Other manufactured products	6+8	55,206	64,984	73,594	71,856	62,391	24.1	19.0	18.8	18.4	16.5
EL											
TOTAL	0-9	10,549	19,148	20,826	17,002	17,248	1.4	1.5	1.3	1.1	1.1
Agricultural products	0+1	1,772	3,011	3,137	2,763	3,059	2.3	2.3	2.3	1.9	2.1
Crude materials	2+4	368	341	338	271	355	1.1	0.8	0.7	0.5	0.7
Energy	3	101	193	239	84	84	0.3	0.5	0.3	0.1	0.1
Chemicals	5	1,332	2,819	3,329	3,030	2,718	1.5	1.6	1.6	1.4	1.1
Machinery and transp. equipment	7	3,354	7,312	7,785	5,954	5,596	1.3	1.3	1.2	0.9	0.9
Other manufactured products	6+8	3,609	5,432	5,975	4,871	5,413	1.5	1.5	1.5	1.2	1.4

(1) With Luxembourg until 1998.

BREAKDOWN BY MEMBER STATE OF GOODS TRADED
EXTRA-EU

IMPORTS

Reporter	SITC rev. 3	Value (Mio ECU/Euro)					Share of EU total by SITC (%)				
		1990	1999	2000	2001	2002	1990	1999	2000	2001	2002
EU											
TOTAL	0-9	404,351	779,825	1,033,436	1,027,955	987,479	100.0	100.0	100.0	100.0	100.0
Agricultural products	0+1	34,699	50,153	54,808	58,289	58,593	100.0	100.0	100.0	100.0	100.0
Crude materials	2+4	31,819	40,266	50,349	48,908	45,639	100.0	100.0	100.0	100.0	100.0
Energy	3	68,802	78,275	149,091	144,978	137,490	100.0	100.0	100.0	100.0	100.0
Chemicals	5	26,442	58,913	71,366	77,533	80,934	100.0	100.0	100.0	100.0	100.0
Machinery and transp. equipment	7	113,054	305,956	394,660	379,951	356,787	100.0	100.0	100.0	100.0	100.0
Other manufactured products	6+8	107,565	224,102	279,555	286,128	277,213	100.0	100.0	100.0	100.0	100.0
B(1)											
TOTAL	0-9	25,396	45,782	60,242	60,865	60,749	6.2	5.8	5.8	5.9	6.1
Agricultural products	0+1	1,839	3,245	3,641	3,674	3,871	5.3	6.4	6.6	6.3	6.6
Crude materials	2+4	2,513	2,855	3,711	3,181	3,171	7.8	7.0	7.3	6.5	6.9
Energy	3	2,652	1,999	4,043	4,528	4,354	3.8	2.5	2.7	3.1	3.1
Chemicals	5	2,628	6,526	7,973	8,546	9,653	9.9	11.0	11.1	11.0	11.9
Machinery and transp. equipment	7	6,004	11,621	15,557	15,974	15,286	5.3	3.7	3.9	4.2	4.2
Other manufactured products	6+8	9,357	19,322	25,134	24,517	24,350	8.6	8.6	8.9	8.5	8.7
DK											
TOTAL	0-9	7,798	12,962	15,659	16,097	15,178	1.9	1.6	1.5	1.5	1.5
Agricultural products	0+1	1,351	2,223	2,567	2,591	2,526	3.8	4.4	4.6	4.4	4.3
Crude materials	2+4	274	503	567	645	659	0.8	1.2	1.1	1.3	1.4
Energy	3	1,065	1,103	1,800	1,549	1,204	1.5	1.4	1.2	1.0	0.8
Chemicals	5	481	723	804	904	912	1.8	1.2	1.1	1.1	1.1
Machinery and transp. equipment	7	2,359	3,766	4,467	4,485	3,926	2.0	1.2	1.1	1.1	1.1
Other manufactured products	6+8	2,001	4,210	5,000	5,138	5,195	1.8	1.8	1.7	1.7	1.8
D											
TOTAL	0-9	101,730	187,667	242,987	242,687	232,189	25.1	24.0	23.5	23.6	23.5
Agricultural products	0+1	7,327	9,157	9,755	9,991	9,807	21.1	18.2	17.7	17.1	16.7
Crude materials	2+4	6,737	7,964	9,872	9,082	8,146	21.1	19.7	19.6	18.5	17.8
Energy	3	10,487	16,747	29,900	29,649	27,448	15.2	21.3	20.0	20.4	19.9
Chemicals	5	6,041	12,273	14,691	15,634	15,551	22.8	20.8	20.5	20.1	19.2
Machinery and transp. equipment	7	32,426	78,507	102,741	101,017	97,589	28.6	25.6	26.0	26.5	27.3
Other manufactured products	6+8	32,778	58,767	70,619	72,345	68,219	30.4	26.2	25.2	25.2	24.6
EL											
TOTAL	0-9	5,036	9,496	14,142	14,505	15,817	1.2	1.2	1.3	1.4	1.6
Agricultural products	0+1	460	549	619	736	966	1.3	1.0	1.1	1.2	1.6
Crude materials	2+4	472	433	540	610	678	1.4	1.0	1.0	1.2	1.4
Energy	3	1,105	1,386	4,138	4,778	4,506	1.6	1.7	2.7	3.2	3.2
Chemicals	5	313	636	747	850	914	1.1	1.0	1.0	1.0	1.1
Machinery and transp. equipment	7	1,478	3,874	4,602	4,003	5,280	1.3	1.2	1.1	1.0	1.4
Other manufactured products	6+8	1,178	2,614	3,434	3,527	3,190	1.0	1.1	1.2	1.2	1.1

BREAKDOWN BY MEMBER STATE OF GOODS TRADED
INTRA-EU

IMPORTS / ARRIVALS

Reporter	SITC rev. 3	Value (Mio ECU/Euro)					Share of EU total by SITC (%)				
		1990	1999	2000	2001	2002	1990	1999	2000	2001	2002
E											
TOTAL	0-9	41,222	87,205	112,303	115,662	106,693	5.7	6.8	7.5	7.6	7.1
Agricultural products	0+1	3,173	7,239	8,665	9,817	9,316	4.1	5.7	6.5	7.0	6.6
Crude materials	2+4	1,923	2,289	3,057	3,125	2,818	6.0	5.7	6.4	6.7	6.1
Energy	3	784	1,046	2,562	2,554	2,371	2.9	2.9	3.9	4.0	3.9
Chemicals	5	5,090	10,990	14,299	15,738	15,483	6.0	6.5	7.1	7.3	6.7
Machinery and transp. equipment	7	18,830	43,998	55,510	55,404	50,155	7.3	8.3	9.0	8.8	8.5
Other manufactured products	6+8	11,321	21,236	27,289	28,275	25,984	4.9	6.2	6.9	7.2	6.8
F											
TOTAL	0-9	130,351	197,981	239,508	239,197	229,987	18.1	15.5	16.0	15.8	15.3
Agricultural products	0+1	12,031	18,410	19,515	20,124	20,493	15.6	14.6	14.6	14.3	14.6
Crude materials	2+4	4,020	4,860	5,729	5,338	5,309	12.7	12.1	12.0	11.5	11.6
Energy	3	4,226	4,681	7,917	7,326	7,228	15.9	13.3	12.1	11.5	11.8
Chemicals	5	15,127	25,064	30,894	30,799	31,080	17.8	14.8	15.3	14.3	13.5
Machinery and transp. equipment	7	51,695	87,628	108,203	109,410	100,434	20.2	16.6	17.5	17.5	17.1
Other manufactured products	6+8	43,110	56,446	66,286	65,471	64,617	18.8	16.5	16.9	16.7	17.1
IRL											
TOTAL	0-9	11,919	27,078	34,380	37,091	36,532	1.6	2.1	2.3	2.4	2.4
Agricultural products	0+1	1,389	2,612	2,787	3,236	3,353	1.8	2.0	2.0	2.3	2.3
Crude materials	2+4	269	485	547	521	509	0.8	1.2	1.1	1.1	1.1
Energy	3	798	853	1,396	1,369	1,296	3.0	2.4	2.1	2.1	2.1
Chemicals	5	1,636	3,413	4,137	4,234	4,413	1.9	2.0	2.0	1.9	1.9
Machinery and transp. equipment	7	3,484	11,142	15,809	17,771	16,866	1.3	2.1	2.5	2.8	2.8
Other manufactured products	6+8	4,031	6,318	7,139	7,473	7,319	1.7	1.8	1.8	1.9	1.9
I											
TOTAL	0-9	88,217	127,285	146,571	146,945	146,157	12.2	9.9	9.8	9.7	9.7
Agricultural products	0+1	11,969	14,862	15,484	15,398	15,330	15.6	11.8	11.6	10.9	10.9
Crude materials	2+4	6,112	6,032	7,100	6,889	6,707	19.3	15.1	14.8	14.8	14.6
Energy	3	1,385	1,181	2,072	1,892	1,980	5.2	3.3	3.1	2.9	3.2
Chemicals	5	12,067	20,302	23,395	23,940	24,808	14.2	12.0	11.6	11.1	10.7
Machinery and transp. equipment	7	33,309	53,488	60,966	61,115	60,648	13.0	10.1	9.8	9.8	10.3
Other manufactured products	6+8	22,163	30,425	35,775	34,799	33,533	9.6	8.9	9.1	8.9	8.8
L											
TOTAL	0-9	:	8,597	10,092	10,902	10,905	:	0.6	0.6	0.7	0.7
Agricultural products	0+1	:	1,037	1,141	1,179	1,223	:	0.8	0.8	0.8	0.8
Crude materials	2+4	:	435	517	604	545	:	1.0	1.0	1.3	1.1
Energy	3	:	372	775	668	684	:	1.0	1.1	1.0	1.1
Chemicals	5	:	904	1,039	1,150	1,106	:	0.5	0.5	0.5	0.4
Machinery and transp. equipment	7	:	2,713	3,091	3,596	3,626	:	0.5	0.5	0.5	0.6
Other manufactured products	6+8	:	2,792	3,189	3,357	3,392	:	0.8	0.8	0.8	0.8
NL											
TOTAL	0-9	67,931	106,662	120,844	120,354	122,618	9.4	8.3	8.1	7.9	8.2
Agricultural products	0+1	7,977	12,028	12,762	13,867	14,294	10.3	9.5	9.5	9.8	10.1
Crude materials	2+4	2,700	4,134	4,886	4,612	4,691	8.5	10.3	10.2	9.9	10.2
Energy	3	2,597	4,364	8,384	7,743	9,156	9.8	12.4	12.8	12.2	15.0
Chemicals	5	7,978	14,057	16,744	17,010	18,102	9.4	8.3	8.3	7.9	7.8
Machinery and transp. equipment	7	21,712	40,860	44,020	42,792	41,886	8.5	7.7	7.1	6.8	7.1
Other manufactured products	6+8	23,986	30,700	33,477	33,674	33,896	10.4	8.9	8.5	8.6	8.9

IMPORTS

Reporter	SITC rev. 3	Value (Mio ECU/Euro)					Share of EU total by SITC (%)				
		1990	1999	2000	2001	2002	1990	1999	2000	2001	2002
E											
TOTAL	0-9	24,961	39,785	56,756	57,015	56,879	6.1	5.1	5.4	5.5	5.7
Agricultural products	0+1	3,235	4,846	5,510	6,025	6,177	9.3	9.6	10.0	10.3	10.5
Crude materials	2+4	2,536	3,715	4,179	4,286	4,061	7.9	9.2	8.2	8.7	8.8
Energy	3	6,873	7,907	17,815	16,752	16,136	9.9	10.1	11.9	11.5	11.7
Chemicals	5	1,614	2,959	3,731	4,064	4,483	6.1	5.0	5.2	5.2	5.5
Machinery and transp. equipment	7	6,587	11,034	13,303	12,664	12,635	5.8	3.6	3.3	3.3	3.5
Other manufactured products	6+8	4,040	9,055	11,527	12,269	12,475	3.7	4.0	4.1	4.2	4.5
F											
TOTAL	0-9	61,029	98,274	127,469	127,717	118,217	15.0	12.6	12.3	12.4	11.9
Agricultural products	0+1	5,164	5,260	5,666	6,005	6,066	14.8	10.4	10.3	10.3	10.3
Crude materials	2+4	3,798	3,521	4,357	4,254	3,858	11.9	8.7	8.6	8.6	8.4
Energy	3	13,339	13,104	24,712	24,162	22,170	19.3	16.7	16.5	16.6	16.1
Chemicals	5	4,414	8,714	9,974	11,346	11,359	16.6	14.7	13.9	14.6	14.0
Machinery and transp. equipment	7	19,134	43,353	52,720	51,165	44,760	16.9	14.1	13.3	13.4	12.5
Other manufactured products	6+8	14,723	23,354	28,967	29,465	28,374	13.6	10.4	10.3	10.2	10.2
IRL											
TOTAL	0-9	4,217	16,804	20,883	19,359	18,477	1.0	2.1	2.0	1.8	1.8
Agricultural products	0+1	266	433	549	549	550	0.7	0.8	1.0	0.9	0.9
Crude materials	2+4	225	324	395	401	402	0.7	0.8	0.7	0.8	0.8
Energy	3	197	428	876	728	509	0.2	0.5	0.5	0.5	0.3
Chemicals	5	388	1,504	1,957	2,112	2,666	1.4	2.5	2.7	2.7	3.2
Machinery and transp. equipment	7	2,369	11,292	13,374	11,687	10,686	2.0	3.6	3.3	3.0	2.9
Other manufactured products	6+8	717	2,354	3,060	3,177	3,110	0.6	1.0	1.0	1.1	1.1
I											
TOTAL	0-9	54,189	79,730	111,935	113,107	110,730	13.4	10.2	10.8	11.0	11.2
Agricultural products	0+1	3,821	4,281	4,868	5,381	5,734	11.0	8.5	8.8	9.2	9.7
Crude materials	2+4	5,954	6,694	8,718	8,314	7,555	18.7	16.6	17.3	16.9	16.5
Energy	3	13,525	12,151	22,921	21,806	21,224	19.6	15.5	15.3	15.0	15.4
Chemicals	5	3,837	6,571	8,081	8,113	8,444	14.5	11.1	11.3	10.4	10.4
Machinery and transp. equipment	7	9,546	19,460	25,030	25,254	24,830	8.4	6.3	6.3	6.6	6.9
Other manufactured products	6+8	12,353	23,082	30,156	32,189	32,179	11.4	10.2	10.7	11.2	11.6
L											
TOTAL	0-9	:	1,928	2,119	2,866	3,001	:	0.2	0.2	0.2	0.3
Agricultural products	0+1	:	54	61	49	51	:	0.1	0.1	0.0	0.0
Crude materials	2+4	:	34	52	51	57	:	0.0	0.1	0.1	0.1
Energy	3	:	0.0	0.0	0.0	4	:	0.0	0.0	0.0	0.0
Chemicals	5	:	60	85	98	87	:	0.1	0.1	0.1	0.1
Machinery and transp. equipment	7	:	1,460	1,468	2,221	1,994	:	0.4	0.3	0.5	0.5
Other manufactured products	6+8	:	313	437	409	352	:	0.1	0.1	0.1	0.1
NL											
TOTAL	0-9	38,675	86,772	115,478	112,604	109,261	9.5	11.1	11.1	10.9	11.0
Agricultural products	0+1	4,203	6,886	7,455	8,208	7,974	12.1	13.7	13.6	14.0	13.6
Crude materials	2+4	3,660	5,230	6,503	6,714	6,505	11.5	12.9	12.9	13.7	14.2
Energy	3	9,573	9,911	16,721	14,838	15,181	13.9	12.6	11.2	10.2	11.0
Chemicals	5	2,854	6,439	8,298	9,082	9,956	10.7	10.9	11.6	11.7	12.3
Machinery and transp. equipment	7	10,006	37,638	51,217	48,315	44,989	8.8	12.3	12.9	12.7	12.6
Other manufactured products	6+8	7,676	20,281	24,881	24,897	24,260	7.1	9.0	8.9	8.7	8.7

BREAKDOWN BY MEMBER STATE OF GOODS TRADED
INTRA-EU

IMPORTS / ARRIVALS

Reporter	SITC rev. 3	Value (Mio ECU/Euro)					Share of EU total by SITC (%)				
		1990	1999	2000	2001	2002	1990	1999	2000	2001	2002
A											
TOTAL	0-9	27,924	48,405	53,932	56,797	55,767	3.8	3.8	3.6	3.7	3.7
Agricultural products	0+1	1,095	3,197	3,339	3,709	3,851	1.4	2.5	2.5	2.6	2.7
Crude materials	2+4	965	1,492	1,748	1,746	1,795	3.0	3.7	3.6	3.7	3.9
Energy	3	464	933	1,663	2,023	2,300	1.7	2.6	2.5	3.2	3.7
Chemicals	5	3,098	5,441	6,065	6,423	6,654	3.6	3.2	3.0	3.0	2.8
Machinery and transp. equipment	7	11,115	20,219	22,233	23,166	22,152	4.3	3.8	3.6	3.7	3.7
Other manufactured products	6+8	11,172	17,045	18,694	19,666	18,913	4.8	4.9	4.7	5.0	5.0
P											
TOTAL	0-9	13,898	29,300	32,494	33,072	31,270	1.9	2.3	2.1	2.1	2.0
Agricultural products	0+1	927	3,045	3,254	3,609	3,370	1.2	2.4	2.4	2.5	2.4
Crude materials	2+4	480	703	794	828	784	1.5	1.7	1.6	1.7	1.7
Energy	3	394	897	1,525	1,377	1,440	1.4	2.5	2.3	2.1	2.3
Chemicals	5	1,532	3,131	3,596	3,838	4,001	1.8	1.8	1.7	1.7	1.7
Machinery and transp. equipment	7	6,059	12,219	12,949	12,809	11,704	2.3	2.3	2.1	2.0	1.9
Other manufactured products	6+8	4,449	9,264	10,224	10,495	9,876	1.9	2.7	2.6	2.6	2.6
FIN											
TOTAL	0-9	12,790	19,697	23,082	23,137	23,387	1.7	1.5	1.5	1.5	1.5
Agricultural products	0+1	488	1,304	1,390	1,448	1,584	0.6	1.0	1.0	1.0	1.1
Crude materials	2+4	560	636	763	741	708	1.7	1.5	1.5	1.5	1.5
Energy	3	434	684	1,075	1,015	952	1.6	1.9	1.6	1.6	1.5
Chemicals	5	1,714	2,623	3,070	3,144	3,352	2.0	1.5	1.5	1.4	1.4
Machinery and transp. equipment	7	5,301	9,022	10,375	10,289	10,241	2.0	1.7	1.6	1.6	1.7
Other manufactured products	6+8	4,285	4,810	5,560	5,703	5,742	1.8	1.4	1.4	1.4	1.5
S											
TOTAL	0-9	27,033	43,551	50,652	46,267	46,474	3.7	3.4	3.3	3.0	3.1
Agricultural products	0+1	1,301	2,801	2,990	3,222	3,663	1.6	2.2	2.2	2.2	2.6
Crude materials	2+4	870	1,057	1,303	1,181	1,248	2.7	2.6	2.7	2.5	2.7
Energy	3	1,355	1,328	2,706	2,195	2,574	5.1	3.7	4.1	3.4	4.2
Chemicals	5	3,110	5,080	5,271	5,437	5,438	3.6	3.0	2.6	2.5	2.3
Machinery and transp. equipment	7	10,542	19,143	22,420	19,715	19,048	4.1	3.6	3.6	3.1	3.2
Other manufactured products	6+8	9,662	10,772	12,196	11,740	12,271	4.2	3.1	3.1	3.0	3.2
UK											
TOTAL	0-9	98,559	162,164	184,129	185,812	192,351	13.6	12.7	12.3	12.3	12.8
Agricultural products	0+1	11,113	17,110	17,891	18,500	19,357	14.4	13.6	13.4	13.1	13.7
Crude materials	2+4	3,341	4,159	4,905	4,966	4,889	10.5	10.4	10.2	10.7	10.7
Energy	3	2,507	2,367	3,435	3,504	3,101	9.4	6.7	5.2	5.5	5.1
Chemicals	5	10,838	21,009	24,614	25,794	27,600	12.7	12.4	12.2	12.0	12.0
Machinery and transp. equipment	7	36,998	75,804	86,750	85,517	86,722	14.5	14.3	14.0	13.7	14.7
Other manufactured products	6+8	31,033	41,389	46,095	47,262	48,716	13.5	12.1	11.7	12.1	12.9

BREAKDOWN BY MEMBER STATE OF GOODS TRADED
EXTRA-EU

IMPORTS

Reporter	SITC rev. 3	Value (Mio ECU/Euro)					Share of EU total by SITC (%)				
		1990	1999	2000	2001	2002	1990	1999	2000	2001	2002
A											
TOTAL	0-9	11,354	18,512	24,451	26,536	27,037	2.8	2.3	2.3	2.5	2.7
Agricultural products	0+1	856	699	783	930	979	2.4	1.3	1.4	1.5	1.6
Crude materials	2+4	899	1,167	1,439	1,364	1,374	2.8	2.8	2.8	2.7	3.0
Energy	3	2,007	1,950	3,239	3,481	3,442	2.9	2.4	2.1	2.4	2.5
Chemicals	5	797	1,417	1,736	2,095	2,263	3.0	2.4	2.4	2.7	2.7
Machinery and transp. equipment	7	3,786	7,318	10,369	11,060	11,369	3.3	2.3	2.6	2.9	3.1
Other manufactured products	6+8	2,977	5,835	6,779	7,414	7,297	2.7	2.6	2.4	2.5	2.6
P											
TOTAL	0-9	5,406	8,206	10,764	10,982	9,380	1.3	1.0	1.0	1.0	0.9
Agricultural products	0+1	947	1,239	1,251	1,306	1,202	2.7	2.4	2.2	2.2	2.0
Crude materials	2+4	715	763	843	827	794	2.2	1.8	1.6	1.6	1.7
Energy	3	1,709	1,638	2,915	2,894	2,578	2.4	2.0	1.9	1.9	1.8
Chemicals	5	251	475	473	548	543	0.9	0.8	0.6	0.7	0.6
Machinery and transp. equipment	7	984	2,459	3,206	3,232	2,255	0.8	0.8	0.8	0.8	0.6
Other manufactured products	6+8	797	1,632	2,050	2,128	1,974	0.7	0.7	0.7	0.7	0.7
FIN											
TOTAL	0-9	8,498	10,435	14,210	13,306	12,800	2.1	1.3	1.3	1.2	1.2
Agricultural products	0+1	500	454	446	426	397	1.4	0.9	0.8	0.7	0.6
Crude materials	2+4	578	1,368	1,749	1,684	1,630	1.8	3.3	3.4	3.4	3.5
Energy	3	2,056	1,831	3,295	3,139	3,093	2.9	2.3	2.2	2.1	2.2
Chemicals	5	576	668	809	820	830	2.1	1.1	1.1	1.0	1.0
Machinery and transp. equipment	7	2,922	4,142	5,483	4,734	4,378	2.5	1.3	1.3	1.2	1.2
Other manufactured products	6+8	1,864	1,967	2,422	2,490	2,450	1.7	0.8	0.8	0.8	0.8
S											
TOTAL	0-9	15,817	20,795	28,257	24,300	24,080	3.9	2.6	2.7	2.3	2.4
Agricultural products	0+1	1,221	1,428	1,547	1,544	1,611	3.5	2.8	2.8	2.6	2.7
Crude materials	2+4	660	976	1,326	1,254	1,302	2.0	2.4	2.6	2.5	2.8
Energy	3	2,543	2,528	4,442	3,914	3,606	3.6	3.2	2.9	2.6	2.6
Chemicals	5	963	1,534	1,881	1,880	1,847	3.6	2.6	2.6	2.4	2.2
Machinery and transp. equipment	7	5,979	8,166	11,565	8,535	8,536	5.2	2.6	2.9	2.2	2.3
Other manufactured products	6+8	4,388	6,023	7,373	7,082	7,080	4.0	2.6	2.6	2.4	2.5
UK											
TOTAL	0-9	75,915	142,676	188,084	186,010	173,684	18.7	18.2	18.1	18.0	17.5
Agricultural products	0+1	6,086	9,397	10,089	10,874	10,680	17.5	18.7	18.4	18.6	18.2
Crude materials	2+4	4,936	4,719	6,101	6,239	5,447	15.5	11.7	12.1	12.7	11.9
Energy	3	8,276	5,593	12,276	12,761	12,035	12.0	7.1	8.2	8.8	8.7
Chemicals	5	3,621	8,415	10,125	11,442	11,426	13.6	14.2	14.1	14.7	14.1
Machinery and transp. equipment	7	22,161	61,866	79,559	75,605	68,274	19.6	20.2	20.1	19.8	19.1
Other manufactured products	6+8	21,946	45,293	57,715	59,081	56,707	20.4	20.2	20.6	20.6	20.4

BREAKDOWN BY MEMBER STATE AND BY PRODUCT OF INTRA-EU AND EXTRA-EU TRADE BALANCES

Valeur (Mio ECU/Euro)

Reporter	SITC rev. 3	Extra-EU					Intra-EU				
		1990	1999	2000	2001	2002	1990	1999	2000	2001	2002
EU											
TOTAL	**0-9**	**-49,187**	**-19,633**	**-91,391**	**-42,629**	**6,317**	:	:	:	:	:
Agricultural products	0+1	-6,753	-6,516	-4,891	-6,723	-6,147	:	:	:	:	:
Crude materials	2+4	-24,851	-24,903	-31,569	-30,725	-25,807	:	:	:	:	:
Energy	3	-59,324	-61,682	-118,842	-119,035	-111,153	:	:	:	:	:
Chemicals	5	15,538	47,738	58,244	64,927	71,588	:	:	:	:	:
Machinery and transp. equipment	7	29,908	45,877	44,482	81,652	94,589	:	:	:	:	:
Other manufactured products	6+8	519	-17,979	-26,386	-21,596	-9,213	:	:	:	:	:
B[1]											
TOTAL	**0-9**	**-5,997**	**-6,042**	**-8,102**	**-8,588**	**1,170**	**-206**	**19,499**	**19,860**	**21,635**	**16,341**
Agricultural products	0+1	-875	-1,537	-1,365	-1,190	-1,404	400	3,502	3,957	3,986	4,086
Crude materials	2+4	-2,012	-1,945	-2,535	-2,150	-2,128	-1,109	-97	-60	-84	-428
Energy	3	-2,124	-781	-1,651	-2,127	-1,817	-2,812	-3,183	-5,724	-5,821	-4,800
Chemicals	5	2	2,857	3,520	3,544	10,758	1,202	5,984	6,427	5,570	-477
Machinery and transp. equipment	7	-1,671	-1,894	-2,019	-2,165	-1,797	1,266	3,111	2,841	5,306	6,133
Other manufactured products	6+8	-201	-2,947	-4,429	-4,668	-2,656	3,395	9,521	11,420	11,645	11,302
DK											
TOTAL	**0-9**	**1,020**	**2,630**	**2,713**	**3,719**	**5,180**	**1,403**	**1,632**	**3,497**	**3,408**	**2,866**
Agricultural products	0+1	867	877	921	1,079	1,076	3,337	3,882	4,306	4,773	4,397
Crude materials	2+4	-20	145	247	185	156	284	77	99	33	50
Energy	3	-955	-836	-1,372	-1,058	-561	139	1,027	2,911	2,115	2,269
Chemicals	5	145	1,387	1,724	2,171	2,212	-1,289	-599	-546	-580	-525
Machinery and transp. equipment	7	472	1,017	1,099	1,627	2,324	-1,131	-3,378	-4,210	-3,684	-4,110
Other manufactured products	6+8	-68	-435	-451	-515	-456	-1,116	-429	-299	-350	-285
D											
TOTAL	**0-9**	**10,939**	**28,944**	**17,088**	**43,982**	**61,265**	**32,739**	**36,258**	**42,042**	**51,513**	**64,961**
Agricultural products	0+1	-3,720	-3,465	-3,119	-3,161	-3,105	-7,577	-8,535	-7,326	-6,953	-6,365
Crude materials	2+4	-5,370	-5,359	-6,758	-6,011	-4,726	-3,444	-2,849	-3,473	-3,365	-3,281
Energy	3	-9,536	-15,022	-27,221	-27,356	-24,943	-6,005	-5,618	-13,398	-13,649	-11,018
Chemicals	5	7,616	17,931	20,427	22,915	19,662	4,418	2,113	3,214	1,076	239
Machinery and transp. equipment	7	26,814	40,369	43,245	63,582	72,859	40,261	51,719	61,018	59,942	67,370
Other manufactured products	6+8	-3,719	-7,105	-10,083	-7,822	-1,504	4,700	7,566	11,120	14,593	20,616
EL											
TOTAL	**0-9**	**-3,042**	**-4,713**	**-7,438**	**-7,758**	**-9,661**	**-6,307**	**-13,546**	**-15,128**	**-12,322**	**-12,457**
Agricultural products	0+1	15	329	438	457	211	-641	-1,555	-1,803	-1,568	-1,888
Crude materials	2+4	-298	-48	-71	-143	-265	55	405	176	155	28
Energy	3	-829	-552	-2,619	-3,657	-3,663	81	-84	-8	90	-2
Chemicals	5	-183	-199	-198	-247	-285	-1,231	-2,506	-2,861	-2,579	-2,278
Machinery and transp. equipment	7	-1,361	-3,226	-3,513	-2,984	-4,303	-3,207	-6,862	-7,327	-5,644	-5,122
Other manufactured products	6+8	-380	-1,045	-1,413	-1,186	-1,123	-1,469	-3,011	-3,283	-2,748	-3,277

(1) With Luxembourg until 1998.

BREAKDOWN BY MEMBER STATE AND BY PRODUCT OF INTRA-EU AND EXTRA-EU TRADE BALANCES

Valeur (Mio ECU/Euro)

Reporter	SITC rev. 3	Extra-EU					Intra-EU				
		1990	1999	2000	2001	2002	1990	1999	2000	2001	2002
E											
TOTAL	**0-9**	**-10,172**	**-11,571**	**-19,637**	**-19,732**	**-18,865**	**-10,353**	**-17,434**	**-24,637**	**-22,687**	**-18,744**
Agricultural products	0+1	-1,311	-1,724	-1,941	-2,272	-2,391	1,051	2,922	3,695	4,272	4,066
Crude materials	2+4	-1,931	-2,750	-2,956	-2,960	-2,665	-420	-407	-224	-249	-48
Energy	3	-6,082	-6,689	-15,425	-14,645	-14,320	75	265	111	-432	-701
Chemicals	5	211	163	362	351	531	-2,904	-5,285	-6,514	-7,000	-6,800
Machinery and transp. equipment	7	-2,731	-1,031	69	45	454	-5,248	-11,458	-16,370	-14,709	-11,554
Other manufactured products	6+8	1,707	12	-2	-312	-511	-2,879	-3,662	-4,790	-4,229	-3,542
F											
TOTAL	**0-9**	**-496**	**16,266**	**8,168**	**13,793**	**17,174**	**-16,243**	**-7,092**	**-20,434**	**-19,632**	**-14,576**
Agricultural products	0+1	1,873	4,116	4,578	3,935	4,223	5,712	5,800	5,164	4,226	4,924
Crude materials	2+4	-2,849	-2,083	-2,713	-2,844	-2,240	952	-421	-294	-169	-306
Energy	3	-11,901	-11,027	-21,223	-20,925	-19,268	-1,638	-840	-2,441	-2,237	-2,382
Chemicals	5	3,659	6,858	8,260	9,458	10,322	-1,075	1,718	-113	83	553
Machinery and transp. equipment	7	6,718	16,203	18,794	23,116	21,356	-7,268	-2,488	-7,099	-6,292	-3,040
Other manufactured products	6+8	2,210	-39	-1,106	-415	210	-13,288	-11,265	-15,922	-15,655	-15,071
IRL											
TOTAL	**0-9**	**-260**	**5,906**	**9,926**	**14,783**	**14,181**	**2,594**	**17,053**	**18,628**	**21,259**	**24,214**
Agricultural products	0+1	741	1,309	1,423	1,268	1,045	1,751	1,936	2,155	1,738	1,806
Crude materials	2+4	-135	-45	-62	-50	-57	299	135	244	269	203
Energy	3	-186	-357	-739	-636	-409	-691	-746	-1,246	-1,163	-1,034
Chemicals	5	604	7,050	10,436	12,512	12,289	320	9,277	10,928	13,544	19,930
Machinery and transp. equipment	7	-1,258	-2,594	-1,611	816	129	1,216	6,017	5,524	6,368	4,333
Other manufactured products	6+8	-132	344	307	621	784	-464	165	278	-441	-1,278
I											
TOTAL	**0-9**	**-4,611**	**12,598**	**4,067**	**11,397**	**13,529**	**-4,651**	**1,407**	**-2,160**	**-2,214**	**-5,051**
Agricultural products	0+1	-1,616	-135	-104	-7	-88	-6,284	-5,157	-5,475	-4,842	-4,265
Crude materials	2+4	-5,125	-5,257	-6,792	-6,449	-5,600	-4,982	-4,305	-5,191	-5,091	-4,900
Energy	3	-12,232	-10,065	-19,220	-18,667	-18,264	-39	-165	-178	242	-108
Chemicals	5	-192	1,711	2,437	2,778	3,099	-6,965	-8,783	-9,355	-8,635	-8,722
Machinery and transp. equipment	7	9,560	16,367	19,017	22,638	23,043	-2,282	-3,682	-4,963	-6,891	-9,016
Other manufactured products	6+8	9,363	16,142	19,172	21,847	20,500	16,257	23,421	23,383	23,627	22,725
L											
TOTAL	**0-9**	**:**	**-806**	**-684**	**-1,339**	**-1,451**	**:**	**-2,023**	**-2,456**	**-1,534**	**-1,642**
Agricultural products	0+1	:	-47	-47	-31	-36	:	-551	-572	-568	-581
Crude materials	2+4	:	-31	-50	-50	-55	:	-346	-426	-500	-377
Energy	3	:	0.0	-0.0	1	-2	:	-367	-767	-652	-631
Chemicals	5	:	10	5	-9	-5	:	-467	-564	-657	-563
Machinery and transp. equipment	7	:	-1,137	-963	-1,693	-1,413	:	-881	-599	187	36
Other manufactured products	6+8	:	376	380	428	469	:	779	677	862	678
NL											
TOTAL	**0-9**	**-18,383**	**-44,697**	**-61,630**	**-57,716**	**-50,544**	**17,259**	**56,348**	**77,722**	**82,523**	**76,765**
Agricultural products	0+1	-84	-1,196	-703	-1,205	-360	8,146	13,106	14,387	14,965	15,359
Crude materials	2+4	-2,616	-2,993	-3,839	-4,122	-3,592	2,764	5,961	6,251	6,862	7,238
Energy	3	-8,835	-8,714	-14,488	-12,797	-12,526	6,384	7,593	12,030	12,637	10,711
Chemicals	5	277	18	-33	-225	-261	4,176	6,290	8,876	9,349	10,284
Machinery and transp. equipment	7	-4,748	-21,384	-30,443	-26,726	-23,675	-3,982	14,935	24,787	26,043	20,769
Other manufactured products	6+8	-4,065	-11,923	-13,872	-14,402	-11,979	-4,780	4,734	7,251	8,481	8,458

BREAKDOWN BY MEMBER STATE AND BY PRODUCT OF INTRA-EU AND EXTRA-EU TRADE BALANCES

Valeur (Mio ECU/Euro)

Reporter	SITC rev. 3	Extra-EU					Intra-EU				
		1990	1999	2000	2001	2002	1990	1999	2000	2001	2002
A											
TOTAL	**0-9**	**-780**	**4,472**	**3,876**	**3,854**	**5,075**	**-5,609**	**-9,407**	**-8,947**	**-8,188**	**-4,680**
Agricultural products	0+1	-355	133	77	251	250	-531	-946	-744	-848	-755
Crude materials	2+4	-462	-484	-682	-582	-515	331	77	6	-17	7
Energy	3	-1,924	-1,613	-2,823	-2,928	-2,818	-215	-612	-1,164	-1,097	-1,053
Chemicals	5	304	1,383	1,505	1,609	1,980	-1,413	-2,476	-2,656	-2,769	-2,746
Machinery and transp. equipment	7	-112	3,091	2,477	2,578	2,518	-2,459	-4,034	-2,646	-2,014	571
Other manufactured products	6+8	1,799	1,954	2,763	2,986	3,568	-1,310	-1,372	-1,589	-1,535	-813
P											
TOTAL	**0-9**	**-3,031**	**-4,341**	**-5,558**	**-5,552**	**-3,852**	**-3,637**	**-10,139**	**-11,320**	**-11,179**	**-9,693**
Agricultural products	0+1	-712	-904	-873	-901	-759	-324	-1,888	-1,949	-2,240	-1,931
Crude materials	2+4	-418	-534	-564	-589	-579	431	107	207	36	-13
Energy	3	-1,586	-1,400	-2,514	-2,591	-2,293	-162	-714	-1,252	-1,174	-1,187
Chemicals	5	-80	-213	-122	-172	-162	-1,034	-2,245	-2,457	-2,740	-2,812
Machinery and transp. equipment	7	-640	-1,512	-1,609	-1,532	-471	-3,936	-5,298	-5,463	-4,740	-3,656
Other manufactured products	6+8	407	209	130	225	391	1,443	-71	-284	-226	-20
FIN											
TOTAL	**0-9**	**-149**	**6,313**	**7,927**	**9,046**	**9,225**	**-138**	**3,191**	**4,698**	**2,787**	**2,331**
Agricultural products	0+1	-159	-39	-2	104	142	-332	-1,004	-1,038	-1,097	-1,217
Crude materials	2+4	34	-499	-660	-560	-441	959	1,288	1,584	1,205	1,274
Energy	3	-2,026	-1,520	-2,793	-2,834	-2,604	-157	-48	124	185	166
Chemicals	5	157	436	536	675	867	-1,110	-1,269	-1,462	-1,589	-1,736
Machinery and transp. equipment	7	357	4,710	6,821	7,653	7,147	-2,102	-801	70	-936	-784
Other manufactured products	6+8	1,479	3,229	4,027	4,007	4,126	2,600	5,332	5,970	5,459	5,082
S											
TOTAL	**0-9**	**1,277**	**12,358**	**13,312**	**14,031**	**15,558**	**974**	**2,944**	**2,120**	**-135**	**-55**
Agricultural products	0+1	-758	-677	-612	-512	-504	-886	-1,624	-1,696	-1,825	-2,135
Crude materials	2+4	250	263	231	156	417	2,281	2,110	2,823	2,391	2,223
Energy	3	-2,250	-1,996	-3,627	-3,040	-2,911	-277	-8	-369	-235	-733
Chemicals	5	267	1,371	1,859	2,039	2,435	-978	-716	-529	-490	-520
Machinery and transp. equipment	7	2,972	10,220	11,885	11,568	11,472	29	244	-1,144	-3,865	-3,102
Other manufactured products	6+8	711	2,153	2,523	2,666	3,393	757	2,889	3,314	3,455	3,165
UK											
TOTAL	**0-9**	**-15,155**	**-36,950**	**-55,418**	**-56,549**	**-51,667**	**-16,860**	**-12,528**	**-7,759**	**-10,767**	**-18,106**
Agricultural products	0+1	-1,930	-3,555	-3,562	-4,538	-4,446	-5,447	-7,796	-8,221	-9,425	-9,844
Crude materials	2+4	-4,077	-3,284	-4,365	-4,557	-3,516	-1,112	-2,090	-2,354	-2,506	-2,288
Energy	3	-5,057	-1,110	-3,127	-5,776	-4,753	3,910	7,468	13,662	14,551	13,702
Chemicals	5	3,479	6,976	7,526	7,529	8,148	-518	-1,008	-1,355	-824	-2,154
Machinery and transp. equipment	7	-1,247	-13,323	-18,767	-16,872	-15,055	-8,200	-2,789	-2,118	-3,004	-4,968
Other manufactured products	6+8	-4,605	-18,905	-24,332	-25,058	-24,426	-8,260	-6,442	-7,379	-9,662	-11,972

TRADE BALANCE (BN ECU/euro)

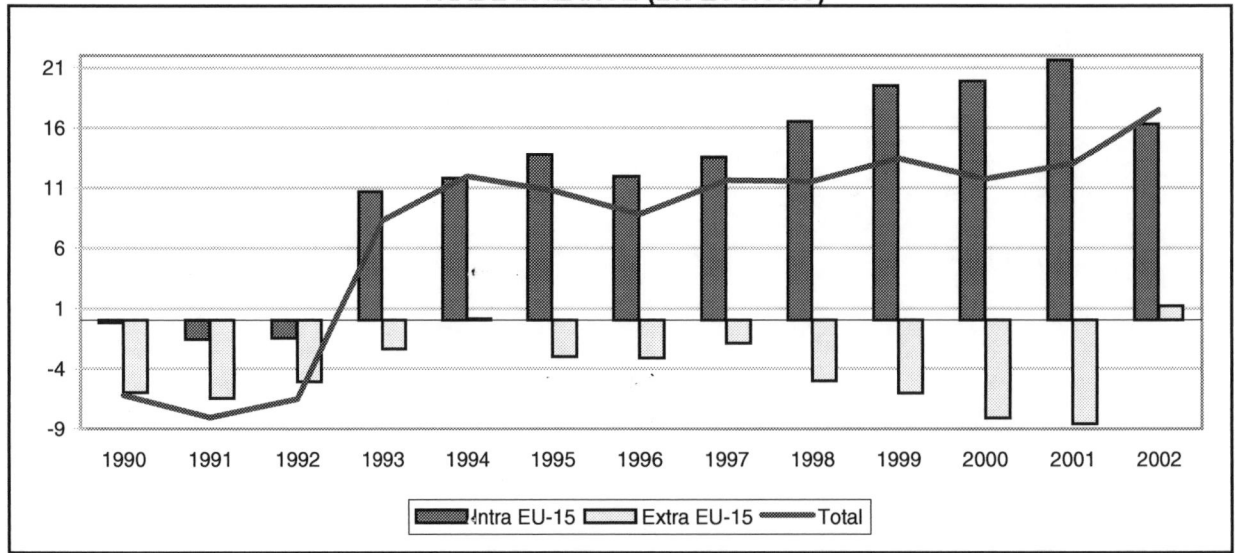

INTRA-EU (BN ECU/euro)

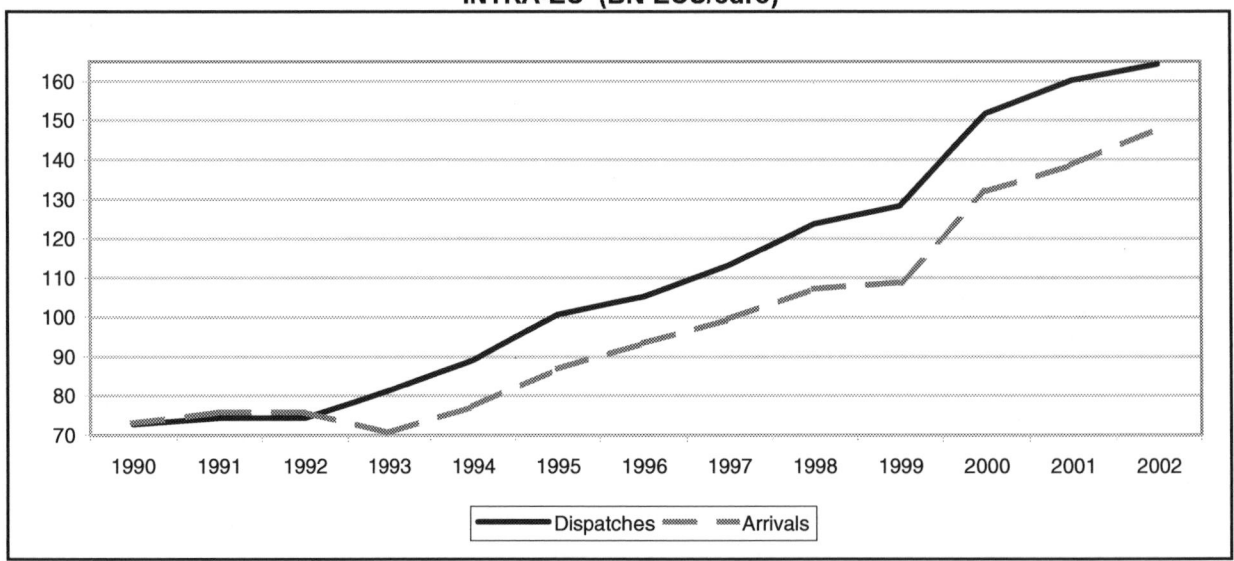

EXTRA-EU (BN ECU/euro)

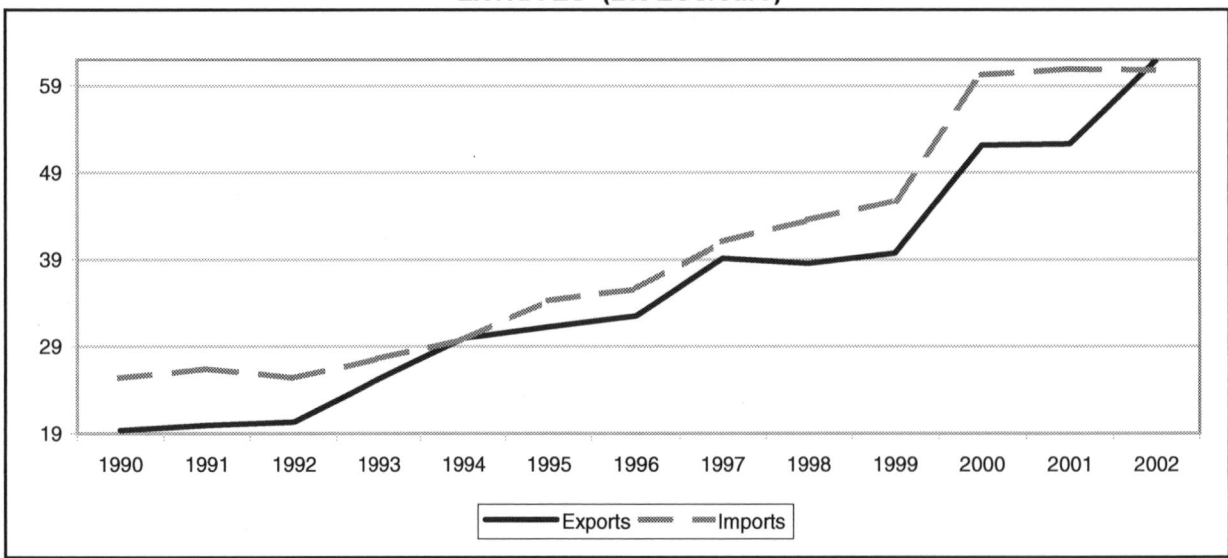

BELGIUM [1]

TRADE BALANCE

INTRA-EU

Value (Mio ECU/Euro)

Year	Intra EU	DK	D	EL	E	F	IRL	I	L	NL	A	P	FIN	S	UK
										Partner					
1980	2,403	320	-205	119	-13	1,586	-46	716	:	-1,248	161	97	15	9	892
1990	-194	252	-2,705	422	859	3,912	-218	1,833	:	-4,868	416	289	72	-835	376
1991	-1,557	184	-255	399	887	2,815	-296	1,323	:	-5,387	524	262	-52	-1,225	-736
1992	-1,438	221	-1,186	452	1,078	2,535	-302	1,285	:	-5,771	565	343	-31	-786	159
1993	10,692	399	2,274	500	1,484	5,750	-619	1,781	:	-1,218	555	456	-43	-828	200
1994	11,833	436	4,557	583	1,772	6,630	-581	1,791	:	-2,748	573	438	-229	-1,489	100
1995	13,788	506	4,196	562	1,610	6,065	-890	1,997	:	-3,451	668	389	-283	-1,286	38
1996	11,977	516	4,202	657	1,918	6,893	-1,213	2,424	:	-4,534	773	409	46	-1,320	1,208
1997	13,552	597	3,831	696	2,347	7,340	-1,671	2,966	:	-5,256	836	373	53	-1,256	2,697
1998	16,545	636	3,338	797	3,021	8,552	-2,901	3,494	:	-4,115	935	571	-60	-1,362	3,639
1999	19,499	695	2,789	910	3,516	8,778	-2,228	3,373	2,509	-4,397	850	342	-57	-1,254	3,672
2000	19,860	770	2,999	983	3,856	11,494	-2,682	3,772	3,063	-7,816	903	115	-135	-1,199	3,738
2001	21,635	829	6,099	1,075	4,309	10,089	-3,931	3,746	2,997	-8,247	928	-357	-84	-1,696	5,879
2002	16,341	768	6,123	1,134	4,327	10,637	-12,946	3,912	2,787	-6,343	1,188	-199	-38	-1,448	6,437

EXTRA-EU

Value (Mio ECU/Euro)

Year	Extra EU	Norway	Switzerland	Russia[2]	Candid. countries	USA	Canada	China	Japan	Hong Kong	Mediterr. Basin	Latin America	OPEC	DAE	ACP
									Partner						
1980	-7,557	-56	664	-370	:	-2,426	-253	-68	-851	106	1,197	-398	-2,615	77	-680
1990	-5,997	-11	595	-832	:	-1,729	-172	-329	-2,175	311	1,118	-1,277	-246	393	-1,220
1991	-6,478	-154	738	-785	:	-2,674	-247	-564	-2,674	358	1,319	-1,105	123	396	-1,037
1992	-5,062	-215	696	-379	:	-2,239	-207	-671	-2,915	506	1,615	-864	815	446	-1,054
1993	-2,368	-701	843	-645	906	-1,107	-59	-650	-2,087	738	2,364	-457	420	1,004	-92
1994	149	-234	728	-613	688	-455	-193	-574	-1,340	792	2,175	-677	532	1,324	-1,140
1995	-3,006	-381	629	-354	863	-3,086	-543	-842	-1,909	627	2,173	-921	545	693	-1,632
1996	-3,123	-400	827	-68	1,589	-3,022	-431	-1,136	-1,384	766	2,445	-1,062	502	998	-1,742
1997	-1,877	-408	1,013	73	2,153	-3,472	-455	-1,523	-1,683	900	2,852	-793	565	929	-1,531
1998	-5,024	-263	1,070	70	2,051	-2,893	-339	-1,642	-2,395	569	2,445	-1,151	429	-526	-1,443
1999	-6,042	-223	1,024	-386	1,486	-2,893	-457	-2,064	-2,796	718	2,580	-1,312	274	-437	-1,733
2000	-8,102	-1,236	1,402	-670	1,722	-2,475	-678	-2,671	-3,529	869	3,109	-1,277	-153	-802	-1,971
2001	-8,588	-1,451	1,326	-687	683	-2,098	-586	-2,625	-3,516	748	2,186	-1,180	833	-1,127	-1,814
2002	1,170	-794	1,209	-591	1,873	4,431	422	-2,730	-4,311	716	1,937	-1,198	239	-484	-1,954

(1) Luxembourg with Belgium until 31.12.1998.
(2) Relates to the external trade with the USSR until 1991 and to the external trade with Russia from 1992 onwards.

BELGIUM [1]

INTRA-EU

Year	Partner														
	Intra EU	DK	D	EL	E	F	IRL	I	L	NL	A	P	FIN	S	UK
EXPORTS / DISPATCHES															
Value (Mio ECU/Euro)															
1980	35,279	554	9,881	197	429	9,020	142	2,566	:	7,060	356	211	167	756	3,941
1990	72,837	832	19,716	566	2,138	18,797	345	6,089	:	12,654	1,111	652	542	1,336	8,060
1994	89,127	1,081	24,810	713	3,462	22,954	482	6,151	:	15,427	1,209	970	490	1,539	9,840
1995	100,674	1,212	27,842	687	3,623	23,708	450	6,872	:	16,952	1,320	925	660	1,796	10,269
1996	105,290	1,255	28,823	821	4,200	25,623	594	7,638	:	18,505	1,518	1,068	833	1,930	12,482
1997	113,166	1,382	29,464	861	4,760	27,056	669	8,360	:	19,464	1,670	1,135	925	2,220	15,202
1998	123,724	1,502	31,498	969	5,785	29,814	888	9,441	:	20,688	1,876	1,425	962	2,586	16,289
1999	128,352	1,521	29,795	1,101	6,646	30,033	1,146	9,366	3,412	21,453	1,896	1,440	990	2,636	16,915
2000	151,813	1,657	34,541	1,310	7,343	35,844	1,619	11,286	4,143	25,758	2,096	1,660	1,121	3,195	20,239
2001	160,262	1,730	38,526	1,412	8,204	36,956	1,661	12,266	4,176	25,893	2,307	1,617	1,179	2,959	21,376
2002	164,305	1,693	42,036	1,392	8,185	36,806	1,756	12,210	4,056	26,320	2,360	1,495	1,155	3,081	21,762
Annual variation (%)															
98/97	9.3	8.7	6.9	12.6	21.5	10.1	32.8	12.9	:	6.2	12.3	25.5	4.0	16.4	7.1
99/98	3.7	1.2	-5.4	13.5	14.8	0.7	29.0	-0.7	:	3.6	1.0	1.0	2.9	1.9	3.8
00/99	18.2	8.9	15.9	19.0	10.4	19.3	41.2	20.5	21.4	20.0	10.5	15.2	13.1	21.2	19.6
01/00	5.5	4.3	11.5	7.7	11.7	3.1	2.6	8.6	0.7	0.5	10.0	-2.6	5.1	-7.3	5.6
02/01	2.5	-2.1	9.1	-1.3	-0.2	-0.4	5.7	-0.4	-2.8	1.6	2.2	-7.5	-1.9	4.0	1.8
Share (%)															
1980	100.0	1.5	28.0	0.5	1.2	25.5	0.4	7.2	:	20.0	1.0	0.5	0.4	2.1	11.1
1990	100.0	1.1	27.0	0.7	2.9	25.8	0.4	8.3	:	17.3	1.5	0.8	0.7	1.8	11.0
1996	100.0	1.1	27.3	0.7	3.9	24.3	0.5	7.2	:	17.5	1.4	1.0	0.7	1.8	11.8
1997	100.0	1.2	26.0	0.7	4.2	23.9	0.5	7.3	:	17.1	1.4	1.0	0.8	1.9	13.4
1998	100.0	1.2	25.4	0.7	4.6	24.0	0.7	7.6	:	16.7	1.5	1.1	0.7	2.0	13.1
1999	100.0	1.1	23.2	0.8	5.1	23.3	0.8	7.2	2.6	16.7	1.4	1.1	0.7	2.0	13.1
2000	100.0	1.0	22.7	0.8	4.8	23.6	1.0	7.4	2.7	16.9	1.3	1.0	0.7	2.1	13.3
2001	100.0	1.0	24.0	0.8	5.1	23.0	1.0	7.6	2.6	16.1	1.4	1.0	0.7	1.8	13.3
2002	100.0	1.0	25.5	0.8	4.9	22.4	1.0	7.4	2.4	16.0	1.4	0.9	0.7	1.8	13.2
IMPORTS / ARRIVALS															
Value (Mio ECU/Euro)															
1980	32,876	233	10,086	79	441	7,434	187	1,850	:	8,308	194	114	152	747	3,049
1990	73,031	579	22,421	143	1,279	14,885	563	4,256	:	17,521	695	363	470	2,171	7,684
1994	77,294	645	20,253	130	1,690	16,323	1,063	4,359	:	18,175	636	532	719	3,029	9,740
1995	86,886	706	23,646	126	2,014	17,642	1,340	4,875	:	20,403	652	535	943	3,082	10,231
1996	93,313	739	24,621	164	2,283	18,730	1,806	5,215	:	23,039	745	659	787	3,250	11,274
1997	99,614	785	25,634	165	2,414	19,716	2,339	5,393	:	24,719	834	762	872	3,476	12,505
1998	107,179	866	28,161	173	2,764	21,262	3,789	5,947	:	24,803	941	854	1,022	3,948	12,650
1999	108,853	826	27,007	191	3,130	21,255	3,374	5,993	903	25,850	1,046	1,098	1,047	3,890	13,242
2000	131,953	887	31,542	328	3,486	24,350	4,301	7,515	1,081	33,575	1,193	1,545	1,256	4,394	16,501
2001	138,626	901	32,427	337	3,895	26,867	5,592	8,520	1,179	34,139	1,379	1,974	1,263	4,656	15,497
2002	147,964	925	35,912	258	3,858	26,169	14,701	8,297	1,269	32,663	1,172	1,693	1,193	4,528	15,324
Annual variation (%)															
98/97	7.5	10.3	9.8	4.5	14.5	7.8	61.9	10.2	:	0.3	12.7	12.0	17.2	13.5	1.1
99/98	1.5	-4.6	-4.0	10.7	13.2	0.0	-10.9	0.7	:	4.2	11.2	28.5	2.4	-1.4	4.6
00/99	21.2	7.4	16.7	71.4	11.3	14.5	27.4	25.3	19.6	29.8	14.0	40.7	19.9	12.9	24.6
01/00	5.0	1.5	2.8	2.8	11.7	10.3	30.0	13.3	9.1	1.6	15.6	27.7	0.5	5.9	-6.0
02/01	6.7	2.7	10.7	-23.3	-0.9	-2.5	162.8	-2.6	7.6	-4.3	-15.0	-14.2	-5.5	-2.7	-1.1
Share (%)															
1980	100.0	0.7	30.6	0.2	1.3	22.6	0.5	5.6	:	25.2	0.5	0.3	0.4	2.2	9.2
1990	100.0	0.7	30.7	0.1	1.7	20.3	0.7	5.8	:	23.9	0.9	0.4	0.6	2.9	10.5
1996	100.0	0.7	26.3	0.1	2.4	20.0	1.9	5.5	:	24.6	0.7	0.7	0.8	3.4	12.0
1997	100.0	0.7	25.7	0.1	2.4	19.7	2.3	5.4	:	24.8	0.8	0.7	0.8	3.4	12.5
1998	100.0	0.8	26.2	0.1	2.5	19.8	3.5	5.5	:	23.1	0.8	0.7	0.9	3.6	11.8
1999	100.0	0.7	24.8	0.1	2.8	19.5	3.0	5.5	0.8	23.7	0.9	1.0	0.9	3.5	12.1
2000	100.0	0.6	23.9	0.2	2.6	18.4	3.2	5.6	0.8	25.4	0.9	1.1	0.9	3.3	12.5
2001	100.0	0.6	23.3	0.2	2.8	19.3	4.0	6.1	0.8	24.6	0.9	1.4	0.9	3.3	11.1
2002	100.0	0.6	24.2	0.1	2.6	17.6	9.9	5.6	0.8	22.0	0.7	1.1	0.8	3.0	10.3

(1) Luxembourg with Belgium until 31.12.1998.

EXTRA-EU

Years	Extra EU	Norway	Switzerland	USSR/ Russia[1]	Candid. countries	USA	Canada	China	Japan	Hong Kong	Mediterr. Basin	Latin America	OPEC	DAE	ACP
						Partner									

EXPORTS
Value (Mio ECU/Euro)

Years	Extra EU	Norway	Switzerland	USSR/ Russia[1]	Candid. countries	USA	Canada	China	Japan	Hong Kong	Mediterr. Basin	Latin America	OPEC	DAE	ACP
1980	11,180	372	1,775	446	:	1,556	129	75	227	280	2,487	625	2,151	654	1,000
1990	19,399	461	1,922	353	:	4,013	404	277	1,238	521	3,134	636	1,680	1,864	1,154
1994	29,958	534	2,395	657	2,226	5,878	506	910	1,543	1,046	4,574	1,378	2,062	3,507	1,116
1995	31,257	524	2,300	804	2,807	4,747	370	674	1,650	906	4,722	1,601	1,758	3,176	1,134
1996	32,512	550	2,425	1,047	3,636	5,840	438	694	1,915	1,032	5,331	1,572	1,857	3,513	1,237
1997	39,143	620	2,604	1,398	4,597	7,598	542	765	1,829	1,295	6,333	1,971	2,311	3,914	1,434
1998	38,538	708	2,642	1,043	5,245	8,519	648	746	1,542	939	6,063	1,969	2,205	2,773	2,005
1999	39,740	717	2,436	636	5,098	8,756	721	888	1,990	1,135	6,417	1,684	2,134	3,160	1,913
2000	52,140	727	3,081	944	6,744	11,924	842	1,340	2,420	1,643	8,458	2,490	2,761	4,434	2,428
2001	52,276	735	3,069	1,210	6,623	11,847	892	1,691	2,197	1,524	7,201	2,759	3,397	4,255	2,452
2002	61,919	802	2,842	1,255	7,603	17,791	1,512	1,989	2,204	1,746	7,636	2,606	3,556	4,436	2,509

Annual variation (%)

Years	Extra EU	Norway	Switzerland	USSR/ Russia[1]	Candid. countries	USA	Canada	China	Japan	Hong Kong	Mediterr. Basin	Latin America	OPEC	DAE	ACP
98/97	-1.5	14.1	1.4	-25.3	14.0	12.1	19.4	-2.5	-15.6	-27.4	-4.2	-0.1	-4.6	-29.1	39.8
99/98	3.1	1.2	-7.7	-39.0	-2.8	2.7	11.2	19.0	29.0	20.8	5.8	-14.4	-3.2	13.9	-4.5
00/99	31.2	1.3	26.4	48.5	32.2	36.1	16.7	50.9	21.5	44.7	31.8	47.8	29.3	40.2	26.8
01/00	0.2	1.1	-0.3	28.1	-1.7	-0.6	5.9	26.1	-9.1	-7.2	-14.8	10.8	23.0	-4.0	0.9
02/01	18.4	9.0	-7.4	3.7	14.7	50.1	69.5	17.6	0.2	14.5	6.0	-5.5	4.6	4.2	2.3

Share (%)

Years	Extra EU	Norway	Switzerland	USSR/ Russia[1]	Candid. countries	USA	Canada	China	Japan	Hong Kong	Mediterr. Basin	Latin America	OPEC	DAE	ACP
1980	100.0	3.3	15.8	3.9	:	13.9	1.1	0.6	2.0	2.5	22.2	5.5	19.2	5.8	8.9
1990	100.0	2.3	9.9	1.8	:	20.6	2.0	1.4	6.3	2.6	16.1	3.2	8.6	9.6	5.9
1996	100.0	1.6	7.4	3.2	11.1	17.9	1.3	2.1	5.8	3.1	16.3	4.8	5.7	10.8	3.8
1997	100.0	1.5	6.6	3.5	11.7	19.4	1.3	1.9	4.6	3.3	16.1	5.0	5.9	9.9	3.6
1998	100.0	1.8	6.8	2.7	13.6	22.1	1.6	1.9	4.0	2.4	15.7	5.1	5.7	7.1	5.2
1999	100.0	1.8	6.1	1.5	12.8	22.0	1.8	2.2	5.0	2.8	16.1	4.2	5.3	7.9	4.8
2000	100.0	1.3	5.9	1.8	12.9	22.8	1.6	2.5	4.6	3.1	16.2	4.7	5.2	8.5	4.6
2001	100.0	1.4	5.8	2.3	12.6	22.6	1.7	3.2	4.2	2.9	13.7	5.2	6.4	8.1	4.6
2002	100.0	1.2	4.5	2.0	12.2	28.7	2.4	3.2	3.5	2.8	12.3	4.2	5.7	7.1	4.0

IMPORTS
Value (Mio ECU/Euro)

Years	Extra EU	Norway	Switzerland	USSR/ Russia[1]	Candid. countries	USA	Canada	China	Japan	Hong Kong	Mediterr. Basin	Latin America	OPEC	DAE	ACP
1980	18,737	428	1,111	816	:	3,982	383	143	1,079	174	1,290	1,023	4,766	577	1,680
1990	25,396	472	1,327	1,185	:	5,742	576	606	3,413	210	2,016	1,912	1,926	1,471	2,374
1994	29,809	768	1,667	1,269	3,077	6,334	699	1,484	2,884	254	2,400	2,055	1,530	2,183	2,255
1995	34,263	905	1,671	1,159	1,944	7,833	913	1,516	3,558	278	2,549	2,522	1,212	2,483	2,766
1996	35,635	950	1,598	1,115	2,047	8,862	868	1,830	3,299	267	2,886	2,633	1,355	2,516	2,978
1997	41,020	1,028	1,592	1,325	2,444	11,070	998	2,288	3,512	396	3,480	2,764	1,746	2,986	2,965
1998	43,563	971	1,572	973	3,194	11,970	987	2,388	3,937	370	3,618	3,120	1,775	3,299	3,448
1999	45,782	939	1,412	1,022	3,612	11,648	1,178	2,952	4,786	417	3,837	2,996	1,860	3,598	3,647
2000	60,242	1,963	1,679	1,614	5,022	14,399	1,520	4,011	5,949	775	5,349	3,767	2,914	5,236	4,399
2001	60,865	2,186	1,743	1,897	5,941	13,945	1,478	4,316	5,713	777	5,016	3,939	2,565	5,382	4,265
2002	60,749	1,596	1,632	1,846	5,730	13,360	1,090	4,719	6,515	1,030	5,699	3,804	3,317	4,920	4,464

Annual variation (%)

Years	Extra EU	Norway	Switzerland	USSR/ Russia[1]	Candid. countries	USA	Canada	China	Japan	Hong Kong	Mediterr. Basin	Latin America	OPEC	DAE	ACP
98/97	6.1	-5.5	-1.2	-26.5	30.6	8.1	-1.0	4.3	12.1	-6.4	3.9	12.8	1.6	10.5	16.2
99/98	5.0	-3.2	-10.2	4.9	13.0	-2.6	19.3	23.6	21.5	12.7	6.0	-3.9	4.7	9.0	5.7
00/99	31.5	108.9	18.9	57.8	39.0	23.6	29.0	35.8	24.2	85.6	39.4	25.7	56.6	45.5	20.6
01/00	1.0	11.3	3.8	17.5	18.2	-3.1	-2.7	7.6	-3.9	0.2	-6.2	4.5	-11.9	2.7	-3.0
02/01	-0.1	-26.9	-6.3	-2.6	-3.5	-4.1	-26.2	9.3	14.0	32.6	13.6	-3.4	29.3	-8.5	4.6

Share (%)

Years	Extra EU	Norway	Switzerland	USSR/ Russia[1]	Candid. countries	USA	Canada	China	Japan	Hong Kong	Mediterr. Basin	Latin America	OPEC	DAE	ACP
1980	100.0	2.2	5.9	4.3	:	21.2	2.0	0.7	5.7	0.9	6.8	5.4	25.4	3.0	8.9
1990	100.0	1.8	5.2	4.6	:	22.6	2.2	2.3	13.4	0.8	7.9	7.5	7.5	5.7	9.3
1996	100.0	2.6	4.4	3.1	5.7	24.8	2.4	5.1	9.2	0.7	8.0	7.3	3.8	7.0	8.3
1997	100.0	2.5	3.8	3.2	5.9	26.9	2.4	5.5	8.5	0.9	8.4	6.7	4.2	7.2	7.2
1998	100.0	2.2	3.6	2.2	7.3	27.4	2.2	5.4	9.0	0.8	8.3	7.1	4.0	7.5	7.9
1999	100.0	2.0	3.0	2.2	7.8	25.4	2.5	6.4	10.4	0.9	8.3	6.5	4.0	7.8	7.9
2000	100.0	3.2	2.7	2.6	8.3	23.9	2.5	6.6	9.8	1.2	8.8	6.2	4.8	8.6	7.3
2001	100.0	3.5	2.8	3.1	9.7	22.9	2.4	7.0	9.3	1.2	8.2	6.4	4.2	8.8	7.0
2002	100.0	2.6	2.6	3.0	9.4	21.9	1.7	7.7	10.7	1.6	9.3	6.2	5.4	8.0	7.3

(1) Relates to the external trade with the USSR until 1991and to the external trade with Russia from 1992 onwards.

DENMARK

TRADE BALANCE (BN ECU/euro)

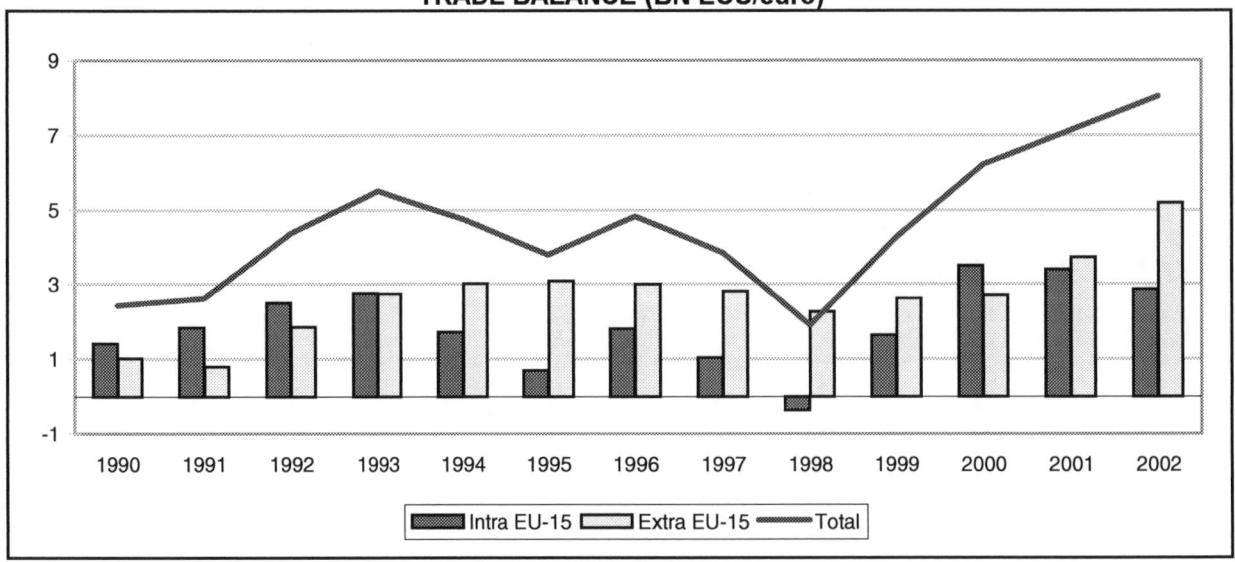

INTRA-EU (BN ECU/euro)

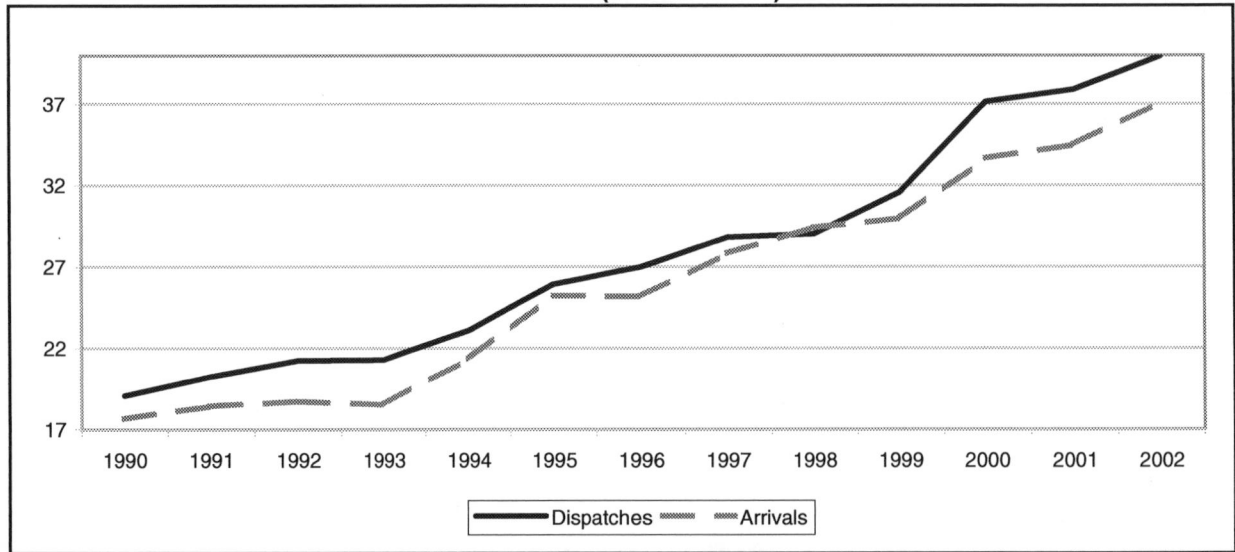

EXTRA-EU (BN ECU/euro)

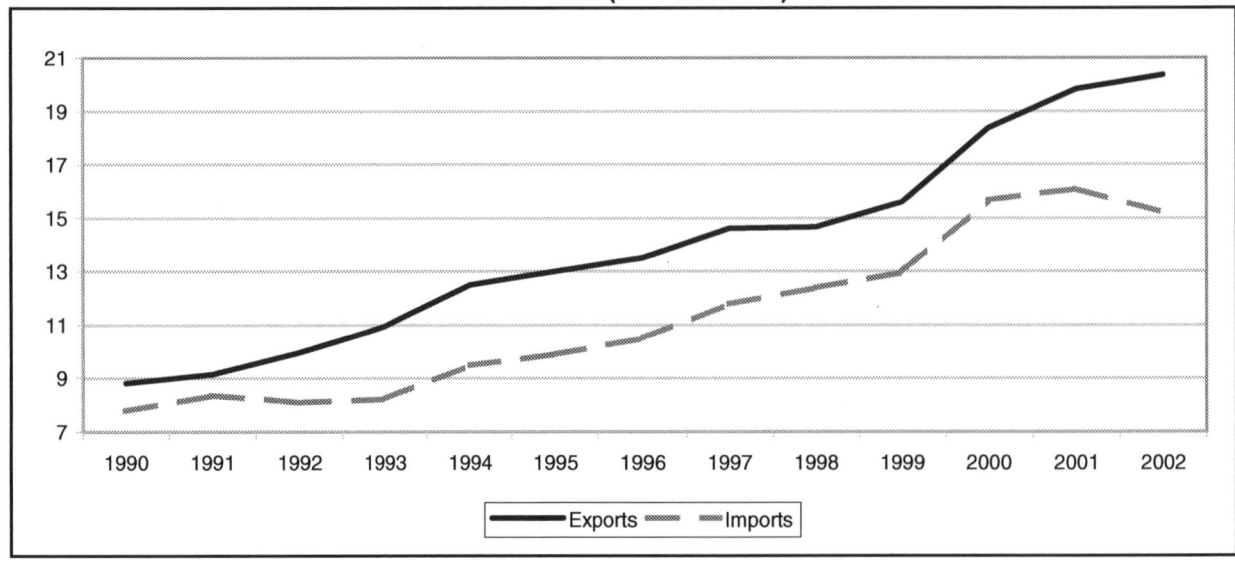

DENMARK

TRADE BALANCE

INTRA-EU

Value (Mio ECU/Euro)

Year	Intra EU	B[1]	D	EL	E	F	IRL	I	L	NL	A	P	FIN	S	UK
															Partner
1980	**-1,442**	**-264**	**-305**	**38**	**1**	**84**	**23**	**233**	**:**	**-624**	**-38**	**-23**	**-271**	**-328**	**33**
1990	**1,414**	**-292**	**-465**	**164**	**230**	**404**	**-7**	**398**	**:**	**-578**	**-39**	**-112**	**-40**	**661**	**1,091**
1991	1,840	-250	434	177	253	148	-32	359	:	-508	-21	-114	-46	511	930
1992	2,514	-273	900	214	280	348	-48	345	:	-445	3	-128	-80	419	979
1993	2,759	-332	1,655	209	241	280	0	146	:	-382	19	-133	-137	260	933
1994	1,731	-451	1,498	200	278	298	-55	26	:	-660	62	-208	-168	-42	951
1995	700	-570	491	220	233	82	-157	-188	:	-1,015	-1	-175	-63	-227	306
1996	1,813	-414	1,138	255	356	275	-191	-18	:	-809	76	-105	130	206	913
1997	1,033	-516	884	283	360	328	-153	-95	:	-1,127	43	-178	20	-71	1,255
1998	-363	-564	136	289	451	73	-130	-141	:	-1,029	45	-141	244	-515	918
1999	1,632	-504	455	331	588	202	131	-135	-5	-1,164	25	-35	352	214	1,176
2000	**3,497**	**-659**	**387**	**364**	**667**	**530**	**134**	**-158**	**85**	**-772**	**-7**	**-41**	**525**	**1,065**	**1,375**
2001	3,408	-711	672	351	620	245	204	-108	83	-807	-32	-2	389	753	1,750
2002	**2,866**	**-873**	**426**	**356**	**956**	**-75**	**213**	**-180**	**96**	**-826**	**-43**	**52**	**570**	**888**	**1,305**

EXTRA-EU

Value (Mio ECU/Euro)

Year	Extra EU	Norway	Switzerland	Russia[2]	Candid. countries	USA	Canada	China	Japan	Hong Kong	Mediterr. Basin	Latin America	OPEC	DAE	ACP
															Partner
1980	**-469**	**180**	**25**	**-233**	**:**	**-345**	**7**	**-14**	**-85**	**-37**	**187**	**-187**	**82**	**-77**	**-8**
1990	**1,020**	**383**	**16**	**77**	**:**	**46**	**32**	**-234**	**69**	**9**	**309**	**-206**	**225**	**-65**	**376**
1991	796	123	35	-58	:	-132	15	-464	244	41	279	-113	467	-130	263
1992	1,865	351	42	-77	:	13	-5	-447	250	62	362	-20	502	138	512
1993	2,745	633	-5	-58	219	470	56	-390	413	93	400	-64	535	18	319
1994	3,021	290	110	61	218	569	76	-395	436	133	258	-7	399	92	463
1995	3,097	69	123	141	245	3	47	-370	592	146	423	55	446	357	435
1996	3,010	83	71	279	391	-6	45	-400	616	201	491	-26	434	470	112
1997	2,821	-163	81	541	435	71	68	-508	652	237	470	-107	416	296	226
1998	2,272	-127	69	362	453	106	123	-621	445	226	512	22	362	92	195
1999	2,630	-136	140	98	221	414	95	-832	725	163	546	7	355	211	235
2000	**2,713**	**-648**	**269**	**123**	**37**	**1,219**	**57**	**-1,005**	**1,219**	**253**	**543**	**50**	**362**	**-239**	**296**
2001	3,719	-182	153	349	-194	1,606	138	-1,013	1,253	261	437	-57	474	96	316
2002	**5,180**	**72**	**194**	**333**	**-19**	**1,932**	**298**	**-932**	**1,110**	**342**	**473**	**-72**	**592**	**297**	**306**

(1)   Luxembourg with Belgium until 31.12.1998.
(2)   Relates to the external trade with the USSR until 1991 and to the external trade with Russia from 1992 onwards.

DENMARK

INTRA-EU

Year	Intra EU	B(1)	D	EL	E	F	IRL	I	L	NL	A	P	FIN	S	UK
EXPORTS / DISPATCHES Value (Mio ECU/Euro)															
1980	**8,214**	**238**	**2,340**	**66**	93	**648**	**64**	**617**	:	**467**	**116**	**40**	**260**	**1,542**	**1,722**
1990	**19,094**	**595**	**5,519**	**217**	**475**	**1,665**	**142**	**1,372**	:	**1,367**	**263**	**170**	**722**	**3,582**	**3,004**
1994	23,089	685	8,497	263	635	1,976	189	1,402	:	1,609	365	193	708	3,431	3,135
1995	25,922	698	8,587	269	646	1,970	200	1,381	:	1,627	354	229	956	3,994	2,875
1996	26,981	834	9,193	312	803	2,215	229	1,588	:	1,795	420	274	1,114	4,580	3,623
1997	28,840	917	9,370	350	888	2,431	313	1,612	:	1,947	419	225	1,173	4,983	4,211
1998	29,050	947	9,197	362	1,040	2,400	321	1,801	:	2,058	461	239	1,339	4,749	4,135
1999	31,599	941	9,542	399	1,214	2,665	651	1,811	44	2,239	481	298	1,510	5,302	4,500
2000	**37,164**	**918**	**10,657**	**451**	**1,347**	**2,984**	**738**	**1,893**	**140**	**2,821**	**509**	**306**	**1,839**	**7,037**	**5,523**
2001	37,915	967	11,531	463	1,399	3,135	799	2,057	150	2,662	512	324	1,715	6,671	5,529
2002	**39,974**	**1,011**	**11,951**	**475**	**1,814**	**3,086**	**892**	**2,022**	**166**	**2,745**	**555**	**371**	**1,897**	**7,119**	**5,869**
Annual variation (%)															
98/97	0.7	3.2	-1.8	3.3	17.1	-1.2	2.3	11.7	:	5.7	9.9	6.1	14.1	-4.6	-1.8
99/98	8.7	-0.6	3.7	10.2	16.6	11.0	102.8	0.5	:	8.7	4.1	24.4	12.7	11.6	8.8
00/99	17.6	-2.4	11.6	13.1	10.9	11.9	13.4	4.5	216.4	25.9	5.8	2.7	21.7	32.7	22.7
01/00	2.0	5.4	8.1	2.5	3.8	5.0	8.2	8.6	7.4	-5.6	0.5	6.0	-6.7	-5.2	0.1
02/01	5.4	4.4	3.6	2.6	29.4	-1.5	11.6	-1.6	10.4	3.1	8.4	14.3	10.5	6.7	6.1
Share (%)															
1980	**100.0**	**2.9**	**28.4**	**0.7**	**1.1**	**7.8**	**0.7**	**7.5**	:	**5.6**	**1.4**	**0.4**	**3.1**	**18.7**	**20.9**
1990	**100.0**	**3.1**	**28.9**	**1.1**	**2.4**	**8.7**	**0.7**	**7.1**	:	**7.1**	**1.3**	**0.8**	**3.7**	**18.7**	**15.7**
1996	100.0	3.0	34.0	1.1	2.9	8.2	0.8	5.8	:	6.6	1.5	1.0	4.1	16.9	13.4
1997	100.0	3.1	32.4	1.2	3.0	8.4	1.0	5.5	:	6.7	1.4	0.7	4.0	17.2	14.6
1998	100.0	3.2	31.6	1.2	3.5	8.2	1.1	6.1	:	7.0	1.5	0.8	4.6	16.3	14.2
1999	100.0	2.9	30.1	1.2	3.8	8.4	2.0	5.7	0.1	7.0	1.5	0.9	4.7	16.7	14.2
2000	**100.0**	**2.4**	**28.6**	**1.2**	**3.6**	**8.0**	**1.9**	**5.0**	**0.3**	**7.5**	**1.3**	**0.8**	**4.9**	**18.9**	**14.8**
2001	100.0	2.5	30.4	1.2	3.6	8.2	2.1	5.4	0.3	7.0	1.3	0.8	4.5	17.5	14.5
2002	**100.0**	**2.5**	**29.8**	**1.1**	**4.5**	**7.7**	**2.2**	**5.0**	**0.4**	**6.8**	**1.3**	**0.9**	**4.7**	**17.8**	**14.6**
IMPORTS / ARRIVALS Value (Mio ECU/Euro)															
1980	**9,656**	**503**	**2,645**	**27**	**94**	**564**	**41**	**385**	:	**1,091**	**154**	**62**	**531**	**1,870**	**1,688**
1990	**17,680**	**887**	**5,984**	**53**	**246**	**1,262**	**149**	**974**	:	**1,946**	**302**	**282**	**761**	**2,921**	**1,913**
1994	21,358	1,137	6,999	63	357	1,678	243	1,376	:	2,269	303	401	876	3,473	2,185
1995	25,221	1,268	8,096	49	413	1,888	357	1,569	:	2,642	355	404	1,019	4,221	2,568
1996	25,169	1,248	8,056	57	447	1,940	420	1,606	:	2,604	343	379	984	4,374	2,710
1997	27,807	1,433	8,486	67	528	2,102	466	1,707	:	3,074	377	404	1,153	5,054	2,956
1998	29,414	1,511	9,062	73	590	2,326	451	1,941	:	3,088	416	380	1,095	5,264	3,217
1999	29,967	1,445	9,087	67	626	2,463	519	1,946	50	3,403	456	333	1,158	5,089	3,324
2000	**33,667**	**1,576**	**10,270**	**87**	**680**	**2,454**	**604**	**2,051**	**55**	**3,593**	**516**	**347**	**1,314**	**5,972**	**4,147**
2001	34,508	1,679	10,858	112	779	2,890	595	2,165	68	3,468	544	326	1,326	5,918	3,778
2002	**37,108**	**1,884**	**11,525**	**119**	**855**	**3,162**	**679**	**2,202**	**70**	**3,571**	**598**	**318**	**1,327**	**6,231**	**4,564**
Annual variation (%)															
98/97	5.7	5.4	6.7	9.1	11.7	10.6	-3.3	13.7	:	0.4	10.4	-5.7	-5.0	4.1	8.8
99/98	1.8	-4.3	0.2	-7.2	6.0	5.8	15.2	0.2	:	10.2	9.5	-12.5	5.7	-3.3	3.3
00/99	12.3	9.0	13.0	29.2	8.6	-0.3	16.3	5.3	11.3	5.5	13.1	4.3	13.4	17.3	24.7
01/00	2.4	6.5	5.7	28.6	14.5	17.7	-1.5	5.5	22.4	-3.4	5.4	-6.0	0.9	-0.9	-8.8
02/01	7.5	12.2	6.1	6.5	9.7	9.3	14.1	1.7	3.2	2.9	9.9	-2.3	0.0	5.2	20.7
Share (%)															
1980	**100.0**	**5.2**	**27.3**	**0.2**	**0.9**	**5.8**	**0.4**	**3.9**	:	**11.2**	**1.5**	**0.6**	**5.4**	**19.3**	**17.4**
1990	**100.0**	**5.0**	**33.8**	**0.2**	**1.3**	**7.1**	**0.8**	**5.5**	:	**11.0**	**1.7**	**1.5**	**4.3**	**16.5**	**10.8**
1996	100.0	4.9	32.0	0.2	1.7	7.7	1.6	6.3	:	10.3	1.3	1.5	3.9	17.3	10.7
1997	100.0	5.1	30.5	0.2	1.8	7.5	1.6	6.1	:	11.0	1.3	1.4	4.1	18.1	10.6
1998	100.0	5.1	30.8	0.2	2.0	7.9	1.6	6.5	:	10.4	1.4	1.2	3.7	17.8	10.9
1999	100.0	4.8	30.3	0.2	2.0	8.2	1.7	6.4	0.1	11.3	1.5	1.1	3.8	16.9	11.0
2000	**100.0**	**4.6**	**30.5**	**0.2**	**2.0**	**7.2**	**1.7**	**6.0**	**0.1**	**10.6**	**1.5**	**1.0**	**3.9**	**17.7**	**12.3**
2001	100.0	4.8	31.4	0.3	2.2	8.3	1.7	6.2	0.1	10.0	1.5	0.9	3.8	17.1	10.9
2002	**100.0**	**5.0**	**31.0**	**0.3**	**2.3**	**8.5**	**1.8**	**5.9**	**0.1**	**9.6**	**1.6**	**0.8**	**3.5**	**16.7**	**12.2**

(1) Luxembourg with Belgium until 31.12.1998.

EXPORTS
Value (Mio ECU/Euro)

Years	Extra EU	Norway	Switzerland	USSR/Russia(1)	Candid. countries	USA	Canada	China	Japan	Hong Kong	Mediterr. Basin	Latin America	OPEC	DAE	ACP
1980	3,981	764	274	70	:	569	75	32	212	31	452	167	511	163	188
1990	8,818	1,582	564	288	:	1,446	150	81	928	127	547	250	575	641	555
1994	12,508	2,160	680	359	1,157	1,856	181	146	1,350	263	657	541	614	1,072	576
1995	12,997	2,234	703	496	1,297	1,528	156	201	1,394	290	705	578	650	1,187	532
1996	13,511	2,455	635	579	1,538	1,637	165	239	1,319	367	748	567	648	1,366	277
1997	14,609	2,486	614	798	1,821	1,989	199	297	1,404	411	798	602	691	1,355	342
1998	14,668	2,521	611	620	2,073	2,163	257	243	1,212	419	868	666	659	1,326	427
1999	15,592	2,525	677	379	2,034	2,615	290	291	1,530	372	954	609	638	1,406	387
2000	18,372	2,804	845	542	2,222	3,320	373	424	1,941	524	1,021	783	734	1,539	481
2001	19,817	2,964	791	772	2,392	3,980	408	457	1,965	502	994	756	835	1,518	522
2002	20,358	3,427	787	702	2,588	3,820	445	541	1,798	572	1,101	654	922	1,606	466

Annual variation (%)

Years	Extra EU	Norway	Switzerland	USSR/Russia(1)	Candid. countries	USA	Canada	China	Japan	Hong Kong	Mediterr. Basin	Latin America	OPEC	DAE	ACP
98/97	0.4	1.4	-0.4	-22.2	13.8	8.7	28.8	-18.4	-13.6	2.0	8.7	10.5	-4.6	-2.1	24.6
99/98	6.2	0.1	10.9	-38.9	-1.8	20.8	13.1	19.9	26.2	-11.2	9.8	-8.6	-3.1	6.0	-9.3
00/99	17.8	11.0	24.7	43.0	9.2	26.9	28.4	45.6	26.8	40.8	7.0	28.6	14.9	9.4	24.3
01/00	7.8	5.7	-6.4	42.4	7.6	19.8	9.4	7.7	1.2	-4.1	-2.6	-3.5	13.8	-1.3	8.6
02/01	2.7	15.6	-0.5	-9.0	8.2	-4.0	8.8	18.4	-8.4	13.9	10.7	-13.3	10.3	5.7	-10.7

Share (%)

Years	Extra EU	Norway	Switzerland	USSR/Russia(1)	Candid. countries	USA	Canada	China	Japan	Hong Kong	Mediterr. Basin	Latin America	OPEC	DAE	ACP
1980	100.0	19.1	6.8	1.7	:	14.2	1.8	0.7	5.3	0.7	11.3	4.2	12.8	4.1	4.7
1990	100.0	17.9	6.3	3.2	:	16.4	1.6	0.9	10.5	1.4	6.2	2.8	6.5	7.2	6.2
1996	100.0	18.1	4.7	4.2	11.3	12.1	1.2	1.7	9.7	2.7	5.5	4.1	4.7	10.1	2.0
1997	100.0	17.0	4.2	5.4	12.4	13.6	1.3	2.0	9.6	2.8	5.4	4.1	4.7	9.2	2.3
1998	100.0	17.1	4.1	4.2	14.1	14.7	1.7	1.6	8.2	2.8	5.9	4.5	4.4	9.0	2.9
1999	100.0	16.1	4.3	2.4	13.0	16.7	1.8	1.8	9.8	2.3	6.1	3.9	4.0	9.0	2.4
2000	100.0	15.2	4.5	2.9	12.0	18.0	2.0	2.3	10.5	2.8	5.5	4.2	3.9	8.3	2.6
2001	100.0	14.9	3.9	3.8	12.0	20.0	2.0	2.3	9.9	2.5	5.0	3.8	4.2	7.6	2.6
2002	100.0	16.8	3.8	3.4	12.7	18.7	2.1	2.6	8.8	2.8	5.4	3.2	4.5	7.8	2.2

IMPORTS
Value (Mio ECU/Euro)

Years	Extra EU	Norway	Switzerland	USSR/Russia(1)	Candid. countries	USA	Canada	China	Japan	Hong Kong	Mediterr. Basin	Latin America	OPEC	DAE	ACP
1980	4,450	584	249	302	:	914	67	45	297	68	265	354	429	240	197
1990	7,798	1,199	548	211	:	1,400	118	315	858	118	238	456	350	706	179
1994	9,487	1,870	570	298	1,877	1,286	105	541	915	130	398	548	214	980	113
1995	9,900	2,164	580	355	1,052	1,525	108	571	802	144	282	523	204	829	98
1996	10,501	2,372	564	299	1,147	1,642	120	639	704	166	257	593	214	896	165
1997	11,788	2,649	532	257	1,386	1,918	131	805	752	174	328	710	275	1,060	117
1998	12,396	2,648	542	259	1,620	2,057	134	864	767	193	356	644	297	1,234	232
1999	12,962	2,661	538	280	1,814	2,202	195	1,123	806	209	408	601	283	1,195	152
2000	15,659	3,451	576	419	2,185	2,101	316	1,429	721	271	478	733	372	1,778	185
2001	16,097	3,146	638	423	2,586	2,374	270	1,470	713	241	556	813	361	1,422	206
2002	15,178	3,356	593	369	2,608	1,888	147	1,473	688	231	627	727	330	1,309	160

Annual variation (%)

Years	Extra EU	Norway	Switzerland	USSR/Russia(1)	Candid. countries	USA	Canada	China	Japan	Hong Kong	Mediterr. Basin	Latin America	OPEC	DAE	ACP
98/97	5.1	0.0	1.7	0.7	16.8	7.2	1.8	7.2	1.9	10.8	8.6	-9.2	8.1	16.4	98.4
99/98	4.5	0.4	-0.7	8.2	11.9	7.0	45.8	30.0	5.0	8.5	14.4	-6.5	-4.6	-3.1	-34.3
00/99	20.8	29.6	7.1	49.5	20.4	-4.5	62.1	27.2	-10.4	29.6	17.2	21.8	31.2	48.7	21.8
01/00	2.7	-8.8	10.7	0.9	18.3	12.9	-14.6	2.8	-1.2	-11.0	16.4	10.8	-2.8	-20.0	11.4
02/01	-5.7	6.6	-7.1	-12.8	0.8	-20.4	-45.6	0.2	-3.4	-4.3	12.7	-10.5	-8.7	-7.9	-22.3

Share (%)

Years	Extra EU	Norway	Switzerland	USSR/Russia(1)	Candid. countries	USA	Canada	China	Japan	Hong Kong	Mediterr. Basin	Latin America	OPEC	DAE	ACP
1980	100.0	13.1	5.5	6.7	:	20.5	1.5	1.0	6.6	1.5	5.9	7.9	9.6	5.3	4.4
1990	100.0	15.3	7.0	2.7	:	17.9	1.5	4.0	11.0	1.5	3.0	5.8	4.4	9.0	2.2
1996	100.0	22.5	5.3	2.8	10.9	15.6	1.1	6.0	6.6	1.5	2.4	5.6	2.0	8.5	1.5
1997	100.0	22.4	4.5	2.1	11.7	16.2	1.1	6.8	6.3	1.4	2.7	6.0	2.3	8.9	0.9
1998	100.0	21.3	4.3	2.0	13.0	16.5	1.0	6.9	6.1	1.5	2.8	5.1	2.3	9.9	1.8
1999	100.0	20.5	4.1	2.1	13.9	16.9	1.5	8.6	6.2	1.6	3.1	4.6	2.1	9.2	1.1
2000	100.0	22.0	3.6	2.6	13.9	13.4	2.0	9.1	4.6	1.7	3.0	4.6	2.3	11.3	1.1
2001	100.0	19.5	3.9	2.6	16.0	14.7	1.6	9.1	4.4	1.4	3.4	5.0	2.2	8.8	1.2
2002	100.0	22.1	3.9	2.4	17.1	12.4	0.9	9.7	4.5	1.5	4.1	4.7	2.1	8.6	1.0

(1) Relates to the external trade with the USSR until 1991and to the external trade with Russia from 1992 onwards.

GERMANY

TRADE BALANCE (BN ECU/euro)

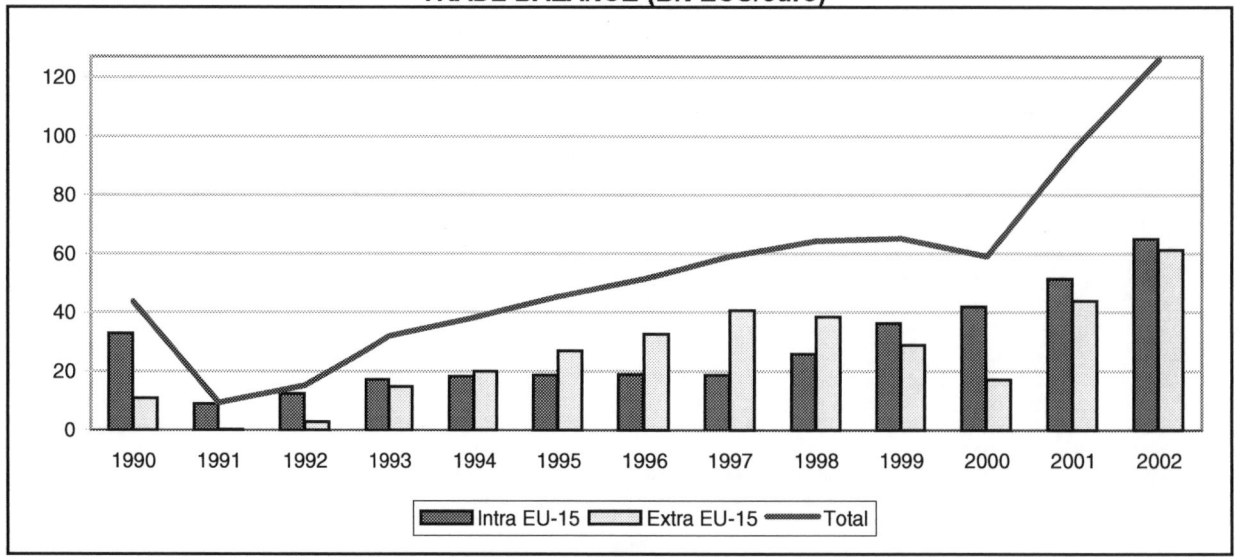

INTRA-EU (BN ECU/euro)

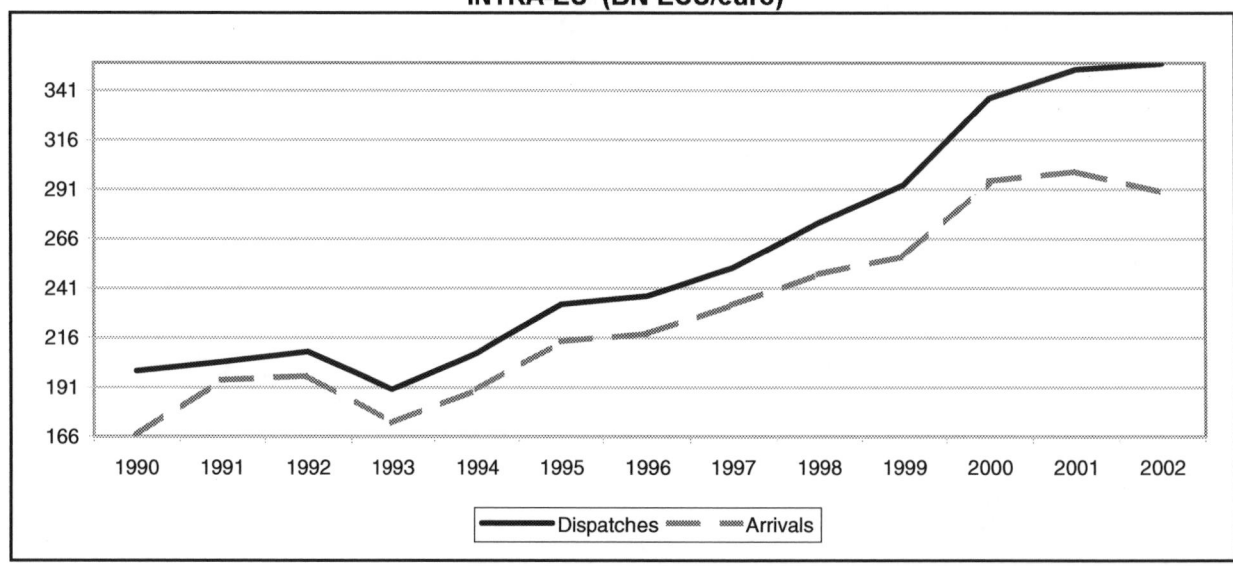

EXTRA-EU (BN ECU/euro)

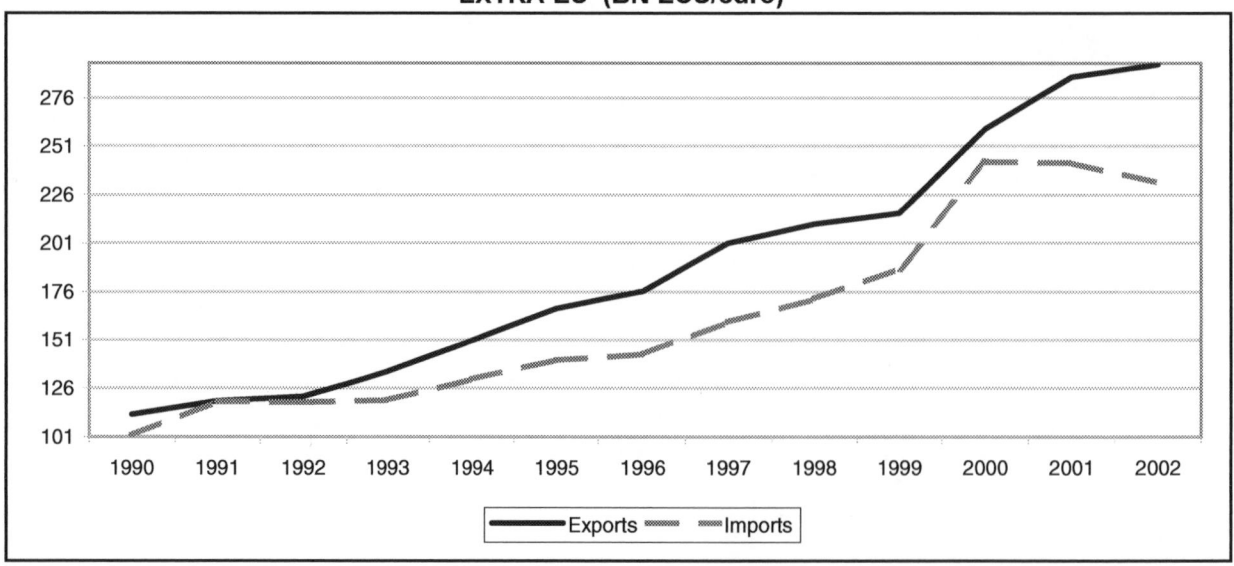

GERMANY

TRADE BALANCE

INTRA-EU

Value (Mio ECU/Euro)

Year	Intra EU	B[1]	DK	EL	E	F	IRL	I	L	NL	A	P	FIN	S	UK
							Partner								
1980	**9,215**	**925**	**315**	**409**	**280**	**3,925**	**-74**	**1,153**	**:**	**-3,044**	**3,732**	**356**	**167**	**1,154**	**-83**
1990	**32,739**	**1,602**	**223**	**1,433**	**4,956**	**9,022**	**-940**	**3,858**	**:**	**-5,977**	**6,238**	**671**	**719**	**1,849**	**9,085**
1991	8,995	-1,323	-878	1,299	4,924	3,931	-1,178	621	:	-10,065	6,099	994	-346	488	4,428
1992	12,371	-179	-1,090	1,937	5,364	4,972	-1,553	1,757	:	-10,106	5,833	690	-416	483	4,678
1993	17,278	2,003	177	1,595	3,168	5,679	-1,654	-200	:	-7,072	5,535	570	-478	215	7,740
1994	18,209	1,487	518	1,377	2,474	6,839	-2,067	593	:	-7,301	5,297	330	-763	938	8,487
1995	18,604	-1,050	583	1,338	2,813	6,546	-2,912	207	:	-9,571	7,847	40	-13	2,712	10,063
1996	18,998	-767	508	1,363	3,209	5,683	-2,729	889	:	-10,381	9,148	231	480	2,679	8,685
1997	18,647	-2,245	393	1,576	3,770	4,736	-2,492	2,575	:	-12,853	8,533	497	365	3,217	10,577
1998	25,976	-948	1,025	1,906	5,825	6,485	-4,704	3,546	:	-13,808	8,787	1,120	648	3,099	12,994
1999	36,258	483	980	2,432	8,700	12,010	-8,068	5,360	661	-14,618	9,299	1,211	1,256	3,596	12,958
2000	**42,042**	**412**	**299**	**3,017**	**11,061**	**15,570**	**-6,948**	**9,603**	**731**	**-21,843**	**11,150**	**1,009**	**1,912**	**3,640**	**12,430**
2001	51,513	-291	1,110	3,474	13,122	18,709	-11,106	12,221	747	-20,555	12,017	1,097	1,544	4,064	15,359
2002	**64,961**	**-6,831**	**1,449**	**3,446**	**14,439**	**19,895**	**-2,462**	**14,085**	**674**	**-19,857**	**11,272**	**1,805**	**1,653**	**4,603**	**20,788**

EXTRA-EU

Value (Mio ECU/Euro)

Year	Extra EU	Norway	Switzerland	Russia[2]	Candid. countries	USA	Canada	China	Japan	Hong Kong	Mediterr. Basin	Latin America	OPEC	DAE	ACP
							Partner								
1980	**-5,670**	**-1,434**	**3,059**	**191**	**:**	**-1,215**	**-544**	**261**	**-2,408**	**-822**	**929**	**524**	**-5,758**	**-1,894**	**-1,793**
1990	**10,939**	**-947**	**7,032**	**703**	**:**	**6,270**	**254**	**-1,647**	**-5,971**	**-806**	**1,350**	**-793**	**2,107**	**-1,413**	**-587**
1991	270	-1,312	5,719	1,799	:	1,464	275	-3,331	-8,489	-837	423	-331	3,251	-2,612	-695
1992	2,900	-1,567	4,713	-521	:	2,125	159	-2,572	-8,654	-80	476	680	4,034	-1,841	-227
1993	14,733	-2,007	4,532	450	3,303	6,306	215	-1,914	-7,058	435	2,084	2,138	2,531	-257	-256
1994	20,081	-2,157	4,890	-1,082	1,727	9,518	338	-2,291	-5,976	1,102	1,940	2,551	2,623	2,198	-764
1995	26,953	-2,334	5,723	-1,513	2,642	9,899	-273	-2,310	-5,920	1,281	3,094	3,128	3,317	4,654	-358
1996	32,627	-3,327	5,040	-1,829	6,574	10,975	-90	-3,150	-4,428	1,644	4,182	3,936	2,492	5,958	-351
1997	40,574	-3,720	5,272	25	8,577	15,661	1,117	-4,871	-6,076	2,336	5,837	5,301	3,408	5,732	-585
1998	38,495	-2,052	5,422	115	9,160	18,174	1,219	-4,832	-8,667	1,545	5,737	7,104	4,361	266	1,393
1999	28,944	-2,675	6,148	-3,020	4,492	21,395	1,219	-5,851	-8,646	1,441	3,956	6,285	3,012	-37	2,058
2000	**17,088**	**-5,762**	**5,519**	**-7,603**	**6,818**	**22,716**	**1,420**	**-7,667**	**-10,348**	**1,897**	**2,766**	**6,415**	**870**	**-1,604**	**1,216**
2001	43,982	-6,155	6,531	-3,920	3,681	29,805	2,468	-5,992	-6,693	2,064	2,295	8,099	5,855	1,398	1,831
2002	**61,265**	**-6,249**	**5,637**	**-1,540**	**4,423**	**33,820**	**3,212**	**-4,563**	**-3,795**	**2,260**	**5,254**	**6,882**	**7,976**	**3,596**	**2,895**

(1)   Luxembourg with Belgium until 31.12.1998.
(2)   Relates to the external trade with the USSR until 1991 and to the external trade with Russia from 1992 onwards.

GERMANY

INTRA-EU

Year	Intra EU	B[1]	DK	EL	E	F	IRL	I	L	NL	A	P	FIN	S	UK
							Partner								

EXPORTS / DISPATCHES
Value (Mio ECU/Euro)

Year	Intra EU	B[1]	DK	EL	E	F	IRL	I	L	NL	A	P	FIN	S	UK
1980	83,926	10,887	2,642	1,495	2,008	18,467	526	11,860	:	13,182	7,629	828	1,311	4,012	9,079
1990	199,231	23,188	5,777	3,083	11,018	40,659	1,330	28,822	:	26,318	17,976	2,874	3,474	8,123	26,589
1994	208,169	24,315	6,713	3,001	11,363	43,173	1,647	27,261	:	27,419	20,653	3,071	2,799	7,966	28,786
1995	232,722	26,236	7,667	2,966	13,772	46,904	1,869	30,363	:	30,491	22,262	3,620	3,689	9,821	33,063
1996	237,061	26,090	7,586	2,928	14,996	45,674	1,806	31,042	:	31,564	23,830	4,276	3,959	9,972	33,338
1997	251,249	26,304	8,157	3,146	16,835	48,069	2,142	33,118	:	32,097	23,762	4,815	4,148	10,502	38,156
1998	274,108	27,568	8,411	3,527	19,528	53,779	2,568	35,813	:	33,974	26,285	5,369	4,866	11,109	41,311
1999	293,371	26,812	8,758	4,158	22,684	58,577	2,921	38,335	2,009	34,354	28,295	5,877	5,811	11,657	43,124
2000	337,380	30,105	9,605	4,665	26,732	67,418	3,628	45,011	2,624	38,994	32,436	6,255	7,005	13,525	49,377
2001	351,612	32,270	10,485	5,144	27,841	69,601	3,946	47,119	2,918	40,011	33,486	6,369	6,682	12,978	52,764
2002	354,792	31,216	10,887	4,976	29,654	69,775	3,985	47,442	2,910	39,539	33,268	6,795	6,642	13,470	54,227

Annual variation (%)

Year	Intra EU	B[1]	DK	EL	E	F	IRL	I	L	NL	A	P	FIN	S	UK
98/97	9.0	4.8	3.1	12.1	15.9	11.8	19.8	8.1	:	5.8	10.6	11.5	17.3	5.7	8.2
99/98	7.0	-2.7	4.1	17.8	16.1	8.9	13.7	7.0	:	1.1	7.6	9.4	19.4	4.9	4.3
00/99	15.0	12.2	9.6	12.1	17.8	15.0	24.2	17.4	30.6	13.5	14.6	6.4	20.5	16.0	14.4
01/00	4.2	7.1	9.1	10.2	4.1	3.2	8.7	4.6	11.1	2.6	3.2	1.8	-4.6	-4.0	6.8
02/01	0.9	-3.2	3.8	-3.2	6.5	0.2	1.0	0.6	-0.2	-1.1	-0.6	6.7	-0.5	3.7	2.7

Share (%)

Year	Intra EU	B[1]	DK	EL	E	F	IRL	I	L	NL	A	P	FIN	S	UK
1980	100.0	12.9	3.1	1.7	2.3	22.0	0.6	14.1	:	15.7	9.0	0.9	1.5	4.7	10.8
1990	100.0	11.6	2.8	1.5	5.5	20.4	0.6	14.4	:	13.2	9.0	1.4	1.7	4.0	13.3
1996	100.0	11.0	3.1	1.2	6.3	19.2	0.7	13.0	:	13.3	10.0	1.8	1.6	4.2	14.0
1997	100.0	10.4	3.2	1.2	6.7	19.1	0.8	13.1	:	12.7	9.4	1.9	1.6	4.1	15.1
1998	100.0	10.0	3.0	1.2	7.1	19.6	0.9	13.0	:	12.3	9.5	1.9	1.7	4.0	15.0
1999	100.0	9.1	2.9	1.4	7.7	19.9	0.9	13.0	0.6	11.7	9.6	2.0	1.9	3.9	14.6
2000	100.0	8.9	2.8	1.3	7.9	19.9	1.0	13.3	0.7	11.5	9.6	1.8	2.0	4.0	14.6
2001	100.0	9.1	2.9	1.4	7.9	19.7	1.1	13.4	0.8	11.3	9.5	1.8	1.9	3.6	15.0
2002	100.0	8.7	3.0	1.4	8.3	19.6	1.1	13.3	0.8	11.1	9.3	1.9	1.8	3.7	15.2

IMPORTS / ARRIVALS
Value (Mio ECU/Euro)

Year	Intra EU	B[1]	DK	EL	E	F	IRL	I	L	NL	A	P	FIN	S	UK
1980	74,711	9,962	2,327	1,086	1,728	14,542	599	10,707	:	16,225	3,897	472	1,144	2,858	9,162
1990	166,492	21,587	5,554	1,649	6,062	31,637	2,270	24,964	:	32,295	11,738	2,203	2,756	6,274	17,503
1994	189,960	22,828	6,196	1,623	8,889	36,334	3,714	26,668	:	34,720	15,357	2,741	3,562	7,028	20,299
1995	214,119	27,287	7,084	1,628	10,959	40,358	4,781	30,155	:	40,062	14,414	3,580	3,701	7,109	23,000
1996	218,063	26,857	7,078	1,565	11,787	39,991	4,535	30,154	:	41,945	14,683	4,045	3,479	7,292	24,653
1997	232,601	28,550	7,764	1,570	13,065	43,333	4,634	30,543	:	44,950	15,229	4,318	3,782	7,285	27,578
1998	248,132	28,516	7,386	1,621	13,703	47,294	7,271	32,268	:	47,782	17,498	4,249	4,217	8,010	28,317
1999	257,113	26,329	7,778	1,726	13,983	46,567	10,989	32,975	1,348	48,972	18,996	4,666	4,555	8,061	30,166
2000	295,338	29,693	9,306	1,648	15,671	51,848	10,577	35,409	1,893	60,837	21,287	5,246	5,093	9,885	36,947
2001	300,100	32,560	9,375	1,669	14,719	50,891	15,051	34,898	2,171	60,566	21,469	5,272	5,138	8,915	37,405
2002	289,831	38,048	9,437	1,530	15,215	49,880	6,448	33,357	2,236	59,396	21,997	4,991	4,989	8,867	33,440

Annual variation (%)

Year	Intra EU	B[1]	DK	EL	E	F	IRL	I	L	NL	A	P	FIN	S	UK
98/97	6.6	-0.1	-4.8	3.2	4.8	9.1	56.9	5.6	:	6.2	14.8	-1.6	11.4	9.9	2.6
99/98	3.6	-7.6	5.3	6.4	2.0	-1.5	51.1	2.1	:	2.4	8.5	9.8	8.0	0.6	6.5
00/99	14.8	12.7	19.6	-4.5	12.0	11.3	-3.7	7.3	40.4	24.2	12.0	12.4	11.8	22.6	22.4
01/00	1.6	9.6	0.7	1.3	-6.0	-1.8	42.3	-1.4	14.6	-0.4	0.8	0.5	0.8	-9.8	1.2
02/01	-3.4	16.8	0.6	-8.3	3.3	-1.9	-57.1	-4.4	3.0	-1.9	2.4	-5.3	-2.8	-0.5	-10.6

Share (%)

Year	Intra EU	B[1]	DK	EL	E	F	IRL	I	L	NL	A	P	FIN	S	UK
1980	100.0	13.3	3.1	1.4	2.3	19.4	0.8	14.3	:	21.7	5.2	0.6	1.5	3.8	12.2
1990	100.0	12.9	3.3	0.9	3.6	19.0	1.3	14.9	:	19.3	7.0	1.3	1.6	3.7	10.5
1996	100.0	12.3	3.2	0.7	5.4	18.3	2.0	13.8	:	19.2	6.7	1.8	1.5	3.3	11.3
1997	100.0	12.2	3.3	0.6	5.6	18.6	1.9	13.1	:	19.3	6.5	1.8	1.6	3.1	11.8
1998	100.0	11.4	2.9	0.6	5.5	19.0	2.9	13.0	:	19.2	7.0	1.7	1.6	3.2	11.4
1999	100.0	10.2	3.0	0.6	5.4	18.1	4.2	12.8	0.5	19.0	7.3	1.8	1.7	3.1	11.7
2000	100.0	10.0	3.1	0.5	5.3	17.5	3.5	11.9	0.6	20.5	7.2	1.7	1.7	3.3	12.5
2001	100.0	10.8	3.1	0.5	4.9	16.9	5.0	11.6	0.7	20.1	7.1	1.7	1.7	2.9	12.4
2002	100.0	13.1	3.2	0.5	5.2	17.2	2.2	11.5	0.7	20.4	7.5	1.7	1.7	3.0	11.5

(1) Luxembourg with Belgium until 31.12.1998.

Years	Extra EU	Norway	Switzerland	USSR/Russia(1)	Candid. countries	USA	Canada	China	Japan	Hong Kong	Mediterr. Basin	Latin America	OPEC	DAE	ACP
EXPORTS															
Value (Mio ECU/Euro)															
1980	54,862	1,591	7,926	3,147	:	8,509	863	823	1,569	423	11,560	4,368	9,038	2,316	2,575
1990	112,669	2,724	18,785	5,063	:	22,855	2,296	1,892	8,500	1,533	12,472	5,297	8,834	9,241	2,605
1994	150,745	3,106	19,266	5,590	22,694	28,146	2,284	5,350	9,315	3,009	13,327	8,460	9,292	16,749	1,854
1995	167,474	3,271	21,188	5,498	28,612	29,159	2,193	5,756	10,058	3,083	14,943	9,368	8,957	19,497	2,212
1996	176,130	3,486	19,798	5,997	33,388	31,469	2,207	5,694	11,099	3,342	16,680	9,536	8,730	20,051	2,023
1997	201,020	3,939	20,281	8,359	40,288	38,984	3,411	5,406	10,426	4,022	19,247	11,920	10,155	20,771	2,298
1998	210,913	4,329	21,679	7,362	46,817	45,579	3,560	6,044	9,297	3,337	19,513	13,758	9,726	16,104	5,583
1999	216,611	3,903	22,807	5,057	46,520	51,425	3,380	6,949	10,367	3,307	19,158	13,176	9,113	16,900	6,411
2000	260,076	4,289	25,596	6,660	57,583	61,765	4,293	9,459	13,195	4,162	22,619	14,431	10,729	21,825	6,839
2001	286,669	4,902	27,489	10,268	60,383	67,824	5,247	12,118	13,103	4,235	21,025	15,717	13,670	22,126	8,203
2002	293,454	4,560	26,634	11,352	65,160	66,596	5,564	14,495	12,171	4,241	22,696	13,842	14,574	22,666	9,015
Annual variation (%)															
98/97	4.9	9.8	6.8	-11.9	16.2	16.9	4.3	11.8	-10.8	-17.0	1.3	15.4	-4.2	-22.4	142.8
99/98	2.7	-9.8	5.2	-31.3	-0.6	12.8	-5.0	14.9	11.5	-0.8	-1.8	-4.2	-6.3	4.9	14.8
00/99	20.0	9.8	12.2	31.6	23.7	20.1	26.9	36.1	27.2	25.8	18.0	9.5	17.7	29.1	6.6
01/00	10.2	14.2	7.3	54.1	4.8	9.8	22.2	28.1	-0.6	1.7	-7.0	8.9	27.4	1.3	19.9
02/01	2.3	-6.9	-3.1	10.5	7.9	-1.8	6.0	19.6	-7.1	0.1	7.9	-11.9	6.6	2.4	9.8
Share (%)															
1980	100.0	2.9	14.4	5.7	:	15.5	1.5	1.5	2.8	0.7	21.0	7.9	16.4	4.2	4.6
1990	100.0	2.4	16.6	4.4	:	20.2	2.0	1.6	7.5	1.3	11.0	4.7	7.8	8.2	2.3
1996	100.0	1.9	11.2	3.4	18.9	17.8	1.2	3.2	6.3	1.8	9.4	5.4	4.9	11.3	1.1
1997	100.0	1.9	10.0	4.1	20.0	19.3	1.6	2.6	5.1	2.0	9.5	5.9	5.0	10.3	1.1
1998	100.0	2.0	10.2	3.4	22.1	21.6	1.6	2.8	4.4	1.5	9.2	6.5	4.6	7.6	2.6
1999	100.0	1.8	10.5	2.3	21.4	23.7	1.5	3.2	4.7	1.5	8.8	6.0	4.2	7.8	2.9
2000	100.0	1.6	9.8	2.5	22.1	23.7	1.6	3.6	5.0	1.6	8.6	5.5	4.1	8.3	2.6
2001	100.0	1.7	9.5	3.5	21.0	23.6	1.8	4.2	4.5	1.4	7.3	5.4	4.7	7.7	2.8
2002	100.0	1.5	9.0	3.8	22.2	22.6	1.8	4.9	4.1	1.4	7.7	4.7	4.9	7.7	3.0
IMPORTS															
Value (Mio ECU/Euro)															
1980	60,532	3,025	4,868	2,956	:	9,724	1,407	562	3,977	1,245	10,631	3,844	14,796	4,210	4,368
1990	101,730	3,671	11,752	4,359	:	16,585	2,042	3,539	14,471	2,340	11,122	6,091	6,726	10,654	3,192
1994	130,664	5,263	14,376	6,672	41,936	18,628	1,946	7,641	15,291	1,907	11,387	5,909	6,669	14,551	2,619
1995	140,521	5,605	15,465	7,011	25,970	19,259	2,467	8,066	15,979	1,802	11,848	6,240	5,640	14,842	2,570
1996	143,503	6,813	14,757	7,826	26,813	20,494	2,297	8,844	15,526	1,699	12,498	5,600	6,239	14,092	2,374
1997	160,446	7,659	15,010	8,334	31,711	23,323	2,294	10,277	16,502	1,686	13,410	6,618	6,747	15,039	2,883
1998	172,418	6,381	16,257	7,247	37,656	27,405	2,340	10,876	17,964	1,791	13,775	6,654	5,365	15,838	4,190
1999	187,667	6,578	16,659	8,077	42,028	30,030	2,161	12,799	19,013	1,866	15,202	6,891	6,100	16,937	4,353
2000	242,987	10,052	20,076	14,263	50,765	39,048	2,873	17,126	23,543	2,265	19,854	8,015	9,859	23,429	5,623
2001	242,687	11,058	20,958	14,188	56,702	38,019	2,779	18,110	19,796	2,171	18,730	7,619	7,814	20,727	6,372
2002	232,189	10,810	20,997	12,891	60,736	32,776	2,352	19,058	15,965	1,981	17,442	6,960	6,598	19,070	6,120
Annual variation (%)															
98/97	7.4	-16.6	8.3	-13.0	18.7	17.5	2.0	5.8	8.8	6.2	2.7	0.5	-20.4	5.3	45.3
99/98	8.8	3.0	2.4	11.4	11.6	9.5	-7.6	17.6	5.8	4.1	10.3	3.5	13.7	6.9	3.8
00/99	29.4	52.8	20.5	76.5	20.7	30.0	32.9	33.8	23.8	21.4	30.6	16.3	61.6	38.3	29.1
01/00	-0.1	10.0	4.3	-0.5	11.6	-2.6	-3.2	5.7	-15.9	-4.1	-5.6	-4.9	-20.7	-11.5	13.3
02/01	-4.3	-2.2	0.1	-9.1	7.1	-13.7	-15.3	5.2	-19.3	-8.7	-6.8	-8.6	-15.5	-7.9	-3.9
Share (%)															
1980	100.0	4.9	8.0	4.8	:	16.0	2.3	0.9	6.5	2.0	17.5	6.3	24.4	6.9	7.2
1990	100.0	3.6	11.5	4.2	:	16.3	2.0	3.4	14.2	2.2	10.9	5.9	6.6	10.4	3.1
1996	100.0	4.7	10.2	5.4	18.6	14.2	1.6	6.1	10.8	1.1	8.7	3.9	4.3	9.8	1.6
1997	100.0	4.7	9.3	5.1	19.7	14.5	1.4	6.4	10.2	1.0	8.3	4.1	4.2	9.3	1.7
1998	100.0	3.7	9.4	4.2	21.8	15.8	1.3	6.3	10.4	1.0	7.9	3.8	3.1	9.1	2.4
1999	100.0	3.5	8.8	4.3	22.3	16.0	1.1	6.8	10.1	0.9	8.1	3.6	3.2	9.0	2.3
2000	100.0	4.1	8.2	5.8	20.8	16.0	1.1	7.0	9.6	0.9	8.1	3.2	4.0	9.6	2.3
2001	100.0	4.5	8.6	5.8	23.3	15.6	1.1	7.4	8.1	0.8	7.7	3.1	3.2	8.5	2.6
2002	100.0	4.6	9.0	5.5	26.1	14.1	1.0	8.2	6.8	0.8	7.5	2.9	2.8	8.2	2.6

(1) Relates to the external trade with the USSR until 1991 and to the external trade with Russia from 1992 onwards.

GREECE

TRADE BALANCE (BN ECU/euro)

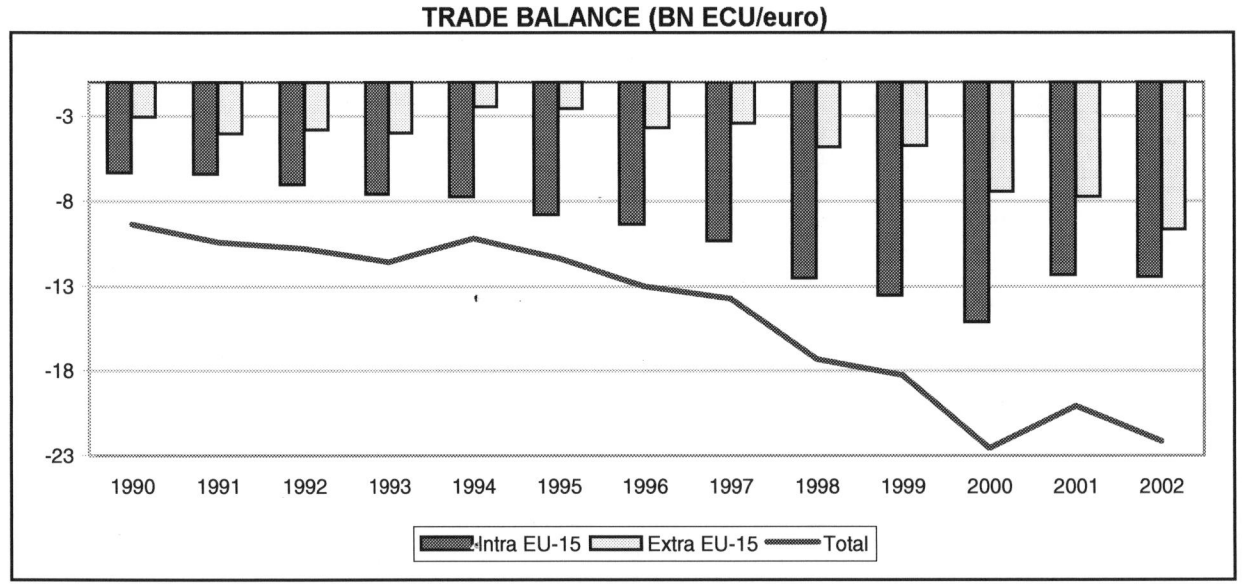

INTRA-EU (BN ECU/euro)

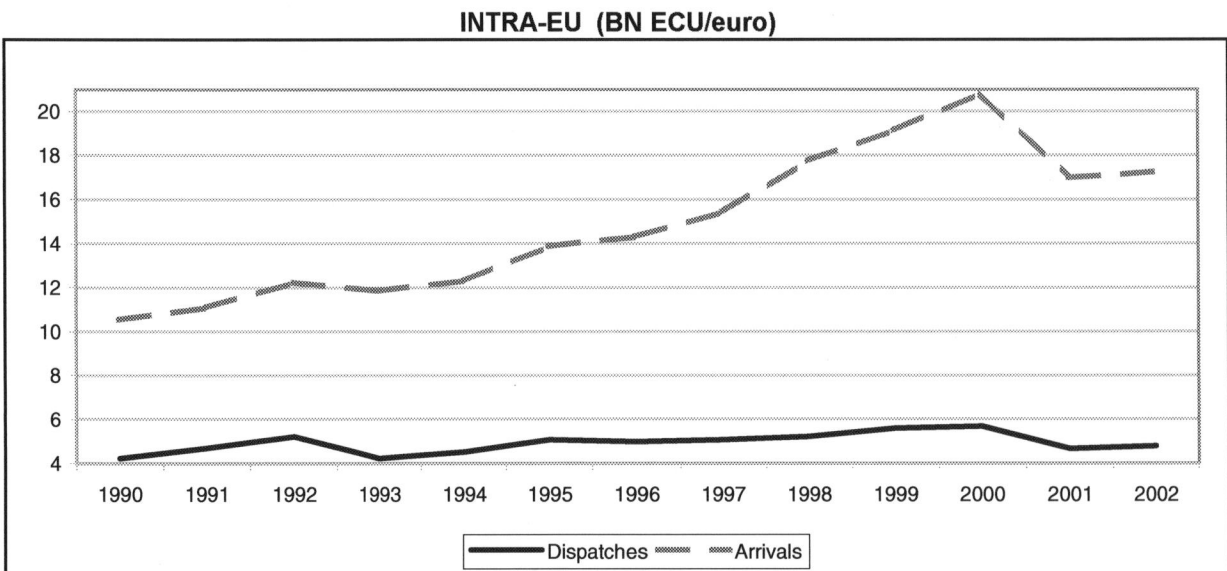

EXTRA-EU (BN ECU/euro)

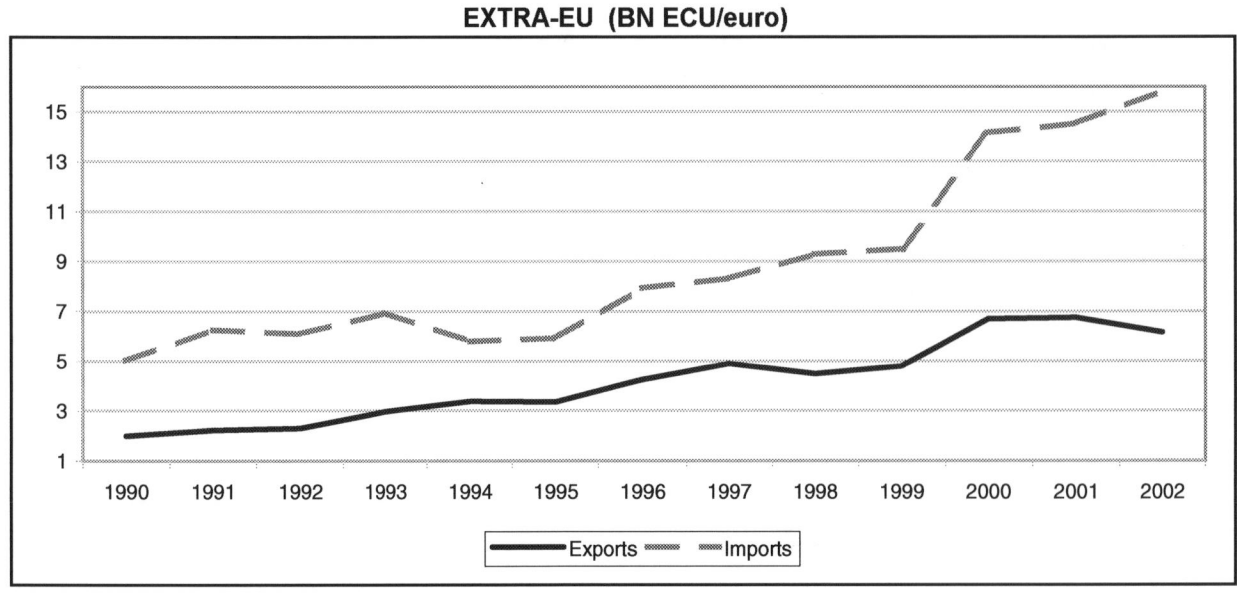

TRADE BALANCE

INTRA-EU

Value (Mio ECU/Euro)

Year	Intra EU	B(1)	DK	D	E	F	IRL	I	L	NL	A	P	FIN	S	UK
								Partner							
1980	-1,547	-82	-13	-413	-48	-195	-24	-261	:	-83	-57	2	-65	-114	-193
1990	-6,307	-454	-147	-1,838	-224	-653	-84	-1,355	:	-830	-122	-49	-74	-118	-360
1991	-6,397	-438	-130	-1,697	-258	-824	-91	-1,301	:	-799	-112	-34	-72	-190	-452
1992	-7,009	-456	-200	-1,961	-225	-908	-95	-1,230	:	-1,065	-151	-43	-67	-167	-475
1993	-7,596	-523	-202	-1,476	-387	-1,037	-125	-1,681	:	-1,063	-94	-29	-80	-167	-732
1994	-7,760	-560	-197	-1,292	-393	-1,036	-129	-1,917	:	-1,150	-76	-33	-105	-217	-655
1995	-8,799	-557	-221	-1,427	-381	-1,165	-177	-2,532	:	-1,152	-91	-19	-110	-192	-776
1996	-9,352	-642	-227	-1,515	-471	-1,316	-168	-2,449	:	-1,161	-136	-26	-116	-202	-923
1997	-10,354	-708	-279	-1,513	-634	-1,662	-159	-2,675	:	-1,214	-141	-49	-145	-273	-893
1998	-12,516	-767	-309	-2,240	-709	-1,866	-152	-3,151	:	-1,380	-151	-39	-267	-411	-1,043
1999	-13,546	-846	-286	-2,716	-670	-2,092	-185	-3,061	-7	-1,532	-180	-50	-330	-411	-1,151
2000	-15,128	-791	-301	-3,175	-834	-2,135	-302	-3,517	-6	-1,770	-201	-30	-423	-554	-1,071
2001	-12,322	-800	-287	-3,063	-689	-1,575	-239	-2,851	-17	-1,495	-176	-12	-258	-351	-509
2002	-12,457	-1,323	-261	-2,887	-999	-1,488	-184	-2,875	-30	-1,586	-177	-17	-273	-292	-664

EXTRA-EU

Value (Mio ECU/Euro)

Year	Extra EU	Norway	Switzerland	Russia(2)	Candid. countries	USA	Canada	China	Japan	Hong Kong	Mediterr. Basin	Latin America	OPEC	DAE	ACP
								Partner							
1980	-2,341	-62	-79	-43	:	-139	-39	-9	-818	-19	-600	-175	-263	-72	-38
1990	-3,042	-39	-189	-182	:	-220	-15	-67	-857	-47	-131	-222	-657	-312	-127
1991	-4,016	-44	-186	-250	:	-345	-21	-135	-1,087	-47	-240	-275	-1,010	-396	-110
1992	-3,796	-10	-222	-113	:	-364	-5	-172	-1,085	-37	-165	-173	-995	-471	-61
1993	-3,993	-42	-256	-275	136	-379	-19	-212	-1,217	-25	-130	-91	-1,022	-602	-61
1994	-2,415	-18	-245	-256	322	-197	-12	-222	-612	-14	172	-126	-647	-339	-71
1995	-2,550	-18	-72	-333	254	-381	-41	-275	-455	-14	364	-252	-564	-457	-83
1996	-3,664	-24	-288	-263	334	-384	-45	-328	-652	-7	536	-217	-1,036	-694	-160
1997	-3,397	-127	-232	-190	330	-388	-51	-370	-750	7	890	-298	-871	-744	-58
1998	-4,812	-43	-350	-204	320	-786	-61	-513	-817	0	633	-178	-1,054	-1,184	-67
1999	-4,713	-17	-400	-261	363	-850	-55	-505	-1,160	-12	1,000	-128	-778	-1,249	-95
2000	-7,438	-148	-348	-916	651	-478	-29	-724	-1,183	-0	1,438	-172	-2,876	-1,610	-119
2001	-7,758	-70	-363	-1,472	489	-469	-15	-892	-894	18	1,167	-306	-2,677	-1,341	-241
2002	-9,661	-45	-403	-2,116	240	-975	-24	-963	-944	-33	765	-381	-1,588	-2,306	-231

(1) Luxembourg with Belgium until 31.12.1998.
(2) Relates to the external trade with the USSR until 1991 and to the external trade with Russia from 1992 onwards.

GREECE

INTRA-EU

Year	Intra EU	B[1]	DK	D	E	F	IRL	I	L	NL	A	P	FIN	S	UK
							EXPORTS / DISPATCHES								
							Value (Mio ECU/Euro)								
1980	1,880	68	33	689	20	275	4	362	:	212	22	14	10	17	154
1990	4,242	128	53	1,374	90	607	10	1,045	:	218	91	16	47	101	459
1994	4,516	129	66	1,671	175	426	25	1,095	:	198	111	31	45	74	470
1995	5,080	162	66	1,853	289	457	27	1,181	:	227	114	50	48	98	510
1996	4,975	138	66	1,670	281	439	26	1,228	:	234	117	64	55	109	548
1997	5,078	146	68	1,798	191	420	23	1,241	:	244	102	37	58	123	624
1998	5,216	158	71	1,780	247	451	37	1,154	:	294	116	48	45	132	675
1999	5,603	180	80	1,717	333	448	39	1,437	1	314	115	53	50	128	697
2000	5,698	200	91	1,645	397	468	41	1,268	6	328	109	82	81	154	821
2001	4,680	109	91	1,246	360	416	40	934	5	269	73	76	55	106	900
2002	4,791	116	72	1,142	275	391	27	929	2	259	79	67	37	99	681
							Annual variation (%)								
98/97	2.7	8.1	5.0	-0.9	28.9	7.5	63.2	-7.0	:	20.4	12.9	27.5	-23.0	6.5	8.2
99/98	7.4	14.3	11.5	-3.5	34.8	-0.7	4.9	24.5	:	6.7	-0.2	10.6	12.4	-2.6	3.2
00/99	1.6	11.2	14.5	-4.2	19.2	4.4	6.0	-11.7	602.2	4.4	-5.3	54.8	61.0	19.9	17.8
01/00	-17.8	-45.3	-0.2	-24.2	-9.3	-11.2	-3.6	-26.3	-4.0	-18.0	-32.8	-6.9	-32.6	-31.2	9.5
02/01	2.3	5.7	-20.6	-8.3	-23.7	-6.0	-31.1	-0.5	-62.7	-3.7	8.0	-11.7	-31.4	-6.3	-24.2
							Share (%)								
1980	100.0	3.6	1.7	36.6	1.0	14.6	0.1	19.2	:	11.2	1.1	0.7	0.5	0.8	8.1
1990	100.0	3.0	1.2	32.4	2.1	14.3	0.2	24.6	:	5.1	2.1	0.3	1.1	2.3	10.8
1996	100.0	2.7	1.3	33.5	5.6	8.8	0.5	24.6	:	4.6	2.3	1.2	1.1	2.1	11.0
1997	100.0	2.8	1.3	35.4	3.7	8.2	0.4	24.4	:	4.8	2.0	0.7	1.1	2.4	12.2
1998	100.0	3.0	1.3	34.1	4.7	8.6	0.7	22.1	:	5.6	2.2	0.9	0.8	2.5	12.9
1999	100.0	3.2	1.4	30.6	5.9	7.9	0.6	25.6	0.0	5.6	2.0	0.9	0.8	2.2	12.4
2000	100.0	3.5	1.5	28.8	6.9	8.2	0.7	22.2	0.0	5.7	1.9	1.4	1.4	2.6	14.4
2001	100.0	2.3	1.9	26.6	7.6	8.8	0.8	19.9	0.1	5.7	1.5	1.6	1.1	2.2	19.2
2002	100.0	2.4	1.5	23.8	5.7	8.1	0.5	19.3	0.0	5.3	1.6	1.4	0.7	2.0	14.2
							IMPORTS / ARRIVALS								
							Value (Mio ECU/Euro)								
1980	3,423	150	46	1,064	69	473	28	649	:	295	80	12	76	132	349
1990	10,549	582	199	3,213	315	1,260	95	2,400	:	1,049	213	65	121	220	819
1994	12,276	690	262	2,963	568	1,461	155	3,012	:	1,348	188	64	150	291	1,124
1995	13,879	719	286	3,279	670	1,622	204	3,713	:	1,379	205	69	158	290	1,286
1996	14,328	780	293	3,185	752	1,755	194	3,677	:	1,394	252	90	171	312	1,471
1997	15,432	854	347	3,311	825	2,081	181	3,916	:	1,459	244	87	203	397	1,517
1998	17,732	925	381	4,020	956	2,317	189	4,305	:	1,674	267	86	312	542	1,718
1999	19,148	1,026	366	4,433	1,003	2,540	224	4,498	8	1,846	296	103	381	539	1,848
2000	20,826	992	392	4,820	1,232	2,604	343	4,786	12	2,098	311	112	503	707	1,893
2001	17,002	910	378	4,310	1,049	1,991	278	3,785	23	1,763	249	88	313	456	1,409
2002	17,248	1,439	333	4,029	1,274	1,879	212	3,804	32	1,844	256	84	311	391	1,345
							Annual variation (%)								
98/97	14.9	8.2	9.6	21.4	15.8	11.3	4.0	9.9	:	14.7	9.6	-0.6	53.8	36.7	13.2
99/98	7.9	10.9	-3.9	10.2	4.8	9.6	18.7	4.4	:	10.2	10.6	19.2	21.9	-0.5	7.5
00/99	8.7	-3.3	7.3	8.7	22.8	2.5	52.9	6.4	48.4	13.6	5.1	8.7	32.3	31.1	2.4
01/00	-18.3	-8.2	-3.7	-10.5	-14.8	-23.5	-18.8	-20.9	90.9	-15.9	-19.6	-21.2	-37.8	-35.5	-25.5
02/01	1.4	58.1	-11.9	-6.5	21.3	-5.6	-23.9	0.5	41.5	4.5	2.6	-4.7	-0.6	-14.2	-4.5
							Share (%)								
1980	100.0	4.3	1.3	31.0	2.0	13.8	0.8	18.9	:	8.6	2.3	0.3	2.2	3.8	10.1
1990	100.0	5.5	1.8	30.4	2.9	11.9	0.8	22.7	:	9.9	2.0	0.6	1.1	2.0	7.7
1996	100.0	5.4	2.0	22.2	5.2	12.2	1.3	25.6	:	9.7	1.7	0.6	1.1	2.1	10.2
1997	100.0	5.5	2.2	21.4	5.3	13.4	1.1	25.3	:	9.4	1.5	0.5	1.3	2.5	9.8
1998	100.0	5.2	2.1	22.6	5.3	13.0	1.0	24.2	:	9.4	1.5	0.4	1.7	3.0	9.6
1999	100.0	5.3	1.9	23.1	5.2	13.2	1.1	23.4	0.0	9.6	1.5	0.5	1.9	2.8	9.6
2000	100.0	4.7	1.8	23.1	5.9	12.5	1.6	22.9	0.0	10.0	1.4	0.5	2.4	3.3	9.0
2001	100.0	5.3	2.2	25.3	6.1	11.7	1.6	22.2	0.1	10.3	1.4	0.5	1.8	2.6	8.2
2002	100.0	8.3	1.9	23.3	7.3	10.8	1.2	22.0	0.1	10.6	1.4	0.4	1.8	2.2	7.7

(1) Luxembourg with Belgium until 31.12.1998.

EXTRA-EU

Years						Partner									
	Extra EU	Norway	Switzerland	USSR/ Russia(1)	Candid. countries	USA	Canada	China	Japan	Hong Kong	Mediterr. Basin	Latin America	OPEC	DAE	ACP

EXPORTS
Value (Mio ECU/Euro)

1980	1,883	5	19	65	:	209	16	9	18	1	670	13	568	14	67
1990	1,995	29	86	102	:	354	37	26	62	9	695	48	250	47	91
1994	3,389	28	89	204	1,042	382	37	15	79	27	1,238	120	314	99	102
1995	3,371	25	264	197	1,148	257	31	13	64	26	1,219	108	199	94	75
1996	4,247	26	86	285	1,257	359	41	38	65	39	1,880	128	273	163	99
1997	4,908	24	183	372	1,502	429	50	51	65	50	2,139	99	256	135	133
1998	4,478	38	76	240	1,574	460	59	16	67	47	1,905	104	243	117	160
1999	4,784	42	87	230	1,619	561	48	18	60	38	2,126	118	237	128	167
2000	6,705	44	95	269	2,499	692	82	33	93	52	3,155	175	313	151	239
2001	6,747	46	125	324	2,539	639	85	49	71	75	2,937	147	396	175	198
2002	6,155	37	92	310	2,212	579	74	60	54	53	2,528	121	435	174	188

Annual variation (%)

98/97	-8.7	59.5	-58.6	-35.4	4.8	7.0	18.7	-69.5	2.9	-6.6	-10.9	4.9	-4.9	-12.8	20.6
99/98	6.8	12.0	15.8	-4.2	2.8	21.9	-18.5	17.5	-11.1	-20.0	11.5	13.1	-2.6	9.0	4.2
00/99	40.1	3.1	8.7	17.1	54.3	23.4	69.0	81.3	55.6	39.0	48.4	48.5	32.0	17.9	43.1
01/00	0.6	6.1	31.3	20.3	1.5	-7.6	3.7	48.4	-24.1	43.9	-6.9	-15.7	26.7	16.0	-16.9
02/01	-8.7	-21.1	-26.0	-4.3	-12.8	-9.2	-12.3	22.0	-23.2	-29.5	-13.9	-17.6	9.8	-0.6	-5.0

Share (%)

1980	100.0	0.2	0.9	3.4	:	11.0	0.8	0.4	0.9	0.0	35.5	0.6	30.1	0.7	3.5
1990	100.0	1.4	4.3	5.0	:	17.7	1.8	1.2	3.1	0.4	34.8	2.4	12.5	2.3	4.5
1996	100.0	0.6	2.0	6.7	29.5	8.4	0.9	0.9	1.5	0.9	44.2	3.0	6.4	3.8	2.3
1997	100.0	0.4	3.7	7.5	30.5	8.7	1.0	1.0	1.3	1.0	43.5	2.0	5.2	2.7	2.7
1998	100.0	0.8	1.6	5.3	35.1	10.2	1.3	0.3	1.5	1.0	42.5	2.3	5.4	2.6	3.5
1999	100.0	0.8	1.8	4.8	33.8	11.7	1.0	0.3	1.2	0.7	44.4	2.4	4.9	2.6	3.4
2000	100.0	0.6	1.4	4.0	37.2	10.3	1.2	0.4	1.3	0.7	47.0	2.6	4.6	2.2	3.5
2001	100.0	0.6	1.8	4.8	37.6	9.4	1.2	0.7	1.0	1.1	43.5	2.1	5.8	2.5	2.9
2002	100.0	0.5	1.5	5.0	35.9	9.4	1.2	0.9	0.8	0.8	41.0	1.9	7.0	2.8	3.0

IMPORTS
Value (Mio ECU/Euro)

1980	4,223	66	98	108	:	348	56	18	836	19	1,270	188	830	86	105
1990	5,036	68	275	284	:	574	52	93	920	56	826	270	906	359	218
1994	5,805	46	334	460	1,439	579	49	236	691	41	1,065	246	961	438	173
1995	5,921	43	336	529	894	638	72	288	519	40	855	359	764	551	158
1996	7,912	50	374	548	923	744	86	367	716	46	1,344	345	1,310	857	258
1997	8,306	151	415	562	1,172	818	101	421	815	43	1,249	397	1,127	879	191
1998	9,289	81	425	444	1,253	1,246	120	529	885	47	1,272	282	1,297	1,301	227
1999	9,496	59	487	491	1,257	1,411	103	523	1,220	50	1,125	246	1,015	1,377	262
2000	14,142	192	443	1,185	1,848	1,170	111	757	1,277	52	1,717	346	3,189	1,761	358
2001	14,505	116	488	1,796	2,050	1,108	100	942	965	57	1,770	453	3,073	1,516	439
2002	15,817	82	496	2,426	1,972	1,554	99	1,023	998	85	1,764	502	2,023	2,480	420

Annual variation (%)

98/97	11.8	-46.0	2.5	-20.9	6.9	52.2	18.5	25.4	8.5	8.1	1.8	-28.9	15.1	48.0	19.3
99/98	2.2	-27.2	14.6	10.6	0.2	13.2	-14.1	-1.0	37.9	6.5	-11.5	-12.8	-21.7	5.8	15.0
00/99	48.9	224.1	-9.1	141.1	47.0	-17.0	7.8	44.6	4.6	4.5	52.5	40.7	214.1	27.8	36.8
01/00	2.5	-39.2	10.2	51.5	10.9	-5.3	-9.9	24.3	-24.3	9.1	3.1	30.8	-3.6	-13.9	22.6
02/01	9.0	-29.9	1.5	35.0	-3.7	40.2	-1.3	8.6	3.4	50.1	-0.3	10.8	-34.1	63.5	-4.3

Share (%)

1980	100.0	1.5	2.3	2.5	:	8.2	1.3	0.4	19.8	0.4	30.0	4.4	19.6	2.0	2.4
1990	100.0	1.3	5.4	5.6	:	11.4	1.0	1.8	18.2	1.1	16.4	5.3	17.9	7.1	4.3
1996	100.0	0.6	4.7	6.9	11.6	9.3	1.0	4.6	9.0	0.5	16.9	4.3	16.5	10.8	3.2
1997	100.0	1.8	4.9	6.7	14.1	9.8	1.2	5.0	9.8	0.5	15.0	4.7	13.5	10.5	2.2
1998	100.0	0.8	4.5	4.7	13.4	13.4	1.2	5.6	9.5	0.5	13.6	3.0	13.9	14.0	2.4
1999	100.0	0.6	5.1	5.1	13.2	14.8	1.0	5.5	12.8	0.5	11.8	2.5	10.6	14.5	2.7
2000	100.0	1.3	3.1	8.3	13.0	8.2	0.7	5.3	9.0	0.3	12.1	2.4	22.5	12.4	2.5
2001	100.0	0.8	3.3	12.3	14.1	7.6	0.6	6.4	6.6	0.3	12.2	3.1	21.1	10.4	3.0
2002	100.0	0.5	3.1	15.3	12.4	9.8	0.6	6.4	6.3	0.5	11.1	3.1	12.7	15.6	2.6

(1) Relates to the external trade with the USSR until 1991and to the external trade with Russia from 1992 onwards.

SPAIN

TRADE BALANCE (BN ECU/euro)

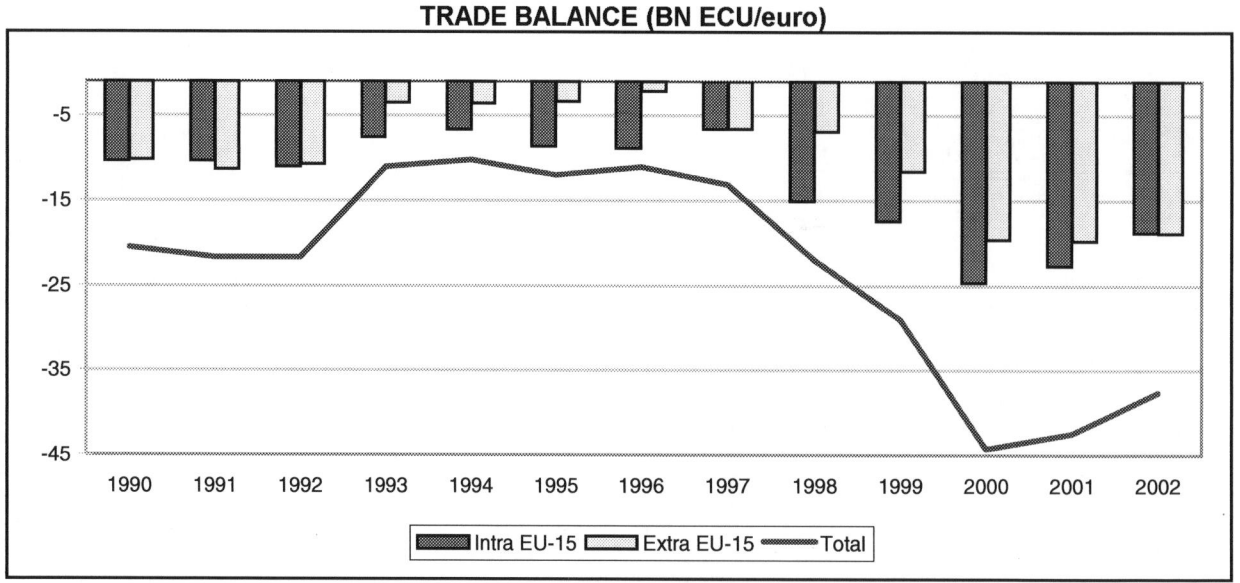

Intra EU-15 ▨ Extra EU-15 ▨ Total ▬

INTRA-EU (BN ECU/euro)

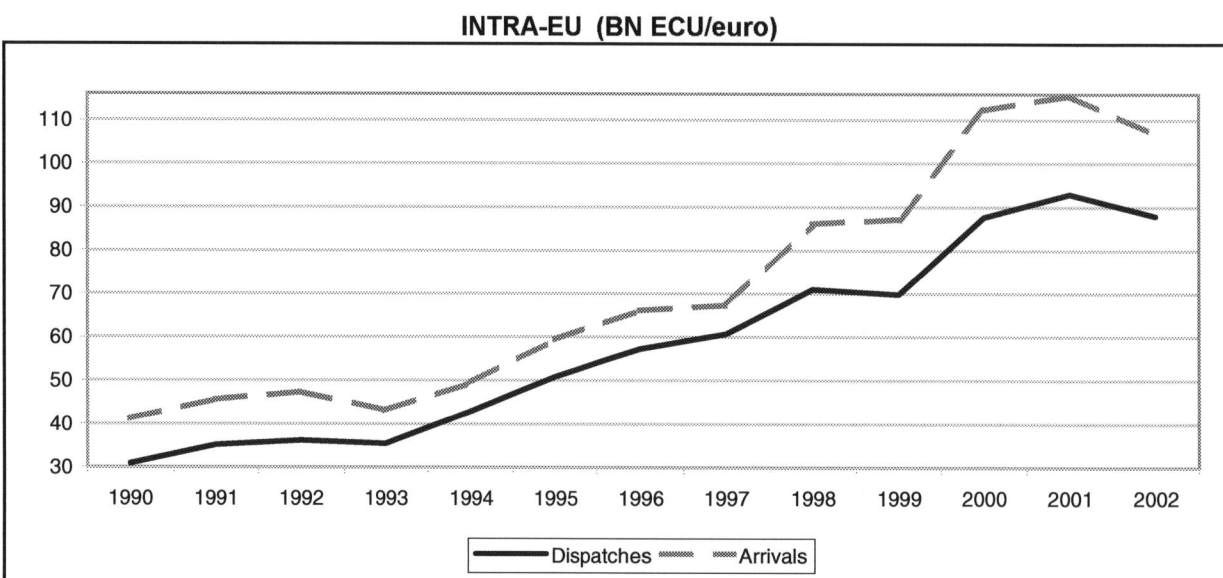

Dispatches ▬ Arrivals ▨

EXTRA-EU (BN ECU/euro)

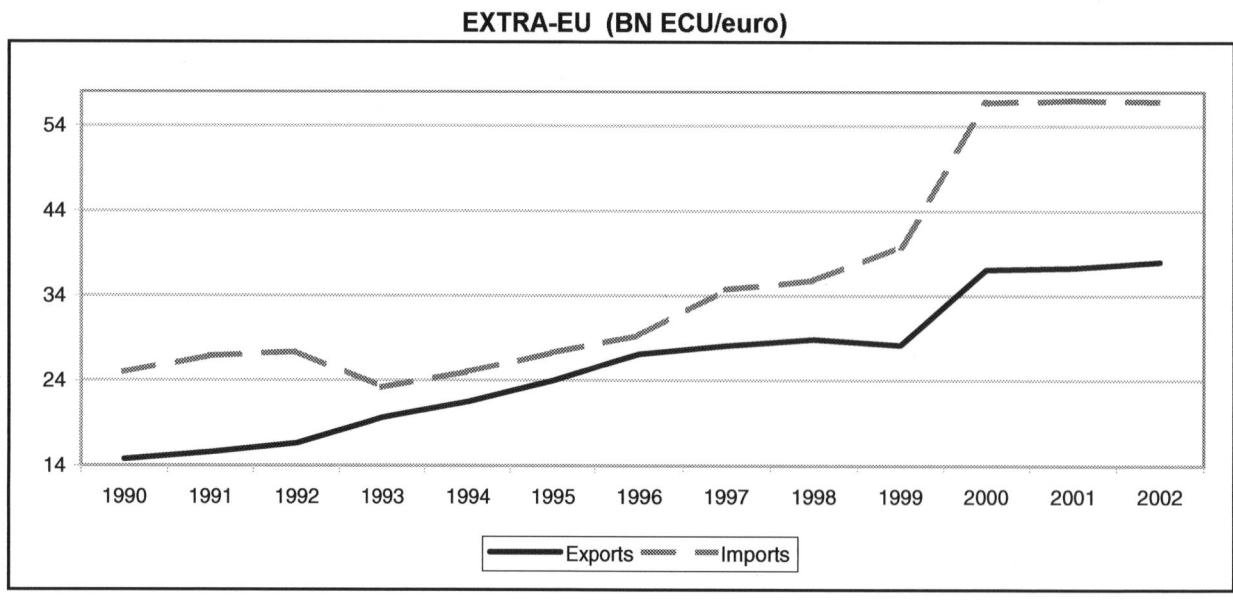

Exports ▬ Imports ▨

TRADE BALANCE

INTRA-EU

Value (Mio ECU/Euro)

Year	Intra EU	B[1]	DK	D	EL	F	IRL	I	L	NL	A	P	FIN	S	UK
1980	**-73**	**11**	**-49**	**-490**	**51**	**448**	**-39**	**-40**	**:**	**47**	**-38**	**292**	**-45**	**-124**	**-95**
1990	**-10,353**	**-670**	**-248**	**-4,978**	**195**	**-872**	**-213**	**-2,013**	**:**	**-703**	**-283**	**966**	**-303**	**-832**	**-399**
1991	-10,359	-609	-164	-3,953	193	-1,450	-219	-1,544	:	-841	-223	1,156	-368	-665	-1,672
1992	-11,041	-823	-286	-4,325	196	-2,050	-351	-1,663	:	-750	-144	1,684	-404	-532	-1,591
1993	-7,563	-936	-263	-3,119	276	-1,528	-344	-857	:	-1,074	-217	1,996	-412	-169	-916
1994	-6,641	-1,060	-232	-2,758	376	-1,095	-422	-846	:	-981	-264	2,720	-428	-436	-1,215
1995	-8,640	-1,225	-243	-2,938	421	-878	-671	-1,743	:	-1,976	-228	3,293	-524	-473	-1,579
1996	-8,841	-1,450	-309	-3,146	461	-1,355	-528	-2,157	:	-2,016	-308	4,265	-498	-656	-1,387
1997	-6,558	-1,380	-185	-3,778	656	-1,888	-792	-582	:	-1,839	-296	5,042	-372	-507	-1,175
1998	-15,117	-2,231	-281	-6,045	740	-3,565	-1,138	-2,836	:	-3,209	-467	5,937	-634	-689	-1,202
1999	-17,434	-2,235	-229	-7,687	760	-4,344	-1,041	-2,457	-56	-2,659	-652	6,007	-654	-1,336	-1,503
2000	**-24,637**	**-2,597**	**-269**	**-10,673**	**969**	**-6,031**	**-1,521**	**-4,110**	**-191**	**-3,520**	**-663**	**7,254**	**-880**	**-1,517**	**-2,087**
2001	-22,687	-2,301	-390	-12,879	1,021	-5,114	-1,546	-4,055	-164	-3,795	-673	8,383	-808	-876	-601
2002	**-18,744**	**-2,274**	**-319**	**-12,636**	**1,081**	**-3,926**	**-1,588**	**-2,354**	**-174**	**-3,768**	**-809**	**7,078**	**-645**	**-810**	**1,487**

EXTRA-EU

Value (Mio ECU/Euro)

Year	Extra EU	Norway	Switzerland	Russia[2]	Candid. countries	USA	Canada	China	Japan	Hong Kong	Mediterr. Basin	Latin America	OPEC	DAE	ACP
1980	**-9,295**	**2**	**-128**	**-133**	**:**	**-2,369**	**-86**	**-37**	**-413**	**-61**	**149**	**-863**	**-5,514**	**-203**	**-468**
1990	**-10,172**	**-35**	**-547**	**-714**	**:**	**-3,022**	**-77**	**-223**	**-2,355**	**-58**	**-180**	**-1,164**	**-3,302**	**-1,116**	**-1,529**
1991	-11,358	-158	-546	-157	:	-3,421	-65	-457	-2,766	-30	-483	-1,302	-3,382	-1,397	-1,454
1992	-10,703	-2	-711	-350	:	-3,180	-180	-822	-2,865	-15	-476	-839	-2,576	-1,588	-1,023
1993	-3,472	132	-711	-458	481	-1,678	-17	-323	-1,718	187	675	271	-1,741	-463	-458
1994	-3,587	-118	-393	-557	424	-1,670	35	-514	-1,355	254	434	775	-2,653	-178	-1,374
1995	-3,355	-15	-449	-683	357	-1,869	-111	-759	-1,270	267	887	467	-2,622	-298	-1,244
1996	-2,167	-322	-260	-565	1,070	-1,734	-67	-1,085	-1,120	399	852	978	-3,750	11	-1,343
1997	-6,594	-163	-525	-361	1,490	-1,819	-44	-1,760	-1,347	577	476	1,389	-4,761	42	-1,906
1998	-6,905	43	-594	-352	1,585	-1,702	-36	-2,080	-2,006	295	1,885	2,079	-3,287	-1,838	-1,535
1999	-11,571	111	-679	-820	1,210	-1,677	-74	-2,727	-2,397	213	886	981	-4,097	-2,216	-1,644
2000	**-19,637**	**-27**	**-787**	**-1,834**	**2,432**	**-1,354**	**-34**	**-3,583**	**-2,628**	**307**	**-426**	**810**	**-10,655**	**-2,618**	**-4,118**
2001	-19,732	-183	-1,150	-1,260	1,004	-1,035	-100	-3,780	-2,232	262	-2,339	831	-9,298	-2,534	-3,453
2002	**-18,865**	**-195**	**-1,274**	**-1,839**	**1,381**	**-275**	**42**	**-3,970**	**-2,313**	**230**	**-929**	**-11**	**-7,531**	**-2,304**	**-3,143**

(1)   Luxembourg with Belgium until 31.12.1998.
(2)   Relates to the external trade with the USSR until 1991 and to the external trade with Russia from 1992 onwards.

SPAIN

INTRA-EU

Year		Partner													
	Intra EU	B(1)	DK	D	EL	F	IRL	I	L	NL	A	P	FIN	S	UK

EXPORTS / DISPATCHES
Value (Mio ECU/Euro)

Year	Intra EU	B(1)	DK	D	EL	F	IRL	I	L	NL	A	P	FIN	S	UK
1980	8,080	401	79	1,532	82	2,469	49	1,170	:	573	56	408	60	151	1,050
1990	30,869	1,329	237	5,824	331	8,965	146	4,624	:	1,984	311	2,656	183	416	3,862
1994	42,970	1,854	394	8,608	565	12,355	263	5,644	:	2,378	507	4,811	211	466	4,914
1995	50,827	2,171	482	10,806	715	14,567	258	6,451	:	2,396	566	5,918	240	637	5,493
1996	57,287	2,386	501	11,749	786	16,247	366	7,047	:	2,622	674	7,080	231	730	6,622
1997	60,718	2,430	587	11,493	854	15,974	366	8,531	:	3,171	733	7,744	340	867	7,091
1998	71,002	2,770	695	13,542	944	19,339	524	9,183	:	3,446	861	9,363	361	1,105	8,367
1999	69,772	2,627	722	12,819	998	18,988	653	8,728	116	3,579	868	9,379	378	1,115	8,149
2000	87,666	3,379	887	15,325	1,315	24,127	883	10,855	149	4,563	1,164	11,855	516	1,251	10,199
2001	92,976	3,719	861	15,387	1,421	25,330	799	11,697	168	4,592	1,165	13,226	476	1,308	11,719
2002	87,949	3,275	921	14,312	1,446	23,803	776	11,649	136	4,029	1,137	11,934	477	1,152	11,989

Annual variation (%)

Year	Intra EU	B(1)	DK	D	EL	F	IRL	I	L	NL	A	P	FIN	S	UK
98/97	16.9	14.0	18.2	17.8	10.4	21.0	43.1	7.6	:	8.6	17.5	20.9	6.3	27.4	18.0
99/98	-1.7	-5.1	3.8	-5.3	5.7	-1.8	24.5	-4.9	:	3.8	0.8	0.1	4.6	0.9	-2.6
00/99	25.6	28.6	22.8	19.5	31.8	27.0	35.1	24.3	28.5	27.5	34.0	26.3	36.6	12.2	25.1
01/00	6.0	10.0	-2.9	0.4	8.0	4.9	-9.4	7.7	12.8	0.6	0.0	11.5	-7.8	4.5	14.9
02/01	-5.4	-11.9	6.9	-6.9	1.7	-6.0	-2.9	-0.4	-19.2	-12.2	-2.3	-9.7	0.2	-11.9	2.3

Share (%)

Year	Intra EU	B(1)	DK	D	EL	F	IRL	I	L	NL	A	P	FIN	S	UK
1980	100.0	4.9	0.9	18.9	1.0	30.5	0.6	14.4	:	7.0	0.6	5.0	0.7	1.8	13.0
1990	100.0	4.3	0.7	18.8	1.0	29.0	0.4	14.9	:	6.4	1.0	8.6	0.5	1.3	12.5
1996	100.0	4.1	0.8	20.5	1.3	28.3	0.6	12.3	:	4.5	1.1	12.3	0.4	1.2	11.5
1997	100.0	4.0	0.9	18.9	1.4	26.3	0.6	14.0	:	5.2	1.2	12.7	0.5	1.4	11.6
1998	100.0	3.9	0.9	19.0	1.3	27.2	0.7	12.9	:	4.8	1.2	13.1	0.5	1.5	11.7
1999	100.0	3.7	1.0	18.3	1.4	27.2	0.9	12.5	0.1	5.1	1.2	13.4	0.5	1.5	11.6
2000	100.0	3.8	1.0	17.4	1.5	27.5	1.0	12.3	0.1	5.2	1.3	13.5	0.5	1.4	11.6
2001	100.0	4.0	0.9	16.5	1.5	27.2	0.8	12.5	0.1	4.9	1.2	14.2	0.5	1.4	12.6
2002	100.0	3.7	1.0	16.2	1.6	27.0	0.8	13.2	0.1	4.5	1.2	13.5	0.5	1.3	13.6

IMPORTS / ARRIVALS
Value (Mio ECU/Euro)

Year	Intra EU	B(1)	DK	D	EL	F	IRL	I	L	NL	A	P	FIN	S	UK
1980	8,105	390	127	2,008	31	2,008	89	1,210	:	526	94	117	105	275	1,125
1990	41,222	1,999	485	10,801	136	9,837	360	6,637	:	2,687	594	1,691	486	1,248	4,260
1994	49,611	2,914	626	11,365	190	13,449	686	6,489	:	3,359	771	2,092	639	902	6,129
1995	59,467	3,396	725	13,744	294	15,446	929	8,194	:	4,372	794	2,626	763	1,110	7,072
1996	66,128	3,836	810	14,894	325	17,602	895	9,204	:	4,638	982	2,815	729	1,386	8,009
1997	67,275	3,809	772	15,271	198	17,861	1,158	9,113	:	5,010	1,029	2,703	711	1,374	8,265
1998	86,119	5,001	975	19,587	203	22,903	1,662	12,019	:	6,655	1,328	3,426	995	1,794	9,570
1999	87,205	4,862	951	20,506	238	23,333	1,694	11,185	172	6,238	1,520	3,372	1,032	2,451	9,652
2000	112,303	5,976	1,155	25,998	346	30,159	2,404	14,965	340	8,083	1,827	4,600	1,396	2,769	12,286
2001	115,662	6,020	1,250	28,266	399	30,443	2,345	15,752	332	8,387	1,838	4,842	1,283	2,184	12,320
2002	106,693	5,549	1,240	26,948	365	27,729	2,363	14,003	309	7,798	1,946	4,857	1,122	1,962	10,502

Annual variation (%)

Year	Intra EU	B(1)	DK	D	EL	F	IRL	I	L	NL	A	P	FIN	S	UK
98/97	28.0	31.2	26.2	28.2	2.8	28.2	43.5	31.8	:	32.8	29.0	26.7	39.9	30.5	15.7
99/98	1.2	-2.7	-2.5	4.6	16.9	1.8	1.9	-6.9	:	-6.2	14.4	-1.5	3.6	36.6	0.8
00/99	28.7	22.8	21.5	26.7	45.5	29.2	41.8	33.7	97.8	29.5	20.1	36.4	35.3	12.9	27.2
01/00	2.9	0.7	8.2	8.7	15.4	0.9	-2.4	5.2	-2.3	3.7	0.5	5.2	-8.0	-21.1	0.2
02/01	-7.7	-7.8	-0.8	-4.6	-8.6	-8.9	0.7	-11.1	-6.7	-7.0	5.9	0.3	-12.5	-10.1	-14.7

Share (%)

Year	Intra EU	B(1)	DK	D	EL	F	IRL	I	L	NL	A	P	FIN	S	UK
1980	100.0	4.8	1.5	24.7	0.3	24.7	1.0	14.9	:	6.4	1.1	1.4	1.2	3.3	13.8
1990	100.0	4.8	1.1	26.2	0.3	23.8	0.8	16.1	:	6.5	1.4	4.1	1.1	3.0	10.3
1996	100.0	5.8	1.2	22.5	0.4	26.6	1.3	13.9	:	7.0	1.4	4.2	1.1	2.0	12.1
1997	100.0	5.6	1.1	22.6	0.2	26.5	1.7	13.5	:	7.4	1.5	4.0	1.0	2.0	12.2
1998	100.0	5.8	1.1	22.7	0.2	26.5	1.9	13.9	:	7.7	1.5	3.9	1.1	2.0	11.1
1999	100.0	5.5	1.0	23.5	0.2	26.7	1.9	12.8	0.1	7.1	1.7	3.8	1.1	2.8	11.0
2000	100.0	5.3	1.0	23.1	0.3	26.8	2.1	13.3	0.3	7.1	1.6	4.0	1.2	2.4	10.9
2001	100.0	5.2	1.0	24.4	0.3	26.3	2.0	13.6	0.2	7.2	1.5	4.1	1.1	1.8	10.6
2002	100.0	5.2	1.1	25.2	0.3	25.9	2.2	13.1	0.2	7.3	1.8	4.5	1.0	1.8	9.8

(1)   Luxembourg with Belgium until 31.12.1998.

EXTRA-EU

Years	Extra EU	Norway	Switzerland	USSR/Russia[1]	Candid. countries	USA	Canada	China	Japan	Hong Kong	Mediterr. Basin	Latin America	OPEC	DAE	ACP
EXPORTS															
Value (Mio ECU/Euro)															
1980	7,168	70	258	188	:	795	106	47	192	27	1,978	1,527	1,936	98	523
1990	14,789	240	706	292	:	2,544	273	230	417	136	2,393	1,636	1,478	599	621
1994	21,507	208	711	250	1,245	2,981	357	656	755	352	3,471	3,679	1,961	1,569	649
1995	23,980	423	789	315	1,632	2,928	344	694	923	380	4,134	3,669	2,076	1,740	743
1996	27,173	301	911	466	2,340	3,371	344	484	898	499	4,406	4,357	2,185	2,099	1,150
1997	28,129	400	959	730	3,108	4,087	408	430	964	719	4,793	5,664	2,466	2,536	1,127
1998	28,877	605	1,083	614	3,516	4,166	434	467	913	460	5,950	6,336	2,662	1,399	1,583
1999	28,214	586	1,014	382	3,479	4,459	444	433	1,069	409	5,789	5,624	2,348	1,452	1,637
2000	37,119	690	1,207	578	5,544	6,052	579	553	1,215	585	8,130	7,023	3,006	1,959	1,855
2001	37,283	564	1,256	743	5,030	5,643	532	634	1,183	506	7,263	7,393	3,240	1,949	2,102
2002	38,013	489	1,281	789	5,962	5,720	640	785	1,038	477	7,914	6,663	3,488	1,978	1,979
Annual variation (%)															
98/97	2.6	51.3	12.8	-15.9	13.1	1.9	6.3	8.6	-5.3	-36.1	24.1	11.8	7.9	-44.8	40.4
99/98	-2.2	-3.1	-6.3	-37.7	-1.0	7.0	2.4	-7.2	17.0	-10.9	-2.7	-11.2	-11.7	3.7	3.4
00/99	31.5	17.7	19.0	51.1	59.3	35.7	30.3	27.8	13.7	43.0	40.4	24.8	27.9	34.9	13.3
01/00	0.4	-18.2	4.1	28.6	-9.2	-6.7	-8.1	14.4	-2.6	-13.5	-10.6	5.2	7.7	-0.5	13.3
02/01	1.9	-13.2	2.0	6.1	18.5	1.3	20.2	23.9	-12.2	-5.7	8.9	-9.8	7.6	1.5	-5.8
Share (%)															
1980	100.0	0.9	3.5	2.6	:	11.0	1.4	0.6	2.6	0.3	27.5	21.3	27.0	1.3	7.2
1990	100.0	1.6	4.7	1.9	:	17.1	1.8	1.5	2.8	0.9	16.1	11.0	9.9	4.0	4.1
1996	100.0	1.1	3.3	1.7	8.6	12.4	1.2	1.7	3.3	1.8	16.2	16.0	8.0	7.7	4.2
1997	100.0	1.4	3.4	2.5	11.0	14.5	1.4	1.5	3.4	2.5	17.0	20.1	8.7	9.0	4.0
1998	100.0	2.0	3.7	2.1	12.1	14.4	1.5	1.6	3.1	1.5	20.6	21.9	9.2	4.8	5.4
1999	100.0	2.0	3.5	1.3	12.3	15.8	1.5	1.5	3.7	1.4	20.5	19.9	8.3	5.1	5.8
2000	100.0	1.8	3.2	1.5	14.9	16.3	1.5	1.4	3.2	1.5	21.9	18.9	8.0	5.2	4.9
2001	100.0	1.5	3.3	1.9	13.4	15.1	1.4	1.6	3.1	1.3	19.4	19.8	8.6	5.2	5.6
2002	100.0	1.2	3.3	2.0	15.6	15.0	1.6	2.0	2.7	1.2	20.8	17.5	9.1	5.2	5.2
IMPORTS															
Value (Mio ECU/Euro)															
1980	16,463	69	385	321	:	3,164	192	85	605	88	1,830	2,390	7,449	300	991
1990	24,961	274	1,253	1,006	:	5,566	349	453	2,772	194	2,573	2,801	4,781	1,715	2,150
1994	25,094	326	1,105	807	1,642	4,651	322	1,169	2,110	98	3,038	2,904	4,614	1,746	2,023
1995	27,335	438	1,238	998	1,275	4,797	455	1,453	2,193	112	3,247	3,201	4,698	2,038	1,987
1996	29,341	624	1,171	1,032	1,270	5,106	411	1,569	2,017	100	3,553	3,379	5,935	2,088	2,494
1997	34,723	563	1,484	1,091	1,618	5,906	451	2,190	2,312	143	4,316	4,275	7,227	2,495	3,033
1998	35,782	562	1,677	966	1,931	5,868	469	2,547	2,919	165	4,065	4,257	5,949	3,238	3,118
1999	39,785	475	1,693	1,202	2,268	6,136	518	3,160	3,466	196	4,904	4,643	6,446	3,667	3,282
2000	56,756	717	1,993	2,412	3,112	7,406	613	4,136	3,843	278	8,556	6,213	13,660	4,577	5,973
2001	57,015	746	2,407	2,003	4,025	6,678	632	4,414	3,415	244	9,602	6,562	12,537	4,482	5,555
2002	56,879	685	2,555	2,627	4,581	5,995	598	4,755	3,351	247	8,843	6,674	11,020	4,282	5,122
Annual variation (%)															
98/97	3.0	-0.2	12.9	-11.4	19.3	-0.6	4.0	16.2	26.2	15.1	-5.8	-0.4	-17.6	29.7	2.8
99/98	11.1	-15.4	0.9	24.3	17.4	4.5	10.4	24.0	18.7	19.1	20.6	9.0	8.3	13.2	5.2
00/99	42.6	50.8	17.7	100.7	37.1	20.6	18.3	30.8	10.8	41.9	74.4	33.8	111.9	24.7	81.9
01/00	0.4	4.1	20.7	-16.9	29.3	-9.8	3.0	6.7	-11.1	-12.2	12.2	5.6	-8.2	-2.0	-6.9
02/01	-0.2	-8.2	6.1	31.1	13.8	-10.2	-5.3	7.7	-1.8	1.1	-7.8	1.7	-12.1	-4.4	-7.8
Share (%)															
1980	100.0	0.4	2.3	1.9	:	19.2	1.1	0.5	3.6	0.5	11.1	14.5	45.2	1.8	6.0
1990	100.0	1.0	5.0	4.0	:	22.2	1.3	1.8	11.1	0.7	10.3	11.2	19.1	6.8	8.6
1996	100.0	2.1	3.9	3.5	4.3	17.4	1.4	5.3	6.8	0.3	12.1	11.5	20.2	7.1	8.4
1997	100.0	1.6	4.2	3.1	4.6	17.0	1.2	6.3	6.6	0.4	12.4	12.3	20.8	7.1	8.7
1998	100.0	1.5	4.6	2.7	5.3	16.3	1.3	7.1	8.1	0.4	11.3	11.8	16.6	9.0	8.7
1999	100.0	1.1	4.2	3.0	5.7	15.4	1.3	7.9	8.7	0.4	12.3	11.6	16.2	9.2	8.2
2000	100.0	1.2	3.5	4.2	5.4	13.0	1.0	7.2	6.7	0.4	15.0	10.9	24.0	8.0	10.5
2001	100.0	1.3	4.2	3.5	7.0	11.7	1.1	7.7	5.9	0.4	16.8	11.5	21.9	7.8	9.7
2002	100.0	1.2	4.4	4.6	8.0	10.5	1.0	8.3	5.8	0.4	15.5	11.7	19.3	7.5	9.0

(1) Relates to the external trade with the USSR until 1991and to the external trade with Russia from 1992 onwards.

FRANCE

TRADE BALANCE (BN ECU/euro)

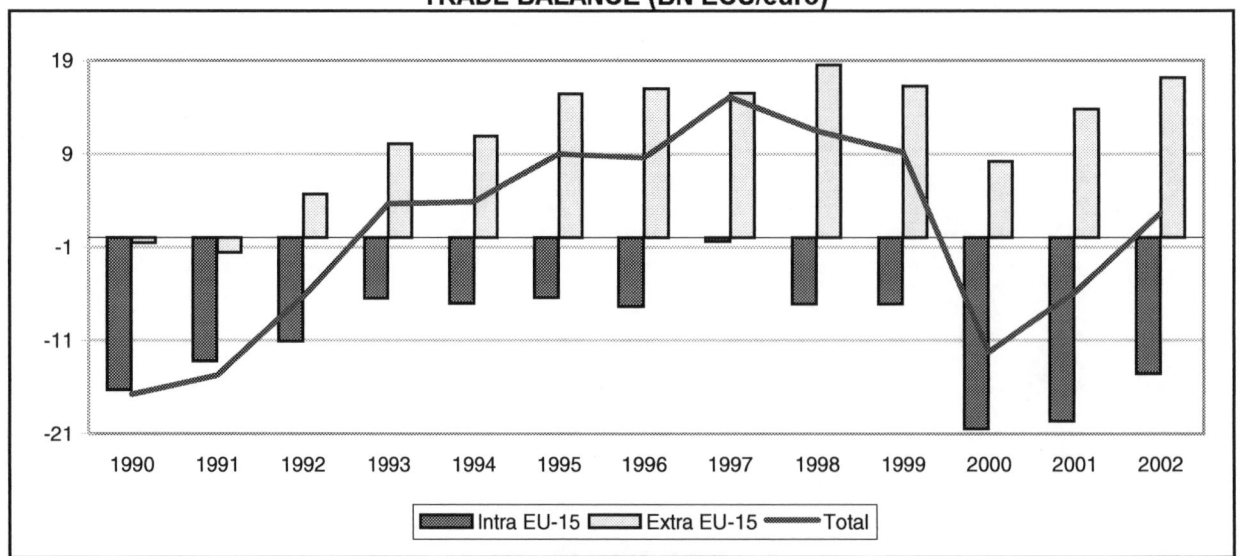

INTRA-EU (BN ECU/euro)

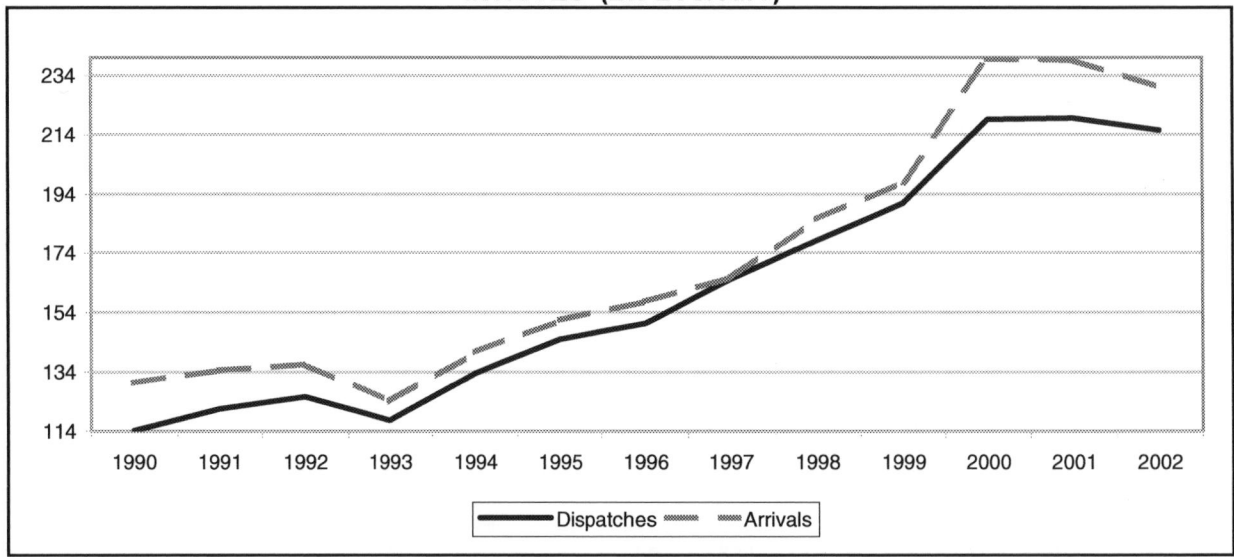

EXTRA-EU (BN ECU/euro)

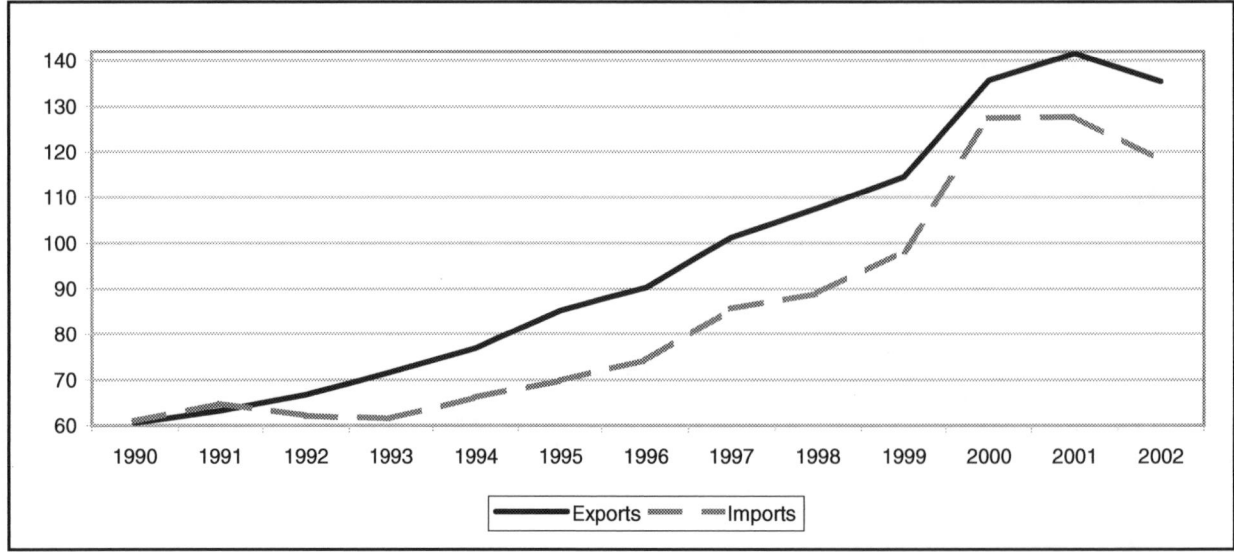

FRANCE

TRADE BALANCE

INTRA-EU

Value (Mio ECU/Euro)

Year	Intra EU	B(1)	DK	D	EL	E	IRL	I	L	NL	A	P	FIN	S	UK
							Partner								
1980	**-6,381**	**-1,454**	**-76**	**-3,625**	**525**	**-554**	**-164**	**846**	**:**	**-1,955**	**218**	**200**	**-190**	**-333**	**180**
1990	**-16,243**	**-4,345**	**-368**	**-7,950**	**660**	**1,973**	**-1,367**	**-2,343**	**:**	**-3,346**	**-175**	**-106**	**-581**	**-738**	**2,442**
1991	-13,172	-4,799	-173	-3,650	707	2,041	-1,294	-1,628	:	-4,526	14	569	-608	-803	977
1992	-11,070	-4,230	-386	-5,403	926	2,840	-1,506	-453	:	-4,328	120	884	-853	-809	2,129
1993	-6,453	-3,116	-217	-3,015	1,014	2,101	-1,497	-951	:	-3,545	309	888	-542	-534	2,653
1994	-7,034	-3,718	-168	-4,854	1,047	2,077	-1,551	-64	:	-4,178	528	831	-519	-195	3,729
1995	-6,438	-3,926	-88	-4,091	1,254	2,297	-1,827	597	:	-4,764	907	741	-383	-159	3,004
1996	-7,365	-3,633	-9	-3,371	1,407	2,713	-1,935	-1,215	:	-5,117	876	691	-351	299	2,280
1997	-417	-3,622	-44	-3,242	1,721	4,286	-1,778	549	:	-5,120	780	1,134	-338	490	4,767
1998	-7,081	-5,594	131	-5,583	1,791	5,043	-2,329	-805	:	-7,118	739	1,202	-410	504	5,347
1999	-7,092	-5,376	-68	-8,009	2,393	7,029	-2,656	-724	9	-7,511	793	1,363	-637	207	5,778
2000	**-20,434**	**-8,564**	**-70**	**-12,940**	**2,107**	**8,128**	**-3,590**	**-945**	**32**	**-10,621**	**440**	**1,460**	**-921**	**196**	**4,564**
2001	-19,632	-7,932	-239	-14,928	2,017	8,404	-2,237	-1,191	-92	-11,638	-168	1,337	-373	414	6,653
2002	**-14,576**	**-7,916**	**-164**	**-14,778**	**1,977**	**8,070**	**-1,961**	**761**	**58**	**-10,909**	**-398**	**1,374**	**-593**	**311**	**9,110**

EXTRA-EU

Value (Mio ECU/Euro)

Year	Extra EU	Norway	Switzerland	Russia(2)	Candid. countries	USA	Canada	China	Japan	Hong Kong	Mediterr. Basin	Latin America	OPEC	DAE	ACP
								Partner							
1980	**-10,569**	**-305**	**1,562**	**-505**	**:**	**-3,377**	**-237**	**-89**	**-1,007**	**-41**	**3,532**	**-42**	**-10,994**	**-642**	**-271**
1990	**-496**	**-1,535**	**2,109**	**-1,294**	**:**	**-3,418**	**406**	**-153**	**-2,044**	**452**	**2,558**	**-888**	**-1,156**	**373**	**582**
1991	-1,554	-1,701	1,787	-1,201	:	-4,667	337	-664	-2,190	508	1,607	-320	-1,245	82	578
1992	4,696	-1,500	1,859	-332	:	-2,539	579	-691	-2,437	780	2,029	371	467	623	1,409
1993	10,097	-1,429	2,144	-881	1,833	-430	301	-1,016	-1,727	1,294	3,718	817	573	1,514	1,110
1994	10,887	-1,532	2,099	-1,217	1,198	-289	94	-819	-1,136	1,587	3,146	1,395	-26	2,542	379
1995	15,438	-1,683	2,470	-1,291	1,570	-665	-57	-1,066	-843	2,546	3,735	809	1,331	4,577	1,319
1996	15,987	-2,333	2,804	-1,355	3,134	-656	297	-1,731	-407	2,383	4,567	1,319	-49	3,509	1,608
1997	15,510	-2,492	2,632	-652	4,371	-1,301	862	-1,474	-957	2,136	5,100	1,996	354	3,583	1,405
1998	18,552	-1,831	2,400	-606	4,333	466	1,016	-2,011	-1,480	2,335	6,540	3,231	1,448	2,745	2,655
1999	16,266	-2,148	3,263	-1,376	4,475	597	1,707	-2,702	-2,293	1,284	6,749	2,332	1,131	95	2,384
2000	**8,168**	**-5,801**	**2,836**	**-2,662**	**5,170**	**3,809**	**757**	**-4,734**	**-3,003**	**1,789**	**6,499**	**2,643**	**-2,240**	**760**	**3,456**
2001	13,793	-5,288	2,567	-2,544	3,688	3,958	1,193	-4,791	-1,834	3,438	4,112	3,081	700	4,042	1,966
2002	**17,174**	**-4,167**	**2,243**	**-2,675**	**4,621**	**3,801**	**692**	**-4,864**	**-1,077**	**2,328**	**5,842**	**2,465**	**3,280**	**2,271**	**1,883**

(1) Luxembourg with Belgium until 31.12.1998.
(2) Relates to the external trade with the USSR until 1991 and to the external trade with Russia from 1992 onwards.

FRANCE

INTRA-EU

Year							Partner									
	Intra EU	B(1)	DK	D	EL	E	IRL	I	L	NL	A	P	FIN	S	UK

EXPORTS / DISPATCHES
Value (Mio ECU/Euro)

Year	Intra EU	B(1)	DK	D	EL	E	IRL	I	L	NL	A	P	FIN	S	UK
1980	46,465	7,488	559	12,843	847	2,244	388	10,017	:	3,903	669	562	315	1,042	5,588
1990	114,108	15,612	1,345	31,735	1,245	10,637	724	19,955	:	9,438	1,469	2,192	844	2,148	16,764
1994	133,624	18,009	1,891	37,259	1,497	14,590	1,231	20,618	:	9,437	2,177	3,064	776	2,344	20,730
1995	145,033	19,091	2,033	41,041	1,744	16,515	1,132	22,322	:	10,214	2,607	3,102	1,049	2,898	21,284
1996	150,299	19,982	2,169	41,178	1,917	18,476	1,189	22,055	:	10,524	2,701	3,270	1,263	3,292	22,283
1997	165,256	20,812	2,296	42,333	2,167	20,527	1,653	24,681	:	11,882	2,728	3,970	1,175	3,713	27,319
1998	178,385	21,441	2,478	46,955	2,243	24,130	1,869	25,823	:	12,722	3,039	4,342	1,348	4,011	27,984
1999	190,889	20,898	2,488	48,523	2,870	27,045	2,130	27,187	1,444	13,607	3,227	4,683	1,377	4,194	30,375
2000	219,074	23,838	2,742	55,232	2,607	31,955	3,099	30,822	2,953	15,008	3,399	5,956	1,723	5,115	33,730
2001	219,565	24,431	2,694	53,708	2,717	31,912	3,163	30,476	2,638	14,226	3,481	7,478	1,895	4,938	35,039
2002	215,411	24,091	2,825	52,673	2,664	31,563	3,047	31,484	2,086	13,534	3,471	5,946	1,646	4,745	34,565

Annual variation (%)

Year	Intra EU	B(1)	DK	D	EL	E	IRL	I	L	NL	A	P	FIN	S	UK
98/97	7.9	3.0	7.9	10.9	3.5	17.5	13.0	4.6	:	7.0	11.3	9.3	14.6	8.0	2.4
99/98	7.0	-2.5	0.4	3.3	27.9	12.0	13.9	5.2	:	6.9	6.2	7.8	2.1	4.5	8.5
00/99	14.7	14.0	10.2	13.8	-9.1	18.1	45.5	13.3	104.4	10.2	5.3	27.1	25.1	21.9	11.0
01/00	0.2	2.4	-1.7	-2.7	4.2	-0.1	2.0	-1.1	-10.6	-5.2	2.4	25.5	10.0	-3.4	3.8
02/01	-1.8	-1.3	4.8	-1.9	-1.9	-1.0	-3.6	3.3	-20.9	-4.8	-0.2	-20.4	-13.1	-3.9	-1.3

Share (%)

Year	Intra EU	B(1)	DK	D	EL	E	IRL	I	L	NL	A	P	FIN	S	UK
1980	100.0	16.1	1.2	27.6	1.8	4.8	0.8	21.5	:	8.3	1.4	1.2	0.6	2.2	12.0
1990	100.0	13.6	1.1	27.8	1.0	9.3	0.6	17.4	:	8.2	1.2	1.9	0.7	1.8	14.6
1996	100.0	13.2	1.4	27.3	1.2	12.2	0.7	14.6	:	7.0	1.7	2.1	0.8	2.1	14.8
1997	100.0	12.5	1.3	25.6	1.3	12.4	1.0	14.9	:	7.1	1.6	2.4	0.7	2.2	16.5
1998	100.0	12.0	1.3	26.3	1.2	13.5	1.0	14.4	:	7.1	1.7	2.4	0.7	2.2	15.6
1999	100.0	10.9	1.3	25.4	1.5	14.1	1.1	14.2	0.7	7.1	1.6	2.4	0.7	2.1	15.9
2000	100.0	10.8	1.2	25.2	1.1	14.5	1.4	14.0	1.3	6.8	1.5	2.7	0.7	2.3	15.3
2001	100.0	11.1	1.2	24.4	1.2	14.5	1.4	13.8	1.2	6.4	1.5	3.4	0.8	2.2	15.9
2002	100.0	11.1	1.3	24.4	1.2	14.6	1.4	14.6	0.9	6.2	1.6	2.7	0.7	2.2	16.0

IMPORTS / ARRIVALS
Value (Mio ECU/Euro)

Year	Intra EU	B(1)	DK	D	EL	E	IRL	I	L	NL	A	P	FIN	S	UK
1980	52,846	8,942	636	16,468	322	2,798	552	9,170	:	5,858	451	361	505	1,375	5,408
1990	130,351	19,957	1,713	39,685	585	8,665	2,091	22,298	:	12,784	1,644	2,298	1,425	2,886	14,322
1994	140,658	21,727	2,058	42,113	450	12,513	2,782	20,682	:	13,615	1,649	2,233	1,295	2,538	17,002
1995	151,471	23,018	2,121	45,132	490	14,218	2,959	21,724	:	14,978	1,700	2,362	1,432	3,057	18,280
1996	157,663	23,615	2,178	44,549	510	15,763	3,124	23,270	:	15,641	1,825	2,579	1,614	2,993	20,003
1997	165,673	24,434	2,340	45,575	445	16,241	3,431	24,132	:	17,002	1,949	2,836	1,514	3,224	22,552
1998	185,466	27,035	2,346	52,538	452	19,087	4,198	26,628	:	19,840	2,299	3,140	1,758	3,507	22,637
1999	197,981	26,273	2,556	56,531	477	20,017	4,786	27,912	1,435	21,119	2,434	3,320	2,014	3,987	24,597
2000	239,508	32,402	2,811	68,173	499	23,827	6,689	31,767	2,921	25,629	2,958	4,496	2,644	4,919	29,166
2001	239,197	32,363	2,932	68,635	700	23,508	5,400	31,667	2,729	25,864	3,649	6,142	2,269	4,524	28,386
2002	229,987	32,007	2,989	67,450	687	23,493	5,007	30,723	2,028	24,443	3,868	4,572	2,239	4,433	25,455

Annual variation (%)

Year	Intra EU	B(1)	DK	D	EL	E	IRL	I	L	NL	A	P	FIN	S	UK
98/97	11.9	10.6	0.2	15.2	1.4	17.5	22.3	10.3	:	16.6	17.9	10.7	16.1	8.7	0.3
99/98	6.7	-2.8	8.9	7.6	5.4	4.8	14.0	4.8	:	6.4	5.8	5.7	14.6	13.6	8.6
00/99	20.9	23.3	9.9	20.5	4.8	19.0	39.7	13.8	103.5	21.3	21.5	35.4	31.2	23.3	18.5
01/00	-0.1	-0.1	4.3	0.6	40.2	-1.3	-19.2	-0.3	-6.5	0.9	23.3	36.5	-14.2	-8.0	-2.6
02/01	-3.8	-1.0	1.9	-1.7	-1.8	0.0	-7.2	-2.9	-25.6	-5.4	6.0	-25.5	-1.3	-1.9	-10.3

Share (%)

Year	Intra EU	B(1)	DK	D	EL	E	IRL	I	L	NL	A	P	FIN	S	UK
1980	100.0	16.9	1.2	31.1	0.6	5.2	1.0	17.3	:	11.0	0.8	0.6	0.9	2.6	10.2
1990	100.0	15.3	1.3	30.4	0.4	6.6	1.6	17.1	:	9.8	1.2	1.7	1.0	2.2	10.9
1996	100.0	14.9	1.3	28.2	0.3	9.9	1.9	14.7	:	9.9	1.1	1.6	1.0	1.8	12.6
1997	100.0	14.7	1.4	27.5	0.2	9.8	2.0	14.5	:	10.2	1.1	1.7	0.9	1.9	13.6
1998	100.0	14.5	1.2	28.3	0.2	10.2	2.2	14.3	:	10.6	1.2	1.6	0.9	1.8	12.2
1999	100.0	13.2	1.2	28.5	0.2	10.1	2.4	14.0	0.7	10.6	1.2	1.6	1.0	2.0	12.4
2000	100.0	13.5	1.1	28.4	0.2	9.9	2.7	13.2	1.2	10.7	1.2	1.8	1.1	2.0	12.1
2001	100.0	13.5	1.2	28.6	0.2	9.8	2.2	13.2	1.1	10.8	1.5	2.5	0.9	1.8	11.8
2002	100.0	13.9	1.2	29.3	0.2	10.2	2.1	13.3	0.8	10.6	1.6	1.9	0.9	1.9	11.0

(1) Luxembourg with Belgium until 31.12.1998.

Years	Extra EU	Norway	Switzerland	USSR/ Russia[1]	Candid. countries	USA	Canada	China	Japan	Hong Kong	Mediterr. Basin	Latin America	OPEC	DAE	ACP
EXPORTS															
Value (Mio ECU/Euro)															
1980	33,686	369	3,759	1,775	:	3,544	490	219	790	199	10,318	2,160	7,094	807	4,646
1990	60,532	745	7,415	1,267	:	10,635	1,596	1,120	3,401	938	9,754	2,385	7,349	4,447	5,168
1994	77,025	849	7,764	1,106	4,815	14,627	1,421	1,831	3,949	1,980	10,897	4,742	7,816	7,571	4,564
1995	85,212	895	8,805	1,423	6,072	13,684	1,468	2,028	4,335	2,960	11,997	4,272	7,709	10,392	5,660
1996	90,307	979	9,178	1,769	8,148	14,592	1,633	1,981	4,275	2,802	13,201	4,564	7,425	9,626	6,377
1997	101,175	1,426	9,391	2,338	9,580	17,981	2,294	3,107	4,376	2,621	14,673	5,881	8,599	10,926	6,212
1998	107,615	1,290	10,358	1,733	10,877	22,030	2,450	3,043	4,223	2,880	16,781	7,060	8,365	10,361	8,226
1999	114,540	1,212	12,546	1,370	11,903	24,086	3,229	3,217	4,331	1,835	17,581	6,319	8,758	8,341	7,935
2000	135,637	1,254	13,033	1,838	14,892	30,492	2,851	3,424	5,475	2,382	19,937	8,320	10,678	10,979	10,508
2001	141,510	1,230	12,727	2,443	14,825	30,931	3,314	3,552	5,488	3,964	19,159	8,852	13,309	12,595	9,851
2002	135,392	1,286	11,153	2,393	16,210	27,505	2,939	3,708	5,615	2,764	19,852	7,267	14,139	10,181	9,382
Annual variation (%)															
98/97	6.3	-9.5	10.3	-25.8	13.5	22.5	6.8	-2.0	-3.4	9.8	14.3	20.0	-2.7	-5.1	32.4
99/98	6.4	-6.0	21.1	-20.9	9.4	9.3	31.7	5.7	2.5	-36.2	4.7	-10.4	4.7	-19.4	-3.5
00/99	18.4	3.4	3.8	34.2	25.1	26.5	-11.7	6.4	26.4	29.8	13.3	31.6	21.9	31.6	32.4
01/00	4.3	-1.9	-2.3	32.8	-0.4	1.4	16.2	3.7	0.2	66.3	-3.9	6.3	24.6	14.7	-6.2
02/01	-4.3	4.5	-12.3	-2.0	9.3	-11.0	-11.3	4.4	2.2	-30.2	3.6	-17.9	6.2	-19.1	-4.7
Share (%)															
1980	100.0	1.0	11.1	5.2	:	10.5	1.4	0.6	2.3	0.5	30.6	6.4	21.0	2.3	13.7
1990	100.0	1.2	12.2	2.0	:	17.5	2.6	1.8	5.6	1.5	16.1	3.9	12.1	7.3	8.5
1996	100.0	1.0	10.1	1.9	9.0	16.1	1.8	2.1	4.7	3.1	14.6	5.0	8.2	10.6	7.0
1997	100.0	1.4	9.2	2.3	9.4	17.7	2.2	3.0	4.3	2.5	14.5	5.8	8.4	10.7	6.1
1998	100.0	1.1	9.6	1.6	10.1	20.4	2.2	2.8	3.9	2.6	15.5	6.5	7.7	9.6	7.6
1999	100.0	1.0	10.9	1.1	10.3	21.0	2.8	2.8	3.7	1.6	15.3	5.5	7.6	7.2	6.9
2000	100.0	0.9	9.6	1.3	10.9	22.4	2.1	2.5	4.0	1.7	14.6	6.1	7.8	8.0	7.7
2001	100.0	0.8	8.9	1.7	10.4	21.8	2.3	2.5	3.8	2.8	13.5	6.2	9.4	8.9	6.9
2002	100.0	0.9	8.2	1.7	11.9	20.3	2.1	2.7	4.1	2.0	14.6	5.3	10.4	7.5	6.9
IMPORTS															
Value (Mio ECU/Euro)															
1980	44,256	674	2,197	2,280	:	6,921	727	308	1,797	240	6,785	2,203	18,088	1,449	4,917
1990	61,029	2,280	5,307	2,562	:	14,053	1,190	1,273	5,445	486	7,196	3,272	8,505	4,074	4,586
1994	66,139	2,381	5,665	2,323	7,233	14,915	1,327	2,649	5,085	393	7,751	3,347	7,842	5,029	4,185
1995	69,774	2,578	6,335	2,714	4,502	14,350	1,525	3,094	5,178	415	8,262	3,462	6,377	5,814	4,340
1996	74,319	3,312	6,374	3,123	5,014	15,248	1,336	3,713	4,681	419	8,634	3,245	7,473	6,117	4,769
1997	85,665	3,917	6,758	2,990	5,209	19,282	1,432	4,581	5,333	485	9,573	3,885	8,245	7,343	4,807
1998	89,062	3,121	7,959	2,339	6,544	21,564	1,435	5,054	5,703	545	10,242	3,829	6,916	7,615	5,571
1999	98,274	3,360	9,283	2,745	7,428	23,490	1,522	5,919	6,623	551	10,832	3,986	7,628	8,246	5,552
2000	127,469	7,055	10,197	4,501	9,722	26,683	2,094	8,158	8,477	593	13,438	5,677	12,918	10,219	7,052
2001	127,717	6,518	10,160	4,987	11,138	26,972	2,120	8,343	7,322	526	15,047	5,772	12,609	8,553	7,885
2002	118,217	5,454	8,910	5,068	11,589	23,703	2,247	8,572	6,692	436	14,011	4,802	10,859	7,910	7,499
Annual variation (%)															
98/97	3.9	-20.3	17.7	-21.7	25.6	11.8	0.1	10.3	6.9	12.3	6.9	-1.4	-16.1	3.7	15.8
99/98	10.3	7.6	16.6	17.3	13.5	8.9	6.1	17.1	16.1	1.1	5.7	4.1	10.2	8.2	-0.3
00/99	29.7	109.9	9.8	63.9	30.8	13.5	37.5	37.8	27.9	7.7	24.0	42.4	69.3	23.9	27.0
01/00	0.1	-7.6	-0.3	10.8	14.5	1.0	1.2	2.2	-13.6	-11.3	11.9	1.6	-2.3	-16.2	11.8
02/01	-7.4	-16.3	-12.3	1.6	4.0	-12.1	5.9	2.7	-8.6	-17.0	-6.8	-16.7	-13.8	-7.5	-4.8
Share (%)															
1980	100.0	1.5	4.9	5.1	:	15.6	1.6	0.6	4.0	0.5	15.3	4.9	40.8	3.2	11.1
1990	100.0	3.7	8.6	4.1	:	23.0	1.9	2.0	8.9	0.7	11.7	5.3	13.9	6.6	7.5
1996	100.0	4.4	8.5	4.2	6.7	20.5	1.7	4.9	6.2	0.5	11.6	4.3	10.0	8.2	6.4
1997	100.0	4.5	7.8	3.4	6.0	22.5	1.6	5.3	6.2	0.5	11.1	4.5	9.6	8.5	5.6
1998	100.0	3.5	8.9	2.6	7.3	24.2	1.6	5.6	6.4	0.6	11.4	4.2	7.7	8.5	6.2
1999	100.0	3.4	9.4	2.7	7.5	23.9	1.5	6.0	6.7	0.5	11.0	4.0	7.7	8.3	5.6
2000	100.0	5.5	7.9	3.5	7.6	20.9	1.6	6.4	6.6	0.4	10.5	4.4	10.1	8.0	5.5
2001	100.0	5.1	7.9	3.9	8.7	21.1	1.6	6.5	5.7	0.4	11.7	4.5	9.8	6.6	6.1
2002	100.0	4.6	7.5	4.2	9.8	20.0	1.9	7.2	5.6	0.3	11.8	4.0	9.1	6.6	6.3

(1) Relates to the external trade with the USSR until 1991and to the external trade with Russia from 1992 onwards.

IRELAND

TRADE BALANCE (BN ECU/euro)

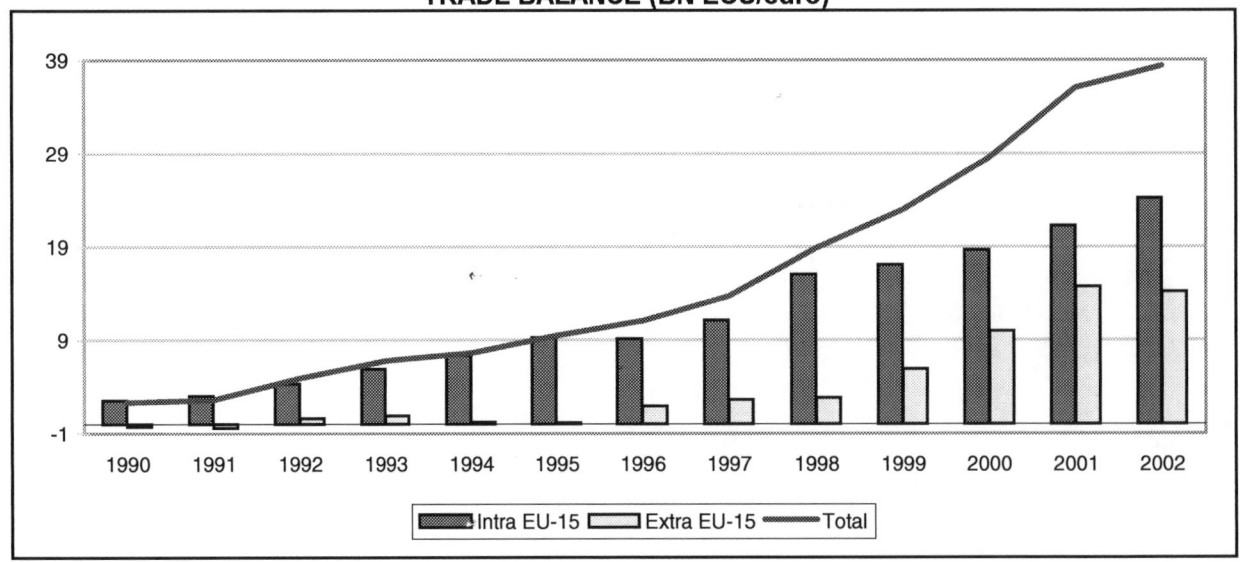

INTRA-EU (BN ECU/euro)

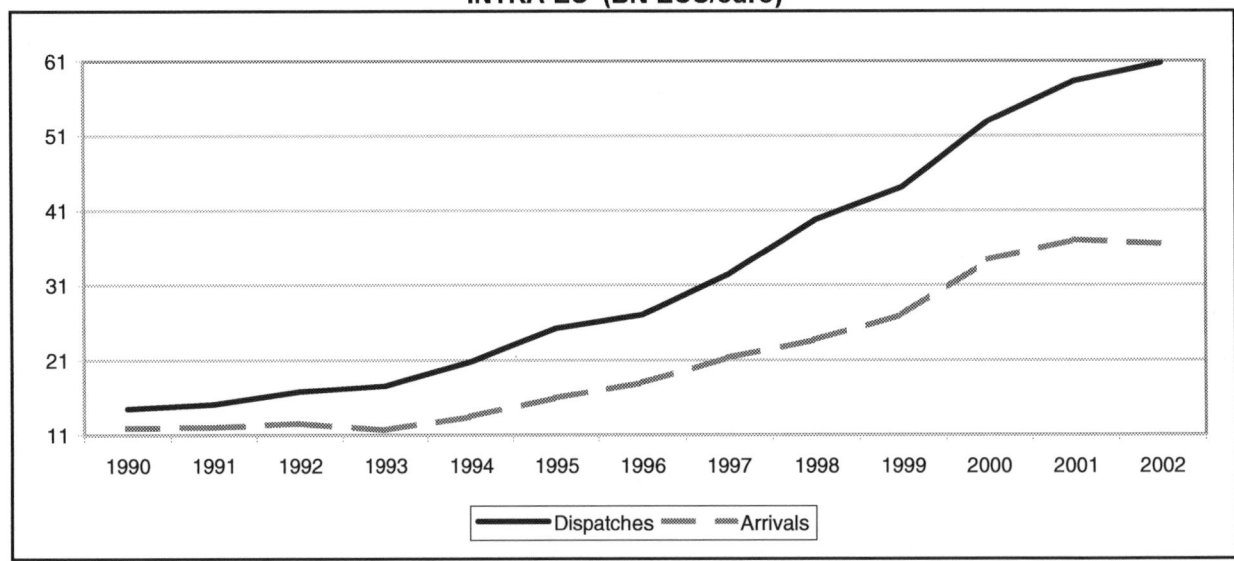

EXTRA-EU (BN ECU/euro)

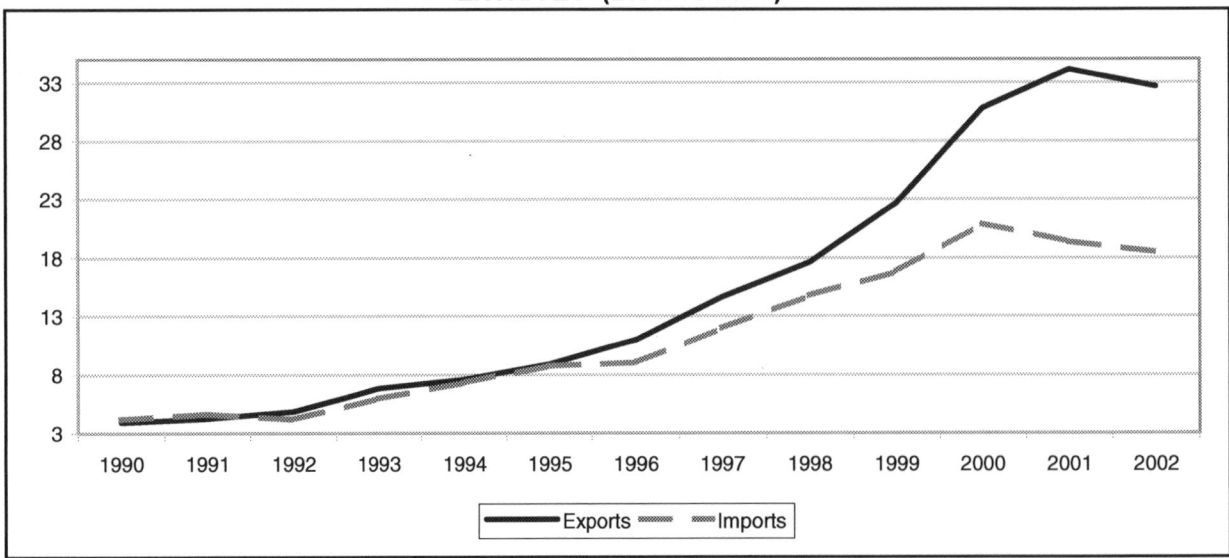

IRELAND

TRADE BALANCE

INTRA-EU

Value (Mio ECU/Euro)

Year	Intra EU	B[1]	DK	D	EL	E	F	I	L	NL	A	P	FIN	S	UK
														Partner	
1980	**-1,473**	**146**	**-7**	**111**	**17**	**3**	**76**	**33**	**:**	**48**	**8**	**0**	**-49**	**-44**	**-1,817**
1990	**2,594**	**450**	**50**	**914**	**79**	**255**	**1,250**	**458**	**:**	**258**	**63**	**33**	**-33**	**147**	**-1,330**
1991	3,038	593	44	1,146	102	317	1,148	455	:	441	52	34	1	96	-1,394
1992	4,312	689	57	1,398	102	391	1,355	517	:	660	49	56	-8	143	-1,097
1993	5,915	718	86	1,938	127	373	1,548	552	:	703	65	59	25	195	-473
1994	7,358	804	122	2,546	133	482	1,918	708	:	895	129	72	105	316	-873
1995	9,296	1,149	251	3,354	192	611	2,290	885	:	1,547	155	81	91	414	-1,094
1996	9,106	1,386	290	3,221	206	561	2,127	889	:	1,676	126	90	61	341	-1,389
1997	11,101	1,908	278	3,894	135	867	2,154	960	:	2,135	124	136	-11	394	-1,444
1998	16,033	3,119	316	6,115	133	1,126	3,305	1,281	:	1,911	237	147	29	722	-1,856
1999	17,053	2,758	257	5,258	215	1,333	3,863	1,722	42	2,678	303	157	268	677	-1,906
2000	**18,628**	**3,054**	**-30**	**6,083**	**265**	**1,403**	**3,833**	**2,132**	**31**	**2,712**	**341**	**147**	**96**	**783**	**-1,825**
2001	21,259	3,393	-76	8,079	285	1,672	2,852	2,224	78	2,161	250	173	107	909	-553
2002	**24,214**	**12,532**	**-139**	**3,009**	**295**	**1,634**	**2,578**	**2,711**	**52**	**1,422**	**116**	**226**	**-76**	**824**	**-592**

EXTRA-EU

Value (Mio ECU/Euro)

Year	Extra EU	Norway	Switzerland	Russia[2]	Candid. countries	USA	Canada	China	Japan	Hong Kong	Mediterr. Basin	Latin America	OPEC	DAE	ACP
									Partner						
1980	**-425**	**-0**	**3**	**2**	**:**	**-306**	**-9**	**-6**	**-152**	**-16**	**227**	**91**	**-83**	**-39**	**13**
1990	**-260**	**54**	**211**	**58**	**:**	**-777**	**37**	**-49**	**-362**	**8**	**145**	**90**	**285**	**-10**	**4**
1991	-392	-75	205	30	:	-842	74	-81	-194	-2	133	79	178	-49	12
1992	676	-113	218	40	:	-209	154	-129	73	-6	123	147	228	-107	6
1993	895	-56	272	43	85	-509	170	-180	-49	19	267	184	339	-369	53
1994	256	-2	349	155	101	-1,260	139	-179	-18	19	327	175	336	-409	15
1995	158	19	462	245	266	-1,170	84	-178	-184	-27	377	181	413	-910	2
1996	1,935	78	501	263	334	-349	120	-181	-108	68	379	188	422	-555	-5
1997	2,656	3	565	281	433	565	35	-260	-542	134	362	301	485	-680	57
1998	2,822	109	848	233	463	1,370	-14	-419	-674	137	541	365	536	-1,593	328
1999	5,906	70	1,375	250	464	3,286	-28	-360	-192	-28	652	361	664	-1,615	405
2000	**9,926**	**-404**	**1,678**	**168**	**924**	**5,237**	**-119**	**-574**	**1,006**	**128**	**925**	**399**	**790**	**-1,133**	**400**
2001	14,783	-208	2,287	219	540	7,066	-33	-376	1,562	336	735	747	836	-86	473
2002	**14,181**	**-124**	**2,512**	**229**	**569**	**7,388**	**89**	**-215**	**898**	**295**	**727**	**427**	**1,213**	**-370**	**419**

(1) Luxembourg with Belgium until 31.12.1998.
(2) Relates to the external trade with the USSR until 1991 and to the external trade with Russia from 1992 onwards.

IRELAND

INTRA-EU

Year	Intra EU	B(1)	DK	D	EL	E	F	I	L	NL	A	P	FIN	S	UK
						Partner									

EXPORTS / DISPATCHES
Value (Mio ECU/Euro)

Year	Intra EU	B(1)	DK	D	EL	E	F	I	L	NL	A	P	FIN	S	UK
1980	4,768	307	45	597	23	54	472	190	:	333	30	15	27	74	2,599
1990	14,513	821	192	2,188	93	399	1,965	825	:	1,075	118	90	100	357	6,288
1994	20,838	1,135	280	4,060	148	673	2,633	1,134	:	1,610	207	128	192	597	8,040
1995	25,274	1,515	431	5,043	207	831	3,271	1,309	:	2,377	214	138	222	658	8,762
1996	27,110	1,806	493	5,076	221	884	3,212	1,401	:	2,604	193	162	212	691	8,682
1997	32,413	2,361	532	5,939	150	1,213	3,794	1,547	:	3,344	198	205	242	752	11,675
1998	39,777	3,650	580	8,561	153	1,527	4,799	1,939	:	3,220	316	232	284	1,076	12,872
1999	44,131	3,434	614	8,011	238	1,827	5,633	2,528	53	4,158	408	249	522	1,093	14,649
2000	53,008	4,105	620	9,393	294	2,122	6,341	3,317	39	4,684	464	257	405	1,335	17,066
2001	58,350	4,431	596	11,671	326	2,283	5,532	3,309	91	4,237	407	302	406	1,354	21,397
2002	60,746	13,525	547	6,755	331	2,239	4,677	3,602	76	3,457	335	360	304	1,200	22,544

Annual variation (%)

Year	Intra EU	B(1)	DK	D	EL	E	F	I	L	NL	A	P	FIN	S	UK
98/97	22.7	54.6	8.9	44.1	2.0	25.9	26.4	25.3	:	-3.7	59.5	13.0	17.5	43.0	10.2
99/98	10.9	-5.9	5.8	-6.4	55.1	19.6	17.3	30.3	:	29.1	29.2	7.0	83.6	1.5	13.8
00/99	20.1	19.5	1.0	17.2	23.5	16.1	12.5	31.2	-26.2	12.6	13.6	3.2	-22.4	22.1	16.4
01/00	10.0	7.9	-3.9	24.2	10.8	7.6	-12.7	-0.2	133.4	-9.5	-12.2	17.8	0.1	1.3	25.3
02/01	4.1	205.2	-8.1	-42.1	1.4	-1.9	-15.4	8.8	-16.1	-18.3	-17.7	19.1	-25.1	-11.3	5.3

Share (%)

Year	Intra EU	B(1)	DK	D	EL	E	F	I	L	NL	A	P	FIN	S	UK
1980	100.0	6.4	0.9	12.5	0.4	1.1	9.9	3.9	:	6.9	0.6	0.3	0.5	1.5	54.5
1990	100.0	5.6	1.3	15.0	0.6	2.7	13.5	5.6	:	7.4	0.8	0.6	0.6	2.4	43.3
1996	100.0	6.6	1.8	18.7	0.8	3.2	11.8	5.1	:	9.6	0.7	0.5	0.7	2.5	32.0
1997	100.0	7.2	1.6	18.3	0.4	3.7	11.7	4.7	:	10.3	0.6	0.6	0.7	2.3	36.0
1998	100.0	9.1	1.4	21.5	0.3	3.8	12.0	4.8	:	8.0	0.7	0.5	0.7	2.7	32.3
1999	100.0	7.7	1.3	18.1	0.5	4.1	12.7	5.7	0.1	9.4	0.9	0.5	1.1	2.4	33.1
2000	100.0	7.7	1.1	17.7	0.5	4.0	11.9	6.2	0.0	8.8	0.8	0.4	0.7	2.5	32.1
2001	100.0	7.5	1.0	20.0	0.5	3.9	9.4	5.6	0.1	7.2	0.6	0.5	0.6	2.3	36.6
2002	100.0	22.2	0.9	11.1	0.5	3.6	7.6	5.9	0.1	5.6	0.5	0.5	0.5	1.9	37.1

IMPORTS / ARRIVALS
Value (Mio ECU/Euro)

Year	Intra EU	B(1)	DK	D	EL	E	F	I	L	NL	A	P	FIN	S	UK
1980	6,242	161	52	486	6	50	396	157	:	285	22	15	76	118	4,416
1990	11,919	371	142	1,274	14	144	715	367	:	817	55	57	133	210	7,618
1994	13,481	331	158	1,514	15	191	715	426	:	715	78	57	88	281	8,913
1995	15,978	365	180	1,689	14	220	981	424	:	829	59	57	131	244	9,856
1996	18,004	420	203	1,855	15	323	1,085	512	:	928	67	72	151	350	10,071
1997	21,312	453	254	2,044	15	345	1,640	586	:	1,209	74	69	253	359	13,120
1998	23,744	531	263	2,446	20	401	1,495	658	:	1,309	79	85	256	354	14,728
1999	27,078	676	356	2,753	23	494	1,771	806	11	1,480	105	92	254	416	16,555
2000	34,380	1,051	650	3,311	29	719	2,507	1,185	8	1,972	123	109	309	552	18,891
2001	37,091	1,038	671	3,592	41	612	2,680	1,085	13	2,076	157	129	299	445	21,950
2002	36,532	993	686	3,746	35	605	2,099	891	24	2,035	219	134	380	376	23,136

Annual variation (%)

Year	Intra EU	B(1)	DK	D	EL	E	F	I	L	NL	A	P	FIN	S	UK
98/97	11.4	17.2	3.5	19.6	31.4	16.0	-8.8	12.2	:	8.2	6.1	23.8	1.1	-1.3	12.2
99/98	14.0	27.2	35.2	12.5	10.6	23.1	18.4	22.4	:	13.0	34.1	7.2	-0.6	17.4	12.4
00/99	26.9	55.4	82.5	20.2	27.8	45.6	41.5	47.1	-20.7	33.2	17.0	19.2	21.8	32.7	14.1
01/00	7.8	-1.2	3.2	8.4	43.2	-14.9	6.8	-8.4	58.6	5.2	27.6	18.0	-3.5	-19.3	16.1
02/01	-1.5	-4.2	2.2	4.3	-14.5	-1.1	-21.6	-17.8	84.1	-1.9	39.0	3.8	27.3	-15.5	5.4

Share (%)

Year	Intra EU	B(1)	DK	D	EL	E	F	I	L	NL	A	P	FIN	S	UK
1980	100.0	2.5	0.8	7.7	0.0	0.8	6.3	2.5	:	4.5	0.3	0.2	1.2	1.8	70.7
1990	100.0	3.1	1.1	10.6	0.1	1.2	6.0	3.0	:	6.8	0.4	0.4	1.1	1.7	63.9
1996	100.0	2.3	1.1	10.3	0.0	1.7	6.0	2.8	:	5.1	0.3	0.4	0.8	1.9	55.9
1997	100.0	2.1	1.1	9.5	0.0	1.6	7.6	2.7	:	5.6	0.3	0.3	1.1	1.6	61.5
1998	100.0	2.2	1.1	10.3	0.0	1.6	6.2	2.7	:	5.5	0.3	0.3	1.0	1.4	62.0
1999	100.0	2.4	1.3	10.1	0.0	1.8	6.5	2.9	0.0	5.4	0.3	0.3	0.9	1.5	61.1
2000	100.0	3.0	1.8	9.6	0.0	2.0	7.2	3.4	0.0	5.7	0.3	0.3	0.9	1.6	54.9
2001	100.0	2.7	1.8	9.6	0.1	1.6	7.2	2.9	0.0	5.5	0.4	0.3	0.8	1.2	59.1
2002	100.0	2.7	1.8	10.2	0.0	1.6	5.7	2.4	0.0	5.5	0.5	0.3	1.0	1.0	63.3

(1) Luxembourg with Belgium until 31.12.1998.

EXPORTS
Value (Mio ECU/Euro)

Years	Extra EU	Norway	Switzerland	USSR/ Russia[1]	Candid. countries	USA	Canada	China	Japan	Hong Kong	Mediterr. Basin	Latin America	OPEC	DAE	ACP
1980	1,333	32	45	36	:	320	78	2	29	5	337	133	267	35	92
1990	3,957	151	316	121	:	1,531	141	6	343	59	232	172	336	240	150
1994	7,586	311	557	174	233	2,327	268	27	895	131	446	270	393	662	183
1995	8,904	360	619	268	423	2,791	253	28	992	115	535	311	468	834	178
1996	10,960	423	675	281	529	3,517	311	40	1,082	172	556	368	469	1,301	196
1997	14,629	507	797	301	687	5,237	306	44	1,458	257	675	462	569	1,871	265
1998	17,605	555	1,152	246	804	7,630	345	75	1,446	295	876	504	631	1,576	573
1999	22,710	588	1,643	259	1,044	10,242	336	122	1,910	333	1,099	579	745	2,252	634
2000	30,809	616	2,040	179	1,659	14,141	394	166	3,190	619	1,463	749	910	3,279	689
2001	34,142	588	2,795	241	1,335	15,523	591	342	3,171	672	1,211	1,162	952	3,658	764
2002	32,659	513	3,093	259	1,226	15,791	507	548	2,461	552	1,071	806	1,351	3,146	673

Annual variation (%)

Years	Extra EU	Norway	Switzerland	USSR/ Russia	Candid. countries	USA	Canada	China	Japan	Hong Kong	Mediterr. Basin	Latin America	OPEC	DAE	ACP
98/97	20.3	9.5	44.4	-18.4	17.0	45.6	12.7	70.6	-0.8	15.0	29.8	9.0	10.9	-15.7	116.2
99/98	29.0	5.9	42.6	5.3	29.8	34.2	-2.7	62.3	32.1	12.6	25.4	14.9	18.0	42.8	10.5
00/99	35.6	4.6	24.1	-30.8	58.8	38.0	17.2	36.8	66.9	85.8	33.0	29.3	22.1	45.5	8.7
01/00	10.8	-4.5	36.9	34.9	-19.5	9.7	50.1	105.8	-0.5	8.5	-17.2	55.1	4.6	11.5	10.7
02/01	-4.3	-12.6	10.6	7.3	-8.1	1.7	-14.1	59.9	-22.3	-17.8	-11.5	-30.6	41.8	-14.0	-11.8

Share (%)

Years	Extra EU	Norway	Switzerland	USSR/ Russia	Candid. countries	USA	Canada	China	Japan	Hong Kong	Mediterr. Basin	Latin America	OPEC	DAE	ACP
1980	100.0	2.4	3.3	2.6	:	24.0	5.8	0.1	2.1	0.3	25.2	9.9	20.0	2.6	6.8
1990	100.0	3.8	7.9	3.0	:	38.6	3.5	0.1	8.6	1.4	5.8	4.3	8.4	6.0	3.7
1996	100.0	3.8	6.1	2.5	4.8	32.0	2.8	0.3	9.8	1.5	5.0	3.3	4.2	11.8	1.7
1997	100.0	3.4	5.4	2.0	4.6	35.7	2.0	0.3	9.9	1.7	4.6	3.1	3.8	12.7	1.8
1998	100.0	3.1	6.5	1.3	4.5	43.3	1.9	0.4	8.2	1.6	4.9	2.8	3.5	8.9	3.2
1999	100.0	2.5	7.2	1.1	4.5	45.0	1.4	0.5	8.4	1.4	4.8	2.5	3.2	9.9	2.7
2000	100.0	1.9	6.6	0.5	5.3	45.9	1.2	0.5	10.3	2.0	4.7	2.4	2.9	10.6	2.2
2001	100.0	1.7	8.1	0.7	3.9	45.4	1.7	1.0	9.2	1.9	3.5	3.4	2.7	10.7	2.2
2002	100.0	1.5	9.4	0.7	3.7	48.3	1.5	1.6	7.5	1.6	3.2	2.4	4.1	9.6	2.0

IMPORTS
Value (Mio ECU/Euro)

Years	Extra EU	Norway	Switzerland	USSR/ Russia	Candid. countries	USA	Canada	China	Japan	Hong Kong	Mediterr. Basin	Latin America	OPEC	DAE	ACP
1980	1,758	33	42	34	:	626	87	8	181	21	110	42	350	75	79
1990	4,217	97	106	63	:	2,307	104	55	706	51	87	82	51	250	146
1994	7,329	313	208	19	264	3,587	129	207	913	112	119	94	57	1,070	168
1995	8,746	341	157	23	158	3,961	169	207	1,176	143	158	129	55	1,744	175
1996	9,025	345	174	18	195	3,866	191	221	1,190	103	177	179	47	1,855	201
1997	11,974	503	232	20	254	4,671	271	304	1,999	123	313	161	84	2,552	209
1998	14,782	446	304	13	342	6,259	359	494	2,120	158	335	139	94	3,169	246
1999	16,804	518	269	9	581	6,957	364	481	2,102	361	447	219	81	3,867	229
2000	20,883	1,020	362	11	735	8,904	513	741	2,184	491	538	350	120	4,412	290
2001	19,359	796	508	23	796	8,457	624	718	1,609	335	476	415	116	3,744	291
2002	18,477	637	581	30	657	8,402	418	763	1,563	256	343	380	139	3,515	254

Annual variation (%)

Years	Extra EU	Norway	Switzerland	USSR/ Russia	Candid. countries	USA	Canada	China	Japan	Hong Kong	Mediterr. Basin	Latin America	OPEC	DAE	ACP
98/97	23.4	-11.2	31.0	-38.8	34.5	33.9	32.2	62.4	6.0	28.4	7.2	-13.8	12.6	24.2	17.7
99/98	13.6	16.0	-11.6	-31.1	69.8	11.1	1.3	-2.5	-0.8	128.6	33.3	57.4	-14.4	22.0	-6.7
00/99	24.2	96.8	34.7	27.6	26.5	27.9	40.9	53.9	3.8	35.8	20.2	59.9	48.7	14.0	26.5
01/00	-7.2	-21.9	40.2	105.6	8.2	-5.0	21.7	-3.0	-26.3	-31.7	-11.4	18.5	-3.1	-15.1	0.4
02/01	-4.5	-19.9	14.4	32.9	-17.4	-0.6	-33.0	6.2	-2.8	-23.5	-27.8	-8.4	19.0	-6.1	-12.6

Share (%)

Years	Extra EU	Norway	Switzerland	USSR/ Russia	Candid. countries	USA	Canada	China	Japan	Hong Kong	Mediterr. Basin	Latin America	OPEC	DAE	ACP
1980	100.0	1.8	2.4	1.9	:	35.6	4.9	0.4	10.2	1.2	6.2	2.3	19.8	4.2	4.4
1990	100.0	2.3	2.5	1.4	:	54.7	2.4	1.3	16.7	1.2	2.0	1.9	1.2	5.9	3.4
1996	100.0	3.8	1.9	0.2	2.1	42.8	2.1	2.4	13.1	1.1	1.9	1.9	0.5	20.5	2.2
1997	100.0	4.2	1.9	0.1	2.1	39.0	2.2	2.5	16.6	1.0	2.6	1.3	0.7	21.3	1.7
1998	100.0	3.0	2.0	0.0	2.3	42.3	2.4	3.3	14.3	1.0	2.2	0.9	0.6	21.4	1.6
1999	100.0	3.0	1.5	0.0	3.4	41.3	2.1	2.8	12.5	2.1	2.6	1.3	0.4	23.0	1.3
2000	100.0	4.8	1.7	0.0	3.5	42.6	2.4	3.5	10.4	2.3	2.5	1.6	0.5	21.1	1.3
2001	100.0	4.1	2.6	0.1	4.1	43.6	3.2	3.7	8.3	1.7	2.4	2.1	0.6	19.3	1.5
2002	100.0	3.4	3.1	0.1	3.5	45.4	2.2	4.1	8.4	1.3	1.8	2.0	0.7	19.0	1.3

(1) Relates to the external trade with the USSR until 1991 and to the external trade with Russia from 1992 onwards.

TRADE BALANCE (BN ECU/euro)

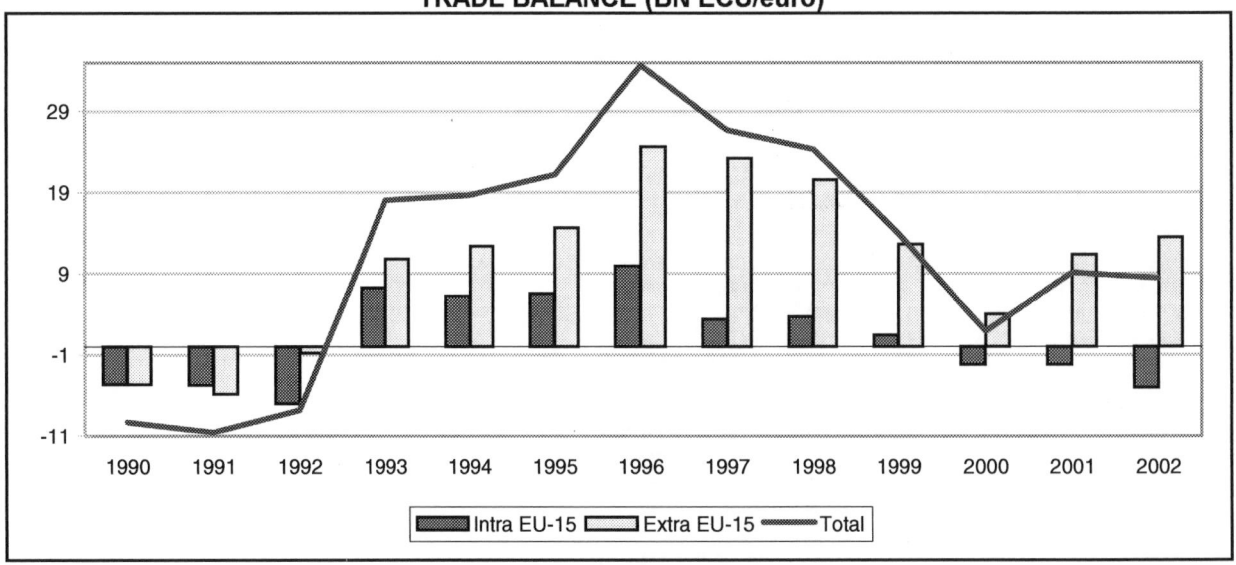

INTRA-EU (BN ECU/euro)

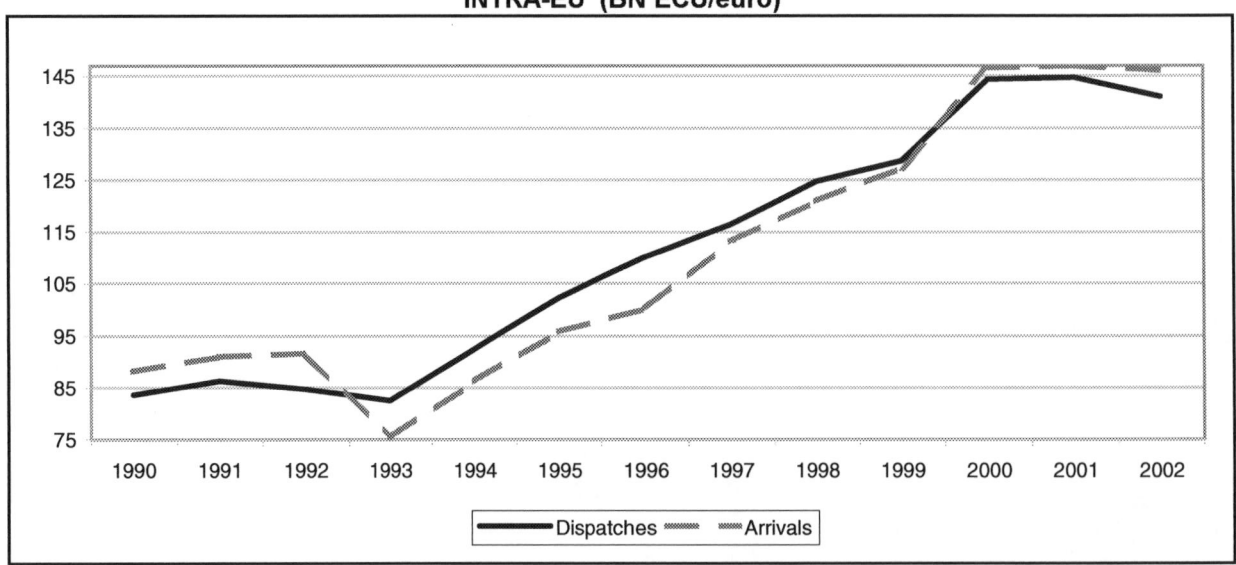

EXTRA-EU (BN ECU/euro)

TRADE BALANCE

INTRA-EU

Value (Mio ECU/Euro)

Year	Intra EU	B[1]	DK	D	EL	E	F	IRL	L	NL	A	P	FIN	S	UK
															Partner
1980	**-4,393**	**-687**	**-242**	**-1,654**	**509**	**-73**	**-1,476**	**-38**	**:**	**-923**	**146**	**151**	**-49**	**-294**	**236**
1990	**-4,651**	**-2,726**	**-408**	**-4,868**	**1,119**	**2,320**	**1,517**	**-586**	**:**	**-4,034**	**-7**	**1,419**	**72**	**-488**	**2,019**
1991	-4,703	-2,529	-392	-2,095	1,276	1,843	-89	-511	:	-4,146	226	1,572	-74	-527	743
1992	-6,979	-2,480	-389	-3,434	1,227	2,194	-952	-607	:	-4,300	218	1,721	-347	-546	717
1993	7,249	-1,575	-264	3,703	1,614	2,035	1,796	-552	:	-3,166	799	1,549	-277	-324	1,910
1994	6,265	-2,002	-48	3,318	1,776	2,003	1,796	-784	:	-3,534	766	1,687	-175	-323	1,783
1995	6,538	-2,488	94	3,328	2,238	2,394	1,805	-746	:	-3,171	534	1,838	-120	-423	1,387
1996	9,972	-2,466	151	4,206	2,524	2,831	3,093	-852	:	-3,689	888	1,822	75	-293	1,929
1997	3,430	-2,904	185	1,430	2,955	2,228	1,295	-1,076	:	-5,362	524	1,989	-25	-483	2,674
1998	3,766	-3,413	135	-520	3,280	3,895	2,507	-1,268	:	-5,725	260	2,226	-281	-640	3,309
1999	1,407	-2,801	184	-2,720	3,175	5,218	2,692	-1,836	-301	-6,598	70	2,381	-548	-807	3,298
2000	**-2,160**	**-3,253**	**279**	**-5,913**	**4,085**	**5,586**	**3,514**	**-1,619**	**-387**	**-8,436**	**-245**	**2,528**	**-1,110**	**-1,188**	**3,851**
2001	-2,214	-3,175	260	-6,951	3,917	5,635	3,988	-1,948	-342	-8,904	-502	2,315	-444	-967	4,880
2002	**-5,051**	**-3,081**	**263**	**-9,308**	**4,300**	**5,062**	**3,288**	**-2,116**	**-390**	**-8,286**	**-1,109**	**1,941**	**-229**	**-906**	**5,444**

EXTRA-EU

Value (Mio ECU/Euro)

Year	Extra EU	Norway	Switzerland	Russia[2]	Candid. countries	USA	Canada	China	Japan	Hong Kong	Mediterr. Basin	Latin America	OPEC	DAE	ACP
															Partner
1980	**-11,305**	**23**	**681**	**-1,296**	**:**	**-2,015**	**-381**	**-130**	**-428**	**-14**	**323**	**-842**	**-5,692**	**-399**	**-869**
1990	**-4,611**	**45**	**-168**	**-1,147**	**:**	**2,915**	**44**	**-679**	**-192**	**935**	**-2,654**	**-1,021**	**-4,588**	**964**	**-426**
1991	-5,800	-42	-467	-1,704	:	1,192	-14	-825	-604	986	-1,795	-466	-4,009	888	-389
1992	-759	-110	-742	-671	:	1,910	-133	-1,003	-763	1,312	-288	398	-1,845	1,437	-178
1993	10,799	-16	-583	-1,849	3,846	4,414	152	-106	-515	1,929	2,599	1,361	-1,213	3,357	453
1994	12,395	27	-795	-2,206	2,780	5,834	239	-706	78	2,446	2,060	1,917	-1,393	4,519	-370
1995	14,697	134	491	-896	3,888	5,267	252	-983	640	2,779	3,755	1,947	-1,568	5,310	-326
1996	24,703	259	1,058	334	6,412	6,427	-34	-966	1,245	3,285	4,621	3,299	-1,864	6,707	-313
1997	23,273	462	81	-377	7,030	7,673	122	-1,666	439	3,320	3,071	4,085	-4,469	5,998	98
1998	20,617	546	-254	-544	6,530	9,211	299	-2,490	-624	2,483	4,393	4,098	-2,340	1,617	-452
1999	12,598	349	-134	-2,487	4,988	10,524	473	-3,167	-1,649	2,257	1,846	3,298	-3,694	1,649	-1,347
2000	**4,067**	**149**	**180**	**-5,815**	**7,108**	**13,142**	**421**	**-4,647**	**-2,083**	**2,872**	**-1,704**	**2,419**	**-12,209**	**2,716**	**-1,049**
2001	11,397	21	239	-4,995	6,578	13,434	1,023	-4,208	-1,573	2,882	-1,854	2,553	-7,845	3,530	-695
2002	**13,529**	**-868**	**-363**	**-4,114**	**6,441**	**13,348**	**1,221**	**-4,289**	**-828**	**2,662**	**85**	**1,203**	**-4,729**	**3,295**	**-731**

(1) Luxembourg with Belgium until 31.12.1998.
(2) Relates to the external trade with the USSR until 1991 and to the external trade with Russia from 1992 onwards.

ITALY

INTRA-EU

Year		Partner														
	Intra EU	B(1)	DK	D	EL	E	F	IRL	L	NL	A	P	FIN	S	UK

EXPORTS / DISPATCHES
Value (Mio ECU/Euro)

Year	Intra EU	B(1)	DK	D	EL	E	F	IRL	L	NL	A	P	FIN	S	UK
1980	31,278	1,866	389	10,270	859	1,069	8,495	152	:	2,070	1,504	366	221	598	3,418
1990	83,566	4,556	1,022	25,397	2,416	6,607	21,883	379	:	4,165	3,258	1,922	837	1,658	9,466
1994	92,528	4,837	1,359	30,781	2,907	7,507	21,184	561	:	4,662	3,925	2,192	637	1,454	10,521
1995	102,384	5,079	1,547	33,545	3,392	8,603	23,141	719	:	5,269	4,244	2,475	813	1,728	11,044
1996	110,161	5,415	1,668	34,552	3,746	9,660	24,704	797	:	5,814	4,669	2,619	952	1,982	12,786
1997	116,528	5,774	1,760	34,923	4,174	11,055	25,948	779	:	6,070	4,832	2,839	1,083	2,123	15,169
1998	124,669	6,010	1,852	36,489	4,387	12,834	28,299	894	:	6,354	5,047	3,117	1,148	2,361	15,876
1999	128,693	5,955	1,895	36,965	4,620	14,250	29,176	1,094	293	6,411	5,228	3,359	1,086	2,409	15,952
2000	144,411	7,208	2,048	39,558	5,414	16,355	33,196	1,890	379	6,965	5,804	3,612	1,167	2,631	18,036
2001	144,731	8,163	2,108	39,220	5,240	16,549	33,007	1,563	525	7,143	5,795	3,558	1,267	2,484	18,085
2002	141,106	8,121	2,030	36,305	5,519	16,824	32,275	1,435	406	6,794	5,811	3,268	1,395	2,534	18,312

Annual variation (%)

Year	Intra EU	B(1)	DK	D	EL	E	F	IRL	L	NL	A	P	FIN	S	UK
98/97	6.9	4.0	5.2	4.4	5.1	16.0	9.0	14.6	:	4.6	4.4	9.7	6.0	11.1	4.6
99/98	3.2	-0.9	2.3	1.3	5.2	11.0	3.0	22.4	:	0.8	3.5	7.7	-5.3	2.0	0.4
00/99	12.2	21.0	8.0	7.0	17.1	14.7	13.7	72.7	29.3	8.6	11.0	7.5	7.4	9.2	13.0
01/00	0.2	13.2	2.9	-0.8	-3.2	1.1	-0.5	-17.3	38.5	2.5	-0.1	-1.4	8.5	-5.5	0.2
02/01	-2.5	-0.5	-3.7	-7.4	5.3	1.6	-2.2	-8.1	-22.5	-4.8	0.2	-8.1	10.1	2.0	1.2

Share (%)

Year	Intra EU	B(1)	DK	D	EL	E	F	IRL	L	NL	A	P	FIN	S	UK
1980	100.0	5.9	1.2	32.8	2.7	3.4	27.1	0.4	:	6.6	4.8	1.1	0.7	1.9	10.9
1990	100.0	5.4	1.2	30.3	2.8	7.9	26.1	0.4	:	4.9	3.8	2.3	1.0	1.9	11.3
1996	100.0	4.9	1.5	31.3	3.4	8.7	22.4	0.7	:	5.2	4.2	2.3	0.8	1.7	11.6
1997	100.0	4.9	1.5	29.9	3.5	9.4	22.2	0.6	:	5.2	4.1	2.4	0.9	1.8	13.0
1998	100.0	4.8	1.4	29.2	3.5	10.2	22.6	0.7	:	5.0	4.0	2.4	0.9	1.8	12.7
1999	100.0	4.6	1.4	28.7	3.5	11.0	22.6	0.8	0.2	4.9	4.0	2.6	0.8	1.8	12.3
2000	100.0	4.9	1.4	27.3	3.7	11.3	22.9	1.3	0.2	4.8	4.0	2.5	0.8	1.8	12.4
2001	100.0	5.6	1.4	27.0	3.6	11.4	22.8	1.0	0.3	4.9	4.0	2.4	0.8	1.7	12.4
2002	100.0	5.7	1.4	25.7	3.9	11.9	22.8	1.0	0.2	4.8	4.1	2.3	0.9	1.7	12.9

IMPORTS / ARRIVALS
Value (Mio ECU/Euro)

Year	Intra EU	B(1)	DK	D	EL	E	F	IRL	L	NL	A	P	FIN	S	UK
1980	35,670	2,553	631	11,923	350	1,141	9,971	190	:	2,993	1,358	215	270	892	3,182
1990	88,217	7,282	1,430	30,264	1,297	4,287	20,366	965	:	8,199	3,264	503	766	2,147	7,447
1994	86,263	6,839	1,407	27,463	1,131	5,504	19,388	1,345	:	8,196	3,159	505	812	1,776	8,737
1995	95,845	7,566	1,453	30,217	1,153	6,209	21,336	1,465	:	8,440	3,710	637	933	2,152	9,657
1996	100,188	7,881	1,517	30,346	1,222	6,828	21,612	1,648	:	9,503	3,782	797	876	2,275	10,857
1997	113,098	8,679	1,575	33,492	1,219	8,827	24,653	1,855	:	11,432	4,307	850	1,108	2,606	12,495
1998	120,903	9,423	1,717	37,009	1,107	8,939	25,793	2,161	:	12,079	4,787	891	1,429	3,001	12,567
1999	127,285	8,756	1,711	39,684	1,444	9,032	26,484	2,930	593	13,009	5,158	978	1,634	3,216	12,655
2000	146,571	10,461	1,769	45,471	1,329	10,769	29,682	3,509	766	15,401	6,049	1,083	2,277	3,819	14,185
2001	146,945	11,338	1,848	46,171	1,323	10,914	29,019	3,511	867	16,047	6,297	1,243	1,711	3,451	13,205
2002	146,157	11,203	1,766	45,613	1,219	11,762	28,987	3,550	797	15,080	6,921	1,327	1,624	3,440	12,868

Annual variation (%)

Year	Intra EU	B(1)	DK	D	EL	E	F	IRL	L	NL	A	P	FIN	S	UK
98/97	6.9	8.5	9.0	10.5	-9.1	1.2	4.6	16.4	:	5.6	11.1	4.7	28.9	15.1	0.5
99/98	5.2	-7.0	-0.3	7.2	30.4	1.0	2.6	35.5	:	7.6	7.7	9.8	14.3	7.1	0.6
00/99	15.1	19.4	3.4	14.5	-7.9	19.2	12.0	19.7	29.0	18.3	17.2	10.7	39.3	18.7	12.0
01/00	0.2	8.3	4.4	1.5	-0.5	1.3	-2.2	0.0	13.1	4.1	4.0	14.7	-24.8	-9.6	-6.9
02/01	-0.5	-1.1	-4.4	-1.2	-7.8	7.7	-0.1	1.1	-8.0	-6.0	9.9	6.6	-5.0	-0.3	-2.5

Share (%)

Year	Intra EU	B(1)	DK	D	EL	E	F	IRL	L	NL	A	P	FIN	S	UK
1980	100.0	7.1	1.7	33.4	0.9	3.1	27.9	0.5	:	8.3	3.8	0.6	0.7	2.5	8.9
1990	100.0	8.2	1.6	34.3	1.4	4.8	23.0	1.0	:	9.2	3.7	0.5	0.8	2.4	8.4
1996	100.0	7.8	1.5	30.2	1.2	6.8	21.5	1.6	:	9.4	3.7	0.7	0.8	2.2	10.8
1997	100.0	7.6	1.3	29.6	1.0	7.8	21.7	1.6	:	10.1	3.8	0.7	0.9	2.3	11.0
1998	100.0	7.7	1.4	30.6	0.9	7.3	21.3	1.7	:	9.9	3.9	0.7	1.1	2.4	10.3
1999	100.0	6.8	1.3	31.1	1.1	7.0	20.8	2.3	0.4	10.2	4.0	0.7	1.2	2.5	9.9
2000	100.0	7.1	1.2	31.0	0.9	7.3	20.2	2.3	0.5	10.5	4.1	0.7	1.5	2.6	9.6
2001	100.0	7.7	1.2	31.4	0.9	7.4	19.7	2.3	0.5	10.9	4.2	0.8	1.1	2.3	8.9
2002	100.0	7.6	1.2	31.2	0.8	8.0	19.8	2.4	0.5	10.3	4.7	0.9	1.1	2.3	8.8

(1) Luxembourg with Belgium until 31.12.1998.

EXTRA-EU

EXPORTS
Value (Mio ECU/Euro)

Years	Extra EU	Norway	Switzerland	USSR/ Russia[1]	Candid. countries	USA	Canada	China	Japan	Hong Kong	Mediterr. Basin	Latin America	OPEC	DAE	ACP
1980	24,838	226	2,472	918	:	2,980	350	185	509	194	8,638	1,916	7,107	677	1,385
1990	49,578	582	6,059	2,095	:	10,198	1,187	764	3,136	1,170	9,637	2,491	5,463	3,848	1,695
1994	68,346	653	6,020	1,822	8,561	12,372	1,463	1,921	3,407	2,637	12,375	5,396	6,123	7,544	1,579
1995	76,335	732	6,617	2,186	10,865	12,809	1,629	2,021	4,065	2,975	13,490	5,880	5,763	8,739	1,718
1996	88,534	973	7,208	2,927	13,413	14,427	1,431	2,209	4,373	3,451	15,585	7,137	6,691	10,165	1,892
1997	95,470	1,204	7,204	3,397	15,449	16,680	1,651	2,231	4,161	3,532	16,977	8,480	7,329	9,949	2,425
1998	94,582	1,151	7,554	2,780	15,995	18,930	1,756	1,835	3,606	2,750	16,717	8,750	7,147	6,585	3,963
1999	92,328	1,013	7,658	1,724	15,518	20,547	1,881	1,834	3,509	2,558	15,767	7,975	6,948	6,910	2,838
2000	116,002	980	8,627	2,521	20,441	26,659	2,343	2,380	4,338	3,269	20,531	8,734	8,504	9,461	3,992
2001	124,504	1,075	9,841	3,539	22,514	26,212	2,578	3,272	4,704	3,277	21,113	8,652	10,268	9,880	3,896
2002	124,259	1,161	9,361	3,801	23,083	25,854	2,462	4,018	4,493	3,089	21,267	7,300	10,763	9,322	3,959

Annual variation (%)

Years	Extra EU	Norway	Switzerland	USSR/ Russia[1]	Candid. countries	USA	Canada	China	Japan	Hong Kong	Mediterr. Basin	Latin America	OPEC	DAE	ACP
98/97	-0.9	-4.3	4.8	-18.1	3.5	13.4	6.3	-17.7	-13.3	-22.1	-1.5	3.1	-2.4	-33.8	63.4
99/98	-2.3	-12.0	1.3	-37.9	-2.9	8.5	7.0	0.0	-2.6	-6.9	-5.6	-8.8	-2.7	4.9	-28.3
00/99	25.6	-3.2	12.6	46.2	31.7	29.7	24.5	29.7	23.6	27.8	30.2	9.5	22.3	36.9	40.6
01/00	7.3	9.7	14.0	40.3	10.1	-1.6	10.0	37.4	8.4	0.2	2.8	-0.9	20.7	4.4	-2.4
02/01	-0.1	7.9	-4.8	7.4	2.5	-1.3	-4.5	22.8	-4.4	-5.7	0.7	-15.6	4.8	-5.6	1.6

Share (%)

Years	Extra EU	Norway	Switzerland	USSR/ Russia[1]	Candid. countries	USA	Canada	China	Japan	Hong Kong	Mediterr. Basin	Latin America	OPEC	DAE	ACP
1980	100.0	0.9	9.9	3.6	:	11.9	1.4	0.7	2.0	0.7	34.7	7.7	28.6	2.7	5.5
1990	100.0	1.1	12.2	4.2	:	20.5	2.3	1.5	6.3	2.3	19.4	5.0	11.0	7.7	3.4
1996	100.0	1.0	8.1	3.3	15.1	16.2	1.6	2.4	4.9	3.8	17.6	8.0	7.5	11.4	2.1
1997	100.0	1.2	7.5	3.5	16.1	17.4	1.7	2.3	4.3	3.6	17.7	8.8	7.6	10.4	2.5
1998	100.0	1.2	7.9	2.9	16.9	20.0	1.8	1.9	3.8	2.9	17.6	9.2	7.5	6.9	4.1
1999	100.0	1.0	8.2	1.8	16.8	22.2	2.0	1.9	3.8	2.7	17.0	8.6	7.5	7.4	3.0
2000	100.0	0.8	7.4	2.1	17.6	22.9	2.0	2.0	3.7	2.8	17.6	7.5	7.3	8.1	3.4
2001	100.0	0.8	7.9	2.8	18.0	21.0	2.0	2.6	3.7	2.6	16.9	6.9	8.2	7.9	3.1
2002	100.0	0.9	7.5	3.0	18.5	20.8	1.9	3.2	3.6	2.4	17.1	5.8	8.6	7.5	3.1

IMPORTS
Value (Mio ECU/Euro)

Years	Extra EU	Norway	Switzerland	USSR/ Russia[1]	Candid. countries	USA	Canada	China	Japan	Hong Kong	Mediterr. Basin	Latin America	OPEC	DAE	ACP
1980	36,143	203	1,791	2,214	:	4,995	732	315	938	207	8,315	2,758	12,800	1,076	2,255
1990	54,189	537	6,226	3,241	:	7,283	1,143	1,444	3,327	235	12,291	3,512	10,051	2,884	2,122
1994	55,951	626	6,815	4,028	11,562	6,538	1,224	2,627	3,329	191	10,315	3,479	7,516	3,025	1,950
1995	61,638	597	6,126	3,082	6,977	7,542	1,377	3,004	3,426	196	9,735	3,933	7,331	3,428	2,043
1996	63,831	714	6,150	2,594	7,001	8,000	1,464	3,175	3,128	166	10,963	3,838	8,555	3,459	2,204
1997	72,197	742	7,123	3,773	8,419	9,007	1,529	3,896	3,721	213	13,906	4,395	11,798	3,950	2,328
1998	73,965	606	7,808	3,324	9,465	9,719	1,458	4,325	4,230	267	12,324	4,651	9,487	4,968	4,415
1999	79,730	664	7,792	4,211	10,530	10,024	1,408	5,001	5,158	300	13,920	4,677	10,643	5,261	4,225
2000	111,935	831	8,447	8,336	13,333	13,517	1,922	7,028	6,421	398	22,235	6,315	20,712	6,745	5,041
2001	113,107	1,054	9,602	8,534	15,936	12,778	1,555	7,481	6,277	395	22,968	6,099	18,113	6,350	4,591
2002	110,730	2,029	9,725	7,915	16,642	12,507	1,241	8,307	5,321	427	21,182	6,097	15,491	6,027	4,690

Annual variation (%)

Years	Extra EU	Norway	Switzerland	USSR/ Russia[1]	Candid. countries	USA	Canada	China	Japan	Hong Kong	Mediterr. Basin	Latin America	OPEC	DAE	ACP
98/97	2.4	-18.3	9.6	-11.9	12.4	7.9	-4.6	11.0	13.6	25.7	-11.3	5.8	-19.5	25.7	89.6
99/98	7.7	9.6	-0.1	26.6	11.2	3.1	-3.4	15.6	21.9	12.4	12.9	0.5	12.1	5.9	-4.2
00/99	40.3	25.2	8.3	97.9	26.6	34.8	36.4	40.5	24.4	32.3	59.7	35.0	94.6	28.2	19.3
01/00	1.0	26.7	13.6	2.3	19.5	-5.4	-19.0	6.4	-2.2	-0.7	3.2	-3.4	-12.5	-5.8	-8.9
02/01	-2.1	92.4	1.2	-7.2	4.4	-2.1	-20.2	11.0	-15.2	8.1	-7.7	0.0	-14.4	-5.0	2.1

Share (%)

Years	Extra EU	Norway	Switzerland	USSR/ Russia[1]	Candid. countries	USA	Canada	China	Japan	Hong Kong	Mediterr. Basin	Latin America	OPEC	DAE	ACP
1980	100.0	0.5	4.9	6.1	:	13.8	2.0	0.8	2.5	0.5	23.0	7.6	35.4	2.9	6.2
1990	100.0	0.9	11.4	5.9	:	13.4	2.1	2.6	6.1	0.4	22.6	6.4	18.5	5.3	3.9
1996	100.0	1.1	9.6	4.0	10.9	12.5	2.2	4.9	4.9	0.2	17.1	6.0	13.4	5.4	3.4
1997	100.0	1.0	9.8	5.2	11.6	12.4	2.1	5.3	5.1	0.2	19.2	6.0	16.3	5.4	3.2
1998	100.0	0.8	10.5	4.4	12.7	13.1	1.9	5.8	5.7	0.3	16.6	6.2	12.8	6.7	5.9
1999	100.0	0.8	9.7	5.2	13.2	12.5	1.7	6.2	6.4	0.3	17.4	5.8	13.3	6.5	5.2
2000	100.0	0.7	7.5	7.4	11.9	12.0	1.7	6.2	5.7	0.3	19.8	5.6	18.5	6.0	4.5
2001	100.0	0.9	8.4	7.5	14.0	11.2	1.3	6.6	5.5	0.3	20.3	5.3	16.0	5.6	4.0
2002	100.0	1.8	8.7	7.1	15.0	11.2	1.1	7.5	4.8	0.3	19.1	5.5	13.9	5.4	4.2

(1) Relates to the external trade with the USSR until 1991 and to the external trade with Russia from 1992 onwards.

LUXEMBOURG

TRADE BALANCE (BN ECU/euro)

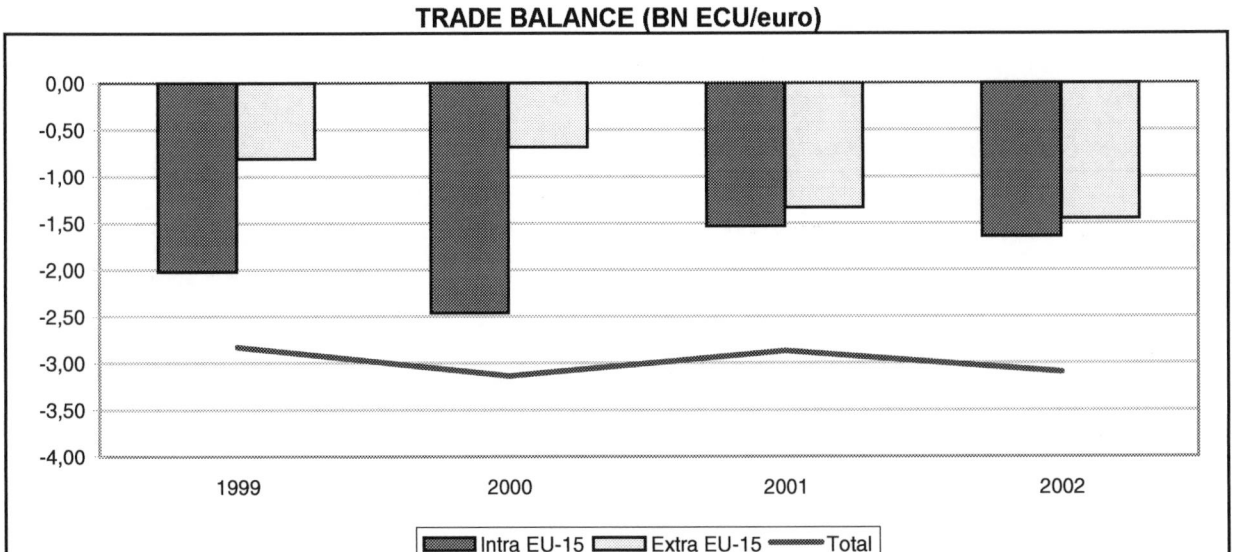

INTRA-EU (BN ECU/euro)

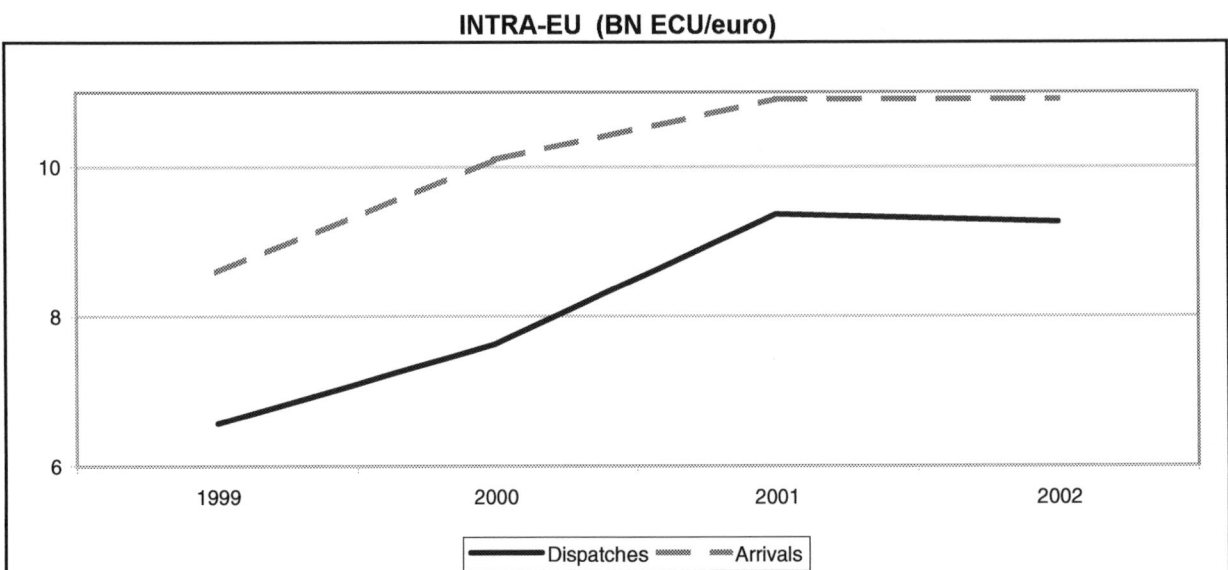

EXTRA-EU (BN ECU/euro)

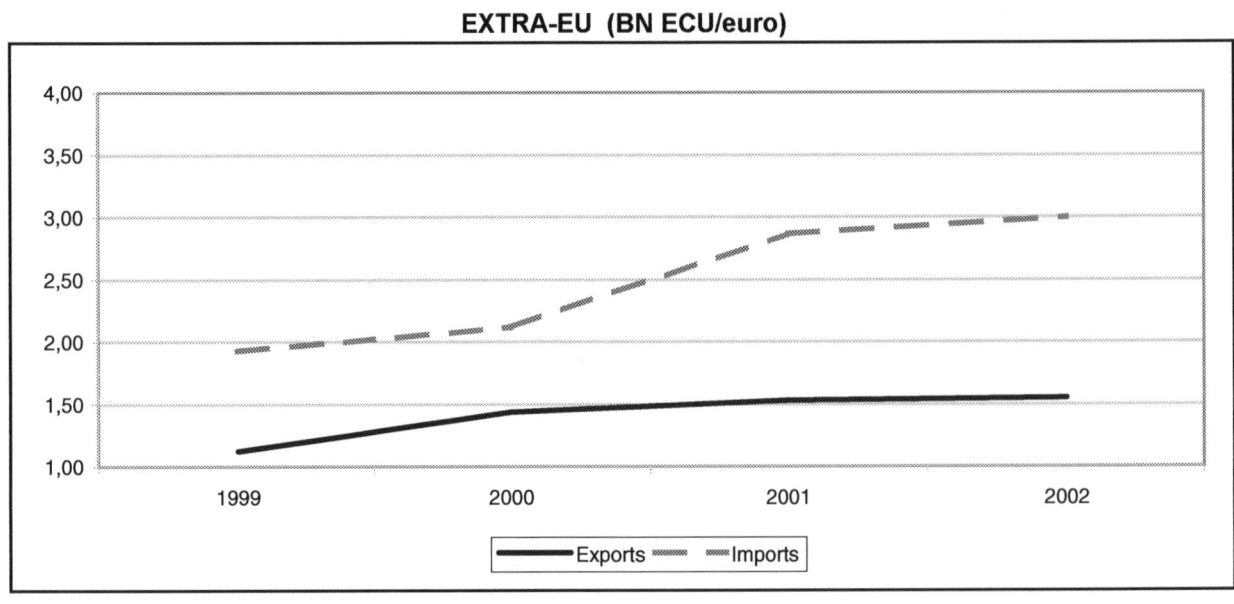

LUXEMBOURG [1]

TRADE BALANCE

INTRA-EU

Value (Mio ECU/Euro)

Year	Intra EU	B[1]	DK	D	EL	E	F	IRL	I	NL	A	P	FIN	S	UK
1980	:	:	:	:	:	:	:	:	:	:	:	:	:	:	:
1990	:	:	:	:	:	:	:	:	:	:	:	:	:	:	:
1991	:	:	:	:	:	:	:	:	:	:	:	:	:	:	:
1992	:	:	:	:	:	:	:	:	:	:	:	:	:	:	:
1993	:	:	:	:	:	:	:	:	:	:	:	:	:	:	:
1994	:	:	:	:	:	:	:	:	:	:	:	:	:	:	:
1995	:	:	:	:	:	:	:	:	:	:	:	:	:	:	:
1996	:	:	:	:	:	:	:	:	:	:	:	:	:	:	:
1997	:	:	:	:	:	:	:	:	:	:	:	:	:	:	:
1998	:	:	:	:	:	:	:	:	:	:	:	:	:	:	:
1999	-2,023	-2,568	17	-683	27	149	441	-22	205	-128	29	32	25	65	387
2000	**-2,456**	**-3,086**	**11**	**-588**	**19**	**171**	**366**	**8**	**257**	**-100**	**18**	**41**	**22**	**78**	**326**
2001	-1,534	-3,053	41	-430	40	139	527	64	498	-198	1	72	107	79	537
2002	**-1,642**	**-2,993**	**53**	**-624**	**45**	**347**	**349**	**11**	**431**	**-161**	**29**	**62**	**102**	**101**	**474**

EXTRA-EU

Value (Mio ECU/Euro)

Year	Extra EU	Norway	Switzerland	Russia[2]	Candid. countries	USA	Canada	China	Japan	Hong Kong	Mediterr. Basin	Latin America	OPEC	DAE	ACP
1980	:	:	:	:	:	:	:	:	:	:	:	:	:	:	:
1990	:	:	:	:	:	:	:	:	:	:	:	:	:	:	:
1991	:	:	:	:	:	:	:	:	:	:	:	:	:	:	:
1992	:	:	:	:	:	:	:	:	:	:	:	:	:	:	:
1993	:	:	:	:	:	:	:	:	:	:	:	:	:	:	:
1994	:	:	:	:	:	:	:	:	:	:	:	:	:	:	:
1995	:	:	:	:	:	:	:	:	:	:	:	:	:	:	:
1996	:	:	:	:	:	:	:	:	:	:	:	:	:	:	:
1997	:	:	:	:	:	:	:	:	:	:	:	:	:	:	:
1998	:	:	:	:	:	:	:	:	:	:	:	:	:	:	:
1999	-806	8	-10	11	128	-639	11	-16	-144	-30	88	-7	8	-222	43
2000	**-684**	**17**	**-112**	**3**	**116**	**-55**	**18**	**-21**	**-135**	**-86**	**99**	**6**	**9**	**-571**	**39**
2001	-1,339	48	9	23	-34	-377	-21	-21	-112	-61	79	18	16	-947	62
2002	**-1,451**	**57**	**98**	**34**	**52**	**-248**	**14**	**-16**	**-91**	**-36**	**42**	**54**	**38**	**-1,028**	**51**

(1) Luxembourg with Belgium until 31.12.1998.
(2) Relates to the external trade with the USSR until 1991 and to the external trade with Russia from 1992 onwards.

LUXEMBOURG (1)

INTRA-EU

Year	Intra EU	B(1)	DK	D	EL	E	F	IRL	I	NL	A	P	FIN	S	UK
							EXPORTS / DISPATCHES								
							Value (Mio ECU/Euro)								
1980	:	:	:	:	:	:	:	:	:	:	:	:	:	:	:
1990	:	:	:	:	:	:	:	:	:	:	:	:	:	:	:
1994	:	:	:	:	:	:	:	:	:	:	:	:	:	:	:
1995	:	:	:	:	:	:	:	:	:	:	:	:	:	:	:
1996	:	:	:	:	:	:	:	:	:	:	:	:	:	:	:
1997	:	:	:	:	:	:	:	:	:	:	:	:	:	:	:
1998	:	:	:	:	:	:	:	:	:	:	:	:	:	:	:
1999	6,574	976	46	1,910	30	217	1,652	14	416	357	112	49	44	99	652
2000	7,636	1,085	66	2,262	26	261	1,880	50	489	457	128	61	43	119	708
2001	9,369	1,171	72	2,682	43	387	2,126	120	709	464	123	99	124	135	1,070
2002	9,263	1,138	80	2,581	47	482	2,176	52	663	472	138	84	114	159	946
							Annual variation (%)								
98/97	:	:	:	:	:	:	:	:	:	:	:	:	:	:	:
99/98	:	:	:	:	:	:	:	:	:	:	:	:	:	:	:
00/99	16.1	11.2	42.6	18.4	-14.1	19.9	13.8	260.2	17.3	27.9	13.6	25.2	-1.9	21.1	8.6
01/00	22.6	7.9	9.8	18.5	66.9	48.5	13.0	138.0	45.1	1.3	-3.9	61.0	191.0	13.2	51.1
02/01	-1.1	-2.8	10.4	-3.7	10.8	24.5	2.3	-56.3	-6.5	1.7	12.2	-15.3	-8.5	17.5	-11.6
							Share (%)								
1980	:	:	:	:	:	:	:	:	:	:	:	:	:	:	:
1990	:	:	:	:	:	:	:	:	:	:	:	:	:	:	:
1996	:	:	:	:	:	:	:	:	:	:	:	:	:	:	:
1997	:	:	:	:	:	:	:	:	:	:	:	:	:	:	:
1998	:	:	:	:	:	:	:	:	:	:	:	:	:	:	:
1999	100.0	14.8	0.6	29.0	0.4	3.3	25.1	0.2	6.3	5.4	1.7	0.7	0.6	1.5	9.9
2000	100.0	14.2	0.8	29.6	0.3	3.4	24.6	0.6	6.3	5.9	1.6	0.8	0.5	1.5	9.2
2001	100.0	12.5	0.7	28.6	0.4	4.1	22.6	1.2	7.5	4.9	1.3	1.0	1.3	1.4	11.4
2002	100.0	12.2	0.8	27.8	0.5	5.2	23.4	0.5	7.1	5.0	1.4	0.9	1.2	1.7	10.2
							IMPORTS / ARRIVALS								
							Value (Mio ECU/Euro)								
1980	:	:	:	:	:	:	:	:	:	:	:	:	:	:	:
1990	:	:	:	:	:	:	:	:	:	:	:	:	:	:	:
1994	:	:	:	:	:	:	:	:	:	:	:	:	:	:	:
1995	:	:	:	:	:	:	:	:	:	:	:	:	:	:	:
1996	:	:	:	:	:	:	:	:	:	:	:	:	:	:	:
1997	:	:	:	:	:	:	:	:	:	:	:	:	:	:	:
1998	:	:	:	:	:	:	:	:	:	:	:	:	:	:	:
1999	8,597	3,544	29	2,593	3	69	1,211	35	211	486	83	17	18	33	264
2000	10,092	4,171	54	2,850	6	89	1,514	43	232	557	109	20	21	42	382
2001	10,902	4,224	31	3,112	3	249	1,599	56	211	662	122	26	17	56	533
2002	10,905	4,131	27	3,205	3	135	1,827	41	232	633	109	22	12	58	472
							Annual variation (%)								
98/97	:	:	:	:	:	:	:	:	:	:	:	:	:	:	:
99/98	:	:	:	:	:	:	:	:	:	:	:	:	:	:	:
00/99	17.3	17.6	88.3	9.9	98.4	30.1	24.9	20.2	9.5	14.7	31.4	23.1	14.4	24.9	44.4
01/00	8.0	1.2	-43.3	9.1	-59.1	178.4	5.6	30.4	-8.7	18.7	11.0	28.7	-16.1	33.7	39.5
02/01	0.0	-2.2	-12.2	2.9	7.8	-45.7	14.2	-26.1	9.5	-4.3	-10.5	-17.2	-33.4	3.7	-11.5
							Share (%)								
1980	:	:	:	:	:	:	:	:	:	:	:	:	:	:	:
1990	:	:	:	:	:	:	:	:	:	:	:	:	:	:	:
1996	:	:	:	:	:	:	:	:	:	:	:	:	:	:	:
1997	:	:	:	:	:	:	:	:	:	:	:	:	:	:	:
1998	:	:	:	:	:	:	:	:	:	:	:	:	:	:	:
1999	100.0	41.2	0.3	30.1	0.0	0.7	14.0	0.4	2.4	5.6	0.9	0.1	0.2	0.3	3.0
2000	100.0	41.3	0.5	28.2	0.0	0.8	15.0	0.4	2.2	5.5	1.0	0.2	0.2	0.4	3.7
2001	100.0	38.7	0.2	28.5	0.0	2.2	14.6	0.5	1.9	6.0	1.1	0.2	0.1	0.5	4.8
2002	100.0	37.8	0.2	29.3	0.0	1.2	16.7	0.3	2.1	5.8	0.9	0.2	0.1	0.5	4.3

(1)   Luxembourg with Belgium until 31.12.1998.

EXTRA-EU

Years	Extra EU	Norway	Switzerland	USSR/Russia[1]	Candid. countries	USA	Canada	China	Japan	Hong Kong	Mediterr. Basin	Latin America	OPEC	DAE	ACP
EXPORTS — Value (Mio ECU/Euro)															
1980	:	:	:	:	:	:	:	:	:	:	:	:	:	:	:
1990	:	:	:	:	:	:	:	:	:	:	:	:	:	:	:
1994	:	:	:	:	:	:	:	:	:	:	:	:	:	:	:
1995	:	:	:	:	:	:	:	:	:	:	:	:	:	:	:
1996	:	:	:	:	:	:	:	:	:	:	:	:	:	:	:
1997	:	:	:	:	:	:	:	:	:	:	:	:	:	:	:
1998	:	:	:	:	:	:	:	:	:	:	:	:	:	:	:
1999	1,123	18	147	16	211	287	37	39	41	12	111	60	36	52	64
2000	**1,435**	**30**	**187**	**21**	**276**	**364**	**54**	**68**	**60**	**21**	**125**	**66**	**52**	**84**	**53**
2001	1,528	56	181	32	286	337	53	60	54	28	132	72	59	92	80
2002	**1,551**	**64**	**218**	**41**	**309**	**296**	**46**	**59**	**46**	**25**	**114**	**62**	**84**	**81**	**69**
Annual variation (%)															
98/97	:	:	:	:	:	:	:	:	:	:	:	:	:	:	:
99/98	:	:	:	:	:	:	:	:	:	:	:	:	:	:	:
00/99	27.8	62.5	26.5	31.2	30.7	26.7	46.9	74.5	43.9	73.1	12.3	9.5	43.5	62.7	-16.8
01/00	6.4	86.5	-2.7	55.4	3.7	-7.3	-2.6	-12.1	-9.3	32.5	5.4	8.0	13.8	9.8	50.5
02/01	1.5	14.3	20.1	28.9	8.0	-12.1	-13.2	-1.2	-14.2	-12.1	-13.3	-13.3	41.9	-11.7	-12.7
Share (%)															
1980	:	:	:	:	:	:	:	:	:	:	:	:	:	:	:
1990	:	:	:	:	:	:	:	:	:	:	:	:	:	:	:
1996	:	:	:	:	:	:	:	:	:	:	:	:	:	:	:
1997	:	:	:	:	:	:	:	:	:	:	:	:	:	:	:
1998	:	:	:	:	:	:	:	:	:	:	:	:	:	:	:
1999	100.0	1.6	13.1	1.3	18.7	25.5	3.2	3.4	3.6	1.1	9.9	5.3	3.2	4.5	5.6
2000	**100.0**	**2.0**	**12.9**	**1.4**	**19.2**	**25.3**	**3.7**	**4.7**	**4.1**	**1.4**	**8.7**	**4.6**	**3.6**	**5.8**	**3.6**
2001	100.0	3.6	11.8	2.0	18.7	22.0	3.4	3.9	3.5	1.8	8.6	4.6	3.8	6.0	5.2
2002	**100.0**	**4.1**	**14.0**	**2.6**	**19.9**	**19.0**	**2.9**	**3.7**	**2.9**	**1.6**	**7.3**	**3.9**	**5.3**	**5.2**	**4.4**
IMPORTS — Value (Mio ECU/Euro)															
1980	:	:	:	:	:	:	:	:	:	:	:	:	:	:	:
1990	:	:	:	:	:	:	:	:	:	:	:	:	:	:	:
1994	:	:	:	:	:	:	:	:	:	:	:	:	:	:	:
1995	:	:	:	:	:	:	:	:	:	:	:	:	:	:	:
1996	:	:	:	:	:	:	:	:	:	:	:	:	:	:	:
1997	:	:	:	:	:	:	:	:	:	:	:	:	:	:	:
1998	:	:	:	:	:	:	:	:	:	:	:	:	:	:	:
1999	1,928	11	157	5	83	926	26	55	185	43	23	68	28	274	21
2000	**2,119**	**13**	**298**	**18**	**160**	**419**	**36**	**89**	**194**	**107**	**26**	**60**	**43**	**655**	**14**
2001	2,866	8	172	9	320	714	74	81	166	89	53	53	43	1,039	18
2002	**3,001**	**7**	**120**	**8**	**257**	**545**	**31**	**74**	**137**	**61**	**72**	**8**	**46**	**1,110**	**19**
Annual variation (%)															
98/97	:	:	:	:	:	:	:	:	:	:	:	:	:	:	:
99/98	:	:	:	:	:	:	:	:	:	:	:	:	:	:	:
00/99	9.9	24.1	89.8	282.3	93.3	-54.7	37.0	60.5	5.0	152.2	13.5	-11.6	51.9	139.0	-35.0
01/00	35.2	-36.5	-42.3	-48.5	100.7	70.4	106.3	-9.0	-14.5	-17.2	104.3	-11.3	0.4	58.6	29.7
02/01	4.7	-13.4	-30.2	-16.5	-19.6	-23.7	-57.6	-7.8	-17.3	-31.7	34.8	-84.5	6.0	6.7	6.8
Share (%)															
1980	:	:	:	:	:	:	:	:	:	:	:	:	:	:	:
1990	:	:	:	:	:	:	:	:	:	:	:	:	:	:	:
1996	:	:	:	:	:	:	:	:	:	:	:	:	:	:	:
1997	:	:	:	:	:	:	:	:	:	:	:	:	:	:	:
1998	:	:	:	:	:	:	:	:	:	:	:	:	:	:	:
1999	100.0	0.5	8.1	0.2	4.2	48.0	1.3	2.8	9.5	2.2	1.1	3.5	1.4	14.2	1.0
2000	**100.0**	**0.6**	**14.0**	**0.8**	**7.5**	**19.7**	**1.6**	**4.1**	**9.1**	**5.0**	**1.2**	**2.8**	**2.0**	**30.9**	**0.6**
2001	100.0	0.2	5.9	0.3	11.1	24.9	2.5	2.8	5.7	3.1	1.8	1.8	1.4	36.2	0.6
2002	**100.0**	**0.2**	**3.9**	**0.2**	**8.5**	**18.1**	**1.0**	**2.4**	**4.5**	**2.0**	**2.3**	**0.2**	**1.5**	**36.9**	**0.6**

(1) Relates to the external trade with the USSR until 1991and to the external trade with Russia from 1992 onwards.

NETHERLANDS

TRADE BALANCE (BN ECU/euro)

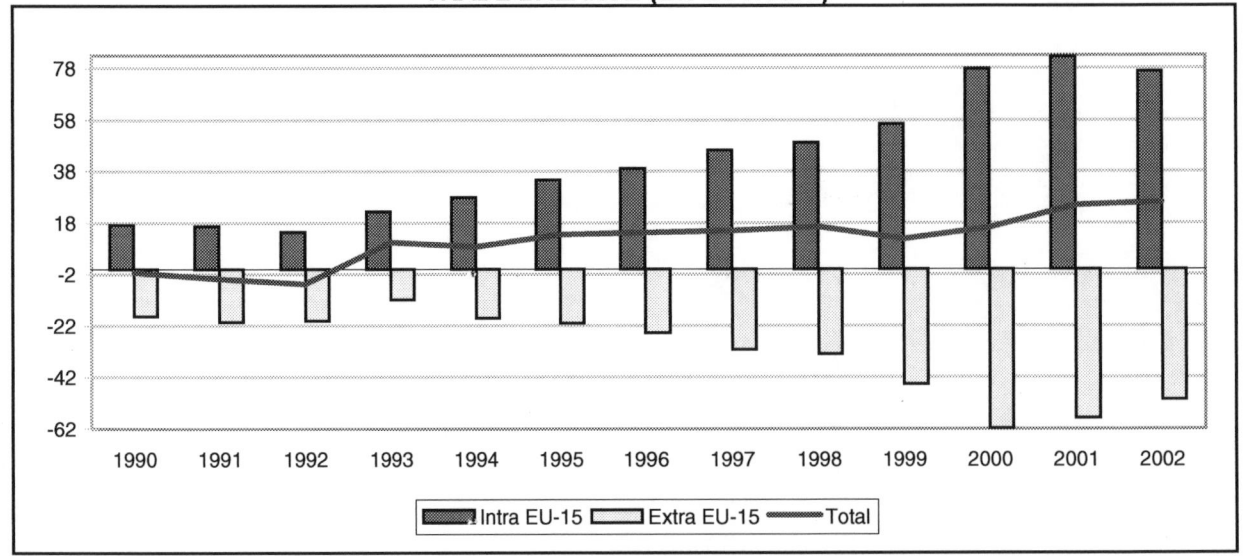

INTRA-EU (BN ECU/euro)

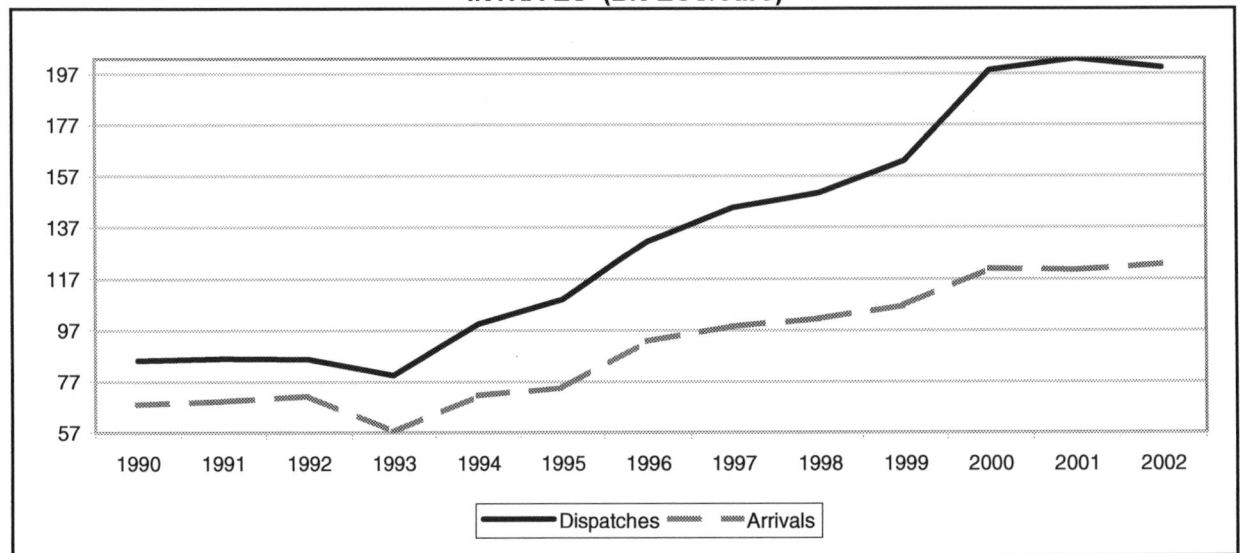

EXTRA-EU (BN ECU/euro)

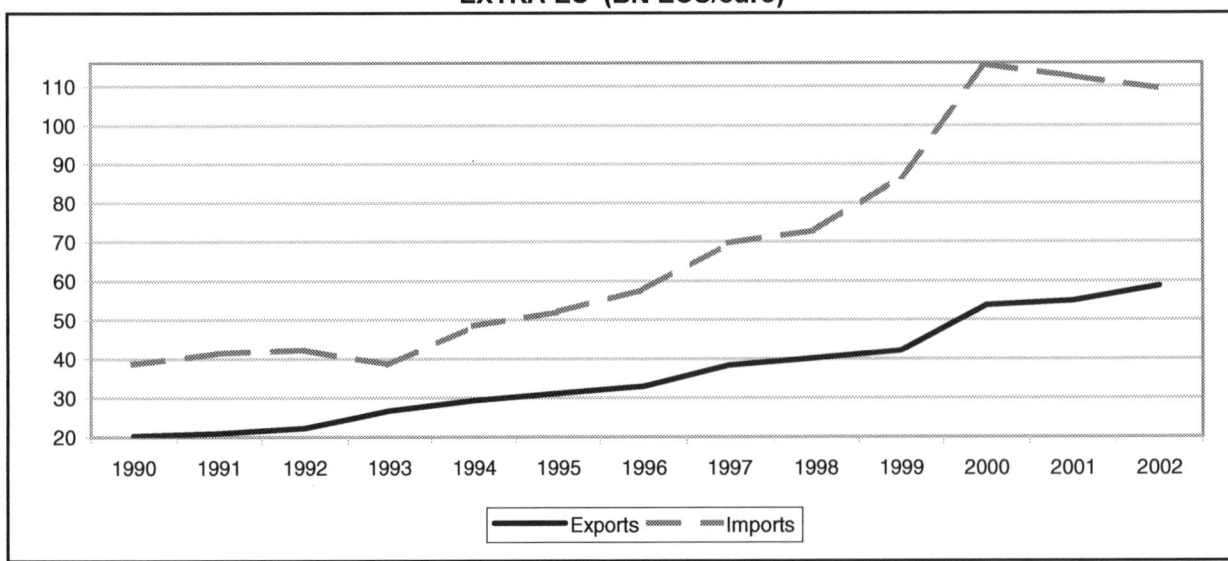

TRADE BALANCE

INTRA-EU

Value (Mio ECU/Euro)

Year	Intra EU	B(1)	DK	D	EL	E	F	IRL	I	L	A	P	FIN	S	UK
1980	8,747	1,559	518	3,619	136	49	1,910	-64	1,325	:	188	72	-150	-89	-325
1990	17,259	1,599	536	3,970	777	1,118	3,700	-290	3,190	:	333	195	-178	-300	2,609
1991	16,730	952	494	5,715	813	1,082	3,710	-194	3,039	:	283	176	-265	-262	1,185
1992	14,441	667	258	4,868	970	1,041	3,200	-526	3,130	:	369	242	-251	-485	958
1993	22,324	3,231	437	9,558	845	861	4,241	-544	2,045	:	428	343	-407	-310	1,595
1994	27,891	4,635	778	10,971	1,088	1,296	5,151	-587	2,920	:	549	347	-553	-725	2,023
1995	34,512	5,283	951	12,694	1,102	1,811	6,662	-663	3,587	:	1,105	364	-8	-261	1,886
1996	39,079	6,058	1,163	15,030	1,129	1,732	7,619	-488	3,712	:	1,318	367	1	-21	2,409
1997	46,341	6,451	1,337	18,668	1,154	1,963	8,116	-667	4,901	:	1,686	574	251	212	2,928
1998	49,212	5,706	1,541	19,392	1,223	2,620	8,896	-1,122	5,544	:	1,783	851	426	56	3,187
1999	56,348	7,818	1,215	20,861	1,448	3,413	10,794	-1,965	6,340	267	1,850	894	479	65	3,595
2000	77,722	11,266	1,388	28,095	1,827	3,491	14,773	-1,986	8,634	180	2,438	1,080	511	987	5,713
2001	82,523	9,459	1,757	28,729	1,774	4,203	14,834	-1,280	9,748	279	2,621	1,152	629	863	11,514
2002	76,765	9,471	1,450	23,535	1,853	4,705	14,339	-1,227	9,341	307	2,226	974	580	442	9,289

EXTRA-EU

Value (Mio ECU/Euro)

Year	Extra EU	Norway	Switzerland	Russia(2)	Candid. countries	USA	Canada	China	Japan	Hong Kong	Mediterr. Basin	Latin America	OPEC	DAE	ACP
1980	-10,931	-313	455	-552	:	-3,531	-275	-91	-811	-158	448	-911	-5,443	-957	-1,722
1990	-18,383	-1,088	614	-1,093	:	-4,355	-318	-856	-3,293	-174	172	-2,741	-4,263	-2,042	-591
1991	-20,416	-337	657	-986	:	-4,922	-556	-1,106	-4,978	-168	-46	-2,642	-4,435	-2,354	-753
1992	-20,021	-849	665	-563	:	-4,942	-289	-1,264	-5,198	-104	-79	-2,244	-3,911	-2,155	-357
1993	-11,788	-856	577	46	766	-4,046	-198	-807	-3,459	-684	802	-1,055	-2,941	-2,053	-3
1994	-19,092	-2,385	695	-19	652	-4,849	-284	-1,135	-3,624	-796	549	-2,663	-4,777	-2,697	-656
1995	-20,957	-2,180	744	-45	817	-6,689	-435	-1,274	-4,005	-827	703	-2,428	-3,360	-3,366	-227
1996	-24,843	-419	570	-215	1,128	-7,477	-441	-1,664	-4,566	-1,031	866	-2,377	-3,650	-4,765	-392
1997	-31,262	-2,807	669	-513	1,543	-9,729	-514	-2,390	-5,499	-1,370	888	-2,564	-3,362	-6,161	-160
1998	-32,855	-871	967	-355	1,712	-9,885	-527	-3,298	-6,873	-2,029	1,032	-2,848	223	-10,696	-127
1999	-44,697	-905	910	-706	1,393	-10,355	-332	-3,884	-7,172	-2,348	988	-3,320	-3,963	-12,099	-629
2000	-61,630	-1,327	1,547	-2,105	2,488	-12,977	-296	-7,589	-8,855	-1,058	977	-4,910	-7,637	-13,359	-455
2001	-57,716	-776	1,544	-2,125	2,279	-12,296	-272	-9,201	-7,833	-525	437	-5,332	-5,103	-13,200	-1,004
2002	-50,544	-3,619	1,595	-1,731	3,227	-9,232	-456	-10,426	-6,961	-500	1,025	-5,440	-3,879	-11,527	-735

(1)   Luxembourg with Belgium until 31.12.1998.
(2)   Relates to the external trade with the USSR until 1991 and to the external trade with Russia from 1992 onwards.

NETHERLANDS

INTRA-EU

Year		Partner													
	Intra EU	B(1)	DK	D	EL	E	F	IRL	I	L	A	P	FIN	S	UK

EXPORTS / DISPATCHES
Value (Mio ECU/Euro)

Year	Intra EU	B(1)	DK	D	EL	E	F	IRL	I	L	A	P	FIN	S	UK
1980	40,832	8,008	998	15,916	352	504	5,617	221	3,071	:	509	225	281	935	4,197
1990	85,189	15,447	1,729	29,512	990	2,623	11,811	645	6,910	:	1,236	811	765	1,874	10,837
1994	99,445	17,624	2,056	36,268	1,270	3,265	13,380	793	6,943	:	1,568	963	794	2,073	12,447
1995	109,016	18,534	2,247	39,018	1,271	3,953	15,069	927	7,640	:	2,065	1,058	1,130	2,868	13,236
1996	131,647	22,439	2,804	47,799	1,366	4,623	17,866	1,151	9,286	:	2,552	1,357	1,330	3,636	15,437
1997	144,870	23,279	2,987	51,445	1,392	5,659	19,391	1,385	10,549	:	2,819	1,559	1,675	4,311	18,416
1998	150,659	23,268	3,153	52,457	1,473	6,566	20,529	1,464	11,201	:	3,028	1,884	1,930	4,557	19,147
1999	163,010	25,468	3,185	55,353	1,677	7,202	22,382	1,523	11,998	534	3,083	1,845	2,085	4,854	21,800
2000	198,566	31,278	3,713	66,638	2,136	8,295	27,123	1,960	14,796	719	3,778	2,216	2,623	5,936	27,296
2001	202,878	29,653	3,626	68,899	2,107	9,040	27,500	2,542	15,970	806	4,163	2,304	2,640	5,251	28,299
2002	199,383	32,231	3,662	64,420	2,214	9,368	26,738	2,571	15,725	777	3,800	2,233	2,687	4,928	27,931

Annual variation (%)

Year	Intra EU	B(1)	DK	D	EL	E	F	IRL	I	L	A	P	FIN	S	UK
98/97	3.9	0.0	5.5	1.9	5.8	16.0	5.8	5.6	6.1	:	7.4	20.8	15.2	5.6	3.9
99/98	8.1	9.4	1.0	5.5	13.8	9.6	9.0	4.0	7.1	:	1.8	-2.0	8.0	6.5	13.8
00/99	21.8	22.8	16.5	20.3	27.4	15.1	21.1	28.7	23.3	34.5	22.5	20.0	25.7	22.3	25.2
01/00	2.1	-5.1	-2.3	3.3	-1.3	8.9	1.3	29.6	7.9	12.0	10.2	3.9	0.6	-11.5	3.6
02/01	-1.7	8.6	0.9	-6.4	5.0	3.6	-2.7	1.1	-1.5	-3.5	-8.7	-3.0	1.7	-6.1	-1.3

Share (%)

Year	Intra EU	B(1)	DK	D	EL	E	F	IRL	I	L	A	P	FIN	S	UK
1980	100.0	19.6	2.4	38.9	0.8	1.2	13.7	0.5	7.5	:	1.2	0.5	0.6	2.2	10.2
1990	100.0	18.1	2.0	34.6	1.1	3.0	13.8	0.7	8.1	:	1.4	0.9	0.8	2.1	12.7
1996	100.0	17.0	2.1	36.3	1.0	3.5	13.5	0.8	7.0	:	1.9	1.0	1.0	2.7	11.7
1997	100.0	16.0	2.0	35.5	0.9	3.9	13.3	0.9	7.2	:	1.9	1.0	1.1	2.9	12.7
1998	100.0	15.4	2.0	34.8	0.9	4.3	13.6	0.9	7.4	:	2.0	1.2	1.2	3.0	12.7
1999	100.0	15.6	1.9	33.9	1.0	4.4	13.7	0.9	7.3	0.3	1.8	1.1	1.2	2.9	13.3
2000	100.0	15.7	1.8	33.5	1.0	4.1	13.6	0.9	7.4	0.3	1.9	1.1	1.3	2.9	13.7
2001	100.0	14.6	1.7	33.9	1.0	4.4	13.5	1.2	7.8	0.3	2.0	1.1	1.3	2.5	13.9
2002	100.0	16.1	1.8	32.3	1.1	4.6	13.4	1.2	7.8	0.3	1.9	1.1	1.3	2.4	14.0

IMPORTS / ARRIVALS
Value (Mio ECU/Euro)

Year	Intra EU	B(1)	DK	D	EL	E	F	IRL	I	L	A	P	FIN	S	UK
1980	32,085	6,449	480	12,297	216	455	3,707	285	1,746	:	321	153	430	1,023	4,522
1990	67,931	13,848	1,193	25,542	212	1,504	8,111	935	3,720	:	903	616	943	2,174	8,229
1994	71,553	12,990	1,278	25,297	181	1,969	8,229	1,380	4,023	:	1,019	616	1,347	2,798	10,424
1995	74,504	13,251	1,296	26,324	169	2,142	8,407	1,590	4,053	:	959	694	1,138	3,129	11,351
1996	92,568	16,380	1,641	32,768	237	2,891	10,248	1,639	5,574	:	1,234	990	1,329	3,657	13,028
1997	98,528	16,828	1,651	32,778	238	3,696	11,275	2,052	5,648	:	1,133	986	1,424	4,100	15,488
1998	101,447	17,562	1,612	33,065	250	3,946	11,632	2,586	5,658	:	1,245	1,033	1,504	4,501	15,960
1999	106,662	17,649	1,971	34,492	228	3,788	11,588	3,488	5,658	268	1,233	951	1,606	4,789	18,206
2000	120,844	20,012	2,325	38,543	309	4,804	12,349	3,947	6,162	539	1,341	1,136	2,112	4,949	21,583
2001	120,354	20,194	1,869	40,170	333	4,838	12,666	3,821	6,222	526	1,543	1,152	2,011	4,388	16,785
2002	122,618	22,760	2,212	40,885	360	4,664	12,399	3,798	6,384	471	1,574	1,259	2,107	4,486	18,642

Annual variation (%)

Year	Intra EU	B(1)	DK	D	EL	E	F	IRL	I	L	A	P	FIN	S	UK
98/97	2.9	4.3	-2.3	0.8	4.9	6.7	3.1	25.9	0.1	:	9.8	4.7	5.6	9.7	3.0
99/98	5.1	0.4	22.2	4.3	-8.7	-3.9	-0.3	34.8	0.0	:	-0.9	-7.9	6.8	6.3	14.0
00/99	13.2	13.3	17.9	11.7	35.2	26.8	6.5	13.1	8.9	101.6	8.7	19.4	31.4	3.3	18.5
01/00	-0.4	0.9	-19.5	4.2	7.6	0.7	2.5	-3.1	0.9	-2.4	15.0	1.4	-4.7	-11.3	-22.2
02/01	1.8	12.7	18.3	1.7	8.2	-3.5	-2.1	-0.6	2.6	-10.5	2.0	9.3	4.7	2.2	11.0

Share (%)

Year	Intra EU	B(1)	DK	D	EL	E	F	IRL	I	L	A	P	FIN	S	UK
1980	100.0	20.1	1.4	38.3	0.6	1.4	11.5	0.8	5.4	:	1.0	0.4	1.3	3.1	14.0
1990	100.0	20.3	1.7	37.6	0.3	2.2	11.9	1.3	5.4	:	1.3	0.9	1.3	3.2	12.1
1996	100.0	17.6	1.7	35.3	0.2	3.1	11.0	1.7	6.0	:	1.3	1.0	1.4	3.9	14.0
1997	100.0	17.0	1.6	33.2	0.2	3.7	11.4	2.0	5.7	:	1.1	1.0	1.4	4.1	15.7
1998	100.0	17.3	1.5	32.5	0.2	3.8	11.4	2.5	5.5	:	1.2	1.0	1.4	4.4	15.7
1999	100.0	16.5	1.8	32.3	0.2	3.5	10.8	3.2	5.3	0.2	1.1	0.8	1.5	4.4	17.0
2000	100.0	16.5	1.9	31.8	0.2	3.9	10.2	3.2	5.0	0.4	1.1	0.9	1.7	4.0	17.8
2001	100.0	16.7	1.5	33.3	0.2	4.0	10.5	3.1	5.1	0.4	1.2	0.9	1.6	3.6	13.9
2002	100.0	18.5	1.8	33.3	0.2	3.8	10.1	3.0	5.2	0.3	1.2	1.0	1.7	3.6	15.2

(1) Luxembourg with Belgium until 31.12.1998.

EXTRA-EU

Years								Partner							
	Extra EU	Norway	Switzerland	USSR/ Russia(1)	Candid. countries	USA	Canada	China	Japan	Hong Kong	Mediterr. Basin	Latin America	OPEC	DAE	ACP

EXPORTS
Value (Mio ECU/Euro)

Years	Extra EU	Norway	Switzerland	USSR/Russia(1)	Candid. countries	USA	Canada	China	Japan	Hong Kong	Mediterr. Basin	Latin America	OPEC	DAE	ACP
1980	12,353	463	1,180	366	:	1,335	141	107	239	97	2,426	669	2,898	458	1,321
1990	20,292	825	1,922	703	:	4,181	450	189	893	321	2,563	822	2,389	1,839	1,342
1994	29,414	976	2,281	1,128	3,183	5,353	544	574	1,372	793	2,906	1,485	2,376	3,769	1,188
1995	31,161	1,127	2,397	1,341	3,818	4,930	523	635	1,580	907	3,186	1,748	2,529	4,125	1,426
1996	32,952	1,074	2,274	1,430	4,390	5,464	498	609	1,732	925	3,611	1,726	2,176	4,512	1,352
1997	38,398	1,259	2,411	1,891	5,419	6,545	556	758	1,753	1,026	4,036	2,099	2,708	5,210	1,538
1998	40,206	1,665	3,067	1,586	6,344	7,187	632	693	1,670	800	4,375	2,183	2,628	4,338	2,399
1999	42,075	1,672	3,316	1,306	6,601	8,096	744	767	2,054	887	4,491	2,024	2,767	4,893	2,178
2000	53,848	1,673	4,008	1,796	8,707	11,053	953	1,116	2,388	1,071	5,639	2,402	3,255	6,928	2,671
2001	54,888	1,881	3,928	2,177	8,548	10,775	994	1,238	2,571	1,018	5,269	2,540	3,922	6,098	3,016
2002	58,717	2,021	4,013	2,593	9,884	11,736	951	1,574	2,423	999	5,944	2,406	4,216	6,191	3,030

Annual variation (%)

Years	Extra EU	Norway	Switzerland	USSR/Russia(1)	Candid. countries	USA	Canada	China	Japan	Hong Kong	Mediterr. Basin	Latin America	OPEC	DAE	ACP
98/97	4.7	32.2	27.2	-16.1	17.0	9.8	13.6	-8.6	-4.7	-22.0	8.3	4.0	-2.9	-16.7	55.9
99/98	4.6	0.3	8.1	-17.6	4.0	12.6	17.7	10.7	23.0	10.8	2.6	-7.3	5.3	12.8	-9.1
00/99	27.9	0.0	20.8	37.4	31.8	36.5	28.1	45.4	16.2	20.7	25.5	18.7	17.6	41.5	22.6
01/00	1.9	12.4	-2.0	21.2	-1.8	-2.5	4.2	10.9	7.6	-4.9	-6.5	5.7	20.4	-11.9	12.9
02/01	6.9	7.4	2.1	19.0	15.6	8.9	-4.3	27.0	-5.7	-1.7	12.8	-5.2	7.5	1.5	0.4

Share (%)

Years	Extra EU	Norway	Switzerland	USSR/Russia(1)	Candid. countries	USA	Canada	China	Japan	Hong Kong	Mediterr. Basin	Latin America	OPEC	DAE	ACP
1980	100.0	3.7	9.5	2.9	:	10.8	1.1	0.8	1.9	0.7	19.6	5.4	23.4	3.7	10.6
1990	100.0	4.0	9.4	3.4	:	20.6	2.2	0.9	4.4	1.5	12.6	4.0	11.7	9.0	6.6
1996	100.0	3.2	6.9	4.3	13.3	16.5	1.5	1.8	5.2	2.8	10.9	5.2	6.6	13.6	4.1
1997	100.0	3.2	6.2	4.9	14.1	17.0	1.4	1.9	4.5	2.6	10.5	5.4	7.0	13.5	4.0
1998	100.0	4.1	7.6	3.9	15.7	17.8	1.5	1.7	4.1	1.9	10.8	5.4	6.5	10.7	5.9
1999	100.0	3.9	7.8	3.1	15.6	19.2	1.7	1.8	4.8	2.1	10.6	4.8	6.5	11.6	5.1
2000	100.0	3.1	7.4	3.3	16.1	20.5	1.7	2.0	4.4	1.9	10.4	4.4	6.0	12.8	4.9
2001	100.0	3.4	7.1	3.9	15.5	19.6	1.8	2.2	4.6	1.8	9.5	4.6	7.1	11.1	5.4
2002	100.0	3.4	6.8	4.4	16.8	19.9	1.6	2.6	4.1	1.7	10.1	4.0	7.1	10.5	5.1

IMPORTS
Value (Mio ECU/Euro)

Years	Extra EU	Norway	Switzerland	USSR/Russia(1)	Candid. countries	USA	Canada	China	Japan	Hong Kong	Mediterr. Basin	Latin America	OPEC	DAE	ACP
1980	23,284	775	725	918	:	4,867	417	197	1,050	255	1,977	1,580	8,341	1,414	3,042
1990	38,675	1,912	1,308	1,796	:	8,536	767	1,046	4,186	494	2,391	3,563	6,652	3,881	1,933
1994	48,506	3,361	1,586	1,147	5,062	10,202	827	1,709	4,996	1,589	2,358	4,148	7,153	6,466	1,844
1995	52,118	3,306	1,653	1,386	3,001	11,619	958	1,908	5,585	1,734	2,483	4,176	5,888	7,491	1,653
1996	57,795	1,494	1,704	1,645	3,262	12,941	939	2,272	6,298	1,956	2,745	4,102	5,827	9,277	1,744
1997	69,659	4,066	1,742	2,404	3,877	16,275	1,070	3,148	7,252	2,396	3,149	4,663	6,071	11,371	1,698
1998	73,061	2,536	2,100	1,941	4,633	17,073	1,159	3,991	8,543	2,829	3,343	5,031	2,404	15,034	2,526
1999	86,772	2,577	2,406	2,012	5,209	18,451	1,076	4,651	9,226	3,235	3,503	5,344	6,729	16,992	2,807
2000	115,478	3,000	2,461	3,901	6,219	24,030	1,249	8,705	11,243	2,129	4,662	7,312	10,892	20,287	3,126
2001	112,604	2,657	2,384	4,302	6,269	23,071	1,266	10,440	10,404	1,543	4,831	7,872	9,024	19,298	4,019
2002	109,261	5,641	2,419	4,324	6,657	20,969	1,406	12,000	9,384	1,500	4,919	7,846	8,095	17,718	3,765

Annual variation (%)

Years	Extra EU	Norway	Switzerland	USSR/Russia(1)	Candid. countries	USA	Canada	China	Japan	Hong Kong	Mediterr. Basin	Latin America	OPEC	DAE	ACP
98/97	4.8	-37.6	20.5	-19.2	19.5	4.9	8.2	26.7	17.8	18.0	6.1	7.9	-60.3	32.2	48.7
99/98	18.7	1.6	14.5	3.6	12.4	8.0	-7.1	16.5	7.9	14.3	4.7	6.2	179.9	13.0	11.1
00/99	33.0	16.4	2.2	93.8	19.3	30.2	16.0	87.1	21.8	-34.1	33.0	36.8	61.8	19.3	11.3
01/00	-2.4	-11.4	-3.1	10.2	0.8	-3.9	1.3	19.9	-7.4	-27.5	3.6	7.6	-17.1	-4.8	28.5
02/01	-2.9	112.2	1.4	0.5	6.1	-9.1	11.1	14.9	-9.8	-2.8	1.8	-0.3	-10.2	-8.1	-6.3

Share (%)

Years	Extra EU	Norway	Switzerland	USSR/Russia(1)	Candid. countries	USA	Canada	China	Japan	Hong Kong	Mediterr. Basin	Latin America	OPEC	DAE	ACP
1980	100.0	3.3	3.1	3.9	:	20.9	1.7	0.8	4.5	1.0	8.4	6.7	35.8	6.0	13.0
1990	100.0	4.9	3.3	4.6	:	22.0	1.9	2.7	10.8	1.2	6.1	9.2	17.2	10.0	4.9
1996	100.0	2.5	2.9	2.8	5.6	22.3	1.6	3.9	10.8	3.3	4.7	7.0	10.0	16.0	3.0
1997	100.0	5.8	2.5	3.4	5.5	23.3	1.5	4.5	10.4	3.4	4.5	6.6	8.7	16.3	2.4
1998	100.0	3.4	2.8	2.6	6.3	23.3	1.5	5.4	11.6	3.8	4.5	6.8	3.2	20.5	3.4
1999	100.0	2.9	2.7	2.3	6.0	21.2	1.2	5.3	10.6	3.7	4.0	6.1	7.7	19.5	3.2
2000	100.0	2.5	2.1	3.3	5.3	20.8	1.0	7.5	9.7	1.8	4.0	6.3	9.4	17.5	2.7
2001	100.0	2.3	2.1	3.8	5.5	20.4	1.1	9.2	9.2	1.3	4.2	6.9	8.0	17.1	3.5
2002	100.0	5.1	2.2	3.9	6.0	19.1	1.2	10.9	8.5	1.3	4.5	7.1	7.4	16.2	3.4

(1) Relates to the external trade with the USSR until 1991and to the external trade with Russia from 1992 onwards.

AUSTRIA

TRADE BALANCE (BN ECU/euro)

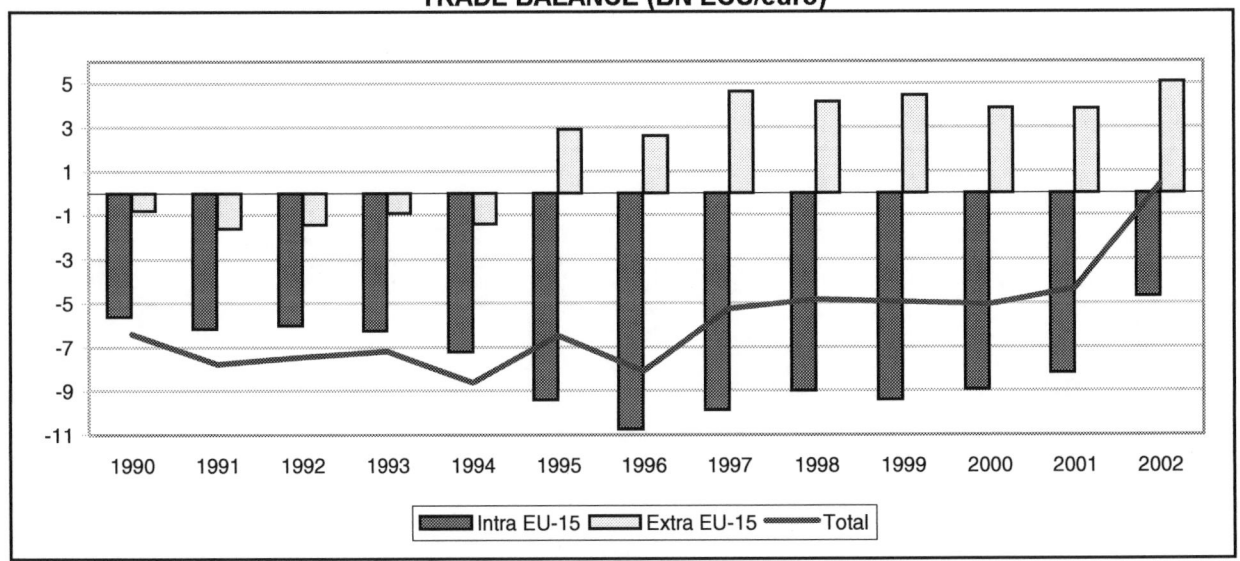

INTRA-EU (BN ECU/euro)

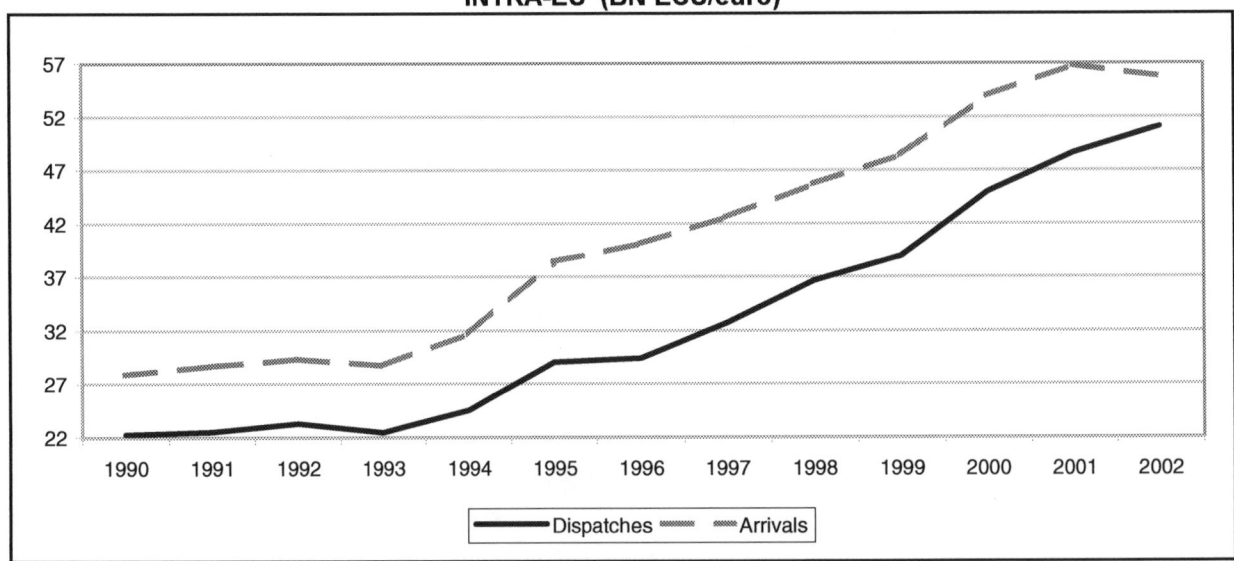

EXTRA-EU (BN ECU/euro)

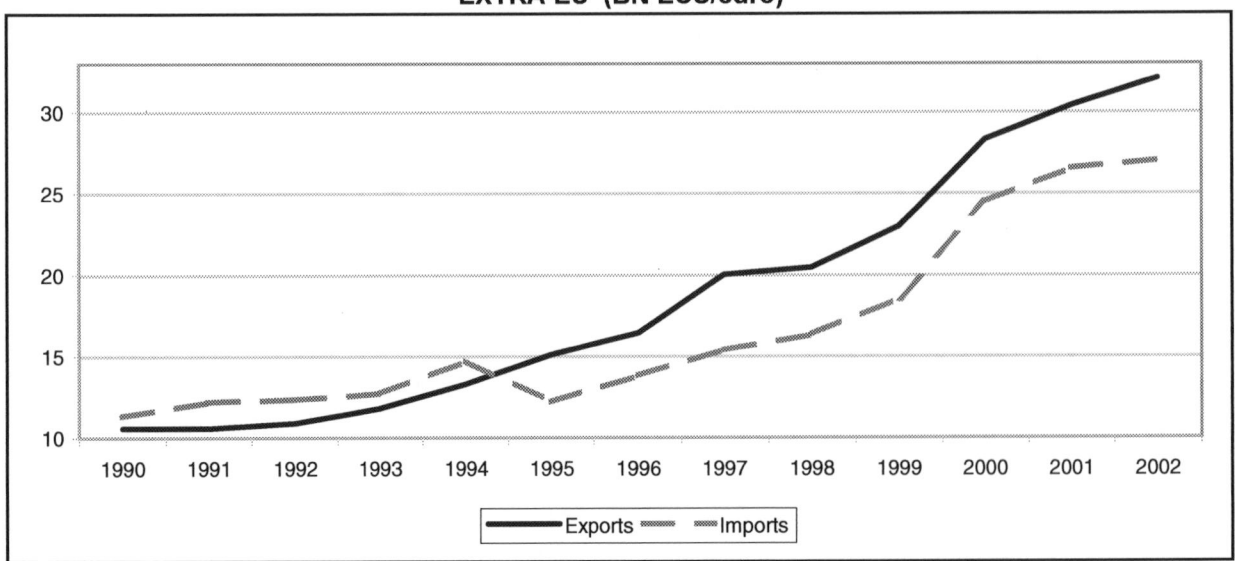

TRADE BALANCE

INTRA-EU

Value (Mio ECU/Euro)

Year	Intra EU	B[1]	DK	D	EL	E	F	IRL	I	L	NL	P	FIN	S	UK
															Partner
1980	**-3,934**	**-173**	**24**	**-3,241**	**62**	**13**	**-257**	**-12**	**-217**	**:**	**-146**	**-5**	**35**	**4**	**-21**
1990	**-5,609**	**-423**	**24**	**-4,975**	**24**	**340**	**-88**	**-89**	**-325**	**:**	**-158**	**-108**	**-14**	**-85**	**266**
1991	-6,164	-531	4	-4,667	31	301	-341	-104	-513	:	-102	-97	-75	-164	94
1992	-6,025	-581	-22	-4,243	53	288	-351	-135	-583	:	-128	-75	-93	-244	89
1993	-6,269	-533	-33	-3,814	11	150	-301	-143	-1,032	:	-184	-78	-87	-213	-13
1994	-7,217	-631	-49	-4,166	10	185	-465	-146	-1,029	:	-272	-98	-121	-287	-147
1995	-9,403	-599	-16	-7,529	113	350	-566	-94	-422	:	-1,174	1	-39	-230	49
1996	-10,724	-440	-33	-8,182	106	412	-492	-95	-663	:	-1,302	14	-52	-165	167
1997	-9,872	-675	16	-8,317	129	499	-390	-88	-247	:	-1,370	40	-33	-64	629
1998	-8,990	-590	71	-7,857	149	791	-366	-129	332	:	-1,673	55	-188	-173	589
1999	-9,407	-631	50	-8,820	202	993	-434	-225	496	-26	-1,654	103	-253	-156	948
2000	**-8,947**	**-856**	**85**	**-9,892**	**233**	**1,139**	**343**	**-240**	**1,107**	**-2**	**-1,613**	**224**	**-376**	**-255**	**1,158**
2001	-8,188	-697	109	-10,661	324	1,142	731	-184	1,270	0	-1,867	214	-265	-94	1,773
2002	**-4,680**	**-798**	**171**	**-9,174**	**382**	**1,361**	**895**	**-152**	**2,137**	**-24**	**-1,613**	**175**	**-113**	**-66**	**2,128**

EXTRA-EU

Value (Mio ECU/Euro)

Year	Extra EU	Norway	Switzerland	Russia[2]	Candid. countries	USA	Canada	China	Japan	Hong Kong	Mediterr. Basin	Latin America	OPEC	DAE	ACP
													Partner		
1980	**-1,029**	**72**	**68**	**-394**	**:**	**-319**	**-22**	**38**	**-324**	**-74**	**321**	**-162**	**-539**	**-130**	**129**
1990	**-780**	**46**	**612**	**-12**	**:**	**-375**	**53**	**-83**	**-1,258**	**-66**	**110**	**-173**	**57**	**-252**	**-66**
1991	-1,612	59	409	-28	:	-680	-0	-142	-1,412	-80	153	-163	88	-281	-141
1992	-1,432	85	362	-44	:	-742	-18	-237	-1,444	-36	297	-91	159	-251	-149
1993	-906	62	420	-107	:	-696	60	-302	-1,294	-10	341	-43	53	-159	-217
1994	-1,394	65	518	-200	:	-707	-82	-445	-1,401	-9	427	-75	-25	-130	-77
1995	2,905	131	326	-178	1,695	-267	59	-114	-274	94	804	170	103	253	-109
1996	2,625	199	222	-241	1,479	-292	1	-227	-108	94	704	311	-116	287	-198
1997	4,621	215	374	-33	2,329	-128	46	-267	-137	153	1,295	486	7	303	-125
1998	4,156	184	390	-130	1,881	208	77	-123	-354	100	1,195	460	282	48	21
1999	4,472	172	883	-179	1,748	110	133	-145	-229	112	1,082	425	210	66	60
2000	**3,876**	**192**	**1,100**	**-421**	**928**	**463**	**45**	**-257**	**-246**	**432**	**1,032**	**444**	**-168**	**389**	**60**
2001	3,854	251	309	-31	92	862	237	-170	-107	95	879	537	204	-7	97
2002	**5,075**	**251**	**450**	**128**	**72**	**1,217**	**270**	**22**	**63**	**519**	**1,422**	**333**	**199**	**197**	**43**

(1) Luxembourg with Belgium until 31.12.1998.
(2) Relates to the external trade with the USSR until 1991 and to the external trade with Russia from 1992 onwards.

AUSTRIA

INTRA-EU

Year	Intra EU	B(1)	DK	D	EL	E	F	IRL	I	L	NL	P	FIN	S	UK
							Partner								

EXPORTS / DISPATCHES
Value (Mio ECU/Euro)

Year	Intra EU	B(1)	DK	D	EL	E	F	IRL	I	L	NL	P	FIN	S	UK
1980	7,277	192	144	3,881	‹:	:	435	20	1,379	:	327	:	116	322	461
1990	22,315	719	306	12,310	189	714	1,562	54	3,231	:	953	134	266	602	1,274
1994	24,563	714	324	14,441	174	812	1,725	81	3,075	:	1,130	163	197	528	1,200
1995	29,036	726	354	16,564	242	879	1,838	93	3,775	:	1,221	168	272	590	1,376
1996	29,405	884	366	17,133	218	1,018	1,962	99	3,838	:	1,188	191	279	603	1,625
1997	32,692	912	397	18,408	233	1,177	2,174	123	4,449	:	1,456	217	310	658	2,177
1998	36,686	1,026	465	20,573	254	1,519	2,576	180	5,047	:	1,399	232	357	678	2,380
1999	38,998	924	476	21,663	301	1,770	2,751	173	5,322	93	1,456	273	377	716	2,702
2000	44,985	1,099	525	24,413	345	1,972	3,281	219	6,464	128	1,760	378	390	862	3,148
2001	48,609	1,366	568	25,528	429	2,038	3,906	245	6,866	170	1,934	411	443	903	3,782
2002	51,087	1,324	601	26,246	498	2,360	3,922	257	7,701	143	2,087	378	508	959	4,086

Annual variation (%)

Year	Intra EU	B(1)	DK	D	EL	E	F	IRL	I	L	NL	P	FIN	S	UK
98/97	12.2	12.4	17.0	11.7	9.1	29.0	18.4	46.1	13.4	:	-3.8	6.6	15.1	2.9	9.3
99/98	6.3	-9.9	2.4	5.2	18.6	16.4	6.8	-3.7	5.4	:	4.0	17.6	5.5	5.6	13.5
00/99	15.3	18.9	10.2	12.6	14.5	11.4	19.2	26.5	21.4	36.9	20.8	38.8	3.4	20.3	16.5
01/00	8.0	24.2	8.1	4.5	24.4	3.3	19.0	12.0	6.2	33.0	9.8	8.6	13.5	4.7	20.1
02/01	5.0	-3.1	5.8	2.8	15.9	15.8	0.4	4.8	12.1	-15.7	7.9	-7.9	14.7	6.2	8.0

Share (%)

Year	Intra EU	B(1)	DK	D	EL	E	F	IRL	I	L	NL	P	FIN	S	UK
1980	100.0	2.6	1.9	53.3	:	:	5.9	0.2	18.9	:	4.4	:	1.5	4.4	6.3
1990	100.0	3.2	1.3	55.1	0.8	3.1	7.0	0.2	14.4	:	4.2	0.6	1.1	2.6	5.7
1996	100.0	3.0	1.2	58.2	0.7	3.4	6.6	0.3	13.0	:	4.0	0.6	0.9	2.0	5.5
1997	100.0	2.7	1.2	56.3	0.7	3.6	6.6	0.3	13.6	:	4.4	0.6	0.9	2.0	6.6
1998	100.0	2.7	1.2	56.0	0.6	4.1	7.0	0.4	13.7	:	3.8	0.6	0.9	1.8	6.4
1999	100.0	2.3	1.2	55.5	0.7	4.5	7.0	0.4	13.6	0.2	3.7	0.6	0.9	1.8	6.9
2000	100.0	2.4	1.1	54.2	0.7	4.3	7.2	0.4	14.3	0.2	3.9	0.8	0.8	1.9	6.9
2001	100.0	2.8	1.1	52.5	0.8	4.1	8.0	0.5	14.1	0.3	3.9	0.8	0.9	1.8	7.7
2002	100.0	2.5	1.1	51.3	0.9	4.6	7.6	0.5	15.0	0.2	4.0	0.7	0.9	1.8	7.9

IMPORTS / ARRIVALS
Value (Mio ECU/Euro)

Year	Intra EU	B(1)	DK	D	EL	E	F	IRL	I	L	NL	P	FIN	S	UK
1980	11,332	364	120	7,169	:	:	693	32	1,596	:	474	:	81	319	483
1990	27,924	1,142	282	17,285	165	374	1,651	143	3,555	:	1,111	242	280	686	1,008
1994	31,781	1,345	373	18,607	164	627	2,190	228	4,104	:	1,402	261	318	815	1,347
1995	38,439	1,325	370	24,093	129	529	2,404	187	4,196	:	2,395	167	310	820	1,327
1996	40,129	1,324	399	25,315	113	606	2,453	194	4,501	:	2,490	177	331	768	1,458
1997	42,564	1,587	382	26,725	104	678	2,564	211	4,697	:	2,826	178	343	722	1,547
1998	45,676	1,616	394	28,430	104	728	2,942	309	4,715	:	3,072	177	546	851	1,791
1999	48,405	1,555	427	30,483	99	776	3,186	398	4,826	120	3,110	170	630	873	1,754
2000	53,932	1,955	441	34,305	111	834	2,938	459	5,357	130	3,374	155	766	1,117	1,990
2001	56,797	2,063	459	36,189	105	895	3,175	429	5,596	170	3,801	197	709	996	2,009
2002	55,767	2,122	430	35,420	116	999	3,027	409	5,564	167	3,701	203	621	1,025	1,957

Annual variation (%)

Year	Intra EU	B(1)	DK	D	EL	E	F	IRL	I	L	NL	P	FIN	S	UK
98/97	7.3	1.8	3.2	6.3	0.6	7.3	14.7	46.6	0.3	:	8.7	-0.3	58.9	17.8	15.7
99/98	5.9	-3.7	8.3	7.2	-5.4	6.5	8.2	28.6	2.3	:	1.2	-4.1	15.4	2.5	-2.0
00/99	11.4	25.7	3.2	12.5	12.8	7.4	-7.7	15.3	10.9	8.6	8.4	-8.9	21.6	28.0	13.4
01/00	5.3	5.5	4.2	5.4	-5.8	7.3	8.0	-6.4	4.4	30.6	12.6	27.2	-7.5	-10.7	0.9
02/01	-1.8	2.8	-6.3	-2.1	10.0	11.6	-4.6	-4.5	-0.5	-1.5	-2.6	3.2	-12.3	2.9	-2.5

Share (%)

Year	Intra EU	B(1)	DK	D	EL	E	F	IRL	I	L	NL	P	FIN	S	UK
1980	100.0	3.2	1.0	63.2	:	:	6.1	0.2	14.0	:	4.1	:	0.7	2.8	4.2
1990	100.0	4.0	1.0	61.8	0.5	1.3	5.9	0.5	12.7	:	3.9	0.8	1.0	2.4	3.6
1996	100.0	3.3	0.9	63.0	0.2	1.5	6.1	0.4	11.2	:	6.2	0.4	0.8	1.9	3.6
1997	100.0	3.7	0.8	62.7	0.2	1.5	6.0	0.4	11.0	:	6.6	0.4	0.8	1.6	3.6
1998	100.0	3.5	0.8	62.2	0.2	1.5	6.4	0.6	10.3	:	6.7	0.3	1.1	1.8	3.9
1999	100.0	3.2	0.8	62.9	0.2	1.6	6.5	0.8	9.9	0.2	6.4	0.3	1.3	1.8	3.6
2000	100.0	3.6	0.8	63.6	0.2	1.5	5.4	0.8	9.9	0.2	6.2	0.2	1.4	2.0	3.6
2001	100.0	3.6	0.8	63.7	0.1	1.5	5.5	0.7	9.8	0.2	6.6	0.3	1.2	1.7	3.5
2002	100.0	3.8	0.7	63.5	0.2	1.7	5.4	0.7	9.9	0.2	6.6	0.3	1.1	1.8	3.5

(1) Luxembourg with Belgium until 31.12.1998.

EXTRA-EU

Years						Partner									
	Extra EU	Norway	Switzerland	USSR/ Russia(1)	Candid. countries	USA	Canada	China	Japan	Hong Kong	Mediterr. Basin	Latin America	OPEC	DAE	ACP

EXPORTS
Value (Mio ECU/Euro)

1980	5,009	132	945	343	:	274	60	62	100	16	1,071	170	701	88	277
1990	10,573	176	2,284	711	:	1,054	247	203	525	135	1,452	212	886	442	192
1994	13,310	211	2,412	553	4,245	1,339	234	273	590	208	1,637	376	810	743	137
1995	15,106	206	2,394	647	5,202	1,312	267	343	593	249	1,946	440	767	1,002	152
1996	16,448	270	2,264	598	5,966	1,462	326	270	712	223	2,216	506	829	1,001	134
1997	20,026	295	2,559	740	7,715	1,956	360	302	661	282	3,002	679	957	1,050	134
1998	20,477	274	2,810	546	8,152	2,308	352	438	526	223	2,938	677	892	835	320
1999	22,984	259	3,671	476	8,748	2,837	399	473	751	238	3,041	627	904	1,017	341
2000	28,327	263	4,591	711	10,308	3,661	531	586	956	537	3,508	774	927	1,514	537
2001	30,390	301	3,968	1,019	10,984	4,064	580	876	947	417	3,867	887	1,311	1,421	633
2002	32,112	295	4,193	1,058	11,809	4,131	544	1,185	981	589	4,428	666	1,153	1,553	586

Annual variation (%)

98/97	2.2	-7.0	9.8	-26.2	5.6	17.9	-2.3	44.8	-20.4	-20.7	-2.1	-0.3	-6.8	-20.4	139.3
99/98	12.2	-5.5	30.6	-12.7	7.3	22.9	13.3	7.8	42.7	6.5	3.4	-7.4	1.4	21.8	6.2
00/99	23.2	1.8	25.0	49.4	17.8	29.0	33.1	23.8	27.3	125.5	15.3	23.5	2.5	48.8	57.6
01/00	7.2	14.4	-13.5	43.1	6.5	10.9	9.2	49.5	-0.9	-22.2	10.2	14.6	41.4	-6.1	17.9
02/01	5.6	-2.1	5.6	3.8	7.5	1.6	-6.1	35.3	3.6	41.0	14.5	-24.9	-12.0	9.3	-7.5

Share (%)

1980	100.0	2.6	18.8	6.8	:	5.4	1.1	1.2	1.9	0.3	21.3	3.3	13.9	1.7	5.5
1990	100.0	1.6	21.6	6.7	:	9.9	2.3	1.9	4.9	1.2	13.7	2.0	8.3	4.1	1.8
1996	100.0	1.6	13.7	3.6	36.2	8.8	1.9	1.6	4.3	1.3	13.4	3.0	5.0	6.0	0.8
1997	100.0	1.4	12.7	3.6	38.5	9.7	1.7	1.5	3.3	1.4	14.9	3.3	4.7	5.2	0.6
1998	100.0	1.3	13.7	2.6	39.8	11.2	1.7	2.1	2.5	1.0	14.3	3.3	4.3	4.0	1.5
1999	100.0	1.1	15.9	2.0	38.0	12.3	1.7	2.0	3.2	1.0	13.2	2.7	3.9	4.4	1.4
2000	100.0	0.9	16.2	2.5	36.3	12.9	1.8	2.0	3.3	1.8	12.3	2.7	3.2	5.3	1.8
2001	100.0	0.9	13.0	3.3	36.1	13.3	1.9	2.8	3.1	1.3	12.7	2.9	4.3	4.6	2.0
2002	100.0	0.9	13.0	3.2	36.7	12.8	1.6	3.6	3.0	1.8	13.7	2.0	3.5	4.8	1.8

IMPORTS
Value (Mio ECU/Euro)

1980	6,038	59	877	737	:	593	82	24	424	89	750	332	1,241	218	148
1990	11,354	131	1,672	723	:	1,429	193	286	1,783	201	1,342	386	830	694	258
1994	14,704	146	1,894	752	3,188	2,046	316	719	1,991	217	1,210	451	836	873	215
1995	12,201	75	2,068	825	3,507	1,579	208	457	866	155	1,142	270	665	749	261
1996	13,823	72	2,042	839	4,487	1,754	325	496	820	130	1,512	195	945	715	332
1997	15,405	79	2,185	774	5,387	2,085	314	570	798	129	1,707	194	950	747	259
1998	16,321	90	2,420	676	6,271	2,100	274	562	880	123	1,744	217	610	787	299
1999	18,512	87	2,788	655	7,001	2,727	266	618	980	127	1,958	202	695	952	280
2000	24,451	72	3,491	1,132	9,380	3,198	486	842	1,202	105	2,476	330	1,095	1,124	477
2001	26,536	50	3,659	1,050	10,891	3,202	343	1,046	1,054	323	2,987	350	1,107	1,428	537
2002	27,037	44	3,743	930	11,737	2,913	274	1,163	918	69	3,006	334	955	1,356	543

Annual variation (%)

98/97	5.9	13.2	10.7	-12.6	16.4	0.7	-12.5	-1.4	10.1	-4.1	2.1	12.1	-35.8	5.2	15.5
99/98	13.4	-3.0	15.1	-3.1	11.6	29.8	-3.0	10.1	11.3	2.6	12.3	-6.9	13.8	20.9	-6.2
00/99	32.0	-17.3	25.2	72.9	33.9	17.2	82.6	36.2	22.6	-17.0	26.4	63.3	57.6	18.1	70.2
01/00	8.5	-30.0	4.8	-7.2	16.1	0.1	-29.4	24.1	-12.3	206.9	20.6	6.0	1.0	26.9	12.4
02/01	1.8	-11.3	2.2	-11.3	7.7	-9.0	-20.0	11.1	-12.9	-78.4	0.6	-4.6	-13.7	-5.0	1.1

Share (%)

1980	100.0	0.9	14.5	12.2	:	9.8	1.3	0.3	7.0	1.4	12.4	5.5	20.5	3.6	2.4
1990	100.0	1.1	14.7	6.3	:	12.5	1.7	2.5	15.6	1.7	11.8	3.3	7.3	6.1	2.2
1996	100.0	0.5	14.7	6.0	32.4	12.6	2.3	3.5	5.9	0.9	10.9	1.4	6.8	5.1	2.4
1997	100.0	0.5	14.1	5.0	34.9	13.5	2.0	3.6	5.1	0.8	11.0	1.2	6.1	4.8	1.6
1998	100.0	0.5	14.8	4.1	38.4	12.8	1.6	3.4	5.3	0.7	10.6	1.3	3.7	4.8	1.8
1999	100.0	0.4	15.0	3.5	37.8	14.7	1.4	3.3	5.2	0.6	10.5	1.0	3.7	5.1	1.5
2000	100.0	0.2	14.2	4.6	38.3	13.0	1.9	3.4	4.9	0.4	10.1	1.3	4.4	4.5	1.9
2001	100.0	0.1	13.7	3.9	41.0	12.0	1.2	3.9	3.9	1.2	11.2	1.3	4.1	5.3	2.0
2002	100.0	0.1	13.8	3.4	43.4	10.7	1.0	4.2	3.3	0.2	11.1	1.2	3.5	5.0	2.0

(1) Relates to the external trade with the USSR until 1991and to the external trade with Russia from 1992 onwards.

PORTUGAL

TRADE BALANCE (BN ECU/euro)

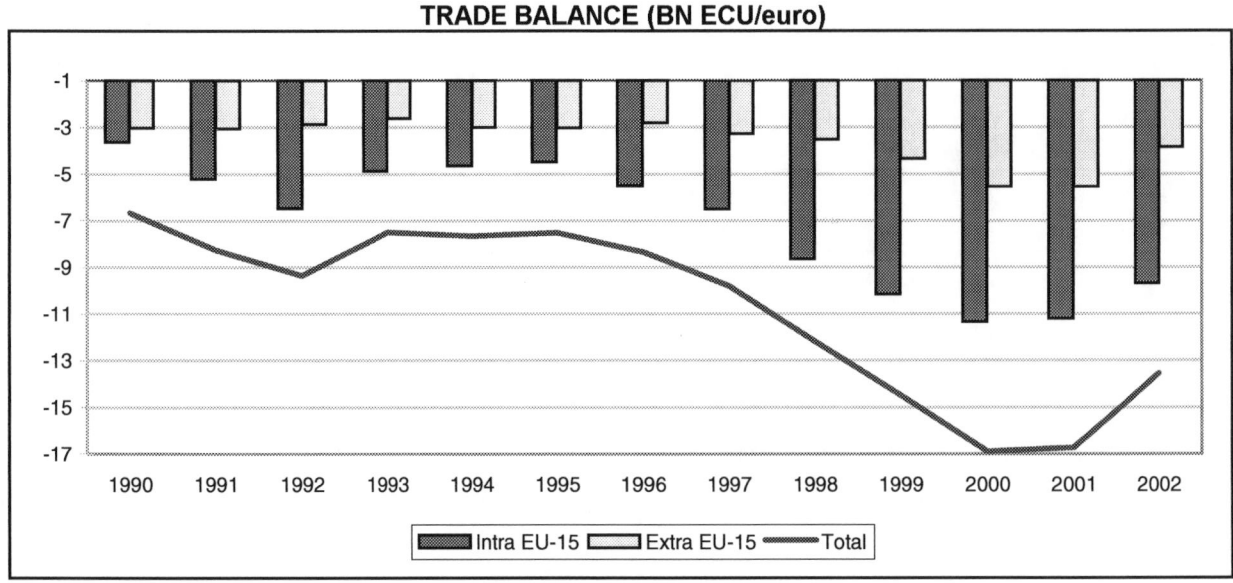

INTRA-EU (BN ECU/euro)

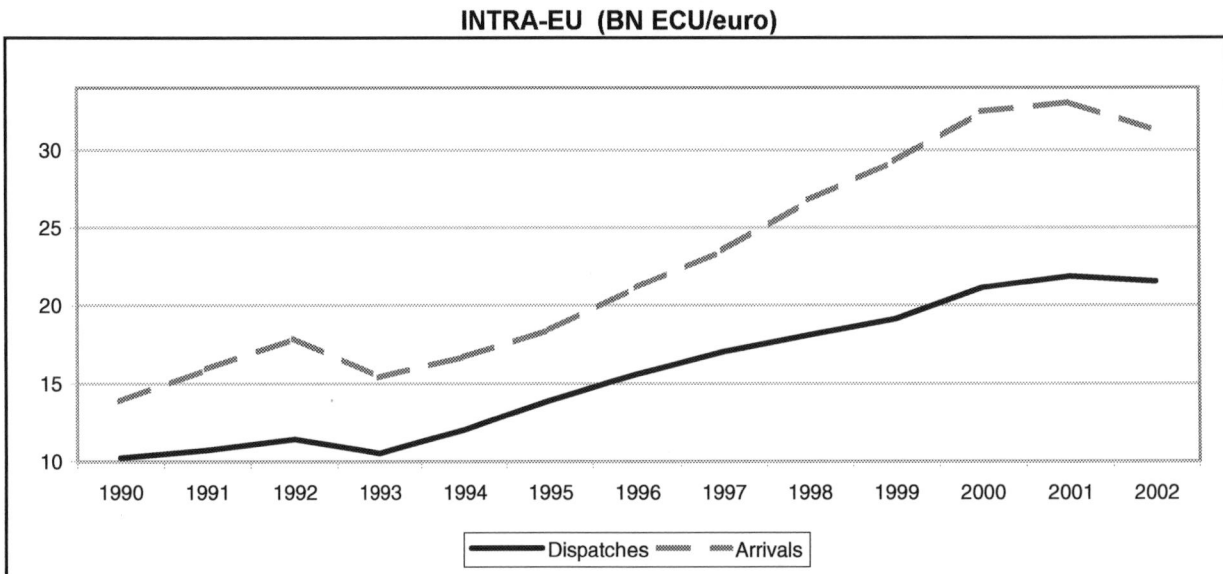

EXTRA-EU (BN ECU/euro)

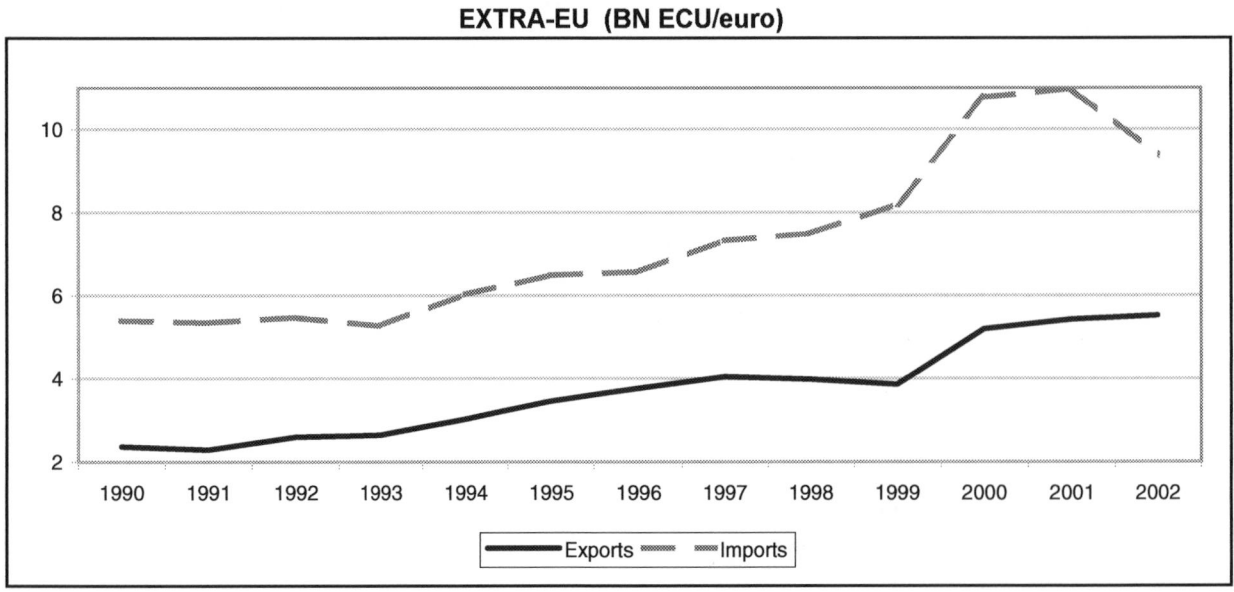

TRADE BALANCE

INTRA-EU

Value (Mio ECU/Euro)

Year	Intra EU	B(1)	DK	D	EL	E	F	IRL	I	L	NL	A	FIN	S	UK
1980	**-1,061**	**-103**	**21**	**-332**	**3**	**-247**	**-134**	**-1**	**-153**	**:**	**-35**	**-0**	**17**	**-3**	**-93**
1990	**-3,637**	**-404**	**105**	**-626**	**40**	**-1,109**	**-230**	**-22**	**-1,408**	**:**	**-372**	**-2**	**74**	**240**	**76**
1991	-5,211	-438	101	-676	36	-1,408	-656	-24	-1,662	:	-545	3	32	199	-175
1992	-6,480	-424	117	-810	51	-1,780	-994	-28	-1,852	:	-831	-30	15	183	-97
1993	-4,876	-318	124	-535	46	-1,795	-636	-62	-1,401	:	-331	-17	-4	91	-38
1994	-4,643	-223	153	-303	40	-2,335	-693	-79	-1,441	:	-169	-11	47	109	260
1995	-4,484	-304	183	175	31	-2,614	-541	-74	-1,516	:	-210	34	9	72	263
1996	-5,529	-120	123	-211	46	-3,471	-317	-62	-1,617	:	-285	54	4	80	234
1997	-6,512	-48	177	-407	51	-4,206	-340	-109	-1,681	:	-413	58	-21	99	318
1998	-8,651	-111	110	-722	43	-4,860	-723	-124	-1,814	:	-621	20	-103	-78	324
1999	-10,139	-88	100	-974	68	-5,312	-1,072	-130	-1,944	-23	-777	10	-129	-90	220
2000	**-11,320**	**247**	**19**	**-1,178**	**22**	**-6,119**	**-1,250**	**-126**	**-2,039**	**-41**	**-868**	**-63**	**-103**	**-102**	**277**
2001	-11,179	125	35	-841	4	-6,862	-1,050	-123	-1,742	-67	-982	-94	-109	-79	600
2002	**-9,693**	**-1**	**5**	**-1,113**	**12**	**-5,958**	**-744**	**-115**	**-1,355**	**-74**	**-818**	**-66**	**-114**	**-78**	**720**

EXTRA-EU

Value (Mio ECU/Euro)

Year	Extra EU	Norway	Switzerland	Russia(2)	Candid. countries	USA	Canada	China	Japan	Hong Kong	Mediterr. Basin	Latin America	OPEC	DAE	ACP
1980	**-2,249**	**30**	**-73**	**-76**	**:**	**-540**	**-30**	**-3**	**-173**	**-0**	**-287**	**-245**	**-1,254**	**-21**	**-58**
1990	**-3,031**	**-27**	**-167**	**18**	**:**	**-137**	**-42**	**-22**	**-372**	**-9**	**-366**	**-618**	**-1,245**	**-192**	**-358**
1991	-3,061	-88	-124	-42	:	-223	-26	-41	-504	-17	-420	-660	-940	-274	-50
1992	-2,867	-171	-137	-30	:	-213	-23	-70	-608	-16	-377	-625	-815	-299	125
1993	-2,625	-150	-130	-118	-13	-78	20	-132	-565	-3	-371	-518	-909	-252	-29
1994	-3,003	-209	-96	-113	-45	-36	42	-130	-533	6	-279	-472	-1,179	-285	-240
1995	-3,029	-136	-37	-145	-65	-27	21	-125	-425	9	-224	-513	-1,121	-426	-335
1996	-2,806	-33	-61	-150	11	-16	-1	-157	-458	16	-232	-423	-1,106	-357	-358
1997	-3,276	-48	-122	-190	22	12	39	-178	-607	21	-176	-547	-1,222	-399	-275
1998	-3,518	-188	-94	-124	-113	126	-4	-250	-825	16	-165	-563	-773	-496	-243
1999	-4,341	-374	-111	-174	-184	81	13	-250	-912	23	-230	-620	-623	-623	-309
2000	**-5,558**	**-429**	**-83**	**-231**	**-312**	**246**	**28**	**-330**	**-941**	**46**	**-337**	**-682**	**-1,931**	**-629**	**-788**
2001	-5,552	-528	-131	-413	-531	-62	47	-291	-706	57	-357	-841	-1,697	-427	-667
2002	**-3,852**	**-266**	**-68**	**-326**	**-555**	**687**	**58**	**-264**	**-626**	**46**	**-312**	**-1,009**	**-1,442**	**-264**	**-264**

(1) Luxembourg with Belgium until 31.12.1998.
(2) Relates to the external trade with the USSR until 1991 and to the external trade with Russia from 1992 onwards.

PORTUGAL

INTRA-EU

Year							Partner								
	Intra EU	B(1)	DK	D	EL	E	F	IRL	I	L	NL	A	FIN	S	UK
EXPORTS / DISPATCHES															
Value (Mio ECU/Euro)															
1980	**2,186**	**104**	**59**	**451**	**10**	**120**	**353**	**12**	**190**	**:**	**157**	**38**	**47**	**150**	**494**
1990	**10,261**	**399**	**275**	**2,118**	**65**	**1,688**	**1,970**	**61**	**524**	**:**	**738**	**145**	**210**	**521**	**1,546**
1994	12,071	550	348	2,858	67	2,187	2,223	75	507	:	813	167	157	367	1,753
1995	13,952	535	387	3,764	70	2,565	2,434	70	577	:	915	177	155	377	1,914
1996	15,623	803	355	4,086	95	2,830	2,783	92	724	:	952	233	155	403	2,098
1997	17,071	938	384	4,190	87	3,080	2,987	94	826	:	1,050	242	165	448	2,568
1998	18,135	1,055	335	4,496	91	3,510	3,135	105	896	:	1,059	215	146	426	2,660
1999	19,161	1,086	333	4,548	119	4,160	3,210	127	960	31	1,015	236	138	417	2,773
2000	**21,173**	**1,566**	**320**	**4,761**	**105**	**5,086**	**3,342**	**139**	**1,046**	**27**	**1,117**	**218**	**135**	**437**	**2,868**
2001	21,893	1,463	292	5,232	103	5,202	3,450	144	1,253	30	1,141	224	131	411	2,812
2002	**21,576**	**1,231**	**271**	**4,978**	**101**	**5,482**	**3,419**	**155**	**1,306**	**26**	**1,023**	**216**	**110**	**400**	**2,850**
Annual variation (%)															
98/97	6.2	12.5	-12.6	7.3	4.7	13.9	4.9	11.1	8.5	:	0.8	-11.1	-11.6	-4.9	3.5
99/98	5.6	2.9	-0.5	1.1	30.9	18.5	2.4	21.1	7.1	:	-4.1	9.7	-5.2	-2.1	4.2
00/99	10.5	44.1	-3.9	4.6	-12.2	22.2	4.1	9.1	8.9	-13.7	9.9	-7.6	-2.4	4.8	3.4
01/00	3.4	-6.5	-8.9	9.8	-1.9	2.2	3.2	3.6	19.7	12.4	2.1	2.5	-2.7	-5.9	-1.9
02/01	-1.4	-15.8	-7.1	-4.8	-1.5	5.3	-0.8	8.0	4.2	-13.2	-10.3	-3.5	-16.3	-2.7	1.3
Share (%)															
1980	**100.0**	**4.7**	**2.7**	**20.6**	**0.4**	**5.4**	**16.1**	**0.5**	**8.7**	**:**	**7.1**	**1.7**	**2.1**	**6.8**	**22.5**
1990	**100.0**	**3.8**	**2.6**	**20.6**	**0.6**	**16.4**	**19.1**	**0.5**	**5.1**	**:**	**7.1**	**1.4**	**2.0**	**5.0**	**15.0**
1996	100.0	5.1	2.2	26.1	0.6	18.1	17.8	0.5	4.6	:	6.0	1.4	0.9	2.5	13.4
1997	100.0	5.4	2.2	24.5	0.5	18.0	17.4	0.5	4.8	:	6.1	1.4	0.9	2.6	15.0
1998	100.0	5.8	1.8	24.7	0.5	19.3	17.2	0.5	4.9	:	5.8	1.1	0.8	2.3	14.6
1999	100.0	5.6	1.7	23.7	0.6	21.7	16.7	0.6	5.0	0.1	5.2	1.2	0.7	2.1	14.4
2000	**100.0**	**7.3**	**1.5**	**22.4**	**0.4**	**24.0**	**15.7**	**0.6**	**4.9**	**0.1**	**5.2**	**1.0**	**0.6**	**2.0**	**13.5**
2001	100.0	6.6	1.3	23.8	0.4	23.7	15.7	0.6	5.7	0.1	5.2	1.0	0.6	1.8	12.8
2002	**100.0**	**5.7**	**1.2**	**23.0**	**0.4**	**25.4**	**15.8**	**0.7**	**6.0**	**0.1**	**4.7**	**0.9**	**0.5**	**1.8**	**13.2**
IMPORTS / ARRIVALS															
Value (Mio ECU/Euro)															
1980	**3,323**	**211**	**39**	**802**	**7**	**376**	**497**	**12**	**359**	**:**	**195**	**39**	**30**	**157**	**598**
1990	**13,898**	**803**	**170**	**2,744**	**25**	**2,797**	**2,199**	**83**	**1,933**	**:**	**1,111**	**147**	**135**	**280**	**1,470**
1994	16,714	773	195	3,161	27	4,522	2,915	154	1,948	:	982	177	110	258	1,492
1995	18,436	839	203	3,589	39	5,179	2,975	144	2,092	:	1,125	143	146	304	1,652
1996	21,152	924	232	4,297	49	6,301	3,099	154	2,341	:	1,237	179	151	323	1,864
1997	23,583	986	207	4,596	36	7,287	3,327	204	2,507	:	1,463	183	187	349	2,251
1998	26,786	1,166	225	5,217	48	8,369	3,858	229	2,709	:	1,679	195	249	504	2,336
1999	29,300	1,174	233	5,522	51	9,472	4,282	257	2,904	54	1,792	226	268	507	2,553
2000	**32,494**	**1,319**	**301**	**5,939**	**83**	**11,205**	**4,592**	**265**	**3,085**	**68**	**1,985**	**281**	**238**	**539**	**2,591**
2001	33,072	1,338	257	6,072	98	12,064	4,500	267	2,994	97	2,123	318	241	490	2,212
2002	**31,270**	**1,232**	**265**	**6,091**	**89**	**11,440**	**4,164**	**271**	**2,660**	**100**	**1,842**	**282**	**224**	**478**	**2,130**
Annual variation (%)															
98/97	13.5	18.2	8.4	13.5	32.2	14.8	15.9	12.2	8.0	:	14.7	6.2	33.2	44.4	3.8
99/98	9.3	0.6	3.8	5.8	5.7	13.1	11.0	12.6	7.1	:	6.7	15.7	7.6	0.6	9.2
00/99	10.9	12.3	29.2	7.5	63.1	18.2	7.2	2.9	6.2	25.9	10.7	24.3	-11.0	6.3	1.4
01/00	1.7	1.4	-14.7	2.2	18.0	7.6	-2.0	0.7	-2.9	42.2	6.9	13.1	1.0	-9.1	-14.6
02/01	-5.4	-7.9	3.2	0.3	-9.2	-5.1	-7.4	1.4	-11.1	2.8	-13.2	-11.1	-6.9	-2.5	-3.6
Share (%)															
1980	**100.0**	**6.3**	**1.1**	**24.1**	**0.2**	**11.3**	**14.9**	**0.3**	**10.7**	**:**	**5.8**	**1.1**	**0.9**	**4.7**	**18.0**
1990	**100.0**	**5.7**	**1.2**	**19.7**	**0.1**	**20.1**	**15.8**	**0.5**	**13.9**	**:**	**7.9**	**1.0**	**0.9**	**2.0**	**10.5**
1996	100.0	4.3	1.0	20.3	0.2	29.7	14.6	0.7	11.0	:	5.8	0.8	0.7	1.5	8.8
1997	100.0	4.1	0.8	19.4	0.1	30.8	14.1	0.8	10.6	:	6.2	0.7	0.7	1.4	9.5
1998	100.0	4.3	0.8	19.4	0.1	31.2	14.4	0.8	10.1	:	6.2	0.7	0.9	1.8	8.7
1999	100.0	4.0	0.7	18.8	0.1	32.3	14.6	0.8	9.9	0.1	6.1	0.7	0.9	1.7	8.7
2000	**100.0**	**4.0**	**0.9**	**18.2**	**0.2**	**34.4**	**14.1**	**0.8**	**9.4**	**0.2**	**6.1**	**0.8**	**0.7**	**1.6**	**7.9**
2001	100.0	4.0	0.7	18.3	0.2	36.4	13.6	0.8	9.0	0.2	6.4	0.9	0.7	1.4	6.6
2002	**100.0**	**3.9**	**0.8**	**19.4**	**0.2**	**36.5**	**13.3**	**0.8**	**8.5**	**0.3**	**5.8**	**0.9**	**0.7**	**1.5**	**6.8**

(1) Luxembourg with Belgium until 31.12.1998.

Years	Extra EU	Norway	Switzerland	USSR/Russia(1)	Candid. countries	USA	Canada	China	Japan	Hong Kong	Mediterr. Basin	Latin America	OPEC	DAE	ACP
EXPORTS Value (Mio ECU/Euro)															
1980	1,231	62	149	37	:	189	31	2	30	5	214	81	68	24	194
1990	2,376	175	249	55	:	622	105	31	137	15	179	71	77	79	470
1994	3,031	151	281	49	107	785	103	15	114	34	323	200	127	149	474
1995	3,467	177	347	53	158	807	98	26	136	41	349	278	113	211	508
1996	3,765	184	317	92	203	854	91	26	141	46	340	299	112	234	616
1997	4,053	178	269	68	263	987	134	42	133	49	378	385	115	216	698
1998	3,980	167	268	39	274	1,065	112	18	114	52	350	401	114	171	738
1999	3,865	156	255	13	291	1,140	102	30	100	59	329	309	113	170	648
2000	5,205	331	269	17	452	1,525	145	53	119	78	454	416	159	244	838
2001	5,429	303	274	23	463	1,539	147	60	109	86	481	489	209	248	912
2002	5,528	210	295	32	530	1,571	140	81	94	69	503	368	196	300	1,019
Annual variation (%)															
98/97	-1.7	-6.4	-0.2	-43.1	4.2	7.8	-16.7	-58.1	-14.7	6.9	-7.3	4.1	-0.7	-20.5	5.8
99/98	-2.8	-6.2	-4.7	-66.9	6.2	7.0	-8.4	73.9	-11.9	13.1	-6.0	-22.8	-0.6	-0.8	-12.2
00/99	34.6	112.0	5.4	30.2	55.2	33.7	42.0	72.8	19.4	30.9	38.0	34.3	40.3	43.4	29.4
01/00	4.3	-8.5	2.0	36.1	2.3	0.8	1.6	14.0	-8.8	11.1	5.9	17.6	31.8	1.6	8.7
02/01	1.8	-30.5	7.4	40.9	14.5	2.0	-4.9	34.0	-13.2	-19.4	4.5	-24.6	-6.1	20.9	11.7
Share (%)															
1980	100.0	5.0	12.1	3.0	:	15.3	2.4	0.1	2.4	0.4	17.3	6.6	5.4	1.9	15.7
1990	100.0	7.3	10.4	2.3	:	26.1	4.4	1.2	5.7	0.6	7.5	2.9	3.2	3.3	19.7
1996	100.0	4.8	8.4	2.4	5.3	22.6	2.4	0.6	3.7	1.2	9.0	7.9	2.9	6.2	16.3
1997	100.0	4.3	6.6	1.6	6.4	24.3	3.3	1.0	3.2	1.2	9.3	9.5	2.8	5.3	17.2
1998	100.0	4.1	6.7	0.9	6.8	26.7	2.8	0.4	2.8	1.3	8.8	10.0	2.8	4.3	18.5
1999	100.0	4.0	6.6	0.3	7.5	29.4	2.6	0.7	2.5	1.5	8.5	8.0	2.9	4.3	16.7
2000	100.0	6.3	5.1	0.3	8.6	29.2	2.7	1.0	2.2	1.4	8.7	7.9	3.0	4.6	16.1
2001	100.0	5.5	5.0	0.4	8.5	28.3	2.7	1.1	2.0	1.5	8.8	9.0	3.8	4.5	16.7
2002	100.0	3.8	5.3	0.5	9.5	28.4	2.5	1.4	1.7	1.2	9.0	6.6	3.5	5.4	18.4
IMPORTS Value (Mio ECU/Euro)															
1980	3,480	32	222	113	:	729	60	5	203	5	501	326	1,321	45	252
1990	5,406	202	416	37	:	759	147	53	509	24	545	689	1,322	271	828
1994	6,034	360	377	162	303	821	60	145	648	28	603	672	1,306	433	714
1995	6,495	313	384	198	224	834	77	151	561	32	573	791	1,234	638	842
1996	6,572	217	379	241	192	870	92	183	599	30	572	722	1,218	591	974
1997	7,328	226	391	258	241	975	95	220	740	28	554	933	1,336	614	973
1998	7,498	355	362	162	387	939	115	267	939	37	516	964	886	668	981
1999	8,206	530	366	187	475	1,059	89	280	1,012	36	559	929	1,074	793	957
2000	10,764	760	352	248	764	1,279	117	382	1,061	32	792	1,098	2,090	873	1,626
2001	10,982	831	406	436	994	1,601	100	351	815	29	838	1,330	1,906	674	1,579
2002	9,380	476	362	358	1,085	883	82	345	721	24	815	1,377	1,639	564	1,284
Annual variation (%)															
98/97	2.3	57.1	-7.2	-37.1	60.7	-3.6	20.8	21.6	26.8	28.3	-6.9	3.4	-33.6	8.6	0.8
99/98	9.4	49.2	0.9	15.2	22.7	12.7	-22.6	4.9	7.8	-1.1	8.4	-3.6	21.2	18.7	-2.4
00/99	31.1	43.4	-3.7	32.5	60.6	20.7	31.4	36.3	4.7	-12.0	41.5	18.1	94.4	10.1	70.0
01/00	2.0	9.3	15.1	75.7	30.1	25.1	-14.3	-8.2	-23.1	-8.4	5.8	21.1	-8.7	-22.7	-2.9
02/01	-14.5	-42.6	-10.6	-17.8	9.2	-44.8	-18.4	-1.8	-11.5	-19.1	-2.8	3.5	-14.0	-16.4	-18.7
Share (%)															
1980	100.0	0.9	6.3	3.2	:	20.9	1.7	0.1	5.8	0.1	14.3	9.3	37.9	1.2	7.2
1990	100.0	3.7	7.6	0.6	:	14.0	2.7	0.9	9.4	0.4	10.0	12.7	24.4	5.0	15.3
1996	100.0	3.3	5.7	3.6	2.9	13.2	1.4	2.7	9.1	0.4	8.7	10.9	18.5	8.9	14.8
1997	100.0	3.0	5.3	3.5	3.2	13.2	1.3	2.9	10.1	0.3	7.5	12.7	18.2	8.3	13.2
1998	100.0	4.7	4.8	2.1	5.1	12.5	1.5	3.5	12.5	0.4	6.8	12.8	11.8	8.9	13.0
1999	100.0	6.4	4.4	2.2	5.7	12.9	1.0	3.4	12.3	0.4	6.8	11.3	13.0	9.6	11.6
2000	100.0	7.0	3.2	2.3	7.0	11.8	1.0	3.5	9.8	0.2	7.3	10.1	19.4	8.1	15.1
2001	100.0	7.5	3.6	3.9	9.0	14.5	0.9	3.1	7.4	0.2	7.6	12.1	17.3	6.1	14.3
2002	100.0	5.0	3.8	3.8	11.5	9.4	0.8	3.6	7.6	0.2	8.6	14.6	17.4	6.0	13.6

(1) Relates to the external trade with the USSR until 1991 and to the external trade with Russia from 1992 onwards.

FINLAND

TRADE BALANCE (BN ECU/euro)

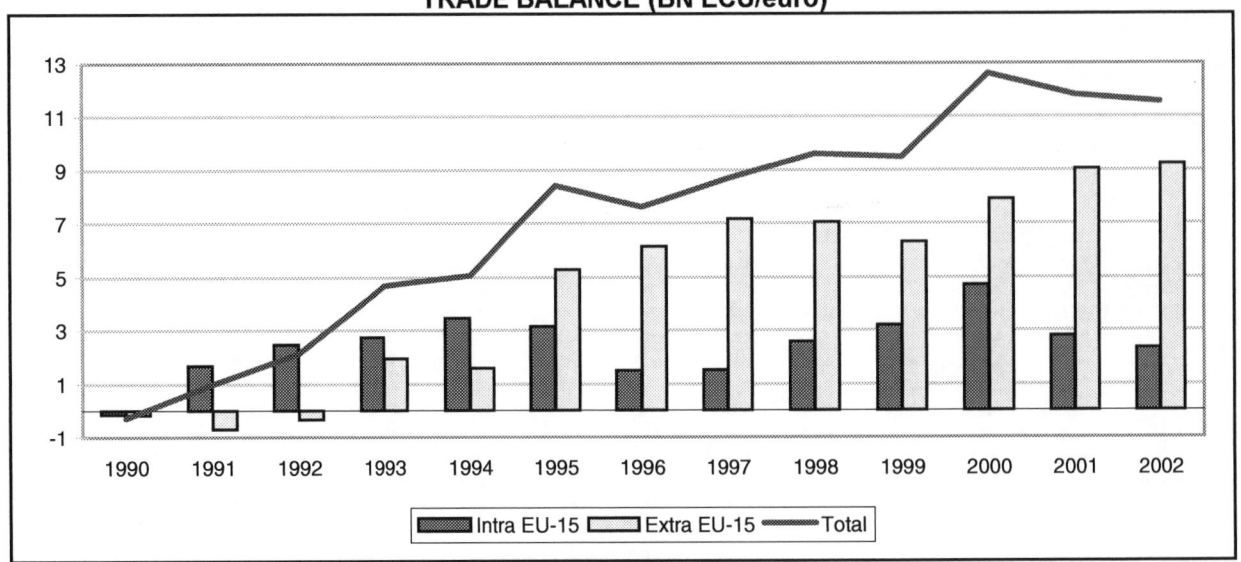

INTRA-EU (BN ECU/euro)

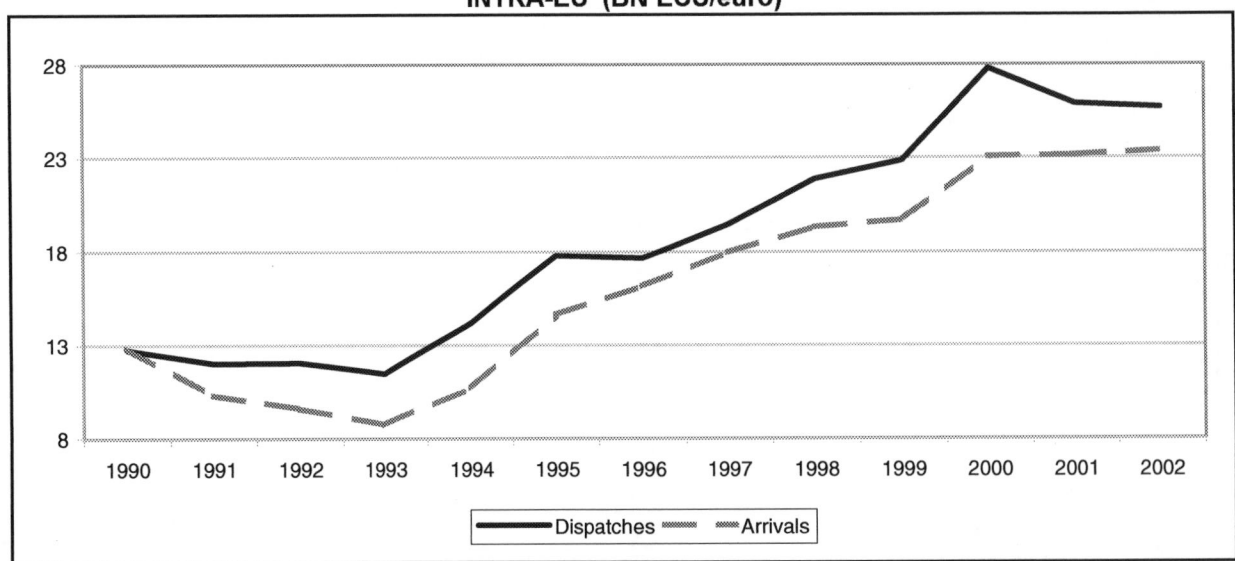

EXTRA-EU (BN ECU/euro)

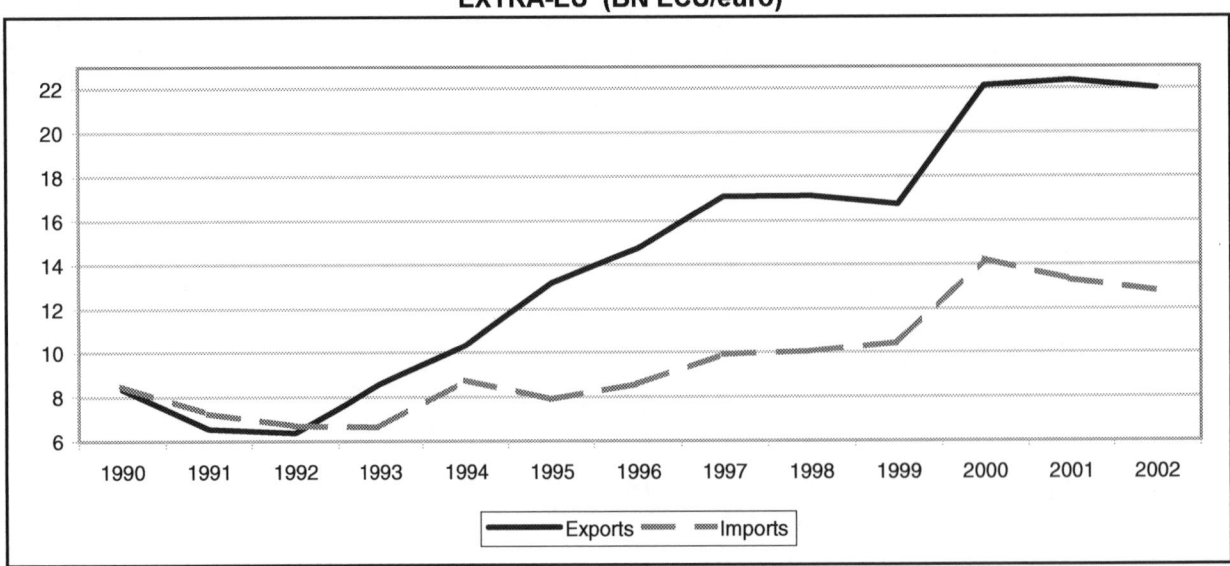

FINLAND

TRADE BALANCE

INTRA-EU

Value (Mio ECU/Euro)

Year	Intra EU	B[1]	DK	D	EL	E	F	IRL	I	L	NL	A	P	S	UK
														Partner	
1980	**455**	**-41**	**86**	**-334**	**47**	**-11**	**117**	**40**	**-24**	**:**	**151**	**-58**	**-20**	**324**	**179**
1990	**-132**	**-151**	**29**	**-1,092**	**43**	**211**	**353**	**11**	**-343**	**:**	**201**	**-62**	**-87**	**188**	**567**
1991	1,688	-2	80	-187	38	316	359	5	-100	:	308	32	-112	415	536
1992	2,474	-11	103	93	72	273	529	-5	125	:	353	33	-76	470	515
1993	2,728	-38	176	41	67	289	425	-1	55	:	426	35	-38	607	686
1994	3,457	-10	248	385	89	299	442	-31	-41	:	567	38	-54	624	901
1995	3,140	179	-176	374	102	459	501	-33	-1	:	5	-8	-34	-300	1,204
1996	1,500	22	-263	157	111	393	374	8	-75	:	-49	16	-4	-157	1,176
1997	1,519	31	-284	-13	152	449	419	54	75	:	-159	56	19	-562	1,553
1998	2,569	68	-522	70	355	566	744	-11	382	:	-134	212	106	-708	1,654
1999	3,191	178	-639	342	296	664	884	-121	481	11	-262	258	132	-446	1,772
2000	**4,698**	**167**	**-915**	**661**	**369**	**825**	**1,247**	**-39**	**1,103**	**-3**	**-351**	**290**	**153**	**-440**	**2,226**
2001	2,787	353	-133	729	283	531	588	-14	474	-3	556	96	98	384	2,306
2002	**2,331**	**244**	**-928**	**-224**	**333**	**746**	**717**	**24**	**342**	**-20**	**-398**	**-30**	**151**	**-1,062**	**2,436**

EXTRA-EU

Value (Mio ECU/Euro)

Year	Extra EU	Norway	Switzerland	Russia[2]	Candid. countries	USA	Canada	China	Japan	Hong Kong	Mediterr. Basin	Latin America	OPEC	DAE	ACP
									Partner						
1980	**-1,481**	**189**	**-16**	**-568**	**:**	**-332**	**-34**	**35**	**-297**	**-29**	**240**	**-98**	**-438**	**-36**	**11**
1990	**-149**	**-74**	**3**	**610**	**:**	**-227**	**62**	**-33**	**-1,073**	**-17**	**314**	**-68**	**206**	**-22**	**76**
1991	-696	-177	48	-596	:	-73	30	6	-783	6	302	-60	120	105	31
1992	-336	-5	8	-529	:	91	18	23	-662	27	283	-117	74	59	-43
1993	1,942	-109	2	-260	:	424	47	0	-568	81	415	-37	406	433	-9
1994	1,598	-142	25	-368	:	306	30	70	-748	159	352	-98	297	565	40
1995	5,285	-28	40	199	1,030	872	103	190	-335	331	500	220	639	1,050	196
1996	6,140	-82	-24	191	1,519	1,166	55	171	-164	428	524	106	830	1,380	8
1997	7,175	88	-61	511	2,040	825	187	252	-454	609	677	76	834	1,731	-3
1998	7,057	303	65	413	2,263	992	158	728	-677	349	821	333	534	668	266
1999	6,313	82	194	-528	2,268	1,469	183	441	-675	367	956	313	437	797	277
2000	**7,927**	**-90**	**322**	**-1,296**	**2,401**	**1,960**	**214**	**527**	**-525**	**377**	**1,259**	**754**	**1,068**	**884**	**383**
2001	9,046	103	192	-605	1,326	3,178	211	398	-206	380	758	688	961	1,264	216
2002	**9,225**	**42**	**262**	**-420**	**1,792**	**2,943**	**269**	**269**	**-24**	**471**	**879**	**518**	**1,225**	**1,020**	**240**

(1) Luxembourg with Belgium until 31.12.1998.
(2) Relates to the external trade with the USSR until 1991 and to the external trade with Russia from 1992 onwards.

FINLAND

INTRA-EU

Year	Intra EU	B[1]	DK	D	EL	E	F	IRL	I	L	NL	A	P	S	UK
					**EXPORTS / DISPATCHES**										
					Value (Mio ECU/Euro)										
1980	5,689	147	355	1,080	:	:	462	62	244	:	434	75	:	1,682	1,147
1990	12,738	431	725	2,604	120	450	1,257	119	641	:	877	228	161	2,944	2,180
1994	14,203	526	845	3,265	142	557	1,219	115	721	:	1,241	258	124	2,671	2,519
1995	17,787	844	880	3,938	155	723	1,337	147	814	:	1,227	256	136	2,913	3,076
1996	17,651	808	975	3,914	165	684	1,420	192	824	:	1,278	281	157	3,469	3,294
1997	19,457	840	1,119	4,033	211	788	1,572	299	1,083	:	1,506	344	205	3,611	3,660
1998	21,889	967	1,088	4,623	396	972	1,986	244	1,488	:	1,759	522	256	3,683	3,652
1999	22,888	1,019	1,116	5,180	341	1,060	2,092	202	1,495	27	1,712	554	277	3,945	3,615
2000	27,780	1,105	1,257	6,246	441	1,286	2,577	283	2,173	34	1,973	648	315	4,643	4,548
2001	25,925	1,181	1,173	5,958	364	1,197	2,220	378	1,751	38	1,880	509	267	4,091	4,637
2002	25,717	1,295	1,156	5,674	401	1,223	2,196	365	1,624	38	2,202	480	289	4,180	4,592
					Annual variation (%)										
98/97	12.5	15.0	-2.8	14.6	87.4	23.3	26.3	-18.5	37.4	:	16.8	51.8	24.7	2.0	-0.2
99/98	4.5	5.3	2.6	12.0	-13.9	8.9	5.3	-16.8	0.4	:	-2.7	6.1	8.2	7.1	-0.9
00/99	21.3	8.4	12.6	20.5	29.2	21.3	23.1	39.6	45.4	27.7	15.2	16.9	14.0	17.6	25.7
01/00	-6.6	6.8	-6.7	-4.6	-17.4	-6.8	-13.8	33.5	-19.4	12.4	-4.7	-21.5	-15.3	-11.8	1.9
02/01	-0.7	9.6	-1.4	-4.7	10.1	2.1	-1.0	-3.2	-7.2	0.2	17.1	-5.5	8.3	2.1	-0.9
					Share (%)										
1980	100.0	2.5	6.2	18.9	:	:	8.1	1.0	4.2	:	7.6	1.3	:	29.5	20.1
1990	100.0	3.3	5.6	20.4	0.9	3.5	9.8	0.9	5.0	:	6.8	1.7	1.2	23.1	17.1
1996	100.0	4.5	5.5	22.1	0.9	3.8	8.0	1.0	4.6	:	7.2	1.5	0.8	19.6	18.6
1997	100.0	4.3	5.7	20.7	1.0	4.0	8.0	1.5	5.5	:	7.7	1.7	1.0	18.5	18.8
1998	100.0	4.4	4.9	21.1	1.8	4.4	9.0	1.1	6.7	:	8.0	2.3	1.1	16.8	16.6
1999	100.0	4.4	4.8	22.6	1.4	4.6	9.1	0.8	6.5	0.1	7.4	2.4	1.2	17.2	15.7
2000	100.0	3.9	4.5	22.4	1.5	4.6	9.2	1.0	7.8	0.1	7.1	2.3	1.1	16.7	16.3
2001	100.0	4.5	4.5	22.9	1.4	4.6	8.5	1.4	6.7	0.1	7.2	1.9	1.0	15.7	17.8
2002	100.0	5.0	4.4	22.0	1.5	4.7	8.5	1.4	6.3 ⊙	0.1	8.5	1.8	1.1	16.2	17.8
					IMPORTS / ARRIVALS										
					Value (Mio ECU/Euro)										
1980	5,232	188	269	1,417	:	:	343	22	256	:	285	134	:	1,354	965
1990	12,870	582	696	3,696	78	239	904	108	984	:	676	289	248	2,756	1,614
1994	10,746	536	597	2,880	53	258	777	146	763	:	673	220	178	2,047	1,618
1995	14,647	665	1,055	3,564	53	264	837	180	815	:	1,222	264	170	3,213	1,872
1996	16,150	785	1,239	3,757	55	290	1,046	184	898	:	1,326	265	162	3,626	2,118
1997	17,938	809	1,404	4,045	60	340	1,152	245	1,008	:	1,665	288	186	4,172	2,108
1998	19,320	899	1,610	4,553	42	406	1,242	255	1,105	:	1,893	310	149	4,391	1,998
1999	19,697	842	1,755	4,839	46	396	1,208	323	1,013	16	1,974	297	144	4,391	1,843
2000	23,082	938	2,172	5,585	72	461	1,331	322	1,071	37	2,325	358	163	5,083	2,322
2001	23,137	828	1,306	5,230	81	666	1,632	392	1,277	41	1,324	413	169	3,707	2,332
2002	23,387	1,051	2,084	5,898	68	478	1,479	342	1,282	59	2,600	510	139	5,242	2,155
					Annual variation (%)										
98/97	7.7	11.1	14.6	12.5	-30.0	19.6	7.7	4.1	9.7	:	13.7	7.4	-19.6	5.2	-5.2
99/98	1.9	-6.4	9.0	6.2	8.9	-2.6	-2.7	26.8	-8.3	:	4.2	-4.2	-3.2	0.0	-7.7
00/99	17.1	11.4	23.7	15.4	57.3	16.5	10.1	-0.4	5.6	133.5	17.7	20.7	12.5	15.7	25.9
01/00	0.2	-11.7	-39.8	-6.3	12.5	44.4	22.6	21.6	19.3	10.6	-43.0	15.3	4.2	-27.0	0.4
02/01	1.0	26.8	59.6	12.7	-15.9	-28.2	-9.3	-12.7	0.3	42.7	96.4	23.5	-18.1	41.4	-7.5
					Share (%)										
1980	100.0	3.5	5.1	27.0	:	:	6.5	0.4	4.9	:	5.4	2.5	:	25.8	18.4
1990	100.0	4.5	5.4	28.7	0.6	1.8	7.0	0.8	7.6	:	5.2	2.2	1.9	21.4	12.5
1996	100.0	4.8	7.6	23.2	0.3	1.7	6.4	1.1	5.5	:	8.2	1.6	1.0	22.4	13.1
1997	100.0	4.5	7.8	22.5	0.3	1.8	6.4	1.3	5.6	:	9.2	1.6	1.0	23.2	11.7
1998	100.0	4.6	8.3	23.5	0.2	2.1	6.4	1.3	5.7	:	9.7	1.6	0.7	22.7	10.3
1999	100.0	4.2	8.9	24.5	0.2	2.0	6.1	1.6	5.1	0.0	10.0	1.5	0.7	22.2	9.3
2000	100.0	4.0	9.4	24.1	0.3	1.9	5.7	1.3	4.6	0.1	10.0	1.5	0.7	22.0	10.0
2001	100.0	3.5	5.6	22.6	0.3	2.8	7.0	1.6	5.5	0.1	5.7	1.7	0.7	16.0	10.0
2002	100.0	4.4	8.9	25.2	0.2	2.0	6.3	1.4	5.4	0.2	11.1	2.1	0.5	22.4	9.2

(1) Luxembourg with Belgium until 31.12.1998.

FINLAND

EXTRA-EU

ears	Extra EU	Norway	Switzerland	USSR/Russia[1]	Candid. countries	USA	Canada	China	Japan	Hong Kong	Mediterr. Basin	Latin America	OPEC	DAE	ACP
EXPORTS															
Value (Mio ECU/Euro)															
980	4,295	425	162	1,791	:	321	48	57	68	9	487	211	451	60	87
990	8,348	627	370	2,630	:	1,213	229	120	297	96	472	289	355	376	182
994	10,352	787	366	1,287	1,689	1,793	167	367	521	295	486	381	392	1,180	128
995	13,168	870	393	1,481	1,842	2,045	210	440	781	425	602	564	685	1,669	269
996	14,737	929	379	1,985	2,334	2,599	184	465	838	524	641	478	941	1,927	151
997	17,112	1,083	368	2,663	3,057	2,571	352	647	690	673	853	580	980	2,226	139
998	17,137	1,286	488	2,334	3,462	2,883	272	1,133	575	482	974	800	665	1,307	441
999	16,747	1,121	600	1,624	3,493	3,179	323	986	669	478	1,129	752	534	1,446	460
000	22,136	1,339	776	2,174	4,370	3,758	360	1,462	862	499	1,478	1,279	1,200	1,905	579
001	22,352	1,241	650	2,832	3,561	4,708	392	1,265	906	472	1,035	1,146	1,131	1,936	447
002	22,025	1,176	661	3,154	3,819	4,273	402	1,226	1,057	539	1,165	993	1,348	1,643	426
Annual variation (%)															
98/97	0.1	18.7	32.5	-12.3	13.2	12.1	-22.4	75.0	-16.5	-28.4	14.1	37.7	-32.1	-41.2	217.1
99/98	-2.2	-12.8	23.0	-30.4	0.8	10.2	18.4	-12.9	16.2	-0.8	15.9	-5.9	-19.7	10.5	4.2
00/99	32.1	19.4	29.3	33.9	25.1	18.2	11.6	48.2	28.8	4.4	30.8	70.0	124.6	31.7	26.0
01/00	0.9	-7.3	-16.1	30.2	-18.5	25.2	8.7	-13.5	5.0	-5.3	-29.9	-10.4	-5.7	1.6	-22.8
02/01	-1.4	-5.1	1.6	11.3	7.2	-9.2	2.7	-3.0	16.7	14.1	12.5	-13.2	19.1	-15.1	-4.7
Share (%)															
1980	100.0	9.8	3.7	41.7	:	7.4	1.1	1.3	1.5	0.2	11.3	4.9	10.5	1.3	2.0
1990	100.0	7.5	4.4	31.5	:	14.5	2.7	1.4	3.5	1.1	5.6	3.4	4.2	4.5	2.1
1996	100.0	6.3	2.5	13.4	15.8	17.6	1.2	3.1	5.6	3.5	4.3	3.2	6.3	13.0	1.0
1997	100.0	6.3	2.1	15.5	17.8	15.0	2.0	3.7	4.0	3.9	4.9	3.3	5.7	13.0	0.8
1998	100.0	7.5	2.8	13.6	20.2	16.8	1.5	6.6	3.3	2.8	5.6	4.6	3.8	7.6	2.5
1999	100.0	6.6	3.5	9.6	20.8	18.9	1.9	5.8	3.9	2.8	6.7	4.4	3.1	8.6	2.7
2000	100.0	6.0	3.5	9.8	19.7	16.9	1.6	6.6	3.8	2.2	6.6	5.7	5.4	8.6	2.6
2001	100.0	5.5	2.9	12.6	15.9	21.0	1.7	5.6	4.0	2.1	4.6	5.1	5.0	8.6	2.0
2002	100.0	5.3	3.0	14.3	17.3	19.3	1.8	5.5	4.8	2.4	5.2	4.5	6.1	7.4	1.9
IMPORTS															
Value (Mio ECU/Euro)															
1980	5,776	236	178	2,359	:	653	82	22	365	38	247	309	890	96	76
1990	8,498	702	367	2,020	:	1,440	167	153	1,369	113	158	357	149	398	106
1994	8,754	929	341	1,655	714	1,486	137	297	1,269	137	134	479	95	616	88
1995	7,883	899	354	1,282	812	1,174	107	250	1,117	94	102	344	46	619	73
1996	8,596	1,011	402	1,793	814	1,433	129	294	1,001	96	117	371	111	547	143
1997	9,937	995	429	2,151	1,017	1,745	164	395	1,144	64	176	504	146	495	142
1998	10,080	983	423	1,921	1,199	1,891	114	406	1,252	132	153	466	132	640	175
1999	10,435	1,040	406	2,151	1,225	1,711	140	545	1,344	111	173	440	97	649	182
2000	14,210	1,429	454	3,471	1,968	1,798	146	935	1,387	122	219	524	132	1,021	197
2001	13,306	1,137	458	3,437	2,235	1,530	181	867	1,112	92	277	458	170	673	231
2002	12,800	1,134	400	3,574	2,027	1,330	134	957	1,081	68	286	476	124	622	186
Annual variation (%)															
98/97	1.4	-1.2	-1.3	-10.7	17.8	8.3	-30.2	2.6	9.4	105.7	-12.8	-7.5	-9.9	29.2	23.4
99/98	3.5	5.7	-4.0	11.9	2.1	-9.5	22.5	34.3	7.3	-16.2	12.6	-5.7	-26.1	1.5	4.1
00/99	36.1	37.4	11.8	61.3	60.6	5.1	3.9	71.5	3.1	9.8	26.8	19.2	35.0	57.2	8.0
01/00	-6.3	-20.4	0.8	-0.9	13.5	-14.9	23.9	-7.2	-19.8	-24.1	26.5	-12.7	29.1	-34.0	17.4
02/01	-3.8	-0.2	-12.7	3.9	-9.2	-13.0	-25.8	10.3	-2.7	-26.1	3.2	3.9	-27.0	-7.4	-19.5
Share (%)															
1980	100.0	4.0	3.0	40.8	:	11.3	1.4	0.3	6.3	0.6	4.2	5.3	15.4	1.6	1.3
1990	100.0	8.2	4.3	23.7	:	16.9	1.9	1.8	16.1	1.3	1.8	4.2	1.7	4.6	1.2
1996	100.0	11.7	4.6	20.8	9.4	16.6	1.4	3.4	11.6	1.1	1.3	4.3	1.2	6.3	1.6
1997	100.0	10.0	4.3	21.6	10.2	17.5	1.6	3.9	11.5	0.6	1.7	5.0	1.4	4.9	1.4
1998	100.0	9.7	4.1	19.0	11.8	18.7	1.1	4.0	12.4	1.3	1.5	4.6	1.3	6.3	1.7
1999	100.0	9.9	3.8	20.6	11.7	16.3	1.3	5.2	12.8	1.0	1.6	4.2	0.9	6.2	1.7
2000	100.0	10.0	3.1	24.4	13.8	12.6	1.0	6.5	9.7	0.8	1.5	3.6	0.9	7.1	1.3
2001	100.0	8.5	3.4	25.8	16.7	11.4	1.4	6.5	8.3	0.6	2.0	3.4	1.2	5.0	1.7
2002	100.0	8.8	3.1	27.9	15.8	10.3	1.0	7.4	8.4	0.5	2.2	3.7	0.9	4.8	1.4

(1) Relates to the external trade with the USSR until 1991 and to the external trade with Russia from 1992 onwards.

SWEDEN

TRADE BALANCE (BN ECU/euro)

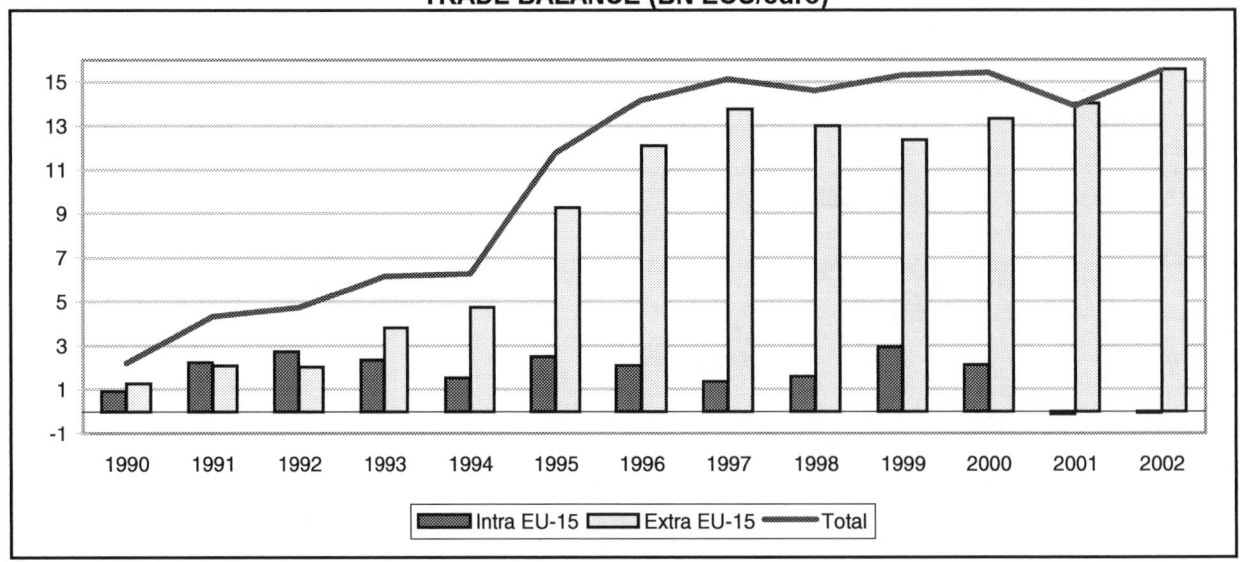

Legend: Intra EU-15 · Extra EU-15 · Total

INTRA-EU (BN ECU/euro)

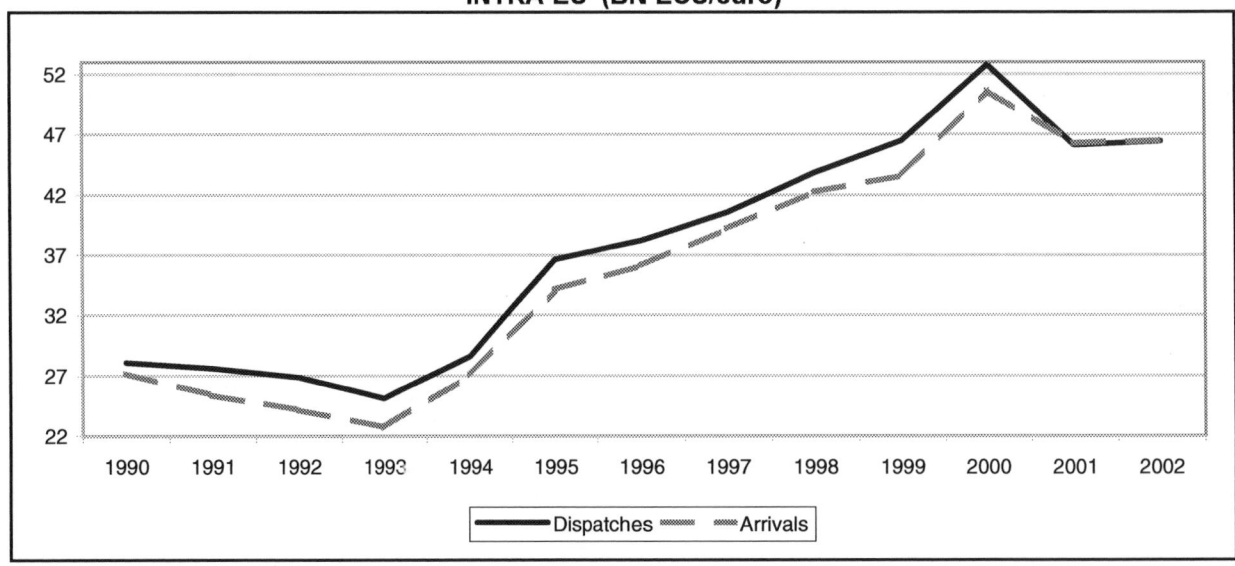

Legend: Dispatches · Arrivals

EXTRA-EU (BN ECU/euro)

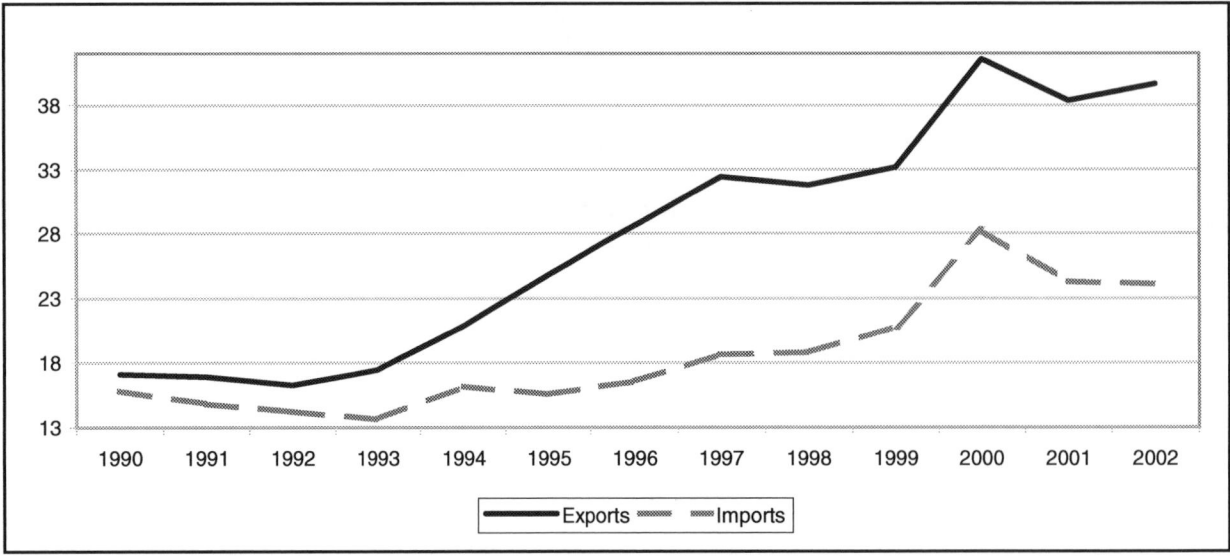

Legend: Exports · Imports

TRADE BALANCE

INTRA-EU

Value (Mio ECU/Euro)

Year	Intra EU	B[1]	DK	D	EL	E	F	IRL	I	L	NL	A	P	FIN	UK
1980	**-1,222**	**-66**	**406**	**-1,416**	**53**	**77**	**259**	**45**	**172**	**:**	**169**	**-32**	**-5**	**-243**	**-641**
1990	**922**	**401**	**-159**	**-2,099**	**76**	**616**	**283**	**-22**	**292**	**:**	**637**	**-20**	**-303**	**122**	**1,098**
1991	2,238	389	80	-802	100	557	501	9	409	:	675	61	-259	-297	815
1992	2,712	467	149	-682	103	423	521	-35	419	:	760	131	-242	-154	850
1993	2,342	502	221	-414	159	276	334	-27	278	:	463	103	-161	-318	927
1994	1,527	916	507	-1,501	193	320	29	-30	195	:	797	97	-226	-434	664
1995	2,503	733	252	-2,137	192	623	349	-315	508	:	-32	110	-96	-159	747
1996	2,078	1,105	290	-1,856	213	811	178	-184	493	:	80	151	-32	506	1,109
1997	1,369	856	338	-2,264	287	822	59	-210	563	:	-18	24	-40	899	1,135
1998	1,583	1,154	681	-2,424	376	995	162	-365	731	:	-107	-39	96	956	936
1999	2,944	1,078	208	-2,132	483	1,669	353	-423	890	-48	79	238	113	734	1,244
2000	**2,120**	**1,225**	**-237**	**-2,690**	**524**	**1,647**	**487**	**-654**	**1,336**	**-58**	**-527**	**211**	**130**	**755**	**1,781**
2001	-135	1,313	-624	-3,032	298	992	-132	-792	778	-99	-174	81	63	850	1,469
2002	**-55**	**1,373**	**-970**	**-3,954**	**255**	**985**	**607**	**-721**	**752**	**-87**	**33**	**86**	**99**	**1,175**	**1,155**

EXTRA-EU

Value (Mio ECU/Euro)

Year	Extra EU	Norway	Switzerland	Russia[2]	Candid. countries	USA	Canada	China	Japan	Hong Kong	Mediterr. Basin	Latin America	OPEC	DAE	ACP
1980	**-467**	**927**	**56**	**-235**	**:**	**-560**	**22**	**-17**	**-430**	**-125**	**456**	**-187**	**-1,477**	**43**	**-190**
1990	**1,277**	**365**	**234**	**-261**	**:**	**180**	**372**	**-149**	**-1,240**	**-174**	**609**	**141**	**495**	**-35**	**91**
1991	2,094	670	263	-133	:	174	315	-242	-1,149	-157	592	147	737	162	33
1992	2,025	993	150	-168	:	211	280	-236	-1,067	-112	338	243	403	127	106
1993	3,811	1,108	60	-84	:	262	281	-173	-771	-39	766	249	393	473	350
1994	4,743	1,556	36	-206	:	404	302	-68	-676	13	739	328	213	795	-8
1995	9,274	1,164	129	-50	601	1,515	417	25	87	212	915	318	220	1,225	45
1996	12,087	1,663	275	-129	1,205	2,094	449	248	598	379	1,304	674	458	1,754	153
1997	13,764	1,868	301	6	1,713	2,356	469	25	300	603	1,538	1,158	705	2,019	91
1998	13,014	2,259	380	93	1,608	2,643	536	220	-160	416	1,688	1,289	725	903	517
1999	12,358	1,587	133	-313	2,052	3,221	538	90	-237	210	2,087	1,458	444	750	432
2000	**13,312**	**840**	**125**	**-357**	**1,714**	**3,362**	**812**	**185**	**-98**	**388**	**2,570**	**1,782**	**495**	**1,141**	**535**
2001	14,031	1,556	205	150	642	4,759	634	-79	566	193	1,333	1,209	673	906	511
2002	**15,558**	**2,338**	**263**	**-207**	**400**	**6,145**	**779**	**-316**	**236**	**173**	**1,282**	**470**	**1,284**	**903**	**666**

(1) Luxembourg with Belgium until 31.12.1998.
(2) Relates to the external trade with the USSR until 1991 and to the external trade with Russia from 1992 onwards.

SWEDEN

INTRA-EU

Year	Intra EU	B[1]	DK	D	EL	E	F	IRL	I	L	NL	A	P	FIN	UK
						Partner									

EXPORTS / DISPATCHES
Value (Mio ECU/Euro)

Year	Intra EU	B[1]	DK	D	EL	E	F	IRL	I	L	NL	A	P	FIN	UK
1980	12,572	722	1,877	2,735	:	:	1,299	121	847	:	1,062	306	:	1,397	2,208
1990	28,120	1,692	3,054	6,374	207	1,135	2,423	253	2,097	:	2,398	599	279	3,056	4,552
1994	28,599	2,420	3,377	6,430	284	922	2,454	330	1,867	:	2,554	633	202	2,298	4,830
1995	36,629	2,462	3,632	7,246	271	1,154	2,915	336	2,053	:	3,097	666	281	2,708	5,335
1996	38,196	2,948	4,197	7,802	291	1,462	3,109	434	2,185	:	3,697	728	344	3,446	6,368
1997	40,549	2,946	4,494	8,096	386	1,578	3,358	457	2,317	:	4,065	741	351	3,907	6,701
1998	43,815	3,403	4,423	8,281	466	1,973	3,749	548	2,675	:	4,332	786	471	3,934	6,800
1999	46,495	3,382	4,434	8,472	581	2,719	4,155	523	2,888	28	4,735	832	507	4,059	7,423
2000	52,772	3,916	5,087	10,064	656	2,678	4,831	591	3,566	30	4,588	921	522	4,796	8,660
2001	46,132	3,789	4,817	8,761	418	2,050	4,230	458	2,935	20	4,131	812	419	4,404	7,325
2002	46,419	3,977	5,029	8,533	383	2,064	4,332	423	2,991	35	4,459	852	435	4,694	6,899

Annual variation (%)

Year	Intra EU	B[1]	DK	D	EL	E	F	IRL	I	L	NL	A	P	FIN	UK
98/97	8.0	15.5	-1.5	2.2	20.5	25.0	11.6	19.8	15.4	:	6.5	6.1	33.9	0.6	1.4
99/98	6.1	-0.6	0.2	2.3	24.6	37.7	10.8	-4.6	7.9	:	9.2	5.8	7.7	3.1	9.1
00/99	13.5	15.8	14.7	18.7	12.9	-1.4	16.2	13.1	23.4	7.3	-3.1	10.6	2.9	18.1	16.6
01/00	-12.5	-3.2	-5.3	-12.9	-36.2	-23.4	-12.4	-22.5	-17.7	-34.2	-9.9	-11.8	-19.8	-8.1	-15.4
02/01	0.6	4.9	4.4	-2.6	-8.4	0.7	2.4	-7.6	1.9	78.6	7.9	5.0	3.7	6.5	-5.8

Share (%)

Year	Intra EU	B[1]	DK	D	EL	E	F	IRL	I	L	NL	A	P	FIN	UK
1980	100.0	5.7	14.9	21.7	:	:	10.3	0.9	6.7	:	8.4	2.4	:	11.1	17.5
1990	100.0	6.0	10.8	22.6	0.7	4.0	8.6	0.8	7.4	:	8.5	2.1	0.9	10.8	16.1
1996	100.0	7.7	10.9	20.4	0.7	3.8	8.1	1.1	5.7	:	9.6	1.9	0.8	9.0	16.6
1997	100.0	7.2	11.0	19.9	0.9	3.8	8.2	1.1	5.7	:	10.0	1.8	0.8	9.6	16.5
1998	100.0	7.7	10.0	18.8	1.0	4.5	8.5	1.2	6.1	:	9.8	1.7	1.0	8.9	15.5
1999	100.0	7.2	9.5	18.2	1.2	5.8	8.9	1.1	6.2	0.0	10.1	1.7	1.0	8.7	15.9
2000	100.0	7.4	9.6	19.0	1.2	5.0	9.1	1.1	6.7	0.0	8.6	1.7	0.9	9.0	16.4
2001	100.0	8.2	10.4	18.9	0.9	4.4	9.1	0.9	6.3	0.0	8.9	1.7	0.9	9.5	15.8
2002	100.0	8.5	10.8	18.3	0.8	4.4	9.3	0.9	6.4	0.0	9.6	1.8	0.9	10.1	14.8

IMPORTS / ARRIVALS
Value (Mio ECU/Euro)

Year	Intra EU	B[1]	DK	D	EL	E	F	IRL	I	L	NL	A	P	FIN	UK
1980	13,781	788	1,469	4,023	:	:	1,038	75	674	:	893	338	:	1,638	2,844
1990	27,198	1,292	3,213	8,473	131	519	2,140	275	1,805	:	1,760	619	582	2,934	3,454
1994	27,071	1,504	2,869	7,931	91	601	2,424	360	1,672	:	1,757	536	429	2,732	4,165
1995	34,125	1,728	3,380	9,383	79	531	2,565	652	1,545	:	3,128	556	377	2,867	4,589
1996	36,118	1,843	3,907	9,658	77	651	2,931	617	1,692	:	3,617	577	376	2,941	5,260
1997	39,180	2,090	4,155	10,359	99	756	3,299	667	1,754	:	4,083	717	392	3,008	5,567
1998	42,232	2,250	3,741	10,705	89	979	3,587	913	1,944	:	4,439	825	375	2,978	5,863
1999	43,551	2,303	4,225	10,605	97	1,050	3,802	946	1,998	77	4,656	594	394	3,325	6,178
2000	50,652	2,691	5,324	12,754	132	1,031	4,345	1,245	2,230	88	5,116	711	392	4,042	6,880
2001	46,267	2,477	5,441	11,793	120	1,058	4,362	1,249	2,157	119	4,305	731	356	3,554	5,857
2002	46,474	2,603	5,999	12,487	128	1,079	3,725	1,144	2,239	123	4,426	766	336	3,519	5,744

Annual variation (%)

Year	Intra EU	B[1]	DK	D	EL	E	F	IRL	I	L	NL	A	P	FIN	UK
98/97	7.7	7.6	-9.9	3.3	-9.6	29.4	8.7	36.9	10.8	:	8.7	15.0	-4.2	-1.0	5.3
99/98	3.1	2.3	12.9	-0.9	8.9	7.2	5.9	3.5	2.7	:	4.8	-28.0	5.0	11.6	5.3
00/99	16.3	16.8	25.9	20.2	35.7	-1.8	14.2	31.6	11.5	15.5	9.8	19.6	-0.3	21.5	11.3
01/00	-8.6	-7.9	2.1	-7.5	-9.1	2.6	0.4	0.3	-3.2	34.5	-15.8	2.8	-9.2	-12.0	-14.8
02/01	0.4	5.1	10.2	5.8	6.7	2.0	-14.5	-8.4	3.8	3.1	2.8	4.8	-5.7	-0.9	-1.9

Share (%)

Year	Intra EU	B[1]	DK	D	EL	E	F	IRL	I	L	NL	A	P	FIN	UK
1980	100.0	5.7	10.6	29.1	:	:	7.5	0.5	4.8	:	6.4	2.4	:	11.8	20.6
1990	100.0	4.7	11.8	31.1	0.4	1.9	7.8	1.0	6.6	:	6.4	2.2	2.1	10.7	12.6
1996	100.0	5.1	10.8	26.7	0.2	1.8	8.1	1.7	4.6	:	10.0	1.5	1.0	8.1	14.5
1997	100.0	5.3	10.6	26.4	0.2	1.9	8.4	1.7	4.4	:	10.4	1.8	1.0	7.6	14.2
1998	100.0	5.3	8.8	25.3	0.2	2.3	8.4	2.1	4.6	:	10.5	1.9	0.8	7.0	13.8
1999	100.0	5.2	9.7	24.3	0.2	2.4	8.7	2.1	4.5	0.1	10.6	1.3	0.9	7.6	14.1
2000	100.0	5.3	10.5	25.1	0.2	2.0	8.5	2.4	4.4	0.1	10.0	1.4	0.7	7.9	13.5
2001	100.0	5.3	11.7	25.4	0.2	2.2	9.4	2.7	4.6	0.2	9.3	1.5	0.7	7.6	12.6
2002	100.0	5.6	12.9	26.8	0.2	2.3	8.0	2.4	4.8	0.2	9.5	1.6	0.7	7.5	12.3

[1] Luxembourg with Belgium until 31.12.1998.

EXTRA-EU

Years						Partner									
	Extra EU	Norway	Switzerland	USSR/ Russia(1)	Candid. countries	USA	Canada	China	Japan	Hong Kong	Mediterr. Basin	Latin America	OPEC	DAE	ACP

EXPORTS
Value (Mio ECU/Euro)

Years	Extra EU	Norway	Switzerland	USSR/Russia(1)	Candid. countries	USA	Canada	China	Japan	Hong Kong	Mediterr. Basin	Latin America	OPEC	DAE	ACP
1980	9,163	2,176	506	302	:	1,191	243	59	254	47	1,241	622	1,145	443	383
1990	17,094	3,751	1,056	331	:	3,897	659	200	948	173	1,031	819	1,006	1,046	281
1994	20,900	4,200	865	342	1,509	4,123	571	845	1,374	301	1,098	1,037	945	1,905	210
1995	24,870	4,350	1,076	488	2,006	4,574	638	852	1,806	443	1,232	1,011	855	2,503	198
1996	28,680	5,631	1,181	571	2,644	5,520	661	1,097	2,137	632	1,627	1,358	1,249	3,055	319
1997	32,426	6,116	1,189	806	3,557	6,052	736	1,079	2,127	902	1,932	1,904	1,519	3,635	272
1998	31,797	6,463	1,299	684	3,867	6,468	775	1,389	1,587	725	2,167	2,020	1,363	2,457	730
1999	33,154	6,217	1,150	468	4,554	7,307	772	1,466	1,912	487	2,584	2,203	1,084	2,441	581
2000	41,568	7,116	1,101	601	5,256	8,919	1,085	2,043	2,640	712	3,274	2,898	1,789	3,534	746
2001	38,330	7,250	1,104	925	4,101	8,918	916	1,729	2,480	444	2,032	2,113	1,924	2,794	813
2002	39,638	7,622	1,163	1,172	4,366	9,885	1,045	1,506	2,082	423	1,992	1,442	2,128	2,697	891

Annual variation (%)

Years	Extra EU	Norway	Switzerland	USSR/Russia(1)	Candid. countries	USA	Canada	China	Japan	Hong Kong	Mediterr. Basin	Latin America	OPEC	DAE	ACP
98/97	-1.9	5.6	9.2	-15.1	8.7	6.8	5.3	28.7	-25.3	-19.5	12.1	6.1	-10.3	-32.4	168.2
99/98	4.2	-3.8	-11.5	-31.5	17.7	12.9	-0.4	5.5	20.5	-32.8	19.2	9.0	-20.4	-0.6	-20.4
00/99	25.3	14.4	-4.2	28.2	15.4	22.0	40.4	39.3	38.0	46.1	26.7	31.5	65.0	44.7	28.5
01/00	-7.7	1.8	0.2	54.0	-21.9	0.0	-15.5	-15.3	-6.0	-37.5	-37.9	-27.0	7.5	-20.9	8.9
02/01	3.4	5.1	5.3	26.6	6.4	10.8	14.1	-12.9	-16.0	-4.7	-1.9	-31.7	10.6	-3.4	9.6

Share (%)

Years	Extra EU	Norway	Switzerland	USSR/Russia(1)	Candid. countries	USA	Canada	China	Japan	Hong Kong	Mediterr. Basin	Latin America	OPEC	DAE	ACP
1980	100.0	23.7	5.5	3.2	:	13.0	2.6	0.6	2.7	0.5	13.5	6.7	12.4	4.8	4.1
1990	100.0	21.9	6.1	1.9	:	22.7	3.8	1.1	5.5	1.0	6.0	4.7	5.8	6.1	1.6
1996	100.0	19.6	4.1	1.9	9.2	19.2	2.3	3.8	7.4	2.2	5.6	4.7	4.3	10.6	1.1
1997	100.0	18.8	3.6	2.4	10.9	18.6	2.2	3.3	6.5	2.7	5.9	5.8	4.6	11.2	0.8
1998	100.0	20.3	4.0	2.1	12.1	20.3	2.4	4.3	4.9	2.2	6.8	6.3	4.2	7.7	2.2
1999	100.0	18.7	3.4	1.4	13.7	22.0	2.3	4.4	5.7	1.4	7.7	6.6	3.2	7.3	1.7
2000	100.0	17.1	2.6	1.4	12.6	21.4	2.6	4.9	6.3	1.7	7.8	6.9	4.3	8.5	1.7
2001	100.0	18.9	2.8	2.4	10.6	23.2	2.3	4.5	6.4	1.1	5.3	5.5	5.0	7.2	2.1
2002	100.0	19.2	2.9	2.9	11.0	24.9	2.6	3.8	5.2	1.0	5.0	3.6	5.3	6.8	2.2

IMPORTS
Value (Mio ECU/Euro)

Years	Extra EU	Norway	Switzerland	USSR/Russia(1)	Candid. countries	USA	Canada	China	Japan	Hong Kong	Mediterr. Basin	Latin America	OPEC	DAE	ACP
1980	9,630	1,249	450	536	:	1,751	222	77	685	172	785	808	2,622	400	573
1990	15,817	3,386	822	593	:	3,717	287	349	2,188	347	421	678	511	1,081	190
1994	16,157	2,644	829	548	1,246	3,719	269	913	2,050	287	359	708	732	1,109	218
1995	15,596	3,186	947	537	1,405	3,059	222	827	1,719	231	317	693	635	1,278	153
1996	16,593	3,968	907	700	1,439	3,426	212	849	1,538	253	323	684	792	1,300	165
1997	18,663	4,248	888	800	1,844	3,696	267	1,053	1,827	299	393	746	814	1,616	181
1998	18,783	4,204	919	591	2,259	3,825	239	1,169	1,747	309	480	732	637	1,554	213
1999	20,795	4,629	1,017	782	2,502	4,086	234	1,376	2,150	277	497	745	641	1,691	148
2000	28,257	6,276	976	958	3,543	5,557	273	1,859	2,738	323	704	1,116	1,295	2,393	211
2001	24,300	5,694	899	775	3,459	4,159	282	1,809	1,914	251	699	903	1,250	1,888	302
2002	24,080	5,283	899	1,379	3,966	3,741	266	1,822	1,846	251	710	973	844	1,794	226

Annual variation (%)

Years	Extra EU	Norway	Switzerland	USSR/Russia(1)	Candid. countries	USA	Canada	China	Japan	Hong Kong	Mediterr. Basin	Latin America	OPEC	DAE	ACP
98/97	0.6	-1.0	3.4	-26.1	22.5	3.4	-10.3	10.9	-4.3	3.4	21.8	-1.8	-21.6	-3.8	17.7
99/98	10.7	10.1	10.6	32.3	10.7	6.8	-2.0	17.6	23.0	-10.2	3.6	1.8	0.5	8.8	-30.3
00/99	35.8	35.5	-4.0	22.5	41.5	35.9	16.4	35.1	27.3	16.8	41.6	49.6	102.0	41.4	42.6
01/00	-14.0	-9.2	-7.9	-19.0	-2.3	-25.1	3.3	-2.6	-30.0	-22.4	-0.6	-19.0	-3.4	-21.0	42.7
02/01	-0.9	-7.2	0.0	77.9	14.6	-10.0	-5.5	0.7	-3.5	0.0	1.5	7.6	-32.4	-5.0	-25.1

Share (%)

Years	Extra EU	Norway	Switzerland	USSR/Russia(1)	Candid. countries	USA	Canada	China	Japan	Hong Kong	Mediterr. Basin	Latin America	OPEC	DAE	ACP
1980	100.0	12.9	4.6	5.5	:	18.1	2.3	0.7	7.1	1.7	8.1	8.3	27.2	4.1	5.9
1990	100.0	21.4	5.1	3.7	:	23.4	1.8	2.2	13.8	2.1	2.6	4.2	3.2	6.8	1.1
1996	100.0	23.9	5.4	4.2	8.6	20.6	1.2	5.1	9.2	1.5	1.9	4.1	4.7	7.8	0.9
1997	100.0	22.7	4.7	4.2	9.8	19.8	1.4	5.6	9.7	1.5	2.1	3.9	4.3	8.6	0.9
1998	100.0	22.3	4.8	3.1	12.0	20.3	1.2	6.2	9.3	1.6	2.5	3.8	3.3	8.2	1.1
1999	100.0	22.2	4.8	3.7	12.0	19.6	1.1	6.6	10.3	1.3	2.3	3.5	3.0	8.1	0.7
2000	100.0	22.2	3.4	3.3	12.5	19.6	0.9	6.5	9.6	1.1	2.4	3.9	4.5	8.4	0.7
2001	100.0	23.4	3.6	3.1	14.2	17.1	1.1	7.4	7.8	1.0	2.8	3.7	5.1	7.7	1.2
2002	100.0	21.9	3.7	5.7	16.4	15.5	1.1	7.5	7.6	1.0	2.9	4.0	3.5	7.4	0.9

(1) Relates to the external trade with the USSR until 1991 and to the external trade with Russia from 1992 onwards.

UNITED KINGDOM

TRADE BALANCE (BN ECU/euro)

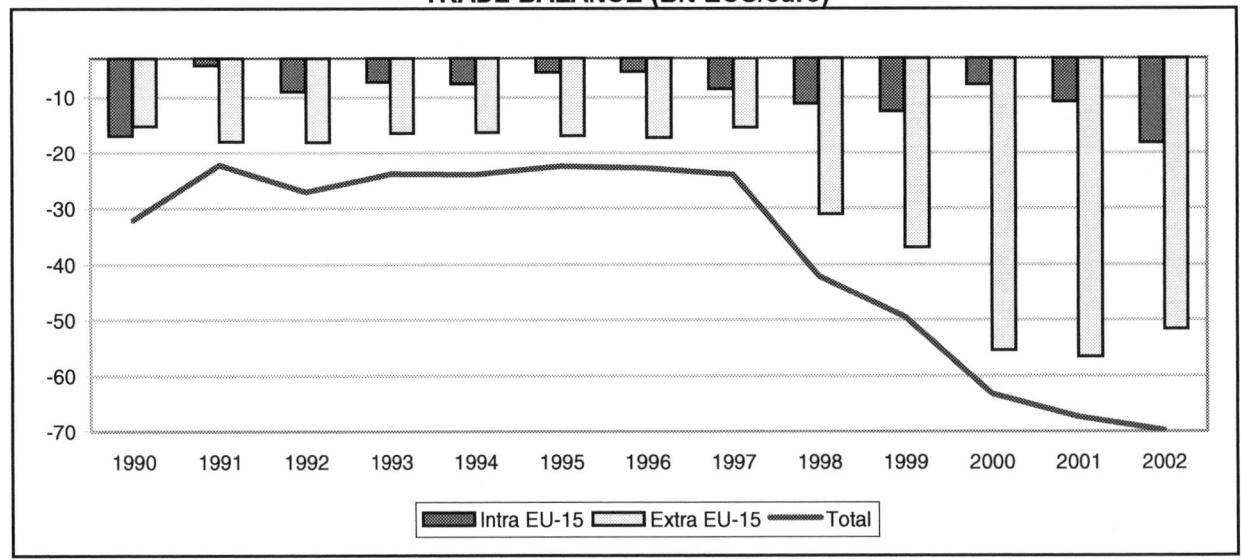

Legend: Intra EU-15 ▨ Extra EU-15 ▢ Total ▬

INTRA-EU (BN ECU/euro)

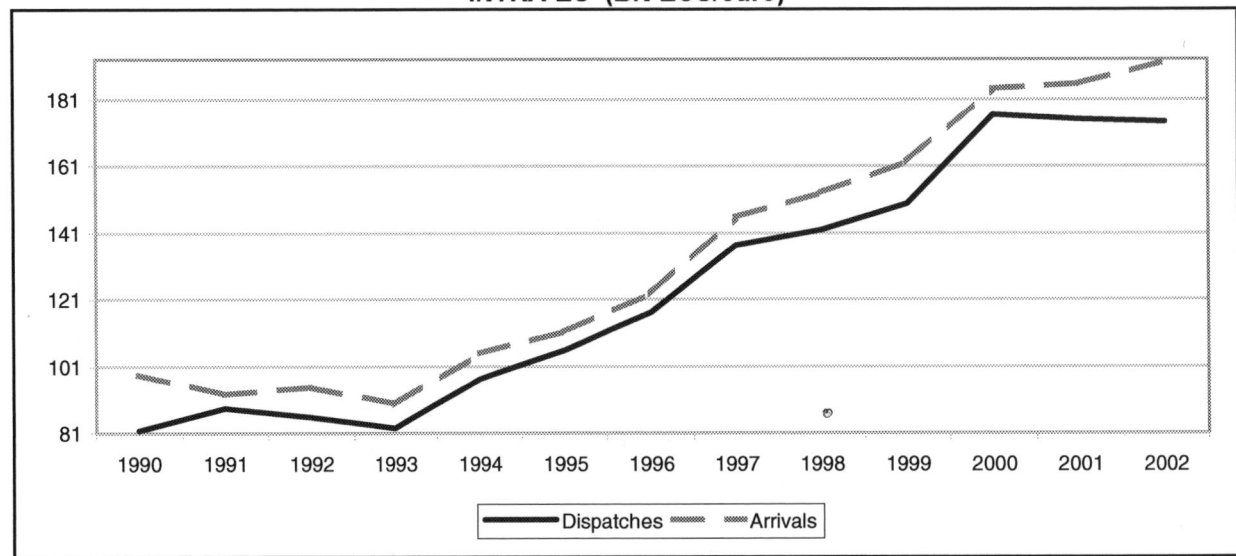

Legend: Dispatches ▬ Arrivals ▬▬

EXTRA-EU (BN ECU/euro)

Legend: Exports ▬ Imports ▬▬

TRADE BALANCE

INTRA-EU

Value (Mio ECU/Euro)

Year	Intra EU	B[(1)]	DK	D	EL	E	F	IRL	I	L	NL	A	P	FIN	S
1980	**1,624**	**315**	**-87**	**-703**	**168**	**-154**	**-196**	**1,547**	**-667**	**:**	**1,584**	**-66**	**86**	**-434**	**233**
1990	**-16,860**	**175**	**-1,195**	**-9,467**	**391**	**1,145**	**-1,395**	**1,112**	**-1,840**	**:**	**-3,065**	**-417**	**-175**	**-1,015**	**-1,115**
1991	-4,315	870	-1,168	-4,703	408	2,317	622	1,209	-537	:	-1,234	-258	66	-976	-931
1992	-8,994	180	-1,139	-5,739	528	1,991	-1,149	781	-1,080	:	-1,070	-241	-4	-913	-1,138
1993	-7,270	296	-612	-4,850	701	1,346	-1,685	1,033	-836	:	-935	-87	165	-934	-873
1994	-7,596	364	-475	-5,943	735	1,811	-1,960	1,704	-936	:	-750	-6	-32	-1,175	-933
1995	-5,512	272	-101	-6,867	763	2,109	-1,407	1,322	-799	:	966	189	40	-945	-596
1996	-5,454	-85	-170	-7,187	951	2,105	-721	2,359	-2,040	:	1,337	83	32	-956	-444
1997	-8,480	-1,233	-395	-7,609	938	2,083	-2,004	3,124	-2,674	:	1,940	-418	-55	-1,381	-455
1998	-11,192	-1,734	-218	-7,320	999	1,872	-2,019	3,001	-2,401	:	-915	-423	-149	-1,329	-371
1999	-12,528	-993	-333	-9,664	1,133	2,268	-1,990	4,008	-2,862	75	-98	-497	-204	-1,445	-963
2000	**-7,759**	**-733**	**-185**	**-9,179**	**1,279**	**3,461**	**486**	**4,878**	**-2,240**	**152**	**-817**	**-494**	**-162**	**-2,090**	**-1,262**
2001	-10,767	-3,005	-594	-8,354	1,018	2,225	-357	7,548	-2,867	-28	-873	-1,083	-44	-2,150	-1,151
2002	**-18,106**	**-2,747**	**-199**	**-14,333**	**967**	**256**	**-577**	**10,057**	**-3,771**	**-233**	**-2,189**	**-1,693**	**-280**	**-2,061**	**-768**

EXTRA-EU

Value (Mio ECU/Euro)

Year	Extra EU	Norway	Switzerland	Russia[(2)]	Candid. countries	USA	Canada	China	Japan	Hong Kong	Mediterr. Basin	Latin America	OPEC	DAE	ACP
1980	**-5,216**	**-1,093**	**703**	**-557**	**:**	**-3,687**	**-1,001**	**-5**	**-1,999**	**-445**	**1,924**	**-65**	**-112**	**-1,153**	**2,121**
1990	**-15,155**	**-3,818**	**-2,496**	**-601**	**:**	**-4,023**	**-254**	**-1,060**	**-5,808**	**68**	**914**	**-1,173**	**2,979**	**-1,489**	**264**
1991	-17,897	-4,002	-2,122	-889	:	-5,004	-313	-1,682	-6,421	213	1,501	-943	3,414	-1,594	344
1992	-18,008	-3,180	-2,708	:	:	-3,365	-558	-2,094	-6,762	472	1,098	-975	3,415	-1,352	251
1993	-16,464	-3,200	-2,954	-269	1,225	-2,160	77	-2,563	-6,927	969	1,853	-620	3,074	-1,338	523
1994	-16,287	-2,137	-3,067	-380	487	-3,360	25	-3,195	-7,767	1,064	1,669	-893	2,493	-1,043	84
1995	-16,886	-2,785	-2,760	-456	1,029	-3,760	-890	-3,572	-7,100	1,216	2,066	-1,217	2,773	-1,467	-3
1996	-17,232	-3,448	-2,027	-518	2,029	-4,989	-662	-4,687	-5,853	1,622	2,307	-1,348	4,396	-2,433	-388
1997	-15,428	-3,060	-2,154	-620	2,670	-6,799	-310	-6,018	-7,118	2,408	3,198	43	7,757	-3,106	165
1998	-30,982	-1,113	-2,597	-972	1,832	-7,945	-304	-7,233	-9,367	1,159	2,534	-70	5,121	-7,852	20
1999	-36,950	-2,252	-3,062	-1,360	634	-2,253	-341	-8,332	-8,758	641	1,818	-1,547	2,527	-8,315	-1,148
2000	**-55,418**	**-5,828**	**-2,885**	**-2,190**	**1,276**	**-1,368**	**-370**	**-11,687**	**-10,848**	**674**	**2,086**	**-2,979**	**2,044**	**-11,183**	**-2,897**
2001	-56,549	-6,096	208	-2,416	-1,514	-4,081	-962	-12,785	-9,052	1,113	666	-3,009	3,039	-7,800	-5,049
2002	**-51,667**	**-5,707**	**-505**	**-2,427**	**-3,051**	**300**	**-513**	**-14,448**	**-7,542**	**729**	**10**	**-3,382**	**2,873**	**-7,153**	**-5,091**

(1)   Luxembourg with Belgium until 31.12.1998.
(2)   Relates to the external trade with the USSR until 1991 and to the external trade with Russia from 1992 onwards.

UNITED KINGDOM

INTRA-EU

Year	Partner														
	Intra EU	B(1)	DK	D	EL	E	F	IRL	I	L	NL	A	P	FIN	S

EXPORTS / DISPATCHES
Value (Mio ECU/Euro)

Year	Intra EU	B(1)	DK	D	EL	E	F	IRL	I	L	NL	A	P	FIN	S
1980	40,929	4,354	1,722	8,506	374	1,179	6,094	4,439	3,167	:	6,410	460	648	874	2,704
1990	81,698	7,867	1,954	17,900	950	4,987	15,024	7,359	7,564	:	10,500	956	1,439	1,431	3,769
1994	97,304	9,448	2,330	22,080	1,197	6,451	17,347	9,188	8,661	:	12,059	1,251	1,625	1,559	4,108
1995	105,945	9,627	2,506	23,693	1,261	7,124	17,829	9,659	9,107	:	14,240	1,256	1,757	1,872	4,662
1996	117,268	10,066	2,720	24,895	1,425	8,120	20,371	11,061	9,626	:	16,008	1,497	2,034	2,123	5,222
1997	137,233	11,676	3,006	29,043	1,528	9,461	23,301	13,889	11,399	:	19,572	1,615	2,482	2,160	6,211
1998	141,805	12,102	3,068	29,807	1,542	10,359	23,917	14,681	12,448	:	18,827	1,731	2,515	2,103	6,401
1999	149,637	13,238	3,127	30,555	1,757	11,147	25,294	16,999	11,790	189	20,238	1,755	2,584	2,043	6,040
2000	176,370	15,714	3,773	36,712	2,004	13,310	29,692	20,841	13,635	364	24,010	1,832	2,669	2,334	6,801
2001	175,045	14,888	3,620	36,873	1,767	13,024	29,953	22,589	13,172	443	22,830	1,907	2,494	2,493	6,236
2002	174,245	15,832	4,351	34,397	1,909	13,318	29,474	25,142	13,418	564	21,918	1,993	2,416	2,276	6,117

Annual variations (%)

Year	Intra EU	B(1)	DK	D	EL	E	F	IRL	I	L	NL	A	P	FIN	S
98/97	3.3	3.6	2.0	2.6	0.9	9.4	2.6	5.6	9.2	:	-3.8	7.1	1.3	-2.6	3.0
99/98	5.5	9.3	1.9	2.5	13.9	7.6	5.7	15.7	-5.2	:	7.4	1.3	2.7	-2.8	-5.6
00/99	17.8	18.6	20.6	20.1	14.0	19.3	17.3	22.5	15.6	92.8	18.6	4.3	3.2	14.2	12.5
01/00	-0.7	-5.2	-4.0	0.4	-11.8	-2.1	0.8	8.3	-3.3	21.5	-4.9	4.1	-6.5	6.8	-8.2
02/01	-0.4	6.3	20.1	-6.7	8.0	2.2	-1.5	11.3	1.8	27.3	-3.9	4.4	-3.1	-8.7	-1.9

Share (%)

Year	Intra EU	B(1)	DK	D	EL	E	F	IRL	I	L	NL	A	P	FIN	S
1980	100.0	10.6	4.2	20.7	0.9	2.8	14.8	10.8	7.7	:	15.6	1.1	1.5	2.1	6.6
1990	100.0	9.6	2.3	21.9	1.1	6.1	18.3	9.0	9.2	:	12.8	1.1	1.7	1.7	4.6
1996	100.0	8.5	2.3	21.2	1.2	6.9	17.3	9.4	8.2	:	13.6	1.2	1.7	1.8	4.4
1997	100.0	8.5	2.1	21.1	1.1	6.8	16.9	10.1	8.3	:	14.2	1.1	1.8	1.5	4.5
1998	100.0	8.5	2.1	21.0	1.0	7.3	16.8	10.3	8.7	:	13.2	1.2	1.7	1.4	4.5
1999	100.0	8.8	2.0	20.4	1.1	7.4	16.9	11.3	7.8	0.1	13.5	1.1	1.7	1.3	4.0
2000	100.0	8.9	2.1	20.8	1.1	7.5	16.8	11.8	7.7	0.2	13.6	1.0	1.5	1.3	3.8
2001	100.0	8.5	2.0	21.0	1.0	7.4	17.1	12.9	7.5	0.2	13.0	1.0	1.4	1.4	3.5
2002	100.0	9.0	2.4	19.7	1.0	7.6	16.9	14.4	7.7	0.3	12.5	1.1	1.3	1.3	3.5

IMPORTS / ARRIVALS
Value (Mio ECU/Euro)

Year	Intra EU	B(1)	DK	D	EL	E	F	IRL	I	L	NL	A	P	FIN	S
1980	39,305	4,039	1,809	9,209	206	1,333	6,290	2,893	3,834	:	4,826	526	562	1,308	2,470
1990	98,559	7,692	3,149	27,367	559	3,842	16,419	6,246	9,404	:	13,564	1,373	1,614	2,446	4,884
1994	104,900	9,084	2,805	28,023	462	4,640	19,307	7,484	9,597	:	12,809	1,257	1,656	2,734	5,042
1995	111,457	9,355	2,607	30,560	498	5,015	19,236	8,337	9,906	:	13,274	1,067	1,717	2,818	5,258
1996	122,722	10,151	2,890	32,082	474	6,015	21,092	8,702	11,666	:	14,670	1,414	2,002	3,079	5,666
1997	145,714	12,910	3,401	36,652	589	7,378	25,305	10,766	14,073	:	17,632	2,033	2,537	3,540	6,666
1998	152,998	13,836	3,286	37,127	542	8,487	25,937	11,680	14,849	:	19,742	2,155	2,665	3,432	6,772
1999	162,164	14,231	3,460	40,219	624	8,880	27,284	12,992	14,652	114	20,336	2,252	2,788	3,488	7,003
2000	184,129	16,446	3,957	45,890	724	9,849	29,205	15,963	15,874	212	24,827	2,326	2,831	4,424	8,063
2001	185,812	17,894	4,214	45,226	749	10,798	30,310	15,041	16,038	471	23,704	2,991	2,538	4,644	7,387
2002	192,351	18,580	4,549	48,730	942	13,062	30,051	15,085	17,189	796	24,107	3,686	2,696	4,337	6,885

Annual variations (%)

Year	Intra EU	B(1)	DK	D	EL	E	F	IRL	I	L	NL	A	P	FIN	S
98/97	4.9	7.1	-3.3	1.2	-8.0	15.0	2.4	8.4	5.5	:	11.9	5.9	5.0	-3.0	1.5
99/98	5.9	2.8	5.2	8.3	15.1	4.6	5.1	11.2	-1.3	:	3.0	4.5	4.6	1.6	3.4
00/99	13.5	15.5	14.3	14.1	16.0	10.9	7.0	22.8	8.3	85.6	22.0	3.2	1.5	26.8	15.1
01/00	0.9	8.8	6.4	-1.4	3.3	9.6	3.7	-5.7	1.0	122.2	-4.5	28.5	-10.3	4.9	-8.3
02/01	3.5	3.8	7.9	7.7	25.7	20.9	-0.8	0.2	7.1	69.0	1.7	23.2	6.2	-6.6	-6.7

Share (%)

Year	Intra EU	B(1)	DK	D	EL	E	F	IRL	I	L	NL	A	P	FIN	S
1980	100.0	10.2	4.6	23.4	0.5	3.3	16.0	7.3	9.7	:	12.2	1.3	1.4	3.3	6.2
1990	100.0	7.8	3.1	27.7	0.5	3.8	16.6	6.3	9.5	:	13.7	1.3	1.6	2.4	4.9
1996	100.0	8.2	2.3	26.1	0.3	4.9	17.1	7.0	9.5	:	11.9	1.1	1.6	2.5	4.6
1997	100.0	8.8	2.3	25.1	0.4	5.0	17.3	7.3	9.6	:	12.1	1.3	1.7	2.4	4.5
1998	100.0	9.0	2.1	24.2	0.3	5.5	16.9	7.6	9.7	:	12.9	1.4	1.7	2.2	4.4
1999 ·	100.0	8.7	2.1	24.8	0.3	5.4	16.8	8.0	9.0	0.0	12.5	1.3	1.7	2.1	4.3
2000	100.0	8.9	2.1	24.9	0.3	5.3	15.8	8.6	8.6	0.1	13.4	1.2	1.5	2.4	4.3
2001	100.0	9.6	2.2	24.3	0.4	5.8	16.3	8.0	8.6	0.2	12.7	1.6	1.3	2.4	3.9
2002	100.0	9.6	2.3	25.3	0.4	6.7	15.6	7.8	8.9	0.4	12.5	1.9	1.4	2.2	3.5

(1) Luxembourg with Belgium until 31.12.1998.

EXTRA-EU

Years	Partner														
	Extra EU	Norway	Switzerland	USSR/ Russia[1]	Candid. countries	USA	Canada	China	Japan	Hong Kong	Mediterr. Basin	Latin America	OPEC	DAE	ACP

EXPORTS
Value (Mio ECU/Euro)

Years	Extra EU	Norway	Switzerland	USSR/Russia[1]	Candid. countries	USA	Canada	China	Japan	Hong Kong	Mediterr. Basin	Latin America	OPEC	DAE	ACP
1980	41,131	1,319	4,844	760	:	7,750	1,262	282	993	904	5,551	1,709	7,552	2,308	4,476
1990	60,760	1,781	3,296	839	:	18,118	2,662	654	3,672	1,769	3,940	1,811	6,814	6,232	4,439
1994	73,181	2,510	2,963	834	3,770	21,724	2,451	1,085	3,826	2,814	4,865	2,730	6,110	9,939	2,655
1995	75,975	2,282	3,149	937	4,776	21,744	2,160	979	4,520	2,996	5,493	2,568	6,460	10,406	2,769
1996	86,337	2,474	4,128	1,106	6,171	23,766	2,378	905	5,185	3,454	6,338	3,007	8,356	11,190	2,842
1997	110,029	3,825	4,196	1,678	7,973	30,277	3,108	1,322	6,050	4,600	7,985	4,451	12,483	13,868	3,430
1998	102,554	4,037	4,095	1,345	7,810	32,156	3,228	1,271	4,790	3,910	7,695	4,513	9,786	10,735	5,533
1999	105,727	3,214	4,547	789	7,408	37,477	3,884	1,838	5,080	3,543	7,616	3,695	7,576	11,429	5,321
2000	132,666	3,443	5,326	1,066	10,301	48,146	5,758	2,391	6,044	4,380	9,823	4,149	8,970	13,738	5,862
2001	129,461	3,018	6,562	1,413	9,233	46,964	5,212	2,744	5,971	4,311	8,337	4,299	9,315	13,134	6,289
2002	122,017	2,860	4,858	1,528	9,812	44,390	5,014	2,364	5,761	3,766	8,738	4,025	8,816	12,012	6,225

Annual variation(%)

Years	Extra EU	Norway	Switzerland	USSR/Russia[1]	Candid. countries	USA	Canada	China	Japan	Hong Kong	Mediterr. Basin	Latin America	OPEC	DAE	ACP
98/97	-6.7	5.5	-2.4	-19.8	-2.0	6.2	3.8	-3.8	-20.8	-14.9	-3.6	1.3	-21.6	-22.5	61.3
99/98	3.0	-20.3	11.0	-41.3	-5.1	16.5	20.3	44.5	6.0	-9.3	-1.0	-18.1	-22.5	6.4	-3.8
00/99	25.4	7.1	17.1	35.1	39.0	28.4	48.2	30.0	18.9	23.6	28.9	12.2	18.4	20.2	10.1
01/00	-2.4	-12.3	23.1	32.5	-10.3	-2.4	-9.4	14.8	-1.2	-1.5	-15.1	3.6	3.8	-4.3	7.2
02/01	-5.7	-5.2	-25.9	8.1	6.2	-5.4	-3.8	-13.8	-3.5	-12.6	4.8	-6.3	-5.3	-8.5	-1.0

Share (%)

Years	Extra EU	Norway	Switzerland	USSR/Russia[1]	Candid. countries	USA	Canada	China	Japan	Hong Kong	Mediterr. Basin	Latin America	OPEC	DAE	ACP
1980	100.0	3.2	11.7	1.8	:	18.8	3.0	0.6	2.4	2.1	13.4	4.1	18.3	5.6	10.8
1990	100.0	2.9	5.4	1.3	:	29.8	4.3	1.0	6.0	2.9	6.4	2.9	11.2	10.2	7.3
1996	100.0	2.8	4.7	1.2	7.1	27.5	2.7	1.0	6.0	4.0	7.3	3.4	9.6	12.9	3.2
1997	100.0	3.4	3.8	1.5	7.2	27.5	2.8	1.2	5.4	4.1	7.2	4.0	11.3	12.6	3.1
1998	100.0	3.9	3.9	1.3	7.6	31.3	3.1	1.2	4.6	3.8	7.5	4.4	9.5	10.4	5.3
1999	100.0	3.0	4.3	0.7	7.0	35.4	3.6	1.7	4.8	3.3	7.2	3.4	7.1	10.8	5.0
2000	100.0	2.5	4.0	0.8	7.7	36.2	4.3	1.8	4.5	3.3	7.4	3.1	6.7	10.3	4.4
2001	100.0	2.3	5.0	1.0	7.1	36.2	4.0	2.1	4.6	3.3	6.4	3.3	7.1	10.1	4.8
2002	100.0	2.3	3.9	1.2	8.0	36.3	4.1	1.9	4.7	3.0	7.1	3.2	7.2	9.8	5.1

IMPORTS
Value (Mio ECU/Euro)

Years	Extra EU	Norway	Switzerland	USSR/Russia[1]	Candid. countries	USA	Canada	China	Japan	Hong Kong	Mediterr. Basin	Latin America	OPEC	DAE	ACP
1980	46,347	2,413	4,141	1,318	:	11,437	2,263	288	2,992	1,349	3,628	1,775	7,664	3,461	2,355
1990	75,915	5,599	5,792	1,439	:	22,141	2,916	1,713	9,480	1,701	3,027	2,984	3,835	7,721	4,175
1994	89,468	4,647	6,030	1,214	6,566	25,083	2,426	4,280	11,593	1,750	3,196	3,622	3,617	10,982	2,571
1995	92,861	5,067	5,910	1,393	3,747	25,504	3,050	4,551	11,620	1,780	3,427	3,785	3,687	11,873	2,773
1996	103,569	5,922	6,154	1,624	4,142	28,755	3,040	5,593	11,038	1,832	4,031	4,354	3,960	13,623	3,230
1997	125,457	6,885	6,350	2,298	5,303	37,076	3,418	7,340	13,169	2,192	4,787	4,408	4,726	16,974	3,265
1998	133,537	5,150	6,692	2,318	5,978	40,101	3,532	8,504	14,157	2,751	5,161	4,583	4,665	18,587	5,513
1999	142,676	5,466	7,609	2,148	6,774	39,730	4,225	10,170	13,838	2,902	5,797	5,242	5,049	19,744	6,469
2000	188,084	9,271	8,211	3,256	9,025	49,515	6,128	14,077	16,892	3,706	7,737	7,128	6,927	24,921	8,759
2001	186,010	9,114	6,353	3,829	10,746	51,046	6,174	15,530	15,022	3,198	7,671	7,308	6,276	20,934	11,338
2002	173,684	8,567	5,363	3,955	12,863	44,091	5,526	16,811	13,303	3,038	8,728	7,407	5,944	19,165	11,316

Annual variation(%)

Years	Extra EU	Norway	Switzerland	USSR/Russia[1]	Candid. countries	USA	Canada	China	Japan	Hong Kong	Mediterr. Basin	Latin America	OPEC	DAE	ACP
98/97	6.4	-25.1	5.3	0.8	12.7	8.1	3.3	15.8	7.5	25.4	7.8	3.9	-1.2	9.5	68.8
99/98	6.8	6.1	13.6	-7.3	13.3	-0.9	19.6	19.5	-2.2	5.4	12.3	14.3	8.2	6.2	17.3
00/99	31.8	69.6	7.9	51.5	33.2	24.6	45.0	38.4	22.0	27.7	33.4	35.9	37.1	26.2	35.3
01/00	-1.1	-1.6	-22.6	17.5	19.0	3.0	0.7	10.3	-11.0	-13.7	-0.8	2.5	-9.3	-15.9	29.4
02/01	-6.6	-5.9	-15.5	3.2	19.6	-13.6	-10.4	8.2	-11.4	-5.0	13.7	1.3	-5.2	-8.4	-0.1

Share (%)

Years	Extra EU	Norway	Switzerland	USSR/Russia[1]	Candid. countries	USA	Canada	China	Japan	Hong Kong	Mediterr. Basin	Latin America	OPEC	DAE	ACP
1980	100.0	5.2	8.9	2.8	:	24.6	4.8	0.6	6.4	2.9	7.8	3.8	16.5	7.4	5.0
1990	100.0	7.3	7.6	1.8	:	29.1	3.8	2.2	12.4	2.2	3.9	3.9	5.0	10.1	5.4
1996	100.0	5.7	5.9	1.5	3.9	27.7	2.9	5.3	10.6	1.7	3.8	4.2	3.8	13.1	3.1
1997	100.0	5.4	5.0	1.8	4.2	29.5	2.7	5.8	10.4	1.7	3.8	3.5	3.7	13.5	2.6
1998	100.0	3.8	5.0	1.7	4.4	30.0	2.6	6.3	10.6	2.0	3.8	3.4	3.4	13.9	4.1
1999	100.0	3.8	5.3	1.5	4.7	27.8	2.9	7.1	9.6	2.0	4.0	3.6	3.5	13.8	4.5
2000	100.0	4.9	4.3	1.7	4.7	26.3	3.2	7.4	8.9	1.9	4.1	3.7	3.6	13.2	4.6
2001	100.0	4.8	3.4	2.0	5.7	27.4	3.3	8.3	8.0	1.7	4.1	3.9	3.3	11.2	6.0
2002	100.0	4.9	3.0	2.2	7.4	25.3	3.1	9.6	7.6	1.7	5.0	4.2	3.4	11.0	6.5

(1) Relates to the external trade with the USSR until 1991and to the external trade with Russia from 1992 onwards.

Candidate countries external trade

BULGARIA

TRADE BALANCE (BN ECU/euro)

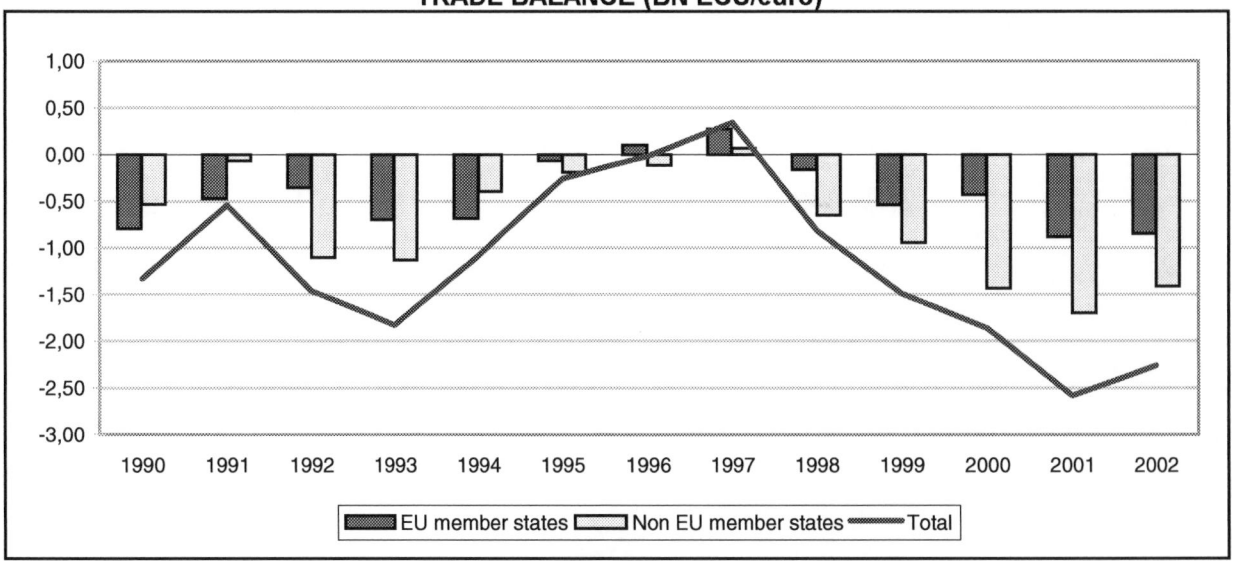

TRADE WITH EU MEMBER STATES (BN ECU/euro)

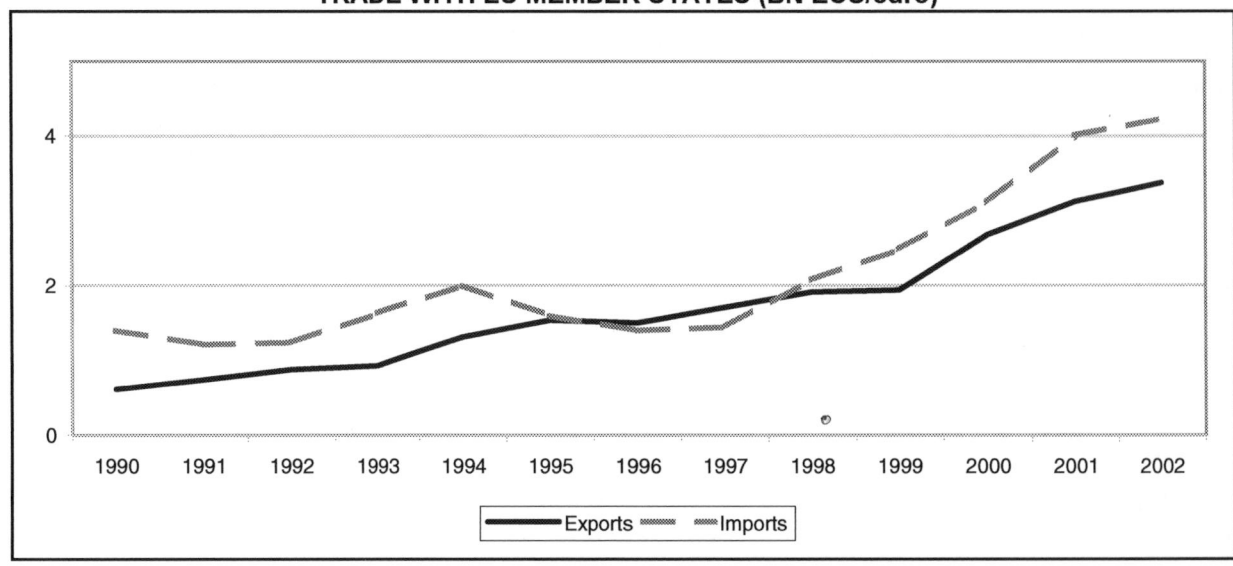

TRADE WITH NON EU MEMBER STATES (BN ECU/euro)

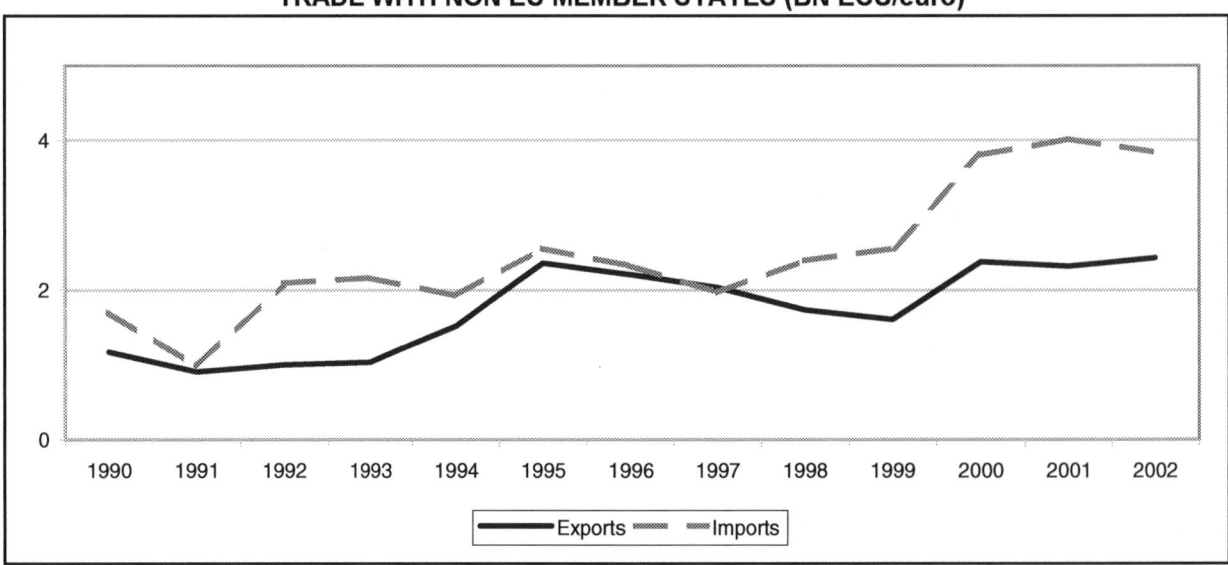

BULGARIE

TRADE BALANCE

EU MEMBER STATES

Value (Mio ECU/Euro)

Year		Partner														
	Intra EU	B(2)	DK	D	EL	E	F	IRL	I	L	NL	A	P	FIN	S	UK
1990	**-792**	**-20**	**-13**	**-505**	**33**	**13**	**-40**	**-3**	**-115**	**:**	**-29**	**-71**	**-2**	**-4**	**-15**	**-22**
1991	-472	-12	-7	-192	38	8	-97	1	-92	:	-14	-68	-2	-8	-20	-8
1992	-358	-48	-1	-158	-78	13	4	-3	14	:	-24	-64	:	-5	-15	1
1993	-698	-15	-14	-249	-130	-26	-17	-2	-77	:	-39	-70	5	-14	-19	-30
1994	-685	11	-9	-260	-170	19	-12	-4	-40	:	-75	-60	-2	-28	-16	-40
1995	-67	6	-11	-183	91	82	-3	-4	84	:	-6	-85	8	-34	-25	15
1996	104	10	-8	-105	119	68	-28	-4	137	:	-9	-57	-3	-25	-19	28
1997	271	:	-18	-66	165	87	-15	-1	176	:	-9	-49	7	-18	-10	15
1998	-162	:	-21	-244	71	63	-74	-0	139	:	-23	-67	4	-28	-30	-16
1999	-543	79	-17	-400	33	31	-99	-13	87	-2	-26	-89	1	-49	-49	-29
2000	**-435**	**232**	**-26**	**-510**	**64**	**3**	**-91**	**-31**	**147**	**-3**	**-26**	**-83**	**-5**	**-40**	**-39**	**-26**
2001	-882	160	-35	-697	41	54	-169	-13	75	2	-59	-67	-3	-49	-71	-51
2002	**-852**	**173**	**-39**	**-621**	**50**	**41**	**-151**	**-10**	**-19**	**-0**	**-63**	**-75**	**-9**	**-29**	**-57**	**-44**

NON EU MEMBER STATES

Value (Mio ECU/euro)

Year		Partner													
	Extra EU	Norway	Switzerland	USSR/Russia(1)	Candid. countries	USA	Canada	China	Japan	Hong Kong	Mediterr. Basin	Latin America	OPEC	DAE	ACP
1990	**-535**	**18**	**-72**	**:**	**:**	**-31**	**-12**	**42**	**-22**	**-9**	**-139**	**-62**	**-233**	**-13**	**19**
1991	-67	-1	-25	:	:	-80	5	48	1	-3	-47	-8	-39	7	14
1992	-1,100	:	-66	:	:	-37	4	6	-34	-8	131	-53	-111	16	18
1993	-1,128	-1	-52	-692	-123	25	10	72	-10	-6	47	-24	-45	-47	24
1994	-396	-1	-55	-172	-140	80	19	22	-1	-18	19	-8	-110	-35	18
1995	-192	1	-54	-801	213	33	9	-4	-19	-2	732	-72	-121	-1	22
1996	-119	1	-34	-958	205	1	15	12	-8	-4	685	-59	1	13	29
1997	68	4	-38	-612	280	-9	32	-6	11	-4	585	-65	-14	14	2
1998	-651	0	-43	-718	185	-85	13	-35	-8	-7	496	-90	-79	-24	-23
1999	-943	5	-24	-864	-24	-43	19	-49	-39	-6	439	-81	-29	-85	-17
2000	**-1,428**	**0**	**-38**	**-1,597**	**-58**	**-0**	**19**	**-62**	**-49**	**-9**	**934**	**-159**	**30**	**-48**	**13**
2001	-1,700	2	-29	-1,494	-135	106	-4	-87	-71	-11	634	-153	-48	-97	11
2002	**-1,410**	**1**	**-5**	**-1,136**	**-86**	**103**	**-1**	**-132**	**-82**	**-14**	**591**	**-143**	**-21**	**-118**	**18**

(1) Relates to the external trade with the USSR until 1991 and to the external trade with Russia from 1992 onwards.
(2) With Luxembourg until 31.12.1998.

BULGARIA

EU MEMBER STATES

Years	Intra EU	B[1]	DK	D	EL	E	F	IRL	I	L	NL	A	P	FIN	S	UK
							Partner									

EXPORTS
Value (Mio ECU/Euro)

Years	Intra EU	B[1]	DK	D	EL	E	F	IRL	I	L	NL	A	P	FIN	S	UK
1990	614	16	4	197	79	28	59	1	104	:	23	35	3	10	8	46
1994	1,315	64	18	353	248	43	119	1	249	:	64	48	5	11	12	82
1995	1,535	64	13	350	281	102	117	1	334	:	78	35	12	10	14	128
1996	1,506	57	14	348	274	88	100	1	388	:	63	40	3	7	13	111
1997	1,712	:	15	359	334	106	106	4	470	:	60	43	16	7	21	104
1998	1,911	:	19	401	336	109	132	8	492	:	71	63	16	8	17	96
1999	1,943	164	21	367	322	101	169	5	519	0	78	64	12	8	19	94
2000	2,684	326	22	474	410	110	253	6	745	0	93	74	12	10	25	125
2001	3,129	280	29	545	501	189	321	9	855	6	89	95	21	8	30	151
2002	3,377	291	28	579	558	204	325	12	935	3	108	101	16	10	32	176

Annual variation (%)

Years	Intra EU	B[1]	DK	D	EL	E	F	IRL	I	L	NL	A	P	FIN	S	UK
98/97	11.5	:	24.5	11.7	0.7	2.4	24.5	105.0	4.7	:	18.5	49.2	2.7	23.0	-19.7	-7.5
99/98	1.6	:	12.8	-8.5	-4.0	-6.8	27.7	-36.2	5.4	:	8.7	0.0	-23.6	-8.6	12.6	-2.6
00/99	38.1	98.8	4.2	29.1	27.1	8.4	49.3	18.3	43.7	-76.4	19.8	17.1	-7.1	32.9	29.2	33.0
01/00	16.5	-14.2	29.2	15.0	22.3	71.9	26.8	54.6	14.7	5,417.0	-3.9	27.9	85.7	-20.6	19.7	20.9
02/01	7.9	4.1	-4.8	6.1	11.3	8.4	1.1	30.0	9.2	-54.2	20.8	6.4	-25.6	20.0	8.1	16.7

Share (%)

Years	Intra EU	B[1]	DK	D	EL	E	F	IRL	I	L	NL	A	P	FIN	S	UK
1990	100.0	2.5	0.7	32.0	12.8	4.5	9.6	0.1	16.9	:	3.7	5.7	0.5	1.6	1.3	7.4
1996	100.0	3.8	0.9	23.1	18.1	5.8	6.6	0.0	25.7	:	4.1	2.6	0.2	0.4	0.8	7.3
1997	100.0	:	0.8	20.9	19.4	6.1	6.2	0.2	27.4	:	3.5	2.4	0.9	0.3	1.2	6.0
1998	100.0	:	0.9	20.9	17.5	5.6	6.9	0.3	25.7	:	3.7	3.3	0.8	0.4	0.8	5.0
1999	100.0	8.4	1.1	18.8	16.5	5.2	8.7	0.2	26.6	0.0	3.9	3.2	0.6	0.3	0.9	4.8
2000	100.0	12.1	0.8	17.6	15.2	4.0	9.4	0.2	27.7	0.0	3.4	2.7	0.4	0.3	0.9	4.6
2001	100.0	8.9	0.9	17.4	16.0	6.0	10.2	0.2	27.3	0.2	2.8	3.0	0.6	0.2	0.9	4.8
2002	100.0	8.6	0.8	17.1	16.5	6.0	9.6	0.3	27.6	0.0	3.1	3.0	0.4	0.2	0.9	5.2

IMPORTS
Value (Mio ECU/Euro)

Years	Intra EU	B[1]	DK	D	EL	E	F	IRL	I	L	NL	A	P	FIN	S	UK
1990	1,406	36	17	702	46	15	100	3	219	:	52	106	5	14	23	68
1994	2,000	52	27	613	418	24	131	5	289	:	139	108	7	38	28	122
1995	1,601	57	24	533	190	21	120	5	250	:	85	120	4	43	38	113
1996	1,403	48	23	453	154	20	128	5	251	:	72	97	6	31	32	83
1997	1,441	:	33	424	169	19	122	4	294	:	69	92	9	25	31	90
1998	2,073	:	40	645	265	45	206	8	353	:	94	130	12	36	47	112
1999	2,486	85	39	766	290	70	268	18	432	3	103	153	11	57	69	123
2000	3,119	94	49	984	345	107	344	37	599	3	119	157	17	50	64	151
2001	4,011	120	64	1,242	461	135	490	22	780	4	148	162	24	57	101	202
2002	4,229	118	67	1,200	508	164	475	21	954	3	171	176	25	38	89	220

Annual variation (%)

Years	Intra EU	B[1]	DK	D	EL	E	F	IRL	I	L	NL	A	P	FIN	S	UK
98/97	43.8	:	20.0	51.9	56.9	135.6	69.2	77.7	20.3	:	36.0	41.4	39.8	46.5	48.6	25.3
99/98	19.9	:	-2.0	18.8	9.3	54.6	30.0	133.9	22.2	:	9.5	17.4	-7.2	57.0	46.9	9.6
00/99	25.4	9.8	25.9	28.3	19.2	53.6	28.4	104.4	38.5	5.2	15.6	2.9	50.0	-12.2	-6.7	22.5
01/00	28.6	28.2	30.9	26.2	33.3	25.8	42.1	-40.9	30.3	54.3	24.2	2.9	45.6	14.4	57.5	34.0
02/01	5.4	-1.3	4.6	-3.4	10.2	21.5	-2.8	-2.7	22.2	-18.4	15.0	8.8	2.3	-32.8	-11.7	8.6

Share (%)

Years	Intra EU	B[1]	DK	D	EL	E	F	IRL	I	L	NL	A	P	FIN	S	UK
1990	100.0	2.5	1.2	49.9	3.2	1.0	7.0	0.2	15.5	:	3.7	7.5	0.3	1.0	1.6	4.8
1996	100.0	3.4	1.6	32.2	11.0	1.4	9.1	0.3	17.8	:	5.1	6.9	0.4	2.2	2.2	5.8
1997	100.0	:	2.2	29.4	11.7	1.3	8.4	0.2	20.3	:	4.8	6.3	0.5	1.7	2.1	6.2
1998	100.0	:	1.9	31.1	12.7	2.1	9.9	0.3	17.0	:	4.5	6.2	0.5	1.7	2.2	5.4
1999	100.0	3.4	1.5	30.8	11.6	2.8	10.7	0.7	17.3	0.1	4.1	6.1	0.4	2.2	2.7	4.9
2000	100.0	2.9	1.5	31.5	11.0	3.4	11.0	1.1	19.1	0.0	3.8	5.0	0.5	1.5	2.0	4.8
2001	100.0	2.9	1.5	30.9	11.4	3.3	12.2	0.5	19.4	0.1	3.6	4.0	0.6	1.4	2.5	5.0
2002	100.0	2.7	1.5	28.3	12.0	3.8	11.2	0.4	22.5	0.0	4.0	4.1	0.5	0.9	2.1	5.1

(1) With Luxembourg until 31.12.1998.

NON EU MEMBER STATES

Years	Extra EU	Norway	Switzerland	USSR/ Russia[1]	Candid. countries	USA	Canada	China	Japan	Hong Kong	Mediterr. Basin	Latin America	OPEC	DAE	ACP
							Partner								
EXPORTS Value (Mio ECU/Euro)															
1990	1,174	22	10	:	:	39	6	73	25	0	251	10	96	28	23
1994	1,525	5	9	265	295	182	23	56	18	2	549	61	56	60	26
1995	2,362	5	22	409	483	124	17	15	14	4	1,044	73	84	51	43
1996	2,208	6	28	378	469	89	21	34	20	1	885	60	65	45	43
1997	2,033	9	24	300	561	105	39	23	33	0	781	49	63	45	26
1998	1,739	6	26	212	559	100	24	8	30	1	747	35	41	27	23
1999	1,609	11	45	176	467	137	29	7	22	1	757	32	45	21	14
2000	2,372	6	51	129	806	207	35	12	19	1	1,311	47	76	43	38
2001	2,319	7	65	134	800	319	21	11	14	1	1,097	43	81	22	38
2002	2,430	8	101	98	952	285	26	13	11	3	1,190	61	81	43	42
Annual variation (%)															
98/97	-14.4	-24.7	7.2	-29.4	-0.2	-4.9	-39.7	-65.0	-8.7	243.6	-4.4	-29.1	-35.0	-40.9	-9.7
99/98	-7.4	71.6	72.5	-16.7	-16.4	37.7	21.1	-16.4	-25.8	43.1	1.3	-9.0	9.3	-21.2	-41.7
00/99	47.4	-42.0	14.0	-26.8	72.5	50.9	22.4	78.0	-12.7	-41.2	73.2	49.3	71.2	104.4	178.7
01/00	-2.2	4.8	27.3	3.6	-0.7	54.1	-38.8	-8.9	-25.1	82.5	-16.3	-8.3	5.3	-49.3	0.2
02/01	4.7	19.0	55.3	-27.0	18.9	-10.5	20.1	23.2	-20.7	171.2	8.4	40.4	0.7	95.7	10.6
Share (%)															
1990	100.0	1.8	0.8	:	:	3.2	0.5	6.1	2.1	0.0	21.3	0.8	8.2	2.4	1.9
1996	100.0	0.2	1.2	17.1	21.2	4.0	0.9	1.5	0.9	0.0	40.0	2.7	2.9	2.0	1.9
1997	100.0	0.4	1.1	14.7	27.5	5.1	1.9	1.1	1.6	0.0	38.4	2.4	3.0	2.2	1.2
1998	100.0	0.3	1.4	12.1	32.1	5.7	1.3	0.4	1.7	0.0	42.9	2.0	2.3	1.5	1.3
1999	100.0	0.6	2.7	10.9	29.0	8.5	1.7	0.4	1.3	0.0	47.0	1.9	2.7	1.3	0.8
2000	100.0	0.2	2.1	5.4	33.9	8.7	1.4	0.5	0.8	0.0	55.2	2.0	3.2	1.8	1.5
2001	100.0	0.2	2.8	5.7	34.5	13.7	0.9	0.4	0.6	0.0	47.3	1.8	3.4	0.9	1.6
2002	100.0	0.3	4.1	4.0	39.1	11.7	1.0	0.5	0.4	0.1	48.9	2.5	3.3	1.7	1.7
IMPORTS Value (Mio ECU/Euro)															
1990	1,709	4	83	:	:	70	19	31	47	9	390	72	329	41	4
1994	1,921	5	64	437	436	101	4	34	18	20	530	69	166	95	8
1995	2,555	4	76	1,210	270	91	8	19	33	6	312	145	205	53	21
1996	2,328	5	62	1,336	264	88	7	23	28	5	199	119	64	31	13
1997	1,965	5	62	912	281	114	7	29	22	5	196	115	77	31	24
1998	2,390	6	69	929	374	185	10	43	38	8	251	125	120	51	46
1999	2,551	6	69	1,041	491	180	9	55	61	7	318	113	74	106	30
2000	3,800	6	89	1,726	865	207	16	74	68	10	377	207	46	91	25
2001	4,019	5	95	1,627	935	213	25	98	86	12	463	197	129	119	27
2002	3,840	7	106	1,233	1,038	182	27	146	94	17	599	204	102	161	24
Annual variation (%)															
98/97	21.6	19.6	11.5	1.9	33.2	62.2	44.1	49.2	72.0	71.2	28.1	9.1	56.9	65.6	91.5
99/98	6.7	-1.7	0.0	11.9	31.4	-2.5	-8.1	29.8	61.3	-12.2	26.4	-9.9	-38.3	107.2	-34.4
00/99	48.9	4.0	29.0	65.8	75.9	15.1	70.6	34.1	12.4	42.1	18.5	83.5	-37.8	-14.3	-18.3
01/00	5.7	-17.5	6.1	-5.7	8.1	2.8	55.5	31.5	25.5	25.0	22.7	-4.8	179.4	30.8	8.2
02/01	-4.4	45.6	12.2	-24.2	10.9	-14.3	6.6	49.3	9.4	38.9	29.3	3.9	-21.0	35.5	-11.2
Share (%)															
1990	100.0	0.2	4.8	:	:	4.0	1.1	1.7	2.7	0.5	22.8	4.2	19.2	2.4	0.2
1996	100.0	0.2	2.6	57.4	11.3	3.7	0.2	0.9	1.1	0.2	8.5	5.1	2.7	1.3	0.5
1997	100.0	0.2	3.1	46.3	14.2	5.7	0.3	1.4	1.1	0.2	9.9	5.8	3.9	1.5	1.2
1998	100.0	0.2	2.8	38.8	15.6	7.7	0.4	1.7	1.5	0.3	10.5	5.2	5.0	2.1	1.9
1999	100.0	0.2	2.7	40.7	19.2	7.0	0.3	2.1	2.3	0.2	12.4	4.4	2.9	4.1	1.1
2000	100.0	0.1	2.3	45.4	22.7	5.4	0.4	1.9	1.7	0.2	9.9	5.4	1.2	2.3	0.6
2001	100.0	0.1	2.3	40.4	23.2	5.3	0.6	2.4	2.1	0.3	11.5	4.8	3.2	2.9	0.6
2002	100.0	0.1	2.7	32.1	27.0	4.7	0.6	3.7	2.4	0.4	15.5	5.3	2.6	4.1	0.6

(1) Relates to the external trade with the USSR until 1991 and to the external trade with Russia from 1992 onwards.

CYPRUS

TRADE BALANCE (BN ECU/euro)

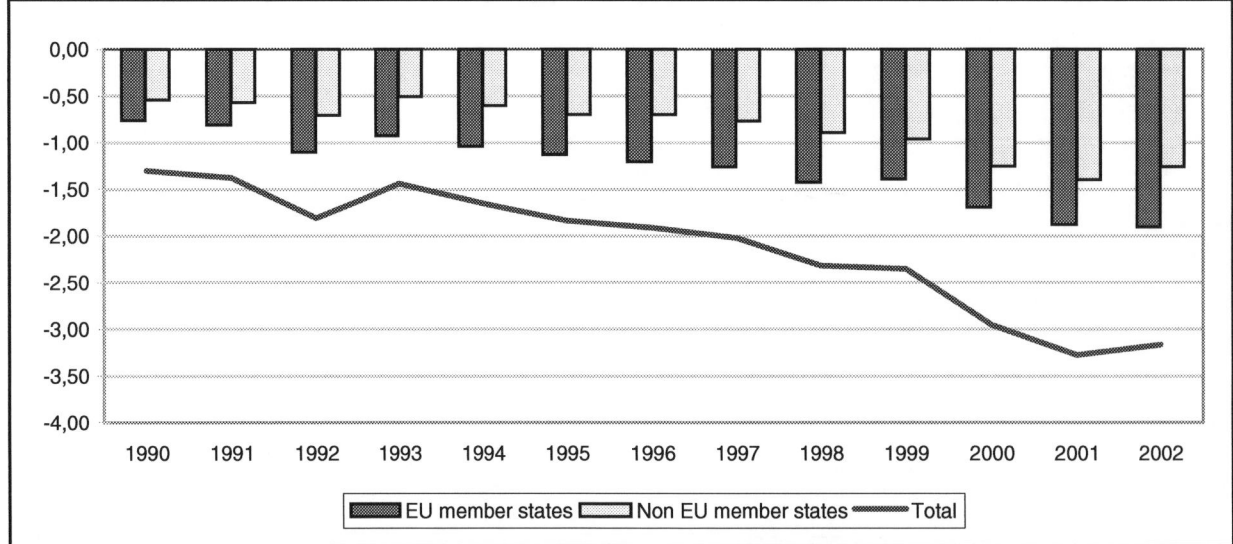

TRADE WITH EU MEMBER STATES (BN ECU/euro)

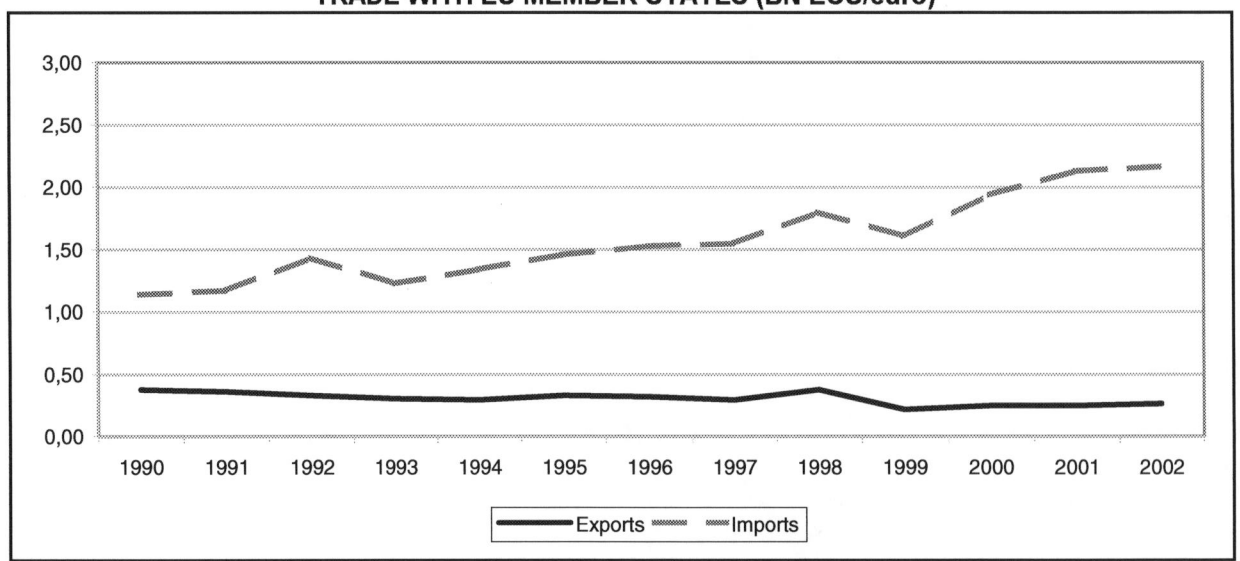

TRADE WITH NON EU MEMBER STATES (BN ECU/euro)

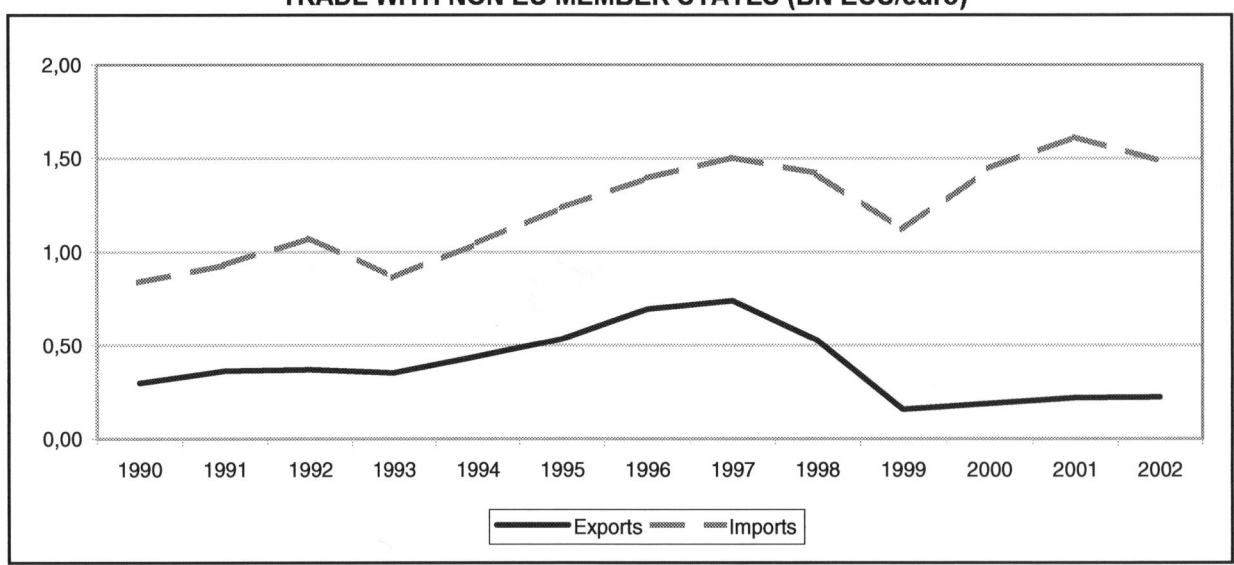

TRADE BALANCE

EU MEMBER STATES

Value (Mio ECU/Euro)

Year								Partner									
	Intra EU	B(2)	DK	D	EL	E	F	IRL	I	L	NL	A	P	FIN	S	UK
1990	**-762**	**-6**	**-16**	**-156**	**-66**	**-37**	**-116**	**-8**	**-190**	:	**-36**	**-15**	**-8**	**-6**	**-26**	**-79**
1991	-808	-8	-21	-178	-82	-27	-64	-13	-203	:	-36	-20	-10	-11	-26	-108
1992	-1,103	-30	-25	-195	-109	-41	-187	-15	-234	:	-47	-33	-12	-8	-29	-140
1993	-927	-13	-22	-137	-124	-33	-113	-17	-216	:	-43	-14	-8	-8	-22	-156
1994	-1,044	-29	-24	-171	-113	-51	-95	-19	-242	:	-65	-10	-10	-14	-30	-171
1995	-1,132	-20	-20	-193	-147	-51	-103	-20	-264	:	-45	-8	-11	-9	-40	-201
1996	-1,208	-16	-21	-173	-163	-67	-109	-15	-270	:	-39	-11	-13	-14	-47	-239
1997	-1,258	:	-20	-159	-154	-80	-126	-14	-254	:	-44	-12	-12	-15	-46	-269
1998	-1,423	:	-19	-249	-176	-113	-153	-17	-298	:	-51	-24	-13	-15	-54	-227
1999	-1,391	-46	-22	-172	-231	-92	-144	-21	-281	-0	-51	-21	-14	-15	-50	-230
2000	**-1,694**	**-63**	**-25**	**-224**	**-291**	**-105**	**-138**	**-28**	**-339**	**-0**	**-76**	**-26**	**-17**	**-46**	**-76**	**-239**
2001	-1,879	-69	-28	-240	-327	-130	-183	-26	-370	-0	-72	-43	-15	-29	-66	-281
2002	**-1,902**	**-44**	**-27**	**-324**	**-370**	**-121**	**-167**	**-26**	**-377**	**-1**	**-69**	**-22**	**-17**	**-30**	**-59**	**-249**

NON EU MEMBER STATES

Value (Mio ECU/euro)

Year								Partner							
	Extra EU	Norway	Switzerland	USSR/Russia(1)	Candid. countries	USA	Canada	China	Japan	Hong Kong	Mediterr. Basin	Latin America	OPEC	DAE	ACP
1990	**-541**	**-6**	**-23**	**-35**	:	**-131**	**-8**	**-14**	**-229**	**-14**	**46**	**-9**	**-23**	**-66**	**4**
1991	-569	-4	-28	-89	:	-160	-8	-22	-243	-11	113	-14	12	-80	-0
1992	-704	-2	-45	-98	:	-203	-13	-33	-267	-14	96	-17	25	-92	4
1993	-509	-17	-29	-70	16	-185	-11	-39	-169	-14	105	-21	34	-86	3
1994	-606	-2	-25	-19	41	-250	-19	-47	-171	-9	67	-35	5	-104	4
1995	-701	1	-28	16	94	-356	-19	-53	-187	-9	24	-34	35	-118	4
1996	-700	0	-25	104	146	-521	-10	-46	-186	-10	-19	-43	46	-92	7
1997	-765	-3	-30	68	77	-606	-9	-53	-171	-9	72	-37	49	-85	16
1998	-892	-2	-34	1	20	-394	-16	-72	-241	-22	30	-35	37	-129	6
1999	-961	-0	-30	-77	-32	-143	-16	-87	-180	-23	-152	-27	-5	-149	2
2000	**-1,256**	**-2**	**-40**	**-152**	**-27**	**-191**	**-13**	**-128**	**-172**	**-25**	**-239**	**-37**	**-1**	**-162**	**-6**
2001	-1,397	13	-45	-133	-57	-268	-9	-146	-182	-25	-272	-47	3	-155	2
2002	**-1,261**	**-10**	**-46**	**-131**	**-44**	**-130**	**-8**	**-162**	**-202**	**-26**	**-229**	**-52**	**3**	**-149**	**5**

(1) Relates to the external trade with the USSR until 1991 and to the external trade with Russia from 1992 onwards.

(2) With Luxembourg until 31.12.1998.

CYPRUS

EU MEMBER STATES

Years	Intra EU	B(1)	DK	D	EL	E	F	IRL	I	L	NL	A	P	FIN	S	UK
							EXPORTS									
						Value (Mio ECU/Euro)										
1990	375	30	2	29	74	7	14	6	11	:	14	5	0	2	4	176
1994	293	22	2	38	62	9	12	3	9	:	11	4	1	1	2	118
1995	326	33	4	37	56	9	13	3	13	:	13	9	1	2	3	131
1996	319	31	3	48	64	7	15	5	17	:	15	5	0	2	3	114
1997	293	:	5	35	79	5	12	7	14	:	13	4	1	2	4	103
1998	375	:	7	32	93	6	11	8	9	:	17	5	2	2	4	144
1999	215	5	7	34	43	4	9	5	12	0	13	4	0	2	5	72
2000	245	5	6	30	58	13	9	6	11	0	13	3	1	1	5	86
2001	247	9	4	29	66	17	8	6	6	0	15	4	0	2	6	74
2002	262	18	4	22	64	12	11	5	12	0	20	5	1	2	6	81
							Annual variation (%)									
98/97	27.9	:	32.0	-10.3	17.6	15.3	-1.9	17.3	-36.2	:	27.2	4.7	171.1	-26.9	15.3	39.5
99/98	-42.6	:	-3.9	6.9	-53.5	-33.2	-18.0	-30.2	27.8	:	-24.5	-2.4	-87.3	7.3	17.0	-50.0
00/99	14.0	-10.5	-12.0	-11.4	34.4	203.5	-6.9	6.7	-4.7	-64.2	2.5	-32.9	135.8	-15.2	-0.3	19.6
01/00	0.7	104.1	-25.8	-2.9	12.8	31.7	-3.2	2.3	-41.4	-80.0	16.9	40.2	-23.1	23.0	35.2	-14.4
02/01	5.7	88.9	-0.2	-23.1	-2.7	-27.7	27.1	-15.7	79.3	150.0	31.1	22.8	64.3	9.7	-6.0	9.3
							Share (%)									
1990	100.0	7.9	0.4	7.8	19.7	1.9	3.7	1.5	2.9	:	3.8	1.3	0.0	0.4	1.1	46.9
1996	100.0	9.7	0.9	15.0	19.9	2.0	4.5	1.5	5.4	:	4.5	1.6	0.1	0.5	1.0	35.7
1997	100.0	:	1.7	11.9	26.9	1.8	3.9	2.2	4.8	:	4.4	1.4	0.2	0.7	1.1	35.2
1998	100.0	:	1.8	8.4	24.8	1.6	3.0	2.0	2.4	:	4.4	1.2	0.4	0.4	1.0	38.4
1999	100.0	2.3	3.0	15.6	20.0	1.9	4.3	2.4	5.3	0.0	5.8	2.0	0.1	0.8	2.1	33.5
2000	100.0	1.8	2.3	12.1	23.6	5.1	3.5	2.3	4.5	0.0	5.2	1.2	0.2	0.6	1.9	35.1
2001	100.0	3.7	1.7	11.7	26.5	6.7	3.3	2.3	2.6	0.0	6.1	1.6	0.1	0.7	2.5	29.8
2002	100.0	6.7	1.6	8.5	24.3	4.5	4.0	1.8	4.4	0.0	7.6	1.9	0.2	0.7	2.2	30.8
							IMPORTS									
							Value (Mio ECU/Euro)									
1990	1,137	36	18	185	140	44	130	14	201	:	50	20	8	8	30	255
1994	1,337	51	26	209	175	60	108	22	250	:	76	14	11	15	32	289
1995	1,458	53	24	230	203	60	116	23	277	:	58	17	11	11	42	333
1996	1,527	47	24	221	226	74	123	20	287	:	54	17	13	16	50	353
1997	1,551	:	25	195	233	85	137	21	268	:	58	17	12	18	50	372
1998	1,799	:	26	280	269	119	164	25	307	:	68	29	15	17	58	371
1999	1,606	51	29	206	274	96	153	26	293	0	64	26	14	17	55	302
2000	1,940	68	30	254	349	118	147	34	350	0	89	29	18	47	81	326
2001	2,127	78	33	269	393	146	191	32	376	0	88	47	16	31	72	354
2002	2,164	62	32	347	434	133	178	31	389	1	89	27	17	32	65	329
							Annual variation (%)									
98/97	15.9	:	4.1	44.0	15.4	40.4	19.5	19.4	14.5	:	17.8	71.3	18.1	-5.4	15.4	-0.3
99/98	-10.6	:	12.0	-26.5	1.8	-19.3	-6.6	5.6	-4.6	:	-6.0	-11.2	-2.9	-0.1	-5.1	-18.4
00/99	20.7	33.3	4.7	23.4	27.2	22.5	-4.2	29.5	19.3	-24.2	40.2	13.7	25.1	183.7	47.2	7.6
01/00	9.6	14.7	7.7	5.6	12.4	24.1	30.3	-3.9	7.4	43.4	-1.9	62.7	-12.3	-34.0	-10.5	8.8
02/01	1.7	-20.7	-2.8	29.1	10.4	-9.0	-6.8	-4.4	3.3	47.8	1.2	-43.2	10.9	1.5	-9.9	-7.1
							Share (%)									
1990	100.0	3.1	1.5	16.2	12.2	3.8	11.3	1.1	17.6	:	4.3	1.7	0.6	0.6	2.6	22.4
1996	100.0	3.0	1.5	14.4	14.8	4.8	8.0	1.2	18.8	:	3.5	1.0	0.8	1.0	3.2	23.1
1997	100.0	:	1.6	12.5	15.0	5.4	8.8	1.3	17.2	:	3.7	1.0	0.8	1.1	3.2	24.0
1998	100.0	:	1.4	15.5	14.9	6.6	9.1	1.3	17.0	:	3.7	1.6	0.8	0.9	3.2	20.6
1999	100.0	3.1	1.8	12.8	17.0	5.9	9.5	1.6	18.2	0.0	3.9	1.5	0.8	1.0	3.4	18.8
2000	100.0	3.5	1.5	13.1	17.9	6.0	7.5	1.7	18.0	0.0	4.6	1.4	0.9	2.4	4.1	16.7
2001	100.0	3.6	1.5	12.6	18.4	6.8	8.9	1.5	17.6	0.0	4.1	2.2	0.7	1.4	3.3	16.6
2002	100.0	2.8	1.4	16.0	20.0	6.1	8.2	1.4	17.9	0.0	4.0	1.2	0.8	1.4	3.0	15.2

(1) With Luxembourg until 31.12.1998.

NON EU MEMBER STATES

Years	Extra EU	Norway	Switzerland	USSR/ Russia[1]	Candid. countries	USA	Canada	China	Japan	Hong Kong	Mediterr. Basin	Latin America	OPEC	DAE	ACP
								EXPORTS							
							Value (Mio ECU/Euro)								
1990	297	2	6	24	:	12	1	0	4	6	142	7	62	10	8
1994	439	2	8	83	80	13	1	1	2	5	172	2	59	13	9
1995	533	5	7	128	144	12	0	1	2	7	138	2	68	12	8
1996	696	4	6	192	202	8	0	0	1	7	167	4	80	17	10
1997	738	1	6	215	123	12	1	0	1	13	220	5	102	23	19
1998	526	3	5	98	72	18	1	0	3	4	204	1	84	18	13
1999	158	4	2	6	13	12	0	0	1	4	57	2	31	10	10
2000	189	2	2	7	17	14	0	1	1	5	63	1	39	13	10
2001	218	22	2	10	22	12	1	1	1	4	55	1	46	13	14
2002	224	3	2	12	23	16	2	1	1	4	67	2	46	14	17
							Annual variation (%)								
98/97	-28.6	151.6	-13.2	-54.4	-40.8	43.5	65.3	-77.5	110.3	-71.0	-7.1	-70.0	-16.8	-22.8	-30.4
99/98	-69.9	15.2	-54.0	-93.9	-81.7	-30.1	-50.0	152.7	-70.8	3.8	-72.0	12.0	-63.8	-46.8	-26.4
00/99	19.6	-39.8	-21.1	22.7	29.8	13.5	-28.1	230.2	-4.1	26.3	10.8	-30.5	28.4	31.3	6.0
01/00	15.0	840.9	-0.1	31.4	27.1	-13.5	201.1	11.4	57.6	-20.5	-12.4	-34.0	17.2	3.1	33.9
02/01	2.7	-87.9	25.5	28.8	6.1	32.7	138.9	13.5	17.5	9.2	21.8	228.4	0.0	7.8	23.8
							Share (%)								
1990	100.0	0.6	1.9	8.1	:	3.9	0.4	0.1	1.1	1.9	47.6	2.3	20.9	3.4	2.6
1996	100.0	0.5	0.9	27.6	29.1	1.1	0.0	0.0	0.1	1.0	23.9	0.5	11.5	2.3	1.4
1997	100.0	0.1	0.7	29.1	16.6	1.6	0.0	0.0	0.1	1.7	29.7	0.6	13.7	3.1	2.5
1998	100.0	0.6	0.9	18.6	13.7	3.3	0.1	0.0	0.5	0.7	38.7	0.2	16.0	3.4	2.5
1999	100.0	2.4	1.4	3.7	8.3	7.8	0.2	0.1	0.5	2.4	36.0	0.9	19.3	6.0	6.2
2000	100.0	1.2	0.9	3.8	9.0	7.4	0.1	0.3	0.4	2.6	33.4	0.5	20.7	6.6	5.4
2001	100.0	10.2	0.8	4.3	10.0	5.6	0.4	0.3	0.5	1.8	25.4	0.3	21.1	5.9	6.4
2002	100.0	1.1	1.0	5.4	10.3	7.2	1.0	0.3	0.6	1.9	30.1	1.0	20.5	6.2	7.7
							IMPORTS								
							Value (Mio ECU/Euro)								
1990	838	8	28	59	:	143	9	14	232	20	95	16	85	76	4
1994	1,045	5	33	102	38	262	20	48	173	14	105	37	54	117	5
1995	1,234	4	35	112	49	367	19	53	189	16	115	36	33	129	3
1996	1,396	3	31	88	57	529	11	47	187	17	185	46	34	109	4
1997	1,503	4	35	147	46	619	10	53	172	22	148	42	53	108	3
1998	1,418	5	39	97	53	412	17	72	244	25	174	36	48	147	8
1999	1,119	4	33	83	46	156	16	87	181	27	209	28	35	159	8
2000	1,445	5	42	160	44	206	13	129	173	30	302	38	40	174	16
2001	1,615	9	47	142	79	280	10	147	183	29	327	47	43	168	12
2002	1,485	13	48	143	67	147	10	163	204	30	297	55	43	163	12
							Annual variation (%)								
98/97	-5.6	24.2	10.1	-34.1	15.5	-33.4	68.1	35.5	41.6	15.0	17.6	-12.7	-10.3	35.4	134.8
99/98	-21.1	-14.7	-15.5	-14.0	-13.6	-62.2	-2.6	21.0	-25.8	7.1	20.4	-22.6	-25.5	8.1	-0.2
00/99	29.1	7.6	27.3	91.5	-3.9	32.2	-19.2	48.3	-4.1	10.3	44.4	33.5	13.9	9.9	110.4
01/00	11.7	98.1	12.0	-11.0	81.3	36.3	-21.3	13.7	5.6	-5.1	8.2	25.9	7.7	-3.4	-27.8
02/01	-8.0	40.8	3.7	0.9	-15.5	-47.6	-2.7	11.3	11.2	6.5	-9.3	15.4	-0.1	-3.4	1.8
							Share (%)								
1990	100.0	0.9	3.3	7.0	:	17.0	1.0	1.6	27.6	2.3	11.3	1.9	10.1	9.0	0.4
1996	100.0	0.2	2.2	6.3	4.0	37.9	0.7	3.3	13.4	1.2	13.2	3.3	2.4	7.8	0.2
1997	100.0	0.2	2.3	9.7	3.0	41.1	0.6	3.5	11.4	1.4	9.8	2.7	3.5	7.2	0.2
1998	100.0	0.3	2.7	6.8	3.7	29.0	1.1	5.0	17.1	1.7	12.2	2.5	3.3	10.3	0.5
1999	100.0	0.3	2.9	7.4	4.0	13.9	1.4	7.7	16.1	2.4	18.7	2.5	3.1	14.1	0.6
2000	100.0	0.3	2.8	11.0	3.0	14.2	0.9	8.9	11.9	2.0	20.9	2.6	2.7	12.0	1.1
2001	100.0	0.5	2.8	8.7	4.9	17.3	0.6	9.0	11.3	1.7	20.2	2.9	2.6	10.4	0.7
2002	100.0	0.8	3.2	9.6	4.5	9.8	0.6	10.9	13.7	2.0	19.9	3.6	2.9	10.9	0.8

(1) Relates to the external trade with the USSR until 1991 and to the external trade with Russia from 1992 onwards.

CZECH REPUBLIC

TRADE BALANCE (BN ECU/euro)

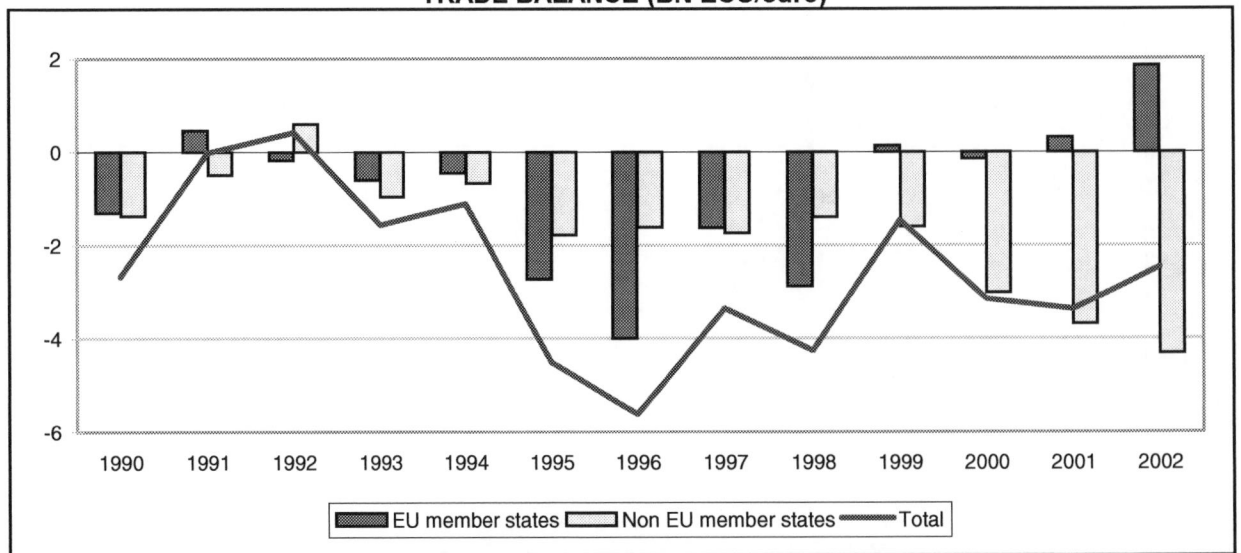

TRADE WITH EU MEMBER STATES (BN ECU/euro)

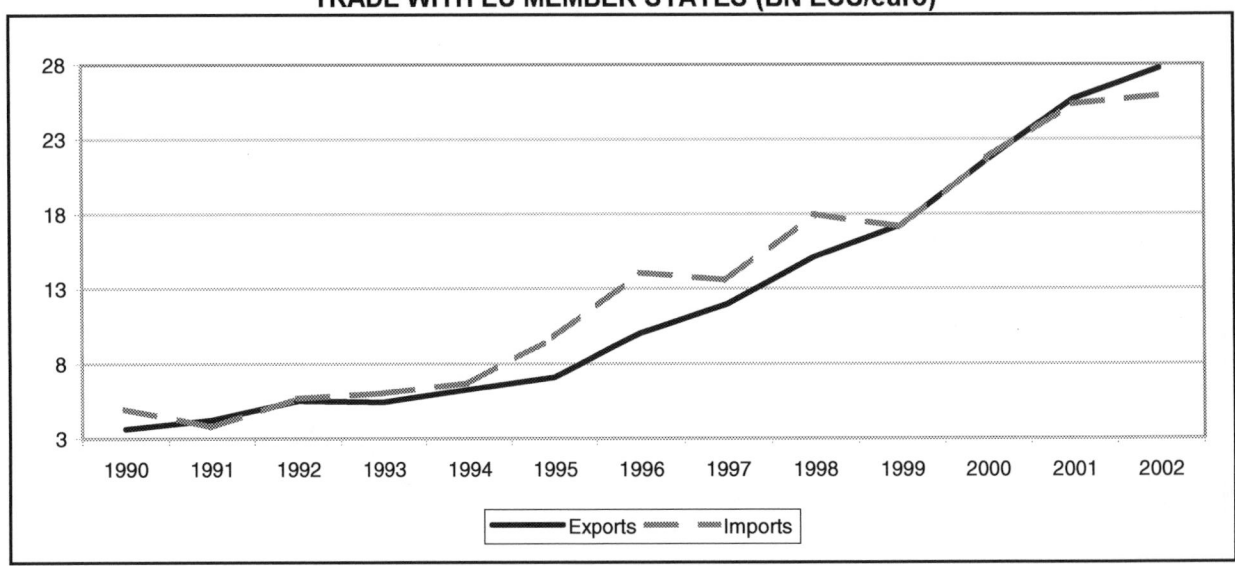

TRADE WITH NON EU MEMBER STATES (BN ECU/euro)

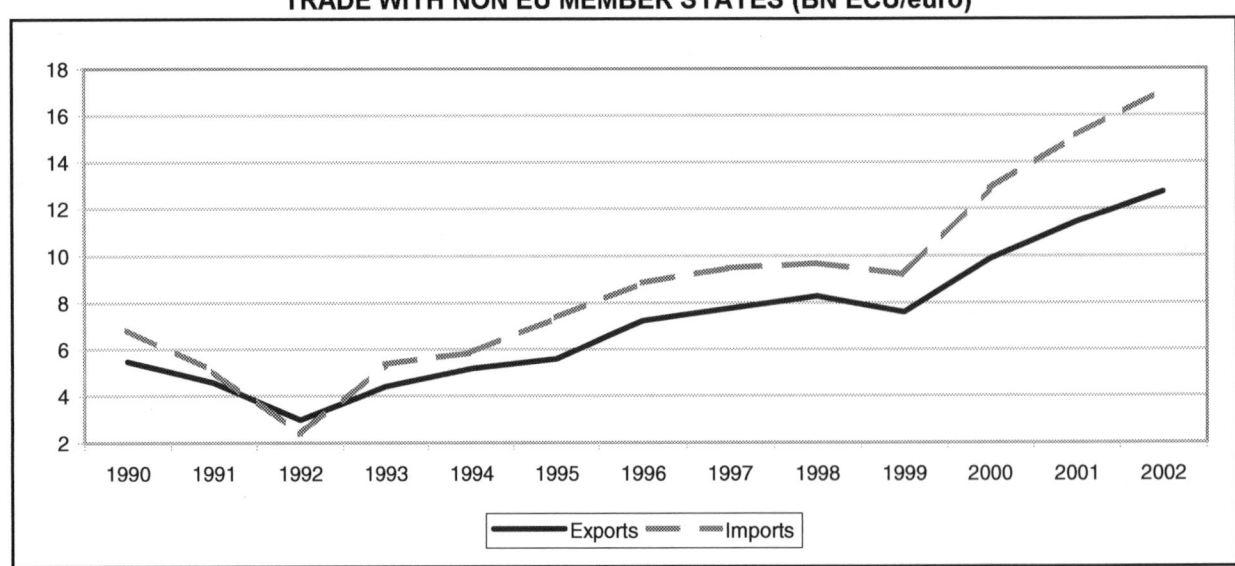

TRADE BALANCE

EU MEMBER STATES

Value (Mio ECU/Euro)

Year	Intra EU	B[2]	DK	D	EL	E	F	IRL	I	L	NL	A	P	FIN	S	UK
1990	**-1,307**	3	-14	-842	44	19	45	-10	29	:	57	-556	6	25	-23	-89
1991	471	41	4	412	11	25	9	-4	96	:	81	-192	4	9	-7	-18
1992	-180	1	-35	234	76	57	-145	-3	17	:	-11	-310	13	-20	-33	-20
1993	-601	-52	-11	-48	36	5	-89	:	-4	:	-81	-270	5	-41	-61	10
1994	-447	-80	-37	310	26	-22	-139	-11	-127	:	-65	-164	9	-20	-81	-47
1995	-2,720	-125	-55	-5	20	-81	-356	-41	-414	:	-108	-264	6	-73	-128	-216
1996	-4,003	-102	-71	-290	34	-155	-422	-65	-717	:	-138	-143	-0	-139	-126	-386
1997	-1,625	30	-53	803	31	-198	-281	-62	-539	6	24	237	12	-166	-63	-189
1998	-2,873	-52	-29	188	24	-70	-356	-54	-458	-4	-84	-27	35	-141	-15	-180
1999	138	-57	-20	1,478	24	22	-463	-68	-521	-9	-31	103	57	-133	-53	-192
2000	**-144**	**-82**	**-35**	**1,434**	**67**	**-115**	**-459**	**-34**	**-610**	**-7**	**-94**	**112**	**62**	**-150**	**-132**	**-102**
2001	312	141	-34	653	78	-96	-357	34	-636	3	67	259	58	-135	-123	399
2002	**1,855**	**-9**	**-32**	**820**	**88**	**-7**	**-176**	**-8**	**-677**	**-17**	**565**	**384**	**58**	**-102**	**-24**	**993**

NON EU MEMBER STATES

Value (Mio ECU/euro)

Year	Extra EU	Norway	Switzerland	USSR/Russia[1]	Candid. countries	USA	Canada	China	Japan	Hong Kong	Mediterr. Basin	Latin America	OPEC	DAE	ACP
1990	**-1,364**	3	-288	-99	:	7	23	-220	16	:	182	-124	113	23	21
1991	-491	8	-119	-1,097	:	-76	21	4	-51	-1	351	-125	-13	-3	-16
1992	604	-1	-79	-2	:	-303	10	31	-96	4	536	-116	236	-16	16
1993	-956	-6	-142	-843	252	-158	-95	167	-147	-11	248	-53	3	-52	0
1994	-666	-6	-148	-660	407	-208	-19	-22	-204	32	314	-34	46	-28	-8
1995	-1,787	-9	-201	-1,083	269	-413	-18	-103	-243	-38	303	-71	53	-161	-9
1996	-1,614	10	-219	-1,240	692	-448	-30	-178	-336	-13	319	-102	69	-174	-28
1997	-1,735	-33	-178	-1,120	951	-523	-32	-320	-423	-23	280	-103	95	-233	-59
1998	-1,393	-26	-214	-973	1,321	-532	-21	-452	-446	-26	328	-81	63	-320	-15
1999	-1,603	-64	-139	-951	1,195	-459	-44	-473	-462	15	332	-76	49	-438	-0
2000	**-3,011**	**-201**	**-124**	**-1,840**	**1,239**	**-520**	**-35**	**-683**	**-542**	**30**	**401**	**-146**	**84**	**-452**	**2**
2001	-3,688	-250	-138	-1,683	1,598	-509	-46	-1,109	-619	27	334	-179	45	-893	-6
2002	**-4,321**	**-215**	**-43**	**-1,407**	**1,766**	**-218**	**-40**	**-1,836**	**-742**	**53**	**472**	**-328**	**199**	**-1,392**	**-30**

(1) Relates to the external trade with the USSR until 1991 and to the external trade with Russia from 1992 onwards.

(2) With Luxembourg until 31.12.1998.

CZECH REPUBLIC

EU MEMBER STATES

Years	Intra EU	B[1]	DK	D	EL	E	F	IRL	I	L	NL	A	P	FIN	S	UK
	Partner															
							EXPORTS									
						Value (Mio ECU/Euro)										
1990	3,661	100	61	1,642	72	49	248	13	290	:	206	556	10	85	89	241
1994	6,289	179	83	3,531	57	112	158	9	531	:	306	855	16	23	92	336
1995	7,083	203	95	4,118	68	115	321	12	519	:	345	843	17	35	109	290
1996	10,051	294	106	6,216	73	127	493	38	568	:	358	1,112	19	71	139	434
1997	11,966	361	117	7,147	75	159	609	47	728	23	488	1,281	34	79	199	610
1998	15,129	462	147	9,047	76	277	794	61	885	32	531	1,478	63	109	317	798
1999	17,290	505	160	10,554	76	419	961	150	900	34	603	1,606	89	108	298	827
2000	21,593	689	171	12,734	130	509	1,268	214	1,191	50	725	1,881	125	131	424	1,352
2001	25,683	1,112	216	14,207	150	668	1,597	266	1,511	69	1,042	2,145	141	159	364	2,035
2002	27,747	961	239	14,790	160	811	1,886	258	1,645	67	1,581	2,251	156	153	452	2,340
						Annual variation (%)										
98/97	26.4	28.0	25.8	26.5	0.4	74.2	30.4	30.6	21.5	38.9	8.9	15.3	85.7	36.7	59.8	30.8
99/98	14.2	9.3	8.8	16.6	0.3	51.4	21.1	145.5	1.7	8.8	13.4	8.6	42.6	-0.9	-6.1	3.6
00/99	24.8	36.3	7.0	20.6	71.3	21.4	31.9	42.2	32.2	45.4	20.2	17.0	40.1	21.3	42.3	63.5
01/00	18.9	61.5	26.6	11.5	14.9	31.2	25.9	24.5	26.8	37.9	43.8	14.0	13.2	21.6	-14.2	50.5
02/01	8.0	-13.6	10.4	4.1	6.6	21.4	18.0	-3.0	8.8	-3.2	51.6	4.9	10.1	-3.6	24.2	14.9
						Share (%)										
1990	100.0	2.7	1.6	44.8	1.9	1.3	6.7	0.3	7.9	:	5.6	15.1	0.2	2.3	2.4	6.5
1996	100.0	2.9	1.0	61.8	0.7	1.2	4.9	0.3	5.6	:	3.5	11.0	0.1	0.7	1.3	4.3
1997	100.0	3.0	0.9	59.7	0.6	1.3	5.0	0.3	6.0	0.1	4.0	10.7	0.2	0.6	1.6	5.0
1998	100.0	3.0	0.9	59.8	0.5	1.8	5.2	0.4	5.8	0.2	3.5	9.7	0.4	0.7	2.0	5.2
1999	100.0	2.9	0.9	61.0	0.4	2.4	5.5	0.8	5.2	0.1	3.4	9.2	0.5	0.6	1.7	4.7
2000	100.0	3.1	0.7	58.9	0.6	2.3	5.8	0.9	5.5	0.2	3.3	8.7	0.5	0.6	1.9	6.2
2001	100.0	4.3	0.8	55.3	0.5	2.5	6.2	1.0	5.8	0.2	4.0	8.3	0.5	0.6	1.4	7.9
2002	100.0	3.4	0.8	53.3	0.5	2.9	6.7	0.9	5.9	0.2	5.6	8.1	0.5	0.5	1.6	8.4
						IMPORTS										
						Value (Mio ECU/Euro)										
1990	4,968	96	75	2,484	28	30	202	23	262	:	149	1,113	5	60	112	330
1994	6,736	259	120	3,221	31	134	297	20	658	:	371	1,019	7	43	173	383
1995	9,803	327	149	4,123	48	196	678	53	934	:	453	1,106	11	107	237	506
1996	14,054	396	177	6,506	39	282	915	102	1,286	:	496	1,255	19	210	265	820
1997	13,591	330	170	6,345	45	357	890	109	1,266	16	464	1,044	21	245	262	799
1998	18,002	513	176	8,859	51	347	1,149	115	1,343	35	615	1,504	27	250	332	978
1999	17,151	561	180	9,076	52	397	1,424	218	1,421	44	633	1,503	32	240	351	1,019
2000	21,737	771	206	11,301	63	624	1,727	248	1,801	57	818	1,768	63	281	556	1,454
2001	25,371	971	251	13,554	71	764	1,954	232	2,147	66	975	1,886	84	293	487	1,637
2002	25,892	970	271	13,970	71	818	2,061	266	2,322	84	1,016	1,867	98	255	476	1,347
						Annual variation (%)										
98/97	32.4	55.3	3.8	39.6	14.7	-2.9	29.1	5.1	6.0	115.4	32.5	44.0	26.7	1.7	26.9	22.3
99/98	-4.7	9.4	2.2	2.4	0.3	14.5	23.9	90.3	5.7	24.7	2.9	-0.1	19.3	-3.7	5.6	4.1
00/99	26.7	37.2	14.2	24.5	21.7	57.0	21.2	13.4	26.7	31.1	29.1	17.6	95.9	16.8	58.4	42.7
01/00	16.7	26.0	21.7	19.9	13.6	22.4	13.1	-6.1	19.2	14.1	19.1	6.6	32.4	4.5	-12.4	12.5
02/01	2.0	-0.1	8.0	3.0	0.1	7.1	5.4	14.6	8.1	27.8	4.1	-1.0	17.0	-12.9	-2.1	-17.6
						Share (%)										
1990	100.0	1.9	1.5	50.0	0.5	0.6	4.0	0.4	5.2	:	2.9	22.3	0.0	1.2	2.2	6.6
1996	100.0	2.8	1.2	46.2	0.2	2.0	6.5	0.7	9.1	:	3.5	8.9	0.1	1.4	1.8	5.8
1997	100.0	2.4	1.2	46.6	0.3	2.6	6.5	0.8	9.3	0.1	3.4	7.6	0.1	1.8	1.9	5.8
1998	100.0	2.8	0.9	49.2	0.2	1.9	6.3	0.6	7.4	0.1	3.4	8.3	0.1	1.3	1.8	5.4
1999	100.0	3.2	1.0	52.9	0.3	2.3	8.3	1.2	8.2	0.2	3.6	8.7	0.1	1.4	2.0	5.9
2000	100.0	3.5	0.9	51.9	0.2	2.8	7.9	1.1	8.2	0.2	3.7	8.1	0.2	1.2	2.5	6.6
2001	100.0	3.8	0.9	53.4	0.2	3.0	7.7	0.9	8.4	0.2	3.8	7.4	0.3	1.1	1.9	6.4
2002	100.0	3.7	1.0	53.9	0.2	3.1	7.9	1.0	8.9	0.3	3.9	7.2	0.3	0.9	1.8	5.2

(1) With Luxembourg until 31.12.1998.

NON EU MEMBER STATES

Years	Extra EU	Norway	Switzerland	USSR/Russia[1]	Candid. countries	USA	Canada	China	Japan	Hong Kong	Mediterr. Basin	Latin America	OPEC	DAE	ACP
EXPORTS — Value (Mio ECU/Euro)																
1990	5,474	34	214	2,370	:	72	37	178	70	:	687	134	222	79	44
1994	5,183	37	165	469	3,086	261	38	73	77	100	479	81	70	213	14
1995	5,570	50	173	456	3,486	232	39	65	64	47	530	80	83	149	20
1996	7,226	67	208	546	4,186	367	47	233	75	82	685	129	158	221	41
1997	7,732	87	245	651	4,599	483	50	236	85	59	694	132	216	201	42
1998	8,262	105	299	584	5,003	526	61	40	74	61	742	149	201	178	93
1999	7,581	95	334	357	4,573	583	52	55	70	74	787	120	193	222	76
2000	**9,849**	**124**	**420**	**420**	**5,645**	**888**	**68**	**72**	**126**	**89**	**1,004**	**173**	**307**	**401**	**83**
2001	11,440	152	513	546	6,645	1,059	67	90	136	98	1,120	210	340	357	90
2002	**12,722**	**183**	**633**	**540**	**7,301**	**1,161**	**69**	**157**	**150**	**122**	**1,356**	**190**	**416**	**396**	**104**
Annual variation (%)																
98/97	6.8	21.7	21.9	-10.3	8.7	8.9	21.8	-82.9	-13.4	4.2	6.9	12.8	-6.5	-11.6	122.8
99/98	-8.2	-9.7	11.5	-38.7	-8.5	10.7	-14.6	36.6	-5.1	20.1	6.1	-19.3	-4.2	24.8	-18.2
00/99	29.9	30.6	25.8	17.5	23.4	52.3	31.4	30.1	79.8	21.4	27.5	44.0	58.9	80.6	9.9
01/00	16.1	22.0	22.2	29.9	17.7	19.2	-1.0	25.5	8.1	9.4	11.5	21.3	11.0	-10.8	8.4
02/01	11.2	20.7	23.3	-1.1	9.8	9.6	2.8	74.3	9.7	24.1	21.0	-9.7	22.2	10.9	14.6
Share (%)																
1990	100.0	0.6	3.9	43.2	:	1.3	0.6	3.2	1.2	:	12.5	2.4	4.0	1.4	0.8
1996	100.0	0.9	2.8	7.5	57.9	5.0	0.6	3.2	1.0	1.1	9.4	1.7	2.1	3.0	0.5
1997	100.0	1.1	3.1	8.4	59.4	6.2	0.6	3.0	1.1	0.7	8.9	1.7	2.7	2.6	0.5
1998	100.0	1.2	3.6	7.0	60.5	6.3	0.7	0.4	0.8	0.7	8.9	1.8	2.4	2.1	1.1
1999	100.0	1.2	4.3	4.7	60.3	7.6	0.6	0.7	0.9	0.9	10.3	1.5	2.5	2.9	0.9
2000	**100.0**	**1.2**	**4.2**	**4.2**	**57.3**	**9.0**	**0.6**	**0.7**	**1.2**	**0.9**	**10.1**	**1.7**	**3.1**	**4.0**	**0.8**
2001	100.0	1.3	4.4	4.7	58.0	9.2	0.5	0.7	1.1	0.8	9.7	1.8	2.9	3.1	0.7
2002	**100.0**	**1.4**	**4.9**	**4.2**	**57.3**	**9.1**	**0.5**	**1.2**	**1.1**	**0.9**	**10.6**	**1.4**	**3.2**	**3.1**	**0.8**
IMPORTS — Value (Mio ECU/Euro)																
1990	6,838	31	502	2,468	:	65	14	398	55	:	506	258	108	55	23
1994	5,849	43	313	1,128	2,679	469	57	94	281	67	164	115	24	241	22
1995	7,357	59	373	1,540	3,217	645	58	168	307	85	227	151	30	310	29
1996	8,841	58	427	1,786	3,494	815	76	411	411	94	366	231	90	395	70
1997	9,467	120	423	1,771	3,648	1,007	82	556	508	82	414	235	121	434	101
1998	9,655	132	513	1,557	3,682	1,059	81	492	519	87	414	230	138	497	108
1999	9,184	159	473	1,308	3,378	1,042	96	528	532	59	455	196	144	660	76
2000	**12,860**	**326**	**543**	**2,260**	**4,406**	**1,409**	**103**	**755**	**668**	**59**	**603**	**319**	**222**	**853**	**81**
2001	15,128	402	651	2,228	5,047	1,569	113	1,198	755	71	786	389	295	1,250	96
2002	**17,043**	**399**	**676**	**1,946**	**5,536**	**1,380**	**109**	**1,992**	**891**	**68**	**883**	**518**	**217**	**1,788**	**134**
Annual variation (%)																
98/97	1.9	10.0	21.2	-12.0	0.9	5.1	-0.5	-11.4	2.1	6.6	0.1	-2.1	14.2	14.5	7.4
99/98	-4.8	20.8	-7.8	-15.9	-8.2	-1.6	18.2	7.3	2.4	-32.5	9.8	-14.8	4.2	32.7	-29.7
00/99	40.0	104.2	14.8	72.7	30.4	35.2	6.9	42.8	25.5	0.3	32.4	63.0	54.3	29.1	7.1
01/00	17.6	23.4	19.8	-1.4	14.5	11.3	9.6	58.7	13.0	19.8	30.3	21.7	32.8	46.5	18.0
02/01	12.6	-0.7	3.8	-12.6	9.6	-12.0	-3.3	66.2	18.0	-3.5	12.3	33.1	-26.4	43.0	39.1
Share (%)																
1990	100.0	0.4	7.3	36.0	:	0.9	0.2	5.8	0.7	:	7.3	3.7	1.5	0.8	0.3
1996	100.0	0.6	4.8	20.2	39.5	9.2	0.8	4.6	4.6	1.0	4.1	2.6	1.0	4.4	0.7
1997	100.0	1.2	4.4	18.7	38.5	10.6	0.8	5.8	5.3	0.8	4.3	2.4	1.2	4.5	1.0
1998	100.0	1.3	5.3	16.1	38.1	10.9	0.8	5.1	5.3	0.9	4.2	2.3	1.4	5.1	1.1
1999	100.0	1.7	5.1	14.2	36.7	11.3	1.0	5.7	5.7	0.6	4.9	2.1	1.5	7.1	0.8
2000	**100.0**	**2.5**	**4.2**	**17.5**	**34.2**	**10.9**	**0.8**	**5.8**	**5.1**	**0.4**	**4.6**	**2.4**	**1.7**	**6.6**	**0.6**
2001	100.0	2.6	4.3	14.7	33.3	10.3	0.7	7.9	4.9	0.4	5.1	2.5	1.9	8.2	0.6
2002	**100.0**	**2.3**	**3.9**	**11.4**	**32.4**	**8.0**	**0.6**	**11.6**	**5.2**	**0.4**	**5.1**	**3.0**	**1.2**	**10.4**	**0.7**

(1) Relates to the external trade with the USSR until 1991 and to the external trade with Russia from 1992 onwards.

ESTONIA

TRADE BALANCE (BN ECU/euro)

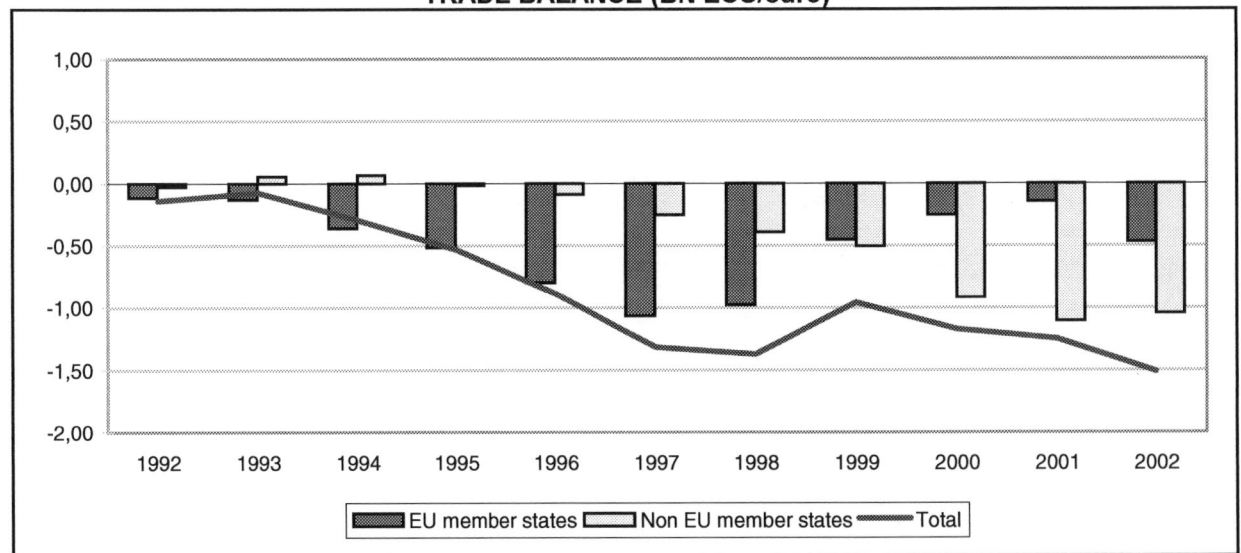

TRADE WITH EU MEMBER STATES (BN ECU/euro)

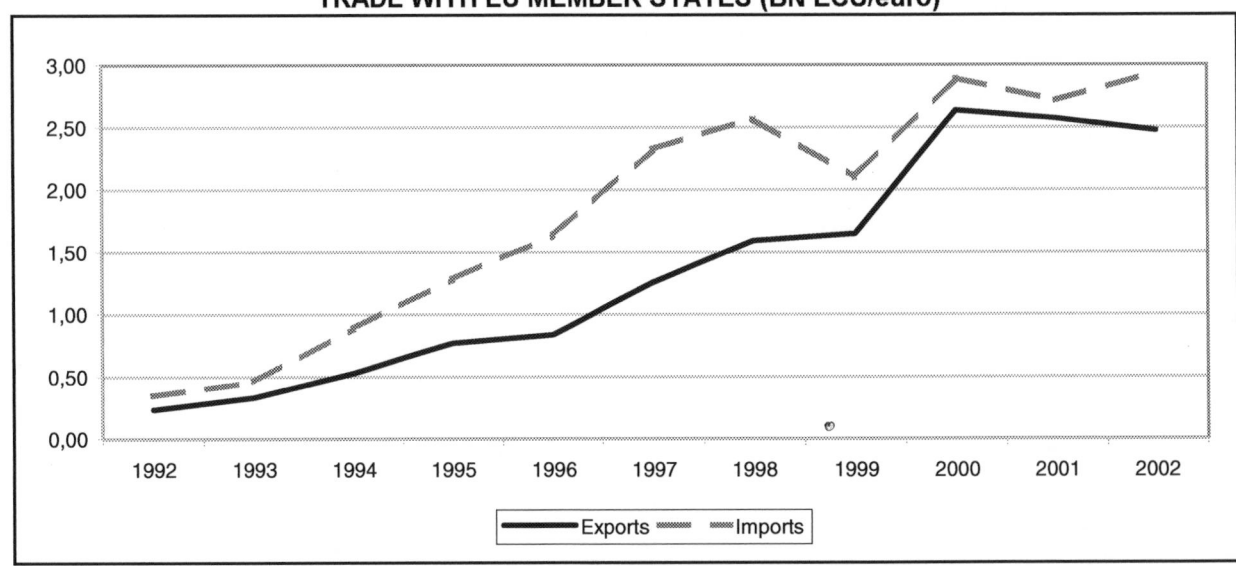

TRADE WITH NON EU MEMBER STATES (BN ECU/euro)

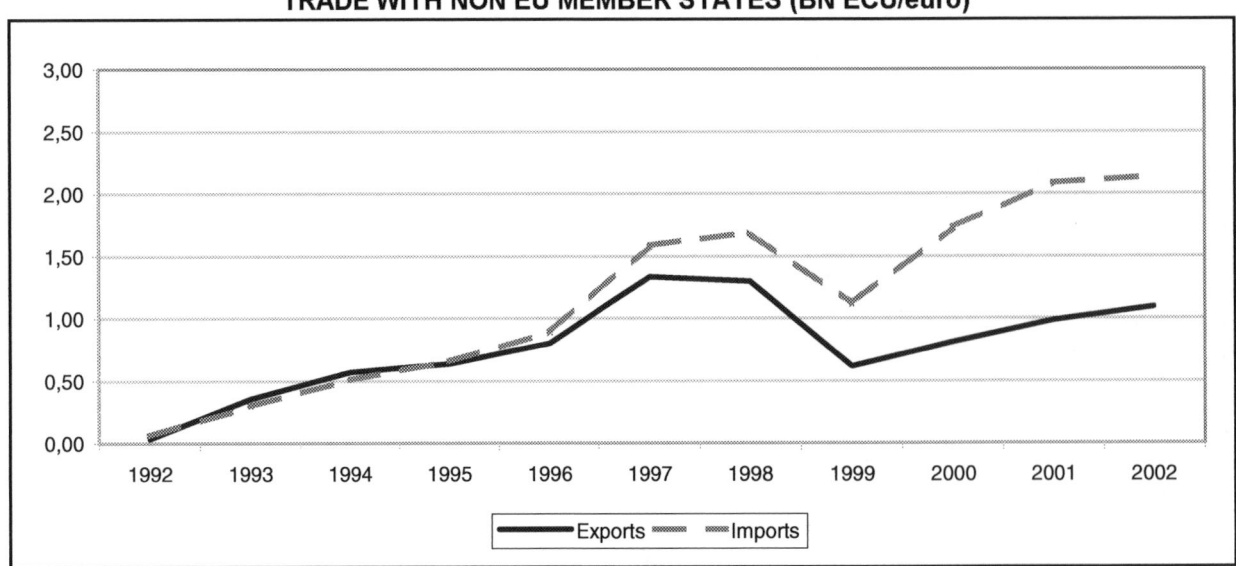

TRADE BALANCE

EU MEMBER STATES

Value (Mio ECU/Euro)

Year		Partner														
	Intra EU	B[(2)]	DK	D	EL	E	F	IRL	I	L	NL	A	P	FIN	S	UK
1990	:	:	:	:	:	:	:	:	:	:	:	:	:	:	:	:
1991	:	:	:	:	:	:	:	:	:	:	:	:	:	:	:	:
1992	-113	:	-0	-36	4	-1	-7	-0	0	:	0	-1	2	-85	5	5
1993	-130	-4	-4	-27	-0	-1	-7	-1	-11	:	0	-0	1	-71	-3	-2
1994	-360	-8	1	-65	-0	-3	-16	-4	-24	:	-8	-7	1	-223	-5	1
1995	-515	-10	-8	-85	-1	-7	-18	-5	-39	:	5	-9	-0	-332	-12	3
1996	-798	-16	-13	-135	-1	-12	-32	-6	-66	:	-24	-10	-2	-436	-17	-27
1997	-1,065	-22	-18	-248	-1	-15	-69	-16	-97	-1	-13	-14	-2	-510	-7	-25
1998	-980	-25	-12	-303	-1	-24	-80	-16	-118	0	-45	-20	-2	-419	96	-4
1999	-455	-30	17	-144	-1	-15	-42	-17	-89	-0	-25	-12	0	-309	167	45
2000	**-255**	**-47**	**3**	**-144**	**-1**	**-21**	**-52**	**-14**	**-98**	**-1**	**-13**	**-15**	**4**	**-153**	**251**	**44**
2001	-144	-66	9	-269	-2	-33	-77	-35	-122	-3	-16	-27	-7	386	76	42
2002	**-467**	**-75**	**38**	**-211**	**-2**	**-24**	**-85**	**-13**	**-196**	**-1**	**-11**	**-36**	**-8**	**32**	**73**	**50**

NON EU MEMBER STATES

Value (Mio ECU/euro)

Year		Partner													
	Extra EU	Norway	Switzerland	USSR/ Russia[(1)]	Candid. countries	USA	Canada	China	Japan	Hong Kong	Mediterr. Basin	Latin America	OPEC	DAE	ACP
1990	:	:	:	:	:	:	:	:	:	:	:	:	:	:	:
1991	:	:	:	:	:	:	:	:	:	:	:	:	:	:	:
1992	-26	5	-1	:	:	-41	:	8	3	:	1	:	:	:	:
1993	55	0	-2	24	49	-8	-1	-1	-29	-1	3	-3	1	-5	10
1994	65	8	-3	20	88	-15	-4	-4	-36	-4	-1	-5	-2	-13	5
1995	-18	10	-12	-65	85	-14	-3	-7	-30	-7	6	-11	-1	-21	3
1996	-87	2	-11	-71	102	-22	-14	-12	-39	-6	4	-12	-5	-46	-9
1997	-254	0	13	-80	189	-98	-8	-19	-117	-6	5	-33	-10	-68	-88
1998	-393	9	3	-90	181	-141	-7	-30	-200	-8	20	-19	-11	-49	-101
1999	-504	25	-26	-183	25	-47	-4	-39	-167	-8	-2	-11	3	-37	-3
2000	**-919**	**18**	**-21**	**-310**	**22**	**-55**	**4**	**-157**	**-273**	**-8**	**1**	**-11**	**4**	**-68**	**-1**
2001	-1,104	52	-22	-288	-49	-42	8	-402	-177	-6	-11	-4	-7	-88	4
2002	**-1,044**	**68**	**-22**	**-254**	**-78**	**-79**	**6**	**-244**	**-182**	**-15**	**-21**	**-19**	**-14**	**-113**	**-6**

(1) Relates to the external trade with the USSR until 1991 and to the external trade with Russia from 1992 onwards.

(2) With Luxembourg until 31.12.1998.

ESTONIA

EU MEMBER STATES

Years	Intra EU	B[1]	DK	D	EL	E	F	IRL	I	L	NL	A	P	FIN	S	UK
							Partner									

EXPORTS
Value (Mio ECU/Euro)

Years	Intra EU	B[1]	DK	D	EL	E	F	IRL	I	L	NL	A	P	FIN	S	UK
1990	:	:	:	:	:	:	:	:	:	:	:	:	:	:	:	:
1994	528	12	38	75	0	1	5	0	10	:	35	2	3	197	120	31
1995	768	21	46	101	0	1	11	3	12	:	66	4	2	303	153	46
1996	835	20	58	115	1	2	19	4	15	:	48	4	3	300	189	57
1997	1,258	30	83	144	1	6	18	7	20	1	87	7	4	406	348	95
1998	1,591	35	105	160	2	7	26	4	21	1	64	13	5	546	482	124
1999	1,644	27	107	192	1	13	32	4	25	0	58	13	6	527	513	127
2000	**2,635**	**31**	**118**	**293**	**3**	**18**	**47**	**11**	**34**	**0**	**85**	**15**	**11**	**1,114**	**706**	**150**
2001	2,567	25	130	256	4	10	40	14	36	0	102	18	5	1,252	518	156
2002	**2,473**	**29**	**162**	**360**	**5**	**22**	**49**	**23**	**39**	**1**	**125**	**20**	**4**	**901**	**558**	**175**

Annual variation (%)

Years	Intra EU	B[1]	DK	D	EL	E	F	IRL	I	L	NL	A	P	FIN	S	UK
98/97	26.4	16.4	27.2	10.8	191.0	22.6	44.3	-46.3	7.9	1.2	-26.8	78.8	31.4	34.4	38.5	30.2
99/98	3.3	-23.1	1.2	20.0	-43.6	78.6	22.2	10.2	19.7	-79.8	-8.5	-0.6	20.8	-3.4	6.2	3.0
00/99	60.2	15.2	10.8	53.0	122.9	43.5	45.3	151.3	35.2	-37.5	45.2	15.0	92.2	111.4	37.7	17.9
01/00	-2.5	-18.5	9.8	-12.5	47.9	-43.2	-13.6	28.4	5.2	132.2	20.9	23.4	-55.1	12.3	-26.5	3.6
02/01	-3.6	17.7	24.4	40.5	24.9	112.4	22.9	61.6	7.2	399.0	21.9	12.1	-26.0	-27.9	7.6	12.6

Share (%)

Years	Intra EU	B[1]	DK	D	EL	E	F	IRL	I	L	NL	A	P	FIN	S	UK
1990	:	:	:	:	:	:	:	:	:	:	:	:	:	:	:	:
1996	100.0	2.4	6.9	13.8	0.1	0.2	2.2	0.5	1.8	:	5.7	0.4	0.3	35.8	22.5	6.7
1997	100.0	2.3	6.5	11.4	0.0	0.4	1.4	0.5	1.5	0.0	6.9	0.5	0.2	32.2	27.6	7.5
1998	100.0	2.1	6.6	10.0	0.1	0.4	1.6	0.2	1.3	0.0	4.0	0.8	0.2	34.3	30.3	7.7
1999	100.0	1.6	6.4	11.6	0.0	0.7	1.9	0.2	1.5	0.0	3.5	0.7	0.3	32.0	31.1	7.7
2000	**100.0**	**1.1**	**4.4**	**11.1**	**0.0**	**0.6**	**1.7**	**0.4**	**1.2**	**0.0**	**3.2**	**0.5**	**0.4**	**42.2**	**26.7**	**5.6**
2001	100.0	0.9	5.0	9.9	0.1	0.4	1.5	0.5	1.4	0.0	3.9	0.7	0.1	48.7	20.1	6.0
2002	**100.0**	**1.1**	**6.5**	**14.5**	**0.1**	**0.8**	**2.0**	**0.9**	**1.5**	**0.0**	**5.0**	**0.8**	**0.1**	**36.4**	**22.5**	**7.0**

IMPORTS
Value (Mio ECU/Euro)

Years	Intra EU	B[1]	DK	D	EL	E	F	IRL	I	L	NL	A	P	FIN	S	UK
1990	:	:	:	:	:	:	:	:	:	:	:	:	:	:	:	:
1994	888	20	37	140	1	4	21	4	34	:	43	9	2	420	125	30
1995	1,283	30	54	186	1	8	28	8	51	:	60	13	2	634	165	43
1996	1,633	36	71	251	2	14	51	10	81	:	72	14	5	736	206	83
1997	2,323	52	101	392	2	21	88	24	117	1	100	22	5	916	355	120
1998	2,571	59	118	462	3	31	107	19	139	1	109	33	6	965	387	127
1999	2,099	56	90	335	2	28	74	21	114	1	84	25	5	836	345	83
2000	**2,890**	**78**	**115**	**437**	**4**	**40**	**98**	**25**	**132**	**1**	**97**	**30**	**7**	**1,266**	**455**	**106**
2001	2,711	91	121	526	5	43	118	49	158	3	118	45	12	866	442	113
2002	**2,941**	**104**	**123**	**571**	**7**	**46**	**134**	**36**	**235**	**2**	**136**	**56**	**11**	**870**	**484**	**125**

Annual variation (%)

Years	Intra EU	B[1]	DK	D	EL	E	F	IRL	I	L	NL	A	P	FIN	S	UK
98/97	10.7	14.4	16.5	17.9	51.7	46.9	21.7	-18.3	19.3	-62.0	8.7	53.7	16.0	5.3	8.8	6.0
99/98	-18.3	-4.6	-23.4	-27.4	-20.0	-11.4	-30.7	8.3	-17.8	0.5	-23.4	-24.4	-14.2	-13.4	-10.7	-34.9
00/99	37.6	38.1	27.5	30.4	56.7	43.8	33.0	18.0	15.4	25.8	16.6	17.6	25.9	51.5	31.7	28.0
01/00	-6.1	17.3	5.3	20.1	47.4	7.9	19.6	95.5	20.1	316.1	21.3	52.3	82.6	-31.6	-2.7	6.9
02/01	8.4	13.9	1.8	8.5	23.6	8.3	13.9	-26.8	48.2	-16.2	14.6	24.5	-7.8	0.4	9.5	10.5

Share (%)

Years	Intra EU	B[1]	DK	D	EL	E	F	IRL	I	L	NL	A	P	FIN	S	UK
1990	:	:	:	:	:	:	:	:	:	:	:	:	:	:	:	:
1996	100.0	2.1	4.3	15.3	0.0	0.8	3.1	0.6	4.9	:	4.3	0.8	0.2	45.0	12.5	5.0
1997	100.0	2.2	4.3	16.8	0.0	0.9	3.7	1.0	5.0	0.0	4.3	0.9	0.2	39.4	15.2	5.1
1998	100.0	2.3	4.5	17.9	0.1	1.2	4.1	0.7	5.4	0.0	4.2	1.2	0.2	37.5	15.0	4.9
1999	100.0	2.6	4.2	15.9	0.1	1.3	3.5	1.0	5.4	0.0	3.9	1.1	0.2	39.8	16.4	3.9
2000	**100.0**	**2.6**	**3.9**	**15.1**	**0.1**	**1.3**	**3.4**	**0.8**	**4.5**	**0.0**	**3.3**	**1.0**	**0.2**	**43.8**	**15.7**	**3.6**
2001	100.0	3.3	4.4	19.3	0.2	1.5	4.3	1.7	5.8	0.1	4.3	1.6	0.4	31.9	16.3	4.1
2002	**100.0**	**3.5**	**4.1**	**19.4**	**0.2**	**1.5**	**4.5**	**1.2**	**7.9**	**0.0**	**4.6**	**1.9**	**0.3**	**29.5**	**16.4**	**4.2**

(1) With Luxembourg until 31.12.1998.

NON EU MEMBER STATES

Years	Extra EU	Norway	Switzerland	USSR/Russia(1)	Candid. countries	USA	Canada	China	Japan	Hong Kong	Mediterr. Basin	Latin America	OPEC	DAE	ACP
							Partner								

EXPORTS
Value (Mio ECU/Euro)

Years	Extra EU	Norway	Switzerland	USSR/Russia(1)	Candid. countries	USA	Canada	China	Japan	Hong Kong	Mediterr. Basin	Latin America	OPEC	DAE	ACP
1990	:	:	:	:	:	:	:	:	:	:	:	:	:	:	:
1994	571	16	5	253	170	20	2	3	5	0	3	1	2	1	8
1995	637	26	4	248	196	34	2	1	7	0	11	1	2	1	7
1996	801	25	19	269	262	36	3	0	12	1	15	1	1	12	8
1997	1,332	42	54	487	422	48	4	2	14	4	22	7	2	27	9
1998	1,296	60	45	384	463	56	5	2	12	3	42	10	4	14	7
1999	615	58	11	76	299	43	3	2	6	4	23	4	9	23	3
2000	809	81	16	82	404	46	11	7	7	5	29	4	12	44	5
2001	983	103	23	101	446	68	16	16	37	7	30	14	12	43	11
2002	1,094	123	27	122	503	82	15	20	13	8	30	3	15	50	12

Annual variation (%)

Years	Extra EU	Norway	Switzerland	USSR/Russia(1)	Candid. countries	USA	Canada	China	Japan	Hong Kong	Mediterr. Basin	Latin America	OPEC	DAE	ACP
98/97	-2.6	42.4	-17.0	-20.9	9.7	17.9	23.2	30.7	-16.1	-37.4	92.5	47.8	111.6	-46.7	-16.4
99/98	-52.5	-2.2	-75.3	-80.2	-35.5	-22.8	-51.4	9.4	-48.3	55.6	-45.4	-56.8	159.2	63.0	-51.5
00/99	31.4	38.3	44.8	7.5	35.4	6.1	325.0	196.4	6.0	20.6	28.5	-9.8	29.3	86.3	56.2
01/00	21.5	27.8	43.0	24.2	10.2	46.6	44.0	139.6	458.3	35.9	1.3	266.4	4.8	-1.0	104.2
02/01	11.3	19.0	16.5	19.8	12.7	21.3	-6.7	24.7	-65.1	24.1	1.1	-77.5	21.3	15.5	6.1

Share (%)

Years	Extra EU	Norway	Switzerland	USSR/Russia(1)	Candid. countries	USA	Canada	China	Japan	Hong Kong	Mediterr. Basin	Latin America	OPEC	DAE	ACP
1990	:	:	:	:	:	:	:	:	:	:	:	:	:	:	:
1996	100.0	3.0	2.4	33.5	32.7	4.4	0.4	0.0	1.4	0.1	1.8	0.1	0.1	1.4	0.9
1997	100.0	3.1	4.0	36.5	31.6	3.5	0.3	0.1	1.0	0.3	1.6	0.5	0.1	2.0	0.6
1998	100.0	4.6	3.4	29.6	35.7	4.3	0.4	0.1	0.9	0.1	3.2	0.7	0.2	1.1	0.5
1999	100.0	9.5	1.7	12.3	48.5	7.0	0.4	0.3	1.0	0.6	3.7	0.6	1.4	3.8	0.5
2000	100.0	10.0	1.9	10.0	50.0	5.6	1.3	0.8	0.8	0.6	3.6	0.4	1.4	5.4	0.6
2001	100.0	10.5	2.3	10.3	45.3	6.8	1.6	1.6	3.7	0.6	3.0	1.4	1.2	4.4	1.1
2002	100.0	11.2	2.4	11.1	45.9	7.4	1.3	1.8	1.1	0.7	2.7	0.2	1.3	4.5	1.0

IMPORTS
Value (Mio ECU/Euro)

Years	Extra EU	Norway	Switzerland	USSR/Russia(1)	Candid. countries	USA	Canada	China	Japan	Hong Kong	Mediterr. Basin	Latin America	OPEC	DAE	ACP
1990	:	:	:	:	:	:	:	:	:	:	:	:	:	:	:
1994	506	9	8	233	82	35	5	7	41	5	4	6	4	14	3
1995	654	16	16	313	111	48	4	8	36	7	6	12	3	22	4
1996	888	23	31	340	161	58	17	13	51	7	11	12	6	58	17
1997	1,585	42	41	567	232	146	12	21	131	11	16	39	11	95	97
1998	1,689	51	42	475	282	197	12	33	212	11	22	29	15	63	108
1999	1,119	33	37	258	274	91	6	42	173	12	24	16	6	60	6
2000	1,727	63	37	391	383	101	7	164	279	13	28	15	8	112	7
2001	2,087	51	45	390	495	110	8	418	214	12	41	18	19	132	7
2002	2,138	55	49	375	580	161	9	265	195	24	51	23	29	163	18

Annual variation (%)

Years	Extra EU	Norway	Switzerland	USSR/Russia(1)	Candid. countries	USA	Canada	China	Japan	Hong Kong	Mediterr. Basin	Latin America	OPEC	DAE	ACP
98/97	6.5	22.2	1.2	-16.2	21.2	35.4	3.2	55.0	62.2	4.5	32.0	-26.1	30.9	-33.5	12.1
99/98	-33.7	-34.7	-12.3	-45.5	-2.8	-54.1	-47.8	27.4	-18.4	9.2	12.0	-46.4	-57.8	-4.6	-94.3
00/99	54.3	87.9	0.7	51.4	39.8	12.0	12.2	293.8	61.3	8.4	16.4	-4.1	30.7	86.4	8.8
01/00	20.8	-18.3	20.8	-0.4	29.3	8.4	13.3	155.4	-23.5	-7.2	44.0	20.4	132.5	17.3	1.1
02/01	2.4	6.7	8.6	-3.7	17.2	46.6	11.6	-36.6	-8.7	93.1	24.0	25.9	52.3	23.5	170.7

Share (%)

Years	Extra EU	Norway	Switzerland	USSR/Russia(1)	Candid. countries	USA	Canada	China	Japan	Hong Kong	Mediterr. Basin	Latin America	OPEC	DAE	ACP
1990	:	:	:	:	:	:	:	:	:	:	:	:	:	:	:
1996	100.0	2.5	3.4	38.2	18.0	6.5	1.9	1.4	5.7	0.8	1.1	1.3	0.6	6.5	1.9
1997	100.0	2.6	2.6	35.7	14.6	9.1	0.7	1.3	8.2	0.6	1.0	2.4	0.7	5.9	6.0
1998	100.0	3.0	2.4	28.1	16.6	11.6	0.7	1.9	12.5	0.6	1.2	1.7	0.8	3.7	6.4
1999	100.0	2.9	3.2	23.0	24.4	8.0	0.5	3.7	15.4	1.0	2.1	1.3	0.5	5.3	0.5
2000	100.0	3.6	2.1	22.6	22.1	5.8	0.4	9.4	16.1	0.7	1.6	0.8	0.4	6.4	0.3
2001	100.0	2.4	2.1	18.6	23.7	5.2	0.3	20.0	10.2	0.5	1.9	0.8	0.9	6.3	0.3
2002	100.0	2.5	2.2	17.5	27.1	7.5	0.4	12.3	9.1	1.0	2.3	1.0	1.3	7.6	0.8

(1) Relates to the external trade with the USSR until 1991 and to the external trade with Russia from 1992 onwards.

HUNGARY

TRADE BALANCE (BN ECU/euro)

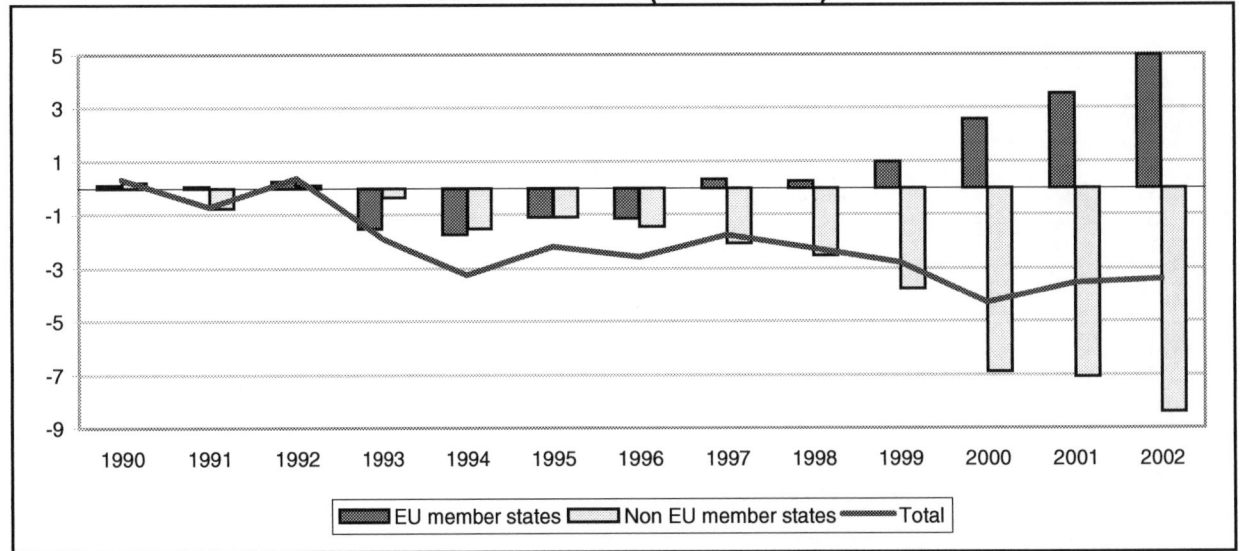

TRADE WITH EU MEMBER STATES (BN ECU/euro)

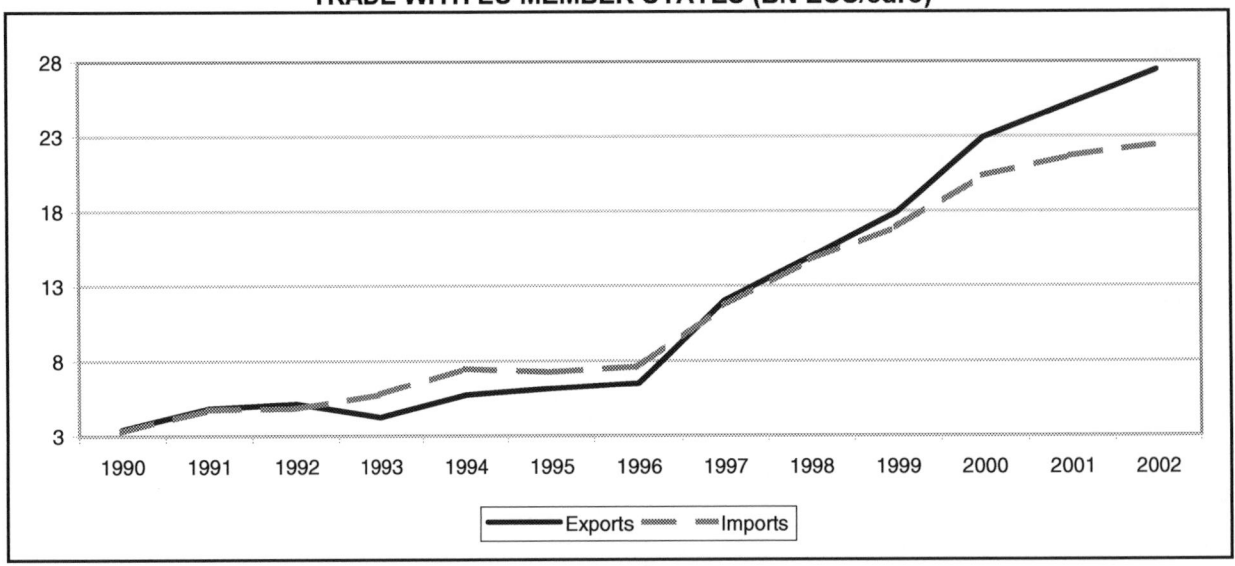

TRADE WITH NON EU MEMBER STATES (BN ECU/euro)

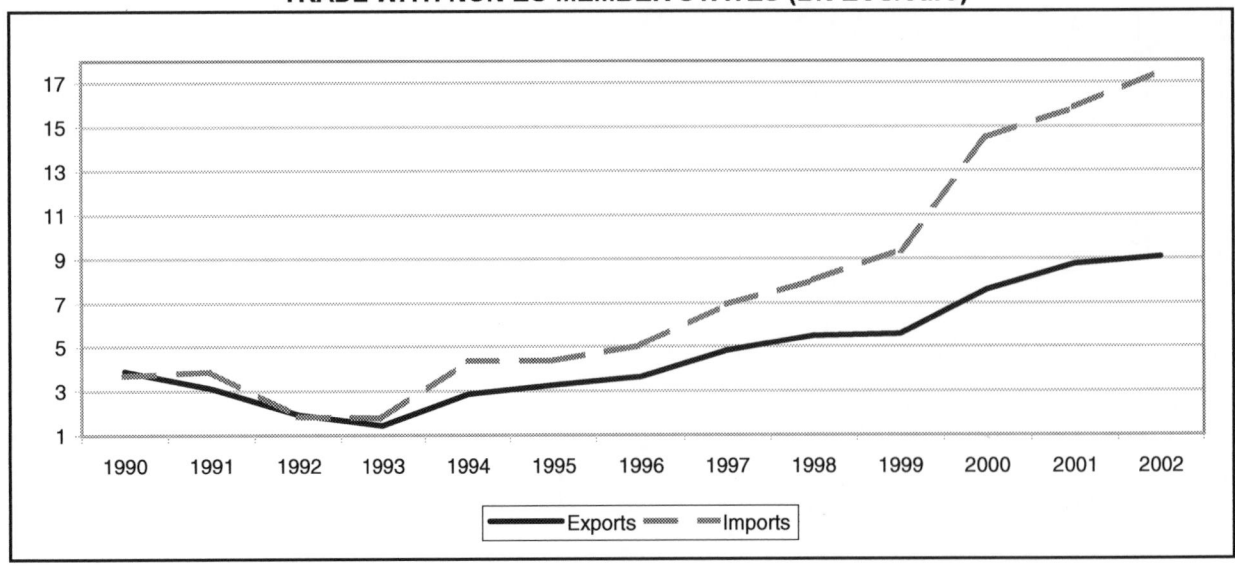

TRADE BALANCE

EU MEMBER STATES

Value (Mio ECU/Euro)

Year	Intra EU	B(2)	DK	D	EL	E	F	IRL	I	L	NL	A	P	FIN	S	UK
1990	**105**	**-28**	**7**	**-64**	**43**	**6**	**63**	**:**	**168**	**:**	**-28**	**-108**	**0**	**29**	**5**	**9**
1991	63	-6	-3	258	18	72	-10	:	-49	:	-80	-39	1	-1	-37	-61
1992	260	15	-9	279	36	45	3	:	248	:	-69	-116	-1	-33	-57	-82
1993	-1,522	-74	-31	-416	20	-34	-93	:	-31	:	-112	-484	-1	-80	-86	-100
1994	-1,743	-94	-45	-323	2	-42	-99	-27	-94	:	-145	-491	-5	-140	-150	-89
1995	-1,097	-90	-45	44	-4	-75	-71	-57	-95	:	-83	-276	-18	-121	-142	-65
1996	-1,145	-100	-50	-4	6	-26	-158	-28	-203	:	-127	-111	-9	-105	-113	-114
1997	320	-30	-51	1,170	28	13	-109	-5	-340	-6	-10	-48	-46	-120	-102	-25
1998	252	-29	-52	1,044	17	-23	-333	127	-556	-9	389	-21	-2	-152	-84	-51
1999	972	27	-30	1,335	20	-57	-176	73	-642	-18	554	-96	21	-212	-80	253
2000	**2,581**	**174**	**-13**	**2,471**	**45**	**-56**	**81**	**-2**	**-823**	**-24**	**891**	**81**	**30**	**-298**	**-125**	**148**
2001	3,534	253	-44	2,745	67	11	268	159	-832	-8	782	-82	87	-176	-52	356
2002	**4,966**	**221**	**-52**	**3,265**	**70**	**142**	**147**	**-62**	**-904**	**-16**	**721**	**-182**	**108**	**-176**	**1,108**	**576**

NON EU MEMBER STATES

Value (Mio ECU/euro)

Year	Extra EU	Norway	Switzerland	USSR/ Russia(1)	Candid. countries	USA	Canada	China	Japan	Hong Kong	Mediterr. Basin	Latin America	OPEC	DAE	ACP
1990	**211**	**6**	**-67**	**224**	**:**	**86**	**15**	**26**	**-54**	**-8**	**241**	**-111**	**-47**	**-45**	**-11**
1991	-763	3	-170	-321	:	18	8	-21	-112	7	222	-68	27	-54	-37
1992	110	1	-109	:	:	14	8	-19	-129	-1	390	-90	123	-49	-5
1993	-349	-2	-161	:	164	-103	-7	-16	-222	-7	155	-109	83	-88	-4
1994	-1,510	-3	-184	-790	-100	-18	1	-73	-253	-10	200	-122	37	-125	-5
1995	-1,095	-0	-156	-777	190	-53	-16	-79	-200	-20	288	-129	121	-174	-5
1996	-1,439	2	-125	-980	116	-82	-19	:	-205	-31	486	-138	56	-201	-61
1997	-2,073	14	-121	-870	196	-158	-46	-242	-523	-31	590	-218	41	-573	-56
1998	-2,524	2	-145	-892	355	42	-39	-370	-797	-70	613	-218	11	-807	-83
1999	-3,771	-13	-117	-1,203	-16	311	-33	-506	-1,005	-82	545	-276	1	-1,142	-58
2000	**-6,889**	**-9**	**-83**	**-2,313**	**7**	**275**	**-40**	**-986**	**-1,677**	**-79**	**738**	**-294**	**-17**	**-1,889**	**-36**
2001	-7,086	7	-98	-2,118	146	115	-25	-1,363	-1,537	-97	800	-274	45	-2,158	-89
2002	**-8,390**	**3**	**-118**	**-1,937**	**-56**	**-202**	**-41**	**-2,045**	**-1,459**	**-177**	**904**	**-276**	**156**	**-2,456**	**6**

(1) Relates to the external trade with the USSR until 1991 and to the external trade with Russia from 1992 onwards.

(2) With Luxembourg until 31.12.1998.

HUNGARY

EU MEMBER STATES

Years	Intra EU	B(1)	DK	D	EL	E	F	IRL	I	L	NL	A	P	FIN	S	UK
							Partner									

EXPORTS
Value (Mio ECU/Euro)

Years	Intra EU	B(1)	DK	D	EL	E	F	IRL	I	L	NL	A	P	FIN	S	UK
1990	3,416	87	46	1,518	65	39	203	:	442	:	114	566	3	75	106	153
1994	5,732	177	43	2,537	35	80	319	6	761	:	228	978	10	61	105	391
1995	6,162	209	44	2,818	37	94	396	11	838	:	286	996	7	44	96	299
1996	6,488	224	42	3,005	47	102	383	8	831	:	277	1,098	10	46	109	302
1997	12,017	410	63	6,267	71	253	634	60	1,037	8	474	1,929	17	81	129	563
1998	14,940	539	87	7,510	66	339	781	224	1,180	9	968	2,181	74	93	187	731
1999	17,902	709	107	9,016	69	383	1,055	235	1,386	6	1,214	2,249	117	86	218	1,053
2000	22,929	954	150	11,370	103	567	1,601	273	1,793	9	1,658	2,647	166	107	277	1,253
2001	25,226	1,110	174	12,098	130	698	2,028	367	2,122	19	1,561	2,688	216	217	335	1,462
2002	27,425	984	218	12,955	140	868	2,070	153	2,107	21	1,554	2,583	232	252	1,577	1,711

Annual variation (%)

Years	Intra EU	B(1)	DK	D	EL	E	F	IRL	I	L	NL	A	P	FIN	S	UK
98/97	24.3	31.5	39.2	19.8	-7.2	34.2	23.2	274.1	13.8	14.5	104.4	13.0	342.5	14.3	44.5	29.7
99/98	19.8	31.6	22.3	20.0	4.5	12.8	35.0	5.0	17.4	-33.1	25.4	3.0	58.4	-7.0	16.3	44.1
00/99	28.0	34.5	40.3	26.1	48.8	47.9	51.8	16.1	29.3	61.0	36.5	17.7	42.2	24.8	27.0	18.9
01/00	10.0	16.3	16.1	6.3	26.2	23.2	26.6	34.4	18.3	105.4	-5.8	1.5	29.6	102.0	21.1	16.6
02/01	8.7	-11.3	25.4	7.0	7.6	24.3	2.0	-58.3	-0.7	6.7	-0.4	-3.9	7.7	16.1	370.9	17.0

Share (%)

Years	Intra EU	B(1)	DK	D	EL	E	F	IRL	I	L	NL	A	P	FIN	S	UK
1990	100.0	2.5	1.3	44.4	1.8	1.1	5.9	:	12.9	:	3.3	16.5	0.0	2.1	3.0	4.4
1996	100.0	3.4	0.6	46.3	0.7	1.5	5.9	0.1	12.8	:	4.2	16.9	0.1	0.7	1.6	4.6
1997	100.0	3.4	0.5	52.1	0.5	2.1	5.2	0.4	8.6	0.0	3.9	16.0	0.1	0.6	1.0	4.6
1998	100.0	3.6	0.5	50.2	0.4	2.2	5.2	1.4	7.9	0.0	6.4	14.5	0.4	0.6	1.2	4.8
1999	100.0	3.9	0.5	50.3	0.3	2.1	5.8	1.3	7.7	0.0	6.7	12.5	0.6	0.4	1.2	5.8
2000	100.0	4.1	0.6	49.5	0.4	2.4	6.9	1.1	7.8	0.0	7.2	11.5	0.7	0.4	1.2	5.4
2001	100.0	4.3	0.6	47.9	0.5	2.7	8.0	1.4	8.4	0.0	6.1	10.6	0.8	0.8	1.3	5.7
2002	100.0	3.5	0.7	47.2	0.5	3.1	7.5	0.5	7.6	0.0	5.6	9.4	0.8	0.9	5.7	6.2

IMPORTS
Value (Mio ECU/Euro)

Years	Intra EU	B(1)	DK	D	EL	E	F	IRL	I	L	NL	A	P	FIN	S	UK
1990	3,312	115	39	1,582	21	33	139	:	274	:	142	674	3	45	101	143
1994	7,474	270	89	2,861	34	122	418	33	855	:	373	1,470	15	201	255	480
1995	7,259	299	89	2,774	41	169	467	68	933	:	370	1,272	26	164	238	364
1996	7,633	324	93	3,008	41	128	541	37	1,034	:	404	1,209	19	151	222	416
1997	11,696	440	114	5,097	43	240	743	65	1,376	14	483	1,978	62	201	231	588
1998	14,688	568	140	6,466	49	363	1,114	97	1,736	18	579	2,202	76	245	271	782
1999	16,930	682	136	7,681	50	440	1,231	162	2,028	24	660	2,344	96	298	297	800
2000	20,348	780	162	8,899	58	623	1,521	275	2,616	34	767	2,565	136	406	401	1,105
2001	21,692	856	218	9,353	63	687	1,760	208	2,955	27	779	2,771	129	393	387	1,106
2002	22,459	763	270	9,690	71	727	1,922	215	3,011	37	833	2,764	124	427	470	1,135

Annual variation (%)

Years	Intra EU	B(1)	DK	D	EL	E	F	IRL	I	L	NL	A	P	FIN	S	UK
98/97	25.5	29.0	22.5	26.8	13.2	50.8	49.9	49.8	26.1	31.8	19.8	11.3	21.5	21.9	17.3	32.9
99/98	15.2	20.1	-2.3	18.7	1.0	21.3	10.5	66.7	16.7	29.7	14.0	6.4	26.1	21.9	9.6	2.3
00/99	20.1	14.4	19.3	15.8	17.9	41.5	23.5	69.7	28.9	41.4	16.1	9.4	41.7	35.9	35.0	38.0
01/00	6.6	9.7	34.0	5.1	7.6	10.3	15.7	-24.2	12.9	-18.5	1.4	8.0	-5.0	-3.1	-3.6	0.0
02/01	3.5	-10.9	24.0	3.6	12.2	5.7	9.2	3.3	1.9	33.3	6.9	-0.2	-3.9	8.7	21.4	2.6

Share (%)

Years	Intra EU	B(1)	DK	D	EL	E	F	IRL	I	L	NL	A	P	FIN	S	UK
1990	100.0	3.4	1.1	47.7	0.6	0.9	4.2	:	8.2	:	4.2	20.3	0.0	1.3	3.0	4.3
1996	100.0	4.2	1.2	39.4	0.5	1.6	7.0	0.4	13.5	:	5.2	15.8	0.2	1.9	2.9	5.4
1997	100.0	3.7	0.9	43.5	0.3	2.0	6.3	0.5	11.7	0.1	4.1	16.9	0.5	1.7	1.9	5.0
1998	100.0	3.8	0.9	44.0	0.3	2.4	7.5	0.6	11.8	0.1	3.9	14.9	0.5	1.6	1.8	5.3
1999	100.0	4.0	0.8	45.3	0.2	2.5	7.2	0.9	11.9	0.1	3.9	13.8	0.5	1.7	1.7	4.7
2000	100.0	3.8	0.7	43.7	0.2	3.0	7.4	1.3	12.8	0.1	3.7	12.6	0.6	1.9	1.9	5.4
2001	100.0	3.9	1.0	43.1	0.2	3.1	8.1	0.9	13.6	0.1	3.5	12.7	0.5	1.8	1.7	5.0
2002	100.0	3.3	1.2	43.1	0.3	3.2	8.5	0.9	13.4	0.1	3.7	12.3	0.5	1.9	2.0	5.0

(1) With Luxembourg until 31.12.1998.

NON EU MEMBER STATES

Years	Extra EU	Norway	Switzerland	USSR/Russia[1]	Candid. countries	USA	Canada	China	Japan	Hong Kong	Mediterr. Basin	Latin America	OPEC	DAE	ACP
						EXPORTS									
					Value (Mio ECU/Euro)										
1990	3,917	16	140	1,510	:	264	23	65	86	11	620	58	208	69	32
1994	2,867	14	134	680	903	361	29	10	77	12	414	40	93	55	3
1995	3,269	17	134	627	1,180	315	16	17	59	15	531	41	189	46	4
1996	3,636	20	153	613	1,296	366	18	:	80	16	734	53	100	53	21
1997	4,846	32	203	857	1,718	546	33	14	90	14	975	62	100	76	30
1998	5,491	29	246	598	2,049	929	56	17	84	11	982	153	97	159	30
1999	5,585	29	276	335	2,010	1,220	27	67	74	20	967	138	102	350	37
2000	7,596	39	370	496	2,809	1,603	43	44	174	38	1,330	165	137	471	62
2001	8,758	57	416	528	3,399	1,703	51	126	193	41	1,512	180	195	376	65
2002	9,078	63	399	482	3,684	1,275	67	164	206	41	1,696	195	340	400	111
					Annual variation (%)										
98/97	13.3	-10.7	21.2	-30.1	19.2	70.0	68.7	18.6	-6.8	-20.5	0.7	147.4	-2.6	108.4	-1.4
99/98	1.7	0.2	12.4	-43.9	-1.9	31.2	-51.4	305.5	-11.4	76.6	-1.5	-9.9	5.4	119.4	24.8
00/99	36.0	35.0	33.8	47.9	39.7	31.4	59.4	-34.4	135.5	95.5	37.4	19.7	33.4	34.7	66.9
01/00	15.2	46.2	12.5	6.3	21.0	6.1	17.3	186.0	10.6	6.5	13.7	9.2	42.4	-20.1	4.3
02/01	3.6	10.6	-4.1	-8.7	8.3	-25.1	31.4	29.9	6.6	0.2	12.1	7.9	74.7	6.3	71.3
					Share (%)										
1990	100.0	0.4	3.5	38.5	:	6.7	0.5	1.6	2.2	0.2	15.8	1.4	5.3	1.7	0.8
1996	100.0	0.5	4.2	16.8	35.6	10.0	0.4	:	2.1	0.4	20.1	1.4	2.7	1.4	0.5
1997	100.0	0.6	4.1	17.6	35.4	11.2	0.6	0.2	1.8	0.2	20.1	1.2	2.0	1.5	0.6
1998	100.0	0.5	4.4	10.8	37.3	16.9	1.0	0.3	1.5	0.2	17.8	2.7	1.7	2.9	0.5
1999	100.0	0.5	4.9	6.0	35.9	21.8	0.4	1.2	1.3	0.3	17.3	2.4	1.8	6.2	0.6
2000	100.0	0.5	4.8	6.5	36.9	21.1	0.5	0.5	2.2	0.5	17.5	2.1	1.7	6.2	0.8
2001	100.0	0.6	4.7	6.0	38.8	19.4	0.5	1.4	2.2	0.4	17.2	2.0	2.2	4.2	0.7
2002	100.0	0.6	4.3	5.3	40.5	14.0	0.7	1.8	2.2	0.4	18.6	2.1	3.7	4.4	1.2
						IMPORTS									
					Value (Mio ECU/Euro)										
1990	3,707	10	207	1,286	:	178	8	39	141	19	379	169	254	114	43
1994	4,377	17	318	1,470	1,003	380	28	83	330	23	214	162	56	180	8
1995	4,365	17	290	1,404	990	368	32	96	259	36	243	170	68	221	9
1996	5,075	18	277	1,592	1,180	448	37	152	285	46	248	192	44	255	82
1997	6,919	18	324	1,727	1,523	705	79	256	613	45	385	280	59	650	86
1998	8,015	27	391	1,490	1,694	888	95	387	881	81	369	371	86	966	113
1999	9,355	42	393	1,539	2,026	909	60	573	1,079	101	422	414	102	1,492	95
2000	14,485	49	453	2,809	2,802	1,328	83	1,031	1,852	117	592	459	154	2,361	98
2001	15,843	50	514	2,645	3,253	1,587	75	1,489	1,730	137	712	454	150	2,534	154
2002	17,468	60	517	2,419	3,740	1,477	107	2,209	1,664	218	792	471	184	2,856	105
					Annual variation (%)										
98/97	15.8	48.5	20.7	-13.7	11.2	25.9	21.0	51.2	43.6	82.1	-3.9	32.5	46.8	48.7	31.1
99/98	16.7	52.2	0.6	3.2	19.6	2.3	-36.9	48.1	22.5	24.1	14.2	11.4	18.1	54.4	-16.2
00/99	54.8	16.8	15.1	82.5	38.2	46.1	38.3	79.8	71.6	15.9	40.3	10.9	51.0	58.2	3.1
01/00	9.3	2.8	13.5	-5.8	16.0	19.4	-9.0	44.4	-6.5	17.2	20.2	-1.1	-2.3	7.3	56.9
02/01	10.2	19.8	0.4	-8.5	14.9	-6.9	42.3	48.3	-3.7	58.3	11.1	3.7	22.5	12.6	-31.4
					Share (%)										
1990	100.0	0.2	5.5	34.6	:	4.8	0.2	1.0	3.7	0.5	10.2	4.5	6.8	3.0	1.1
1996	100.0	0.3	5.4	31.3	23.2	8.8	0.7	2.9	5.6	0.9	4.8	3.7	0.8	5.0	1.6
1997	100.0	0.2	4.6	24.9	22.0	10.1	1.1	3.6	8.8	0.6	5.5	4.0	0.8	9.3	1.2
1998	100.0	0.3	4.8	18.5	21.1	11.0	1.1	4.8	10.9	1.0	4.6	4.6	1.0	12.0	1.4
1999	100.0	0.4	4.2	16.4	21.6	9.7	0.6	6.1	11.5	1.0	4.5	4.4	1.0	15.9	1.0
2000	100.0	0.3	3.1	19.3	19.3	9.1	0.5	7.1	12.7	0.8	4.0	3.1	1.0	16.2	0.6
2001	100.0	0.3	3.2	16.6	20.5	10.0	0.4	9.3	10.9	0.8	4.4	2.8	0.9	15.9	0.9
2002	100.0	0.3	2.9	13.8	21.4	8.4	0.6	12.6	9.5	1.2	4.5	2.6	1.0	16.3	0.6

(1) Relates to the external trade with the USSR until 1991 and to the external trade with Russia from 1992 onwards.

LATVIA

TRADE BALANCE (BN ECU/euro)

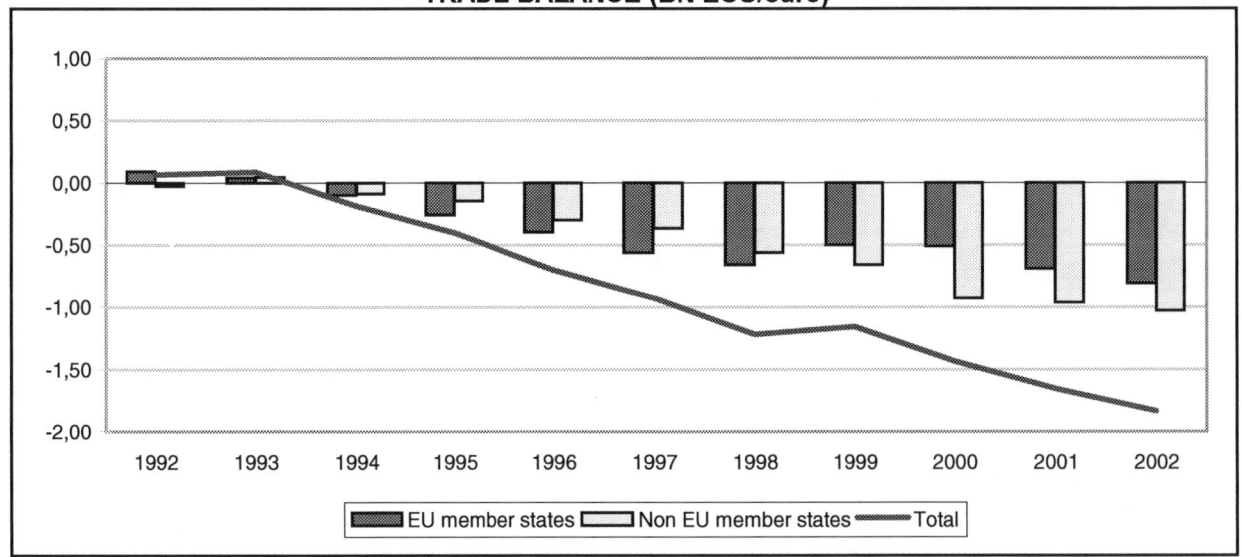

TRADE WITH EU MEMBER STATES (BN ECU/euro)

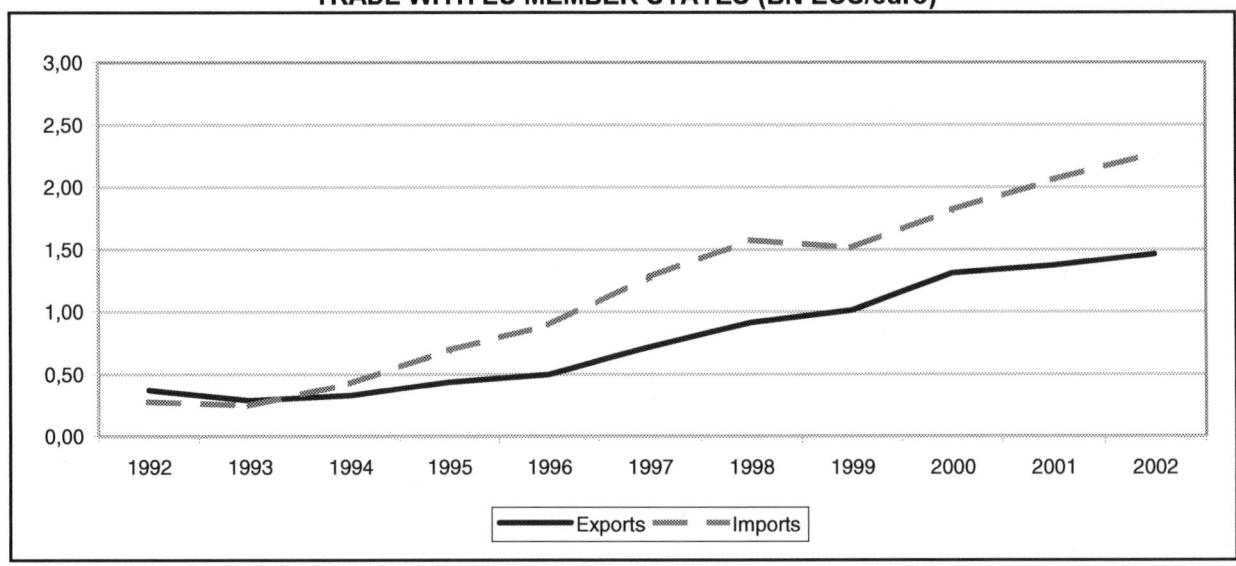

TRADE WITH NON EU MEMBER STATES (BN ECU/euro)

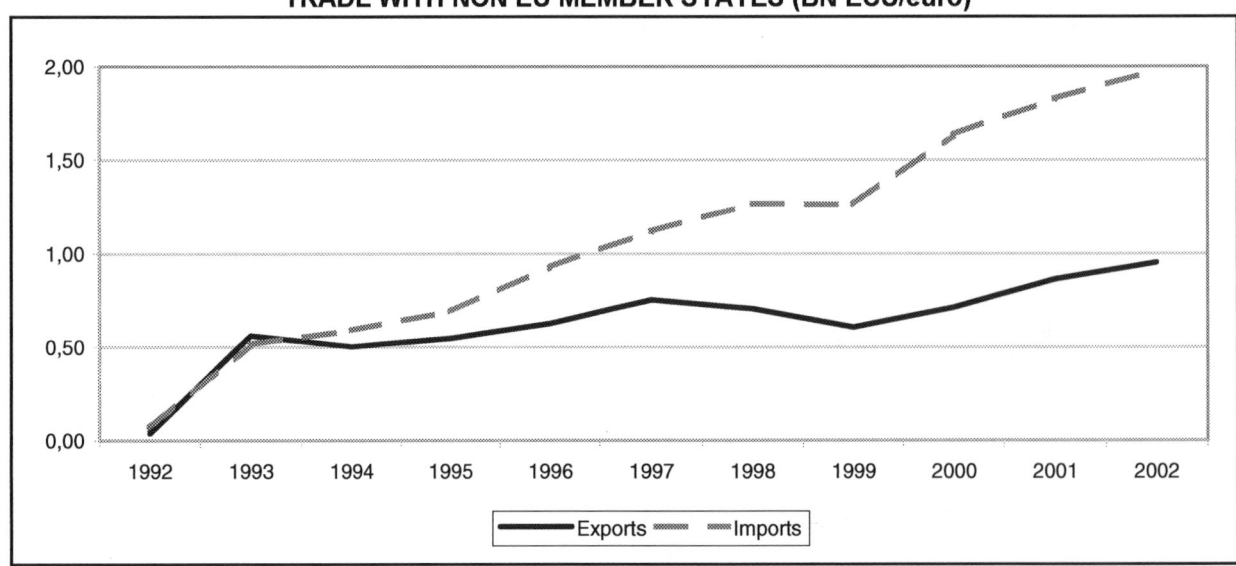

LATVIA

7B

TRADE BALANCE

EU MEMBER STATES

Value (Mio ECU/Euro)

Year	Intra EU	B[2]	DK	D	EL	E	F	IRL	I	L	NL	A	P	FIN	S	UK
														Partner		
1990	:	:	:	:	:	:	:	:	:	:	:	:	:	:	:	:
1991	:	:	:	:	:	:	:	:	:	:	:	:	:	:	:	:
1992	91	30	-3	20	-3	-1	33	4	6	:	5	-1	2	-27	7	17
1993	42	7	-9	-32	0	-1	2	0	5	:	61	-3	0	-20	8	23
1994	-98	-7	-11	-54	-0	-4	-4	6	-11	:	-1	10	2	-69	-10	56
1995	-257	-8	-16	-59	-2	-4	-11	7	-18	:	-19	-12	0	-100	-8	56
1996	-399	-18	-19	-73	-2	-6	-15	-3	-32	:	-36	-11	-0	-126	-56	80
1997	-563	-23	-19	-146	-3	-11	-27	-3	-54	-0	-47	-13	-1	-189	-45	140
1998	-658	-39	-15	-182	-4	-11	-40	-5	-65	-1	-36	-23	-2	-212	-19	138
1999	-500	-28	-9	-147	-5	-11	-59	-10	-76	-0	-52	-27	-1	-221	-28	176
2000	**-511**	**-36**	**-7**	**-195**	**-6**	**-26**	**-69**	**7**	**-96**	**-2**	**-39**	**-24**	**-3**	**-260**	**-15**	**259**
2001	-691	-44	-17	-295	-7	-31	-52	4	-120	-1	-45	-31	-4	-263	-41	256
2002	**-807**	**-57**	**-7**	**-361**	**-3**	**-36**	**-63**	**3**	**-127**	**-3**	**-53**	**-45**	**-2**	**-287**	**-18**	**254**

NON EU MEMBER STATES

Value (Mio ECU/euro)

Year	Extra EU	Norway	Switzerland	USSR/ Russia[1]	Candid. countries	USA	Canada	China	Japan	Hong Kong	Mediterr. Basin	Latin America	OPEC	DAE	ACP
									Partner						
1990	:	:	:	:	:	:	:	:	:	:	:	:	:	:	:
1991	:	:	:	:	:	:	:	:	:	:	:	:	:	:	:
1992	-28	6	-1	-18	:	-39	:	1	10	:	-1	:	:	:	:
1993	46	1	-2	-0	-50	-5	-0	9	2	-1	-2	-2	5	16	6
1994	-88	-1	5	-38	-60	-13	-0	3	-11	-1	-2	-16	-3	2	3
1995	-143	7	-10	-55	-78	-14	-2	-1	-5	-1	-3	-8	-0	-3	0
1996	-299	-17	-18	-110	-157	-34	-4	-2	-1	-1	8	-22	5	2	-1
1997	-364	-27	-22	-66	-238	-35	-6	-4	-3	1	4	-18	8	13	0
1998	-560	-31	-37	-139	-305	-11	-4	-13	-3	5	5	-6	2	10	4
1999	-658	-34	-52	-186	-354	35	0	-14	-2	2	-16	4	2	-13	-0
2000	**-924**	**-22**	**-53**	**-317**	**-446**	**7**	**12**	**-26**	**4**	**-2**	**2**	**0**	**20**	**-21**	**18**
2001	-964	-18	-61	-229	-547	-8	-4	-28	9	2	4	13	44	-14	5
2002	**-1,031**	**-14**	**-72**	**-233**	**-650**	**37**	**4**	**-42**	**12**	**3**	**1**	**3**	**29**	**-16**	**1**

(1) Relates to the external trade with the USSR until 1991 and to the external trade with Russia from 1992 onwards.

(2) With Luxembourg until 31.12.1998.

193

LATVIA

EU MEMBER STATES

Years	Intra EU	B(1)	DK	D	EL	E	F	IRL	I	L	NL	A	P	FIN	S	UK
							Partner									

EXPORTS
Value (Mio ECU/Euro)

Years	Intra EU	B(1)	DK	D	EL	E	F	IRL	I	L	NL	A	P	FIN	S	UK
1990	:	:	:	:	:	:	:	:	:	:	:	:	:	:	:	:
1994	327	4	13	88	0	1	12	8	8	:	16	17	2	20	58	81
1995	433	9	18	136	0	1	8	11	11	:	20	3	0	32	93	91
1996	495	12	40	157	0	4	11	4	12	:	22	5	0	27	74	126
1997	716	18	57	203	0	5	19	7	13	0	36	5	1	23	122	212
1998	915	18	82	252	0	10	28	9	29	0	56	10	1	35	166	218
1999	1,010	23	99	272	1	10	30	12	27	0	57	10	1	30	172	266
2000	**1,306**	**26**	**118**	**347**	**1**	**10**	**36**	**33**	**31**	**0**	**80**	**13**	**1**	**39**	**219**	**351**
2001	1,367	28	129	372	1	15	43	26	41	1	82	14	1	51	213	350
2002	**1,459**	**26**	**138**	**374**	**4**	**16**	**49**	**23**	**52**	**0**	**92**	**15**	**6**	**56**	**255**	**353**

Annual variation (%)

Years	Intra EU	B(1)	DK	D	EL	E	F	IRL	I	L	NL	A	P	FIN	S	UK
98/97	27.7	-0.1	44.1	24.3	-28.0	91.7	45.9	27.9	115.6	42.8	57.9	109.6	1.3	52.0	35.9	3.1
99/98	10.4	31.0	20.0	7.9	238.5	-1.0	7.8	24.7	-6.6	755.0	1.0	2.3	83.1	-12.1	3.5	21.8
00/99	29.2	13.8	19.1	27.4	-30.1	4.4	22.8	175.5	15.2	-7.0	41.7	28.6	9.0	27.5	26.9	32.0
01/00	4.7	7.7	9.5	7.1	11.9	53.6	18.5	-21.4	31.2	261.6	2.4	4.6	-10.7	31.0	-2.5	-0.3
02/01	6.7	-6.8	6.9	0.5	300.8	6.9	13.4	-11.2	27.4	-88.0	11.7	7.7	473.0	10.2	19.5	0.7

Share (%)

Years	Intra EU	B(1)	DK	D	EL	E	F	IRL	I	L	NL	A	P	FIN	S	UK
1990	:	:	:	:	:	:	:	:	:	:	:	:	:	:	:	:
1996	100.0	2.3	8.1	31.6	0.0	0.8	2.2	0.7	2.5	:	4.4	0.9	0.0	5.4	15.0	25.3
1997	100.0	2.4	7.9	28.3	0.0	0.7	2.6	1.0	1.8	0.0	4.9	0.6	0.0	3.1	17.0	29.5
1998	100.0	1.9	9.0	27.5	0.0	1.0	3.0	1.0	3.1	0.0	6.1	1.0	0.0	3.7	18.1	23.8
1999	100.0	2.2	9.7	26.9	0.1	0.9	2.9	1.1	2.6	0.0	5.6	0.9	0.1	3.0	17.0	26.3
2000	**100.0**	**2.0**	**9.0**	**26.5**	**0.0**	**0.7**	**2.7**	**2.4**	**2.3**	**0.0**	**6.1**	**0.9**	**0.0**	**2.9**	**16.7**	**26.8**
2001	100.0	2.0	9.4	27.2	0.0	1.1	3.1	1.8	2.9	0.0	6.0	0.9	0.0	3.7	15.5	25.6
2002	**100.0**	**1.8**	**9.4**	**25.6**	**0.2**	**1.1**	**3.3**	**1.5**	**3.5**	**0.0**	**6.3**	**1.0**	**0.4**	**3.8**	**17.4**	**24.1**

IMPORTS
Value (Mio ECU/Euro)

Years	Intra EU	B(1)	DK	D	EL	E	F	IRL	I	L	NL	A	P	FIN	S	UK
1990	:	:	:	:	:	:	:	:	:	:	:	:	:	:	:	:
1994	425	11	24	142	0	5	16	2	19	:	16	8	0	89	67	25
1995	690	17	34	195	2	5	20	4	29	:	39	15	0	132	101	34
1996	894	30	60	230	2	10	26	6	44	:	58	16	1	153	131	46
1997	1,279	41	76	349	3	16	46	10	67	1	82	18	1	211	168	71
1998	1,573	57	98	434	4	21	68	14	93	1	92	32	3	246	186	81
1999	1,510	51	107	420	7	21	89	21	103	0	109	37	2	252	201	90
2000	**1,817**	**62**	**125**	**542**	**7**	**36**	**105**	**25**	**127**	**2**	**119**	**37**	**4**	**299**	**234**	**92**
2001	2,058	72	146	667	7	46	95	22	161	2	127	45	5	314	254	94
2002	**2,266**	**84**	**145**	**736**	**6**	**53**	**112**	**20**	**179**	**3**	**145**	**60**	**8**	**343**	**273**	**99**

Annual variation (%)

Years	Intra EU	B(1)	DK	D	EL	E	F	IRL	I	L	NL	A	P	FIN	S	UK
98/97	22.9	39.2	28.1	24.3	33.0	33.2	48.9	35.9	38.7	86.1	12.0	81.2	114.0	16.4	10.8	13.1
99/98	-4.0	-9.3	10.1	-3.2	61.2	-0.5	30.9	51.9	10.6	-50.0	18.0	13.3	-21.4	2.1	8.1	11.9
00/99	20.2	21.1	16.1	29.1	10.9	72.8	18.3	17.8	22.5	392.6	9.5	0.7	98.0	18.8	16.3	2.0
01/00	13.2	15.6	16.6	22.9	2.2	28.4	-9.9	-12.3	27.1	-16.3	6.7	21.5	36.5	4.9	8.8	2.6
02/01	10.1	16.6	-0.1	10.3	-13.1	13.8	17.9	-8.4	11.1	42.4	14.0	32.5	53.2	9.4	7.4	4.9

Share (%)

Years	Intra EU	B(1)	DK	D	EL	E	F	IRL	I	L	NL	A	P	FIN	S	UK
1990	:	:	:	:	:	:	:	:	:	:	:	:	:	:	:	:
1996	100.0	3.3	6.6	25.7	0.2	1.1	2.8	0.7	4.9	:	6.5	1.7	0.0	17.1	14.6	5.1
1997	100.0	3.1	5.9	27.2	0.2	1.2	3.5	0.8	5.2	0.0	6.4	1.3	0.0	16.5	13.0	5.5
1998	100.0	3.5	6.2	27.5	0.2	1.3	4.3	0.8	5.9	0.0	5.8	2.0	0.1	15.6	11.8	5.1
1999	100.0	3.3	7.1	27.8	0.4	1.3	5.8	1.4	6.8	0.0	7.1	2.4	0.1	16.6	13.2	5.9
2000	**100.0**	**3.4**	**6.8**	**29.8**	**0.4**	**1.9**	**5.7**	**1.3**	**6.9**	**0.1**	**6.5**	**2.0**	**0.2**	**16.4**	**12.8**	**5.0**
2001	100.0	3.4	7.0	32.4	0.3	2.2	4.6	1.0	7.8	0.0	6.1	2.1	0.2	15.2	12.3	4.5
2002	**100.0**	**3.6**	**6.4**	**32.4**	**0.2**	**2.3**	**4.9**	**0.8**	**7.9**	**0.1**	**6.3**	**2.6**	**0.3**	**15.1**	**12.0**	**4.3**

(1) With Luxembourg until 31.12.1998.

NON EU MEMBER STATES

Years	Extra EU	Norway	Switzerland	USSR/Russia(1)	Candid. countries	USA	Canada	China	Japan	Hong Kong	Mediterr. Basin	Latin America	OPEC	DAE	ACP
							Partner								

EXPORTS
Value (Mio ECU/Euro)

Years	Extra EU	Norway	Switzerland	USSR/Russia(1)	Candid. countries	USA	Canada	China	Japan	Hong Kong	Mediterr. Basin	Latin America	OPEC	DAE	ACP
1990	:	:	:	:	:	:	:	:	:	:	:	:	:	:	:
1994	503	5	11	234	90	10	1	4	3	0	6	2	1	6	6
1995	547	17	3	245	125	13	1	0	3	0	7	1	1	1	1
1996	625	8	4	260	155	8	0	1	3	0	21	0	7	6	1
1997	752	9	12	309	209	21	1	2	4	2	23	4	10	19	2
1998	705	12	8	197	254	47	4	0	4	6	39	13	7	24	6
1999	604	13	7	106	246	92	7	0	4	4	18	7	6	5	2
2000	**711**	**17**	**8**	**85**	**327**	**76**	**21**	**0**	**9**	**0**	**38**	**5**	**24**	**1**	**21**
2001	860	32	7	131	391	64	5	2	14	5	48	22	48	11	8
2002	**949**	**40**	**10**	**142**	**425**	**104**	**11**	**3**	**19**	**6**	**54**	**12**	**34**	**12**	**4**

Annual variation (%)

Years	Extra EU	Norway	Switzerland	USSR/Russia(1)	Candid. countries	USA	Canada	China	Japan	Hong Kong	Mediterr. Basin	Latin America	OPEC	DAE	ACP
98/97	-6.3	43.3	-37.4	-36.3	21.3	120.2	268.5	-99.5	-4.2	179.1	68.5	213.2	-28.7	22.8	178.8
99/98	-14.3	5.5	-2.4	-45.9	-3.1	95.8	51.7	1,175.0	2.1	-38.8	-52.9	-49.1	-16.4	-77.4	-65.7
00/99	17.7	28.8	4.5	-20.2	33.1	-17.1	204.4	122.5	123.9	-91.2	104.2	-22.1	318.2	-72.9	876.4
01/00	21.0	86.2	-3.4	54.0	19.4	-15.7	-75.0	711.0	52.4	1,403.6	28.2	308.1	100.6	647.6	-61.6
02/01	10.3	26.5	27.4	8.3	8.6	62.7	105.7	66.9	38.7	29.7	12.0	-42.9	-29.7	14.8	-55.7

Share (%)

Years	Extra EU	Norway	Switzerland	USSR/Russia(1)	Candid. countries	USA	Canada	China	Japan	Hong Kong	Mediterr. Basin	Latin America	OPEC	DAE	ACP
1990	:	:	:	:	:	:	:	:	:	:	:	:	:	:	:
1996	100.0	1.2	0.6	41.5	24.8	1.2	0.0	0.1	0.5	0.0	3.3	0.0	1.1	0.9	0.1
1997	100.0	1.1	1.6	41.0	27.8	2.8	0.1	0.2	0.5	0.2	3.1	0.5	1.2	2.5	0.2
1998	100.0	1.7	1.0	27.9	36.0	6.6	0.6	0.0	0.5	0.8	5.5	1.9	0.9	3.3	0.8
1999	100.0	2.1	1.2	17.6	40.7	15.2	1.1	0.0	0.6	0.6	3.0	1.1	0.9	0.8	0.3
2000	**100.0**	**2.3**	**1.0**	**11.9**	**46.0**	**10.7**	**2.8**	**0.0**	**1.2**	**0.0**	**5.3**	**0.7**	**3.3**	**0.2**	**2.9**
2001	100.0	3.6	0.8	15.2	45.4	7.4	0.5	0.2	1.6	0.5	5.6	2.5	5.5	1.2	0.9
2002	**100.0**	**4.2**	**1.0**	**14.9**	**44.7**	**10.9**	**1.1**	**0.3**	**2.0**	**0.6**	**5.7**	**1.3**	**3.5**	**1.2**	**0.3**

IMPORTS
Value (Mio ECU/Euro)

Years	Extra EU	Norway	Switzerland	USSR/Russia(1)	Candid. countries	USA	Canada	China	Japan	Hong Kong	Mediterr. Basin	Latin America	OPEC	DAE	ACP
1990	:	:	:	:	:	:	:	:	:	:	:	:	:	:	:
1994	590	6	6	271	151	23	1	1	14	2	8	19	4	4	3
1995	690	11	13	300	203	27	2	1	8	2	10	8	1	4	1
1996	925	25	22	370	312	42	5	3	4	1	13	23	2	4	2
1997	1,117	36	34	375	448	56	8	5	7	1	19	22	2	6	2
1998	1,265	44	44	335	559	58	8	13	7	1	34	20	5	13	2
1999	1,261	48	59	292	600	56	7	14	6	1	34	2	4	18	2
2000	**1,635**	**39**	**61**	**402**	**773**	**69**	**8**	**26**	**5**	**3**	**36**	**5**	**4**	**22**	**3**
2001	1,825	49	68	359	938	72	9	30	5	2	45	9	4	25	3
2002	**1,980**	**54**	**82**	**374**	**1,074**	**67**	**7**	**45**	**7**	**3**	**54**	**10**	**5**	**28**	**3**

Annual variation (%)

Years	Extra EU	Norway	Switzerland	USSR/Russia(1)	Candid. countries	USA	Canada	China	Japan	Hong Kong	Mediterr. Basin	Latin America	OPEC	DAE	ACP
98/97	13.3	21.4	30.1	-10.5	24.7	2.8	7.4	131.9	-1.4	35.9	82.1	-11.9	130.7	123.4	-2.7
99/98	-0.3	8.5	33.7	-12.9	7.4	-2.9	-20.8	12.9	-12.0	-5.9	-0.5	-87.6	-15.6	37.2	20.0
00/99	29.6	-18.9	3.1	37.6	28.7	22.0	25.6	82.6	-20.0	109.8	5.7	113.7	10.8	23.0	45.2
01/00	11.6	27.7	11.6	-10.5	21.4	4.7	15.0	17.0	-9.2	-3.8	23.0	66.6	-3.3	10.7	-19.3
02/01	8.5	8.8	19.9	4.2	14.4	-7.1	-28.4	49.0	52.7	25.2	20.3	13.0	14.2	13.8	12.6

Share (%)

Years	Extra EU	Norway	Switzerland	USSR/Russia(1)	Candid. countries	USA	Canada	China	Japan	Hong Kong	Mediterr. Basin	Latin America	OPEC	DAE	ACP
1990	:	:	:	:	:	:	:	:	:	:	:	:	:	:	:
1996	100.0	2.7	2.3	39.9	33.7	4.4	0.4	0.2	0.4	0.0	1.4	2.4	0.1	0.4	0.2
1997	100.0	3.2	3.0	33.5	40.0	5.0	0.6	0.4	0.6	0.0	1.6	1.9	0.1	0.5	0.1
1998	100.0	3.4	3.4	26.4	44.1	4.5	0.6	0.9	0.5	0.1	2.7	1.5	0.3	1.0	0.1
1999	100.0	3.7	4.6	23.1	47.5	4.4	0.5	1.1	0.4	0.0	2.7	0.1	0.3	1.4	0.1
2000	**100.0**	**2.3**	**3.7**	**24.5**	**47.2**	**4.2**	**0.5**	**1.5**	**0.3**	**0.1**	**2.2**	**0.3**	**0.2**	**1.3**	**0.1**
2001	100.0	2.7	3.7	19.6	51.4	3.9	0.5	1.6	0.2	0.1	2.4	0.4	0.2	1.3	0.1
2002	**100.0**	**2.7**	**4.1**	**18.9**	**54.2**	**3.3**	**0.3**	**2.2**	**0.3**	**0.1**	**2.7**	**0.4**	**0.2**	**1.4**	**0.1**

(1) Relates to the external trade with the USSR until 1991 and to the external trade with Russia from 1992 onwards.

LITHUANIA

TRADE BALANCE (BN ECU/euro)

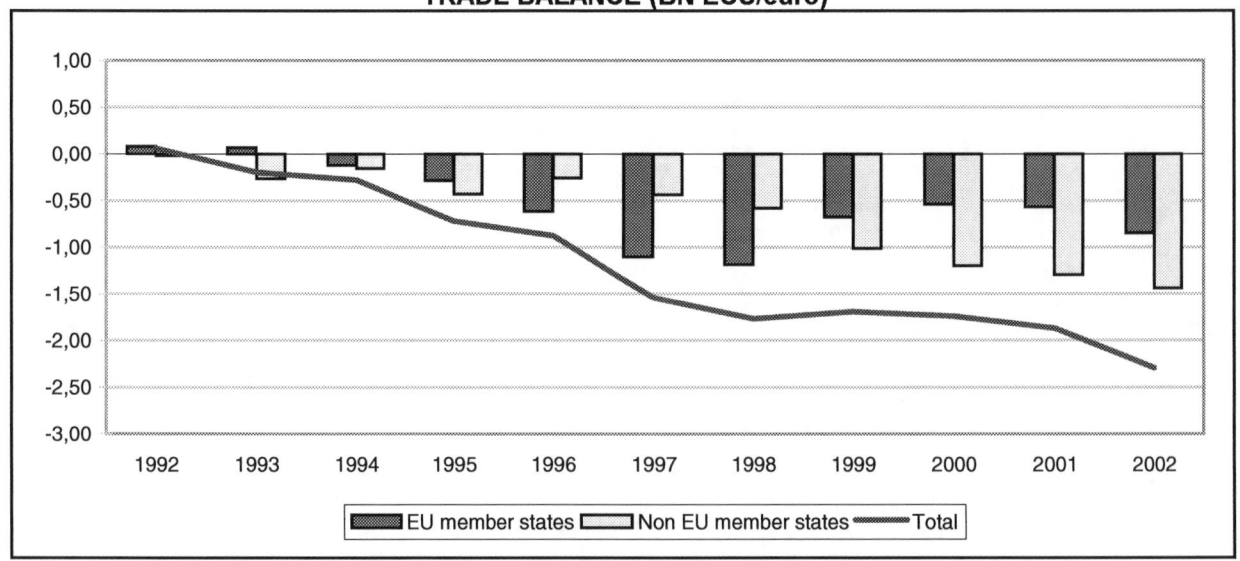

TRADE WITH EU MEMBER STATES (BN ECU/euro)

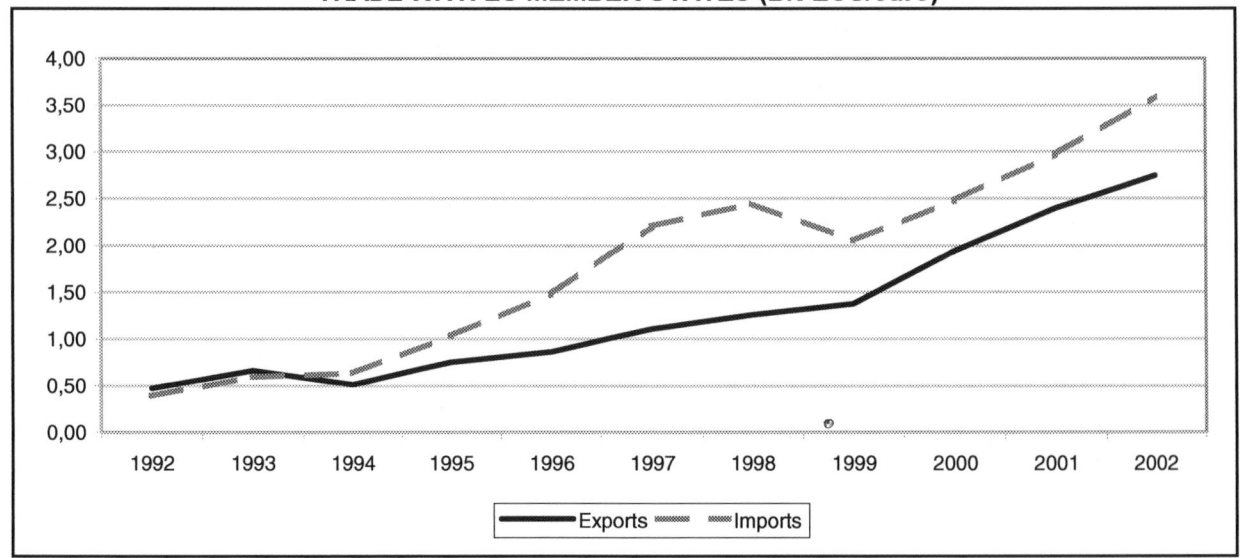

TRADE WITH NON EU MEMBER STATES (BN ECU/euro)

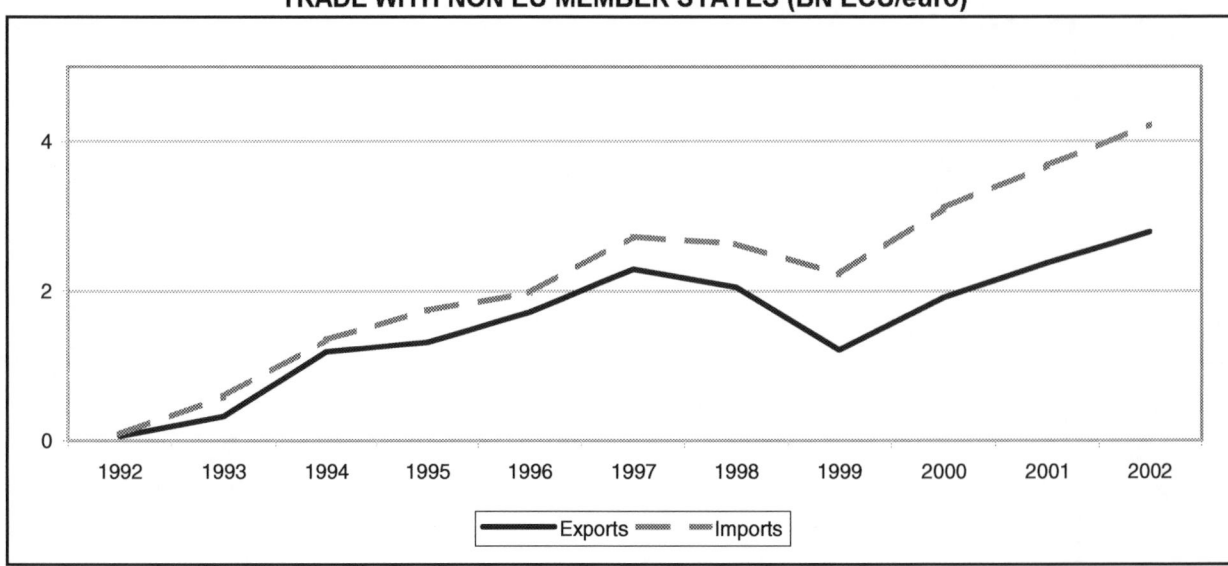

TRADE BALANCE

EU MEMBER STATES

Value (Mio ECU/Euro)

Year	Intra EU	B[2]	DK	D	EL	E	F	IRL	I	L	NL	A	P	FIN	S	UK
1990	:	:	:	:	:	:	:	:	:	:	:	:	:	:	:	:
1991	:	:	:	:	:	:	:	:	:	:	:	:	:	:	:	:
1992	81	:	15	5	18	3	-1	0	1	:	-1	-23	2	-16	17	61
1993	69	12	6	-134	-1	37	-14	-1	-15	:	47	-2	2	-23	6	148
1994	-125	-2	-22	-77	0	10	-15	-0	-22	:	36	-7	-3	-41	6	12
1995	-286	-20	-42	-102	-1	6	-11	18	-26	:	29	-18	-1	-70	-26	-22
1996	-616	-35	-66	-207	-1	7	-34	10	-43	:	-15	-22	12	-104	-65	-51
1997	-1,104	-37	-141	-506	-18	6	-12	-14	-125	-4	-37	-17	:	-127	-97	25
1998	-1,187	-54	-61	-505	-6	-25	-64	2	-88	-4	-33	-22	-7	-136	-104	-76
1999	-681	-45	1	-283	-5	-19	-30	7	-74	-4	-4	-24	-5	-112	-35	-49
2000	**-540**	**-53**	**20**	**-276**	**-5**	**-16**	**-62**	**-10**	**-112**	**-8**	**60**	**-25**	**-0**	**-98**	**-18**	**64**
2001	-570	-63	21	-521	-6	-18	-83	-17	-179	-8	-14	-39	-9	-90	-24	483
2002	**-852**	**-50**	**55**	**-788**	**8**	**-47**	**-75**	**-20**	**-231**	**-11**	**-8**	**-51**	**-3**	**-120**	**-28**	**516**

NON EU MEMBER STATES

Value (Mio ECU/euro)

Year	Extra EU	Norway	Switzerland	USSR/Russia[1]	Candid. countries	USA	Canada	China	Japan	Hong Kong	Mediterr. Basin	Latin America	OPEC	DAE	ACP
1990	:	:	:	:	:	:	:	:	:	:	:	:	:	:	:
1991	:	:	:	:	:	:	:	:	:	:	:	:	:	:	:
1992	-20	2	-3	:	:	-34	:	2	5	:	0	:	:	:	:
1993	-268	-0	-3	-241	55	-39	1	8	21	1	5	0	:	0	:
1994	-157	-3	-19	-303	73	-28	2	2	-2	3	-6	1	16	2	17
1995	-432	-11	8	-448	-55	-38	-10	-1	-5	0	-6	-19	-3	5	2
1996	-261	-18	-51	-287	-96	-54	-15	-3	3	-9	-8	-0	-7	-34	-3
1997	-438	-20	-24	-428	-101	-90	-4	-42	-68	-3	-17	-30	-5	-74	-3
1998	-579	-26	-8	-546	-54	-54	-6	-51	-93	-5	-21	-21	-8	-43	-10
1999	-1,012	-2	-16	-724	-30	-56	-7	-58	-60	-4	-23	-20	-7	-76	-9
2000	**-1,198**	**1**	**-6**	**-1,306**	**350**	**53**	**-4**	**-88**	**-88**	**-2**	**15**	**-25**	**-10**	**-101**	**-7**
2001	-1,297	4	-30	-1,291	417	-21	0	-132	-102	-8	-4	-44	-9	-137	-8
2002	**-1,439**	**19**	**28**	**-1,118**	**204**	**-42**	**16**	**-190**	**-155**	**5**	**-13**	**-37**	**-8**	**-186**	**-38**

(1) Relates to the external trade with the USSR until 1991 and to the external trade with Russia from 1992 onwards.

(2) With Luxembourg until 31.12.1998.

EU MEMBER STATES

Years	Intra EU	B[1]	DK	D	EL	E	F	IRL	I	L	NL	A	P	FIN	S	UK
								Partner								

EXPORTS
Value (Mio ECU/Euro)

Years	Intra EU	B[1]	DK	D	EL	E	F	IRL	I	L	NL	A	P	FIN	S	UK
1990	:	:	:	:	:	:	:	:	:	:	:	:	:	:	:	:
1994	513	13	30	195	1	15	20	2	32	:	89	5	1	16	53	39
1995	750	22	55	298	1	17	35	23	40	:	101	10	10	22	53	65
1996	864	26	66	337	1	26	40	33	67	:	82	14	15	25	44	88
1997	1,107	62	95	418	2	57	122	2	63	0	107	21	:	24	74	194
1998	1,258	43	135	434	1	38	115	19	137	1	82	22	1	28	86	115
1999	1,371	48	174	436	1	37	130	25	109	0	99	25	2	28	117	141
2000	**1,940**	**62**	**201**	**578**	**1**	**47**	**174**	**9**	**91**	**0**	**194**	**16**	**11**	**51**	**180**	**324**
2001	2,402	73	223	624	1	66	166	11	97	0	148	13	7	71	187	716
2002	**2,746**	**102**	**295**	**583**	**24**	**54**	**234**	**14**	**154**	**0**	**168**	**12**	**11**	**67**	**242**	**785**

Annual variation (%)

Years	Intra EU	B[1]	DK	D	EL	E	F	IRL	I	L	NL	A	P	FIN	S	UK
98/97	13.6	-30.5	42.0	3.8	-26.4	-33.8	-5.7	757.5	117.2	505.8	-22.8	7.4	:	17.1	15.2	-40.8
99/98	8.9	10.5	28.6	0.5	-55.1	-2.2	12.6	28.4	-20.5	-52.2	19.8	13.6	268.3	-0.5	36.0	23.3
00/99	41.4	28.9	15.5	32.4	53.4	27.3	34.3	-63.7	-16.7	-35.3	96.8	-36.6	393.4	84.2	54.4	129.5
01/00	23.8	18.6	10.9	7.9	9.7	41.2	-4.9	20.6	6.8	198.1	-23.9	-17.7	-37.9	37.3	3.5	120.8
02/01	14.3	39.2	32.2	-6.5	2,391.4	-18.2	41.2	33.5	58.9	2.1	13.5	-10.0	70.4	-4.9	29.6	9.5

Share (%)

Years	Intra EU	B[1]	DK	D	EL	E	F	IRL	I	L	NL	A	P	FIN	S	UK
1990	:	:	:	:	:	:	:	:	:	:	:	:	:	:	:	:
1996	100.0	3.0	7.6	38.9	0.1	2.9	4.6	3.7	7.7	:	9.5	1.5	1.7	2.8	5.0	10.1
1997	100.0	5.6	8.6	37.7	0.1	5.1	11.0	0.2	5.7	0.0	9.6	1.8	:	2.1	6.7	17.5
1998	100.0	3.4	10.7	34.5	0.1	2.9	9.1	1.5	10.9	0.0	6.5	1.7	0.0	2.2	6.8	9.1
1999	100.0	3.4	12.6	31.8	0.0	2.6	9.4	1.7	7.9	0.0	7.2	1.8	0.1	2.0	8.5	10.3
2000	**100.0**	**3.1**	**10.3**	**29.8**	**0.0**	**2.4**	**8.9**	**0.4**	**4.6**	**0.0**	**10.0**	**0.8**	**0.5**	**2.6**	**9.2**	**16.7**
2001	100.0	3.0	9.2	25.9	0.0	2.7	6.8	0.4	4.0	0.0	6.1	0.5	0.2	2.9	7.7	29.8
2002	**100.0**	**3.7**	**10.7**	**21.2**	**0.8**	**1.9**	**8.5**	**0.5**	**5.6**	**0.0**	**6.1**	**0.4**	**0.4**	**2.4**	**8.8**	**28.5**

IMPORTS
Value (Mio ECU/Euro)

Years	Intra EU	B[1]	DK	D	EL	E	F	IRL	I	L	NL	A	P	FIN	S	UK
1990	:	:	:	:	:	:	:	:	:	:	:	:	:	:	:	:
1994	638	15	51	272	1	5	35	2	54	:	54	12	4	58	47	28
1995	1,036	42	97	399	2	11	46	5	66	:	72	28	11	92	79	86
1996	1,480	61	132	544	2	19	74	23	110	:	97	35	4	129	109	139
1997	2,211	99	236	924	19	51	135	16	188	4	144	38	:	150	171	169
1998	2,446	97	196	939	7	63	179	17	225	5	115	45	8	164	190	190
1999	2,052	93	173	719	6	55	159	18	183	4	103	49	7	140	152	190
2000	**2,480**	**114**	**181**	**854**	**6**	**63**	**236**	**19**	**203**	**9**	**134**	**41**	**11**	**150**	**199**	**260**
2001	2,972	136	203	1,145	7	85	249	28	276	8	162	52	16	161	211	234
2002	**3,599**	**152**	**240**	**1,371**	**16**	**101**	**308**	**35**	**385**	**12**	**176**	**63**	**14**	**187**	**270**	**269**

Annual variation (%)

Years	Intra EU	B[1]	DK	D	EL	E	F	IRL	I	L	NL	A	P	FIN	S	UK
98/97	10.6	-1.8	-16.9	1.6	-61.5	21.7	32.7	10.3	20.0	30.3	-19.6	18.4	:	8.8	11.2	12.5
99/98	-16.0	-4.8	-11.5	-23.3	-23.0	-11.4	-10.8	3.1	-18.7	-15.5	-10.8	9.8	-5.2	-14.6	-20.0	0.0
00/99	20.8	23.2	4.4	18.7	8.4	13.0	48.4	4.5	10.8	111.1	30.3	-17.0	50.8	7.1	30.6	36.9
01/00	19.8	19.4	11.8	34.0	18.5	35.0	5.1	49.4	35.9	-6.8	20.3	28.5	48.5	7.5	5.9	-10.2
02/01	21.0	11.0	18.4	19.7	114.9	19.7	24.0	23.5	39.2	47.8	8.6	20.3	-9.9	16.3	28.1	15.1

Share (%)

Years	Intra EU	B[1]	DK	D	EL	E	F	IRL	I	L	NL	A	P	FIN	S	UK
1990	:	:	:	:	:	:	:	:	:	:	:	:	:	:	:	:
1996	100.0	4.1	8.9	36.7	0.1	1.2	5.0	1.5	7.4	:	6.5	2.3	0.2	8.7	7.3	9.4
1997	100.0	4.4	10.6	41.7	0.8	2.3	6.0	0.7	8.4	0.1	6.4	1.6	:	6.8	7.7	7.6
1998	100.0	3.9	8.0	38.3	0.3	2.5	7.3	0.7	9.2	0.1	4.7	1.8	0.3	6.6	7.7	7.7
1999	100.0	4.5	8.4	35.0	0.2	2.7	7.7	0.8	8.9	0.1	5.0	2.3	0.3	6.8	7.4	9.2
2000	**100.0**	**4.6**	**7.3**	**34.4**	**0.2**	**2.5**	**9.5**	**0.7**	**8.1**	**0.3**	**5.4**	**1.6**	**0.4**	**6.0**	**8.0**	**10.5**
2001	100.0	4.5	6.8	38.5	0.2	2.8	8.3	0.9	9.2	0.2	5.4	1.7	0.5	5.4	7.0	7.8
2002	**100.0**	**4.2**	**6.6**	**38.1**	**0.4**	**2.8**	**8.5**	**0.9**	**10.6**	**0.3**	**4.8**	**1.7**	**0.4**	**5.2**	**7.4**	**7.4**

(1) With Luxembourg until 31.12.1998.

NON EU MEMBER STATES

Years								Partner							
	Extra EU	Norway	Switzerland	USSR/ Russia(1)	Candid. countries	USA	Canada	China	Japan	Hong Kong	Mediterr. Basin	Latin America	OPEC	DAE	ACP

EXPORTS
Value (Mio ECU/Euro)

Years	Extra EU	Norway	Switzerland	USSR/ Russia	Candid. countries	USA	Canada	China	Japan	Hong Kong	Mediterr. Basin	Latin America	OPEC	DAE	ACP
1990	:	:	:	:	:	:	:	:	:	:	:	:	:	:	:
1994	1,191	10	6	481	314	11	4	2	2	3	8	5	20	6	19
1995	1,313	13	51	421	324	16	1	0	2	4	23	6	2	15	2
1996	1,716	11	29	615	437	19	5	0	12	1	24	5	1	17	1
1997	2,292	16	23	836	524	55	5	3	12	1	40	14	4	25	6
1998	2,052	17	51	549	622	94	4	1	10	1	39	22	3	22	4
1999	1,211	31	41	151	564	116	4	1	8	0	41	21	2	6	1
2000	1,912	46	48	238	1,015	193	12	2	13	1	90	20	2	10	3
2001	2,376	66	29	449	1,181	192	18	2	20	1	92	8	7	14	8
2002	2,786	137	97	628	1,194	187	31	3	14	39	194	19	8	58	10

Annual variation (%)

Years	Extra EU	Norway	Switzerland	USSR/ Russia	Candid. countries	USA	Canada	China	Japan	Hong Kong	Mediterr. Basin	Latin America	OPEC	DAE	ACP
98/97	-10.5	5.6	121.0	-34.3	18.7	72.1	-22.5	-43.1	-20.9	-28.9	-2.6	56.8	-33.0	-10.5	-41.8
99/98	-40.9	86.1	-18.3	-72.5	-9.3	23.3	-11.5	-50.4	-14.3	-72.4	3.5	-5.3	-23.9	-72.7	-62.4
00/99	57.8	49.0	15.4	57.7	79.8	65.8	244.3	122.0	56.5	605.7	120.1	-3.9	3.0	72.9	137.5
01/00	24.2	41.9	-38.9	88.9	16.4	-0.4	42.6	26.8	51.6	0.5	2.5	-57.4	202.7	33.5	138.3
02/01	17.2	107.3	234.7	39.7	1.1	-2.4	77.6	47.7	-30.2	3,053.0	111.1	129.0	21.6	320.9	33.4

Share (%)

Years	Extra EU	Norway	Switzerland	USSR/ Russia	Candid. countries	USA	Canada	China	Japan	Hong Kong	Mediterr. Basin	Latin America	OPEC	DAE	ACP
1990	:	:	:	:	:	:	:	:	:	:	:	:	:	:	:
1996	100.0	0.6	1.7	35.8	25.4	1.1	0.2	0.0	0.6	0.0	1.4	0.3	0.0	0.9	0.0
1997	100.0	0.6	0.9	36.4	22.8	2.3	0.2	0.1	0.5	0.0	1.7	0.6	0.1	1.0	0.2
1998	100.0	0.8	2.4	26.7	30.3	4.5	0.1	0.0	0.4	0.0	1.9	1.0	0.1	1.0	0.1
1999	100.0	2.5	3.4	12.4	46.5	9.5	0.2	0.0	0.6	0.0	3.3	1.7	0.1	0.4	0.1
2000	100.0	2.4	2.4	12.4	53.0	10.0	0.6	0.0	0.6	0.0	4.6	1.0	0.1	0.5	0.1
2001	100.0	2.7	1.2	18.9	49.6	8.0	0.7	0.0	0.8	0.0	3.8	0.3	0.2	0.5	0.3
2002	100.0	4.9	3.4	22.5	42.8	6.7	1.1	0.1	0.4	1.3	6.9	0.6	0.2	2.0	0.3

IMPORTS
Value (Mio ECU/Euro)

Years	Extra EU	Norway	Switzerland	USSR/ Russia	Candid. countries	USA	Canada	China	Japan	Hong Kong	Mediterr. Basin	Latin America	OPEC	DAE	ACP
1990	:	:	:	:	:	:	:	:	:	:	:	:	:	:	:
1994	1,348	13	24	784	241	39	2	1	4	0	14	4	4	4	2
1995	1,745	24	43	870	379	53	11	1	7	3	29	25	4	11	0
1996	1,978	30	80	903	532	73	20	3	9	10	32	6	8	51	4
1997	2,731	36	47	1,264	625	145	9	45	80	4	57	44	9	99	9
1998	2,631	42	59	1,095	677	148	10	53	103	5	61	43	11	65	13
1999	2,223	33	57	875	594	172	10	59	69	4	64	40	9	82	11
2000	3,110	46	54	1,544	665	140	17	89	101	4	74	44	12	111	10
2001	3,673	62	59	1,740	764	212	17	134	122	9	96	52	16	151	16
2002	4,224	117	70	1,746	990	229	15	193	169	34	207	56	16	244	48

Annual variation (%)

Years	Extra EU	Norway	Switzerland	USSR/ Russia	Candid. countries	USA	Canada	China	Japan	Hong Kong	Mediterr. Basin	Latin America	OPEC	DAE	ACP
98/97	-3.6	18.0	25.5	-13.3	8.2	2.5	11.4	17.0	28.7	30.1	5.9	-2.3	18.4	-34.4	49.0
99/98	-15.4	-21.6	-2.1	-20.1	-12.2	15.6	0.1	12.0	-33.2	-19.0	5.4	-6.2	-19.5	27.6	-19.0
00/99	39.8	37.0	-5.7	76.4	11.9	-18.6	61.6	51.0	47.8	-14.2	16.0	10.1	35.6	35.0	-6.0
01/00	18.1	36.6	8.7	12.7	14.8	52.1	2.8	50.2	20.3	142.9	28.7	17.3	29.9	35.8	54.2
02/01	15.0	88.2	19.1	0.3	29.6	7.7	-13.0	44.1	38.1	282.0	117.0	7.6	3.1	61.3	209.6

Share (%)

Years	Extra EU	Norway	Switzerland	USSR/ Russia	Candid. countries	USA	Canada	China	Japan	Hong Kong	Mediterr. Basin	Latin America	OPEC	DAE	ACP
1990	:	:	:	:	:	:	:	:	:	:	:	:	:	:	:
1996	100.0	1.4	4.0	45.6	26.9	3.6	1.0	0.1	0.4	0.5	1.6	0.2	0.4	2.5	0.2
1997	100.0	1.3	1.7	46.2	22.8	5.3	0.3	1.6	2.9	0.1	2.0	1.6	0.3	3.6	0.3
1998	100.0	1.6	2.2	41.6	25.7	5.6	0.3	2.0	3.9	0.1	2.3	1.6	0.4	2.4	0.5
1999	100.0	1.4	2.5	39.3	26.7	7.7	0.4	2.6	3.0	0.1	2.8	1.8	0.4	3.7	0.4
2000	100.0	1.4	1.7	49.6	21.3	4.4	0.5	2.8	3.2	0.1	2.3	1.4	0.3	3.5	0.3
2001	100.0	1.6	1.5	47.3	20.7	5.7	0.4	3.6	3.3	0.2	2.6	1.4	0.4	4.1	0.4
2002	100.0	2.7	1.6	41.3	23.4	5.4	0.3	4.5	3.9	0.8	4.9	1.3	0.3	5.7	1.1

(1) Relates to the external trade with the USSR until 1991 and to the external trade with Russia from 1992 onwards.

MALTA

TRADE BALANCE (BN ECU/euro)

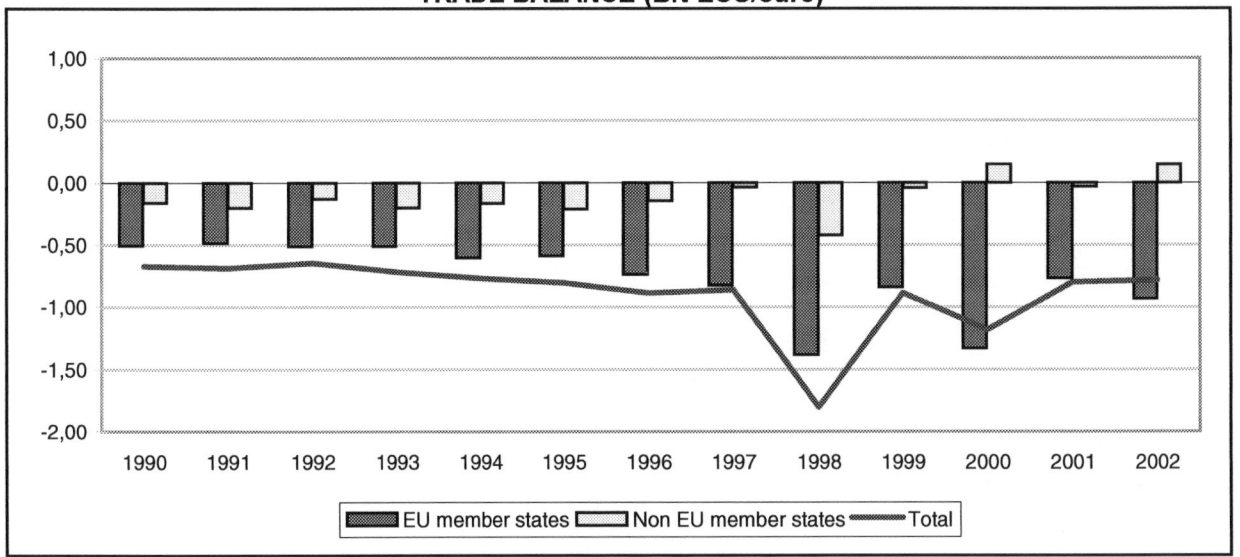

TRADE WITH EU MEMBER STATES (BN ECU/euro)

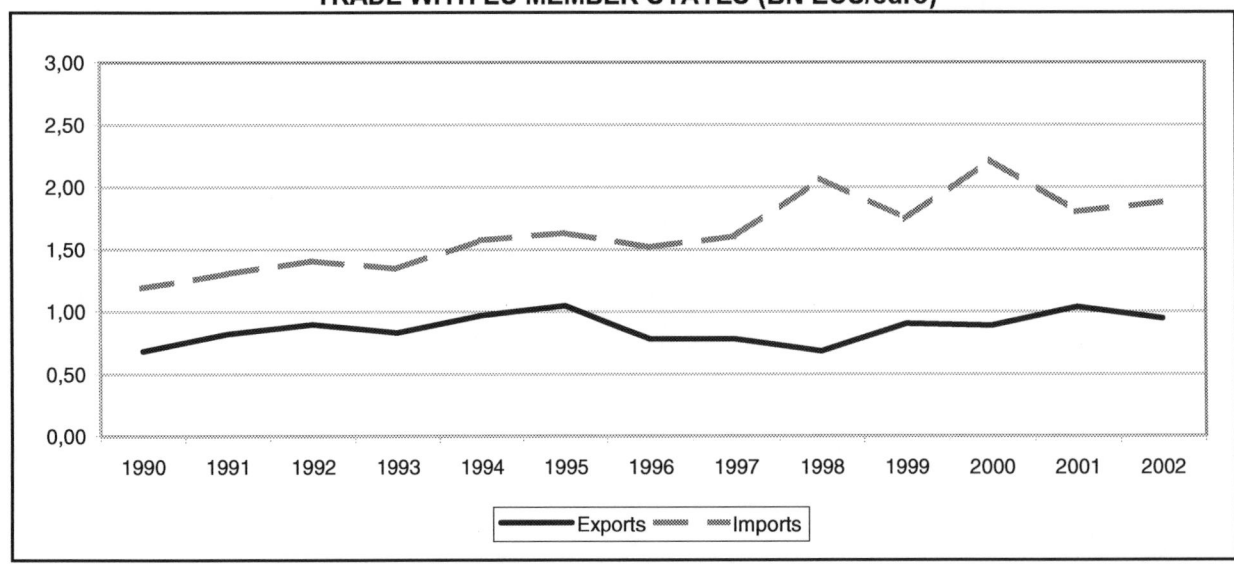

TRADE WITH NON EU MEMBER STATES (BN ECU/euro)

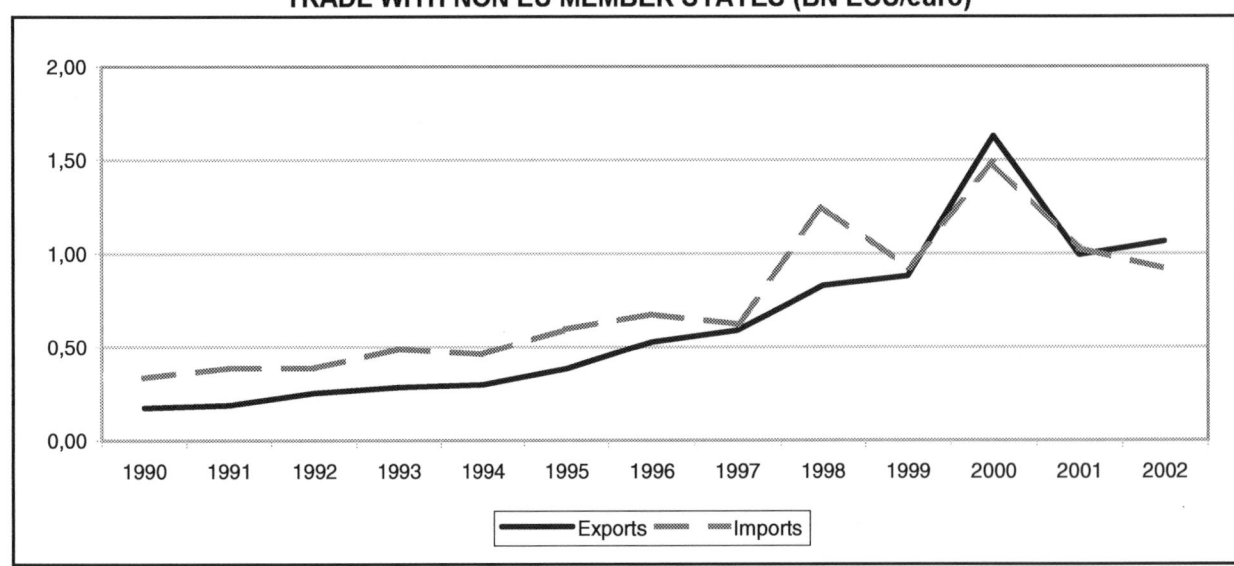

TRADE BALANCE

EU MEMBER STATES

Value (Mio ECU/Euro)

Year	Intra EU	B(2)	DK	D	EL	E	F	IRL	I	L	NL	A	P	FIN	S	UK
1990	**-507**	**-2**	**-11**	**2**	**-13**	**-21**	**-49**	**-9**	**-194**	**:**	**-27**	**-19**	**-5**	**-3**	**-6**	**-149**
1991	-484	-2	-10	-12	-13	-21	40	-15	-222	:	-33	-9	-5	-2	-2	-179
1992	-510	-3	-9	-25	-11	-22	-6	-16	-198	:	-37	-8	-10	-5	-4	-155
1993	-513	-3	-12	-83	-13	-24	-35	-16	-133	:	-20	-8	-4	-2	-4	-156
1994	-602	5	-12	-176	-16	-30	-43	-14	-52	:	-23	-8	-5	-3	-6	-219
1995	-588	24	-14	-54	-13	-41	-9	-17	-174	:	-29	-9	-4	-2	-6	-241
1996	-738	11	-13	-9	-13	-39	-144	-16	-259	:	-34	-7	-4	-2	-7	-199
1997	-824	28	-15	-30	-15	-45	-95	-18	-373	-0	-26	-10	-6	-2	-5	-215
1998	-1,383	11	-20	-80	-17	-95	-259	-21	-630	-1	-56	-10	-1	-1	-7	-197
1999	-842	28	-15	-34	-11	-47	-228	-17	-355	-0	-29	-13	-3	4	-4	-119
2000	**-1,332**	**10**	**-18**	**-48**	**-14**	**-56**	**-487**	**-32**	**-529**	**0**	**-44**	**-22**	**-5**	**20**	**-4**	**-103**
2001	-765	31	-16	31	-14	-63	-81	-17	-455	-0	-39	-25	-5	13	-12	-113
2002	**-934**	**42**	**-18**	**3**	**-17**	**-57**	**-226**	**-13**	**-519**	**-1**	**-42**	**-19**	**-4**	**4**	**-10**	**-57**

NON EU MEMBER STATES

Value (Mio ECU/euro)

Year	Extra EU	Norway	Switzerland	USSR/Russia(1)	Candid. countries	USA	Canada	China	Japan	Hong Kong	Mediterr. Basin	Latin America	OPEC	DAE	ACP
1990	**-161**	**-1**	**-10**	**2**	**:**	**-17**	**-2**	**:**	**-56**	**-9**	**-16**	**-18**	**5**	**-20**	**1**
1991	-200	-2	-10	-17	:	-27	-2	-13	-69	-9	3	-22	43	-33	12
1992	-132	-1	-8	-0	:	12	-1	-18	-73	-8	-4	-11	29	-24	9
1993	-204	-8	-19	-0	-14	-75	3	-18	-43	-9	3	-14	29	-41	8
1994	-166	-3	-40	-3	-28	-7	12	-14	-37	-10	-17	-13	32	-47	24
1995	-213	12	-15	-7	-30	4	5	-5	-44	-11	-64	-14	-24	-73	6
1996	-147	-6	-21	-10	-21	33	19	-27	-31	-10	-83	-11	-44	-11	7
1997	-36	-5	-23	-8	-10	40	26	-26	-27	-9	7	-15	28	10	1
1998	-423	-2	-26	-57	-109	17	15	-23	-96	-14	-55	2	31	-115	-1
1999	-43	-18	-22	-1	-39	171	1	-41	-25	-9	-46	-12	-7	-24	2
2000	**150**	**-6**	**115**	**-12**	**-34**	**334**	**14**	**-59**	**28**	**3**	**-42**	**-14**	**0**	**-187**	**8**
2001	-32	-2	-30	-20	-24	84	-10	-59	2	19	19	-20	67	20	6
2002	**149**	**1**	**11**	**-29**	**-23**	**10**	**-4**	**-60**	**0**	**30**	**25**	**-12**	**73**	**211**	**9**

(1) Relates to the external trade with the USSR until 1991 and to the external trade with Russia from 1992 onwards.
(2) With Luxembourg until 31.12.1998.

MALTA

EU MEMBER STATES

Years	Intra EU	B(1)	DK	D	EL	E	F	IRL	I	L	NL	A	P	FIN	S	UK
							Partner									

EXPORTS
Value (Mio ECU/Euro)

Years	Intra EU	B(1)	DK	D	EL	E	F	IRL	I	L	NL	A	P	FIN	S	UK
1990	681	22	3	182	1	3	62	1	306	:	16	1	0	0	4	79
1994	972	29	3	185	1	6	128	2	491	:	25	2	2	0	2	97
1995	1,044	51	2	220	3	4	179	2	444	:	23	2	4	0	2	110
1996	780	49	2	198	2	2	205	3	171	:	25	3	2	1	2	115
1997	782	55	3	194	1	4	278	4	82	0	33	3	2	1	2	118
1998	682	62	2	181	2	20	185	4	82	0	15	5	5	1	2	115
1999	903	62	4	233	2	7	281	4	91	0	32	2	2	6	4	172
2000	885	52	4	255	2	11	212	4	89	1	29	2	4	23	5	193
2001	1,037	68	5	285	1	11	348	2	74	0	30	3	5	18	4	183
2002	943	75	4	230	2	14	243	5	78	0	26	2	6	9	6	243

Annual variation (%)

Years	Intra EU	B(1)	DK	D	EL	E	F	IRL	I	L	NL	A	P	FIN	S	UK
98/97	-12.7	11.4	-37.8	-6.7	42.6	357.2	-33.1	-19.1	0.0	112.7	-55.7	93.2	197.9	15.6	1.5	-2.1
99/98	32.3	0.6	83.9	28.5	15.8	-65.7	51.6	4.5	11.4	-86.6	117.7	-62.4	-53.8	396.2	81.0	49.0
00/99	-2.0	-16.9	16.3	9.2	-22.7	56.6	-24.5	9.2	-2.6	1,477.5	-7.9	-14.4	58.6	257.2	27.0	12.3
01/00	17.1	31.1	27.1	11.8	-57.8	5.8	63.6	-51.5	-17.0	-64.9	3.5	81.9	25.5	-20.9	-20.4	-5.2
02/01	-9.0	10.5	-25.1	-19.0	153.9	22.0	-30.1	124.7	5.8	-92.9	-13.6	-27.8	25.5	-49.4	41.4	32.8

Share (%)

Years	Intra EU	B(1)	DK	D	EL	E	F	IRL	I	L	NL	A	P	FIN	S	UK
1990	100.0	3.1	0.4	26.7	0.1	0.4	9.1	0.2	44.9	:	2.3	0.1	0.0	0.0	0.6	11.5
1996	100.0	6.3	0.2	25.3	0.2	0.2	26.2	0.4	21.8	:	3.1	0.3	0.2	0.1	0.2	14.7
1997	100.0	7.0	0.4	24.8	0.1	0.5	35.4	0.5	10.4	0.0	4.2	0.3	0.2	0.1	0.2	15.0
1998	100.0	9.0	0.2	26.5	0.2	2.9	27.1	0.5	11.9	0.0	2.1	0.7	0.7	0.1	0.3	16.9
1999	100.0	6.8	0.4	25.8	0.2	0.7	31.1	0.4	10.1	0.0	3.5	0.2	0.2	0.7	0.4	19.0
2000	100.0	5.8	0.4	28.7	0.2	1.2	24.0	0.4	10.0	0.0	3.3	0.1	0.4	2.5	0.5	21.8
2001	100.0	6.5	0.5	27.4	0.0	1.1	33.5	0.1	7.1	0.0	2.9	0.2	0.4	1.7	0.3	17.6
2002	100.0	7.9	0.4	24.4	0.2	1.4	25.7	0.4	8.2	0.0	2.7	0.2	0.6	0.9	0.5	25.8

IMPORTS
Value (Mio ECU/Euro)

Years	Intra EU	B(1)	DK	D	EL	E	F	IRL	I	L	NL	A	P	FIN	S	UK
1990	1,188	24	14	181	14	24	111	10	500	:	43	20	6	3	10	228
1994	1,574	24	15	362	17	36	172	15	542	:	48	10	6	3	8	316
1995	1,632	28	17	273	16	46	188	19	618	:	52	11	8	2	8	350
1996	1,518	39	15	207	15	41	349	19	430	:	59	10	6	3	9	315
1997	1,606	28	18	224	16	50	373	22	455	1	59	12	8	3	7	332
1998	2,065	51	22	262	19	115	444	25	712	1	70	15	6	2	9	312
1999	1,744	34	19	267	13	54	509	21	446	1	60	14	6	2	8	291
2000	2,216	41	22	302	16	67	699	36	618	1	73	24	9	3	9	296
2001	1,802	37	22	254	15	75	428	19	528	1	70	28	10	5	15	296
2002	1,876	32	22	227	18	71	469	17	597	1	69	21	10	5	16	300

Annual variation (%)

Years	Intra EU	B(1)	DK	D	EL	E	F	IRL	I	L	NL	A	P	FIN	S	UK
98/97	28.5	83.1	21.3	16.6	15.3	132.4	19.1	11.6	56.3	51.3	19.4	26.9	-20.9	-26.2	34.6	-6.0
99/98	-15.5	-33.7	-13.8	1.8	-28.6	-53.0	14.6	-14.3	-37.3	-49.0	-13.9	-6.3	-2.3	-7.6	-13.3	-6.8
00/99	27.0	22.4	19.6	13.3	20.5	23.4	37.2	69.9	38.5	38.3	21.6	62.3	51.9	36.9	18.1	1.9
01/00	-18.7	-10.7	-3.0	-16.0	-8.8	12.2	-38.7	-48.0	-14.5	-22.3	-5.3	20.6	12.5	74.2	65.8	0.0
02/01	4.1	-12.4	1.2	-10.4	26.7	-5.0	9.5	-6.2	13.0	34.1	-1.2	-25.4	3.7	4.7	0.6	1.4

Share (%)

Years	Intra EU	B(1)	DK	D	EL	E	F	IRL	I	L	NL	A	P	FIN	S	UK
1990	100.0	1.9	1.2	15.2	1.1	2.0	9.3	0.8	42.0	:	3.5	1.6	0.4	0.2	0.8	19.1
1996	100.0	2.5	1.0	13.6	0.9	2.7	22.9	1.2	28.3	:	3.8	0.6	0.3	0.2	0.5	20.7
1997	100.0	1.7	1.1	13.9	1.0	3.0	23.2	1.3	28.3	0.0	3.6	0.7	0.4	0.1	0.4	20.6
1998	100.0	2.4	1.0	12.6	0.8	5.5	21.5	1.1	34.4	0.0	3.3	0.7	0.2	0.0	0.4	15.1
1999	100.0	1.9	1.0	15.2	0.7	3.1	29.1	1.2	25.5	0.0	3.4	0.8	0.3	0.1	0.4	16.6
2000	100.0	1.8	1.0	13.6	0.7	3.0	31.5	1.6	27.8	0.0	3.3	1.0	0.3	0.1	0.4	13.3
2001	100.0	2.0	1.2	14.0	0.8	4.1	23.7	1.0	29.3	0.0	3.8	1.5	0.5	0.2	0.8	16.4
2002	100.0	1.7	1.1	12.1	0.9	3.7	25.0	0.9	31.8	0.0	3.6	1.1	0.5	0.2	0.8	16.0

(1)   With Luxembourg until 31.12.1998.

NON EU MEMBER STATES

Years	Extra EU	Norway	Switzerland	USSR/Russia(1)	Candid. countries	USA	Canada	China	Japan	Hong Kong	Mediterr. Basin	Latin America	OPEC	DAE	ACP
EXPORTS															
Value (Mio ECU/Euro)															
1990	**175**	**1**	**4**	**26**	**:**	**34**	**1**	**:**	**1**	**0**	**51**	**0**	**58**	**29**	**8**
1994	297	1	3	3	7	98	14	0	10	1	51	1	79	65	29
1995	382	14	7	2	3	139	7	18	13	0	36	4	46	110	9
1996	526	2	10	1	16	185	22	0	40	1	44	2	53	171	10
1997	588	3	6	1	25	218	32	1	50	2	85	3	76	154	4
1998	826	20	2	10	17	282	20	1	7	1	120	9	81	294	5
1999	880	3	11	0	9	396	7	0	48	6	62	2	64	311	7
2000	**1,629**	**3**	**172**	**0**	**20**	**727**	**26**	**2**	**101**	**19**	**52**	**5**	**60**	**469**	**17**
2001	993	2	4	0	34	433	4	1	65	36	74	4	78	329	18
2002	**1,064**	**3**	**53**	**0**	**38**	**289**	**4**	**6**	**62**	**49**	**103**	**6**	**100**	**455**	**19**
Annual variation (%)															
98/97	40.5	663.0	-74.2	1,192.5	-30.3	29.2	-37.6	98.2	-86.7	-11.2	41.8	178.4	6.8	91.0	12.4
99/98	6.5	-85.8	593.5	-99.8	-49.0	40.6	-62.7	-72.2	619.2	320.7	-48.7	-79.6	-20.6	6.0	57.4
00/99	85.0	-6.9	1,447.6	2,616.6	120.1	83.5	261.2	324.8	111.3	221.4	-16.3	168.0	-6.3	50.6	133.6
01/00	-39.0	-26.7	-97.9	-83.0	72.4	-40.5	-83.0	-11.2	-35.3	85.3	43.0	-20.4	29.4	-29.9	4.0
02/01	7.1	58.2	1,421.5	16.8	13.7	-33.2	-12.7	285.8	-4.1	35.8	39.3	50.7	28.5	38.5	2.6
Share (%)															
1990	**100.0**	**0.4**	**2.1**	**15.0**	**:**	**19.4**	**0.4**	**:**	**0.4**	**0.0**	**29.2**	**0.2**	**33.0**	**16.5**	**4.6**
1996	100.0	0.4	1.9	0.2	3.0	35.2	4.2	0.0	7.5	0.1	8.3	0.3	10.0	32.4	1.9
1997	100.0	0.4	1.0	0.1	4.2	37.0	5.3	0.1	8.5	0.2	14.4	0.5	12.8	26.1	0.7
1998	100.0	2.4	0.1	1.2	2.1	34.1	2.3	0.1	0.8	0.1	14.5	1.0	9.7	35.5	0.5
1999	100.0	0.3	1.2	0.0	1.0	45.0	0.8	0.0	5.4	0.6	6.9	0.2	7.2	35.3	0.8
2000	**100.0**	**0.1**	**10.5**	**0.0**	**1.2**	**44.6**	**1.6**	**0.0**	**6.1**	**1.1**	**3.1**	**0.2**	**3.6**	**28.7**	**1.0**
2001	100.0	0.1	0.3	0.0	3.3	43.5	0.4	0.1	6.5	3.6	7.4	0.3	7.8	33.0	1.8
2002	**100.0**	**0.2**	**5.0**	**0.0**	**3.6**	**27.1**	**0.3**	**0.5**	**5.8**	**4.6**	**9.6**	**0.5**	**9.3**	**42.7**	**1.7**
IMPORTS															
Value (Mio ECU/Euro)															
1990	**336**	**2**	**13**	**24**	**:**	**51**	**3**	**9**	**57**	**9**	**67**	**19**	**52**	**49**	**8**
1994	463	4	44	6	35	105	3	14	47	11	68	14	47	112	5
1995	595	2	23	9	34	135	3	23	57	11	100	18	71	183	3
1996	674	8	31	11	37	152	3	27	70	11	127	13	97	181	4
1997	624	8	29	9	35	178	6	27	77	10	78	18	48	144	3
1998	1,249	23	28	68	127	265	5	25	102	15	175	7	50	408	6
1999	923	21	33	1	48	225	7	42	73	15	107	14	71	336	5
2000	**1,479**	**9**	**56**	**12**	**54**	**393**	**12**	**61**	**73**	**16**	**94**	**19**	**60**	**656**	**9**
2001	1,025	4	34	20	57	349	14	60	64	17	55	23	11	309	12
2002	**915**	**2**	**42**	**29**	**61**	**279**	**8**	**66**	**62**	**19**	**77**	**18**	**27**	**244**	**9**
Annual variation (%)															
98/97	100.3	186.2	-5.9	688.6	256.5	48.7	-18.5	-8.6	32.1	44.9	125.5	-60.4	3.9	183.9	84.9
99/98	-26.0	-6.3	19.9	-98.3	-62.4	-15.0	46.8	69.1	-29.0	-2.8	-38.5	95.5	42.0	-17.7	-6.2
00/99	60.2	-57.1	69.7	1,029.9	13.2	74.4	83.2	45.7	0.1	11.0	-12.5	34.0	-15.9	95.3	77.6
01/00	-30.7	-60.4	-40.4	65.5	6.7	-11.1	19.4	-0.8	-12.5	7.3	-41.5	26.1	-82.0	-52.8	30.9
02/01	-10.6	-38.4	24.6	42.3	6.5	-20.0	-42.7	8.4	-2.1	7.1	40.7	-24.4	155.7	-21.0	-25.4
Share (%)															
1990	**100.0**	**0.6**	**3.9**	**7.0**	**:**	**15.2**	**0.8**	**2.5**	**17.0**	**2.7**	**20.0**	**5.5**	**15.5**	**14.4**	**2.2**
1996	100.0	1.2	4.6	1.6	5.5	22.6	0.4	4.0	10.4	1.6	18.9	1.9	14.4	26.8	0.5
1997	100.0	1.2	4.7	1.3	5.6	28.5	0.8	4.3	12.3	1.6	12.4	2.8	7.7	23.0	0.4
1998	100.0	1.8	2.2	5.4	10.1	21.2	0.3	1.9	8.1	1.2	14.0	0.5	3.9	32.6	0.4
1999	100.0	2.3	3.6	0.1	5.1	24.3	0.7	4.5	7.8	1.5	11.6	1.5	7.6	36.3	0.5
2000	**100.0**	**0.6**	**3.8**	**0.8**	**3.6**	**26.5**	**0.8**	**4.1**	**4.9**	**1.1**	**6.3**	**1.2**	**4.0**	**44.3**	**0.6**
2001	100.0	0.3	3.2	1.9	5.6	34.0	1.4	5.9	6.1	1.7	5.3	2.2	1.0	30.1	1.1
2002	**100.0**	**0.2**	**4.5**	**3.1**	**6.6**	**30.4**	**0.9**	**7.1**	**6.7**	**2.0**	**8.4**	**1.9**	**2.9**	**26.6**	**0.9**

(1) Relates to the external trade with the USSR until 1991 and to the external trade with Russia from 1992 onwards.

POLAND

TRADE BALANCE (BN ECU/euro)

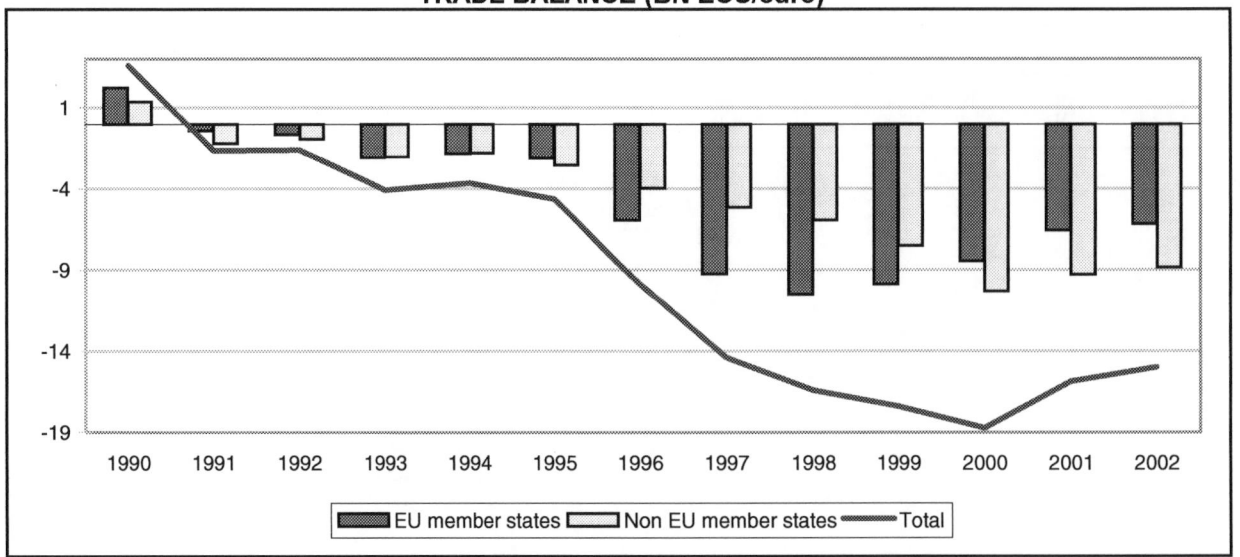

TRADE WITH EU MEMBER STATES (BN ECU/euro)

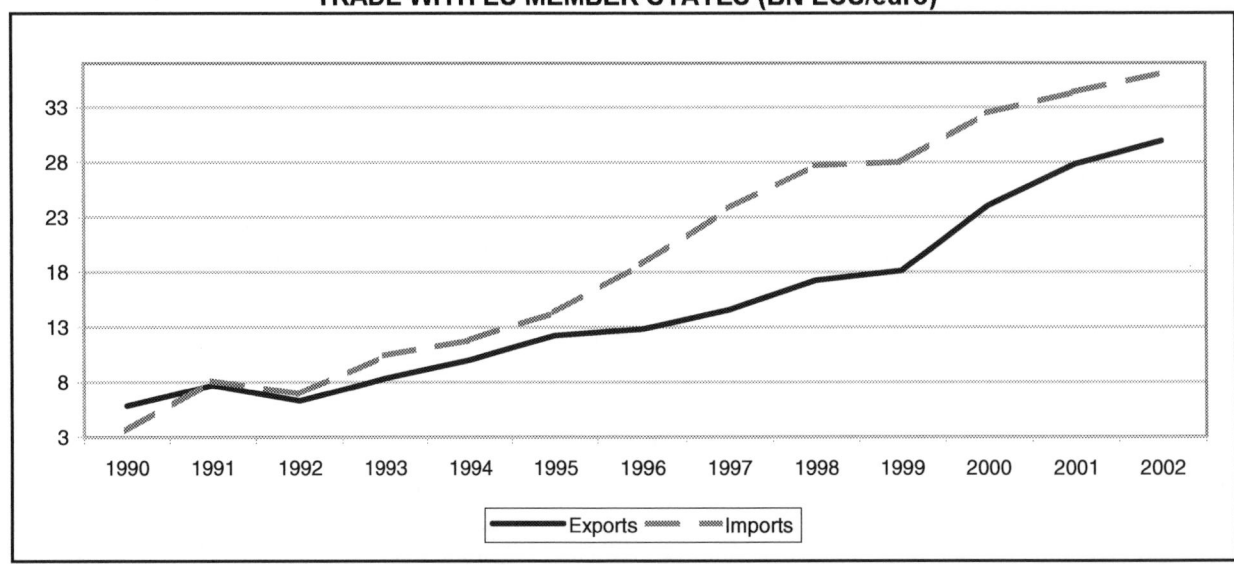

TRADE WITH NON EU MEMBER STATES (BN ECU/euro)

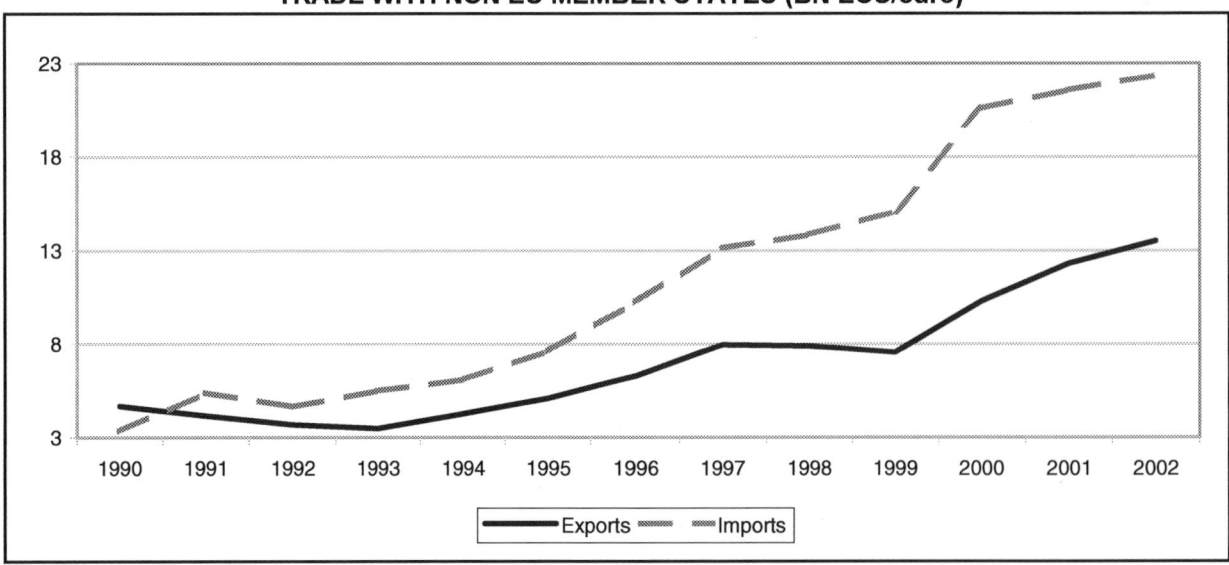

TRADE BALANCE

EU MEMBER STATES

Value (Mio ECU/Euro)

Year	Intra EU	B[2]	DK	D	EL	E	F	IRL	I	L	NL	A	P	FIN	S	UK
1990	**2,239**	**82**	**108**	**1,269**	**40**	**39**	**132**	**27**	**-211**	:	**150**	**12**	**6**	**78**	**143**	**364**
1991	-408	-111	-14	-117	-5	-59	-44	23	-121	:	-58	-321	:	30	73	307
1992	-638	267	7	385	-4	-50	-151	22	-249	:	51	:	5	-79	30	-341
1993	-2,057	-55	-31	-124	14	-129	-179	-3	-622	:	-40	-234	7	-160	-98	-405
1994	-1,814	-96	27	188	6	-137	-240	-19	-806	:	17	-148	15	-182	-140	-298
1995	-2,092	-155	41	796	12	-171	-460	-74	-1,038	:	-22	-190	8	-144	-251	-448
1996	-5,911	-270	-54	-590	83	-400	-750	-98	-1,836	:	-192	-261	-7	-233	-326	-966
1997	-9,239	-495	-61	-1,499	12	-667	-1,203	-130	-2,353	-39	-290	-336	-38	-351	-587	-1,193
1998	-10,480	-562	-127	-1,969	28	-722	-1,519	-158	-2,444	-64	-390	-312	-73	-478	-610	-1,077
1999	-9,876	-506	15	-1,640	-7	-674	-1,645	-152	-2,349	-48	-262	-310	-91	-539	-724	-943
2000	**-8,441**	**-370**	**78**	**-720**	**1**	**-744**	**-1,627**	**-211**	**-2,238**	**-51**	**-151**	**-339**	**49**	**-708**	**-589**	**-822**
2001	-6,567	-287	58	394	-9	-775	-1,641	-209	-2,456	-43	-91	-278	111	-611	-407	-321
2002	**-6,154**	**-213**	**190**	**-150**	**2**	**-776**	**-1,449**	**-208**	**-2,493**	**-39**	**-104**	**-321**	**173**	**-607**	**-138**	**-19**

NON EU MEMBER STATES

Value (Mio ECU/euro)

Year	Extra EU	Norway	Switzerland	USSR/ Russia[1]	Candid. countries	USA	Canada	China	Japan	Hong Kong	Mediterr. Basin	Latin America	OPEC	DAE	ACP
1990	**1,349**	**-44**	**101**	**243**	:	**183**	**39**	**24**	**-74**	**-7**	**390**	**91**	**40**	**65**	**24**
1991	-1,211	-152	62	-614	:	-12	20	-7	-151	-99	272	51	-401	-243	39
1992	-938	-140	-81	-440	:	-169	-12	-79	-194	-40	242	72	-183	-107	52
1993	-2,035	-238	-120	-535	-55	-477	-22	-49	-238	-36	100	14	-237	-132	-5
1994	-1,808	-218	-177	-434	60	-212	-6	-207	-263	-11	151	-84	-210	-144	-56
1995	-2,529	-189	-226	-523	-102	-394	-35	-328	-332	-27	65	-141	-153	-267	-76
1996	-3,957	-59	-261	-688	-321	-853	-77	-553	-436	-38	-36	-378	-44	-576	-62
1997	-5,148	-175	-395	-469	-509	-1,086	-81	-775	-599	-40	-46	-411	-17	-1,105	-202
1998	-5,933	-144	-391	-688	-295	-902	-128	-984	-773	-28	3	-357	-99	-1,544	-252
1999	-7,499	-100	-463	-1,848	-351	-840	-79	-1,019	-829	-8	-75	-264	-59	-1,750	-93
2000	**-10,292**	**-70**	**-437**	**-4,077**	**-336**	**-1,278**	**-4**	**-1,393**	**-1,071**	**14**	**71**	**-360**	**33**	**-1,552**	**-2**
2001	-9,291	-96	-417	-3,750	-138	-952	-1	-1,604	-1,025	-8	-154	-557	87	-1,572	-13
2002	**-8,835**	**55**	**-419**	**-3,264**	**290**	**-769**	**21**	**-1,978**	**-1,031**	**-12**	**-289**	**-499**	**5**	**-1,674**	**-149**

(1) Relates to the external trade with the USSR until 1991 and to the external trade with Russia from 1992 onwards.

(2) With Luxembourg until 31.12.1998.

POLAND

EU MEMBER STATES

Years	Intra EU	B[(1)]	DK	D	EL	E	F	IRL	I	L	NL	A	P	FIN	S	UK
							Partner									

EXPORTS
Value (Mio ECU/Euro)

Years	Intra EU	B[(1)]	DK	D	EL	E	F	IRL	I	L	NL	A	P	FIN	S	UK
1990	5,864	184	188	2,687	61	75	345	43	316	:	335	412	7	168	280	763
1994	10,029	359	462	5,170	55	149	579	55	720	:	854	319	23	253	373	658
1995	12,246	431	526	6,711	73	191	626	42	860	:	985	374	29	270	444	701
1996	12,804	479	585	6,629	144	197	847	51	1,069	:	921	381	30	248	459	757
1997	14,590	489	667	7,481	87	253	1,004	63	1,336	8	1,061	422	24	293	538	853
1998	17,214	618	692	9,128	115	348	1,188	65	1,486	19	1,207	493	35	227	602	979
1999	18,090	712	788	9,265	91	389	1,246	74	1,679	23	1,353	519	40	247	634	1,031
2000	24,018	1,012	927	11,978	108	549	1,784	97	2,167	28	1,733	693	217	250	936	1,539
2001	27,824	1,241	1,039	13,819	138	647	2,177	116	2,168	35	1,900	816	290	334	1,094	2,010
2002	29,915	1,411	1,201	14,070	160	768	2,624	132	2,395	48	1,949	799	387	302	1,411	2,258

Annual variation (%)

Years	Intra EU	B[(1)]	DK	D	EL	E	F	IRL	I	L	NL	A	P	FIN	S	UK
98/97	17.9	26.5	3.6	22.0	32.4	37.5	18.3	2.7	11.1	134.5	13.7	16.7	42.3	-22.4	11.9	14.7
99/98	5.0	15.1	13.8	1.5	-21.1	11.8	4.8	14.6	13.0	21.1	12.0	5.2	17.1	8.5	5.2	5.2
00/99	32.7	42.1	17.7	29.2	19.3	40.9	43.2	31.2	29.0	19.6	28.1	33.5	435.9	1.2	47.6	49.3
01/00	15.8	22.6	12.0	15.3	27.2	17.9	22.0	19.3	0.0	25.6	9.5	17.6	33.7	33.9	16.8	30.5
02/01	7.5	13.6	15.6	1.8	15.8	18.7	20.5	14.0	10.4	35.7	2.6	-2.0	33.5	-9.6	29.0	12.3

Share (%)

Years	Intra EU	B[(1)]	DK	D	EL	E	F	IRL	I	L	NL	A	P	FIN	S	UK
1990	100.0	3.1	3.2	45.8	1.0	1.2	5.8	0.7	5.3	:	5.7	7.0	0.1	2.8	4.7	13.0
1996	100.0	3.7	4.5	51.7	1.1	1.5	6.6	0.3	8.3	:	7.1	2.9	0.2	1.9	3.5	5.9
1997	100.0	3.3	4.5	51.2	0.5	1.7	6.8	0.4	9.1	0.0	7.2	2.8	0.1	2.0	3.6	5.8
1998	100.0	3.5	4.0	53.0	0.6	2.0	6.9	0.3	8.6	0.1	7.0	2.8	0.2	1.3	3.4	5.6
1999	100.0	3.9	4.3	51.2	0.5	2.1	6.8	0.4	9.2	0.1	7.4	2.8	0.2	1.3	3.5	5.6
2000	100.0	4.2	3.8	49.8	0.4	2.2	7.4	0.4	9.0	0.1	7.2	2.8	0.9	1.0	3.8	6.4
2001	100.0	4.4	3.7	49.6	0.4	2.3	7.8	0.4	7.7	0.1	6.8	2.9	1.0	1.2	3.9	7.2
2002	100.0	4.7	4.0	47.0	0.5	2.5	8.7	0.4	8.0	0.1	6.5	2.6	1.2	1.0	4.7	7.5

IMPORTS
Value (Mio ECU/Euro)

Years	Intra EU	B[(1)]	DK	D	EL	E	F	IRL	I	L	NL	A	P	FIN	S	UK
1990	3,624	101	80	1,417	21	37	213	16	527	:	185	400	1	90	138	398
1994	11,842	455	435	4,982	49	286	819	73	1,526	:	837	467	8	435	513	956
1995	14,337	586	485	5,915	61	362	1,087	116	1,898	:	1,008	564	20	413	695	1,149
1996	18,715	749	639	7,219	61	596	1,597	149	2,905	:	1,113	642	37	481	785	1,722
1997	23,828	984	728	8,980	75	920	2,207	193	3,689	48	1,351	758	63	643	1,125	2,046
1998	27,693	1,180	819	11,097	88	1,070	2,707	222	3,930	83	1,597	805	107	705	1,212	2,056
1999	27,966	1,218	773	10,906	98	1,064	2,891	226	4,028	71	1,614	829	132	786	1,358	1,973
2000	32,459	1,382	850	12,698	107	1,293	3,411	309	4,405	79	1,884	1,032	168	958	1,525	2,361
2001	34,391	1,528	981	13,426	147	1,422	3,818	325	4,624	78	1,991	1,093	179	945	1,501	2,331
2002	36,069	1,624	1,011	14,220	158	1,545	4,073	341	4,888	86	2,053	1,120	215	909	1,549	2,277

Annual variation (%)

Years	Intra EU	B[(1)]	DK	D	EL	E	F	IRL	I	L	NL	A	P	FIN	S	UK
98/97	16.2	19.9	12.4	23.5	17.5	16.3	22.6	15.5	6.5	74.7	18.2	6.2	71.4	9.6	7.6	0.4
99/98	0.9	3.2	-5.6	-1.7	11.8	-0.6	6.8	1.7	2.4	-14.3	1.0	2.9	22.8	11.3	12.0	-4.0
00/99	16.0	13.4	9.9	16.4	9.1	21.5	17.9	36.4	9.3	10.2	16.7	24.4	27.5	21.9	12.3	19.6
01/00	5.9	10.5	15.4	5.7	37.2	9.9	11.9	5.3	4.9	-0.1	5.6	5.9	6.7	-1.2	-1.5	-1.2
02/01	4.8	6.3	3.0	5.9	7.7	8.6	6.6	4.7	5.6	9.8	3.1	2.4	19.5	-3.8	3.1	-2.2

Share (%)

Years	Intra EU	B[(1)]	DK	D	EL	E	F	IRL	I	L	NL	A	P	FIN	S	UK
1990	100.0	2.7	2.2	39.1	0.5	1.0	5.8	0.4	14.5	:	5.1	11.0	0.0	2.4	3.7	10.9
1996	100.0	4.0	3.4	38.5	0.3	3.1	8.5	0.7	15.5	:	5.9	3.4	0.1	2.5	4.1	9.2
1997	100.0	4.1	3.0	37.6	0.3	3.8	9.2	0.8	15.4	0.1	5.6	3.1	0.2	2.7	4.7	8.5
1998	100.0	4.2	2.9	40.0	0.3	3.8	9.7	0.8	14.1	0.3	5.7	2.9	0.3	2.5	4.3	7.4
1999	100.0	4.3	2.7	38.9	0.3	3.8	10.3	0.8	14.4	0.2	5.7	2.9	0.4	2.8	4.8	7.0
2000	100.0	4.2	2.6	39.1	0.3	3.9	10.5	0.9	13.5	0.2	5.8	3.1	0.5	2.9	4.6	7.2
2001	100.0	4.4	2.8	39.0	0.4	4.1	11.1	0.9	13.4	0.2	5.7	3.1	0.5	2.7	4.3	6.7
2002	100.0	4.5	2.8	39.4	0.4	4.2	11.2	0.9	13.5	0.2	5.6	3.1	0.5	2.5	4.2	6.3

(1) With Luxembourg until 31.12.1998.

NON EU MEMBER STATES

Years	Extra EU	Norway	Switzerland	USSR/ Russia(1)	Candid. countries	USA	Canada	China	Japan	Hong Kong	Mediterr. Basin	Latin America	OPEC	DAE	ACP
EXPORTS Value (Mio ECU/Euro)															
1990	**4,687**	**45**	**556**	**1,624**	:	**296**	**47**	**152**	**87**	**5**	**616**	**153**	**260**	**94**	**34**
1994	4,282	96	142	784	936	499	53	53	32	51	446	195	148	232	112
1995	5,097	112	159	973	1,394	476	51	27	33	40	422	176	159	225	108
1996	6,290	236	178	1,303	1,655	444	67	27	41	34	421	162	219	339	120
1997	7,955	191	154	1,902	2,118	599	75	30	52	19	483	188	264	283	95
1998	7,896	206	188	1,428	2,703	685	84	62	41	12	660	222	183	104	94
1999	7,553	322	173	668	2,949	711	93	123	40	21	621	265	185	290	218
2000	**10,285**	**369**	**266**	**943**	**4,042**	**1,092**	**176**	**107**	**67**	**52**	**915**	**337**	**310**	**388**	**248**
2001	12,289	452	313	1,182	4,961	951	188	201	73	43	982	356	365	293	438
2002	**13,511**	**769**	**345**	**1,415**	**5,654**	**1,163**	**191**	**220**	**76**	**32**	**1,136**	**320**	**333**	**264**	**311**
Annual variation (%)															
98/97	-0.7	7.8	21.7	-24.9	27.6	14.3	10.9	108.0	-19.9	-38.5	36.5	17.9	-30.8	-63.3	-1.0
99/98	-4.3	56.1	-7.9	-53.2	9.0	3.8	11.6	99.4	-2.3	79.5	-5.9	19.2	1.5	178.9	131.2
00/99	36.1	14.7	53.8	41.1	37.0	53.5	87.8	-13.0	67.3	149.5	47.4	27.4	67.3	33.8	13.9
01/00	19.4	22.4	17.5	25.3	22.7	-12.9	6.8	87.2	8.3	-17.5	7.3	5.4	17.5	-24.3	76.1
02/01	9.9	70.0	10.1	19.6	13.9	22.3	1.7	9.2	3.4	-25.1	15.6	-10.0	-8.6	-9.9	-28.9
Share (%)															
1990	**100.0**	**0.9**	**11.8**	**34.6**	:	**6.3**	**1.0**	**3.2**	**1.8**	**0.1**	**13.1**	**3.2**	**5.5**	**2.0**	**0.7**
1996	100.0	3.7	2.8	20.7	26.3	7.0	1.0	0.4	0.6	0.5	6.6	2.5	3.4	5.3	1.9
1997	100.0	2.4	1.9	23.9	26.6	7.5	0.9	0.3	0.6	0.2	6.0	2.3	3.3	3.5	1.1
1998	100.0	2.6	2.3	18.0	34.2	8.6	1.0	0.7	0.5	0.1	8.3	2.8	2.3	1.3	1.1
1999	100.0	4.2	2.2	8.8	39.0	9.4	1.2	1.6	0.5	0.2	8.2	3.5	2.4	3.8	2.8
2000	**100.0**	**3.5**	**2.5**	**9.1**	**39.2**	**10.6**	**1.7**	**1.0**	**0.6**	**0.5**	**8.8**	**3.2**	**3.0**	**3.7**	**2.4**
2001	100.0	3.6	2.5	9.6	40.3	7.7	1.5	1.6	0.5	0.3	7.9	2.8	2.9	2.3	3.5
2002	**100.0**	**5.6**	**2.5**	**10.4**	**41.8**	**8.6**	**1.4**	**1.6**	**0.5**	**0.2**	**8.4**	**2.3**	**2.4**	**1.9**	**2.3**
IMPORTS Value (Mio ECU/Euro)															
1990	**3,338**	**90**	**455**	**1,380**	:	**114**	**9**	**128**	**161**	**12**	**226**	**62**	**220**	**29**	**10**
1994	6,090	313	319	1,218	877	712	60	260	295	61	295	279	358	376	168
1995	7,626	301	385	1,496	1,497	870	86	355	365	67	357	317	312	491	184
1996	10,247	294	439	1,991	1,976	1,297	144	579	477	73	457	541	264	915	182
1997	13,103	366	549	2,371	2,627	1,686	157	805	650	59	529	599	281	1,388	297
1998	13,828	350	579	2,115	2,998	1,587	212	1,046	814	40	657	579	281	1,647	346
1999	15,052	422	636	2,515	3,300	1,551	173	1,142	869	28	695	528	245	2,040	311
2000	**20,577**	**440**	**703**	**5,019**	**4,378**	**2,370**	**180**	**1,500**	**1,139**	**38**	**844**	**698**	**277**	**1,940**	**250**
2001	21,580	548	730	4,932	5,099	1,903	188	1,805	1,098	51	1,136	913	278	1,866	450
2002	**22,347**	**714**	**764**	**4,678**	**5,364**	**1,933**	**169**	**2,197**	**1,107**	**44**	**1,425**	**819**	**328**	**1,938**	**460**
Annual variation (%)															
98/97	5.5	-4.4	5.4	-10.7	14.1	-5.8	34.9	29.8	25.2	-32.4	24.1	-3.3	-0.1	18.6	16.5
99/98	8.8	20.6	9.9	18.9	10.0	-2.2	-18.2	9.2	6.7	-28.8	5.9	-8.6	-12.9	23.8	-10.1
00/99	36.7	4.2	10.5	99.5	32.6	52.7	3.8	31.3	31.0	32.3	21.4	32.0	13.2	-4.8	-19.6
01/00	4.8	24.6	3.8	-1.7	16.4	-19.6	4.8	20.2	-3.5	36.2	34.5	30.8	0.3	-3.8	80.0
02/01	3.5	30.2	4.6	-5.1	5.1	1.5	-10.0	21.7	0.7	-13.4	25.4	-10.3	18.2	3.8	2.1
Share (%)															
1990	**100.0**	**2.6**	**13.6**	**41.3**	:	**3.4**	**0.2**	**3.8**	**4.8**	**0.3**	**6.7**	**1.8**	**6.5**	**0.8**	**0.3**
1996	100.0	2.8	4.2	19.4	19.2	12.6	1.4	5.6	4.6	0.7	4.4	5.2	2.5	8.9	1.7
1997	100.0	2.7	4.1	18.0	20.0	12.8	1.1	6.1	4.9	0.4	4.0	4.5	2.1	10.5	2.2
1998	100.0	2.5	4.1	15.2	21.6	11.4	1.5	7.5	5.8	0.2	4.7	4.1	2.0	11.9	2.5
1999	100.0	2.8	4.2	16.7	21.9	10.3	1.1	7.5	5.7	0.1	4.6	3.5	1.6	13.5	2.0
2000	**100.0**	**2.1**	**3.4**	**24.3**	**21.2**	**11.5**	**0.8**	**7.2**	**5.5**	**0.1**	**4.1**	**3.3**	**1.3**	**9.4**	**1.2**
2001	100.0	2.5	3.3	22.8	23.6	8.8	0.8	8.3	5.0	0.2	5.2	4.2	1.2	8.6	2.0
2002	**100.0**	**3.1**	**3.4**	**20.9**	**24.0**	**8.6**	**0.7**	**9.8**	**4.9**	**0.1**	**6.3**	**3.6**	**1.4**	**8.6**	**2.0**

(1) Relates to the external trade with the USSR until 1991 and to the external trade with Russia from 1992 onwards.

ROMANIA

TRADE BALANCE (BN ECU/euro)

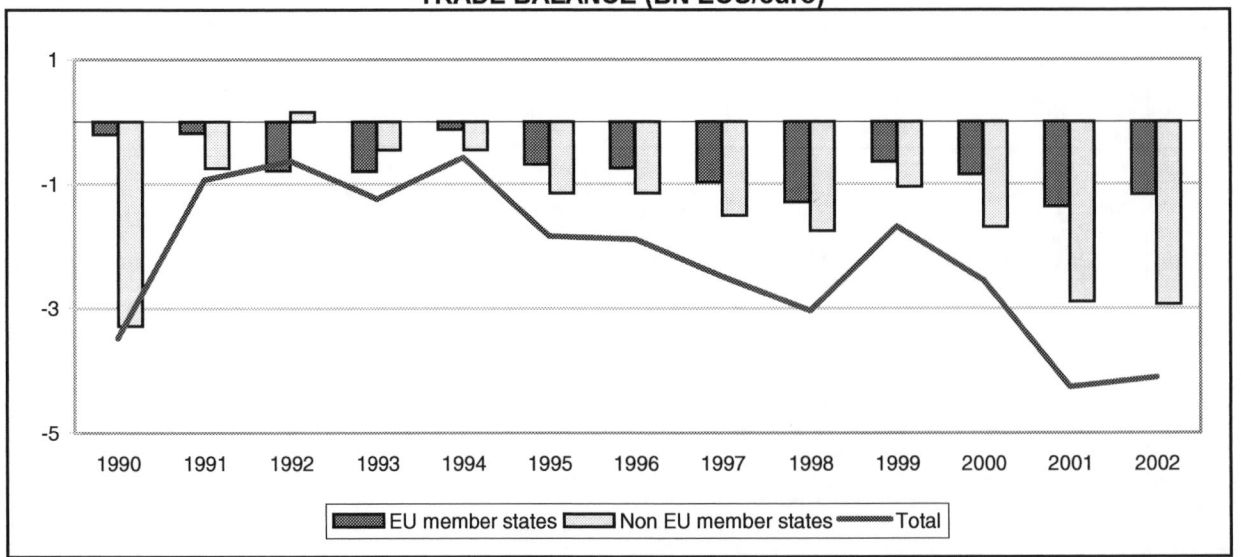

TRADE WITH EU MEMBER STATES (BN ECU/euro)

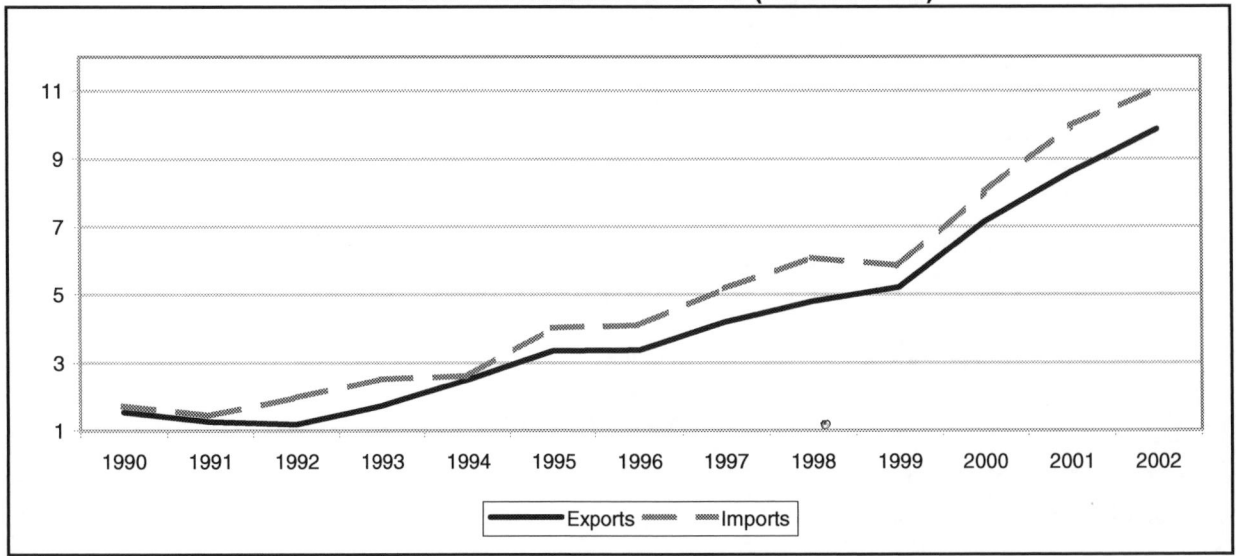

TRADE WITH NON EU MEMBER STATES (BN ECU/euro)

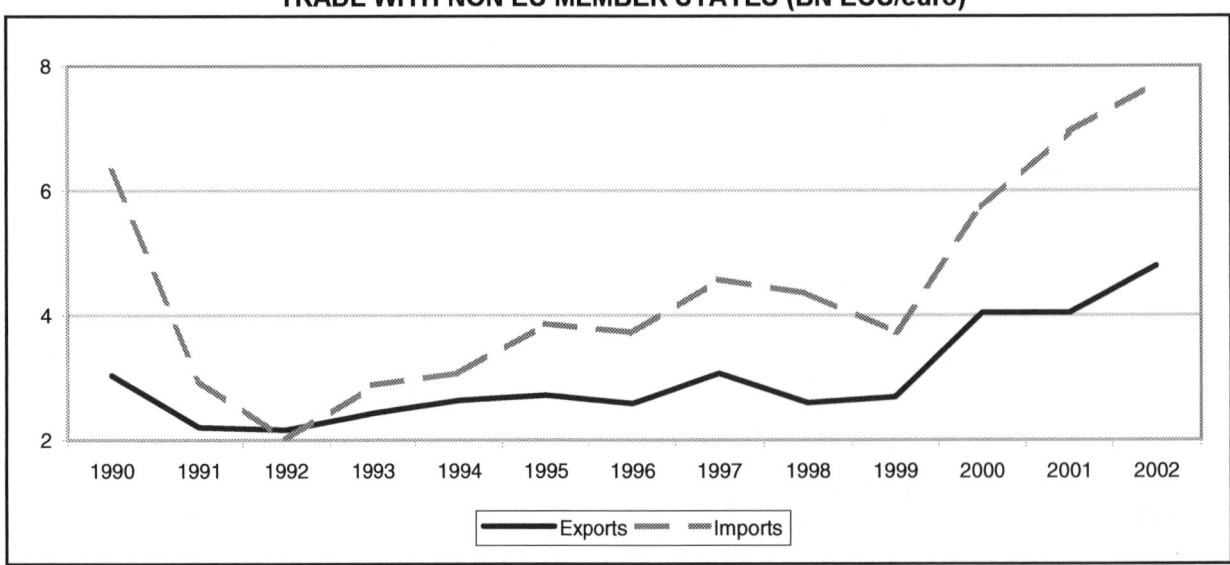

ROMANIA

TRADE BALANCE

EU MEMBER STATES

Value (Mio ECU/Euro)

Year	Intra EU	B(2)	DK	D	EL	E	F	IRL	I	L	NL	A	P	FIN	S	UK
1990	**-199**	**3**	**-7**	**-414**	**10**	**16**	**4**	**-12**	**311**	**:**	**5**	**-77**	**-3**	**6**	**9**	**-51**
1991	-182	-13	-7	-103	-34	4	-23	-3	3	:	97	-91	1	-2	5	-16
1992	-792	-21	-13	-289	29	14	-155	-6	-186	:	-40	-72	0	-2	-22	-29
1993	-793	-9	-36	-283	13	-11	-245	-9	-175	:	47	-77	-0	-10	-10	12
1994	-123	21	-28	-146	50	12	-12	-6	27	:	47	-67	0	-18	-2	-2
1995	-684	-6	-27	-155	48	16	-22	-12	5	:	-9	-100	4	-12	-24	-30
1996	-742	-26	-44	-130	15	10	-15	-14	-98	:	92	-98	-3	-18	-15	-21
1997	-974	:	-25	-220	3	8	-112	-13	39	:	53	-85	7	-16	-73	-42
1998	-1,291	:	-37	-233	14	-23	-232	-22	-40	:	47	-59	3	-30	-82	-55
1999	-641	-30	-36	-254	17	-0	-158	-35	-31	-3	87	-56	12	-39	-86	-31
2000	**-853**	**-22**	**-30**	**-329**	**-56**	**-19**	**-80**	**-32**	**-109**	**-6**	**46**	**-88**	**5**	**-51**	**-63**	**-20**
2001	-1,362	-71	-44	-655	-12	-44	-56	6	-298	-6	70	-110	-13	-50	-106	29
2002	**-1,169**	**-68**	**-54**	**-512**	**132**	**-90**	**-84**	**-58**	**-241**	**0**	**49**	**-182**	**-17**	**-50**	**-120**	**127**

NON EU MEMBER STATES

Value (Mio ECU/euro)

Year	Extra EU	Norway	Switzerland	USSR/ Russia(1)	Candid. countries	USA	Canada	China	Japan	Hong Kong	Mediterr. Basin	Latin America	OPEC	DAE	ACP
1990	**-3,280**	**3**	**-93**	**-746**	**:**	**-109**	**6**	**-80**	**6**	**5**	**-311**	**-81**	**-1,412**	**39**	**30**
1991	-744	2	-101	10	:	-14	-5	5	39	28	-27	-66	-565	19	37
1992	155	-2	-26	:	:	-114	-13	99	-17	-8	115	-30	-387	-7	41
1993	-449	-1	-26	-465	60	-259	-31	279	-4	:	308	-28	-349	60	78
1994	-448	-0	-87	-652	140	-226	-9	184	-4	2	446	-45	-171	98	135
1995	-1,149	-9	-108	-817	-97	-168	-9	68	-31	-23	321	-39	-33	-120	42
1996	-1,144	5	-98	-875	32	-154	-19	-10	-46	-11	574	-112	-96	-238	77
1997	-1,510	40	-90	-973	-82	-113	-48	-64	-81	-7	568	-130	77	-406	51
1998	-1,750	24	-76	-874	-484	-161	-9	-138	-54	-23	450	-95	116	-253	45
1999	-1,045	23	-62	-617	-57	-50	-10	-101	-88	-5	598	-111	126	-281	32
2000	**-1,694**	**17**	**-99**	**-1,121**	**79**	**-22**	**-21**	**-96**	**-169**	**-0**	**934**	**-225**	**210**	**-282**	**67**
2001	-2,894	47	-129	-1,227	-648	-154	-26	-183	-152	17	614	-239	206	-272	30
2002	**-2,940**	**72**	**-88**	**-1,306**	**-854**	**56**	**-1**	**-176**	**-218**	**214**	**554**	**-228**	**307**	**-281**	**21**

(1) Relates to the external trade with the USSR until 1991 and to the external trade with Russia from 1992 onwards.

(2) With Luxembourg until 31.12.1998.

ROMANIA

EU MEMBER STATES

Years	Intra EU	B[1]	DK	D	EL	E	F	IRL	I	L	NL	A	P	FIN	S	UK
							EXPORTS									
						Value (Mio ECU/Euro)										
1990	1,540	46	5	509	68	33	158	1	408	:	123	56	1	7	26	100
1994	2,497	88	7	830	119	47	265	2	671	:	183	82	2	3	29	168
1995	3,351	177	12	1,097	158	78	350	4	955	:	183	119	7	5	30	181
1996	3,368	94	10	1,091	136	73	339	3	1,015	:	255	126	8	4	32	177
1997	4,199	:	14	1,244	154	73	403	6	1,460	:	232	156	12	5	41	261
1998	4,793	:	20	1,416	177	74	425	6	1,614	:	272	220	15	9	40	265
1999	5,219	141	16	1,414	204	100	498	3	1,858	0	307	228	24	3	41	381
2000	7,155	192	30	1,763	352	123	789	39	2,516	1	356	273	26	3	132	561
2001	8,588	215	32	1,986	352	200	1,024	71	3,167	1	429	382	23	5	68	632
2002	9,864	233	27	2,293	413	216	1,121	16	3,670	7	461	446	34	7	70	849
						Annual variation (%)										
98/97	14.1	:	40.8	13.8	14.5	1.8	5.4	-4.8	10.5	:	17.0	40.8	24.3	65.2	-1.4	1.4
99/98	8.8	:	-17.8	0.0	15.6	34.4	17.2	-45.6	15.1	:	13.1	3.6	62.6	-63.9	1.8	43.9
00/99	37.0	35.5	84.0	24.6	72.3	23.2	58.4	1,172.5	35.4	41.4	15.7	19.9	7.2	7.1	223.4	47.1
01/00	20.0	12.3	7.9	12.6	0.1	62.3	29.7	82.9	25.8	156.9	20.7	39.5	-10.3	33.9	-48.1	12.5
02/01	14.8	7.9	-15.3	15.4	17.1	8.2	9.5	-77.4	15.8	402.6	7.4	16.8	48.8	57.0	2.0	34.4
						Share (%)										
1990	100.0	2.9	0.3	33.0	4.3	2.1	10.2	0.0	26.4	:	7.9	3.6	0.0	0.4	1.6	6.4
1996	100.0	2.7	0.3	32.3	4.0	2.1	10.0	0.1	30.1	:	7.5	3.7	0.2	0.1	0.9	5.2
1997	100.0	:	0.3	29.6	3.6	1.7	9.5	0.1	34.7	:	5.5	3.7	0.2	0.1	0.9	6.2
1998	100.0	:	0.4	29.5	3.6	1.5	8.8	0.1	33.6	:	5.6	4.5	0.3	0.1	0.8	5.5
1999	100.0	2.7	0.3	27.1	3.9	1.9	9.5	0.0	35.5	0.0	5.8	4.3	0.4	0.0	0.7	7.3
2000	100.0	2.6	0.4	24.6	4.9	1.7	11.0	0.5	35.1	0.0	4.9	3.8	0.3	0.0	1.8	7.8
2001	100.0	2.5	0.3	23.1	4.1	2.3	11.9	0.8	36.8	0.0	4.9	4.4	0.2	0.0	0.7	7.3
2002	100.0	2.3	0.2	23.2	4.1	2.1	11.3	0.1	37.2	0.0	4.6	4.5	0.3	0.0	0.7	8.6
							IMPORTS									
						Value (Mio ECU/Euro)										
1990	1,740	42	12	923	58	17	154	13	96	:	118	133	4	1	17	150
1994	2,620	67	35	976	68	36	277	8	644	:	136	149	2	21	31	171
1995	4,035	184	38	1,252	110	61	373	16	950	:	192	219	3	17	53	211
1996	4,110	119	54	1,220	121	62	355	17	1,113	:	163	223	11	22	46	198
1997	5,172	:	39	1,464	151	65	515	19	1,421	:	179	241	5	21	114	303
1998	6,084	:	57	1,648	163	97	657	28	1,653	:	225	279	12	38	122	320
1999	5,860	171	52	1,668	187	100	656	38	1,888	3	220	284	12	42	127	412
2000	8,007	214	59	2,092	408	142	869	70	2,625	6	310	361	21	54	195	581
2001	9,950	287	76	2,642	365	244	1,080	66	3,465	7	360	491	37	55	174	602
2002	11,033	301	81	2,805	281	306	1,206	74	3,912	7	412	628	52	57	190	722
						Annual variation (%)										
98/97	17.6	:	43.8	12.6	7.8	49.9	27.6	48.5	16.3	:	25.3	15.8	129.8	84.0	6.9	5.5
99/98	-3.6	:	-8.2	1.1	14.7	2.5	-0.1	35.1	14.2	:	-2.3	1.7	-1.1	9.0	4.1	28.8
00/99	36.6	24.9	14.3	25.4	118.3	42.2	32.4	86.3	38.9	83.9	40.8	27.0	74.8	29.9	54.1	40.8
01/00	24.2	33.8	28.7	26.2	-10.4	71.3	24.2	-7.0	32.0	17.0	16.2	36.1	73.7	0.6	-10.7	3.7
02/01	10.8	4.9	6.5	6.1	-22.8	25.6	11.6	12.4	12.8	-8.4	14.5	27.8	41.2	4.4	9.1	19.8
						Share (%)										
1990	100.0	2.4	0.6	53.0	3.3	0.9	8.8	0.7	5.5	:	6.7	7.6	0.2	0.0	0.9	8.6
1996	100.0	2.9	1.3	29.6	2.9	1.5	8.6	0.4	27.0	:	3.9	5.4	0.2	0.5	1.1	4.8
1997	100.0	:	0.7	28.2	2.9	1.2	9.9	0.3	27.4	:	3.4	4.6	0.1	0.4	2.1	5.8
1998	100.0	:	0.9	27.0	2.6	1.6	10.7	0.4	27.1	:	3.6	4.5	0.1	0.6	1.9	5.2
1999	100.0	2.9	0.8	28.4	3.1	1.7	11.1	0.6	32.2	0.0	3.7	4.8	0.2	0.7	2.1	7.0
2000	100.0	2.6	0.7	26.1	5.0	1.7	10.8	0.8	32.7	0.0	3.8	4.5	0.2	0.6	2.4	7.2
2001	100.0	2.8	0.7	26.5	3.6	2.4	10.8	0.6	34.8	0.0	3.6	4.9	0.3	0.5	1.7	6.0
2002	100.0	2.7	0.7	25.4	2.5	2.7	10.9	0.6	35.4	0.0	3.7	5.6	0.4	0.5	1.7	6.5

(1) With Luxembourg until 31.12.1998.

NON EU MEMBER STATES

Years	Extra EU	Norway	Switzerland	USSR/Russia(1)	Candid. countries	USA	Canada	China	Japan	Hong Kong	Mediterr. Basin	Latin America	OPEC	DAE	ACP
					EXPORTS										
					Value (Mio ECU/Euro)										
1990	3,039	6	70	1,166	:	270	22	121	74	6	511	86	191	53	41
1994	2,632	9	38	175	581	160	33	235	45	17	802	89	244	169	147
1995	2,717	9	50	121	577	153	23	136	27	5	1,009	129	214	183	80
1996	2,582	19	30	118	610	142	17	73	30	8	1,017	138	172	118	111
1997	3,062	54	40	220	730	276	31	39	33	13	1,065	114	322	150	67
1998	2,598	42	47	73	742	286	55	21	21	9	979	125	237	54	77
1999	2,689	39	46	44	1,035	291	23	34	18	9	1,063	77	178	78	60
2000	4,039	46	60	97	1,659	408	38	93	17	17	1,531	90	279	135	115
2001	4,045	82	53	93	1,486	398	40	100	20	34	1,423	136	352	165	116
2002	4,786	120	75	43	1,581	627	50	216	12	242	1,547	90	396	367	106
					Annual variation (%)										
98/97	-15.1	-22.2	16.5	-66.8	1.6	3.7	76.5	-47.2	-34.5	-27.5	-8.0	9.6	-26.2	-63.9	15.6
99/98	3.5	-7.5	-3.2	-39.4	39.3	1.6	-57.7	66.0	-13.9	-0.4	8.6	-38.3	-24.9	43.4	-21.7
00/99	50.1	19.5	32.2	119.5	60.3	40.1	66.7	171.8	-5.1	83.9	44.0	16.8	56.3	73.0	91.5
01/00	0.1	76.4	-12.9	-4.3	-10.4	-2.4	4.5	7.0	13.6	98.4	-7.0	50.8	26.2	22.4	0.1
02/01	18.3	46.0	42.7	-53.7	6.3	57.5	25.3	116.8	-38.3	608.0	8.6	-33.9	12.6	123.0	-7.9
					Share (%)										
1990	100.0	0.2	2.3	38.3	:	8.8	0.7	3.9	2.4	0.1	16.8	2.8	6.2	1.7	1.3
1996	100.0	0.7	1.1	4.5	23.6	5.4	0.6	2.8	1.1	0.3	39.3	5.3	6.6	4.5	4.3
1997	100.0	1.7	1.3	7.1	23.8	9.0	1.0	1.2	1.0	0.4	34.7	3.7	10.5	4.9	2.1
1998	100.0	1.6	1.8	2.8	28.5	11.0	2.1	0.7	0.8	0.3	37.6	4.8	9.1	2.0	2.9
1999	100.0	1.4	1.6	1.6	38.4	10.8	0.8	1.2	0.6	0.3	39.5	2.8	6.6	2.8	2.2
2000	100.0	1.1	1.4	2.3	41.0	10.0	0.9	2.3	0.4	0.4	37.9	2.2	6.8	3.3	2.8
2001	100.0	2.0	1.2	2.2	36.7	9.8	0.9	2.4	0.4	0.8	35.1	3.3	8.6	4.0	2.8
2002	100.0	2.5	1.5	0.8	33.0	13.0	1.0	4.5	0.2	5.0	32.3	1.8	8.2	7.6	2.2
					IMPORTS										
					Value (Mio ECU/Euro)										
1990	6,319	4	164	1,912	:	379	16	202	68	1	822	167	1,603	13	12
1994	3,080	9	126	828	441	386	42	51	48	14	356	134	414	72	12
1995	3,865	18	158	938	674	321	33	69	58	28	688	167	248	302	38
1996	3,726	14	129	993	579	296	36	84	76	19	443	249	268	356	34
1997	4,571	14	131	1,193	812	389	79	103	114	20	497	244	246	556	16
1998	4,348	18	123	947	1,227	448	63	158	76	32	529	221	122	307	32
1999	3,734	16	107	661	1,092	340	33	136	107	15	465	188	52	359	29
2000	5,732	30	160	1,218	1,581	430	59	189	186	18	597	315	68	416	49
2001	6,938	35	181	1,320	2,134	551	66	282	171	17	809	375	145	436	86
2002	7,725	47	163	1,349	2,435	571	51	392	230	28	993	319	89	649	85
					Annual variation (%)										
98/97	-4.8	33.1	-5.6	-20.6	51.0	15.0	-19.6	53.2	-33.6	59.3	6.4	-9.4	-50.4	-44.8	97.8
99/98	-14.1	-14.4	-13.1	-30.1	-10.9	-23.9	-47.2	-14.2	41.2	-54.5	-12.0	-14.6	-57.3	17.0	-9.6
00/99	53.5	88.2	48.8	84.1	44.7	26.1	78.0	39.2	74.6	19.1	28.2	67.1	31.8	15.8	70.3
01/00	21.0	17.6	13.5	8.3	35.0	28.3	11.7	49.4	-8.0	-1.4	35.6	19.0	112.5	4.8	76.6
02/01	11.3	36.4	-9.8	2.2	14.1	3.5	-22.6	39.0	34.1	60.8	22.6	-15.0	-38.5	48.6	-1.0
					Share (%)										
1990	100.0	0.0	2.5	30.2	:	5.9	0.2	3.1	1.0	0.0	13.0	2.6	25.3	0.2	0.1
1996	100.0	0.3	3.4	26.6	15.5	7.9	0.9	2.2	2.0	0.5	11.8	6.6	7.1	9.5	0.9
1997	100.0	0.3	2.8	26.0	17.7	8.5	1.7	2.2	2.4	0.4	10.8	5.3	5.3	12.1	0.3
1998	100.0	0.4	2.8	21.7	28.2	10.2	1.4	3.6	1.7	0.7	12.1	5.0	2.7	7.0	0.7
1999	100.0	0.4	2.8	17.7	29.2	9.1	0.8	3.6	2.8	0.3	12.4	5.0	1.3	9.6	0.7
2000	100.0	0.5	2.7	21.2	27.5	7.4	1.0	3.2	3.2	0.3	10.4	5.4	1.1	7.2	0.8
2001	100.0	0.5	2.6	19.0	30.7	7.9	0.9	4.0	2.4	0.2	11.6	5.4	2.0	6.2	1.2
2002	100.0	0.6	2.1	17.4	31.5	7.3	0.6	5.0	2.9	0.3	12.8	4.1	1.1	8.3	1.0

(1) Relates to the external trade with the USSR until 1991 and to the external trade with Russia from 1992 onwards.

SLOVAKIA

TRADE BALANCE (BN ECU/euro)

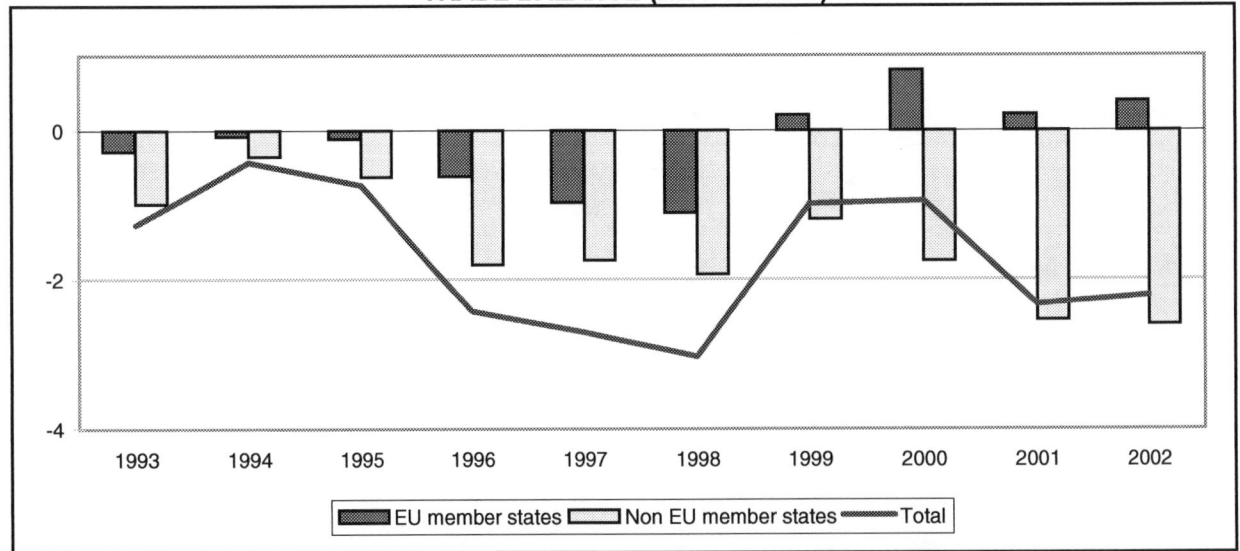

TRADE WITH EU MEMBER STATES (BN ECU/euro)

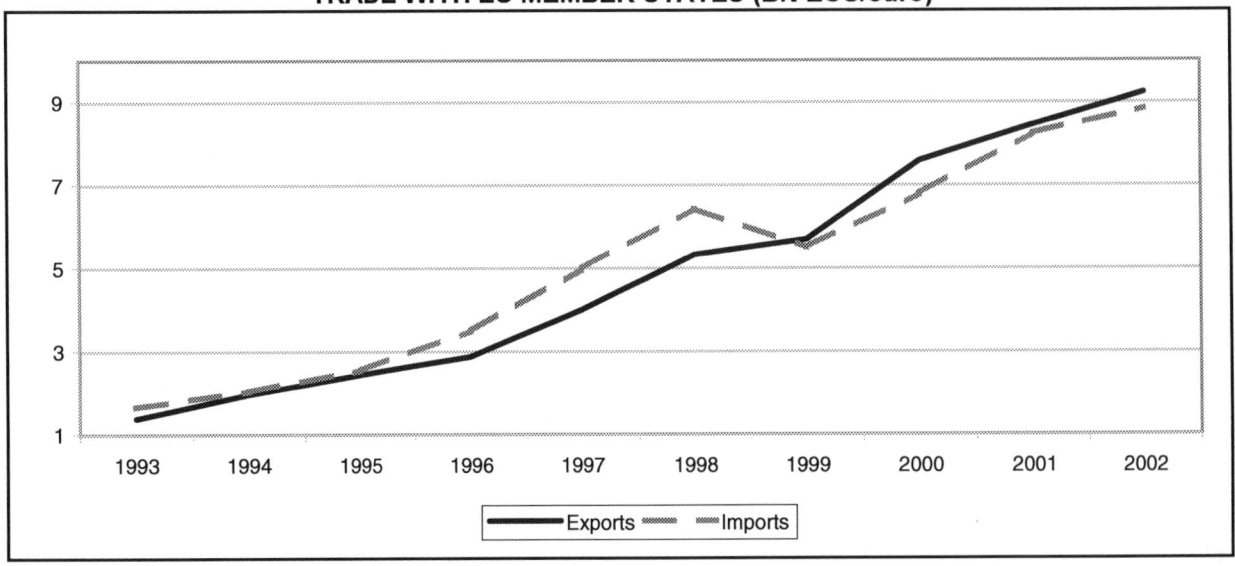

TRADE WITH NON EU MEMBER STATES (BN ECU/euro)

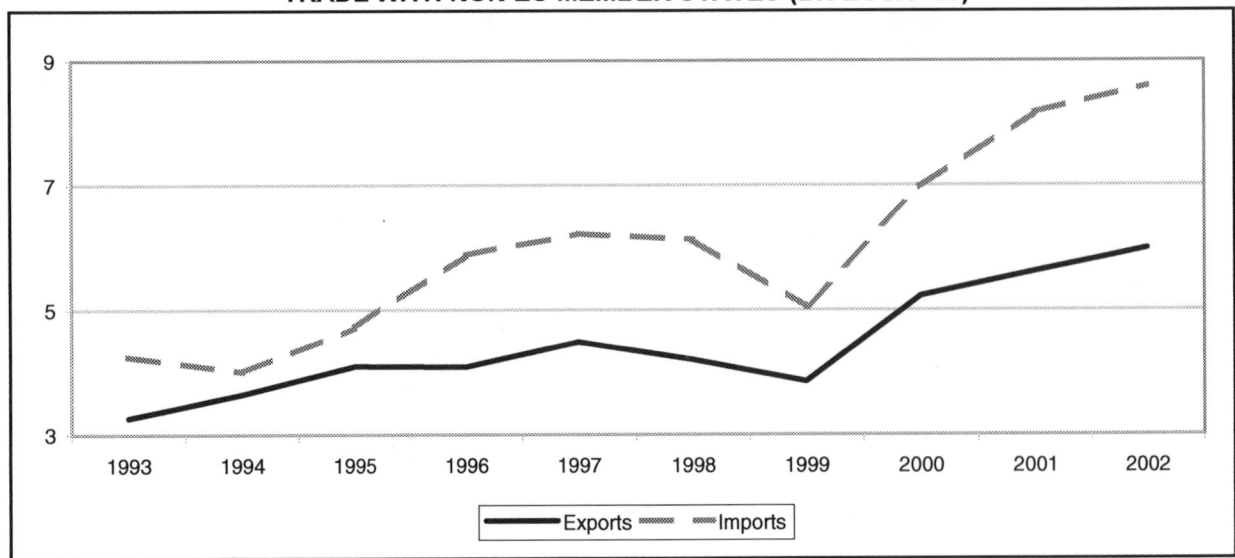

TRADE BALANCE

EU MEMBER STATES

Value (Mio ECU/Euro)

Year								Partner								
	Intra EU	B(2)	DK	D	EL	E	F	IRL	I	L	NL	A	P	FIN	S	UK
1990	:	:	:	:	:	:	:	:	:	:	:	:	:	:	:	:
1991	:	:	:	:	:	:	:	:	:	:	:	:	:	:	:	:
1992	:	:	:	:	:	:	:	:	:	:	:	:	:	:	:	:
1993	-280	-4	-19	30	2	-9	-15	-6	-51	:	-4	-139	1	-29	-12	-27
1994	-77	-5	-21	140	8	-4	-41	-9	-25	:	-2	-57	3	-33	-7	-26
1995	-110	-20	-21	180	10	-5	-50	-11	-25	:	-11	-51	4	-33	-40	-39
1996	-622	-43	-29	95	16	-40	-154	-18	-224	:	-41	-21	3	-51	-45	-69
1997	-973	-21	-38	-225	11	-40	-205	-24	-154	0	-64	43	-1	-56	-69	-131
1998	-1,109	11	-39	-541	6	-46	-166	-22	-147	-2	-48	116	-7	-55	-48	-119
1999	207	26	-10	-123	4	-65	50	-20	92	7	110	258	-1	-55	3	-68
2000	**801**	**47**	**-9**	**-33**	**13**	**-206**	**132**	**-28**	**325**	**20**	**126**	**525**	**-0**	**-35**	**19**	**-96**
2001	216	64	-10	-267	63	-224	-82	-41	199	40	154	457	-2	-45	-17	-75
2002	**393**	**0**	**28**	**-14**	**22**	**-303**	**-136**	**-41**	**429**	**12**	**155**	**430**	**-26**	**-44**	**-35**	**-84**

NON EU MEMBER STATES

Value (Mio ECU/euro)

Year								Partner							
	Extra EU	Norway	Switzerland	USSR/ Russia(1)	Candid. countries	USA	Canada	China	Japan	Hong Kong	Mediterr. Basin	Latin America	OPEC	DAE	ACP
1990	:	:	:	:	:	:	:	:	:	:	:	:	:	:	:
1991	:	:	:	:	:	:	:	:	:	:	:	:	:	:	:
1992	:	:	:	:	:	:	:	:	:	:	:	:	:	:	:
1993	-987	-10	-46	-945	38	-55	-9	28	-61	-10	138	-34	29	11	-0
1994	-352	-1	-48	-867	571	-84	20	-15	-70	-15	139	-10	23	36	5
1995	-628	-4	-71	-971	585	-99	-2	-36	-96	-26	160	-30	43	-54	-0
1996	-1,799	-7	-64	-1,433	141	-161	-16	-40	-150	-19	127	-40	37	-202	-13
1997	-1,736	-9	-60	-1,282	165	-212	-11	-103	-180	-23	147	-32	23	-104	0
1998	-1,925	11	-40	-1,157	48	-255	-19	-145	-200	-14	106	-33	3	-135	-15
1999	-1,196	14	10	-1,178	454	-133	-10	-130	-155	-5	127	-13	7	-162	14
2000	**-1,746**	**25**	**44**	**-2,231**	**1,007**	**-94**	**-2**	**-181**	**-219**	**-5**	**188**	**-19**	**18**	**-180**	**-2**
2001	-2,547	8	4	-2,287	635	-134	-3	-245	-252	-10	175	-55	3	-276	-6
2002	**-2,607**	**27**	**-48**	**-2,047**	**435**	**-150**	**3**	**-324**	**-170**	**-14**	**211**	**-79**	**-16**	**-325**	**-7**

(1) Relates to the external trade with the USSR until 1991 and to the external trade with Russia from 1992 onwards.

(2) With Luxembourg until 31.12.1998.

SLOVAKIA

EU MEMBER STATES

Years	Intra EU	B[1]	DK	D	EL	E	F	IRL	I	L	NL	A	P	FIN	S	UK
							EXPORTS									
						Value (Mio ECU/Euro)										
1990	:	:	:	:	:	:	:	:	:	:	:	:	:	:	:	:
1994	1,967	71	17	962	17	33	95	4	242	:	100	295	6	18	33	72
1995	2,451	72	22	1,233	20	47	131	4	316	:	115	326	7	29	45	86
1996	2,872	88	25	1,474	26	43	147	6	340	:	131	420	7	26	31	107
1997	4,006	141	25	2,014	28	67	204	10	510	5	169	610	10	30	41	141
1998	5,316	201	27	2,754	24	91	328	15	685	5	218	714	9	36	73	145
1999	5,699	191	46	2,653	23	86	460	13	847	10	295	771	10	39	87	168
2000	**7,590**	**269**	**59**	**3,443**	**32**	**110**	**597**	**14**	**1,181**	**34**	**342**	**1,074**	**16**	**51**	**124**	**243**
2001	8,445	339	67	3,819	91	174	556	17	1,247	44	397	1,146	31	55	116	347
2002	**9,231**	**317**	**111**	**3,962**	**51**	**248**	**637**	**19**	**1,635**	**18**	**464**	**1,172**	**29**	**74**	**130**	**362**
							Annual variation (%)									
98/97	32.7	42.7	9.5	36.7	-13.6	35.9	60.4	52.2	34.5	5.0	28.5	17.0	-6.4	18.6	78.1	3.1
99/98	7.1	-5.0	68.8	-3.6	-3.3	-5.1	40.3	-8.3	23.5	84.9	35.3	7.9	5.5	10.3	18.6	16.0
00/99	33.1	40.6	28.6	29.7	38.2	27.8	29.9	3.0	39.4	245.8	15.9	39.3	67.0	29.8	42.7	44.4
01/00	11.2	26.0	12.7	10.8	184.1	57.3	-6.8	20.6	5.5	28.5	16.2	6.7	93.5	7.4	-6.1	42.6
02/01	9.3	-6.4	67.1	3.7	-43.6	42.9	14.5	13.6	31.1	-58.9	16.7	2.2	-6.3	34.2	12.3	4.4
							Share (%)									
1990	:	:	:	:	:	:	:	:	:	:	:	:	:	:	:	:
1996	100.0	3.0	0.8	51.3	0.8	1.4	5.1	0.2	11.8	:	4.5	14.6	0.2	0.9	1.0	3.7
1997	100.0	3.5	0.6	50.2	0.6	1.6	5.0	0.2	12.7	0.1	4.2	15.2	0.2	0.7	1.0	3.5
1998	100.0	3.7	0.5	51.8	0.4	1.7	6.1	0.2	12.8	0.1	4.0	13.4	0.1	0.6	1.3	2.7
1999	100.0	3.3	0.8	46.5	0.4	1.5	8.0	0.2	14.8	0.1	5.1	13.5	0.1	0.6	1.5	2.9
2000	**100.0**	**3.5**	**0.7**	**45.3**	**0.4**	**1.4**	**7.8**	**0.1**	**15.5**	**0.4**	**4.5**	**14.1**	**0.2**	**0.6**	**1.6**	**3.2**
2001	100.0	4.0	0.7	45.2	1.0	2.0	6.5	0.1	14.7	0.5	4.7	13.5	0.3	0.6	1.3	4.1
2002	**100.0**	**3.4**	**1.2**	**42.9**	**0.5**	**2.6**	**6.9**	**0.2**	**17.7**	**0.1**	**5.0**	**12.6**	**0.3**	**0.7**	**1.4**	**3.9**
							IMPORTS									
							Value (Mio ECU/Euro)									
1990	:	:	:	:	:	:	:	:	:	:	:	:	:	:	:	:
1994	2,044	77	37	821	9	37	137	13	268	:	102	353	3	51	40	98
1995	2,561	92	43	1,052	10	52	181	15	341	:	127	376	3	62	85	125
1996	3,494	131	54	1,378	9	83	301	24	564	:	173	441	4	77	76	176
1997	4,979	162	63	2,239	16	107	410	34	664	5	234	567	11	86	110	272
1998	6,425	191	66	3,295	18	137	494	36	833	8	265	598	16	91	121	264
1999	5,492	165	56	2,776	20	151	410	34	754	3	185	513	11	94	83	237
2000	**6,789**	**222**	**68**	**3,476**	**19**	**316**	**465**	**42**	**856**	**14**	**215**	**549**	**17**	**86**	**105**	**339**
2001	8,229	276	77	4,085	27	397	638	58	1,048	5	243	689	33	99	133	421
2002	**8,839**	**317**	**83**	**3,976**	**29**	**551**	**773**	**60**	**1,207**	**7**	**309**	**742**	**55**	**117**	**165**	**447**
							Annual variation (%)									
98/97	29.0	17.3	5.1	47.1	7.9	27.7	20.5	8.1	25.4	50.3	13.5	5.4	45.3	5.9	9.8	-2.8
99/98	-14.5	-13.2	-15.1	-15.7	10.1	10.5	-17.0	-6.6	-9.3	-60.5	-30.3	-14.2	-34.0	3.3	-30.8	-10.4
00/99	23.6	34.3	21.6	25.2	-3.2	108.9	13.5	23.5	13.4	378.6	16.4	7.0	56.8	-8.8	25.3	43.4
01/00	21.2	24.1	12.2	17.5	44.3	25.7	37.1	38.6	22.4	-68.2	12.9	25.4	97.3	16.0	27.0	24.2
02/01	7.4	15.0	8.7	-2.6	5.3	38.6	21.2	3.3	15.2	43.5	26.9	7.7	68.7	17.9	24.4	5.9
							Share (%)									
1990	:	:	:	:	:	:	:	:	:	:	:	:	:	:	:	:
1996	100.0	3.7	1.5	39.4	0.2	2.3	8.6	0.6	16.1	:	4.9	12.6	0.1	2.1	2.1	5.0
1997	100.0	3.2	1.2	44.9	0.3	2.1	8.2	0.6	13.3	0.1	4.6	11.3	0.2	1.7	2.2	5.4
1998	100.0	2.9	1.0	51.2	0.2	2.1	7.6	0.5	12.9	0.1	4.1	9.3	0.2	1.4	1.8	4.1
1999	100.0	3.0	1.0	50.5	0.3	2.7	7.4	0.6	13.7	0.0	3.3	9.3	0.1	1.7	1.5	4.3
2000	**100.0**	**3.2**	**1.0**	**51.2**	**0.2**	**4.6**	**6.8**	**0.6**	**12.6**	**0.2**	**3.1**	**8.0**	**0.2**	**1.2**	**1.5**	**4.9**
2001	100.0	3.3	0.9	49.6	0.3	4.8	7.7	0.7	12.7	0.0	2.9	8.3	0.3	1.2	1.6	5.1
2002	**100.0**	**3.5**	**0.9**	**44.9**	**0.3**	**6.2**	**8.7**	**0.6**	**13.6**	**0.0**	**3.4**	**8.3**	**0.6**	**1.3**	**1.8**	**5.0**

(1) With Luxembourg until 31.12.1998.

NON EU MEMBER STATES

Years	Extra EU	Norway	Switzerland	USSR/ Russia(1)	Candid. countries	USA	Canada	China	Japan	Hong Kong	Mediterr. Basin	Latin America	OPEC	DAE	ACP
						Partner									

EXPORTS
Value (Mio ECU/Euro)

Years	Extra EU	Norway	Switzerland	USSR/ Russia(1)	Candid. countries	USA	Canada	China	Japan	Hong Kong	Mediterr. Basin	Latin America	OPEC	DAE	ACP
1990	:	:	:	:	:	:	:	:	:	:	:	:	:	:	:
1994	3,648	5	42	233	2,692	91	31	20	5	1	211	54	43	89	19
1995	4,096	10	53	253	3,087	82	15	13	13	1	265	46	62	44	19
1996	4,083	7	76	243	2,992	94	9	31	15	1	258	39	58	37	12
1997	4,486	10	99	294	3,229	139	30	9	11	2	303	50	47	18	18
1998	4,201	32	143	181	3,175	115	15	4	11	2	281	48	30	12	16
1999	3,856	32	149	97	2,900	140	14	6	13	4	262	52	34	21	42
2000	5,221	51	221	115	3,954	184	16	10	13	7	372	55	53	45	33
2001	5,617	34	216	144	4,347	181	18	14	12	8	419	39	43	40	29
2002	5,983	51	191	152	4,472	220	24	43	153	7	522	23	38	47	23

Annual variation (%)

Years	Extra EU	Norway	Switzerland	USSR/ Russia(1)	Candid. countries	USA	Canada	China	Japan	Hong Kong	Mediterr. Basin	Latin America	OPEC	DAE	ACP
98/97	-6.3	236.4	45.1	-38.3	-1.6	-17.3	-47.8	-60.5	-2.6	-13.2	-7.3	-4.6	-36.3	-31.8	-6.4
99/98	-8.2	-1.4	4.4	-46.6	-8.6	21.6	-6.4	47.2	21.3	155.8	-6.7	8.6	13.1	71.4	157.5
00/99	35.3	58.5	47.7	18.8	36.3	32.0	10.4	85.2	1.9	60.6	41.9	5.6	54.8	112.4	-22.0
01/00	7.5	-33.0	-2.0	25.3	9.9	-1.8	12.5	38.4	-5.2	18.9	12.5	-28.7	-17.9	-12.3	-12.3
02/01	6.5	48.9	-11.5	5.3	2.8	21.5	33.7	202.0	1,126.6	-7.1	24.8	-42.0	-12.0	18.8	-19.9

Share (%)

Years	Extra EU	Norway	Switzerland	USSR/ Russia(1)	Candid. countries	USA	Canada	China	Japan	Hong Kong	Mediterr. Basin	Latin America	OPEC	DAE	ACP
1990	:	:	:	:	:	:	:	:	:	:	:	:	:	:	:
1996	100.0	0.1	1.8	5.9	73.2	2.2	0.2	0.7	0.3	0.0	6.3	0.9	1.4	0.9	0.2
1997	100.0	0.2	2.1	6.5	71.9	3.0	0.6	0.2	0.2	0.0	6.7	1.1	1.0	0.4	0.3
1998	100.0	0.7	3.4	4.3	75.5	2.7	0.3	0.0	0.2	0.0	6.6	1.1	0.7	0.2	0.3
1999	100.0	0.8	3.8	2.5	75.1	3.6	0.3	0.1	0.3	0.1	6.7	1.3	0.8	0.5	1.0
2000	100.0	0.9	4.2	2.2	75.7	3.5	0.3	0.1	0.2	0.1	7.1	1.0	1.0	0.8	0.6
2001	100.0	0.6	3.8	2.5	77.3	3.2	0.3	0.2	0.2	0.1	7.4	0.6	0.7	0.7	0.5
2002	100.0	0.8	3.1	2.5	74.7	3.6	0.4	0.7	2.5	0.1	8.7	0.3	0.6	0.7	0.3

IMPORTS
Value (Mio ECU/Euro)

Years	Extra EU	Norway	Switzerland	USSR/ Russia(1)	Candid. countries	USA	Canada	China	Japan	Hong Kong	Mediterr. Basin	Latin America	OPEC	DAE	ACP
1990	:	:	:	:	:	:	:	:	:	:	:	:	:	:	:
1994	4,001	6	89	1,100	2,121	174	11	35	76	16	72	64	20	53	14
1995	4,724	15	125	1,223	2,503	181	17	49	109	27	105	76	19	98	19
1996	5,882	15	140	1,676	2,850	255	25	70	165	20	131	79	21	239	25
1997	6,222	19	159	1,576	3,064	351	40	112	191	25	156	82	24	123	17
1998	6,126	21	183	1,338	3,128	369	34	149	210	16	174	81	27	147	32
1999	5,052	18	139	1,275	2,445	272	24	136	168	9	135	65	27	183	28
2000	6,967	26	177	2,346	2,947	278	18	191	233	11	184	74	35	225	35
2001	8,164	26	212	2,431	3,712	314	21	260	264	18	244	94	40	316	35
2002	8,590	23	239	2,198	4,038	370	21	366	323	21	312	102	54	372	30

Annual variation (%)

Years	Extra EU	Norway	Switzerland	USSR/ Russia(1)	Candid. countries	USA	Canada	China	Japan	Hong Kong	Mediterr. Basin	Latin America	OPEC	DAE	ACP
98/97	-1.5	15.3	15.1	-15.1	2.0	5.2	-14.9	32.4	9.9	-35.5	11.6	-1.5	12.5	20.2	84.1
99/98	-17.5	-14.5	-23.8	-4.7	-21.8	-26.2	-29.2	-8.7	-20.0	-41.7	-22.8	-19.7	1.9	24.3	-10.1
00/99	37.9	42.3	26.8	84.0	20.5	2.0	-26.8	40.5	38.2	22.8	36.8	14.4	28.0	22.7	23.7
01/00	17.1	-1.7	20.2	3.6	25.9	13.0	17.9	35.8	13.5	57.6	32.4	26.9	14.8	40.2	-1.1
02/01	5.2	-9.5	12.5	-9.5	8.7	17.5	-0.8	41.0	22.4	17.1	27.7	8.7	33.8	17.9	-14.2

Share (%)

Years	Extra EU	Norway	Switzerland	USSR/ Russia(1)	Candid. countries	USA	Canada	China	Japan	Hong Kong	Mediterr. Basin	Latin America	OPEC	DAE	ACP
1990	:	:	:	:	:	:	:	:	:	:	:	:	:	:	:
1996	100.0	0.2	2.3	28.4	48.4	4.3	0.4	1.1	2.7	0.3	2.2	1.3	0.3	4.0	0.4
1997	100.0	0.2	2.5	25.3	49.2	5.6	0.6	1.8	3.0	0.4	2.5	1.3	0.3	1.9	0.2
1998	100.0	0.3	2.9	21.8	51.0	6.0	0.5	2.4	3.4	0.2	2.8	1.3	0.4	2.4	0.5
1999	100.0	0.3	2.7	25.2	48.4	5.3	0.4	2.6	3.3	0.1	2.6	1.2	0.5	3.6	0.5
2000	100.0	0.3	2.5	33.6	42.3	3.9	0.2	2.7	3.3	0.1	2.6	1.0	0.5	3.2	0.5
2001	100.0	0.3	2.6	29.7	45.4	3.8	0.2	3.1	3.2	0.2	2.9	1.1	0.4	3.8	0.4
2002	100.0	0.2	2.7	25.5	47.0	4.3	0.2	4.2	3.7	0.2	3.6	1.1	0.6	4.3	0.3

(1) Relates to the external trade with the USSR until 1991 and to the external trade with Russia from 1992 onwards.

SLOVENIA

TRADE BALANCE (BN ECU/euro)

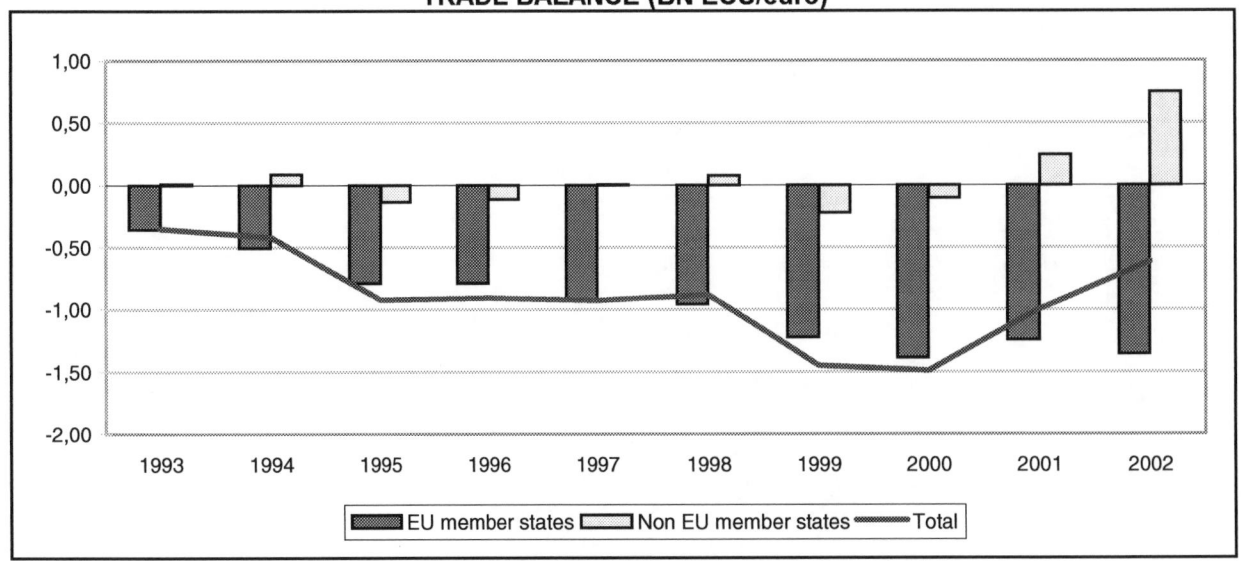

TRADE WITH EU MEMBER STATES (BN ECU/euro)

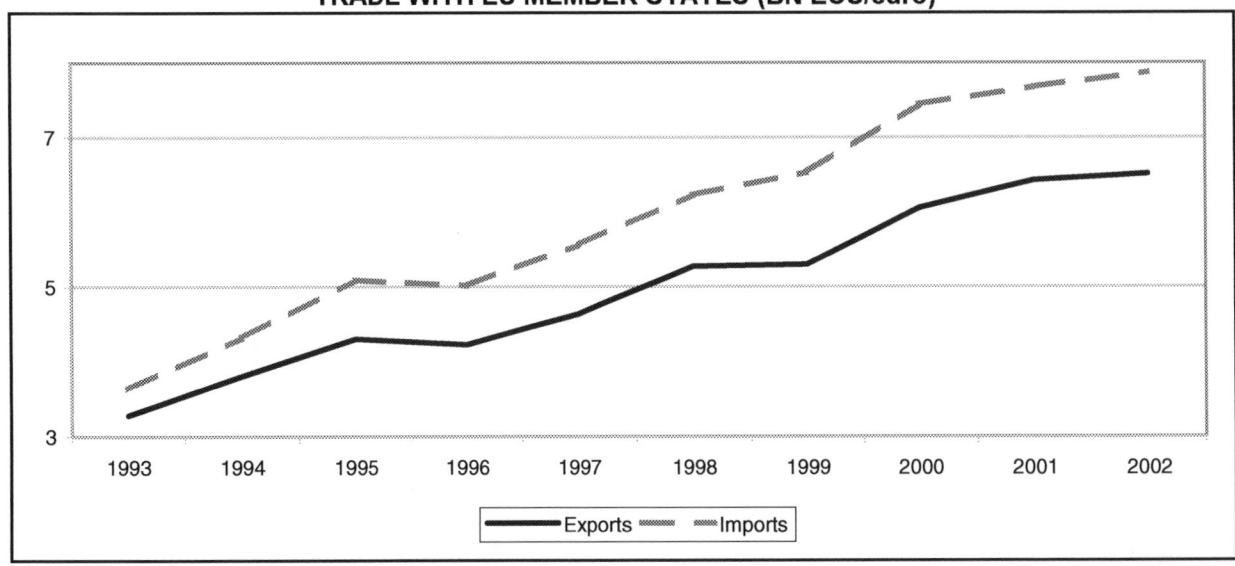

TRADE WITH NON EU MEMBER STATES (BN ECU/euro)

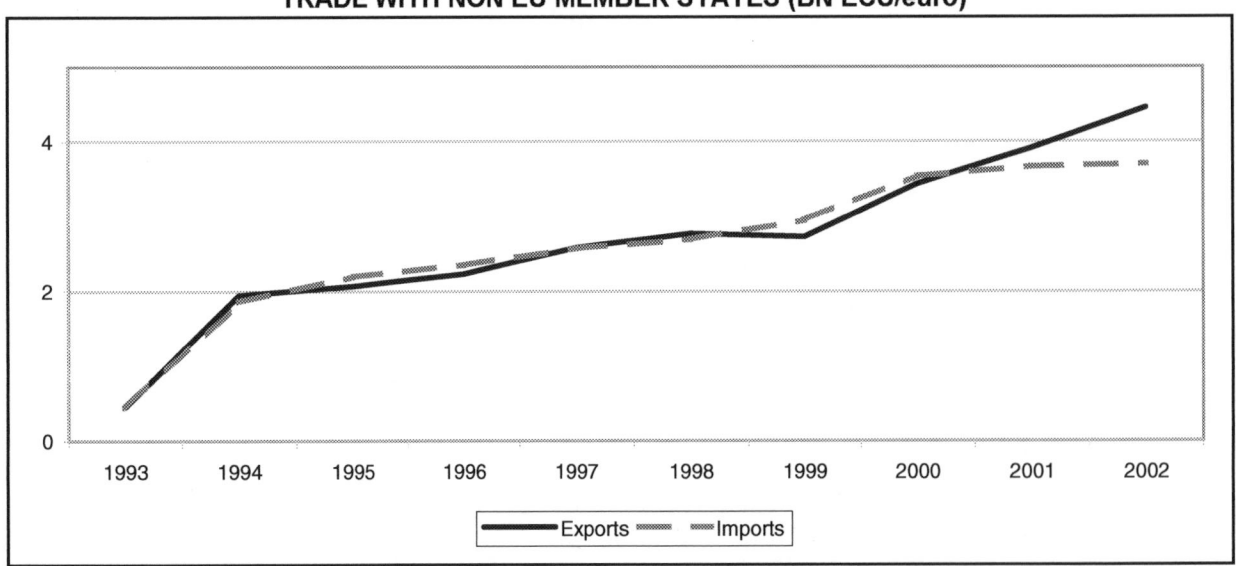

TRADE BALANCE

EU MEMBER STATES

Value (Mio ECU/Euro)

Year	Intra EU	B[2]	DK	D	EL	E	F	IRL	I	L	NL	A	P	FIN	S	UK
1990	:	:	:	:	:	:	:	:	:	:	:	:	:	:	:	:
1991	:	:	:	:	:	:	:	:	:	:	:	:	:	:	:	:
1992	:	:	:	:	:	:	:	:	:	:	:	:	:	:	:	:
1993	-358	-11	-1	147	11	-19	5	-2	-252	:	-27	-214	-2	-13	-17	39
1994	-505	-48	-0	280	9	-67	-22	-10	-281	:	-57	-321	2	-28	-28	66
1995	-787	-122	-3	231	16	-139	-89	-2	-305	:	-68	-294	3	-16	-32	30
1996	-790	-64	4	395	8	-99	-257	-19	-386	:	-55	-224	6	-15	-44	-37
1997	-929	-56	7	464	8	-129	-455	-18	-271	-8	-68	-197	2	-20	-47	-80
1998	-958	2	19	441	3	-146	-454	-27	-392	-12	-74	-164	-1	-21	-69	-64
1999	-1,226	-15	24	521	0	-148	-573	-28	-484	-8	-60	-173	1	-34	-117	-130
2000	**-1,388**	**-53**	**31**	**493**	**3**	**-195**	**-456**	**-26**	**-628**	**-16**	**-67**	**-192**	**4**	**-39**	**-113**	**-134**
2001	-1,243	-64	34	536	-3	-195	-503	-27	-714	-22	-47	-170	-0	-32	-33	-3
2002	**-1,360**	**-74**	**29**	**499**	**-15**	**-240**	**-455**	**-25**	**-747**	**-21**	**-58**	**-182**	**3**	**-45**	**-19**	**-10**

NON EU MEMBER STATES

Value (Mio ECU/euro)

Year	Extra EU	Norway	Switzerland	USSR/ Russia[1]	Candid. countries	USA	Canada	China	Japan	Hong Kong	Mediterr. Basin	Latin America	OPEC	DAE	ACP
1990	:	:	:	:	:	:	:	:	:	:	:	:	:	:	:
1991	:	:	:	:	:	:	:	:	:	:	:	:	:	:	:
1992	:	:	:	:	:	:	:	:	:	:	:	:	:	:	:
1993	6	9	-49	39	-12	102	10	2	1	-13	0	-8	:	-13	-1
1994	85	-13	-82	99	-150	44	5	-26	-90	-7	326	-52	10	-45	-13
1995	-134	-17	-98	49	-200	-22	-7	-36	-104	-6	356	-42	-12	-60	-4
1996	-116	-44	-86	71	-134	-62	-6	-33	-113	-5	397	-58	-46	-99	-7
1997	4	-14	-80	68	-173	-36	-4	-67	-128	-9	506	-59	-55	-69	-8
1998	77	-17	-83	53	-120	-39	-54	-95	-146	-8	711	-39	16	-136	-10
1999	-224	-4	-119	-28	-180	-33	-31	-115	-168	-8	681	-35	-7	-184	-9
2000	**-104**	**-34**	**-65**	**-41**	**-198**	**-31**	**-42**	**-133**	**-167**	**-10**	**784**	**-41**	**-42**	**-166**	**-2**
2001	245	-2	-62	1	-268	-58	-23	-164	-149	-7	1,061	-39	-33	-168	-10
2002	**748**	**7**	**-5**	**51**	**-135**	**-36**	**-9**	**-215**	**-135**	**-5**	**1,332**	**-100**	**36**	**-185**	**-3**

(1) Relates to the external trade with the USSR until 1991 and to the external trade with Russia from 1992 onwards.

(2) With Luxembourg until 31.12.1998.

SLOVENIA

EU MEMBER STATES

Years	Intra EU	B(1)	DK	D	EL	E	F	IRL	I	L	NL	A	P	FIN	S	UK
							Partner									

EXPORTS
Value (Mio ECU/Euro)

Years	Intra EU	B(1)	DK	D	EL	E	F	IRL	I	L	NL	A	P	FIN	S	UK
1990	:	:	:	:	:	:	:	:	:	:	:	:	:	:	:	:
1994	3,816	100	27	1,738	14	30	493	5	776	:	84	314	6	11	42	175
1995	4,311	113	32	1,917	24	32	521	13	926	:	90	409	7	14	45	175
1996	4,231	63	37	2,005	18	35	471	3	869	:	98	434	10	15	43	127
1997	4,638	75	48	2,171	21	46	409	5	1,101	1	109	499	11	16	49	132
1998	5,272	141	67	2,292	20	61	666	4	1,117	3	127	549	11	17	58	143
1999	5,302	125	74	2,466	23	71	460	8	1,102	9	135	584	11	16	57	160
2000	**6,057**	**106**	**89**	**2,575**	**26**	**91**	**672**	**15**	**1,289**	**5**	**164**	**714**	**17**	**25**	**66**	**203**
2001	6,432	112	97	2,715	33	100	703	15	1,290	3	172	773	17	30	82	290
2002	**6,509**	**97**	**97**	**2,714**	**36**	**116**	**734**	**14**	**1,323**	**8**	**183**	**774**	**22**	**27**	**97**	**268**

Annual variation (%)

Years	Intra EU	B(1)	DK	D	EL	E	F	IRL	I	L	NL	A	P	FIN	S	UK
98/97	13.6	87.5	39.7	5.5	-3.2	32.2	63.1	-8.4	1.4	252.7	16.8	10.1	-2.9	6.0	18.4	8.4
99/98	0.5	-10.8	10.7	7.6	10.6	15.9	-30.9	93.4	-1.3	188.1	6.3	6.3	0.0	-4.9	-1.8	11.6
00/99	14.2	-15.1	19.3	4.4	15.1	27.7	46.1	87.7	16.9	-49.6	21.2	22.2	52.2	52.4	15.6	26.6
01/00	6.1	5.2	9.7	5.4	25.4	10.3	4.5	-2.1	0.0	-35.8	5.3	8.3	-1.2	23.2	23.6	42.8
02/01	1.2	-13.4	-0.7	0.0	9.7	15.6	4.5	-10.2	2.5	162.6	5.8	0.0	31.8	-11.1	18.6	-7.4

Share (%)

Years	Intra EU	B(1)	DK	D	EL	E	F	IRL	I	L	NL	A	P	FIN	S	UK
1990	:	:	:	:	:	:	:	:	:	:	:	:	:	:	:	:
1996	100.0	1.4	0.8	47.3	0.4	0.8	11.1	0.0	20.5	:	2.3	10.2	0.2	0.3	1.0	3.0
1997	100.0	1.6	1.0	46.8	0.4	1.0	8.8	0.0	23.7	0.0	2.3	10.7	0.2	0.3	1.0	2.8
1998	100.0	2.6	1.2	43.4	0.3	1.1	12.6	0.0	21.1	0.0	2.4	10.4	0.2	0.3	1.1	2.7
1999	100.0	2.3	1.4	46.5	0.4	1.3	8.6	0.1	20.7	0.1	2.5	11.0	0.2	0.3	1.0	3.0
2000	**100.0**	**1.7**	**1.4**	**42.5**	**0.4**	**1.5**	**11.0**	**0.2**	**21.2**	**0.0**	**2.7**	**11.7**	**0.2**	**0.4**	**1.0**	**3.3**
2001	100.0	1.7	1.5	42.2	0.5	1.5	10.9	0.2	20.0	0.0	2.6	12.0	0.2	0.4	1.2	4.5
2002	**100.0**	**1.4**	**1.4**	**41.6**	**0.5**	**1.7**	**11.2**	**0.2**	**20.3**	**0.1**	**2.8**	**11.8**	**0.3**	**0.4**	**1.4**	**4.1**

IMPORTS
Value (Mio ECU/Euro)

Years	Intra EU	B(1)	DK	D	EL	E	F	IRL	I	L	NL	A	P	FIN	S	UK
1990	:	:	:	:	:	:	:	:	:	:	:	:	:	:	:	:
1994	4,321	149	27	1,458	5	97	515	15	1,058	:	141	635	4	38	70	109
1995	5,098	235	35	1,687	8	172	610	15	1,232	:	158	703	4	30	77	145
1996	5,021	127	33	1,610	10	134	728	23	1,255	:	153	658	4	31	87	164
1997	5,567	131	41	1,707	13	176	864	23	1,371	9	177	695	10	36	97	212
1998	6,230	138	48	1,850	17	208	1,120	31	1,509	15	201	713	12	38	127	208
1999	6,528	140	50	1,945	23	219	1,033	36	1,586	17	195	757	10	50	175	290
2000	**7,445**	**159**	**57**	**2,083**	**24**	**286**	**1,128**	**41**	**1,917**	**21**	**230**	**906**	**13**	**63**	**180**	**337**
2001	7,675	176	63	2,178	36	295	1,205	42	2,004	25	219	944	17	62	115	292
2002	**7,869**	**170**	**67**	**2,216**	**51**	**356**	**1,190**	**39**	**2,070**	**29**	**240**	**956**	**19**	**72**	**116**	**278**

Annual variation (%)

Years	Intra EU	B(1)	DK	D	EL	E	F	IRL	I	L	NL	A	P	FIN	S	UK
98/97	11.9	5.3	17.9	8.3	31.0	18.2	29.6	34.2	10.0	68.7	13.6	2.6	26.3	4.8	31.6	-2.1
99/98	4.7	1.3	3.8	5.1	30.1	5.6	-7.7	17.2	5.1	16.0	-2.5	6.1	-16.7	31.7	37.3	39.5
00/99	14.0	13.3	14.0	7.0	4.2	30.5	9.2	12.9	20.8	20.4	17.8	19.6	32.1	26.2	2.8	16.2
01/00	3.0	10.9	10.0	4.5	52.8	3.1	6.8	3.3	4.5	19.0	-4.6	4.1	25.8	-2.2	-36.0	-13.2
02/01	2.5	-3.3	6.6	1.7	41.2	20.5	-1.2	-7.7	3.2	17.0	9.5	1.2	10.8	16.7	1.1	-4.7

Share (%)

Years	Intra EU	B(1)	DK	D	EL	E	F	IRL	I	L	NL	A	P	FIN	S	UK
1990	:	:	:	:	:	:	:	:	:	:	:	:	:	:	:	:
1996	100.0	2.5	0.6	32.0	0.1	2.6	14.5	0.4	24.9	:	3.0	13.0	0.0	0.6	1.7	3.2
1997	100.0	2.3	0.7	30.6	0.2	3.1	15.5	0.4	24.6	0.1	3.1	12.4	0.1	0.6	1.7	3.8
1998	100.0	2.2	0.7	29.6	0.2	3.3	17.9	0.4	24.2	0.2	3.2	11.4	0.1	0.6	2.0	3.3
1999	100.0	2.1	0.7	29.8	0.3	3.3	15.8	0.5	24.3	0.2	2.9	11.6	0.1	0.7	2.6	4.4
2000	**100.0**	**2.1**	**0.7**	**27.9**	**0.3**	**3.8**	**15.1**	**0.5**	**25.7**	**0.2**	**3.0**	**12.1**	**0.1**	**0.8**	**2.4**	**4.5**
2001	100.0	2.2	0.8	28.3	0.4	3.8	15.7	0.5	26.1	0.3	2.8	12.2	0.2	0.8	1.4	3.8
2002	**100.0**	**2.1**	**0.8**	**28.1**	**0.6**	**4.5**	**15.1**	**0.4**	**26.3**	**0.3**	**3.0**	**12.1**	**0.2**	**0.9**	**1.4**	**3.5**

(1) With Luxembourg until 31.12.1998.

NON EU MEMBER STATES

Years	Extra EU	Norway	Switzerland	USSR/Russia[1]	Candid. countries	USA	Canada	China	Japan	Hong Kong	Mediterr. Basin	Latin America	OPEC	DAE	ACP
							EXPORTS Value (Mio ECU/Euro)								
1990	:	:	:	:	:	:	:	:	:	:	:	:	:	:	:
1994	1,946	12	50	222	303	210	35	5	15	4	923	21	67	29	8
1995	2,066	9	57	233	364	200	28	4	16	9	995	26	57	25	9
1996	2,233	9	55	235	418	194	26	6	15	10	1,095	29	56	30	5
1997	2,578	12	64	289	506	215	24	5	14	7	1,231	41	77	29	8
1998	2,772	15	68	213	617	225	32	7	9	6	1,380	48	104	20	15
1999	2,726	17	84	122	677	244	21	12	12	6	1,369	35	86	37	11
2000	**3,437**	**19**	**111**	**210**	**865**	**295**	**22**	**16**	**13**	**6**	**1,651**	**50**	**83**	**51**	**22**
2001	3,915	19	108	315	921	276	22	13	14	8	1,904	56	98	50	25
2002	**4,453**	**22**	**180**	**320**	**1,066**	**299**	**28**	**23**	**16**	**8**	**2,108**	**35**	**140**	**57**	**29**
							Annual variation (%)								
98/97	7.4	17.7	6.3	-26.3	21.9	4.8	30.0	30.7	-31.8	-14.5	12.1	17.3	33.8	-29.1	86.8
99/98	-1.6	16.9	24.1	-42.7	9.7	8.0	-34.8	82.4	29.2	6.3	-0.8	-25.6	-17.1	80.8	-29.0
00/99	26.0	9.1	31.8	72.4	27.7	21.0	6.4	31.2	9.7	-0.5	20.6	41.6	-3.2	38.7	101.9
01/00	13.9	0.3	-2.3	50.1	6.4	-6.5	-2.4	-20.2	3.8	18.7	15.3	10.5	18.1	-2.2	13.2
02/01	13.7	17.7	66.4	1.3	15.6	8.4	29.4	81.4	16.5	11.8	10.6	-36.6	42.1	13.2	16.0
							Share (%)								
1990	:	:	:	:	:	:	:	:	:	:	:	:	:	:	:
1996	100.0	0.4	2.4	10.5	18.7	8.6	1.1	0.2	0.6	0.4	49.0	1.3	2.5	1.3	0.2
1997	100.0	0.4	2.4	11.1	19.6	8.3	0.9	0.1	0.5	0.2	47.7	1.5	3.0	1.1	0.3
1998	100.0	0.5	2.4	7.6	22.2	8.1	1.1	0.2	0.3	0.2	49.8	1.7	3.7	0.7	0.5
1999	100.0	0.6	3.0	4.4	24.8	8.9	0.7	0.4	0.4	0.2	50.2	1.3	3.1	1.3	0.3
2000	**100.0**	**0.5**	**3.2**	**6.1**	**25.1**	**8.5**	**0.6**	**0.4**	**0.3**	**0.1**	**48.0**	**1.4**	**2.4**	**1.4**	**0.6**
2001	100.0	0.4	2.7	8.0	23.5	7.0	0.5	0.3	0.3	0.1	48.6	1.4	2.5	1.2	0.6
2002	**100.0**	**0.4**	**4.0**	**7.1**	**23.9**	**6.7**	**0.6**	**0.5**	**0.3**	**0.1**	**47.3**	**0.7**	**3.1**	**1.2**	**0.6**
							IMPORTS Value (Mio ECU/Euro)								
1990	:	:	:	:	:	:	:	:	:	:	:	:	:	:	:
1994	1,861	25	132	124	453	167	29	31	105	11	598	73	58	74	21
1995	2,200	26	155	184	564	222	35	40	120	14	639	68	69	84	13
1996	2,349	53	142	164	552	256	32	39	128	15	697	88	102	129	13
1997	2,575	26	144	221	679	251	29	72	142	16	725	100	133	97	16
1998	2,695	31	151	160	737	264	86	101	155	14	670	86	88	157	26
1999	2,949	21	203	150	857	277	52	127	180	14	688	70	93	221	19
2000	**3,540**	**53**	**175**	**251**	**1,063**	**326**	**64**	**149**	**181**	**16**	**867**	**91**	**125**	**217**	**24**
2001	3,670	20	170	315	1,189	334	45	177	163	14	844	95	132	218	34
2002	**3,705**	**15**	**186**	**269**	**1,201**	**335**	**36**	**238**	**151**	**14**	**776**	**135**	**104**	**241**	**32**
							Annual variation (%)								
98/97	4.6	19.3	4.8	-27.5	8.6	5.3	198.2	39.9	9.2	-9.2	-7.5	-13.2	-33.8	61.0	61.2
99/98	9.4	-33.0	34.6	-6.3	16.2	4.8	-39.9	25.3	15.8	-0.7	2.7	-18.8	5.7	41.1	-23.8
00/99	20.0	150.7	-13.7	67.7	24.0	17.6	23.8	16.8	0.5	10.8	26.0	30.3	34.5	-1.9	22.9
01/00	3.6	-61.2	-2.8	25.3	11.8	2.2	-29.7	18.9	-9.9	-10.0	-2.6	3.6	5.2	0.6	42.9
02/01	0.9	-26.9	8.9	-14.6	1.0	0.2	-19.1	34.3	-7.0	-5.5	-8.0	41.9	-20.9	10.5	-7.0
							Share (%)								
1990	:	:	:	:	:	:	:	:	:	:	:	:	:	:	:
1996	100.0	2.2	6.0	6.9	23.5	10.8	1.3	1.6	5.4	0.6	29.6	3.7	4.3	5.4	0.5
1997	100.0	1.0	5.5	8.5	26.3	9.7	1.1	2.8	5.5	0.6	28.1	3.8	5.1	3.7	0.6
1998	100.0	1.1	5.6	5.9	27.3	9.8	3.1	3.7	5.7	0.5	24.8	3.2	3.2	5.8	0.9
1999	100.0	0.7	6.8	5.0	29.0	9.3	1.7	4.3	6.0	0.4	23.3	2.3	3.1	7.5	0.6
2000	**100.0**	**1.4**	**4.9**	**7.0**	**30.0**	**9.2**	**1.8**	**4.1**	**5.0**	**0.4**	**24.4**	**2.5**	**3.5**	**6.1**	**0.6**
2001	100.0	0.5	4.6	8.5	32.3	9.0	1.2	4.8	4.4	0.3	22.9	2.5	3.5	5.9	0.9
2002	**100.0**	**0.4**	**5.0**	**7.2**	**32.4**	**9.0**	**0.9**	**6.4**	**4.0**	**0.3**	**20.9**	**3.6**	**2.8**	**6.5**	**0.8**

(1) Relates to the external trade with the USSR until 1991 and to the external trade with Russia from 1992 onwards.

TURKEY

TRADE BALANCE (BN ECU/euro)

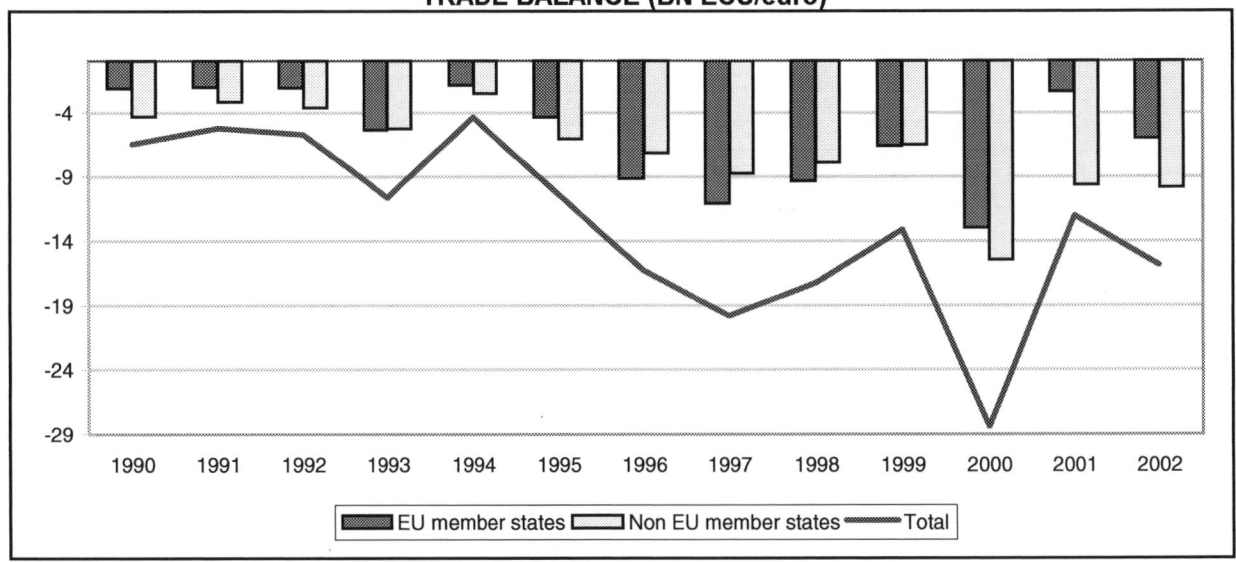

TRADE WITH EU MEMBER STATES (BN ECU/euro)

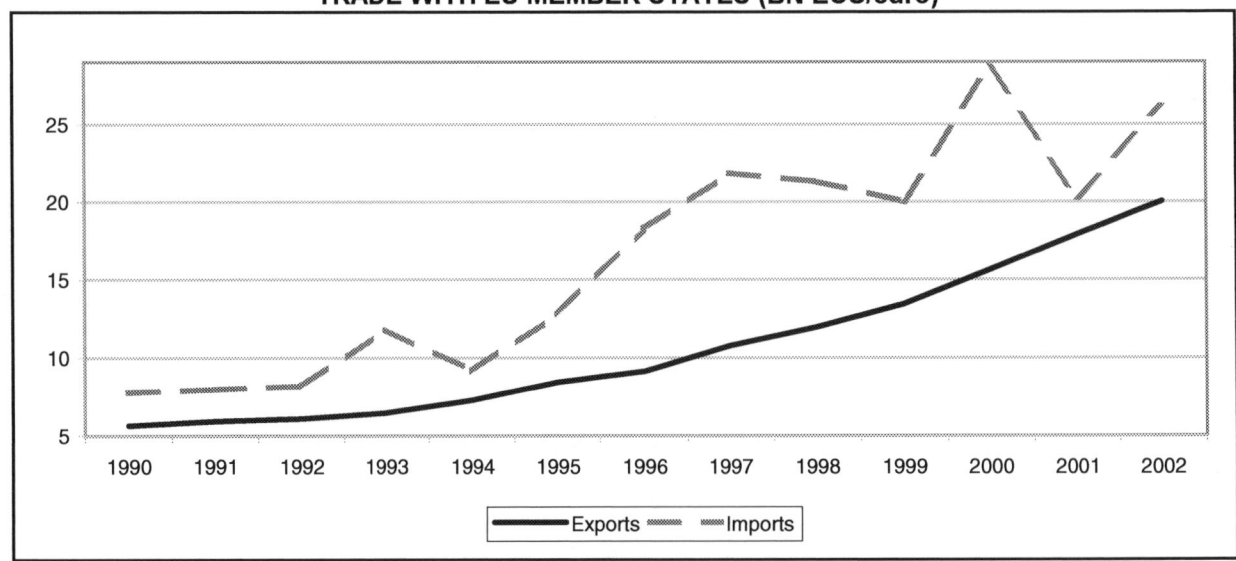

TRADE WITH NON EU MEMBER STATES (BN ECU/euro)

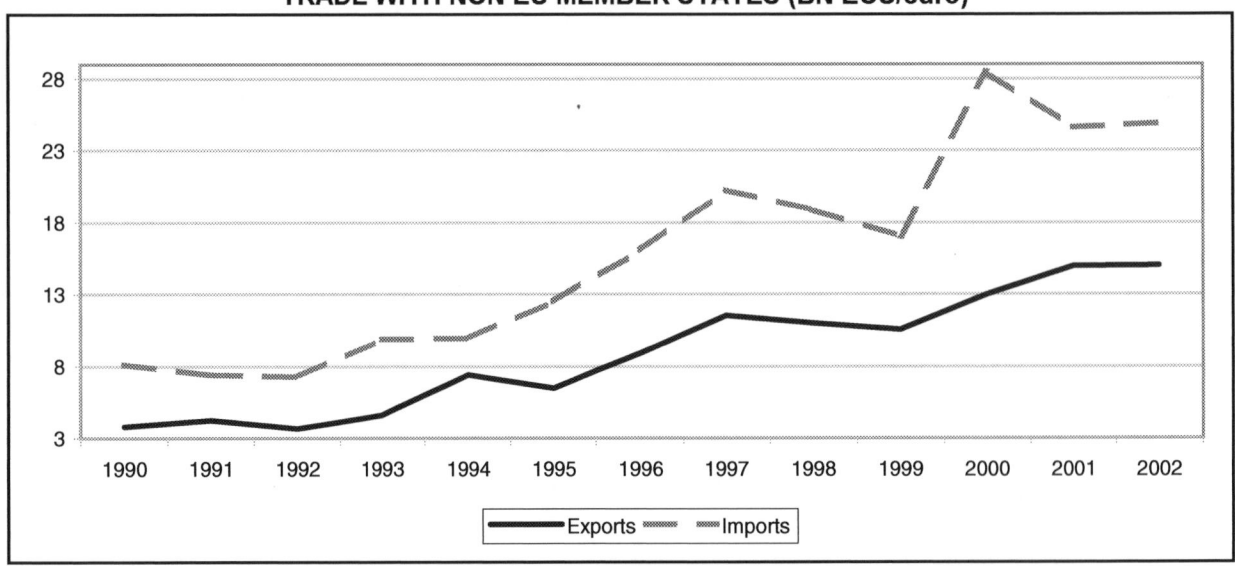

TURKEY

TRADE BALANCE

EU MEMBER STATES

Value (Mio ECU/Euro)

Year	Intra EU	B(2)	DK	D	EL	E	F	IRL	I	L	NL	A	P	FIN	S	UK
1990	**-2,143**	**-166**	**-12**	**-346**	**8**	**-115**	**-474**	**-29**	**-488**	:	**-108**	**-57**	**21**	**-62**	**-105**	**-211**
1991	-2,034	-193	-7	146	54	-67	-434	-19	-705	:	-135	-88	20	-61	-149	-395
1992	-2,110	-199	-9	-72	44	-17	-417	-21	-752	:	-153	-41	14	-79	-107	-301
1993	-5,353	-334	-45	-749	-2	-197	-1,009	-42	-1,544	:	-301	-79	-2	-136	-307	-606
1994	-1,869	-135	-4	242	54	-123	-462	-57	-820	:	-100	32	1	-94	-166	-236
1995	-4,348	-352	-42	-391	7	-178	-736	-111	-1,327	:	-266	-14	-10	-152	-315	-531
1996	-9,135	-503	-19	-2,086	-31	-526	-1,351	-68	-2,215	:	-549	-206	-7	-167	-426	-980
1997	-11,077	-574	-25	-2,450	-105	-742	-1,588	-106	-2,670	:	-624	-182	0	-255	-662	-1,095
1998	-9,337	-465	-4	-1,652	53	-680	-1,527	-151	-2,344	:	-501	-276	67	-323	-709	-827
1999	-6,624	-478	-8	-399	117	-462	-1,442	-137	-1,403	:	-369	-188	94	-412	-1,196	-341
2000	**-12,956**	**-1,104**	**23**	**-2,207**	**44**	**-1,062**	**-2,012**	**-295**	**-2,645**	:	**-785**	**-246**	**100**	**-705**	**-1,327**	**-733**
2001	-2,385	-326	84	24	252	-128	-436	-258	-1,267	:	-166	-88	245	-255	-369	302
2002	**-6,031**	:	:	:	:	:	:	:	:	:	:	:	:	:	:	:

NON EU MEMBER STATES

Value (Mio ECU/euro)

Year	Extra EU	Norway	Switzerland	USSR/Russia(1)	Candid. countries	USA	Canada	China	Japan	Hong Kong	Mediterr. Basin	Latin America	OPEC	DAE	ACP
1990	**-4,308**	**-14**	**-188**	**-534**	:	**-1,028**	**-94**	**-81**	**-683**	**-33**	**-163**	:	**-1,252**	:	:
1991	-3,178	-11	-197	-300	:	-1,097	-81	-49	-701	-38	472	:	-765	:	:
1992	-3,625	-21	-397	-461	:	-1,341	-37	-1	-771	-23	276	:	-987	-124	:
1993	-5,277	-38	-373	-889	365	-2,012	-76	214	-1,253	27	296	:	-743	27	:
1994	-2,520	-46	-198	-196	100	-772	-51	84	-655	137	682	-175	-867	132	4
1995	-6,043	-16	-441	-317	114	-1,688	-151	-360	-929	60	68	-444	-1,119	-357	14
1996	-7,167	-29	-589	-330	-139	-1,514	-193	-392	-997	14	-139	-491	-1,776	-800	-45
1997	-8,719	-76	-700	-106	-33	-2,058	-173	-658	-1,684	69	-379	-542	-1,369	-1,206	19
1998	-7,874	-42	-695	-709	97	-1,647	-18	-718	-1,716	6	579	-483	-731	-1,704	83
1999	-6,494	-81	-454	-1,655	-50	-621	-26	-808	-1,190	-25	600	-268	-1,036	-1,336	68
2000	**-15,425**	**-194**	**-713**	**-3,533**	**-830**	**-840**	**-89**	**-1,355**	**-1,603**	**-40**	**-1,036**	**-410**	**-3,008**	**-2,228**	**-136**
2001	-9,623	-201	-1,096	-2,810	-107	-176	48	-802	-1,324	52	-286	-129	-2,395	-1,352	-292
2002	**-9,830**	**-197**	**-1,027**	**-3,199**	:	**1**	**74**	**-1,014**	**-830**	**-66**	**-195**	**-173**	**-2,474**	**-1,283**	**-311**

(1) Relates to the external trade with the USSR until 1991 and to the external trade with Russia from 1992 onwards.
(2) With Luxembourg until 31.12.1998.

TURKEY

EU MEMBER STATES

Years	Intra EU	B[(1)]	DK	D	EL	E	F	IRL	I	L	NL	A	P	FIN	S	UK
							Partner									

EXPORTS
Value (Mio ECU/Euro)

Years	Intra EU	B[(1)]	DK	D	EL	E	F	IRL	I	L	NL	A	P	FIN	S	UK
1990	**5,652**	**244**	**68**	**2,423**	**109**	**156**	**579**	**19**	**869**	:	**342**	**140**	**35**	**20**	**63**	**585**
1994	7,309	312	77	3,308	142	196	763	28	869	:	522	209	37	26	72	747
1995	8,461	345	102	3,850	161	276	790	36	1,114	:	563	210	46	32	81	868
1996	9,144	392	118	4,101	188	294	836	48	1,148	:	606	230	60	36	96	993
1997	10,803	500	152	4,631	265	390	1,027	77	1,224	:	686	264	87	44	128	1,327
1998	11,982	597	177	4,857	329	461	1,159	80	1,382	:	787	270	138	52	165	1,527
1999	13,449	584	186	5,131	382	720	1,476	128	1,579	:	870	292	160	62	169	1,709
2000	**15,666**	**702**	**237**	**5,588**	**475**	**773**	**1,785**	**223**	**1,930**	:	**940**	**317**	**199**	**81**	**214**	**2,201**
2001	17,913	769	303	5,967	530	1,063	2,106	163	2,584	:	993	379	321	80	237	2,419
2002	:	:	:	:	:	:	:	:	:	:	:	:	:	:	:	:

Annual variation (%)

Years	Intra EU	B[(1)]	DK	D	EL	E	F	IRL	I	L	NL	A	P	FIN	S	UK
98/97	10.9	19.4	16.4	4.8	24.2	18.0	12.8	3.0	12.9	:	14.7	2.0	58.3	19.4	29.0	15.0
99/98	12.2	-2.1	4.8	5.6	16.2	56.2	27.3	60.3	14.2	:	10.4	8.3	15.6	19.8	2.3	11.9
00/99	16.4	20.0	27.3	8.9	24.1	7.4	20.9	74.6	22.2	:	8.1	8.5	24.5	30.2	26.6	28.7
01/00	14.3	9.5	27.9	6.7	11.6	37.5	17.9	-26.9	33.8	:	5.5	19.3	61.0	-2.0	10.6	9.8
02/01	:	:	:	:	:	:	:	:	:	:	:	:	:	:	:	:

Share (%)

Years	Intra EU	B[(1)]	DK	D	EL	E	F	IRL	I	L	NL	A	P	FIN	S	UK
1990	**100.0**	**4.3**	**1.2**	**42.8**	**1.9**	**2.7**	**10.2**	**0.3**	**15.3**	:	**6.0**	**2.4**	**0.6**	**0.3**	**1.1**	**10.3**
1996	100.0	4.2	1.2	44.8	2.0	3.2	9.1	0.5	12.5	:	6.6	2.5	0.6	0.3	1.0	10.8
1997	100.0	4.6	1.4	42.8	2.4	3.6	9.5	0.7	11.3	:	6.3	2.4	0.8	0.4	1.1	12.2
1998	100.0	4.9	1.4	40.5	2.7	3.8	9.6	0.6	11.5	:	6.5	2.2	1.1	0.4	1.3	12.7
1999	100.0	4.3	1.3	38.1	2.8	5.3	10.9	0.9	11.7	:	6.4	2.1	1.1	0.4	1.2	12.7
2000	**100.0**	**4.4**	**1.5**	**35.6**	**3.0**	**4.9**	**11.3**	**1.4**	**12.3**	:	**6.0**	**2.0**	**1.2**	**0.5**	**1.3**	**14.0**
2001	100.0	4.2	1.6	33.3	2.9	5.9	11.7	0.9	14.4	:	5.5	2.1	1.7	0.4	1.3	13.5
2002	:	:	:	:	:	:	:	:	:	:	:	:	:	:	:	:

IMPORTS
Value (Mio ECU/Euro)

Years	Intra EU	B[(1)]	DK	D	EL	E	F	IRL	I	L	NL	A	P	FIN	S	UK
1990	**7,795**	**410**	**80**	**2,768**	**101**	**271**	**1,053**	**48**	**1,356**	:	**450**	**198**	**14**	**82**	**168**	**796**
1994	9,178	447	81	3,065	88	320	1,226	85	1,689	:	622	177	36	120	238	984
1995	12,809	697	144	4,241	153	453	1,526	148	2,441	:	829	225	55	184	396	1,399
1996	18,279	895	137	6,187	220	820	2,187	115	3,363	:	1,155	436	67	203	522	1,972
1997	21,880	1,074	177	7,081	369	1,132	2,615	184	3,894	:	1,310	446	87	299	790	2,422
1998	21,319	1,062	181	6,509	276	1,141	2,686	230	3,726	:	1,288	546	71	375	874	2,353
1999	20,073	1,062	194	5,530	265	1,181	2,918	265	2,982	:	1,239	480	66	474	1,365	2,050
2000	**28,622**	**1,806**	**214**	**7,795**	**431**	**1,836**	**3,797**	**518**	**4,575**	:	**1,725**	**563**	**99**	**786**	**1,541**	**2,934**
2001	20,298	1,095	219	5,942	278	1,192	2,541	421	3,851	:	1,159	466	76	334	606	2,117
2002	:	:	:	:	:	:	:	:	:	:	:	:	:	:	:	:

Annual variation (%)

Years	Intra EU	B[(1)]	DK	D	EL	E	F	IRL	I	L	NL	A	P	FIN	S	UK
98/97	-2.5	-1.1	2.0	-8.0	-25.2	0.8	2.7	25.4	-4.3	:	-1.7	22.3	-18.0	25.6	10.6	-2.8
99/98	-5.8	0.0	7.2	-15.0	-3.8	3.5	8.6	15.0	-19.9	:	-3.7	-12.0	-7.0	26.4	56.1	-12.9
00/99	42.5	70.0	10.1	40.9	62.2	55.3	30.0	95.5	53.4	:	39.2	17.3	49.9	65.7	12.9	43.1
01/00	-29.0	-39.3	2.4	-23.7	-35.4	-35.0	-33.0	-18.7	-15.8	:	-32.8	-17.2	-23.8	-57.5	-60.7	-27.8
02/01	:	:	:	:	:	:	:	:	:	:	:	:	:	:	:	:

Share (%)

Years	Intra EU	B[(1)]	DK	D	EL	E	F	IRL	I	L	NL	A	P	FIN	S	UK
1990	**100.0**	**5.2**	**1.0**	**35.5**	**1.2**	**3.4**	**13.5**	**0.6**	**17.3**	:	**5.7**	**2.5**	**0.1**	**1.0**	**2.1**	**10.2**
1996	100.0	4.8	0.7	33.8	1.2	4.4	11.9	0.6	18.3	:	6.3	2.3	0.3	1.1	2.8	10.7
1997	100.0	4.9	0.8	32.3	1.6	5.1	11.9	0.8	17.7	:	5.9	2.0	0.3	1.3	3.6	11.0
1998	100.0	4.9	0.8	30.5	1.2	5.3	12.5	1.0	17.4	:	6.0	2.5	0.3	1.7	4.1	11.0
1999	100.0	5.2	0.9	27.5	1.3	5.8	14.5	1.3	14.8	:	6.1	2.3	0.3	2.3	6.7	10.2
2000	**100.0**	**6.3**	**0.7**	**27.2**	**1.5**	**6.4**	**13.2**	**1.8**	**15.9**	:	**6.0**	**1.9**	**0.3**	**2.7**	**5.3**	**10.2**
2001	100.0	5.3	1.0	29.2	1.3	5.8	12.5	2.0	18.9	:	5.7	2.2	0.3	1.6	2.9	10.4
2002	:	:	:	:	:	:	:	:	:	:	:	:	:	:	:	:

(1) With Luxembourg until 31.12.1998.

NON EU MEMBER STATES

Years									Partner						
	Extra EU	Norway	Switzerland	USSR/ Russia[1]	Candid. countries	USA	Canada	China	Japan	Hong Kong	Mediterr. Basin	Latin America	OPEC	DAE	ACP
EXPORTS Value (Mio ECU/Euro)															
1990	**3,806**	**31**	**230**	**414**	:	**757**	**50**	**7**	**184**	**28**	**883**	:	**1,322**	:	:
1994	7,419	30	201	682	719	1,276	66	301	157	199	1,431	112	1,526	487	69
1995	6,454	41	182	616	1,014	1,156	73	51	137	166	1,204	81	1,309	483	93
1996	8,610	46	224	1,168	790	1,300	79	53	131	173	1,675	104	1,462	613	107
1997	11,178	77	280	1,821	1,046	1,781	104	39	127	208	1,998	175	1,598	756	210
1998	10,809	90	217	1,218	1,384	2,003	139	34	100	131	2,801	211	1,465	331	326
1999	10,540	84	251	552	1,007	2,266	140	34	114	92	2,636	239	1,539	400	341
2000	**12,991**	**87**	**258**	**700**	**1,260**	**3,370**	**186**	**105**	**162**	**123**	**2,820**	**262**	**1,730**	**531**	**367**
2001	14,955	78	269	1,032	1,591	3,463	192	224	138	164	3,330	369	2,190	508	494
2002	**15,015**	**137**	**266**	**696**	:	**3,614**	**271**	**253**	**159**	**157**	**3,448**	**345**	**2,145**	**464**	**497**
Annual variation (%)															
98/97	-3.3	17.8	-22.4	-33.1	32.3	12.4	34.0	-12.5	-20.9	-37.3	40.2	20.5	-8.3	-56.1	55.3
99/98	-2.4	-6.7	15.3	-54.6	-27.2	13.1	0.4	-1.2	13.3	-29.4	-5.9	12.9	5.0	20.6	4.5
00/99	23.2	2.8	2.8	26.8	25.1	48.7	33.5	208.8	42.3	33.6	6.9	9.8	12.4	32.8	7.7
01/00	15.1	-10.3	4.4	47.3	26.2	2.7	2.9	113.5	-14.6	33.1	18.0	40.8	26.6	-4.3	34.5
02/01	0.4	75.9	-1.3	-32.5	:	4.3	41.0	12.8	15.1	-4.0	3.5	-6.4	-2.0	-8.7	0.6
Share (%)															
1990	**100.0**	**0.8**	**6.0**	**10.8**	:	**19.8**	**1.3**	**0.1**	**4.8**	**0.7**	**23.1**	:	**34.7**	:	:
1996	100.0	0.5	2.6	13.5	9.1	15.0	0.9	0.6	1.5	2.0	19.4	1.2	16.9	7.1	1.2
1997	100.0	0.6	2.5	16.2	9.3	15.9	0.9	0.3	1.1	1.8	17.8	1.5	14.2	6.7	1.8
1998	100.0	0.8	2.0	11.2	12.8	18.5	1.2	0.3	0.9	1.2	25.9	1.9	13.5	3.0	3.0
1999	100.0	0.8	2.3	5.2	9.5	21.5	1.3	0.3	1.0	0.8	25.0	2.2	14.5	3.7	3.2
2000	**100.0**	**0.6**	**1.9**	**5.3**	**9.6**	**25.9**	**1.4**	**0.8**	**1.2**	**0.9**	**21.7**	**2.0**	**13.3**	**4.0**	**2.8**
2001	100.0	0.5	1.8	6.8	10.6	23.1	1.2	1.4	0.9	1.0	22.2	2.4	14.6	3.3	3.3
2002	**100.0**	**0.9**	**1.7**	**4.6**	:	**24.0**	**1.8**	**1.6**	**1.0**	**1.0**	**22.9**	**2.2**	**14.2**	**3.0**	**3.3**
IMPORTS Value (Mio ECU/Euro)															
1990	**8,114**	**45**	**418**	**948**	:	**1,784**	**144**	**87**	**867**	**61**	**1,046**	:	**2,574**	**142**	:
1994	9,939	76	399	879	619	2,048	117	217	811	62	750	287	2,393	355	65
1995	12,497	57	622	933	900	2,844	225	411	1,066	106	1,135	525	2,428	840	79
1996	15,154	72	889	1,456	910	2,526	260	500	1,090	160	1,815	567	3,182	1,060	147
1997	19,681	157	971	1,912	1,090	3,839	275	697	1,809	144	2,411	699	2,986	1,560	197
1998	18,114	132	912	1,926	755	3,641	158	753	1,826	126	2,005	693	2,194	1,606	243
1999	17,033	166	705	2,207	1,057	2,887	165	842	1,303	117	2,036	507	2,575	1,735	272
2000	**28,416**	**281**	**971**	**4,233**	**2,090**	**4,210**	**276**	**1,460**	**1,765**	**163**	**3,856**	**672**	**4,737**	**2,759**	**503**
2001	24,578	278	1,366	3,842	1,698	3,638	144	1,026	1,463	112	3,616	498	4,585	1,860	786
2002	**24,845**	**334**	**1,293**	**3,895**	:	**3,613**	**197**	**1,267**	**989**	**224**	**3,643**	**518**	**4,619**	**1,746**	**808**
Annual variation (%)															
98/97	-7.9	-15.7	-6.1	0.7	-30.7	-5.1	-42.4	8.0	0.9	-12.5	-16.8	-0.8	-26.5	2.9	23.8
99/98	-5.9	24.9	-22.7	14.5	39.9	-20.6	4.4	11.7	-28.6	-6.8	1.5	-26.9	17.3	8.0	11.8
00/99	66.8	69.6	37.7	91.8	97.7	45.8	66.6	73.4	35.4	39.2	89.4	32.5	84.0	58.9	84.8
01/00	-13.5	-0.8	40.6	-9.2	-18.7	-13.5	-47.8	-29.7	-17.1	-31.0	-6.2	-25.9	-3.2	-32.5	56.0
02/01	1.0	20.0	-5.3	1.3	:	-0.6	36.8	23.4	-32.4	98.8	0.7	4.0	0.7	-6.1	2.8
Share (%)															
1990	**100.0**	**0.5**	**5.1**	**11.6**	:	**21.9**	**1.7**	**1.0**	**10.6**	**0.7**	**12.8**	:	**31.7**	**1.7**	:
1996	100.0	0.4	5.8	9.6	6.0	16.6	1.7	3.3	7.1	1.0	11.9	3.7	20.9	6.9	0.9
1997	100.0	0.7	4.9	9.7	5.5	19.5	1.3	3.5	9.1	0.7	12.2	3.5	15.1	7.9	0.9
1998	100.0	0.7	5.0	10.6	4.1	20.0	0.8	4.1	10.0	0.6	11.0	3.8	12.1	8.8	1.3
1999	100.0	0.9	4.1	12.9	6.2	16.9	0.9	4.9	7.6	0.6	11.9	2.9	15.1	10.1	1.5
2000	**100.0**	**0.9**	**3.4**	**14.8**	**7.3**	**14.8**	**0.9**	**5.1**	**6.2**	**0.5**	**13.5**	**2.3**	**16.6**	**9.7**	**1.7**
2001	100.0	1.1	5.5	15.6	6.9	14.8	0.5	4.1	5.9	0.4	14.7	2.0	18.6	7.5	3.1
2002	**100.0**	**1.3**	**5.2**	**15.6**	:	**14.5**	**0.7**	**5.0**	**3.9**	**0.9**	**14.6**	**2.0**	**18.5**	**7.0**	**3.2**

(1) Relates to the external trade with the USSR until 1991 and to the external trade with Russia from 1992 onwards.

ICELAND

TRADE BALANCE (BN ECU/euro)

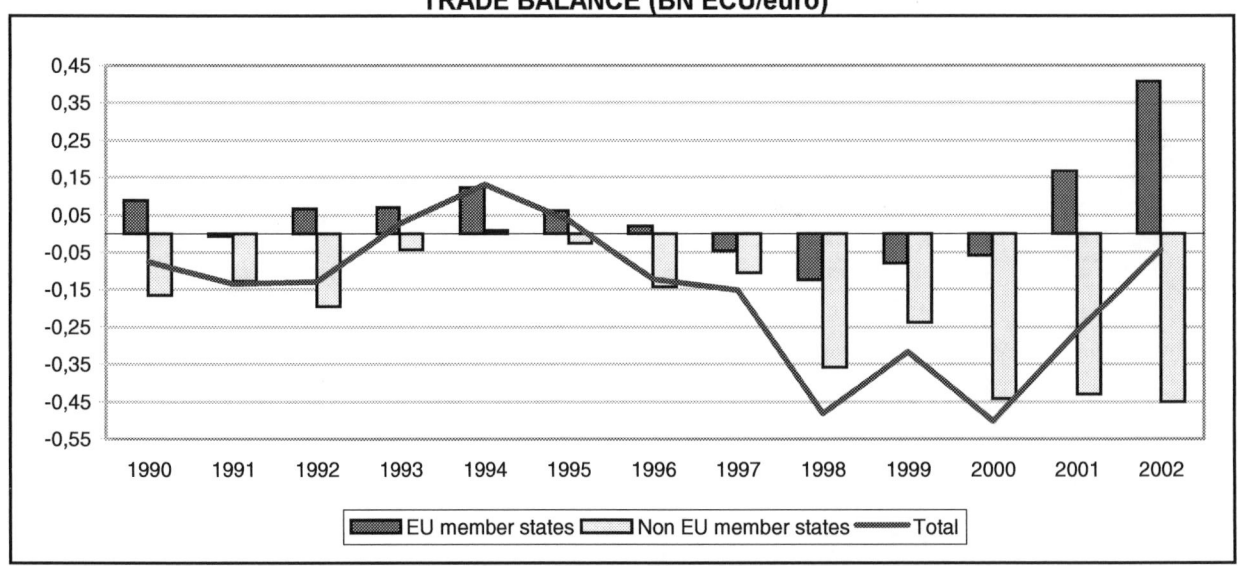

TRADE WITH EU MEMBER STATES (BN ECU/euro)

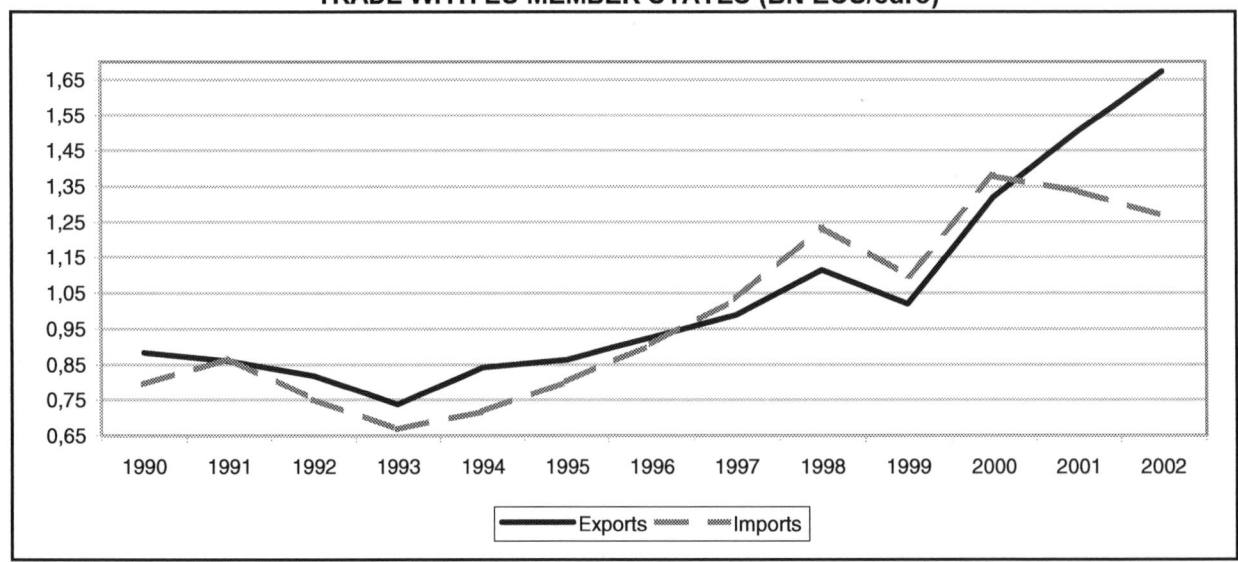

TRADE WITH NON EU MEMBER STATES (BN ECU/euro)

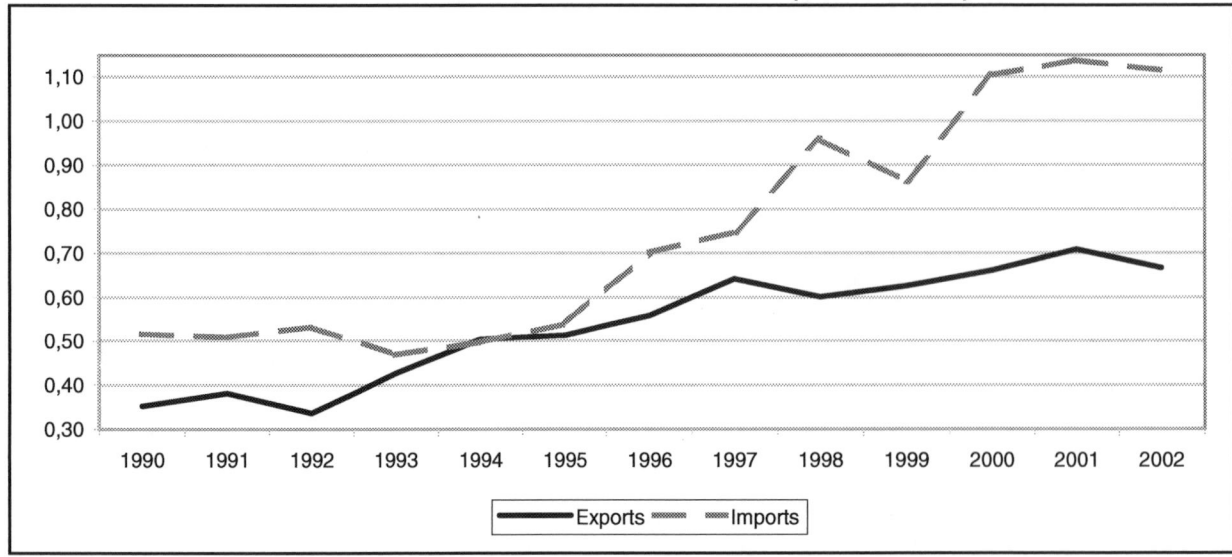

ICELAND

TRADE BALANCE

EU MEMBER STATES

Value (Mio ECU/Euro)

Year	Intra EU	B[1]	DK	D	EL	E	F	IRL	I	L	NL	A	P	FIN	S	UK
1980	**-67**	**-11**	**-44**	**-6**	**9**	**16**	**-1**	**-1**	**14**	**:**	**-58**	**-3**	**14**	**-0**	**-37**	**41**
1990	**88**	**-11**	**-51**	**-12**	**11**	**50**	**72**	**-4**	**-5**	**:**	**-111**	**-7**	**32**	**-10**	**-78**	**211**
1991	-6	-13	-67	-28	8	38	76	-6	-2	:	-118	-11	40	-18	-85	178
1992	67	-6	-49	-28	12	42	73	-7	-13	:	-73	-8	19	-11	-71	186
1993	69	-3	-41	-6	8	43	59	-8	-16	:	-43	-8	8	-14	-64	155
1994	123	0	-23	37	10	46	57	-10	-8	:	-55	-6	3	-11	-72	155
1995	61	-3	-18	35	10	29	36	-11	-16	:	-51	-6	13	-18	-76	136
1996	21	-11	-27	17	9	30	47	-14	-23	:	-42	-8	27	-12	-89	119
1997	-46	-18	-61	4	9	42	44	-18	-29	3	-61	-9	31	-10	-101	128
1998	-124	-24	-76	5	7	42	36	-25	-42	1	-60	-11	51	-23	-124	112
1999	-80	-13	-86	-37	10	48	14	-24	-40	0	-7	-12	61	-25	-109	129
2000	**-59**	**-9**	**-116**	**39**	**12**	**44**	**2**	**-28**	**-47**	**-2**	**-29**	**-13**	**93**	**-21**	**-141**	**145**
2001	167	-15	-124	27	12	71	8	-25	-49	-2	79	-13	110	-27	-122	220
2002	**406**	**-6**	**-96**	**180**	**16**	**79**	**12**	**-29**	**-40**	**-1**	**111**	**-10**	**91**	**-19**	**-118**	**235**

NON EU MEMBER STATES

Value (Mio ECU/euro)

Year	Extra EU	Norway	Switzerl-and	USSR/Russia[2]	Candid. countries	USA	Canada	China	Japan	Hong Kong	Mediterr. Basin	Latin America	OPEC	DAE	ACP
1980	**14**	**-43**	**16**	**-35**	**:**	**76**	**-6**	**:**	**-19**	**:**	**39**	**-0**	**46**	**:**	**45**
1990	**-164**	**-48**	**36**	**-32**	**:**	**-66**	**-3**	**-6**	**1**	**-8**	**-1**	**-5**	**8**	**-16**	**8**
1991	-127	-57	30	-39	:	14	-6	-8	-12	-9	5	-6	9	-17	9
1992	-196	-161	18	-17	:	19	-9	-9	14	-8	-5	9	9	-22	9
1993	-43	-102	24	-25	-10	82	-1	-12	47	-6	-0	-4	9	-20	10
1994	8	-138	9	-19	-12	88	4	-16	143	-6	-3	-4	6	-25	8
1995	-25	-92	14	-23	-30	58	10	-16	98	-7	-2	-1	4	-15	7
1996	-143	-162	6	-25	-40	25	3	-20	82	-7	-1	3	4	-17	20
1997	-105	-115	10	-15	-13	63	1	-18	20	-9	-2	7	8	-25	11
1998	-358	-119	46	-25	-48	-20	8	-24	-30	-10	-8	-5	-1	-52	12
1999	-238	-107	36	-28	-43	27	10	-30	-16	-10	1	-4	7	-44	-4
2000	**-443**	**-123**	**15**	**-42**	**-80**	**-34**	**9**	**-35**	**-11**	**-10**	**-13**	**-26**	**12**	**-44**	**-8**
2001	-430	-81	38	-32	-75	-48	-2	-62	-5	-7	-10	-62	11	-34	-13
2002	**-450**	**-95**	**8**	**-83**	**:**	**-5**	**1**	**-55**	**3**	**-6**	**-15**	**-6**	**30**	**-37**	**7**

(1) With Luxembourg until 31.12.1998.
(2) Relates to the external trade with the USSR until 1991 and to the external trade with Russia from 1992 onwards.

ICELAND

EU MEMBER STATES

Years	Intra EU	B[1]	DK	D	EL	E	F	IRL	I	L	NL	A	P	FIN	S	UK
							EXPORTS									
							Value (Mio ECU/Euro)									
1980	345	5	14	65	9	23	17	1	31	:	7	1	32	19	14	109
1990	884	14	63	159	12	62	113	1	36	:	27	2	44	12	22	317
1994	841	25	88	175	11	63	99	2	32	:	22	2	17	13	14	277
1995	863	24	108	188	11	50	93	2	28	:	41	2	25	7	18	265
1996	927	20	107	192	10	58	100	2	28	:	53	1	38	14	19	283
1997	988	18	93	213	10	71	103	3	29	4	55	2	43	19	18	309
1998	1,114	17	94	257	8	86	116	7	29	3	70	2	66	13	16	325
1999	1,019	24	80	204	11	86	91	5	30	1	98	3	76	8	16	314
2000	1,320	33	84	330	13	89	99	5	31	0	151	3	110	14	19	372
2001	1,505	32	95	335	14	121	88	3	29	1	245	3	124	15	24	410
2002	1,674	37	109	438	17	124	87	4	32	1	256	3	103	22	25	414
							Annual variation (%)									
98/97	12.7	-2.0	1.0	20.6	-19.3	21.5	12.2	138.9	2.5	-21.9	27.3	16.3	53.0	-32.1	-13.7	5.1
99/98	-8.5	40.9	-14.8	-20.9	37.3	0.1	-21.7	-31.2	0.8	-52.2	40.3	33.3	15.1	-34.5	-1.4	-3.4
00/99	29.4	32.9	5.7	62.0	21.9	3.1	9.3	-0.6	3.7	-65.4	54.7	-0.3	44.6	66.4	22.7	18.6
01/00	14.0	-1.6	12.4	1.5	3.1	35.3	-11.3	-33.1	-6.6	30.0	62.4	21.4	12.7	9.1	23.7	10.2
02/01	11.1	16.3	15.5	30.6	25.3	2.7	-1.1	17.1	10.2	18.1	4.4	-14.7	-16.8	42.5	5.3	1.0
							Share (%)									
1980	100.0	1.3	4.0	18.9	2.5	6.5	4.7	0.1	9.1	:	1.9	0.1	9.2	5.6	4.0	31.5
1990	100.0	1.5	7.1	18.0	1.3	6.9	12.7	0.1	4.0	:	3.0	0.2	4.9	1.3	2.5	35.8
1996	100.0	2.1	11.5	20.6	1.0	6.2	10.7	0.2	3.0	:	5.7	0.1	4.1	1.5	2.0	30.5
1997	100.0	1.7	9.3	21.5	0.9	7.1	10.4	0.3	2.9	0.3	5.5	0.1	4.3	1.9	1.8	31.2
1998	100.0	1.5	8.3	23.1	0.7	7.7	10.4	0.6	2.6	0.2	6.2	0.1	5.9	1.1	1.4	29.1
1999	100.0	2.4	7.8	19.9	1.0	8.4	8.9	0.4	2.9	0.1	9.5	0.2	7.4	0.8	1.5	30.7
2000	100.0	2.4	6.3	24.9	1.0	6.7	7.5	0.3	2.3	0.0	11.4	0.1	8.3	1.0	1.4	28.1
2001	100.0	2.1	6.2	22.2	0.9	8.0	5.8	0.2	1.9	0.0	16.2	0.2	8.2	1.0	1.5	27.2
2002	100.0	2.2	6.5	26.1	1.0	7.4	5.1	0.2	1.8	0.0	15.3	0.1	6.1	1.2	1.5	24.7
							IMPORTS									
							Value (Mio ECU/Euro)									
1980	412	15	58	71	0	7	17	1	17	:	65	3	18	20	51	68
1990	796	24	114	171	1	12	41	5	41	:	138	10	12	22	100	106
1994	719	25	111	138	1	17	43	12	40	:	77	8	15	23	86	122
1995	802	27	126	153	1	22	57	13	44	:	92	8	12	25	94	129
1996	906	32	134	175	1	28	53	16	52	:	96	10	12	26	108	164
1997	1,035	36	154	210	1	29	59	21	58	1	115	11	12	29	119	180
1998	1,238	42	170	252	1	44	80	33	71	2	129	13	15	35	140	212
1999	1,099	37	166	241	1	38	77	29	69	1	105	14	15	33	125	184
2000	1,379	41	200	291	1	45	97	33	78	2	180	16	17	35	160	226
2001	1,338	47	218	308	1	50	80	28	78	3	166	16	14	43	146	190
2002	1,267	43	205	257	1	45	75	33	72	2	145	13	12	40	143	180
							Annual variation (%)									
98/97	19.6	16.8	10.2	20.1	22.3	50.9	35.2	55.5	23.4	86.5	12.2	24.0	20.8	22.2	17.4	17.7
99/98	-11.2	-9.8	-2.2	-4.3	4.5	-13.1	-3.2	-10.6	-2.4	-50.0	-18.8	6.8	1.6	-6.5	-10.6	-13.1
00/99	25.4	9.6	20.7	20.6	6.3	16.2	25.4	12.2	12.8	121.8	71.1	9.8	11.2	6.0	28.3	22.8
01/00	-2.9	14.7	9.0	5.8	1.5	11.2	-17.5	-12.8	-0.5	7.6	-7.2	1.3	-17.5	21.1	-9.0	-16.1
02/01	-5.2	-9.0	-5.9	-16.3	0.4	-10.2	-6.3	15.6	-7.2	-28.7	-12.7	-17.5	-16.0	-5.1	-2.0	-5.5
							Share (%)									
1980	100.0	3.6	14.0	17.2	0.0	1.6	4.2	0.3	4.2	:	15.7	0.8	4.3	4.7	12.4	16.5
1990	100.0	3.0	14.2	21.4	0.1	1.4	5.0	0.6	5.1	:	17.3	1.2	1.4	2.7	12.6	13.3
1996	100.0	3.4	14.8	19.3	0.0	3.0	5.8	1.8	5.7	:	10.5	1.0	1.2	2.9	11.9	18.1
1997	100.0	3.4	14.8	20.2	0.1	2.8	5.6	2.0	5.5	0.1	11.1	1.0	1.1	2.8	11.5	17.4
1998	100.0	3.3	13.6	20.3	0.1	3.5	6.4	2.6	5.7	0.1	10.4	1.0	1.2	2.8	11.3	17.1
1999	100.0	3.4	15.0	21.9	0.1	3.4	7.0	2.6	6.3	0.0	9.5	1.2	1.3	3.0	11.3	16.7
2000	100.0	2.9	14.5	21.0	0.1	3.2	7.0	2.3	5.6	0.1	13.0	1.1	1.2	2.5	11.6	16.4
2001	100.0	3.5	16.3	23.0	0.1	3.7	5.9	2.1	5.8	0.1	12.4	1.1	1.0	3.1	10.9	14.1
2002	100.0	3.3	16.1	20.3	0.1	3.5	5.9	2.5	5.6	0.1	11.4	1.0	0.9	3.1	11.2	14.1

(1) With Luxembourg until 31.12.1998.

NON EU MEMBER STATES

Years	Extra EU	Norway	Switzerla-nd	USSR/Russia[1]	Candid. countries	USA	Canada	China	Japan	Hong Kong	Mediterr. Basin	Latin America	OPEC	DAE	ACP
						Partner									

EXPORTS
Value (Mio ECU/Euro)

Years	Extra EU	Norway	Switzerland	USSR/Russia[1]	Candid. countries	USA	Canada	China	Japan	Hong Kong	Mediterr. Basin	Latin America	OPEC	DAE	ACP
1980	315	11	23	36	:	143	4	:	10	:	68	10	46	:	45
1990	352	18	52	32	:	124	4	0	75	0	5	3	8	2	9
1994	505	38	24	8	3	198	17	0	193	1	1	4	8	4	8
1995	514	45	30	8	6	171	23	2	156	0	2	7	7	29	8
1996	559	55	29	15	10	177	17	1	146	1	5	11	7	32	22
1997	642	91	50	29	20	232	20	7	108	0	5	16	12	30	13
1998	601	83	79	19	17	225	27	7	83	0	3	11	13	17	14
1999	625	83	59	5	22	252	29	5	89	1	14	5	12	19	13
2000	661	80	43	9	22	246	34	13	107	1	7	6	18	27	21
2001	709	116	73	8	36	233	24	10	78	1	8	7	27	26	30
2002	666	98	35	9	:	256	20	15	79	2	7	6	37	9	47

Annual variations (%)

Years	Extra EU	Norway	Switzerland	USSR/Russia[1]	Candid. countries	USA	Canada	China	Japan	Hong Kong	Mediterr. Basin	Latin America	OPEC	DAE	ACP
98/97	-6.4	-8.7	59.2	-34.4	-13.0	-2.7	34.5	-0.6	-23.4	-43.9	-46.8	-27.2	11.1	-42.1	5.8
99/98	4.1	0.6	-24.9	-71.8	24.0	11.8	8.4	-27.8	7.8	356.5	371.2	-56.4	-7.9	7.5	-11.8
00/99	5.6	-4.0	-28.3	65.9	-0.9	-2.3	17.7	186.7	20.2	57.0	-45.5	16.3	51.8	40.9	64.4
01/00	7.2	45.7	71.7	-8.8	67.0	-5.4	-28.7	-23.2	-26.9	-5.7	9.0	21.5	52.3	-1.8	44.5
02/01	-6.0	-15.5	-52.5	11.9	:	10.2	-18.2	47.8	0.8	127.5	-14.1	-15.3	33.0	-66.3	57.0

Share (%)

Years	Extra EU	Norway	Switzerland	USSR/Russia[1]	Candid. countries	USA	Canada	China	Japan	Hong Kong	Mediterr. Basin	Latin America	OPEC	DAE	ACP
1980	100.0	3.5	7.2	11.4	:	45.5	1.2	:	3.1	:	21.4	3.0	14.5	:	14.4
1990	100.0	5.1	14.8	9.0	:	35.2	1.0	0.0	21.2	0.1	1.4	0.8	2.3	0.4	2.4
1996	100.0	9.9	5.2	2.7	1.8	31.6	3.0	0.1	26.1	0.1	0.8	1.9	1.2	5.6	3.9
1997	100.0	14.1	7.7	4.5	3.1	36.0	3.0	1.0	16.7	0.0	0.8	2.4	1.8	4.7	2.0
1998	100.0	13.7	13.2	3.2	2.9	37.5	4.4	1.0	13.7	0.0	0.4	1.8	2.1	2.9	2.3
1999	100.0	13.3	9.5	0.8	3.4	40.2	4.6	0.7	14.2	0.0	2.1	0.7	1.9	3.0	2.0
2000	100.0	12.1	6.4	1.3	3.2	37.2	5.1	2.0	16.2	0.1	1.1	0.8	2.7	4.0	3.1
2001	100.0	16.4	10.3	1.1	5.0	32.8	3.4	1.4	11.0	0.1	1.1	0.9	3.8	3.6	4.2
2002	100.0	14.7	5.2	1.3	:	38.5	2.9	2.2	11.8	0.2	1.0	0.8	5.4	1.3	7.0

IMPORTS
Value (Mio ECU/Euro)

Years	Extra EU	Norway	Switzerland	USSR/Russia[1]	Candid. countries	USA	Canada	China	Japan	Hong Kong	Mediterr. Basin	Latin America	OPEC	DAE	ACP
1980	301	54	7	71	:	68	9	1	29	4	28	10	0	9	0
1990	516	66	16	64	:	190	7	6	74	8	7	8	0	18	1
1994	497	176	15	27	15	110	13	16	50	6	4	8	2	29	0
1995	539	137	16	31	36	113	13	18	59	7	4	8	2	43	1
1996	701	218	24	40	51	152	15	21	64	8	6	8	3	49	2
1997	747	205	40	44	33	168	18	24	88	9	8	9	3	56	2
1998	959	201	33	45	66	246	19	30	112	10	11	17	14	69	3
1999	864	190	23	34	65	225	19	35	105	10	12	9	5	63	17
2000	1,103	203	27	51	102	279	25	49	118	11	20	32	6	70	29
2001	1,139	197	35	41	111	280	26	73	84	8	18	69	16	60	43
2002	1,116	193	26	93	:	261	19	70	76	8	22	12	6	45	40

Annual variations (%)

Years	Extra EU	Norway	Switzerland	USSR/Russia[1]	Candid. countries	USA	Canada	China	Japan	Hong Kong	Mediterr. Basin	Latin America	OPEC	DAE	ACP
98/97	28.2	-1.8	-16.6	0.5	97.6	46.1	1.3	24.1	28.2	7.4	48.3	85.2	334.1	24.7	11.9
99/98	-9.8	-5.7	-29.2	-24.3	-1.5	-8.5	0.3	14.5	-6.4	2.0	11.7	-47.5	-63.1	-9.9	554.0
00/99	27.7	6.9	16.5	50.1	56.8	24.3	34.5	41.4	11.9	4.2	59.6	259.9	26.6	12.4	68.7
01/00	3.2	-2.8	27.8	-19.8	9.2	0.2	2.8	48.3	-28.9	-22.7	-7.5	116.4	153.8	-14.4	49.4
02/01	-2.0	-1.8	-24.0	127.8	:	-6.7	-27.1	-3.5	-9.5	-3.7	19.5	-82.5	-60.5	-24.4	-6.5

Share (%)

Years	Extra EU	Norway	Switzerland	USSR/Russia[1]	Candid. countries	USA	Canada	China	Japan	Hong Kong	Mediterr. Basin	Latin America	OPEC	DAE	ACP
1980	100.0	17.9	2.2	23.6	:	22.4	3.1	0.3	9.7	1.2	9.4	3.2	0.0	2.9	0.0
1990	100.0	12.7	3.0	12.3	:	36.7	1.4	1.1	14.2	1.5	1.2	1.5	0.0	3.4	0.1
1996	100.0	31.0	3.3	5.6	7.2	21.6	2.0	2.9	9.1	1.1	0.8	1.1	0.3	6.9	0.3
1997	100.0	27.4	5.2	5.9	4.4	22.4	2.4	3.2	11.7	1.2	1.0	1.2	0.4	7.4	0.3
1998	100.0	21.0	3.4	4.6	6.8	25.6	1.9	3.1	11.7	1.0	1.1	1.7	1.4	7.2	0.2
1999	100.0	21.9	2.7	3.9	7.5	26.0	2.1	4.0	12.1	1.1	1.4	1.0	0.5	7.2	1.9
2000	100.0	18.3	2.4	4.5	9.2	25.3	2.2	4.4	10.6	0.9	1.8	2.8	0.5	6.3	2.5
2001	100.0	17.3	3.0	3.5	9.7	24.6	2.2	6.3	7.3	0.7	1.6	6.0	1.4	5.2	3.7
2002	100.0	17.3	2.3	8.2	:	23.4	1.6	6.2	6.7	0.7	1.9	1.0	0.5	4.0	3.5

(1) Relates to the external trade with the USSR until 1991 and to the external trade with Russia from 1992 onwards.

NORWAY

TRADE BALANCE (BN ECU/euro)

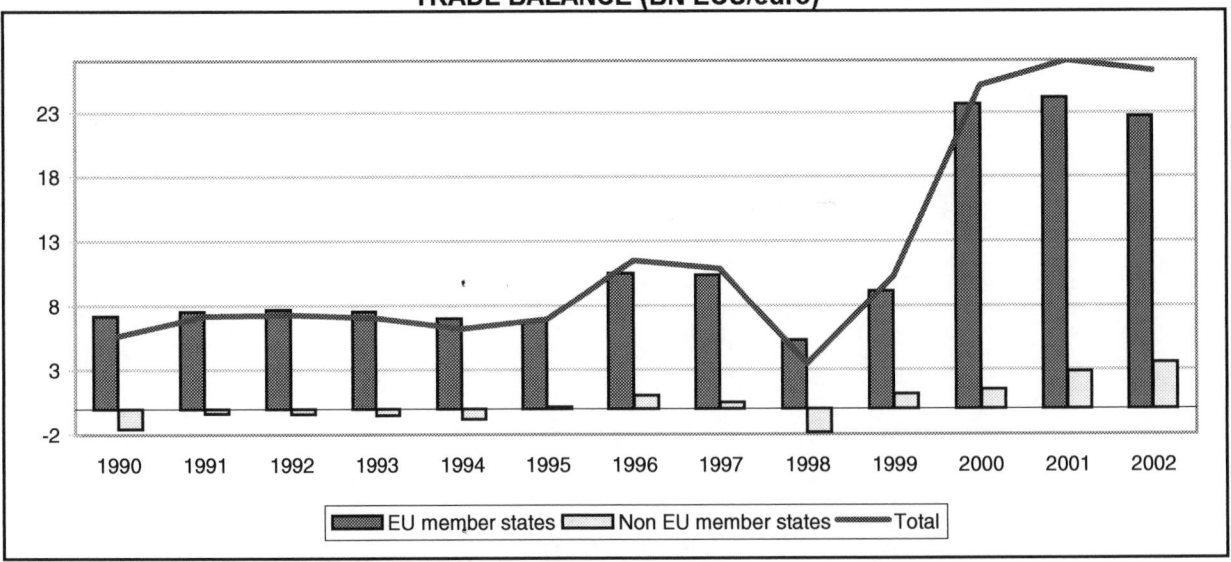

TRADE WITH EU MEMBER STATES (BN ECU/euro)

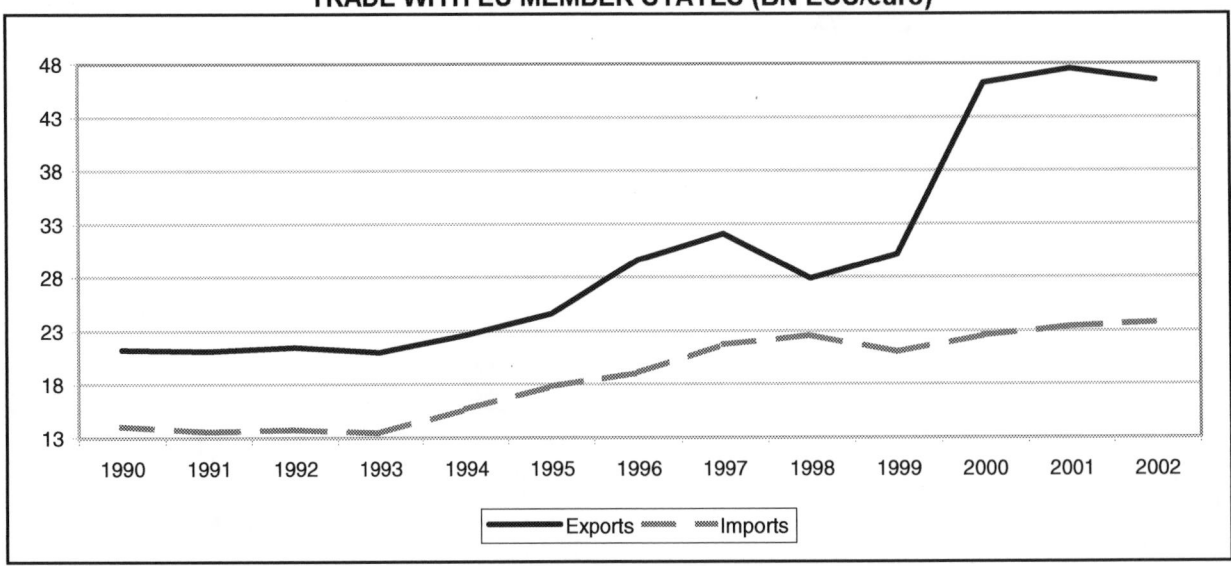

TRADE WITH NON EU MEMBER STATES (BN ECU/euro)

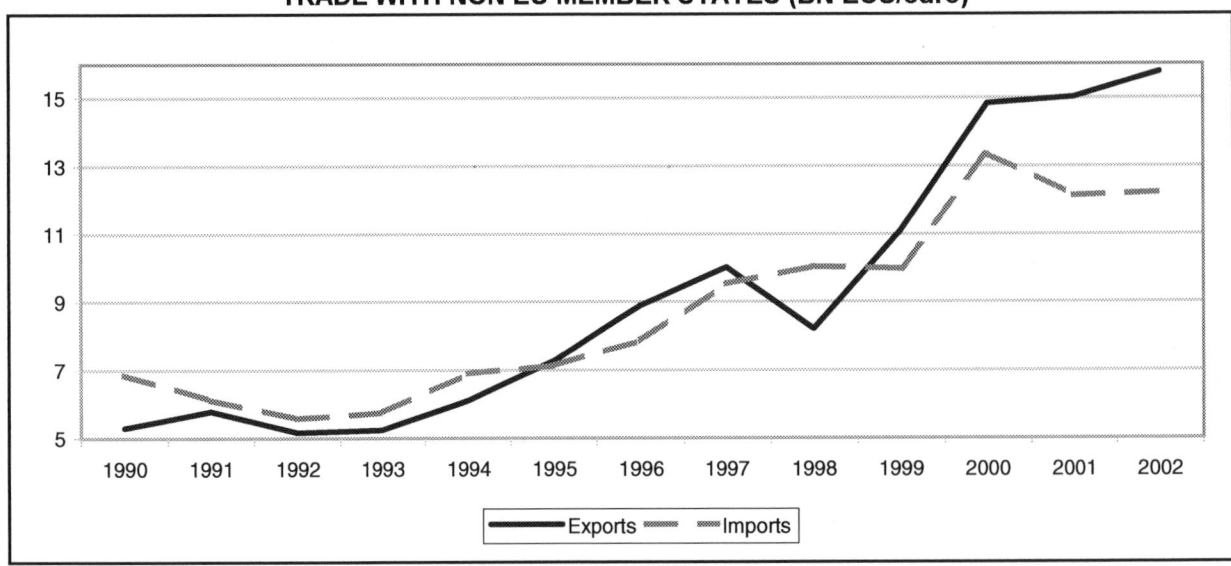

TRADE BALANCE

EU MEMBER STATES

Value (Mio ECU/Euro)

Year		Partner														
	Intra EU	B[1]	DK	D	EL	E	F	IRL	I	L	NL	A	P	FIN	S	UK
1980	**2,528**	**-274**	**-195**	**565**	**55**	**-26**	**-136**	**-4**	**-86**	**:**	**78**	**-96**	**-43**	**-238**	**-799**	**3,728**
1990	**7,174**	**85**	**-124**	**-76**	**14**	**20**	**1,285**	**-73**	**10**	**:**	**1,294**	**-105**	**-52**	**72**	**-221**	**5,044**
1991	7,533	152	60	101	49	73	1,304	45	-71	:	1,100	-118	0	180	-347	5,005
1992	7,701	316	-35	726	4	88	1,321	75	31	:	1,173	-140	23	-17	-563	4,699
1993	7,528	181	-299	668	13	8	1,286	44	-3	:	1,468	-118	45	22	-536	4,749
1994	6,964	279	-291	411	32	162	1,413	82	30	:	1,790	-111	46	32	-625	3,714
1995	6,791	271	-285	326	131	69	1,377	-85	-7	:	1,925	-112	53	-109	-707	3,944
1996	10,492	531	-330	679	45	354	2,257	-23	5	:	3,076	-121	44	-121	-1,037	5,133
1997	10,345	641	-36	-25	47	-267	2,445	131	-40	10	3,496	-176	54	-124	-1,162	5,351
1998	5,286	270	-163	-105	147	149	1,847	51	-510	9	2,114	-165	132	-151	-1,403	3,052
1999	9,130	249	-150	744	40	167	2,317	152	-267	14	2,596	-150	283	-133	-856	4,388
2000	**23,607**	**1,282**	**132**	**1,284**	**129**	**184**	**4,984**	**547**	**21**	**25**	**5,713**	**-90**	**268**	**99**	**-15**	**10,350**
2001	24,106	1,521	-249	2,880	219	383	5,762	465	-8	21	4,983	-166	385	-44	-503	9,998
2002	**22,665**	**1,147**	**-526**	**3,079**	**103**	**519**	**5,718**	**248**	**459**	**2**	**4,217**	**-173**	**283**	**-36**	**-953**	**9,729**

NON EU MEMBER STATES

Value (Mio ECU/euro)

Year		Partner													
	Extra EU	Iceland	Switzerl- and	USSR/ Russia[2]	Candid. countries	USA	Canada	China	Japan	Hong Kong	Mediterr. Basin	Latin America	OPEC	DAE	ACP
1980	**-1,342**	**39**	**-101**	**14**	**:**	**-622**	**-238**	**44**	**-328**	**-41**	**83**	**-2**	**-112**	**-56**	**112**
1990	**-1,547**	**44**	**-116**	**-158**	**:**	**95**	**164**	**-47**	**-480**	**-135**	**29**	**-357**	**278**	**-124**	**-911**
1991	-349	56	-117	-201	:	-294	218	-113	-441	-154	50	-65	28	-114	101
1992	-410	142	-140	:	:	-239	289	-180	-752	-65	194	3	122	-108	152
1993	-508	95	-160	-212	210	146	157	-214	-576	-53	140	11	88	-27	-45
1994	-787	132	-131	-414	157	170	506	-321	-874	-62	129	-40	55	-61	-19
1995	134	80	-176	-307	113	291	668	-333	-391	-29	179	48	128	30	-204
1996	1,028	134	-211	-238	149	1,105	976	-386	-338	-36	191	111	88	-253	-218
1997	492	98	-170	-309	153	533	1,453	-432	-506	-13	122	-45	24	41	-407
1998	-1,828	96	-262	-290	-67	649	649	-530	-678	-2	5	-94	62	-188	-207
1999	1,113	146	-176	-474	-30	1,093	1,482	-366	-174	21	227	-221	18	-116	-207
2000	**1,478**	**132**	**-190**	**-683**	**-134**	**2,067**	**2,687**	**-784**	**-576**	**64**	**255**	**-247**	**98**	**-621**	**-245**
2001	2,886	37	-227	-571	-55	2,629	1,647	-358	-288	76	329	-94	128	-59	178
2002	**3,552**	**31**	**-194**	**-388**	**-449**	**3,257**	**1,513**	**-969**	**-89**	**-10**	**181**	**-63**	**107**	**294**	**399**

(1) With Luxembourg until 31.12.1998.
(2) Relates to the external trade with the USSR until 1991 and to the external trade with Russia from 1992 onwards.

NORWAY

EU MEMBER STATES

Years	Intra EU	B(1)	DK	D	EL	E	F	IRL	I	L	NL	A	P	FIN	S	UK
EXPORTS Value (Mio ECU/Euro)																
1980	11,134	137	555	2,251	64	65	305	27	195	:	489	55	28	215	1,237	5,511
1990	21,228	584	1,289	2,962	63	242	2,084	110	685	:	2,137	99	182	734	3,093	6,964
1994	22,635	867	1,369	3,598	65	397	2,349	352	832	:	2,767	118	256	868	2,703	6,095
1995	24,634	994	1,604	3,807	163	539	2,481	295	875	:	3,039	139	285	876	3,148	6,390
1996	29,620	1,223	1,760	4,295	76	736	3,394	342	1,037	:	4,280	136	273	848	3,573	7,647
1997	32,064	1,272	2,173	4,235	83	669	3,725	504	1,136	32	4,830	143	306	894	3,780	8,281
1998	27,883	992	2,055	4,389	187	799	3,156	453	873	30	3,618	132	364	977	3,526	6,323
1999	30,150	984	2,045	4,853	87	835	3,683	571	946	30	4,182	129	508	978	3,979	7,354
2000	46,192	1,972	2,511	5,716	209	949	6,477	1,062	1,201	43	7,169	188	496	1,427	5,470	13,316
2001	47,512	2,219	2,365	7,534	271	980	7,652	1,011	1,215	44	6,576	151	591	1,225	5,107	12,834
2002	46,419	1,896	2,374	7,891	157	1,074	7,433	778	1,878	26	5,932	152	480	1,179	4,699	12,392
Annual variation (%)																
98/97	-13.0	-21.9	-5.4	3.6	124.8	19.4	-15.2	-10.0	-23.1	-7.0	-25.0	-7.9	19.0	9.3	-6.7	-23.6
99/98	8.1	-0.7	-0.5	10.5	-53.5	4.5	16.6	25.9	8.3	-0.1	15.6	-2.2	39.4	0.0	12.8	16.3
00/99	53.2	100.3	22.8	17.7	140.2	13.6	75.8	85.9	26.9	44.4	71.4	45.8	-2.2	45.8	37.4	81.0
01/00	2.8	12.4	-5.8	31.8	29.8	3.2	18.1	-4.8	1.1	1.1	-8.2	-19.3	19.1	-14.1	-6.6	-3.6
02/01	-2.3	-14.5	0.3	4.7	-41.9	9.6	-2.8	-23.0	54.5	-39.9	-9.7	0.2	-18.7	-3.7	-7.9	-3.4
Share (%)																
1980	100.0	1.2	4.9	20.2	0.5	0.5	2.7	0.2	1.7	:	4.3	0.4	0.2	1.9	11.1	49.4
1990	100.0	2.7	6.0	13.9	0.2	1.1	9.8	0.5	3.2	:	10.0	0.4	0.8	3.4	14.5	32.8
1996	100.0	4.1	5.9	14.4	0.2	2.4	11.4	1.1	3.5	:	14.4	0.4	0.9	2.8	12.0	25.8
1997	100.0	3.9	6.7	13.2	0.2	2.0	11.6	1.5	3.5	0.1	15.0	0.4	0.9	2.7	11.7	25.8
1998	100.0	3.5	7.3	15.7	0.6	2.8	11.3	1.6	3.1	0.1	12.9	0.4	1.3	3.5	12.6	22.6
1999	100.0	3.2	6.7	16.0	0.2	2.7	12.2	1.8	3.1	0.0	13.8	0.4	1.6	3.2	13.1	24.3
2000	100.0	4.2	5.4	12.3	0.4	2.0	14.0	2.2	2.6	0.0	15.5	0.4	1.0	3.0	11.8	28.8
2001	100.0	4.6	4.9	15.8	0.5	2.0	16.1	2.1	2.5	0.0	13.8	0.3	1.2	2.5	10.7	27.0
2002	100.0	4.0	5.1	16.9	0.3	2.3	16.0	1.6	4.0	0.0	12.7	0.3	1.0	2.5	10.1	26.6
IMPORTS Value (Mio ECU/Euro)																
1980	8,606	412	750	1,686	9	91	440	31	282	:	411	151	71	454	2,035	1,783
1990	14,054	499	1,414	3,038	49	222	799	183	675	:	843	204	234	662	3,314	1,920
1994	15,671	588	1,660	3,187	33	235	935	270	802	:	977	229	211	836	3,328	2,380
1995	17,843	723	1,889	3,481	32	469	1,104	380	882	:	1,113	251	231	985	3,855	2,446
1996	19,127	692	2,090	3,616	31	382	1,137	366	1,033	:	1,203	256	229	969	4,609	2,514
1997	21,719	631	2,210	4,260	36	936	1,280	374	1,176	22	1,333	319	252	1,017	4,943	2,930
1998	22,597	722	2,218	4,494	40	650	1,309	402	1,383	21	1,504	296	232	1,128	4,930	3,271
1999	21,020	736	2,195	4,110	47	668	1,365	419	1,213	16	1,587	279	225	1,111	4,835	2,966
2000	22,585	691	2,379	4,432	80	765	1,493	515	1,180	18	1,456	277	228	1,328	5,486	2,966
2001	23,406	697	2,614	4,654	52	597	1,889	545	1,223	23	1,593	318	206	1,269	5,610	2,836
2002	23,754	749	2,900	4,812	55	555	1,715	530	1,419	24	1,715	325	197	1,216	5,652	2,663
Annual variation (%)																
98/97	4.0	14.4	0.3	5.4	9.9	-30.5	2.2	7.6	17.5	-3.7	12.7	-7.1	-7.5	10.8	-0.2	11.6
99/98	-6.9	1.8	-1.0	-8.5	18.4	2.7	4.2	4.2	-12.2	-24.9	5.4	-5.9	-3.2	-1.5	-1.9	-9.3
00/99	7.4	-6.0	8.3	7.8	68.5	14.5	9.3	22.6	-2.6	13.5	-8.2	-0.5	1.3	19.5	13.4	0.0
01/00	3.6	0.9	9.8	5.0	-34.6	-22.0	26.5	6.0	3.6	24.8	9.3	14.5	-9.8	-4.4	2.2	-4.3
02/01	1.4	7.3	10.9	3.4	4.9	-6.9	-9.2	-2.8	16.0	7.3	7.6	2.3	-4.0	-4.2	0.7	-6.0
Share (%)																
1980	100.0	4.7	8.7	19.5	0.1	1.0	5.1	0.3	3.2	:	4.7	1.7	0.8	5.2	23.6	20.7
1990	100.0	3.5	10.0	21.6	0.3	1.5	5.6	1.3	4.8	:	5.9	1.4	1.6	4.7	23.5	13.6
1996	100.0	3.6	10.0	18.9	0.1	1.9	5.9	1.9	5.3	:	6.2	1.3	1.1	5.0	24.0	13.1
1997	100.0	2.9	10.1	19.6	0.1	4.3	5.8	1.7	5.4	0.1	6.1	1.4	1.1	4.6	22.7	13.4
1998	100.0	3.1	9.8	19.8	0.1	2.8	5.7	1.7	6.1	0.0	6.6	1.3	1.0	4.9	21.8	14.4
1999	100.0	3.4	10.4	19.5	0.2	3.1	6.4	1.9	5.7	0.0	7.5	1.3	1.0	5.2	23.0	14.1
2000	100.0	3.0	10.5	19.6	0.3	3.3	6.6	2.2	5.2	0.0	6.4	1.2	1.0	5.8	24.2	13.1
2001	100.0	2.9	11.1	19.8	0.2	2.5	8.0	2.3	5.2	0.0	6.8	1.3	0.8	5.4	23.9	12.1
2002	100.0	3.1	12.2	20.2	0.2	2.3	7.2	2.2	5.9	0.1	7.2	1.3	0.8	5.1	23.7	11.2

(1) With Luxembourg until 31.12.1998.

NON EU MEMBER STATES

Years	Extra EU	Iceland	Switzerland	USSR/Russia(1)	Candid. countries	USA	Canada	China	Japan	Hong Kong	Mediterr. Basin	Latin America	OPEC	DAE	ACP
						EXPORTS									
						Value (Mio ECU/Euro)									
1980	**2,183**	**54**	**98**	**81**	:	**397**	**55**	**62**	**106**	**11**	**326**	**270**	**298**	**73**	**394**
1990	**5,308**	**65**	**197**	**136**	:	**1,752**	**625**	**81**	**442**	**50**	**302**	**223**	**397**	**336**	**359**
1994	6,104	168	180	105	500	1,865	955	114	548	72	299	286	150	473	315
1995	7,268	127	172	146	602	1,963	1,205	142	567	129	381	391	220	912	199
1996	8,912	197	170	218	664	2,852	1,560	159	713	104	397	500	187	860	220
1997	10,019	192	196	302	811	2,636	1,992	274	850	131	424	478	192	1,145	244
1998	8,209	184	184	240	821	2,231	1,212	225	821	147	362	426	207	916	230
1999	11,087	235	194	165	883	3,403	2,035	504	1,108	155	549	384	166	1,054	186
2000	**14,825**	**225**	**217**	**205**	**1,028**	**5,037**	**3,701**	**290**	**1,071**	**211**	**582**	**443**	**245**	**1,162**	**365**
2001	15,014	161	241	293	1,241	5,191	2,699	746	987	197	647	565	267	1,204	610
2002	**15,777**	**135**	**273**	**342**	**1,293**	**5,531**	**2,271**	**986**	**1,039**	**119**	**573**	**480**	**265**	**1,455**	**904**
						Annual variation (%)									
98/97	-18.0	-4.5	-6.2	-20.6	1.3	-15.3	-39.1	-17.8	-3.3	12.0	-14.5	-10.8	7.6	-20.0	-5.5
99/98	35.0	27.7	5.6	-31.1	7.5	52.5	67.8	124.1	34.8	5.4	51.5	-9.9	-19.7	15.0	-19.3
00/99	33.7	-4.0	11.8	23.8	16.4	48.0	81.9	-42.3	-3.3	36.3	5.9	15.4	47.7	10.2	96.7
01/00	1.2	-28.6	11.2	43.0	20.6	3.0	-27.0	156.7	-7.8	-6.7	11.1	27.5	8.8	3.5	66.9
02/01	5.0	-16.2	13.0	16.8	4.2	6.5	-15.8	32.2	5.2	-39.3	-11.4	-15.0	-0.5	20.8	48.2
						Share (%)									
1980	**100.0**	**2.4**	**4.4**	**3.6**	:	**18.1**	**2.5**	**2.8**	**4.8**	**0.4**	**14.9**	**12.3**	**13.6**	**3.3**	**18.0**
1990	**100.0**	**1.2**	**3.7**	**2.5**	:	**33.0**	**11.7**	**1.5**	**8.3**	**0.9**	**5.6**	**4.1**	**7.4**	**6.3**	**6.7**
1996	100.0	2.2	1.9	2.4	7.4	32.0	17.5	1.7	7.9	1.1	4.4	5.6	2.0	9.6	2.4
1997	100.0	1.9	1.9	3.0	8.0	26.3	19.8	2.7	8.4	1.3	4.2	4.7	1.9	11.4	2.4
1998	100.0	2.2	2.2	2.9	10.0	27.1	14.7	2.7	10.0	1.7	4.4	5.1	2.5	11.1	2.8
1999	100.0	2.1	1.7	1.4	7.9	30.6	18.3	4.5	9.9	1.3	4.9	3.4	1.4	9.5	1.6
2000	**100.0**	**1.5**	**1.4**	**1.3**	**6.9**	**33.9**	**24.9**	**1.9**	**7.2**	**1.4**	**3.9**	**2.9**	**1.6**	**7.8**	**2.4**
2001	100.0	1.0	1.6	1.9	8.2	34.5	17.9	4.9	6.5	1.3	4.3	3.7	1.7	8.0	4.0
2002	**100.0**	**0.8**	**1.7**	**2.1**	**8.1**	**35.0**	**14.3**	**6.2**	**6.5**	**0.7**	**3.6**	**3.0**	**1.6**	**9.2**	**5.7**
						IMPORTS									
						Value (Mio ECU/Euro)									
1980	**3,525**	**15**	**199**	**67**	:	**1,019**	**292**	**18**	**434**	**52**	**243**	**272**	**410**	**129**	**282**
1990	**6,855**	**21**	**314**	**294**	:	**1,657**	**462**	**129**	**922**	**186**	**272**	**580**	**119**	**459**	**1,270**
1994	6,891	36	311	519	343	1,695	449	435	1,422	134	170	325	95	533	334
1995	7,133	47	349	453	490	1,672	537	475	958	158	201	343	92	882	403
1996	7,883	62	381	456	516	1,748	584	546	1,051	139	206	390	99	1,113	438
1997	9,527	94	366	611	657	2,103	538	705	1,355	144	302	523	168	1,104	651
1998	10,037	88	446	530	888	2,400	563	755	1,500	149	358	520	144	1,104	437
1999	9,974	88	370	639	913	2,310	553	870	1,282	134	322	605	148	1,169	392
2000	**13,347**	**93**	**408**	**888**	**1,162**	**2,971**	**1,014**	**1,075**	**1,647**	**147**	**327**	**690**	**147**	**1,783**	**610**
2001	12,128	124	469	864	1,296	2,562	1,052	1,104	1,275	121	318	659	139	1,263	432
2002	12,225	103	467	730	1,742	2,274	758	1,955	1,128	129	392	543	158	1,160	505
						Annual variation (%)									
98/97	5.3	-6.9	21.7	-13.3	35.0	14.1	4.5	6.9	10.6	3.1	18.5	-0.4	-13.8	0.0	-32.7
99/98	-0.6	0.7	-16.9	20.6	2.7	-3.7	-1.7	15.3	-14.5	-9.7	-9.9	16.3	2.4	5.9	-10.3
00/99	33.8	5.2	10.1	38.8	27.3	28.6	83.4	23.4	28.4	9.4	1.4	14.1	-0.4	52.4	55.5
01/00	-9.1	33.0	14.9	-2.6	11.4	-13.7	3.7	2.6	-22.5	-17.4	-2.7	-4.5	-5.7	-29.1	-29.1
02/01	0.8	-16.4	-0.3	-15.5	34.4	-11.2	-27.8	77.1	-11.5	6.4	23.3	-17.5	14.0	-8.1	16.8
						Share (%)									
1980	**100.0**	**0.4**	**5.6**	**1.8**	:	**28.9**	**8.2**	**0.5**	**12.3**	**1.4**	**6.9**	**7.7**	**11.6**	**3.6**	**7.9**
1990	**100.0**	**0.3**	**4.5**	**4.2**	:	**24.1**	**6.7**	**1.8**	**13.4**	**2.7**	**3.9**	**8.4**	**1.7**	**6.7**	**18.5**
1996	100.0	0.7	4.8	5.7	6.5	22.1	7.4	6.9	13.3	1.7	2.6	4.9	1.2	14.1	5.5
1997	100.0	0.9	3.8	6.4	6.9	22.0	5.6	7.4	14.2	1.5	3.1	5.4	1.7	11.5	6.8
1998	100.0	0.8	4.4	5.2	8.8	23.9	5.6	7.5	14.9	1.4	3.5	5.1	1.4	10.9	4.3
1999	100.0	0.8	3.7	6.4	9.1	23.1	5.5	8.7	12.8	1.3	3.2	6.0	1.4	11.7	3.9
2000	**100.0**	**0.6**	**3.0**	**6.6**	**8.7**	**22.2**	**7.5**	**8.0**	**12.3**	**1.0**	**2.4**	**5.1**	**1.1**	**13.3**	**4.5**
2001	100.0	1.0	3.8	7.1	10.6	21.1	8.6	9.0	10.5	0.9	2.6	5.4	1.1	10.4	3.5
2002	**100.0**	**0.8**	**3.8**	**5.9**	**14.2**	**18.6**	**6.2**	**15.9**	**9.2**	**1.0**	**3.2**	**4.4**	**1.2**	**9.4**	**4.1**

(1) Relates to the external trade with the USSR until 1991 and to the external trade with Russia from 1992 onwards.

SWITZERLAND

TRADE BALANCE (BN ECU/euro)

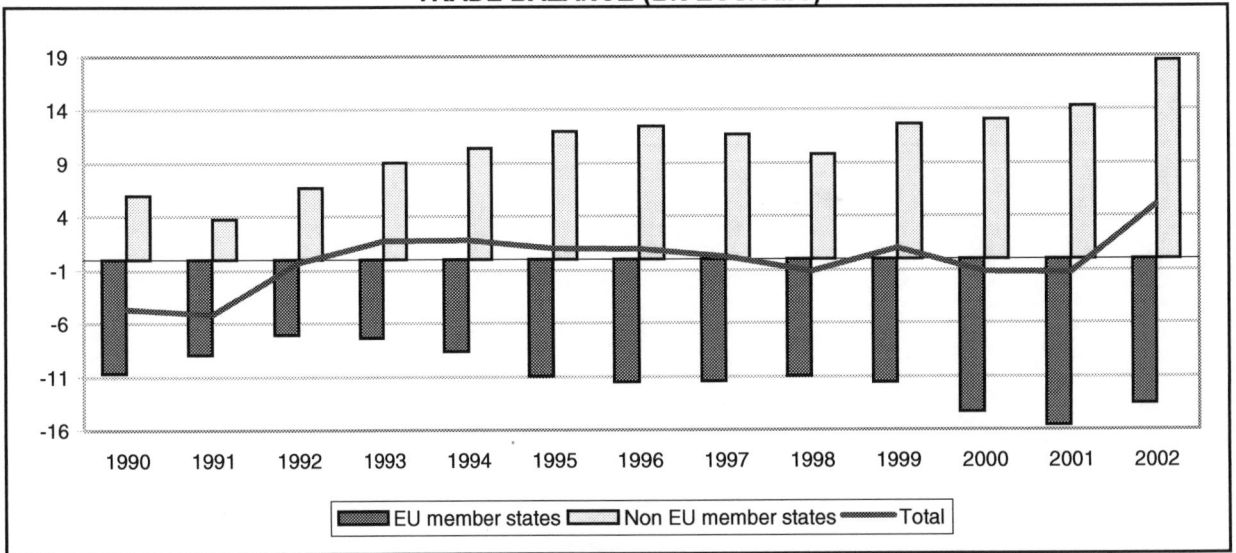

TRADE WITH EU MEMBER STATES (BN ECU/euro)

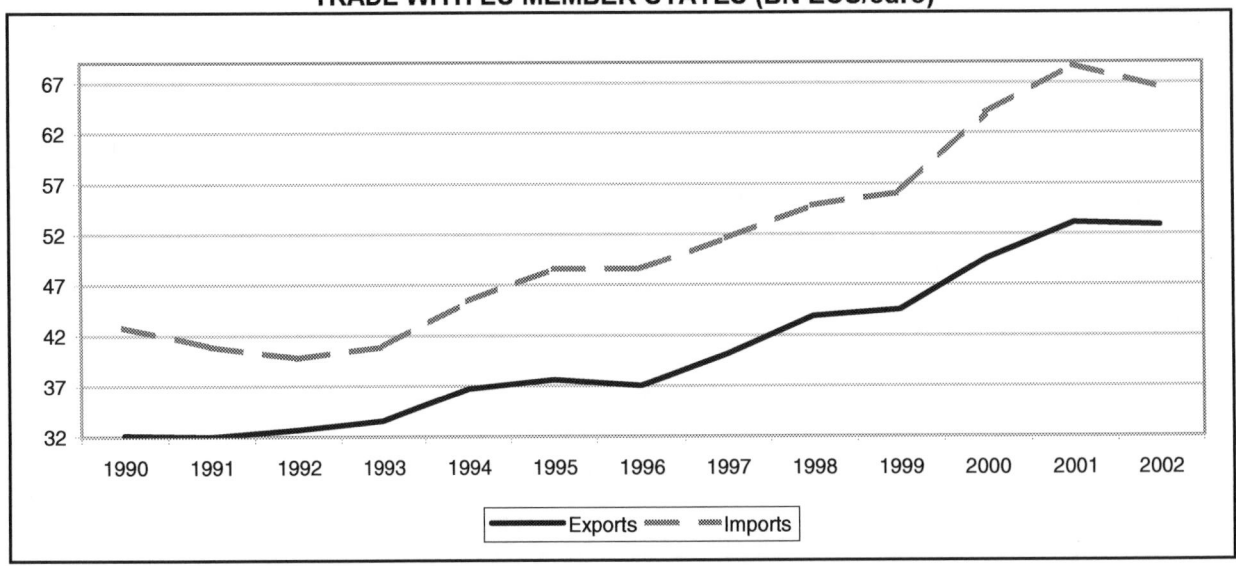

TRADE WITH NON EU MEMBER STATES (BN ECU/euro)

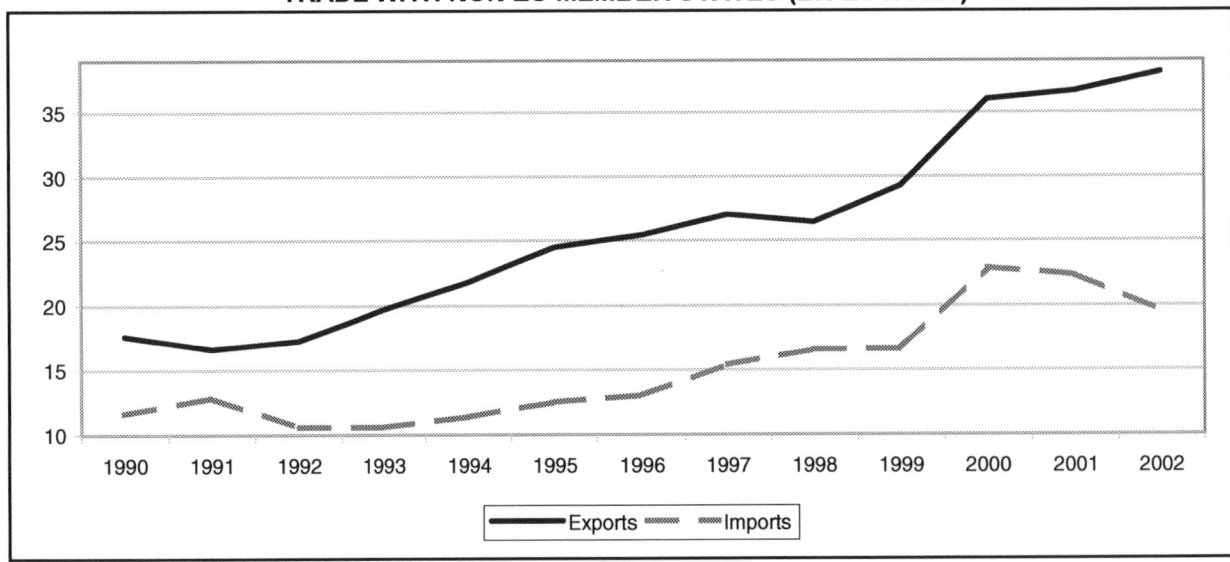

SWITZERLAND

TRADE BALANCE

EU MEMBER STATES

Value (Mio ECU/Euro)

Year	Intra EU	B[1]	DK	D	EL	E	F	IRL	I	L	NL	A	P	FIN	S	UK
1980	**-6,476**	**-401**	**17**	**-3,006**	**100**	**139**	**-1,244**	**-27**	**-837**	**:**	**-464**	**36**	**95**	**22**	**-88**	**-819**
1990	**-10,689**	**-819**	**5**	**-7,401**	**173**	**418**	**-1,101**	**-221**	**-1,303**	**:**	**-893**	**-302**	**160**	**3**	**-230**	**822**
1991	-8,922	-685	16	-5,755	196	488	-1,059	-195	-1,045	:	-846	-177	153	-58	-264	310
1992	-7,043	-572	7	-5,112	247	514	-689	-231	-660	:	-861	-133	157	-20	-148	458
1993	-7,360	-504	-10	-4,611	268	358	-773	-278	-878	:	-871	-65	120	14	-72	-58
1994	-8,657	-694	-2	-4,925	270	370	-849	-314	-1,256	:	-1,086	-240	107	-42	-145	149
1995	-10,959	-801	19	-6,278	276	413	-1,262	-389	-1,517	:	-1,153	-389	94	-54	-245	326
1996	-11,530	-716	-30	-5,448	283	324	-1,635	-515	-1,994	:	-1,301	-547	113	8	-105	34
1997	-11,432	-871	-24	-5,219	349	567	-1,251	-895	-1,562	:	-1,726	-468	165	63	-114	-446
1998	-10,959	-813	-67	-5,564	497	785	-1,021	-962	-1,479	:	-1,520	-620	181	-10	-63	-303
1999	-11,588	-614	-76	-6,263	454	911	-2,046	-1,141	-1,273	-15	-1,424	-512	219	-172	-151	-114
2000	**-14,308**	**-1,009**	**-59**	**-7,330**	**459**	**876**	**-1,434**	**-1,771**	**-1,598**	**73**	**-2,413**	**-505**	**201**	**-279**	**-172**	**-282**
2001	-15,560	-1,009	-23	-8,427	501	1,237	-1,398	-3,080	-1,507	22	-2,269	-402	234	-174	83	-333
2002	**-13,562**	**-682**	**-70**	**-8,856**	**555**	**1,295**	**-363**	**-2,895**	**-1,499**	**-30**	**-1,745**	**-498**	**231**	**-179**	**-13**	**474**

NON EU MEMBER STATES

Value (Mio ECU/euro)

Year	Extra EU	Iceland	Norway	USSR/ Russia[2]	Candid. countries	USA	Canada	China	Japan	Hong Kong	Mediterr. Basin	Latin America	OPEC	DAE	ACP
1980	**1,651**	**-14**	**85**	**-481**	**:**	**-220**	**35**	**45**	**-311**	**154**	**1,028**	**413**	**575**	**194**	**196**
1990	**5,989**	**-39**	**-49**	**355**	**:**	**650**	**230**	**-0**	**-20**	**779**	**1,282**	**530**	**880**	**1,465**	**-30**
1991	3,765	-16	0	-300	:	1	148	-107	-207	676	892	524	938	1,322	45
1992	6,726	-15	13	-27	:	1,040	189	-137	-293	1,012	916	859	1,300	1,768	178
1993	9,079	-22	94	-27	990	1,461	233	-82	-132	1,223	1,176	928	1,462	2,330	119
1994	10,436	-16	135	-40	945	1,642	226	-182	362	1,536	1,029	1,058	1,060	2,955	57
1995	11,991	-27	135	-98	1,184	1,334	233	-153	483	1,361	1,179	814	1,166	3,176	0
1996	12,486	-16	188	29	1,328	1,268	240	-224	884	1,307	1,416	971	778	3,142	-115
1997	11,669	-34	181	-296	1,673	1,432	232	-378	838	1,519	1,831	1,327	815	3,480	-134
1998	9,849	-12	246	-497	1,584	2,634	126	-538	807	1,147	1,648	1,505	808	1,215	-102
1999	12,632	-26	150	-827	1,454	4,020	208	-506	885	1,409	1,530	1,410	781	2,774	19
2000	**13,082**	**-33**	**155**	**-2,109**	**1,550**	**4,401**	**432**	**-575**	**1,193**	**1,894**	**1,642**	**1,399**	**554**	**3,634**	**-210**
2001	14,298	-27	207	-2,605	1,634	4,339	575	-390	1,319	2,224	1,568	1,655	972	4,056	-71
2002	**18,576**	**-10**	**170**	**-440**	**1,760**	**5,239**	**746**	**-109**	**1,745**	**2,492**	**1,526**	**1,278**	**1,373**	**4,440**	**105**

(1) With Luxembourg until 31.12.1998.
(2) Relates to the external trade with the USSR until 1991 and to the external trade with Russia from 1992 onwards.

SWITZERLAND

EU MEMBER STATES

Years	Intra EU	B(1)	DK	D	EL	E	F	IRL	I	L	NL	A	P	FIN	S	UK
							Partner									
EXPORTS Value (Mio ECU/Euro)																
1980	12,976	673	236	4,187	129	387	1,959	38	1,671	:	594	975	172	170	439	1,347
1990	32,142	1,152	541	11,099	249	1,086	4,963	99	4,452	:	1,359	1,856	381	374	822	3,709
1994	36,771	1,469	635	13,870	345	1,180	5,434	230	4,399	:	1,595	2,120	395	334	834	3,931
1995	37,638	1,361	705	14,293	357	1,283	5,655	163	4,630	:	1,636	2,190	431	367	852	3,716
1996	37,068	1,452	618	13,890	355	1,332	5,478	181	4,588	:	1,599	1,890	440	378	887	3,981
1997	40,172	1,590	623	15,032	420	1,654	6,104	234	5,015	:	1,759	2,059	466	441	880	3,896
1998	43,869	1,604	628	16,210	572	1,990	6,743	330	5,418	:	2,059	2,204	496	490	965	4,161
1999	44,525	1,527	622	17,017	533	2,191	6,966	319	5,992	107	2,374	2,419	524	443	998	4,127
2000	49,604	1,657	674	18,748	546	2,432	7,726	362	6,723	226	2,667	2,673	532	519	1,058	4,945
2001	53,099	1,796	730	19,870	603	2,889	8,238	448	7,308	165	2,796	2,961	581	527	1,067	5,083
2002	52,900	1,944	685	19,002	647	3,093	8,508	603	7,645	111	2,789	3,097	551	495	1,006	4,779
Annual variation (%)																
98/97	9.2	0.8	0.7	7.8	36.1	20.3	10.4	40.9	8.0	:	17.0	7.0	6.5	11.0	9.6	6.8
99/98	1.4	-4.8	-0.9	4.9	-6.8	10.1	3.3	-3.4	10.5	:	15.2	9.7	5.6	-9.4	3.4	-0.8
00/99	11.4	8.5	8.2	10.1	2.4	10.9	10.8	13.5	12.2	110.4	12.3	10.5	1.3	17.1	6.0	19.8
01/00	7.0	8.4	8.3	5.9	10.3	18.7	6.6	23.7	8.7	-27.0	4.8	10.7	9.2	1.5	0.8	2.7
02/01	-0.3	8.2	-6.1	-4.3	7.3	7.0	3.2	34.8	4.6	-32.3	-0.2	4.5	-5.2	-6.1	-5.7	-5.9
Share (%)																
1980	100.0	5.1	1.8	32.2	0.9	2.9	15.0	0.2	12.8	:	4.5	7.5	1.3	1.3	3.3	10.3
1990	100.0	3.5	1.6	34.5	0.7	3.3	15.4	0.3	13.8	:	4.2	5.7	1.1	1.1	2.5	11.5
1996	100.0	3.9	1.6	37.4	0.9	3.5	14.7	0.4	12.3	:	4.3	5.0	1.1	1.0	2.3	10.7
1997	100.0	3.9	1.5	37.4	1.0	4.1	15.1	0.5	12.4	:	4.3	5.1	1.1	1.0	2.1	9.6
1998	100.0	3.6	1.4	36.9	1.3	4.5	15.3	0.7	12.3	:	4.6	5.0	1.1	1.1	2.1	9.4
1999	100.0	3.4	1.3	38.2	1.1	4.9	15.6	0.7	13.4	0.2	5.3	5.4	1.1	0.9	2.2	9.2
2000	100.0	3.3	1.3	37.7	1.1	4.9	15.5	0.7	13.5	0.4	5.3	5.3	1.0	1.0	2.1	9.9
2001	100.0	3.3	1.3	37.4	1.1	5.4	15.5	0.8	13.7	0.3	5.2	5.5	1.0	0.9	2.0	9.5
2002	100.0	3.6	1.2	35.9	1.2	5.8	16.0	1.1	14.4	0.2	5.2	5.8	1.0	0.9	1.9	9.0
IMPORTS Value (Mio ECU/Euro)																
1980	19,452	1,074	218	7,194	28	248	3,203	65	2,508	:	1,058	939	77	148	527	2,165
1990	42,831	1,971	536	18,500	76	668	6,063	320	5,756	:	2,253	2,157	221	372	1,052	2,887
1994	45,428	2,163	637	18,794	75	810	6,283	544	5,656	:	2,680	2,360	288	376	980	3,781
1995	48,598	2,162	686	20,572	81	870	6,916	552	6,147	:	2,788	2,579	337	421	1,097	3,390
1996	48,598	2,168	648	19,338	72	1,007	7,113	696	6,582	:	2,900	2,437	327	370	993	3,947
1997	51,604	2,461	647	20,251	71	1,087	7,355	1,129	6,577	:	3,485	2,527	301	378	993	4,342
1998	54,828	2,417	695	21,774	74	1,205	7,764	1,292	6,897	:	3,579	2,823	315	500	1,028	4,464
1999	56,112	2,141	698	23,279	79	1,280	9,012	1,460	7,265	123	3,797	2,931	306	615	1,148	4,241
2000	63,912	2,666	732	26,079	87	1,556	9,159	2,133	8,321	153	5,080	3,179	331	798	1,230	5,227
2001	68,659	2,806	753	28,297	101	1,652	9,636	3,527	8,815	143	5,065	3,363	347	702	984	5,416
2002	66,462	2,626	755	27,858	92	1,798	8,872	3,498	9,144	142	4,534	3,595	319	674	1,019	4,305
Annual variation (%)																
98/97	6.2	-1.8	7.4	7.5	4.5	10.8	5.5	14.4	4.8	:	2.6	11.7	4.7	32.2	3.4	2.8
99/98	2.3	-11.4	0.4	6.9	6.2	6.2	16.0	12.9	5.3	:	6.1	3.8	-3.0	23.1	11.7	-4.9
00/99	13.9	24.4	4.8	12.0	10.5	21.5	1.6	46.1	14.5	24.7	33.7	8.4	8.1	29.7	7.1	23.2
01/00	7.4	5.2	2.8	8.5	16.0	6.1	5.2	65.3	5.9	-6.6	-0.2	5.8	4.8	-12.0	-20.0	3.6
02/01	-3.2	-6.4	0.2	-1.5	-9.3	8.8	-7.9	-0.8	3.7	-0.5	-10.4	6.8	-7.9	-3.9	3.5	-20.5
Share (%)																
1980	100.0	5.5	1.1	36.9	0.1	1.2	16.4	0.3	12.8	:	5.4	4.8	0.3	0.7	2.7	11.1
1990	100.0	4.6	1.2	43.1	0.1	1.5	14.1	0.7	13.4	:	5.2	5.0	0.5	0.8	2.4	6.7
1996	100.0	4.4	1.3	39.7	0.1	2.0	14.6	1.4	13.5	:	5.9	5.0	0.6	0.7	2.0	8.1
1997	100.0	4.7	1.2	39.2	0.1	2.1	14.2	2.1	12.7	:	6.7	4.8	0.5	0.7	1.9	8.4
1998	100.0	4.4	1.2	39.7	0.1	2.1	14.1	2.3	12.5	:	6.5	5.1	0.5	0.9	1.8	8.1
1999	100.0	3.8	1.2	41.4	0.1	2.2	16.0	2.6	12.9	0.2	6.7	5.2	0.5	1.0	2.0	7.5
2000	100.0	4.1	1.1	40.8	0.1	2.4	14.3	3.3	13.0	0.2	7.9	4.9	0.5	1.2	1.9	8.1
2001	100.0	4.0	1.0	41.2	0.1	2.4	14.0	5.1	12.8	0.2	7.3	4.8	0.5	1.0	1.4	7.8
2002	100.0	3.9	1.1	41.9	0.1	2.7	13.3	5.2	13.7	0.2	6.8	5.4	0.4	1.0	1.5	6.4

(1) With Luxembourg until 31.12.1998.

NON EU MEMBER STATES

Years	Extra EU	Norway	Iceland	USSR/Russia(1)	Candid. countries	USA	Canada	China	Japan	Hong Kong	Mediterr. Basin	Latin America	OPEC	DAE	ACP
						EXPORTS Value (Mio ECU/Euro)									
1980	8,240	184	6	217	:	1,542	180	100	547	400	1,960	938	1,507	638	465
1990	17,648	265	14	579	:	4,014	402	236	2,390	1,292	2,018	1,139	1,552	2,632	373
1994	21,833	297	12	268	1,569	5,421	405	525	2,293	1,953	1,938	1,639	1,765	4,138	347
1995	24,513	315	11	231	1,962	5,239	481	538	2,417	1,778	2,080	1,458	1,956	4,770	308
1996	25,491	347	18	265	2,137	5,666	503	542	2,549	1,701	2,451	1,577	1,683	4,772	296
1997	27,053	328	16	362	2,591	7,035	494	574	2,711	1,948	2,808	1,913	1,894	5,178	311
1998	26,459	408	39	323	2,713	7,716	538	499	2,707	1,581	2,552	2,182	1,713	3,911	389
1999	29,282	313	16	222	2,753	9,327	606	619	3,033	1,819	2,729	2,109	1,645	4,547	418
2000	35,955	337	18	358	3,300	11,435	804	903	3,710	2,470	3,206	2,436	2,019	6,012	378
2001	36,625	403	19	552	3,530	10,646	912	1,104	3,564	2,674	3,158	2,629	2,349	6,186	458
2002	38,091	367	22	601	3,868	11,104	1,055	1,395	3,530	3,054	3,125	2,365	2,726	6,495	584
						Annual variation (%)									
98/97	-2.1	24.3	146.0	-10.8	4.7	9.6	8.9	-13.0	-0.1	-18.8	-9.0	14.0	-9.5	-24.4	25.1
99/98	10.6	-23.2	-58.5	-31.3	1.4	20.8	12.7	24.0	12.0	15.0	6.9	-3.3	-3.9	16.2	7.3
00/99	22.7	7.8	13.8	61.4	19.8	22.5	32.5	45.9	22.3	35.7	17.4	15.5	22.6	32.2	-9.5
01/00	1.8	19.3	4.7	54.1	6.9	-6.8	13.4	22.2	-3.9	8.2	-1.4	7.9	16.3	2.8	21.2
02/01	4.0	-8.9	15.3	8.9	9.5	4.3	15.6	26.3	-0.9	14.1	-1.0	-10.0	16.0	4.9	27.3
						Share (%)									
1980	100.0	2.2	0.0	2.6	:	18.7	2.1	1.2	6.6	4.8	23.7	11.3	18.2	7.7	5.6
1990	100.0	1.5	0.0	3.2	:	22.7	2.2	1.3	13.5	7.3	11.4	6.4	8.7	14.9	2.1
1996	100.0	1.3	0.0	1.0	8.3	22.2	1.9	2.1	9.9	6.6	9.6	6.1	6.6	18.7	1.1
1997	100.0	1.2	0.0	1.3	9.5	26.0	1.8	2.1	10.0	7.2	10.3	7.0	7.0	19.1	1.1
1998	100.0	1.5	0.1	1.2	10.2	29.1	2.0	1.8	10.2	5.9	9.6	8.2	6.4	14.7	1.4
1999	100.0	1.0	0.0	0.7	9.4	31.8	2.0	2.1	10.3	6.2	9.3	7.2	5.6	15.5	1.4
2000	100.0	0.9	0.0	0.9	9.1	31.8	2.2	2.5	10.3	6.8	8.9	6.7	5.6	16.7	1.0
2001	100.0	1.0	0.0	1.5	9.6	29.0	2.4	3.0	9.7	7.3	8.6	7.1	6.4	16.8	1.2
2002	100.0	0.9	0.0	1.5	10.1	29.1	2.7	3.6	9.2	8.0	8.2	6.2	7.1	17.0	1.5
						IMPORTS Value (Mio ECU/Euro)									
1980	6,589	98	21	698	:	1,762	145	55	858	246	932	525	932	444	269
1990	11,659	314	53	223	:	3,364	172	236	2,410	513	736	609	672	1,167	403
1994	11,397	161	28	308	624	3,779	179	707	1,931	416	909	581	705	1,183	290
1995	12,522	180	38	329	778	3,906	248	691	1,934	417	901	644	790	1,595	308
1996	13,005	159	34	236	809	4,398	262	767	1,665	394	1,035	606	904	1,630	411
1997	15,384	147	50	658	918	5,602	262	952	1,872	430	977	586	1,079	1,699	445
1998	16,610	161	51	820	1,129	5,082	412	1,037	1,900	435	904	677	905	2,696	491
1999	16,650	163	42	1,048	1,300	5,307	398	1,125	2,148	410	1,198	698	864	1,773	399
2000	22,873	183	52	2,467	1,751	7,033	372	1,478	2,517	576	1,564	1,037	1,464	2,378	588
2001	22,327	195	46	3,157	1,896	6,308	337	1,495	2,245	450	1,590	974	1,377	2,130	529
2002	19,515	196	32	1,041	2,108	5,866	308	1,504	1,785	562	1,599	1,087	1,353	2,054	479
						Annual variation (%)									
98/97	7.9	9.7	2.6	24.5	23.0	-9.2	57.1	8.9	1.4	1.1	-7.4	15.5	-16.1	58.7	10.2
99/98	0.2	1.1	-17.1	27.8	15.1	4.4	-3.3	8.5	13.0	-5.6	32.4	3.0	-4.4	-34.2	-18.7
00/99	37.3	11.9	21.5	135.3	34.6	32.5	-6.5	31.3	17.1	40.5	30.5	48.5	69.4	34.1	47.5
01/00	-2.3	6.9	-10.1	27.9	8.2	-10.3	-9.5	1.1	-10.8	-21.9	1.6	-6.1	-5.9	-10.4	-10.0
02/01	-12.5	0.5	-31.2	-67.0	11.1	-7.0	-8.3	0.6	-20.4	24.9	0.5	11.6	-1.7	-3.5	-9.5
						Share (%)									
1980	100.0	1.4	0.3	10.5	:	26.7	2.2	0.8	13.0	3.7	14.1	7.9	14.1	6.7	4.0
1990	100.0	2.6	0.4	1.9	:	28.8	1.4	2.0	20.6	4.3	6.3	5.2	5.7	10.0	3.4
1996	100.0	1.2	0.2	1.8	6.2	33.8	2.0	5.8	12.8	3.0	7.9	4.6	6.9	12.5	3.1
1997	100.0	0.9	0.3	4.2	5.9	36.4	1.7	6.1	12.1	2.7	6.3	3.8	7.0	11.0	2.8
1998	100.0	0.9	0.3	4.9	6.7	30.5	2.4	6.2	11.4	2.6	5.4	4.0	5.4	16.2	2.9
1999	100.0	0.9	0.2	6.2	7.8	31.8	2.3	6.7	12.9	2.4	7.1	4.1	5.1	10.6	2.3
2000	100.0	0.7	0.2	10.7	7.6	30.7	1.6	6.4	11.0	2.5	6.8	4.5	6.4	10.3	2.5
2001	100.0	0.8	0.2	14.1	8.4	28.2	1.5	6.6	10.0	2.0	7.1	4.3	6.1	9.5	2.3
2002	100.0	1.0	0.1	5.3	10.8	30.0	1.5	7.7	9.1	2.8	8.1	5.5	6.9	10.5	2.4

(1) Relates to the external trade with the USSR until 1991 and to the external trade with Russia from 1992 onwards.

Periods	Belg.-Lux.	Denmark	Germany	Greece	Spain	France	Ireland	Italy	Netherlands
1973	47.801	7.416	3.276	36.952	71.813	5.468	0.502	716.461	3.428
1975	45.569	7.123	3.049	39.994	70.271	5.319	0.560	809.547	3.135
1977	40.883	6.856	2.648	42.155	86.824	5.606	0.654	1,006.790	2.800
1979	40.165	7.208	2.511	50.757	91.973	5.830	0.669	1,138.430	2.749
1981	41.295	7.923	2.514	61.623	102.676	6.040	0.691	1,263.180	2.775
1982	44.712	8.157	2.376	65.342	107.558	6.431	0.690	1,323.780	2.614
1983	45.438	8.132	2.270	78.088	127.503	6.771	0.715	1,349.930	2.537
1984	45.442	8.146	2.238	88.416	126.569	6.872	0.726	1,381.380	2.523
1985	44.914	8.019	2.226	105.739	129.135	6.795	0.715	1,447.990	2.511
1986	43.798	7.936	2.128	137.425	137.456	6.800	0.734	1,461.880	2.401
1987	43.041	7.885	2.072	156.269	142.165	6.929	0.775	1,494.910	2.334
1988	43.428	7.952	2.074	167.576	137.601	7.036	0.776	1,537.330	2.335
1989	43.381	8.049	2.070	178.841	130.406	7.024	0.777	1,510.470	2.335
1990	42.426	7.856	2.052	201.412	129.411	6.914	0.768	1,521.980	2.312
1991	42.223	7.909	2.051	225.216	128.469	6.973	0.768	1,533.240	2.311
1992	41.593	7.809	2.020	247.026	132.526	6.848	0.761	1,595.520	2.275
1993	40.471	7.594	1.936	268.568	149.124	6.634	0.800	1,841.230	2.175
1994	39.656	7.543	1.924	288.026	158.918	6.583	0.794	1,915.060	2.158
1995	38.552	7.328	1.874	302.989	163.000	6.525	0.816	2,130.143	2.099
1996	39.299	7.359	1.910	305.546	160.748	6.493	0.793	1,958.960	2.140
1997	40.533	7.484	1.964	309.355	165.887	6.613	0.748	1,929.300	2.211
1998	40.621	7.499	1.969	330.731	167.184	6.601	0.786	1,943.650	2.220
1999	40.340	7.436	1.956	325.763	166.386	6.560	0.788	1,936.270	2.204
2000	40.340	7.454	1.956	336.630	166.386	6.560	0.788	1,936.270	2.204
2001	40.340	7.452	1.956	340.750	166.386	6.560	0.788	1,936.270	2.204
2002	40.340	7.430	1.956	340.750	166.386	6.560	0.788	1,936.270	2.204

	Austria	Portugal	Finland	Sweden	United Kingdom	Iceland	Norway	Switzerland	USA	Japan
1973	:	30.267	:	:	0.502	:	:	3.892	1.232	333.222
1975	21.547	31.436	4.544	5.141	0.560	1.904	6.472	3.200	1.241	360.733
1977	18.842	43.620	4.593	5.119	0.654	2.271	6.076	2.739	1.141	305.807
1979	18.310	67.014	5.322	5.872	0.646	4.840	6.937	2.279	1.370	300.461
1981	17.715	68.495	4.793	5.635	0.553	8.033	6.387	2.187	1.116	245.379
1982	16.699	78.007	4.707	6.143	0.560	12.021	6.313	1.986	0.980	243.546
1983	15.969	98.689	4.948	6.821	0.587	21.984	6.491	1.868	0.890	211.354
1984	15.735	115.680	4.724	6.511	0.591	24.879	6.417	1.848	0.789	187.089
1985	15.643	130.252	4.694	6.521	0.589	31.639	6.511	1.856	0.763	180.559
1986	14.964	147.089	4.980	6.996	0.672	40.408	7.278	1.761	0.984	164.997
1987	14.571	162.616	5.065	7.310	0.705	44.606	7.765	1.718	1.154	166.598
1988	14.586	170.059	4.944	7.242	0.664	50.755	7.700	1.728	1.182	151.459
1989	14.570	173.413	4.723	7.099	0.673	62.852	7.604	1.800	1.102	151.938
1990	14.440	181.109	4.855	7.520	0.714	74.033	7.948	1.762	1.273	183.660
1991	14.431	178.614	5.002	7.479	0.701	73.002	8.017	1.772	1.239	166.493
1992	14.217	174.714	5.807	7.533	0.738	74.574	8.042	1.818	1.298	164.223
1993	13.624	188.370	6.696	9.122	0.780	79.253	8.310	1.730	1.171	130.148
1994	13.540	196.896	6.191	9.163	0.776	83.106	8.374	1.621	1.190	121.322
1995	13.182	196.105	5.708	9.332	0.829	84.685	8.286	1.546	1.308	123.012
1996	13.434	195.761	5.828	8.515	0.814	84.656	8.197	1.568	1.270	138.084
1997	13.824	198.589	5.881	8.651	0.692	80.439	8.019	1.644	1.134	137.077
1998	13.854	201.695	5.982	8.916	0.676	79.698	8.466	1.622	1.121	146.415
1999	13.760	200.482	5.946	8.808	0.659	77.182	8.310	1.600	1.066	121.317
2000	13.760	200.482	5.946	8.445	0.610	72.585	8.113	1.558	0.924	99.475
2001	13.760	200.482	5.946	9.255	0.622	87.417	8.048	1.510	0.896	108.682
2002	13.760	200.482	5.946	9.161	0.629	86.194	7.509	1.467	0.946	118.091

(1) The ECU is a basket monetary unit based on the market exchange rates of certain quantity of each European Union currency weighted on the basis of the average gross national product over the years and of the intra-EU trade of each Member State. The rates used here are averages of the daily rates.

ECU/EURO EXCHANGE RATE [1]

CANDIDATE COUNTRIES TO THE MEMBERSHIP OF THE EU

Periods	Bulgaria	Cyprus	Czech Rep.	Estonia	Hungary	Latvia	Lithuania
1990	0.004	0.582	:	:	130.522	:	:
1991	0.034	0.573	:	:	142.202	:	:
1992	0.051	0.584	:	:	172.777	0.896	2.143
1993	0.032	0.583	34.169	15.491	107.611	0.794	5.087
1994	0.064	0.584	34.151	15.396	125.030	0.664	4.732
1995	0.088	0.592	34.773	14.990	164.545	0.690	5.232
1996	0.225	0.592	34.457	15.276	193.741	0.700	5.079
1997	1.973	0.583	35.930	15.715	211.654	0.659	4.536
1998	1.969	0.577	36.320	15.753	240.573	0.660	4.484
1999	1.956	0.579	36.884	15.647	252.767	0.626	4.264
2000	1.953	0.574	35.600	15.647	260.045	0.559	3.695
2001	1.948	0.576	34.068	15.647	256.591	0.560	3.582
2002	1.949	0.575	30.807	15.647	242.958	0.581	3.460

	Malta	Poland	Romania	Slovakia	Slovenia	Turkey
1990	0.404	1.962	46.257	:	:	3,329.060
1991	0.400	2.017	145.370	:	36.969	5,153.290
1992	0.413	2.975	673.713	:	98.434	8,930.950
1993	0.447	2.122	885.825	36.032	132.486	12,879.300
1994	0.449	2.702	1,971.560	38.118	152.766	35,535.300
1995	0.461	3.170	2,947.120	38.865	154.880	59,912.100
1996	0.458	3.422	3,922.190	39.380	171.778	103,214.000
1997	0.438	3.911	8,111.500	38.106	180.996	171,848.000
1998	0.435	3.918	9,984.880	39.541	185.958	293,736.000
1999	0.426	4.227	16,345.200	44.123	194.473	447,237.000
2000	0.404	4.008	19,921.800	42.602	206.613	574,816.000
2001	0.403	3.672	26,004.000	43.300	217.980	1,102,430.000
2002	0.409	3.858	31,273.800	42.691	225.980	1,440,760.000

(1) The ECU is a basket monetary unit based on the market exchange rates of certain quantity of each European Union currency weighted on the basis of the average gross national product over the years and of the intra-EU trade of each Member State. The rates used here are averages of the daily rates.

PRODUCT LIST : SITC REV. 3

0 Food and live animals

00 Live animals other than animals of division 03

01 Meat and meat preparations
02 Dairy products and birds' eggs
03 Fish (not marine mammals), crustaceans, molluscs and aquatic invertebrates and preparations thereof

04 Cereals and cereal preparations
05 Vegetables and fruit
06 Sugars, sugar preparations and honey
07 Coffee, tea, cocoa, spices, and manufactures thereof
08 Feeding stuff for animals (not including unmilled cereals)
09 Miscellaneous edible products and preparations

1 Beverages and tobacco

11 Beverages
12 Tobacco and tobacco manufactures

2 Crude materials, inedible, except fuels

21 Hides, skins and fur skins, raw
22 Oil seeds and oleaginous fruits
23 Crude rubber (including synthetic and reclaimed)
24 Cork and wood
25 Pulp and waste paper
26 Textile fibres (other than wool tops and other combed wool), and their wastes (not manufactured into yarn or fabric)
27 Crude fertilizers, other than those of division 56, and crude minerals (excluding coal, petroleum and precious stones)
28 Metalliferous ores and metal scrap
29 Crude animal and vegetable materials, n.e.s.

3 Mineral fuels, lubricants and related materials

32 Coal, coke and briquettes
33 Petroleum, petroleum products and related materials
34 Gas, natural and manufactured
35 Electric current

4 Animal and vegetable oils, fats and waxes

41 Animal oils and fats
42 Fixed vegetable fats and oils, crude, refined or fractionated
43 Animal or vegetable fats and oils, processed; waxes of animal or vegetable origin; inedible mixtures or preparations of animal or vegetable fats and oils, n.e.s

5 Chemicals and related products, n.e.s

51 Organic chemicals
52 Inorganic chemicals
53 Dyeing, tanning and colouring materials
54 Medical and pharmaceutical products
55 Essential oils and resinoids and perfume materials; toilet, polishing and cleaning preparations
56 Fertilizers (other than those of group 272)
57 Plastics in primary forms
58 Plastics in non–primary forms
59 Chemical materials and products, n.e.s

6 Manufactured goods classified chiefly by material

60 Complete industrial plant appropriate to section 6
61 Leather, leather manufacture, n.e.s, and dressed fur skins
62 Rubber manufacture, n.e.s
63 Cork and wood manufacture (excluding furniture)
64 Paper, paperboard and articles of paper pulp, of paper or of paperboard
65 Textile yarn, fabrics, made–up articles, n.e.s, and related products
66 Non–metallic mineral manufactures, n.e.s
67 Iron and steel
68 Non–ferrous metals
69 Manufacture of metals, n.e.s

7 Machinery and transport equipment

70 Complete industrial plant appropriate to section 7
71 Power–generating machinery and equipment
72 Machinery specialized for particular industries
73 Metal working machinery
74 General industrial machinery and equipment, n.e.s, and machine parts, n.e.s
75 Office machines and automatic data–processing machines
76 Telecommunications and sound recording and reproducing apparatus and equipment
77 Electrical machinery, apparatus and appliances, n.e.s and electrical parts thereof (including non–electrical counterparts n.e.s of electrical household type equipment)
78 Road vehicles (including air–cushion vehicles)
79 Other transport equipment

8 Miscellaneous manufactured articles

80 Complete industrial plant appropriate to section 8
81 Prefabricated buildings; sanitary plumbing, heating and lighting fixtures and fittings, n.e.s
82 Furniture and parts thereof; bedding, mattresses, mattress supports, cushions and similar stuffed furnishings
83 Travel goods, handbags and similar containers
84 Articles of apparel and clothing accessories
85 Footwear
87 Professional, scientific and controlling instruments and apparatus, n.e.s
88 Photographic apparatus, equipment and supplies and optical goods, n.e.s; watches and clocks
89 Miscellaneous manufactured articles, n.e.s

9 Commodities and transactions not classified elsewhere in SITC

91 Postal packages not classified according to kind
93 Special transactions and commodities not classified according to kind
94 Complete industrial plant, not elsewhere specified
96 Coin (other than gold coin) not being legal tender
97 Gold, non–monetary (excluding gold, ores and concentrates)

5100 Europe

| | 5110 | European Union (15) |

| | 5190 | Other European countries |

5110 European Union (15)

AT	038	Austria	GR	009	Greece
BE	017	Belgium	IE	007	Ireland
DE	004	Germany	IT	005	Italy
DK	008	Denmark	LU	018	Luxembourg
ES	011	Spain	NL	003	Netherlands
FI	032	Finland	PT	010	Portugal
FR	001	France	SE	030	Sweden
GB	006	United Kingdom		5910	Miscellaneous (countries not specified) intra

5190 Other European countries

AD	043	Andorra	LV	054	Latvia
AL	070	Albania	MD	074	Moldova (Republic of)
BA	093	Bosnia and Herzegovina	MK	096	Former Yugoslav Republic of Macedonia
BG	068	Bulgaria	MT	046	Malta
BY	073	Belarus	NO	028	Norway
CH	039	Switzerland	PL	060	Poland
CY	600	Cyprus	RO	066	Romania
CZ	061	Czech Republic	RU	075	Russian Federation
EE	053	Estonia	SI	091	Slovenia
FO	041	Faroe Islands	SK	063	Slovakia
GI	044	Gibraltar	SM	047	San Marino
HR	092	Croatia	TR	052	Turkey
HU	064	Hungary	UA	072	Ukraine
IS	024	Iceland	VA	045	Holy See
LI	037	Liechtenstein	YU	094	Yugoslavia
LT	055	Lithuania			

5200 Africa

| | 5210 | North Africa |

| | 5290 | Other African countries |

5210 North Africa

DZ	208	Algeria	TN	212	Tunisia
EG	220	Egypt	XC	021	Ceuta
LY	216	Lybian Arab Jamahiriya	XL	023	Melilla
MA	204	Morocco			

5290 Other African countries

AO	330	Angola	ML	232	Mali
BF	236	Burkina Faso	MR	228	Mauritania
BI	328	Burundi	MU	373	Mauritius
BJ	284	Benin	MW	386	Malawi
BW	391	Botswana	MZ	366	Mozambique
CD	322	Congo (Democratic Republic of)	NA	389	Namibia
CF	306	Central African Republic	NE	240	Niger
CG	318	Congo	NG	288	Nigeria
CI	272	Côte d'Ivoire	RW	324	Rwanda
CM	302	Cameroon	SC	355	Seychelles
CV	247	Cape Verde	SD	224	Sudan
DJ	338	Djibouti	SH	329	Saint Helena
ER	336	Eritrea	SL	264	Sierra Leone
ET	334	Ethiopia	SN	248	Senegal
GA	314	Gabon	SO	342	Somalia
GH	276	Ghana	ST	311	São Tomé and Principe
GM	252	Gambia	SZ	393	Swaziland
GN	260	Guinea	TD	244	Chad

GQ	310	Equatorial Guinea		TG	280	Togo
GW	257	Guinea-Bissau		TZ	352	Tanzania (United Republic of)
IO	357	British Indian Ocean Territory		UG	350	Uganda
KE	346	Kenya		YT	377	Mayotte
KM	375	Comoros		ZA	388	South Africa
LR	268	Liberia		ZM	378	Zambia
LS	395	Lesotho		ZW	382	Zimbabwe
MG	370	Madagascar				

5300   America

	5310	North America			5330	South America
	5320	Central America and Caribbean				

5310   North America

CA	404	Canada		PM	408	Saint Pierre and Miquelon
GL	406	Greenland		US	400	United States

5320   Central America and Caribbean

AG	459	Antigua and Barbuda		HT	452	Haiti
AI	446	Anguilla		JM	464	Jamaica
AN	478	Netherlands Antilles		KN	449	St Kitts and Nevis
AW	474	Aruba		KY	463	Cayman Islands
BB	469	Barbados		LC	465	St Lucia
BM	413	Bermuda		MS	470	Montserrat
BS	453	Bahamas		MX	412	Mexico
BZ	421	Belize		NI	432	Nicaragua
CR	436	Costa Rica		PA	442	Panama
CU	448	Cuba		SV	428	El Salvador
DM	460	Dominica		TC	454	Turks and Caicos Islands
DO	456	Dominican Republic		TT	472	Trinidad and Tobago
GD	473	Grenada		VC	467	St Vincent and the Grenadines
GT	416	Guatemala		VG	468	Virgin Islands (British)
HN	424	Honduras		VI	457	Virgin Islands (US)

5330   South America

AR	528	Argentina		GY	488	Guyana
BO	516	Bolivia		PE	504	Peru
BR	508	Brazil		PY	520	Paraguay
CL	512	Chile		SR	492	Suriname
CO	480	Colombia		UY	524	Uruguay
EC	500	Ecuador		VE	484	Venezuela
FK	529	Falkland Islands				

5400   Asia

	5410	Near and Middle Eastern countries			5490	Other Asian countries

5410   Near and Middle Eastern countries

AE	647	United Arab Emirates		KW	636	Kuwait
AM	077	Armenia		LB	604	Lebanon
AZ	078	Azerbaijan		OM	649	Oman
BH	640	Bahrain		PS	625	Occupied Palestinian Territory
GE	076	Georgia		QA	644	Qatar
IL	624	Israel		SA	632	Saudi Arabia
IQ	612	Iraq		SY	608	Syrian Arab Republic
IR	616	Iran (Islamic Republic of)		YE	653	Yemen
JO	628	Jordan				

5490   Other Asian countries

AF	660	Afghanistan		MM	676	Myanmar
BD	666	Bangladesh		MN	716	Mongolia
BN	703	Brunei Darussalam		MO	743	Macao
BT	675	Bhutan		MV	667	Maldives

CN	720	China (People's Republic of)	MY	701	Malaysia
HK	740	Hong Kong	NP	672	Nepal
ID	700	Indonesia	PH	708	Philippines
IN	664	India	PK	662	Pakistan
JP	732	Japan	SG	706	Singapore
KG	083	Kyrgyzstan	TH	680	Thailand
KH	696	Cambodia	TJ	082	Tajikistan
KP	724	Korea (Democratic People's Republic of)	TL	626	East Timor
KR	728	Korea (Republic of)	TM	080	Turkmenistan
KZ	079	Kazakhstan	TW	736	Taiwan
LA	684	Lao People's Democratic Republic	UZ	081	Uzbekistan
LK	669	Sri Lanka	VN	690	Viet-Nam

5500   Oceania and Polar regions

	5510	Australia and New Zealand		5590	Other countries of Oceania and Polar regions

5510   Australia and New Zealand

AU	800	Australia	NF	836	Norfolk Island
CC	833	Cocos Islands (or Keeling Islands)	NU	838	Niue
CK	837	Cook Islands	NZ	804	New Zealand
CX	834	Christmas Island	TK	839	Tokelau
HM	835	Heard Island and McDonald Islands			

5590   Other countries of Oceania and Polar regions

AQ	891	Antarctica	PF	822	French Polynesia
AS	830	American Samoa	PG	801	Papua New Guinea
BV	892	Bouvet Island	PN	813	Pitcairn
FJ	815	Fiji	PW	825	Palau
FM	823	Micronesia (Federated States of)	SB	806	Solomon Islands
GS	893	South Georgia and South Sandwich Islands	TF	894	French Southern Territories
GU	831	Guam	TO	817	Tonga
KI	812	Kiribati	TV	807	Tuvalu
MH	824	Marshall Islands	UM	832	United States Minor Outlying Islands
MP	820	Northern Mariana Islands	VU	816	Vanuatu
NC	809	New Caledonia	WF	811	Wallis and Futuna
NR	803	Nauru	WS	819	Samoa

1021 EFTA
European Free Trade Association

CH	039	Switzerland		LI	037	Liechtenstein
IS	024	Iceland		NO	028	Norway

1031 ACP
African, Caribbean and Pacific countries, signatories to the Partnership Agreement

AG	459	Antigua and Barbuda		LS	395	Lesotho
AO	330	Angola		MG	370	Madagascar
BB	469	Barbados		MH	824	Marshall Islands
BF	236	Burkina Faso		ML	232	Mali
BI	328	Burundi		MR	228	Mauritania
BJ	284	Benin		MU	373	Mauritius
BS	453	Bahamas		MW	386	Malawi
BW	391	Botswana		MZ	366	Mozambique
BZ	421	Belize		NA	389	Namibia
CD	322	Congo (Democratic Republic of)		NE	240	Niger
CF	306	Central African Republic		NG	288	Nigeria
CG	318	Congo		NR	803	Nauru
CI	272	Côte d'Ivoire		NU	838	Niue
CK	837	Cook Islands		PG	801	Papua New Guinea
CM	302	Cameroon		PW	825	Palau
CV	247	Cape Verde		RW	324	Rwanda
DJ	338	Djibouti		SB	806	Solomon Islands
DM	460	Dominica		SC	355	Seychelles
DO	456	Dominican Republic		SD	224	Sudan
ER	336	Eritrea		SL	264	Sierra Leone
ET	334	Ethiopia		SN	248	Senegal
FJ	815	Fiji		SO	342	Somalia
FM	823	Micronesia (Federated States of)		SR	492	Suriname
GA	314	Gabon		ST	311	São Tomé and Principe
GD	473	Grenada		SZ	393	Swaziland
GH	276	Ghana		TD	244	Chad
GM	252	Gambia		TG	280	Togo
GN	260	Guinea		TO	817	Tonga
GQ	310	Equatorial Guinea		TT	472	Trinidad and Tobago
GW	257	Guinea-Bissau		TV	807	Tuvalu
GY	488	Guyana		TZ	352	Tanzania (United Republic of)
HT	452	Haiti		UG	350	Uganda
JM	464	Jamaica		VC	467	St Vincent and the Grenadines
KE	346	Kenya		VU	816	Vanuatu
KI	812	Kiribati		WS	819	Samoa
KM	375	Comoros		ZA	388	South Africa
KN	449	St Kitts and Nevis		ZM	378	Zambia
LC	465	St Lucia		ZW	382	Zimbabwe
LR	268	Liberia				

1051 Mediterranean basin countries

AL	070	Albania		MA	204	Morocco
BA	093	Bosnia and Herzegovina		MK	096	Former Yugoslav Republic of Macedonia
CY	600	Cyprus		MT	046	Malta
DZ	208	Algeria		PS	625	Occupied Palestinian Territory
EG	220	Egypt		SI	091	Slovenia
GI	044	Gibraltar		SY	608	Syrian Arab Republic
HR	092	Croatia		TN	212	Tunisia
IL	624	Israel		TR	052	Turkey
JO	628	Jordan		XC	021	Ceuta
LB	604	Lebanon		XL	023	Melilla
LY	216	Lybian Arab Jamahiriya		YU	094	Yugoslavia

1053 OPEC
Organisation of Petroleum Exporting Countries

AE	647	United Arab Emirates	LY	216	Lybian Arab Jamahiriya
DZ	208	Algeria	NG	288	Nigeria
ID	700	Indonesia	QA	644	Qatar
IQ	612	Iraq	SA	632	Saudi Arabia
IR	616	Iran (Islamic Republic of)	VE	484	Venezuela
KW	636	Kuwait			

1055 MEDA
Mediterranean countries in the Euro-Mediterranean Partnership

CY	600	Cyprus	MA	204	Morocco
DZ	208	Algeria	MT	046	Malta
EG	220	Egypt	PS	625	Occupied Palestinian Territory
IL	624	Israel	SY	608	Syrian Arab Republic
JO	628	Jordan	TN	212	Tunisia
LB	604	Lebanon	TR	052	Turkey

1058 Latin American countries

AR	528	Argentina	HN	424	Honduras
BO	516	Bolivia	HT	452	Haiti
BR	508	Brazil	MX	412	Mexico
CL	512	Chile	NI	432	Nicaragua
CO	480	Colombia	PA	442	Panama
CR	436	Costa Rica	PE	504	Peru
CU	448	Cuba	PY	520	Paraguay
DO	456	Dominican Republic	SV	428	El Salvador
EC	500	Ecuador	UY	524	Uruguay
GT	416	Guatemala	VE	484	Venezuela

1110 European Union (15)

AT	038	Austria	GR	009	Greece
BE	017	Belgium	IE	007	Ireland
DE	004	Germany	IT	005	Italy
DK	008	Denmark	LU	018	Luxembourg
ES	011	Spain	NL	003	Netherlands
FI	032	Finland	PT	010	Portugal
FR	001	France	SE	030	Sweden
GB	006	United Kingdom		5910	Miscellaneous (countries not specified) intra

1120 CEEC
Central and Eastern European countries

AL	070	Albania	LV	054	Latvia
BA	093	Bosnia and Herzegovina	MK	096	Former Yugoslav Republic of Macedonia
BG	068	Bulgaria	PL	060	Poland
CZ	061	Czech Republic	RO	066	Romania
EE	053	Estonia	SI	091	Slovenia
HR	092	Croatia	SK	063	Slovakia
HU	064	Hungary	YU	094	Yugoslavia
LT	055	Lithuania			

1130 Candidate countries

BG	068	Bulgaria	MT	046	Malta
CY	600	Cyprus	PL	060	Poland
CZ	061	Czech Republic	RO	066	Romania
EE	053	Estonia	SI	091	Slovenia
HU	064	Hungary	SK	063	Slovakia
LT	055	Lithuania	TR	052	Turkey
LV	054	Latvia			

1310 NAFTA
North American Free Trade Agreement

CA	404	Canada		US	400	United States
MX	412	Mexico				

1330 MERCOSUR
South American Common Market

AR	528	Argentina		PY	520	Paraguay
BR	508	Brazil		UY	524	Uruguay

1415 DAEs
Dynamic Asian economies

HK	740	Hong Kong		SG	706	Singapore
KR	728	Korea (Republic of)		TH	680	Thailand
MY	701	Malaysia		TW	736	Taiwan

1811 Extra-european Union (15)

5190	Other European countries		5400	Asia
5200	Africa		5500	Oceania and Polar regions
5300	America		5920	Miscellaneous (countries not specified) extra

1815 CIS
Commonwealth of Independent States

AM	077	Armenia		MD	074	Moldova (Republic of)
AZ	078	Azerbaijan		RU	075	Russian Federation
BY	073	Belarus		TJ	082	Tajikistan
GE	076	Georgia		TM	080	Turkmenistan
KG	083	Kyrgyzstan		UA	072	Ukraine
KZ	079	Kazakhstan		UZ	081	Uzbekistan

1820 OECD excluding E.U.
Organisation for Economic Cooperation and Development, excluding E.U.

AU	800	Australia		KR	728	Korea (Republic of)
CA	404	Canada		MX	412	Mexico
CC	833	Cocos Islands (or Keeling Islands)		NF	836	Norfolk Island
CH	039	Switzerland		NO	028	Norway
CX	834	Christmas Island		NZ	804	New Zealand
CZ	061	Czech Republic		PL	060	Poland
HM	835	Heard Island and McDonald Islands		SK	063	Slovakia
HU	064	Hungary		TR	052	Turkey
IS	024	Iceland		US	400	United States
JP	732	Japan		VI	457	Virgin Islands (US)

European Commission

External and intra-European Union trade — Statistical yearbook — Data 1958-2002

Luxembourg: Office for Official Publications of the European Communities

2003 — 249 pp. — 21 x 29.7 cm

Theme 6: External trade
Collection: Detailed tables

ISBN 92-894-4302-2
ISSN 1606-3481

Price (excluding VAT) in Luxembourg: EUR 29.50

.... Eurostat **Data Shops**

DANMARK

Danmarks Statistik
Bibliotek og Information
Eurostat Data Shop
Sejrøgade 11
DK-2100 København Ø
Tlf. (45) 39 17 30 30
Fax (45) 39 17 30 03
E-post: bib@dst.dk
URL: http://www.dst.dk/bibliotek

DEUTSCHLAND

Statistisches Bundesamt
Eurostat Data Shop Berlin
Otto-Braun-Straße 70-72
(Eingang: Karl-Marx-Allee)
D-10178 Berlin
Tel. (49) 1888-644 94 27/28
(49) 611 75 94 27
Fax (49) 1888-644 94 30
E-Mail: datashop@destatis.de
URL: http://www.eu-datashop.de/

ESPAÑA

INE
Eurostat Data Shop
Paseo de la Castellana, 183
Despacho 011B
Entrada por Estébanez
Calderón
E-28046 Madrid
Tel. (34) 915 839 167 / 915 839
500
Fax (34) 915 830 357
E-mail:
datashop.eurostat@ine.es
URL: http://www.ine.es/prodyser/
datashop/index.html
Member of the MIDAS Net

FRANCE

INSEE Info service
Eurostat Data Shop
195, rue de Bercy
Tour Gamma A
F-75582 Paris Cedex 12
Tél. (33) 1 53 17 88 44
Fax (33) 1 53 17 88 22
E-mail: datashop@insee.fr
Member of the MIDAS Net

ITALIA - ROMA

ISTAT
Centro di informazione
statistica — Sede di Roma
Eurostat Data Shop
Via Cesare Balbo, 11a
I-00184 Roma
Tel. (39) 06 46 73 32 28
Fax (39) 06 46 73 31 01/07
E-mail: datashop@istat.it
URL:
http://www.istat.it/Prodotti-e/
Allegati/Eurostatdatashop.html
Member of the MIDAS Net

ITALIA - MILANO

ISTAT
Ufficio regionale per la
Lombardia
Eurostat Data Shop
Via Fieno, 3
I-20123 Milano
Tel. (39) 02 80 61 32 460
Fax (39) 02 80 61 32 304
E-mail: mileuro@tin.it
URL:
http://www.istat.it/Prodotti-e/
Allegati/Eurostatdatashop.html
Member of the MIDAS Net

NEDERLAND

Centraal Bureau voor de
Statistiek
Eurostat Data Shop —
Voorburg
Postbus 4000
2270 JM Voorburg
Nederland
Tel. (31-70) 337 49 00
Fax (31-70) 337 59 84
E-mail: datashop@cbs.nl
URL: www.cbs.nl/eurodatashop

PORTUGAL

Eurostat Data Shop Lisboa
INE/Serviço de Difusão
Av. António José de Almeida, 2
P-1000-043 Lisboa
Tel. (351) 21 842 61 00
Fax (351) 21 842 63 64
E-mail: data.shop@ine.pt

SUOMI/FINLAND

Statistics Finland
Eurostat Data Shop Helsinki
Tilastokirjasto
PL 2B
FIN-00022 Tilastokeskus
Työpajakatu 13 B, 2. kerros,
Helsinki
P. (358-9) 17 34 22 21
F. (358-9) 17 34 22 79
Sähköposti: datashop@stat.fi
URL:
http://tilastokeskus.fi/tk/kk/data
shop/

SVERIGE

Statistics Sweden
Information service
Eurostat Data Shop
Karlavägen 100
Box 24 300
S-104 51 Stockholm
Tfn (46-8) 50 69 48 01
Fax (46-8) 50 69 48 99
E-post: infoservice@scb.se
URL: http://www.scb.se/tjanster/
datashop/datashop.asp

UNITED KINGDOM

Eurostat Data Shop
Office for National Statistics
Room 1.015
Cardiff Road
Newport NP10 8XG
South Wales
United Kingdom
Tel. (44-1633) 81 33 69
Fax (44-1633) 81 33 33
E-mail:
eurostat.datashop@ons.gov.uk

NORGE

Statistics Norway
Library and Information Centre
Eurostat Data Shop
Kongens gate 6
Boks 8131 Dep.
N-0033 Oslo
Tel. (47) 21 09 46 42/43
Fax (47) 21 09 45 04
E-mail: Datashop@ssb.no
URL: http://www.ssb.no/
biblioteket/datashop/

SCHWEIZ/SUISSE/SVIZZERA

Statistisches Amt des Kantons
Zürich
Eurostat Data Shop
Bleicherweg 5
CH-8090 Zürich
Tel. (41) 1 225 12 12
Fax (41) 1 225 12 99
E-Mail: datashop@statistik.zh.ch
URL: http://www.statistik.zh.ch

USA

Haver Analytics
Eurostat Data Shop
60 East 42nd Street
Suite 3310
New York, NY 10165
Tel. (1-212) 986 93 00
Fax (1-212) 986 69 81
E-mail: eurodata@haver.com
URL: http://www.haver.com/

EUROSTAT HOME PAGE
www.europa.eu.int/comm/eurostat/

MEDIA SUPPORT
EUROSTAT
(only for professional journalists)
Postal address:
Jean Monnet building
L-2920 Luxembourg
Office: BECH A4/017 —
5, rue Alphonse Weicker
L-2721 Luxembourg
Tel. (352) 43 01-33408
Fax (352) 43 01-35349
E-mail:
eurostat-mediasupport@cec.eu.int